I0747970

THE
SHAHNAMEH
VOLUME III

THE SHAHNAMEH

VOLUME III

Hakim Abul-Ghassem Ferdowsi

Translated by Josiane Cohanim

GIROUETTE BOOKS

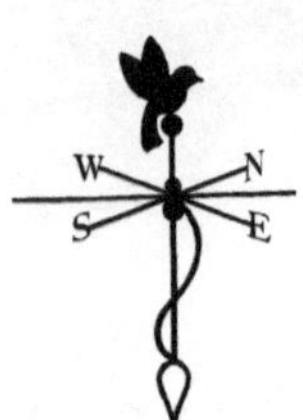

Girouette Books

"Should the inquiry be reliable,
Two thousand years passed on this book...
I therefore acclaim the blessed scribe
Who carved the road for later poets.
From him we inherit a glorious book,
A royal jewel to place upon the throne. "

CONTENTS

VOLUME THREE

PART SIXTEEN

The Reign of Kay Khosrow
The Great Battle Between Kay Khosrow & Afraasiyaab

PART NINETEEN

The Seven Stages of Esfandiar's Quest

The Battle of Esfandiar and Rostam

The Adventure of Rostam and Shaghaad

PART TWENTY

The Ninety-Nine-Year Reign of Bahman, Son of Esfandiar

The Thirty-Two-Year Reign of Homay, Daughter of Bahman

The Twelve-Year Reign of Daaraab, Son of Bahman and Homay

The Fourteen-Year Reign of Dara, son of Daaraab

PART TWENTY-ONE

The Fourteen-Year Reign of Eskandar

Appendix:

PREFACE

"Should one search deeply from the perspective
Of Eternal Wisdom, one will discern
And understand the true meaning of man…
You, who stand there,
You, whose origins stem from far beyond the two worlds,
You, who have been nurtured and cherished by many,
The essence of your being is most precious,
Yet your evolution is the slowest." (Volume I)

Volume Three begins with the battle of eleven Iranian heroes and
their Tooranian counterparts. Throughout his reign, Kay Khosrow
is driven by his desire to avenge the death of his father, Siaavoosh,
at the direction of King Afraasiyaab. We witness many conflicts
between Iran and Tooran as their two opposing kings and their heroes
continue to confront each other. The forces of good prevail: Iran's king
Kay Khosrow successfully completes his mission on earth and kills
Tooran's evil ruler, Afraasiyaab. Thereafter, no longer wishing to rule,
Kay Khosrow relinquishes the throne and crown to one of his army
leaders, Lohraasp, and vanishes into nature. At this point, we are
introduced to a new religion, Zoroastrianism, and the worship of fire.
In addition, we have the opportunity to read the thousand verses by
the poet Daghighi that Ferdowsi inserted into his poem.

Upon reaching old age, Lohraasp abdicates to spend his remaining
years in worship at the fire temple. There follows a succession of
kings: Goshtaasp, Bahman, Daaraab, Dara, and Esfandiar. Homay,
Bahman's daughter, becomes the first ruling queen of Iran. The
story of her reign is highlighted by a colorful account, reminiscent of
biblical tales, in which she abandons her son on a river bank, wishing
to keep his existence a secret. We learn the circumstances surrounding
his survival, his childhood, and his reign.

Two mighty heroes come face to face: Rostam and Esfandiar,
Goshtaasp's son. Esfandiar is a prince and an important warrior hero
equal in strength to Rostam. There is potential for them to unite and
become allies, but Esfandiar is manipulated by his father into battling
Rostam and tragically loses his life. In the scenes with Esfandiar,
Rostam holds firm to his values and refuses to allow Esfandiar to
restrain him in chains to deliver him to his father as ordered. Rostam
would rather kill a prince than succumb to shackles.

In Volume One, Rostsam declares:
"I was born free; I am a slave to no one.
I am merely the servant of the Divine Creator.
My eyes are fixed on my path and my duties,
And, above all, my eyes are fixed on world order."

Now he says to Esfandiar:
"Treasure and land belonged to me
When Goshtaasp was a mere blacksmith in Rum...
How dare he tell you to enchain me
When not even the lofty sky has the ability to bind me?
From my childhood to my declining years,
I have never been submitted to such degradation.
I shall neither act in shame nor beg for mercy.
For me to ask forgiveness would be humiliating.
Not even the subject of our discussion is worthy of my status."

This section raises many questions in the mind of the reader: do
Rostam's words reflect a dominating pride, or is he staying true to his
own free spirit? The price is high: A prince dies a death that leads to
our hero's demise. What has happened to Rostam's staunch loyalty to
king and kingship? Why does he refuse to be bound up and taken to
the king? Is Rostam's power waning? Is his relationship with kingship
weakening, or is his allegiance to the essence of who he is more
valuable to him? Just as Rostam allowed his son to die to protect the
king and the ideal of kingship, perhaps in this instance he risks the life
of a prince as well as his own to preserve his integrity. This Rostam
is a more evolved, more complex Rostam, one who wrestles with his
inner demons. We must also keep in mind that Ferdowsi's characters
are far from perfect, that even Rostam the hero is flawed, succumbing
to excessive eating and drinking, and ego-driven behavior. Soon after
the episode with Esfandiar, Rostam, weakened, dies at the hands of
his own brother, Shaghaad.

PREFACE

This volume concludes with the reign of Eskandar, an adaptation of
the life of Alexander the Great and his invasion and occupation of the
Persian Empire. Upon the murder of King Dara, executed by his two
viziers, the conqueror Eskandar ascends the throne of Iran. He then
marries and seeks the four wonders possessed by the Indian ruler
Keid. Later, Eskandar the explorer travels the world in an epic pursuit
of adventure and immortality, tirelessly searching for the fountain of
youth and the elixir of life. The stories in the present volume end with
the death of Eskandar and his burial.

Some of the most lyrical passages in Ferdowsi's long poem are those
dedicated to nature, its cycle of four seasons, and its cosmic motions
of day and night, sun and moon, sunrise and sunset:

"Once the shining sun reveals its face as it adorns the earth
And places on its head the crown under the sign of the ram,
East and west are both pleased.
Mountains are filled with the rolling din of thunder,
The edges of streams are blanketed with tulips and narcissus.
Narcissus provide delights, tulips restore patience,
The flower of the spikenard causes anguish,
And the pomegranate tree blesses one with fineries."

Beyond his reverence for nature, Ferdowsi spends a not insignificant
amount of time with questions on human existence and destiny. He
tells us that we have choices in life: We can choose freedom, light,
love, truth, justice, and virtue, or we can succumb to human flaws,
such as greed and corruption, thus aligning ourselves with darkness
and Ahriman, the opponent of light. When we unite with the truth,
with wisdom, and with the divine, we rise. When we align with
darkness, we fail, lose our path, and fall into the trap of attachments
and the acquisition of worldly possessions.

"Life is a vast ocean with unseen, undiscovered depths.
No one ever finds the keys to its treasures and mysteries.
Even if you unlock one or two, you may want for more,
But fate rubs out of your life every day that you have lived…
Enjoy what you have, and do not dwell on greed,
For it will only serve to tarnish the luster of your being."

Beyond the visible world, there is a mysterious non-physical realm to
be explored, although we are told we will never fully comprehend its
magnitude, its beauty, its vastness. The human journey is a search for

answers to the most profound questions concerning our existence on earth and the idea of finding balance in the integration of the material and the imperceptible.

"I have heard this from a wise man:
What do we know of the secrets of creation?
How can we ever grasp the magnitude of such mysteries?" (Volume I)

About This Translation

This translation is based on two editions of *The Shahnameh*: the original Persian text edited by Dr. Seyed Mohammad Dabir Siaghi (2007), and a French edition, *Le livre des rois*, translated by Mr. Jules Mohl (1878).

Although Ferdowsi uses the past tense for his stories, it seemed more natural to narrate the English translation in the present tense. This provides a sense of continuity and permanence, as if the values he upholds cannot be constricted into a specific time frame.

Spelling and Pronunciation

In order to transfer text from Persian to English, we have used a simple form of transliteration. While it may vary from the more common methods, it makes sense to us and, we hope, will to the reader. In this approach, names of characters and places are spelled based on their pronunciation in Persian, rather than on their Romanized equivalent. For example, Zoroaster is *Zartosht*, Alexander is *Eskandar*, China is *Chin*, and Rome is *Rum*.

Most of the sounds for long syllables are pronounced as in English:
1. Aah sounds, as in "fall," are spelled *aa*, as in *Zaal* or *Rudaabeh*, except when a word ends in *ah*, as in *shah*, or *an*, as in *Iran, Tooran,* or *Nariman.* Some exceptions include *Baarmaan* and *Hoomaan.* One phonetic exception is in the second syllable of *Ghaaran* which has the *a* sound as in "fan."

2. Oo sounds as in "fool" are most often spelled *oo*, as in *Tooran* or *Fereydoon*. A few exceptions are *Zu* and *Tous*.

3. Ee sounds, as in "feel," are spelled *ee* as in *beed* and *deev*. At times we revert to *-i-* as in *Giv*.

Persian Words

The Persian language offers a unique perspective that requires careful consideration when translating into English. Finding an accurate English equivalent is often a daunting task. A number of words, such as *farr, kherrad,* and *ayeen,* are almost impossible to translate accurately. We have attempted to provide corresponding English words in footnotes and in the glossary; however, these may not completely capture the essence of the original words.

The absence of pronouns in Persian can lead to the use of vague terms such as "it", "this", or "that" to refer to a person or an object. This translation avoids pronouns when it comes to Yazdan, the divine Creator, and Sooroosh, the archangel. In the case of Simorgh, the mystical bird, we chose feminine pronouns to convey nurturing and maternal qualities.

VOLUME THREE

From the Battle of the Eleven Heroes
to the Death of Eskandar

PART FIFTEEN

The Battle of the Eleven Heroes

1 | The Beginning of the Story

No matter what happens, life will pass,
And fortune, good or bad, will reach an end.

If you cinch your waist in readiness to travel down
The path of greed, life will appear long and harsh.
On the other hand, you are better off
Taking the road of righteousness,
Even if you must snatch it from the dragon's jaws.
I know that a slave to passions,
A seeker of war and battle, will not be blessed.

Furthermore, this fugitive world
Does not stop its onward march for anyone,
Whether one's dwelling is opulent or narrow.
The worshipper of greed and enmity
Will never be praised in the world.

When, in the garden, the slender figure of the cypress tree
Leans to the side, its bright light grows dim,
Its leaves wither, its roots dry out,
Its head droops low as it plucks itself from the soil
To blend with and return to the earth.
At such a time the world echoes with fears and worries.

A man of wisdom will flow through life in peace.
If you remain on the earth at length,
Your body's weariness will make you long to leave.

Life is a vast ocean with unseen, undiscovered depths.
No one ever finds the keys to its treasures and mysteries.
Even if you unlock one or two, you may want for more,
But fate rubs out of your life every day that you have lived.

No matter how carefree you may be,
You must have three indispensable elements:
Food, clothing, and a place to rest,
Necessities that leave you in a constant state
Of need and greed, further increasing your suffering.

Your condition is such that the world
Will never fall into your possession.
If you know that you will not live forever,
Why sacrifice your cherished soul in pursuit of things?
A man of sense and wisdom desires only contentment.

Enjoy what you have, and do not dwell on greed,
For it will only serve to tarnish the luster of your being.

2 | Afraasiyaab Assembles an Army

Now that we have reached the end of the tale of Bijan,
I shall mention once again the name of Afraasiyaab.
I shall recount his woes as he returns from the battlefield,
Where Rostam rendered the world black for him.

From what I have heard, the heart of the Tooranian king
Continuously reels with pain, desire, and greed.
He rushes to Khalokh[1] without pause,
Ashamed and not wishing to show his face,
His heart full of pain and worry.
He enters his palace with his skilled and wise men:
Piran, his advisor; Garsivaz,
Gharaakhan, Shiddeh, and Garsivan;
Hoomaan, Golbaad, and Farshidvard;
Rooeen, son of Piran, a battling whale.

Afraasiyaab unloads his heart, exposes past incidents,
And says, "Since I set the royal crown on my head,
The sun and moon have shone over me.
I have ruled over the most powerful men.
No one ever prompted me to flee.
Even during the time of Manoochehr Shah,
Iran-Zamin could not overcome Tooran-Zamin.
The Iranians today dare threaten my life
With a night assault within the limits of my own palace.
Weak men act in the way of warriors:
Like deer marching up to a lion's lair in defiance,
Like a pigeon flying right up to a falcon,

◇◇◇◇◇◇◇◇◇◇◇◇◇
1 Khalokh: A town in the land of Tooran.

PART FIFTEEN

Like gold seeking vengeance on cutting shears.

"We must gear ourselves for quick retribution
Or else we shall have to resign
And watch our land be given over to destruction.
My goal is to send messengers to all corners
Of the kingdom to gather thousands and thousands
Of riders from Tooran and Chin, strapped for battle,
To surround the Iranian host and fight everywhere."

After the king's speech, the wise men offer advice:
"We must cross the Jayhoon, sound the kettledrums
Upon the vast desert, gather an army in the city of Amu.[2]
We must do so in haste, by day and by night,
Without the luxury of a moment's waste.
This is the right place to engage in battle and bloodshed,
Where we must charge and assault Giv and Rostam.
They are proud heroes, conquerors of lands,
Brandishing swords doused in poison."

At these words, Afraasiyaab shines on his throne,
Beaming with joy and relief.
He blesses his wise men and heroes
According to the customs of war.
He summons a minister and dictates his command.
He dispatches envoys with letters to the Emperor of Chin,[3]
To the King of Khotan, and to rulers of every province.
He demands the hastening of troops everywhere,
For his thoughts have a tight grip on war,
And the memory of Rostam pulls at his heart.

Two weeks pass.
Armies from Chin and Khotan arrive in Tooran-Zamin.
The earth moves like a shimmering sea;
The surface of fields disappears beneath the mass of men.

Afraasiyaab summons to the cities herds of horses
Freely wandering through pastures.
He opens treasuries transferred secretly from father to son.

◇◇◇◇◇◇◇◇◇◇◇◇◇
2 Amu: A city near Amu Darya or the Jayhoon River.
3 The Emperor of Chin, or Faghfoor: Title given to the rulers of Chin, or China; gener-
ally allies of Afraasiyaab and subsequent rulers of Turks or Tooran-Zamin.

He reaches into pouches for dinars to distribute all around.

Soon the army is fully equipped and lacks for nothing.
Afraasiyaab selects fifty thousand brave men,
Men eager for battle and ready for war.
He says to Shiddeh, his courageous son
Who holds his head higher than the boldest lions,
"I entrust this army, ready to engage in battle, to you.
Go to war in the land of Khaarazm,[4]
Position yourself as its border's guardian,
And maintain yourself strapped for battle."

He then commands Piran to select fifty thousand
Additional Chini warriors and tells him,
"Advance toward the capital of Iran,
And seize the throne of the young king.
Refrain from talks of peace and amity.
Remain focused on war and enmity.
The one who mixes fire with water
Will injure both, one and the other."

The two noble and prudent heroes,
One aged and wise, the other young and bold,
Depart, enlightened by the king's advice.
The old man's nature is quiet and calm,
While the young man is full of trepidation.
Both are furnished with timpani, gold, mace, and sword,
And escorted by the sound of weapons,
Loud as the roar of thunder.

3 | Kay Khosrow Sends Goodarz
To Fight the Tooranians

The cruel Afraasiyaab, seed of an evil race,
Heart set on vengeance, enjoys neither rest nor sleep.
In the hopes of washing away his shame,
He sends troops left and right to stir up war.
He dips in poison the steel of spears,
Advancing three hundred thousand Tooranian riders,

◇◇◇◇◇◇◇◇◇◇◇◇◇◇◇
4 Khaarazm: In present-day Tajikistan and Afghanistan.

Armed for battle, toward the land of Iran.
They cross the Jayhoon, forcing its flows to simmer
And its spume to rise to the firmament.

The beat of drums deprives his men of sleep.
The blow of clarions and the din of bells
Trouble the Tooranians, who feel as if
Their hearts leap out of their chests.
If this host were to travel to Iran,
Its bravest lions would be in a constant state of agitation.

Afraasiyaab entrusts the border of Iran to Piran,
Stationing numerous troops there.
Finally, he sends fifty thousand battling horsemen
To the border of Khaarazm,
Under the command of Shiddeh of lion heart,
Whose sword strikes flames with terror.
This is a host as strong as an army of drunken elephants,
Its weight capable of leveling out mountains.

If a ruler plants the tree of injustice, he might as well
Abandon his empire, his fortune, and his throne.

News reaches the world king Khosrow
That an army from Tooran has entered the land of Iran.
With reports from his spies, he sits to deliberate
His mind full of thoughts, then he speaks to say,
"Leaders of sense, I have heard from wise men that
At the moment the moon of Tooran exhibits its face
In all its glory, it will be destroyed by the sun of Iran.
It is when the black serpent raises its head
To crawl before the stick that it is decidedly crushed."

Khosrow summons his wise men
And communicates to them the reports.
The king's leading advisors sit at his side:
Men such as Zaal and Rostam, Goodarz, Giv,
Shiddush, Rohaam, and Farhaad the brave;
Bijan, Ashkesh, Gostaham, Gorgeen, Zangueh
And Gojdaham; Tous, Nozar's proud son;
And Fariborz, noble offspring of Kaavoos.
The army leaders surround the world king in secrecy,
Ready to serve him as his loyal subjects.

The triumphant king says to his heroes,
"The Turks aim to seize the crown and throne.
Now that the enemy has mustered an army,
Now that it has honed its claws,
We must not lose time and at once prepare for war."

He asks for the blare of trumpets at the palace gates,
Brazen timpani placed on the backs of elephants.
He travels from palace to square.
His throne is lifted to sit atop an elephant.
The king climbs upon it and gives the signal
For departure by pitching the ball into a cup.[5]

You would think that the world is covered
In a layer of indigo, so dark is the air.
The earth dons all sorts of colors.
The army's brave men appear like leopards,
Mace in hand, hearts full of thoughts for battle.
The earth sags beneath the weight,
Like the sea fiercely tossing waves about.

A voice rises from the palace: "O great Iranian heroes,
Anyone skilled in the use of rein, stirrup, and weapon
Must not linger home but must prepare to march off."

Khosrow summons war riders, brave and able,
From the lands of Rum and India.
He calls for noble Taazian fighters
Outfitted for battle in the manner of wild lions,
And three hundred thousand desert riders
Strapped and armed with spears.

The king's envoys ride to the most remote corners,
Bearing the message that anyone who does not appear
Before him within the span of forty days
Will not have the honor of receiving a headdress.

Two weeks later, the entire empire resounds
With the clash of troops, just as the king wished for.
All the provinces are in a state of expectancy,
And a great hum makes the earth vibrate.

◇◇◇◇◇◇◇◇◇◇◇◇◇◇
5 Pitch a ball into a cup: A signal that calls for war.

PART FIFTEEN

One early morning, at the hour of the rooster's call,
The din of timpani rings out.
Great men from every land organize their troops
In rows before the royal palace.

Khosrow opens ancient treasures
And distributes coins to the army.
Enriched by the king's wealth and by his gold,
Warriors set golden diadems on their heads.
They appear with armor and trappings,
Forming a colossal mass of steel,
Broad and as bulky as a mountain.

Once the host is fully equipped,
Khosrow's heart is freed from worry.
First, he selects among the illustrious army
Thirty thousand sword-bearing cavaliers.
He entrusts them to Rostam, to whom he says,
"O illustrious warrior, lead these troops to Sistan
And then to India to fight my enemy.
Advance toward Ghaznein,[6] in the direction of Barein,[7]
Where you will find your crown, throne, and seal.
Once you have cleansed the land of the enemy's presence,
The leopard and the herds will have the chance
To drink from the same source.
Entrust Faraamarz with diadem and seal.
Let him select his troops.
He will make your kingdom blossom.
Let the din of trumpets, clarions, and timpani resound.
Do not linger in Kashmir or Kabol,
For the war against Afraasiyaab
Will warrant me neither food nor peace."

He then assigns the lands of Alaanan[8] and Ghoz Castle
To Lohraasp and says to him, "O hero of noble lineage,
Depart with a host as large as a mountain.
Select your troops among Iranian warriors.
Take riders skilled in battle to vanquish the enemy."

◇◇◇◇◇◇◇◇◇◇◇◇◇
6 Ghaznein: A city in Iran-Zamin, in present-day Afghanistan.
7 Barein: A city in Iran-Zamin.
8 Alaanan: Land in Iran-Zamin; Manoochehr's army captures the fortress of Alaanan
to bar Salm from taking shelter in it.

He orders Ashkesh to drive troops to Khaarazm,
Thirty-thousand bounding lions
Armed with spears, preceded by timpani,
An army resembling a fierce pack of wolves.
He says to him, "Set up camp in the land of Khaarazm,
Where you will launch a battle against Shiddeh."

Finally, the king places Goodarz at the head
Of the fourth army and directs him with exhortation:
"O brave man of heroic lineage,
Leave now with valuable chiefs from Iran
Such as Gorgeen, Zangueh, and Gostaham;
Shiddush, Farhaad, Khorraad, and Giv;
The leader Goraazeh, and the valiant Rohaam."
He commands them to cinch their waists for battle
And to depart without delay for the land of Tooran.

Upon the king's order,
Warriors and noblemen mount their horses.
Goodarz, son of Kashvaad,
Places himself at the head of troops.

The king says to him,
"Take your leave, strapped and prepared for war.
Refrain from executing the slightest injustice.
Keep at a distance from cultivated land.
Do not harm anyone who does not seek a dispute,
For the Creator condemns misdeeds.
This world is an illusion,
And our passage through it is merely transitory.
When you lead your army into the land of Tooran,
Do not surrender your heart
To fits of anger and your head to the blaze of fire.
Do not follow the example of Tous and lose yourself.
Refrain from sounding the timpani at every instant.
Always proceed with justice, and at all times,
Remember Yazdan, Donor of all that is good.
Send a man of experience to meet with Piran,
A cautious man who forgets nothing.
Let Piran listen to wise advice
And don for him the veil of friendship."

The army chief replies to the king,
"Your command is more inspiring than the moon itself.
I shall march as you direct.
You are king and world master, and I am at your service."

The earth resounds with the blast of clarions
And the clatter of troops as they march off in single file.
The air dims from the dust scattered by the horses' hooves.

Sixty elephants precede the host,
Making the earth buckle under their weight.
From these war elephants, four are bound in trappings,
With howdahs on their backs belonging to the king,
And a golden throne and crown, emblems of royalty.

Khosrow instructs Goodarz to take the golden seat.
Then he orders their departure,
Deeming as a good omen the dust rising to the sky.
He says, "We shall reduce Piran to smoke,
Like the dust scattered by these elephants."

The army sets in motion, as instructed by the king,
And marches from stage to stage
And place to place without facing obstacles.

4 | Giv Takes a Message From Goodarz to Piran

Once Goodarz approaches Raibad,[9]
He selects chiefs from among the Iranians,
One thousand spear-holding warriors ready for battle.
In addition, ten eloquent, noble riders
Are singled out from the army elite.

Then he summons Giv to head the troops
And conveys to him the king's demands:
"O my cautious son, your head surpasses many.
I have mustered a host for you,
Each soldier able to rule a nation.
Lead this convoy to Piran's side.

◇◇◇◇◇◇◇◇◇◇◇◇◇
9 Raibad: A city in Tooran-Zamin.

Speak to him and listen to his reply.
Tell him, 'I have entered the land of Tooran
          With an army, as dictated by my king.
          You are fully aware of your words and your actions.
          Remember peaceful times, as well as turbulent ones
          When noblemen, the king and his entire land
          Committed the most vicious crime.
          Remember when the illustrious Fereydoon
          Closed his eyes on the world, his heart wounded,
          His eyes' lashes inundated with tears.
          Remember when Iran and its king bewailed,
          And the moon no longer shone as it dwelt
          In a state of mourning over the death of Iraj.
          All these troubles were instigated by Salm and Toor.
          You, alone among the Turks, expressed affection.
          But your character was wrongfully assessed,
          And your reputation is inauthentic and false.
          I discern in your heart neither compassion nor peace.

          'Khosrow, king full of mercy, asked me
          To address you with sweet and gentle words.
          He told me to remind you that,
          During the time of Siaavoosh,
          You never leaned toward bad deeds,
          That he always regarded you with utmost respect,
          Certain of your innocence in his father's murder.
          All your sins up until now toward the world king
          Will be cast aside and forgiven,
          And honored by the Shah as good deeds.
          You must not perish at my hands,
          For all your actions are in the past.

          'Also think that in the course of the war against
          Afraasiyaab, fate may prepare a quick end for you.
          Iran's noblemen and my son relate to you my advice.
          Tell them what you know; ask them your questions.
          If your heart and tongue speak in agreement,
          You can envisage your worries as a thing of the past
          And your life as if spared.
          Your land and your family will prosper,
          And your head will not fall prey to my sword's tip.
          But if you give way to the suspicion of betrayal,

Your life will not be spared by the king.
We shall have in this war neither rest nor sleep.
I shall charge with my mace on the battlefield,
Go after Afraasiyaab, and that is sufficient.

'My king will not need many troops to seek vengeance.
If you wish to follow my advice, point by point,
If you agree to my wise words,
Extract yourself from the gathering of leaders.
Leave the side of those who gave birth to this hatred,
Who rolled up their sleeves to spill blood,
Who reached out to pluck out Siaavoosh's life,
For the injustice of this act weighs heavily on men.
Bind them up like dogs and surrender them to me
To take before the king, who will decide their fate,
Whether to show mercy or send them to be executed.

'The world master has written their names in books.
Have you never heard the great story
That the wild lion told the wolf?
          "Providence reserves a seat level with the dust
          For the one who raises his hand to shed royal blood."
Furthermore, all your wealth
Will be the adversary of your dim heart.
Send me your noble stallions, your jewels and brocade,
Your dinars, your gold, your diadems, helmets and swords,
Your trappings, your armors and Indian daggers,
Your weapons, troops, gold and silver,
Send them to me with no exceptions.
Send what you have received unfairly from men,
What you have amassed through your crimes.
Use these to buy back your heart
And assure a quick remedy to your ailments.

'Among this wealth, I shall send to the world king
The pieces that are worthy of him.
I shall distribute the rest to the army
As a way to atone for your sins.
Finally, send me your son, guardian of throne and seal,
As well as your two brothers, army leaders,
Who stretch their necks as high as the moon.
Once you hand over as hostages these three men

From your illustrious family,
I shall then trust your sincerity.
The tree of loyalty will bear your fruit.

'Observe now these two paths stretched before you.
Take the one that leads to King Khosrow.
Go to the shah with your family,
Bask in the shadow of his affection.
Pluck from your heart any bond to Afraasiyaab.
Refuse to see him even at night in dream.
I promise you that our king will raise your head
As high as the shining sun.
No one knows better than you the love in his heart
And how his actions are never unworthy of a ruler.

'But if fear of the Tooranian king
Prevents you from traveling to Iran-Zamin,
Then secretly leave Tooran, travel to the city of Chaadj,
Take your seat on your throne of poplar wood,
And make your crown shine over the land.
If, on the other hand, you feel devoted to Afraasiyaab,
Return to his court. Do not remain here to fight us,
For you must not pretend to measure yourself against me.
I possess the strength of a lion and the claws of a leopard.
I shall completely destroy the fortune of the Turks.
My arrow is a cloud dripping a thick shower of poison.

'Now if this does not deter you,
If you still wish to fight and march against Iran,
Then your head is full of evil thoughts and treachery.
If you think you can withstand the voracious lion,
Then prepare your weapons, rise, and advance toward us.
Once the two hosts form their ranks, then the line
Between the guilty and innocent will be incontestable.
If you fail to listen to my advice,
You will regret it for the rest of your days.
This remorse will not serve you well when the sword
Of providence turns up to harvest your head.'"

In this way speaks Goodarz, noble world hero,
Asking his son to repeat his discourse, word for word.

5 | Giv Visits Piran in Viseh-Guerd

After having committed Goodarz's bitter words
To memory, Giv takes leave of his father,
He takes off in the direction of Balkh, where he stops
To send a messenger ahead as Goodarz instructed.

At the descent of night, he gathers his escort,
Exits Balkh, and takes the direction of Viseh-Guerd,
Where Piran awaits with an army
To seize the throne and crown.

As soon as the envoy arrives at the side of Piran,
The latter recognizes him as a member of the Iranian host.
The messenger reveals that Giv is in Balkh,
Accompanied by renowned heroes.

Piran listens eagerly to his words.
His men shout and holler.
He calls for the sound of trumpets and timpani.
The horses' hooves turn the earth as black as ebony.

One hundred ten thousand eager cavaliers assemble.
He leaves two-thirds in place
And marches off with the most skilled.
On the banks of the River Jayhoon, Piran sets up camp
And aligns his troops to create a massive wall of spears.
There he meets Giv, son of Goodarz.

They remain two weeks discussing a just course of action.
The Iranians propose options as Piran listens to them,
But the bad faith of the Turks bares a wicked face.

As the Iranian army's brave men
Unfurl their tongues' eloquence, Piran deploys
A rider in haste to Afraasiyaab with a brief message:
"Goodarz, son of Kashvaad, army leader,
Shelters beneath his helm the throne of Iran.
He has sent to my side as envoy Giv, his dear son,
The most powerful man of his land.
But my heart and my ear follow only your command,
And my life warrants blind obedience to you."

Once this message is delivered,
The leader of Tooran selects an army of brave warriors.
He sends thirty thousand sword-bearing men to Piran
And says to him, "Draw the blade of vengeance.
Free the earth from the burden of the Iranians.
We must allow neither Goodarz nor Giv to survive,
Neither Rohaam the warrior, nor Farhaad or Gorgeen.
I shall gather around me a great number of riders,
Eager to conquer the throne
And convert the land of Iran into a flood of blood.
With the guidance and assistance of my brave leaders,
I shall destroy Kay Khosrow once and for all!"

Witness to the number of bloodthirsty troops,
Piran's sense of strength is fortified,
And he can breathe only battle and feud.
He banishes from his heart any vestiges of virtue
And abandons himself completely to violence.
This man, naturally good, becomes wild and ferocious.
He hollers and shouts and thinks of nothing but war.

He says to Giv, "Stand up and leave!
Return to your army leader.
From four sides troops are coming to my aid,
All eager to snatch the throne of Iran.
Tell Goodarz not to ask anything of me
That wise men would disapprove of.
His first demand is for me to surrender
A certain number of our men and heroes.
How could that be possible?
Next, he expects me to cast aside weapons,
Horses and troops, throne and crown,
My brother, so dear to me, my cherished son, my hero.
How someone so wise speak such nonsense?
I prefer death to such a life, and, although
I am a prince, I shall become a slave.
The story goes that a leopard coming upon
A fight with a brave lion once said,
        'Better shed blood in battle than live a life of shame.'
Furthermore, I received word from my king,
And an army has already arrived at my side,
Geared up and ready to engage in battle."

After receipt of this reply,
Giv returns with escort and illustrious heroes.

The moment Giv departs, Piran, the leader,
Prepares for battle, shouting the cry of war.
He takes the road, and, once approaching Konaabad,[10]
He makes his army descend to the foot of the mountain.

6 | The Two Armies Form Their Lines of Battle

Giv arrives at his father's side
And reports the reply, point by point.
He says to Goodarz,
"Take your army to a place where we can fight,
For Piran's unjust heart is not intent on peace.
We have relayed to him all your words.
But the Turks' betrayal exposed itself in full light.
Piran dispatched an envoy on camelback to Afraasiyaab
To give an account of the circumstances:
The arrival of Goodarz and Giv, their desire to fight,
And how he has hastened reinforcements.
Afraasiyaab immediately sent an army that crossed
The River Jayhoon just as we were on our way back.
Now, out of vengeance, he has placed war timpani
On the backs of elephants, prepared to initiate war."

Goodarz replies to Giv, "Piran is weary of life.
I expected this from such an evil man.
Yet we were obliged to communicate with him
At the king's order. We had no choice.
The shah wished to test Piran's loyalty.
I was telling the king a story
When he commanded me to set the army in motion.
I was telling him to pluck from his heart
Any remnant of affection for this man
Whose words do not conform to his heart's sentiments.
Piran clearly directs his love to the Turks,
And all that remains for our king
Is to renounce his faith in him.

◇◇◇◇◇◇◇◇◇◇◇◇◇
10 Konaabad: A city in Tooran-Zamin.

The bold Piran followed Giv in haste,
Rushing his army's march, fierce as a lion."

Once Goodarz learns of the army's approach,
He exits the city of Raibad to the beat of timpani.
Streaming from behind the mountain, he emerges
Onto the vast plain, fixing his troops to camp there.

As Piran drives his army out of Konaabad,
The light of day dims. He brings to the desert
A mass of troops, as large as a mountain,
And his divisions descend, one after the other,
One hundred thousand Turk riders sheathed in armor
And strapped for battle, sporting steel helmets.
They are eager to engage in war,
With spear in one hand, Indian sword in the other.

The blare of trumpets resounds.
One would think the mountain trembles
From Raibad to Konaabad.
The earth disappears beneath armed men.
Mountain and plain turn black.
The dust of the riders dims the light of day.
The air solidifies into an iron mass,
A sort of armor, from the points of spears.
Lances shimmer like stars; swords blaze like the sun.
The earth appears to be made of steel, the clouds of dust.
Heroes' voices boom in echoes.

Goodarz observes the Tooranian army, beneath which
The earth swells and bends like an ocean surge.
Banners and army corps line up, one after the other,
Until they are swallowed by the descending night gloom.

At dusk, elephants are placed strategically to block the road.
Fires are lit on both sides.
Such is the cry of heroes, eager for battle,
That one might think the earth is permeated by Ahrimans.
From hem to sleeve, one discerns only enemy troops.
The beating of drums splits open the hearts of rocks,
Enveloped by a night that is pitch black.

As daybreak climbs to peek above the mountain,

PART FIFTEEN

The leader of the Iranian host straddles a fresh horse,
Places himself at the head of the army
To assign each warrior his post.

To the right stands the mountain,
The struggle of the brave unable to make it budge.
To the left flows a river of fresh water,
So beautiful in proximity, as if body to soul.

Behind the spear riders are infantrymen
With shields and arrows able to puncture steel armor,
Each bow draped around an arm,
Each heart boiling over with avenging blood.

Behind them are cavaliers heavily equipped,
Swords stealing their luster from the fire's core.
Further behind these troops is a mass of elephants
Beneath whose weight the ground caves in.

In the midst of the army surges the blessed banner,
Resplendent like the moon with countless precious stones.
The sight of the purple swords,
Gleaming beneath the Kaaviani standard,
Makes one think the sky sows stars in the dark of night.

Goodarz decks his army like paradise, and he plants
The tree of vengeance in the king's garden of allegiance.
He entrusts the right wing to Fariborz
While Hojir takes the rear with supplies and baggage.
Goraazeh, from the seed of Giv,
And Zavaareh, guardian of Kianian throne,
Hasten to assist Fariborz, placing their troops beside his.

Then Goodarz says to Rohaam,
"O great hero, glory of the Kianian crown and throne,
Go with your riders to the left wing, where you will shine
Like a Nowruz sun under the sign of the ram.
You will illuminate the army with your splendor.
You will take it beneath your wing,
And like a fierce lion, you will battle heroes
With this shining, man-devouring sword."

Rohaam departs with his escort,

At the head of which is Gostaham, followed by Gojdaham
And Fooroohal, whose shots fly to reach the firmament.

Goodarz commands Giv to take ten thousand cavaliers,
Riding horses clad in steel, and assigns him the rearguard,
A post worthy of the most eager warriors.
Two brave men, Gorgeen and Zangueh of Shaavaran,
Escort Giv on his way.

Then Goodarz sends three hundred men with banners
To guard the host on the river's edge and other places.

At the mountain is a banner with three hundred noble riders.
A sentinel is posted on its crest who stretches his neck,
Day and night, to spy on the Tooranian army,
Whose eyes are so piercing he can identify,
From a distance, the legs of an ant crossing the road.
At the sound of his cry, the leader would rise.

Finally, Goodarz lays down the battlefield in a manner
As to give sun and moon the urge to take part in war.
With an army chief so worthy of command,
His troops fear nothing, not even a valiant whale.

Goodarz then takes his post to stake out
The enemy's undertakings against his army.
He plants before him the banner, delight of dim hearts,
And assigns posts to those who lead the core.
Bringing together the heroes,
He places Shiddush behind him and Farhaad ahead.
Positioned at the center of his warriors,
The leader Goodarz waves the Kaaviani banner,
So glorious it outshines sun and moon.

From afar, Piran observes the enemy host,
Its war apparatus, its aligned troops whose dim hearts
Have not yet experienced the rusting effects of worry.
They have no knowledge yet of these ravines, mountains,
Fields, and plains so covered with spears standing on end,
And horses' reins interwoven through and through.

The leader Piran is shaken by a wave of fury,
Cursing the eclipsed sun of his fortune.

He then glances over at his own army
And deems the battlefield no longer suitable for him.
He sees neither the space for battle nor the place for ranks,
And, in his rage, he strikes his hands together.

He endeavors to fix everything, as one must
When it comes down to waging war.
From among his glorious troops,
He picks the ones most ready to fight,
And from Afraasiyaab's men,
Those exhibiting the most ardor for vengeance.
He assembles a corps of thirty thousand men,
Armed with swords and ready for battle,
Entrusting the heart of these avid troops to Hoomaan.

He summons Andariman and Akhvaast,
The support and leadership of the army,
Handing them the left wing,
Composed of a corps of thirty thousand warriors.
Lahaak the brave and Farshidvard form the right wing,
Along with thirty thousand men of courage.
The earth in its entirety is blackened by steel.

He sends Zangaleh the valiant, Kolbaad,
And Sepahram, the hero reserved for a day of need,
Along with ten thousand renowned spear-holding men,
To form a corps at the rear, holders of piercing daggers.
Rooeen, the indomitable, is to stand ambush in the forest
With ten thousand warriors from Khotan,
Placing himself in their midst like a lion.
He sends sentinels to the river's edge and to the mountainside
To frighten the leader of Iran and make him tremble for his fate.
If he were to reach beyond the battlefield,
Rooeen would then attack him from behind like a pouncing lion.

Sentinels are placed on mountain heights to gaze out,
Day and night, and as soon as an Iranian rider
Is visible in the distance, swinging his horse's reins,
Appearing to be on the verge of attacking,
The sentinel is to call out and stir up the army camp.

7 | Bijan Asks Permission to Engage in Battle

Two armies come face to face,
Composed of eager, distinguished warriors.
They remain so still for three days and three nights
You would think not a single man stirs or moves his lips.

Goodarz says, "If I leave my post and advance
Toward the Tooranians, an army corps will pounce on me,
And I shall clutch nothing but a fistful of wind."

Day and night, he stands at the army head,
Hoping to foresee an outcome from sun and moon,
Searching for the opportune day to take action,
When the tempest of war would rise,
Rendering the combatants' eyes blind with dust.

He says to his heart, "May I gain the upper hand!
May I fling my army onto the Tooranians,
Like a fierce and vicious hurricane!"

On his side, Piran observes keenly, rage stirring his heart,
Waiting for the moment when Goodarz will advance.
Having failed to secure the rear, troops hiding in ambush
Find a way to take them from behind.

On the fourth day, Bijan rushes from the rear
To the vanguard and presents himself before his father.
His suit's collar in shreds, tossing dust to the sky,
He says to Giv, "O father full of experience,
How can you so foolishly maintain yourself motionless?
The fifth day is upon us, and nothing is happening,
Neither by day nor by night. All we do is rest.
The sun has not yet witnessed either the drawing of swords
Or the dust of our motions stirring the air.
Riders are geared for war, helmets are secured on heads,
But it is as if no blood flows through their veins.
The weight of their armor bears down on them.
After the glorious Rostam, there is no one in all of Iran
With the horsemanship skills of Goodarz.

PART FIFTEEN

But since he returned from the battle of Pashan,[11]
With all its carnage on the vast field,
To the battle of Laadan[12], where he witnessed
The fall of a great number of his sons
And the plunge of the fortune of the Iranians,
Goodarz's heart is broken, he has lost his way,
And he no longer wishes to take part in war.

"One must consider his old age.
His sights are set on the dome of sky,
And he who has a vast army
Spends his time counting the stars around the moon.
The blood coursing through his limbs has dried up.
He is too weak to fight with valiant men.
It is not the aged Goodarz who surprises me
But the Goodarz whose thoughts
No longer celebrate his land.

"It is you, O father, who surprises me,
You, from whom lions borrow their courage.
Two armies have their eyes fixed on you.
Show them some ardor, ignite your wrath.
At this time, when the world is warm, the air serene,
The army is in want of the command to fight.
Once the fair season has eluded us,
Once the earth is frozen hard as steel,
Our hands will be solidly bound to our spears.
We will have the snow beneath us, the war before us.
Who among our heroes will then have the will to fight?
If you fear an ambush, if you fear vengeance seekers,
Give me one thousand select brave riders.
We shall convert their ambush into dust
And fling their heads beyond the surface of the moon."

Giv smiles at Bijan's speech
And showers his heroic son with praise.
He addresses the Justice Giver:
"I am grateful that you have given me a son
Who distinguishes between good and bad,

◇◇◇◇◇◇◇◇◇◇◇◇◇
11 Battle of Pashan: Battle where the Iranians lost heavily to the Tooranians.
12 Battle of Laadan: Battle where the Iranians lost heavily to the Tooranians.

And for having endowed him with strength,
With noble thoughts, and with compassion,
Making him wise in all things and passionate for battle.
I am grateful that this valiant young man,
The son of a warrior hero, has been returned to me.
A lion once said to his mate,
> 'If our son lacks courage,
> We shall snatch our affection from him.
> We shall break the bonds uniting us to him.
> May the waters of the sea serve him as father
> And the dust as mother!'

"You, my son, do not denounce your grandfather.
He has much experience and is far wiser than we are.
Commander of this vast army,
He is a man accustomed to world affairs,
Who needs no advice from others.
If our riders suffer from the weight of their armor,
The Turks do not live in the folds of luxury.
They are miserable; they are losing their minds.
Their eyes are filled with tears,
Their hearts seething with blood.
The old, cunning Goodarz wishes to force the Turks
To advance and be the first to adopt an offensive.
As soon as they turn their backs to the mountain,
He will ambush them.
The troops eager for war will fall upon them.
You will then witness how Goodarz's mace
Will sweep over the entire border.
He is watching the rotation of the sky,
To see in it our good and bad omens.
Once the propitious day has arrived,
He will decidedly free the earth of our enemy."

To his illustrious father, Bijan replies, "O noble leader,
If my blessed grandfather wishes to give us permission,
We shall refrain from donning our Rumi coats of mail.
I shall cast aside armor and helmet.
I shall drink wine until my pale cheeks
Absorb a deep ruby color.
Should the world hero need me, instantly
I shall cinch my waist and strap myself for battle."

8 | Hoomaan Asks Permission to Engage in Battle

In the camp of Turks, the brave Hoomaan stomps over
To his brother like a fierce lion and cries out to him,
"O warrior, Afraasiyaab promised us war,
But we have reached the fifth day,
And though we are strapped and ready,
We stand impatient on this field.
Iron erodes our sides with the desire for vengeance.
Our hearts and eyes are fastened on the land of Iran.
Why do you stare into the enemy's face?
What thoughts does your heart foster?
Reveal them to me.
If you wish to fight, then engage in battle.
If you wish to withdraw, then do not linger here,
For your honor suffers, O great hero,
And you will incite young and old to laugh at us.

"This host is here to engage in war.
We find ourselves dishonored and pale of cheeks.
Had we taken action, we would have colored
The earth crimson as a blooming rose with blood.
But we have not lost a single illustrious rider,
And our troops have no warrior of Rostam's race.
If you wish to refrain from spilling blood,
You have no need for such a host.
Select a valiant warrior, entrust him to me,
And observe the developments on this battlefield."

At these words, Hoomaan retorts, "Do not act in haste!
Do not lose your temper with me!
Know, my brother, that the warrior advancing toward us
With a vast army is the leader of warriors
From the court of Kay Khosrow, a bold and mighty hero.
No one carries his head higher than the Iranian monarch,
Not even our own king!
Secondly, I know no warlord in the king's court
Equal in rank to Goodarz or as proud, as valiant,
As wise of counsel, and as cautious in his ventures.

"Thirdly, his heart is burdened by grief.
He is eager to avenge the deaths of his many sons,

Whom we left deprived of heads
On a ground tinted with blood from end to end.
As long as his soul dwells in his body, he will not cease
To writhe like a coiling serpent to find a way to retaliate.
Fourthly, he has centralized his host
At the junction of two mountains.
We can find no path leading to them.
Reflect on this, for it is not an easy feat.
We must find a way to bring them out of their shelter.
Let us be patient until they tire and are the first
To make a move and emerge toward us.

"Once Goodarz leads his troops out of the mountains,
I shall inflict on him an ominous shower of shots.
We shall raise around them a wall of steel
And, like fierce lions, extract life from them.
We shall do as we please to elevate our names to the sun.
You are the support and leader of the king's army.
You sport your diadem higher than the circle of Saturn.
How then could a man who has no need to pursue fame
Allow himself to be conquered by greed?
Besides, none of the brave Iranian warriors
Will come forward to fight the bellowing leopard.
If they were to select, from among their soldiers,
An unknown, ambitious man,
Eager to fight you in vengeance,
If you were to unroll the surface of the earth before him,
Such an act would not win you fame.
The Iranians would suffer no grave injury,
While our valiant Turks would feel disheartened
And feeble should the enemy spill your blood."

Hoomaan weighs his brother's words carefully.
Now certain of Piran's foolishness, he retorts,
"None of the Iranian cavaliers will dare
Measure himself against my person.
Your nature leads you to mercy,
While mine leads me to battle.
If you entertain no thought of contention,
If the fire of courage is extinguished in your heart,
I shall saddle my stallion of speed,
And at the dawn of day I shall incite the fight."

9 | Hoomaan Challenges Rohaam

Hoomaan returns to his quarters, teeth clenched,
A wild boar honing its tusks.
At the crack of dawn, he rises and mounts his horse
In the manner of a raging lion.
Escorted by an interpreter,
He presents himself before the Iranian army,
Heart engulfed in zeal, head yearning for vengeance.

Piran learns that his brother has departed to fight.
Overwhelmed with dread,
He feels the world contract around him.
His heart pounds with concern for Hoomaan,
And he repeats a story he remembers from his father:
"A wise man must act with caution in all matters
And not allow anger to rush him to engage in war.
A foolish man, quick to lose his temper,
Will sink into a state of misery.
If pearls were to drop from such a brainless head,
They would be devoid of value.
Since Hoomaan allowed himself to fall prey to anger,
I do not envisage any good coming out of this affair.
May the World Master come to his aid!
I see for him no other way out."

On the battlefield, Hoomaan, son of Viseh,
Ready to stir up a fight, confronts Goodarz's troops.
The patrol of the round espies him and his band of riders.
He advances toward the interpreter
As the Iranians look on with concern.

The patrol asks the interpreter, "Why does this warrior
Venture foolishly, rushing onto the field like a courier,
With mace in hand and noose on saddle?
Where does he wish to go on his horse of speed?"

The interpreter replies to the Iranians,
"The time is upon us to make use of sword, mace,
And arrow, for this renowned warrior
Of lion heart challenges you to a fight.
His name is Hoomaan, leader of the family of Viseh,

Who sheaths his sword inside a lion's heart."
As the Iranians observe his mace, armor, and royal stance,
Their hands equipped with spear abstain from battle
Out of sheer respect for the renowned hero.
They retreat before him, turn to the interpreter, and say,
"Go speak to Hoomaan in the language of Turks
And repeat to him all that we say.
Tell him we wish to abstain from fighting against him.
Tell him, 'Goodarz does not grant us permission.
        If you are keen on battle, the way is clear for you
        To present yourself before the glorious leader.'"

They point out to Hoomaan the noble army chiefs.
They show him where each, great and small, stands
And indicate to him who commands the right wing
And who is in command of the left.

The leader of the sentries sends a swift rider
To tell the hero that Hoomaan has exited his camp
Like a leopard and is arriving to fight.

Hoomaan passes the line of sentries, approaches Rohaam,
And shouts, "O son of the blessed army leader,
Mount your horse and advance between the two hosts.
You direct the army's left wing.
You are the support of Iran's leader and the claws of lions.
You must measure yourself against me.
Choose a field, either on the river's edge or on the mountainside.
If you refuse to accept my challenge,
Then may Gostaham and Fooroohal do so.
Who among your brave men wishes
To stand up to me with sword, spear, and mace?
Anyone who accepts my challenge will be met with a fate
That will make his feet lose hold of the ground,
For the lion's heart and the leopard's skin
Split open at the sight of my sword."

Rohaam replies, "O famous hero, eager for battle,
I imagined you as the most sensible of Turks.
I took you for a different sort of man.
You show up alone on the battlefield.
You expose yourself bravely before a vast host.

You think there is not, in the entire world,
A rider wielding sword to match your skills.
Reflect on this Kianian saying
And borrow wisdom from it to save your head.
Remember a story from the past,
And raise your neck higher toward freedom:
          'Whoever flings himself in battle first
          Need not find the way back.'

"All those whose names you mentioned
Are eager to accept your offer of contention.
But none of them can do so
Without the order of the royal army leader.
If you wish to engage in battle,
Then why don't you ask the eminent Goodarz
For permission to measure our strength against yours?
Once it is granted, we shall welcome your affronts."

Hoomaan retorts, "Do not utter such foolishness!
Do not seek an excuse to evade me.
You deem this spear a mere spindle.
You are neither a rider
Nor a warrior apt to execute vengeance."

10 | Hoomaan Challenges Fariborz

Then Hoomaan rushes like a raging elephant
To the army core with his interpreter
And approaches Fariborz.
He hollers, "O man of ill repute,
You lower your head before men of high standing.
You once had riders, elephants,
Golden boots, and Kaaviani banner.
You were forced to restore them to the Tooranians.
The warriors of Iran do not consider you brave.
You were born a prince but became a low-ranking man.
You should strap yourself like a slave.
You are the brother of the noble Siaavoosh.
You are of higher birth than your leader.
You must now come and face me on the battlefield.
You are worthy of conflict. Prepare yourself for it.

My lineage goes back to Toor, King of Tooran-Zamin,
And, like you, I come from a noble, royal race.
Come and face me in the arena; confront our troops.
Once you march against me, your name
Will rise all the way to the shining sun.
But if a fight against me does not suit you,
Check and see where Zavaareh and Goraazeh stand.
Bring to me one of the renowned Iranian warriors."

Fariborz replies, "Do not seek battle with a vicious lion!
Such is the outcome of a clash: One is happy and victorious,
While the other is vanquished and sad.
When you triumph, you must fear pending trouble,
For the sublime dome of sky never spins with constancy.
A quarreling man acts in such a way that, in the end,
His home remains vacant and uninhabited.
If the king seized my banner, he had the right to do so.
He entrusts whomever he wishes
With his elephants and army
In all the wars, since the time of Kay Ghobaad.

"The leader Goodarz, son of Kashvaad, was the one
Who placed the crown of power on royal heads,
The one ready and strapped for war
Only to move the world to blossom in peace.
Goodarz is a constant figure at the head of the army.
From father to son, members of his family
Have been loyal subjects, fierce warriors,
And great defenders of throne and crown.
In the end, it will be his mace
That will bring down your army leader.
He has the right to command us, lead us in war.
His share will be the return of either shame or glory.
Should he allow me to measure myself against you,
He will place a salve on my body's wounds.
You will see how I wash away my disgrace
When I step onto the battlefield!"

Hoomaan replies, "Enough!
Your speech has no power against actions.
Why do you hope to shun war
With a blunt sword only able to cut grass?

Should you assail me with your measly mace,
It will cause little impact on my armor and helmet."

11 | Hoomaan Challenges Goodarz

Hoomaan takes off so impetuously
He takes on the appearance of a wicked deev.
Strapped for battle to exact retribution,
He approaches Goodarz, son of Kashvaad,
And yells out, "O proud, arrogant leader,
I have knowledge of your message to Kay Khosrow
And of the fact that you have driven your army here.
I know of the king's counsel, his gifts, and your oath,
Which you have conveyed to Piran the leader.
I am aware that your son Giv, the army's support,
Has intruded upon the Tooranian camp
Disguised as a messenger to spy on us.
I know of your oath sworn by king, sun, and moon,
By throne and crown, to wipe out Piran
As soon as your eyes fall on him on the battlefield.

"You have equipped your army like a raging lion,
Desiring battle with all of your will.
But now you take shelter behind the ridge,
Eyes aghast, like a timid mountain goat.
You resemble a wild animal hunted by a lion,
A deer seeking a narrow corner of the forest,
Too fearful of death to claim fame and glory.
Lead, for once, your army to the field.
Why do you conceal it behind the mountains?
Is this what you promised Kay Khosrow,
To use these heights as ramparts in times of war?"

Goodarz retorts, "Spend some time in reflection
So that your words may deserve an answer!
No one in this army wishes to reply to you.
In your ignorance, you blame this on me.
Let me tell you that, as it is the king's command,
I am bound by oath and duty to obey.
I have come with a vast host,
With valiant leaders plucked from Iran-Zamin,

But you hold yourselves back in the forest
Like aging, cowardly foxes fearful of the hunter.
You rely on tricks and artifice,
Then run away before noose, mace, and spear.
Guard yourselves from acts of heroism
Or from provoking us, for the fox
Dares not venture out to assail a fierce lion!"

After hearing Goodarz out,
Hoomaan leaps like a lion onto the battlefield
And retorts, "If you do not engage in a fight with me,
It has nothing to do with your status.
Ever since you witnessed the battle of Pashan,
You have avoided every opportunity
To measure yourself against the Tooranians.
In the war of Laadan, you had the chance
To experience my skills and my strength.
You have often witnessed my fearlessness,
And you have praised me on the battlefield.
But if it is as you say, if you wish to remain loyal
To your words, then select a soldier from your host
And send him to fight against me on this field.

"I have challenged Fariborz and Rohaam.
I have spanned your entire host in search of a warrior,
But none has advanced to contend with me.
They stand subject to the commands of Goodarz.
Accosting them was ineffective.
You are the man who says that, on the day of battle,
You will cover the mountain with tulips of blood.
Find someone to test his hand against me
And use his heavy mace vengefully.
You have a great number of illustrious sons and heroes
Who are ready, their waists cinched for battle.
Summon one of them to oppose me.
Why do you prolong a fight if your humor is warlike?"

The famed leader reflects for a long time:
"Who among my men is able to grapple with him?
If I send a raging lion, one of my noble warriors,
He will kill the enemy on this battlefield,
And no other Turk will dare come to fight.

Hoomaan's warriors will tremble with grief.
Heartbroken, they will no longer seek conflicts.
Piran's army will remain in the Mountain of Konaabad,
And our hands will be tied and useless.
Better then to refrain from giving in to a clash.
Better for us to cut the road for them in an ambush,
Unless he triumphs, and his host confronts us in war."

Goodarz finally says to Hoomaan, "Leave!
You are brisk in speech and lacking in experience!
As soon as you opened your mouth to speak,
I knew what you were about to say
And what you wished to hide.
Is there no one among the Turks with the slightest sense,
No one who knows how to take advice
And to find contentment in his own reflections?
Do you not know that a raging lion, on the day of battle,
Does not sully his claws with the blood of a fox?

"Furthermore, when two armies are equipped as
These are, standing tall with pride and earnestness,
Would we allow two men to fight
While the others impatiently bite their fingers?
You must make your host advance and strike en masse.
Return now to your camp!
Hold your head high before your leader!
Tell him you enticed the Iranians,
But they did not move to action.
Tell him they did nothing more than emit a sigh.
Then your name will expand among the ranks,
And Piran will fulfill all your wishes."

His voice unnerving, Hoomaan replies,
"Who then are your heroes and army chiefs?
I remember a story told by world ruler Afraasiyaab:
'If you long for the Kianian throne, resist temptation.
But if you persist, then do not turn your face
Away from the burning flame.'
You do not wish to fight,
But should you wish to collect roses,
Be aware of stems fraught with thorns.
Have you no man of lion heart willing

To measure himself against me before the two hosts?
You seek to cast me aside by way of deceit and ruse,
But if you knew me, you would realize that I am not one
To allow myself to be taken by the likes of you!"

The noblemen, eager for battle, plead with Goodarz:
"This is not reasonable!
Send one of us to defy this miserable Turk!"

Goodarz replies, "Today is not the day to fight!"

Hoomaan, weary of speech, is overtaken by anger.
Like a valiant lion, he turns his back on the leader.
All the while snickering, he runs to the camp guard,
Binds his bow, and strikes four riders,
Flinging them to the ground.
Once the army guardians spot this proud Tooranian
Shooting at them from afar, they leave the path open
And flee without any attempt to strike back.

Hoomaan charges to the heights like a drunken man,
And the mountain bends at the strength of his cries.
He makes his spear twirl above his head
And bellows, "Hoomaan is the victorious hero!"

The sound of brazen trumpets rises into the air.
The warriors of the Turkish host rub their helmets
Against the sphere of the moon.

Witnessing Hoomaan's triumphant departure,
Goodarz stands astonished at his audacity.
His heart is overcome with shame,
An embarrassment that fills him with anger.
So humiliated does he feel before his warriors
That sweat crawls down his back.
Yet he is able to draw a happy omen from this occurrence.
He says, "They are the ones who provoke the bloodshed.
Misfortune falls on those who indulge in evil deeds."

He observes the heroes to assess which ones
Would be willing to engage in fight.

12 | Bijan Learns of Hoomaan's Deeds

Bijan hears the news of Hoomaan's arrival,
How he approached his grandfather like a lion;
Stirred up the troops left and right,
Challenging them to contend with him;
How he turned his back in anger and disdain
At the fact that no one accepted a confrontation;
How he brutally struck four cavaliers down.

Bijan enters a fit of rage, assuming a leopard's stance.
Restless and eager to get his hands on Hoomaan,
He demands a horse of elephant strength
To be saddled, the one he rides in times of battle.
He dons his Rumi coat of mail,
Clasps the girth of his black stallion, Shabrang,
And charges toward Giv in a great surge of fury,
Wishing to argue with his father.

He says to Giv, "O father, have I not revealed to you,
Point by point, the way Goodarz has lost his mind?
Do you not perceive, from the manner in which he acts,
That he is not the same man?
His reasoning is overtaken by fear.
His heart simmers and overflows with blood.
His state of being results from the immense grief
Caused by the death of his many sons, and the way
Their heads were severed, and his troops destroyed.
The proof of his foolhardiness is evident:
Here comes a Turk wishing to assail our warriors.
He appears before my grandfather, brandishing his spear,
Hollering like a mad elephant.
Not a single rider from our glorious army can fight him,
To lift him by the tip of his spear as one skewers poultry.
O my dear and caring father, I plead with you,
Dress my shoulders in Siaavoosh's armor!
I must be the one to challenge Hoomaan and none other.
Only I am able to pulverize this man into dust."

Giv says to his son, "O wise offspring, listen to me:
I have already warned you not to act in haste
Or to denounce Goodarz.

He has more experience and more wisdom than us.
Besides, he is the leader of this glorious army.
He is surrounded by riders full of courage,
Well able to stand against this elephant.
You fill my heart with grief, for I fear it is merely
Youth's impulse that foolishly sweeps over you,
Making you raise your head and rush to me,
Consumed by such a degree of passion.
I do not consent to your demand.
Do not speak further of this matter."

Bijan says to him, "Since you do not wish to help me,
Since you show no interest in elevating my glory,
I shall plead to the army leader.
I shall be strapped, hand placed on my chest,
Eager to contend with Hoomaan."

He hurls his horse forward, turns his back on his father,
And calmly rides in the direction of Goodarz.
He approaches him, praises him, and, heart wounded,
Says to him, "O hero and protector of the king,
Master of the earth, adornment of the throne,
You have experience in all matters.
While I have little reason, I am confused by your strategy.
You have turned this field into a garden,
And your heart has ceased to occupy itself
With the struggle against the Turks.
Today is the seventh day that we are here.
Why do we stand inactive day and night?
The sun does not witness the swords of heroes.
The dust sits unstirred and motionless on the ground.

"What astonishes me even more is that a lone Turk,
A man led astray and dedicated to destruction,
Left his army's ranks to come here.
Yazdan, Giver of good, has extracted an evil warrior
From the Tooranian camp to make him perish at your hand.
Yet you allowed someone captured in the trap to flee.
I cannot comprehend your intentions.
Did you think that if he dies, Piran would refrain from war?
Do not rely on the idea that they will march their army forth.
Here I am. I have washed my hands in blood.

Here I am, strapped and ready to fight Hoomaan.
If the hero allows me, I shall attack like a wild lion.
May the leader command Giv to dress me
In the brave Siaavoosh's armor, helmet, and Rumi mail.
May he allow me to unfasten the clasps."

Goodarz deems Bijan's words wise and reasonable.
He commends him joyfully, showers him with blessings,
And says, "May fortune never abandon you!
From the moment you sat on this saddle of leopard skin,
Whales have refrained from attack,
Lions have retracted their claws.
You fling yourself bravely into the midst of battles,
Victorious like a lion in every struggle.
But before you rush to defy Hoomaan,
Reflect on your ability to overcome him,
For he is an evil, cursed man, an Ahriman in a fight.
He resembles a mountain dressed in armor of steel.
You are young.
The sky's revolutions over you have been few.
Are you not fond of life? Sit tight.
Allow me to send a skilled lion to charge at Hoomaan
Like thunder and assail him with a shower of shots,
Like a fierce cloud of hail, to pin his steel helm to his head."

Bijan replies, "O noble hero,
A man with heart must be young, skilled, and strong.
If you have not seen me in the battle against Foorood,
Then this is the time to put me to the test.
In the battle of Pashan, I rushed daringly across the arena,
Confronting the enemy at all times,
Never allowing them to glimpse my back.
Life has no value for me if I am less valiant than another.
If you sanction me from measuring
My strength against Hoomaan,
I shall complain about the hero to the king
And, from here on, lay a hand on neither helmet nor belt."

Goodarz laughs, and, pleased with this young man
Who resembles a noble cypress tree, he says to him,
"Happy is the star shining on Giv's fortune,
For he has a son as spirited as you!

I remember and celebrate the blessed day
When your pure mother gave birth to you!
Since your fists first unfolded, lion claws grew feeble.
I shall allow you this fight against Hoomaan
Hoping that your good fortune will serve you as guide.
In the name of Yazdan, World Master,
In the name of the victories of the king of brave men,
May your hands break this Ahriman
And bring him to his end!
May Piran witness a great defeat
And refrain from further hunting fame and glory!

"I shall tell Giv to hand over to you
The famous coat of mail, and if you are blessed
With victory, your glory will expand significantly.
The most celebrated noblemen will rush to your side.
I shall place you above Giv and Farhaad.
I shall give you treasure and troops,
A throne, and a diadem more magnificent than theirs."

In this manner speaks grandfather to grandson.
Goodarz is full of ingenuity and good sense.
The young Bijan dismounts and bows low
To kiss the ground and praise his grandfather.

Goodarz asks for Giv, speaks to him of the young man
And of the royal coat of mail requested by Bijan.

The son replies to his father, "O world hero,
In all the world, this child is the pride of my heart.
His life is not of little worth. I wish not to lose sight
Of him by sending him into the dragon's maw."

Goodarz says, "My dear son, we must think differently,
For while Bijan is young and has little experience,
He is guided in all matters by sense and wisdom.
Besides, here is the place where one must fight.
It is time to flood the surface of the earth
And wash away Ahrimans with torrents of blood.
When it comes to avenging Siaavoosh and obeying the king,
One must not give thought to family kinship.
Even if it were to shower a rain of mace and sword,
We must not be stingy with our lives.

It would be shameful to soften Bijan's passion
And prevent him from acquiring fame and glory,
For a young man who makes a habit of cowardice
Will always bear a lowly soul and a troubled mind."

Giv, aware that he has no means
To force Goodarz into yielding,
Attempts once again to influence his son
In an effort to deter him from the draw of war.

But Bijan replies with an accusation,
"You wish to cover my name with shame."

Then Giv says to Goodarz, "O world hero,
At the time battle endangers life, nothing should matter,
Neither son nor shame, neither treasure nor host,
Neither king nor army command.
I stand at the eve of a perilous journey.
Why should I give up my life if he wishes to fight?
Does he not have armor?
He has a coat of mail. Why should he ask for mine?"

The warring son replies to his father,
"I have no need for your armor.
Do you think that all brave men
Require your armor to exhibit valor?
Those who hold their heads high
Will seek fame and glory, even if
Siaavoosh's armor did not loom over the battlefield!"

Bijan charges out of the army's core, distancing himself
From the ranks and closing in on the arena.

13 | Giv Equips Bijan With Siaavoosh's Armor

Once Bijan removes himself from the center forces,
Giv's heart leaps with trepidation.
Remorseful, he sheds blood tears and laments,
"Observe how vast is a father's love and sorrow!"

He raises his head toward the sky,
His heart unsteady with blood,

His spirit drained by a deep weariness.
He addresses Yazdan, Justice Dispenser,
"O World Master, have pity on my wounded heart.
Do not set it ablaze by Bijan's death.
My eyes' tears plunge to the ground,
Turning the dust into mud at my feet.
Return to me my child, O Creator.
Turn him away from his fatal hour!"

The warrior hero leaps forth, heart troubled
And overwhelmed by pity for his young son.
He thinks, "What a fool I have been to cause him grief!
Why did I not meet his demands?
If he is killed at the hands of Hoomaan,
What good will do me armor, sword, and belt?
I shall remain in a state of pain and anger,
My heart burdened by anguish,
My eyes forever brimful of tears."

He rushes like a whirlwind of dust,
Appears before his son, and says,
"Why do you aggrieve me so?
You lose your temper when the order is for peace.
The black serpent leaps to action on the day of battle
When he wishes to draw the whale out of the water.
The moon shines at a time when the sun is concealed.
You wish to charge at Hoomaan, you refuse to obey me,
You wish to act in accordance with your own fervor,
Yet you ignore the mandate of your destiny."

Bijan replies, "O valiant father,
Do not distract my heart from avenging Siaavoosh!
Hoomaan is made of neither steel nor bronze.
He is neither a mad elephant nor Ahriman.
He is a man of war, and I too am eager to fight.
I swear by my fortune that I shall not retreat before him.
Perhaps a different fate is written for me,
But destiny is in the hands of the World Master.
If what is meant to be unfolds,
Then do not surrender your heart to pain.
Do not allow yourself to be brought down!"

PART FIFTEEN

Hearing these words from his brave son,
An unyielding lion strapped for battle,
Giv dismounts his swift horse and presents Bijan
With Siaavoosh's steed and armor.
He says to him, "Since you wish to fight,
A wish that overrules any sense of caution,
Climb upon this charger of speed.
It will roll up the earth beneath you.
You will have need for this armor
Since your fight is with a wily Ahriman."

Bijan leaps off his own horse,
As swift as wind, to bestride the royal steed.
He clasps Siaavoosh's armor around his waist
And seizes the powerful, princely mace.
He searches the army for an interpreter
Able to speak the language of the Turks.
Then he takes off like a bounding lion,
Belt tight in eagerness to avenge Siaavoosh's death.

He springs into Hoomaan's camp
To witness a sight as vast as a mountain in ebullience.
His armor illuminates the entire desert,
And his horse is more massive than an elephant.

Bijan commands the interpreter to holler loud
At the enemy and say, "If you wish to fight,
Come here, to the spot where Bijan stands in defiance!"

Hoomaan says to Bijan,
 "Why do you launch your horse into this meadow?
If some misfortune befalls Afraasiyaab,
You will repent and merit the curses of Tooran-Zamin."

Bijan replies, "Your ill nature has given rise to this enmity,
For you are the one to blame for our troubles.
Praise to Yazdan, my shelter,
For having led you before me on this battlefield.
Veer your horse's reins in my direction,
Since the desire for vengeance makes your blood simmer.
Select the place you wish to fight.
And stand before me on mountain, plain, or valley,
Or any place of your choosing across army lines,

As you seek to aggrandize your name
And rank before family, friend, and foe.
Now, pray tell, what is your wish?"

Hoomaan laughs and retorts,
"O wretched one, you exhibit tremendous confidence.
Have you grown weary of life and body?
I shall return you to your army in such a state
That Giv will be deeply tortured.
I shall quickly separate your head from your torso,
Just as I have done in the past
To numerous brave warriors of your house.
You fling yourself beneath my claws,
And I shall pluck you off,
Like a falcon snatches a pheasant out of a tree.
The pheasant shrieks, blood dripping from its eyes,
While the falcon shreds the flesh off its limbs.
But what can I do now that night is approaching?
Leave under the protection of darkness.
Like an eagle, I shall return to my troops,
And, at the break of day, I shall present myself to Piran.
Then I shall return and find you,
Holding my head high, ready for combat."

Bijan replies, "Go! May Ahriman precede you as guide!
May a ditch open up behind you!
If you appear tomorrow on the battlefield,
Neither king nor army will ever set eyes on you again.
I shall fling your head so far that you will never
Have a chance to manage a host."

At nightfall, they turn their backs on each other
To withdraw into their respective camps.
They spend the night lying restless in sleep,
Hearts troubled by thoughts of an imminent fight.

14 | Hoomaan Arrives to Fight Bijan

As daybreak unveils its light over the mountain,
And night withdraws the folds of its black cloak,
Hoomaan dresses in battle armor,

Approaches Piran, and recounts everything:
How he challenged Bijan, son of Giv,
And prepared for battle in the middle of the night.

Then he calls an interpreter from the army ranks,
Bids him to climb upon a horse of speed,
And rides to the battlefield, where he awaits Bijan,
Eyes fixed on the road.

At the same time, Bijan readies himself for battle.
Firmly saddled on his horse, Shabaahang, he advances
Like a valiant leopard, accompanied by his interpreter.
His chest is covered with a warrior hero's coat of mail.
On his head shines the royal helmet.

He says to Hoomaan, "O feeble man, remember,
Last night I let you depart with your head?
Today, my sword will separate it from your torso
And engulf the earth with your blood!
You will then remember the story
The wild mountain goat told the antelope:
        'Were the entire desert covered in silk,
        I would not approach at the point
        Where my foot evades the trap.
        I shall remember that!'"

Hoomaan retorts, "Today, Giv will be struck
At the heart and deprived of his brave son!
Do you wish to fight on Mount Konaabad,
Or would you rather take it to Raibad,
Where no one, neither Iranian nor Tooranian,
May have the chance to come to our aid?"

Bijan replies, "So much meaningless talk!
You may attack me wherever you wish!"

They launch their horses to stir up the dust.
They take out their war bows and mark their shots.
These two men, ready to spill blood,
Hold their heads higher than the moon
While their dimmed hearts share the hatred
And the longing for vengeance that stirs their kings.

They ride from the mountains of Konaabad to the plain.
They arrive at a field where no one has ever set foot.
There are no vultures crossing its skies,
And its ground is vacant of paw prints.
One cannot perceive, far and wide,
A single man from either host able to rescue them.

They vow to each other to refrain
From attacking the interpreters without reason.
The one who survives this battle is to set them free
So that they may recount to the king
The will of the sky's rotations, the outcome of battle,
And the tragedies unfolding on this blood-soaked field.

Once agreed, the brave warriors set foot
To the ground to secure their mail fastenings.
They saddle their steeds, as swift as wind,
Their hearts full of wrath and hatred.
They prepare their bows diligently,
Then charge onto the battlefield.

They strap their steel-tipped arrows
And stretch their bows until the two ends meet.
After depleting their supply of arrows,
They deploy spears, wielding the reins, left and right.
Their armor falls to pieces beneath the heavy blows.
It will soon be determined which warrior lacks strength
And may be betrayed by fortune's spins.

Their mouths gape with thirst.
Their bodies are in desperate need of drink and rest.
At the end, they pause to catch their breath
And to toss water on the ardent fires of thirst.
Then they seize shield and double-edged sword.
One would think the day of resurrection has arrived.

Sparks flare from helmet and blade,
Like lightning from a dark cloud.
Steel clashes on steel, causing injury.
The blows of swords fall on these men like surging flames.
Though unable to consummate the bloodshed,
Their hearts do not grow weary from the strain.

After sword, they carry on brutally with mace.
In the end, they test the strength of their bare hands,
Each hoping to succeed in dismounting the other.
They grab each other by the belt
So that the stronger man may lift the weaker one
And toss him to the ground as if discarding a vile thing.
The strength of these warrior heroes and the force
Of their efforts make the straps of their belts snap.
Still, they remain in the saddle,
And neither succeeds in conquering the other.

Finally, they dismount, two brave men, fierce as lions.
They rest while their mediators tend to the horses.
After a moment's pause, despite their deep fatigue,
They rise again and resume the wrestling match.

In this way, from the rise of dawn to the moment
The setting sun casts long shadows across the land,
The two bloodthirsty leaders continue to fight,
Driven one moment by hope and another by fear.
But never does either one entertain the thought
Or the possibility of renouncing vengeance.
Mouths and tongues are scorched,
Limbs are drenched in sweat from the sun's brutal heat.
They end the day on common ground,
Agreeing to dash to a fresh spring of water.

Bijan drinks his fill, rises with difficulty,
And addresses Yazdan, Donor of all good.
His body shakes with fatigue,
Like willow branches quivering in the wind.
His heart despairs for his sweet life.

He says to Yazdan, "O Creator,
You are familiar with my deeds, public and hidden.
If you deem my cause just, my right to win this battle,
Then do not take my strength from me,
But help me conserve my self-control."

15 | Hoomaan Dies at the Hands of Bijan

Hoomaan reappears, heartbroken like a crow,
Face black as a smoking lamp from aching.

Wounded as they are, the two heroes resume the fight,
Marching toward each other, proud as leopards.
They measure their strength, one against the other.
At times. Bijan touches the ground, at times Hoomaan.
In turn, they make use of strength as well as skill.

In the end, the sublime sky reveals its will.
Hoomaan is stronger than Bijan,
But when the sun of fortune dims,
Value itself becomes a fault.

Bijan reaches for Hoomaan like a fierce leopard.
He grabs his neck with his left hand, his thigh with his right,
And forces the back of his huge body to yield.
Lifting him up high, he flings him onto the ground.
Immediately, his hand reaches for his dagger.
He shoves the other's head against the ground,
Cuts it off in one fell swoop, and kicks away
The detached corpse as if kicking a lifeless dragon.

The desert floods with torrents of blood
As Hoomaan's body rolls in the dust.
Astounded, Bijan observes it, large as an elephant
And as tall as a cypress tree, lumbered down on the ground.

He turns his eyes away to address the Creator:
"O World Master, you are above time and space.
You are above the sky's rotation.
Human wisdom admits this truth: You are sole Creator.
I have no part in the merits of this high deed,
For I did not have the courage to battle an elephant.
I severed Hoomaan's head to avenge the death of Siaavoosh
As well as the blood of seventy of my father's brothers.
May Hoomaan's soul be slave to mine!
May his body be torn to bits by lions' claws!"

He fastens Hoomaan's head to Shabrang's saddle strap
And abandons the corpse in the dust,

PART FIFTEEN

The armor undone, the belt ripped,
The body in one place, the head in another.

This world, from end to end, is nothing but deception.
In times of challenge, it does not come to assist.
In the midst of despair, its appearance
Is not in accordance with its actions.
It is not worth surrendering your heart to it.

Once Hoomaan, son of Viseh, is dead,
Both interpreters rush to Bijan to offer homage
In the manner of brahmins[13] before an idol from Chin.

Glancing around, Bijan realizes that he has no choice
But to pass before the Tooranian troops on his way to camp.
He fears that these men, always ready to fight,
Have grown aware of the battle just fought
And might throw themselves on him like a mountain.
Wounded and weak as he is,
He would not be able to withstand so many troops.

He takes off Siaavoosh's armor, dons Hoomaan's coat of mail,
And climbs on the dead one's massive horse,
Waving the banner of the Tooranian leader.
He takes the road, all the while blessing the field,
His propitious fate, and this fortunate land.

Hoomaan's interpreter, having witnessed
His leader's misfortune, trembles fiercely before Bijan.
The latter reassures him: "Do not be alarmed.
I promised to spare you, and my oath binds me to you.
Go now to your army and recount all my deeds."

The interpreter immediately rushes off.
Bijan runs to Mount Konaabad with banded bow in hand.

The Turkish sentinels spot from afar the banner
And weapons of the leader of Tooran.
They spring up at the sight and shout with joy.

The chief of flagships sends to Piran

◇◇◇◇◇◇◇◇◇◇◇◇◇
13 Brahmin: Priest, guide or teacher of the Hindu caste.

A rider as swift as smoke to tell him
That Hoomaan returns triumphant from the battlefield,
That the proud banner of Iran has been destroyed,
And that Bijan lies in dust, drowning in his own blood.

The troops cry out in jubilation
And listen attentively for Hoomaan's footsteps.
But their joy is foolish, for it is snuffed out by despair,
Followed by a hail of flames.

Hoomaan's interpreter reaches the Turkish camp
And recounts the scene he witnessed.
At the news of the tarnished glory of their king,
A great clamor rises from the camp.
The heroes remove their helmets
As their world dims, its sparkle obscured.

Bijan returns to camp and to the shelter of the throne.
He lowers his black banner.
The Iranian sentinels, witness to this gesture,
Turn their gaze toward the hero
And shout out from the top of their tower.

The chief of flagships dispatches to Goodarz
A speedy rider as messenger to tell him
That Bijan arrives victorious as a lion,
Swinging the overturned black banner.
Before this moment, Giv found himself distraught,
Sobbing at the sight of anyone approaching and
Running in every direction, asking for news of his son.
As soon as he hears of the return, he rushes to him,
Dismounts at the sight of his cherished features,
Rolls around on the ground, and tosses dust
On his head, praising Yazdan, Justice Giver.

He draws his valiant son close in a tight embrace.
Then they both take the direction of Goodarz,
Leader of the king's armies,
All the while sanctifying the Creator.

As soon as Bijan spots his grandfather from afar,
He jumps off his chestnut-colored horse.
His armor is soiled with blood,

His forehead crusted with dust.
He detaches Hoomaan's head
From the saddle strap and presents it to Goodarz
With the weapons and horse of the valiant Tooranian.

The warrior leader Goodarz is so proud of Bijan,
It is as if he exhales his soul before him.
He thanks Yazdan for his lucky star
And for the fortune that watched over Bijan.
Goodarz orders his treasurer to bring royal robes,
Garments embroidered in gold, with figures
And precious gems, a crown and belt shining like the sun,
Ten horses with golden bridles,
And ten slaves with golden belts.

He gives the lot to Bijan and says to him,
"Since the days of Saam, the lion,
No one has tamed dragons as you have.
You have saved this army with your sword.
With your bare hand, you have clutched
And wrung the heart of the King of Turks.
Our brave men now resemble lions,
And their horses leap beneath their weight.

16 | Nastihan Attacks by Night and Is Killed

On his side, Piran is overwhelmed by fury,
His heart wounded with a throbbing ache,
His eyes flooding with abundant tears.

He sends someone to speak to the renowned Nastihan,
Always ready to rescue others, and exclaims,
"We must engage in battle!
We must rush to avenge your brother,
Charge at night against the Iranians,
And cover the surface of the earth with blood,
Its floods as wide as the River Jayhoon.
Bring on ten thousand skilled riders,
Strapped and dressed in battle armor.
Only then will you succeed in avenging Hoomaan
And place enemy heads beneath the shears of death!"

Nastihan replies, "I am ready to force
A deluge of blood onto the earth
And make it flow as wide as the River Jayhoon!"

As two-thirds of the night drifts away,
The desert echoes with the motion of troops.
The Turks prepare for an attack,
Hoping to once again elevate their heads with glory.

Nastihan drives his vengeful army near the Iranian camp.
At dawn, a sentry spots him from his tower.
He shouts to his aides,
"A Tooranian host is speeding toward us!"

Spies immediately rush to Goodarz and say,
"An army comes our way like a quiet body of water.
Troops advance silently as if unable to speak.
This can only be the way of a surprise night attack.
The warrior leader must decide on a course of action."

Goodarz commands his men to remain attentive and awake:
"Keep an ear out for the slightest sound or motion
Coming from the Tooranian camp.
We must immediately spot an approach."

Then he summons Bijan, son of Giv,
Brave warrior always ready to strike.
He says to him, "Your star is auspicious,
And your ventures are victorious.
Your name shatters your opponents' hearts.
Take among my brave heroes and noblemen
As many riders as you may need.
Go as a lion to meet this oncoming garrison
And bring the sky down to verge to the ground."

Bijan selects one thousand brave cavaliers eager for battle.
Soon the two armies advance, one against the other,
Full of hatred and impatient to fight.
At the moment they raise their maces,
A black cloud descends to spread across the earth.
From it rises a somber dust that envelops
The Tooranians and renders them invisible.

PART FIFTEEN

At the sight of this darkness stealing the Turks from sight,
The leader Bijan calls for the drawing of warrior bows.

He approaches Nastihan,
Catches sight of the banner of the family of Viseh.
He extends his chest and shoots an arrow
Into Nastihan's horse.
Fatally struck, the beast collapses in agony.

Avid for glory, Bijan leaps on Nastihan,
Strikes his helmet with his mace,
And makes his brains spew out.

He says to the Iranians, "Any warrior strapped for battle
Who refuses to make use of mace or sword
Will be forced to defer to my bow.
The Turks are a handsome group with fair faces,
But they have no courage when it comes to war."

The Iranians gain valor. They raise their shining swords.
The air turns the color of rust; the earth is a sea of blood.
They fight like elephants.
Corpses deprived of heads pile up on the vast field.
Two-thirds of the Turks fall, trampled beneath
Their steeds, each drowning in his own blood.
The remaining Tooranian soldiers flee back to camp.

Upon their return, Piran notices the absence of his brother.
The world dims before his eyes. He addresses his spies:
"We must send a rider to the Iranian camp to look
For signs of my brother Nastihan, or else I shall resort
To plucking out my eyes from my lowly head!"

Immediately, they dispatch a rider to survey the arena.
He soon returns in haste and says, "Nastihan lies dead
On the field, with other brave Tooranian warriors.
His head is cut off, tossed aside like a crushed elephant.
His body is black and blue, battered
And broken by heavy blows of mace."

At these words, an agitated Piran loses his mind.
He tears out his hair, sheds copious tears,
Shreds his Rumi robes to bits,

And suffers the loss of appetite, rest, and sleep.
He breaks down into sobs and laments,
"O World Creator, I have always been on your side.
What crimes have I committed?
Why do you deprive me of my arm's strength?
My star and sun have dimmed.
Alas, this lion tamer, hero vanquisher!
Alas, this man so young, so bold, so brave!
My noble brother, dearer to me than my own life,
My hero Hoomaan, leader of the family of Viseh,
Nastihan, the lion bellowing in battle,
In whose hand a leopard is no more than a fox.
Who will now be the champion on this battlefield?
For I must lead my army to war."

Piran asks for brazen trumpets to be played
And timpani placed on the backs of elephants.
The air turns indigo, the earth ebony.
The army emerges out of the folds of Mount Konaabad,
Marching in the direction of the plain.
Both sun and moon lose their sparkle.

The leader of Iran asks for the blare of trumpets
As he leads his troops forward to take their positions.
In the midst of them flies the banner of Kaaveh,
Encircled by blue swords.
Each noble warrior, eager for battle,
Raises his spear and bull-headed mace.

The two armies battle from the first light of day
To the hour when the world dips in darkness.
This war is more savage than any prior war.

At the advent of night, troops go to their camps
Filled with hatred and plotting new struggles.

The leader of Iran enters Raibad.
His heart full of worry, he reflects,
"Today, we have engaged in battle
And killed a number of their chiefs.
I suppose Piran will quickly send a rider
To the King of Tooran in a desperate cry for help.
I must do the same and send word to Kay Khosrow."

17 | Goodarz Asks Kay Khosrow for Help

Goodarz calls a scribe and says to him,
"I shall relay a message to you in secrecy.
If you open your lips to utter a word,
Your tongue will bring destruction onto your head."

He commands him to write a letter to the king
To acquaint him with the army's efforts,
The conflicts they overcame, and Piran's arguments.
The letter covers the offers of alliance, peace, and amity
Received by Giv, as well as the reply given by Piran,
The demise and fall of Hoomaan and Nastihan,
Two noblemen, and Piran's valiant advisors.
It recounts the emergence of the Iranian host
Out of the mountain of Konaabad,
The fight and the outcome of battle.
Finally, it covers the subject of Hoomaan and Nastihan,
And the high deeds of Bijan on the day of battle:
How he dealt with the mace-bearing Tooranians.

Next, Goodarz speaks of Afraasiyaab in the letter:
His approach with his host to the edge of the river.
He adds, "O glorious King, you know that
If he crosses the Jayhoon and enters our land,
We have no power to fight him
Unless Khosrow decides to support the troops
And gives them newfound hope and strength.
If Piran fails to muster additional legions,
I shall inform you and ask for your command.
Furthermore, send news to me of Rostam, deev-binder,
As well as Lohraasp and Ashkesh, the wise."

Once the seal is affixed to the letter,
They place a royal saddle on a speedy horse,
And they bring out a great number of additional steeds.

Goodarz summons his son Hojir,
A young warrior mature in wisdom.
He says to him, "My enlightened son,
Give your heart fully to this matter.
This is your time to achieve fame and grandeur.

Take this letter to the king, as swift as wind.
Travel day and night without pause."

After Goodarz embraces his son,
Hojir takes leave of his blessed father, exits the tent,
And selects two relatives from the army as escort.

Hojir gallops off, stopping only to leap on a fresh horse.
He remains in the saddle day and night
Until he arrives at the royal court on the seventh day.

The sentry informs Kay Khosrow of the arrival of riders.
The king sends an escort of leaders to receive the guests.
At the sight of Hojir, they ask,
"O warrior hero of long lineage, O lion vanquisher,
What news have you for the world king?"

They invite him into the royal pavilion with his horse.
Hojir enters and, once in the presence of Kay Khosrow,
He dismounts and bows low to the ground.

Kay Khosrow invites him to sit next to him.
He asks for news of his father,
Of Goodarz and the noble warriors.

Hojir exchanges greetings from everyone
And shares the news relating to the army and the troops.
Then the awakened youth hands the letter to the king.

They call for a scribe, and, after the reading,
The king finds Hojir's mouth full of shining rubies.[14]
Then he asks the treasurer for gold and coins,
Dinars and silk brocade.
They pour pouches of gold and silver over Hojir
In such abundance that his body and head disappear.
In addition, they give him a golden royal robe,
A bejeweled crown, and ten stallions with golden saddles.
Hojir's companions are presented with treasure and dinars.

Hojir and the noblemen sit with the shah,

◇◇◇◇◇◇◇◇◇◇◇◇◇
14 Mouth full of jewels or gold: Meaning that his or her words are valuable (pearls of
wisdom).

Reveling in drink and song.
For one full day and one full night,
They discuss matters great and small.

Once night descends, Khosrow washes his head and body,
Then presents himself before the Creator
Dressed in a special robe, eyes brimming with tears.
He lowers his head in a bow to praise the Justice Giver.
He appeals for victory, grace, and strength for his kingdom.
Asking to remain in possession of the crown and throne,
He laments about Afraasiyaab, his eyes tearing from grief.

He then returns to the royal court, a tall cypress tree,
And sits on his throne in splendor and glory.

18 | Khosrow's Reply to Goodarz's Letter

Khosrow summons a writer full of good judgment
And speaks to him wisely.
He asks him to write a reply to Goodarz's letter
In which he communicates a message
At times gracious, at times stern.

After extolling the Creator,
Khosrow praises the warrior hero:
"May you remain always joyous!
You are my army's most fortunate leader.
You are a man of sense, in all matters a good advisor,
In all times eager for battle.
You are master of mace and purple sword.
You elevate the Kaaviani banner high in the sky.
Praise be to Yazdan for rewarding our men with victory!
Good fortune looked down on you,
As our enemy was swiftly reduced to dust.

"You tell me first that you sent Giv to Piran's side,
With great men and brave advisors to give excellent advice,
But that your views did not make an impression on him,
For he did not wish to agree to a peace accord.
You write of his refusal,
Thus granting you permission to fight.

He told a story full of vengeance and acrimony.
Any man who lacks compassion and decency
And succumbs to transgression
Will surrender his soul to pain and suffering.
I knew that Piran's heart would never relinquish hate.
Yet, because of his past high deeds,
I wished to avoid acts of hostility toward him.

"Now the sky has overtly shown the direction
Of Piran's devotion: It is exclusive to the land of Tooran.
He considers Afraasiyaab as reigning world ruler.
He will never withdraw his affections from him.
This man is so haunted by his wants and desires
That he is blind to the path of wisdom.
Do not waste time trying to reason with him.
Your efforts will be unavailing.
One cannot force grass to grow on a solid boulder.
Still, I acclaim you for speaking to him with kindness,
For gentle and amiable words are befitting noble Iranians.

"Furthermore, you mentioned the attack you launched,
Our star of good fortune,
The favorable spins of sun and moon,
The efforts you exerted on the field with your heavy mace.
I am sure your valor will grant you victory in war.
With such a grandfather, your grandson can only triumph.
Lions give birth to strong and valiant offspring.
This warrior hero is as noble and glorious as his father.
Since your fight is in the name of justice,
You will undoubtedly be blessed with divine help.
Your strength and courage come from the Creator.
Remember that, and always remain grateful.

"Thirdly, you tell me that Afraasiyaab
Is about to cross the Jayhoon with his vast host,
Propelled to such action by a message from Piran.
These are the facts you convey to me.
I shall now reply, O thoughtful, cautious friend.
As leader of my troops, you are worthy of every venture!
Know that Afraasiyaab's arrival at the River Jayhoon
Is not with the aim of leading an offensive.

He holds his army there, waiting for the Tarkhan[15]
To send troops from Chin and beyond.

"Fourthly, our leaders have taken over
The land of Tooran-Zamin and invaded its borders.
We have powerful chiefs: Lohraasp, the fighting Ashkesh,
And Rostam, the support of warriors.
Afraasiyaab, once aware of their presence,
Has driven his army to the River Jayhoon.
If he vacates his position,
He will surrender his land to the enemy.

"In the fifth place, you ask for news of the heroes
For whom your heart is full of affection.
May you always be the escort of good fortune!
Rostam has stirred the dust of destruction
All the way to India and Kashmir.
The prudent Ashkesh is stationed at Khaarazm,
From where rises a single war cry.
Shiddeh fled before him in battle
And is turning toward the land of Gorganj.
The lands of Alaanan and Ghoz,[16]
Where Lohraasp and his army stand,
Have been evacuated and are now under our control.
If Afraasiyaab were to lead his army against us,
If he were to cross the Jayhoon,
Our brave troops would fall upon him, and
He would find himself holding nothing but wind.

"Be assured that he will not abandon his beautiful land
And his flourishing kingdom because of Piran's pleas.
He will not surrender his realm by marching on,
For he knows that the enemy would seize it.
He cannot open his lips to speak
Without my awareness of his words.
May the day be cursed when he crosses the river
With his troops and triumphs over us in battle!
But none of us will ever witness this dark day.
I shall command the leader Tous

◇◇◇◇◇◇◇◇◇◇◇◇◇◇

15 Tarkhan: A title the Turks and Iranians use to refer to rulers who fight with the
Tooranian army against Iran-Zamin.
16 Ghoz: A city in Iran-Zamin

To immediately place timpani on elephants,
To capture and secure Dahestan, Gorgan,[17]
And the entire region, thus raising his head to the sun.

"I shall leave soon after Tous, with elephants and throne,
To support you and reinforce your army.
As for you, do not worry. Go and battle Piran.
Put your troops in order and engage in war.
Now that he has lost Hoomaan and Nastihan,
He is left with nothing but wind.
If he provokes one of our renowned men,
Allow them to advance and accept the challenge.
If Piran defies you, do not be timid,
But speed toward him like a lion.
Do not fear an attack by Afraasiyaab.
Revive your courage, and do not turn your back on him.
You will conquer him in battle if you keep your heart strong.

"I hope fortune shines on my destiny.
I think that once I lead my troops behind yours,
Once I arrive on the battlefield,
You will have advanced against them.
You will have gained a certain victory,
Your goal having reached the shining sun.
From that time on, we shall be exempt from battle,
And our affairs will prosper."

The king adds many greetings
To the troops from Kaavoos and Tous.
Then he affixes his seal on the letter, hands it over
To the messenger, and showers him with blessings.

19 | Khosrow Equips an Army

As soon as Hojir takes leave of him,
Khosrow summons his writer.
His heart full of love for his army,
He feels he must engage in war.

---

17 Gorgan: A city in the north of Iran, capital of the Golestan province.

He says, "If Afraasiyaab sets his host in motion,
If they cross the Jayhoon,
Our troops will be forced to retreat.
My only option will be to withdraw."

He immediately calls Tous, leader of Nozar's family,
And orders him to swiftly engage in a campaign
And march toward Dahestan with his troops
To take hold of the plains of Khaarazm,
To watch over Ashkesh on the day of battle,
And to fight as a leopard would fight.

The rising sounds of timpani, clarions, and trumpets
Resound above Tous's palace gates.
The commander sets his army in motion.
The earth disappears beneath the horses' hooves.
You would think the revolving sun
Would stop in its tracks for fear of these riders.

For two weeks, an army crossing the border of Iran
Eclipses the light of sun and moon.
News spreads through the world that the winning ruler
Is about to engage in a war campaign.

As soon as Tous departs,
The King of Iran quickly prepares to take the road
With one hundred thousand noble warriors,
Full of pride, selected from among his bravest.
He takes the direction of Goodarz with troops,
With elephants and drums, clarions and timpani,
With the crown and the throne of the King of Kings.

Hojir marches proudly, full speed ahead, heart full of joy,
Having been shoaled with presents, kindness, and honors.
He travels swiftly, rolling the earth beneath him.
As he nears Goodarz's tent enclosure,
He hears the din of trumpets rising to the sky.
Everyone leaves camp to come to his advance.
Noblemen strapped with golden belts invite him in.

Hojir presents himself before the illustrious Goodarz,
Recounts his observations at the court of the King of Kings,
How amiably he was received, the promises made to him,

How noble are the depths of the king's affection
For his army, and how his face brightened
With cheer upon hearing the message.

Then he produces the world king's letter
And places it in Goodarz's hand,
Repeating the greetings relayed by the brave leaders.

Goodarz listens and lifts the letter to his eyes.
He breaks its seal and hands it to his scribe.
The leader invokes divine grace on the king
And kisses the ground as a sign of obeisance.
He remains standing all night long,
Holding counsel with his son Hojir.

At daybreak, he sits and opens his court.
Army leaders enter right away, sporting helmets.
Hojir places the letter of the king of good fortune
Before the scribe, who reads it to the warriors,
Revealing the instructions of Kay Khosrow.

The troops sing the praises of the caring world king.
The leader summons the army treasurers and takes
A seat in the audience hall ready to hand out dinars.
He summons herds of horses from the mountains.
He opens his treasury to distribute gold and silver,
Swords, belts, armor, golden helmets, and crowns.
Since the time for battle is drawing near,
He lavishes the army with wealth,
Catering to the riders and infantrymen.

He gathers an army as vast as a mountain.
The earth bends beneath the weight of war steeds.
The hearts of lions tremble in fear at the sight
Of men covered in steel, gold, and silver.

Goodarz commands them to prepare for battle
And maintain heart, eyes, and ears fixed on vengeance.
They parade, army corps by army corps,
Forming a mass as large as a mountain.
Their valiant leader observes this multitude.
He sees the earth dimming, the sky obscuring.

He says, "From the time of the mighty Jamsheed,
No army has so covered a space and battlefield
With such an abundance of horse, armor,
Gold and silver, war elephants and brave lions.
If I remain in the favor of the Creator,
I shall whip my horse's reins from here to the land of Chin."

He says this, then asks for his advisors.
He sits with them, listening to music and drinking gaily
While holding counsel on the upcoming battle.

20 | Piran's Letter to Goodarz

Once aware of the actions of the Iranian leader,
Piran's heart fills with grave concern.
He seeks a solution in deception and guile,
And asks a wise man for advice.
Then, as a last resource, he summons a scribe
To compose a letter addressed to the hero Goodarz.

He begins the letter in praise of Yazdan,
Sanctuary against the deev's ambush.
Then he adds, "I secretly implore the World Creator
To remove all sentiment of hostility between our two hosts.
O Goodarz, if you had hopes of filling
The world with hatred and war, you must
Be satisfied, for you have now reached your goal.
What do you say? How shall we proceed?
Consider how many of my brave lions,
Members of my clan, you have deprived of heads,
Tossing their headless corpses into the dust.

"Have you no fear of Yazdan?
Have you renounced all sense of compassion and reason?
Now that you have triumphed, be weary of vengeance.
Do not be so hasty to spill blood!
Consider how many have perished on both sides!
The time has come to show clemency,
To break from the execution of vengeance,
And to aspire to make peace.
Why cut off the heads of living men

To avenge the death of only one?

"Bygone times are long gone, never to return.
Do not sow seeds of vengeance!
Do not tire your mind and use up your body!
Renounce the shedding of innocent blood!
Anyone who promotes a reputation of cruelty,
His name will be damned after his death.
Once your dark mane of hair turns white,
You have little hope left to live for long.
I fear our armies' fight on this battlefield.
I fear not a single soul will survive from either host.
Life will fly away while hatred will forever remain.

"Besides, who knows which party will prevail,
Which will see its fortunes dim,
And which is destined to light up the world?
If by seeking war and carnage,
And assailing me on this battlefield, you hope
To benefit Iran-Zamin, tell me so right away.
I shall dispatch an envoy to Afraasiyaab
So that he may agree to divide the world
And we may leave behind us our hatred,
As it happened during the time of King Manoochehr,
When he resolved to apportion the world.
Point out all the regions within the borders of Iran
That the Turks have occupied, and we shall evacuate.
Point out any land, populated or uninhabited,
That Kay Khosrow, giver of justice, may deem necessary.

"In the first instance, I shall retreat into the mountains
To concede to you the lands of Gharchehgan.[18]
After that, we shall include Taleghan within Iran-Zamin
And its surrounding region, all the way to Faariaab,
As well as the nation of Balkh, all the way to Andaraab,
In addition to the five cities up to Baamian, the fortunate
Land of Goozganan[19] named by the world master.
Finally, yours will be the territory extending
From the gate of Balkh to Badakhshan,

◇◇◇◇◇◇◇◇◇◇◇◇◇
18 Gharchehgan: Land near Gharcheh.
19 Faariaab, Andaraab, Baamian, Goozganan: Cities in present-day Afghanistan.

Where there remain vestiges of your past domination.
The border will run even higher, embracing the fields
Of Amu and Zam, with Khotan, Shangan, Tarmaz,
Viseh-Guerd[20] and Bukhara,
Along with the entire surrounding properties as far as Sughd,
The ownership of which no one will dispute.

"I shall cede to Rostam, the destroyer, the entire Nimrooz,
Recall the Tooranian troops stationed nearby,
And have them travel westward.
I shall withdraw my companies to the land of India
And thus close the door of enmity.
I shall surrender to you a stretch of land
Comprised of Kashmir, Kabol, Kandahar,
And regions in between, all the way to Sindh.
On the side where the brave Lohraasp stands,
I shall renounce the lands of Alaanan and Ghozdej.

"I shall hand over the territory from this border
To the summit of Mount Ghaaf to Kay Khosrow,
Without a fight or a contest,
As well as the land presently occupied by Ashkesh.
Once this is done, I shall recall my troops
And swear an oath to discard any remnant of hostility.
You know that on our side, we act with righteousness,
As my heart is full of affection and loyalty.
I shall send a message to the King of Tooran
That we no longer have reason to engage in war.
In turn, you write a letter to Khosrow,
In the spirit of humanity, to show us the face of peace.
Accept my words with grace rather than
With the longing to fight and to shed further blood.
Once we conclude the treaty, I shall send to Khosrow
Plenty of wealth, assuming that he will block
His army from exercising a new vengeance.

"Once the matter is settled, I shall set free
The hostages and distribute vast treasure.
I shall conclude this treaty with humanity

◇◇◇◇◇◇◇◇◇◇◇◇◇◇
20 Amu, Zam, Khotan, Shangan, Tarmaz, Viseh-Guerd: Cities near the border be-
tween Iran-Zamin and Tooran-Zamin.

And loyalty, according to the laws of faith.
I shall shut the eye of vengeance that the wicked Toor
And the fierce Salm opened violently long ago.
Their actions led to the death of the glorious Iraj
And overwhelmed Fereydoon with grief.

"Ask of me anything within the realm of reason,
Then write to Khosrow about me.
Do not think my peaceful words rise from weariness,
For I speak only from the point of compassion
And pursue nothing but a commendable goal.
I hold more treasure and men than you,
And my reputation of courage is greater than yours.
Yet my heart is consumed by affection for my troops
And for this coldblooded spreading of carnage.
I seek to extinguish these feelings of retribution.

"Besides, I hold before my eyes fear of the Creator,
Who does not approve of wicked acts
That would perturb an entire generation.
If you spurn my words, if you seek a fight to the death,
If you deem me guilty,
Me, who is the picture of innocence,
Because justice and injustice
Are one and the same in your eyes
And you wish only to prolong vengeance,
Then select a number of mace-bearing Iranian warriors.
I too shall seek in my army suitable brave men,
And we shall pit them against each other
With their leaders upon the battlefield.

"Yet, even better, you and I shall measure
Ourselves against each other so that the innocent
May avoid an assault and ensuing bloodbath.
I shall bring before you those you deem culpable
And for whom your heart fosters resentment,
But then you must swear the following oath:
If you succeed in spilling my blood,
If the good fortune of the Tooranians succumbs,
You will refrain from attacking my troops.
You will not set fire to my land and palace.
You will free my warriors, allow them to travel

PART FIFTEEN

To Tooran-Zamin without the threat of ambush.

"Conversely, if I were to gain victory,
If my star of good fortune delivers the world to me,
Then the Iranians would have no cause to worry.
I would not hold it against them.
I shall grant them the freedom to return
To the land of Iran and to their king.
And from here on, I shall make sure
That not a single warrior will perish.
His life and his treasure will remain intact.
Finally, if you do not accept these terms
And persist in fighting en masse according to the rules,
Then have your army advance.
You will be the one accountable in the other world
For the blood spilled in this struggle."

He fastens the letter with a string and calls Rooeen,
His noble son of brazen build
Who may boast a high position in his counsel.
Piran says to him, "Travel to Goodarz,
Wager with him wisely, and listen to his reply."

Rooeen leaves his renowned father's side
And takes off with ten cavaliers full of caution.
Clear-sighted, he charges up to the hero's tents
To be announced by the chamberlain.

Piran's son enters and, at the sight of Goodarz,
Crosses his arms over his chest and bows his head.

The leader rises and embraces him eagerly.
He asks for news of Piran and of army, king, and land.

Rooeen draws out the letter in haste,
Hands it over, and delivers the message.
A scribe arrives, skims over the letter,
And communicates its contents to Goodarz.

Once the letter is read, the noblemen are astounded
By the soft words, the sound advice,
The mention of good deeds,
And the humane treaty proposed by the wise Piran.

Goodarz says to Rooeen,
"O son of the army chief, noble young man,
You must first receive hospitality from us.
Then you may ask for a reply to the letter."

In a banquet room worthy of a king,
A new tent is erected, ornate with Rumi brocade.
Musicians and dishes are summoned.

Goodarz's heart is filled with concern.
He sits with an advisor to prepare his reply.
For seven days, he is engaged
In composing the letter, with music and wine,
An assembly and the messenger by his side.

21 | Goodarz's Reply to Piran's Letter

On the eighth day, at dawn,
The leader of Khosrow's host summons a scribe
And orders him to write a reply that would plant
A new tree in the garden of vengeance.

He begins in praise of Yazdan,
Then he takes on every mention, point by point:
"I have read your letter from beginning to end
And understand your demands.
Rooeen related to me your messages,
All that you wished him to convey to me.
I am surprised by your gentle and sweet letter.
Your heart and tongue do not appear to be neighbors.
Your mind is not in its right judgment.
You employ language that is soft and flowery.
Anyone who has not a penetrating mind
Would consider you a man full of humanity.
But you are like cursed barren lands from afar,
With the false appearance of a serene lake
As the sun beats down on them.

"This is not the time for ruse, cunning, or guile.
It is the time to reach for mace, noose, and spear.
I desire neither affection nor peace from you.

This is neither the time to reply nor the hour to speak.
Now is the moment for the vengeance of war!
Think of the way the sky revolves,
And recognize that one must not deceive
But prepare treaties to speak about humanity.
The will of the World Master is to be determined.
Who will be given strength, power, and victory?
Nevertheless, listen to my reply
And remember that wisdom leads to happiness.

"First, you speak of your feelings of affection.
You speak of the divine and of the reversals of fortune.
You say you have no wish to engage in battle,
That wars sadden and distress your heart.
But your tongue was not in accord with your heart
At the moment when the words brushed your lips.
If justice guided you, you would not have initiated
Bloodshed when Giv came your way with his escort.
Before any hostility was articulated,
He spoke to you on all the points of dispute.

"Nonetheless, you prepared your army for war,
Drawing out troops from every corner!
You scampered from region to region.
You instigated the struggle.
Reason comes to you far too late.
Had you sooner followed its path,
You would have the chance to welcome peace.
But your nature is ill-intentioned,
And your tendency leans toward heinous acts.
How can an evil nature lead you on the path to wisdom?
Spiteful deeds are the essence of your race,
Which only revels in offense and injury.
You know how the blessed Iraj suffered
At the hands of Toor for the sake of throne and crown.
It is through Salm and Toor that evil entered the world,
Injustice and vengeance stretching far and wide!

"Fereydoon, who, in his grief, cursed them day and night,
Found consolation and support only
By placing his hope in Yazdan, Justice Giver.
Manoochehr came and evened the score.

If Toor was driven by evil, he suffered its consequences.
Afraasiyaab inherited the bad nature of these foolish rulers.
He instigated wars against Manoochehr,
Nozar, and Kay Ghobaad.
He brought down calamities on Kay Kaavoos
And destroyed the inhabited lands of Iran-Zamin.
Then he ignited new hatred by killing Siaavoosh.
I did not see you contemplate justice
When this innocent man surrendered his sweet life.

"How many brave Iranian warriors, masters of crown
And throne, have perished in these wars?
You ask me how an aged man like me
Can strap himself to fight and shed blood?
O skilled and cunning man,
You have experienced good and ill fortune.
Know that Yazdan has granted me a long life
And a destiny that glorifies my exploits.
On the day of battle, I shall propel the dust
Of the land of Tooran to soar as high as the sun.
My only worry is that Yazdan will snatch my soul
Before I can trample your nation beneath my feet.

"Thirdly, you reproach me for lacking
Fear of the divine and lacking reflection because
In my foolishness I spill so much blood,
That in the end the misfortune will be mine.
But if I allow myself to be swayed by your gentle words
And to return without a fight,
Then the Creator, on the day of judgment,
Would demand an account of my deeds and would say,
        'I endowed you with command,
            Force, treasure, and courage.
            Why are you not leading the Iranians
            To avenge the death of Siaavoosh?'
The Justice Giver would question me
On the gratuitous deaths of my seventy noble sons.
What would I answer then?
How would I explain my reasons for repudiating war?

"Fourthly, O aged army leader, you speak of Siaavoosh.
You say that one must not deprive the living of life

For one lone man who has languished into dust.
But when I remember your atrocious acts,
The torments you inflicted upon our hearts,
The anguish you caused our rulers,
The treaties you violated, the wars you initiated,
And the wrongs you have often stirred up,
When I remember all of that, how can I make peace
With someone who deems acts of evil as good?

"In the fifth place, you wish to make a pact
That would close the path of war,
A pact in which you surrender to Kay Khosrow
The great leaders of Tooran-Zamin as hostages
Along with vast treasure.
But know, O support of Tooran's army,
That the king has commanded otherwise.
We are to engage in war, to spill blood,
And to avenge the death of Siaavoosh.
If I disobey Kay Khosrow, world master,
I shall have cause to blush deeply before the Creator.
Furthermore, if you hope for Kay Khosrow
To yield to your words, then send to him, in haste,
Hostages and treasures, whatever they may be.
Send them under the guidance of Lahaak and Rooeen,
As they will find the road open to Iran-Zamin.

"In the sixth place, you propose to return to Khosrow
The cities and cultivated lands belonging to Iran-Zamin
And to recall to your side the occupying troops.
But Yazdan has placed me in a position
Where I need not accept this plan.
If you are not aware of it, I shall reveal to you this secret:
Lands from the west to the border of Khazar
Are under the occupation of Lohraasp.
In the south, from Nimrooz to the land of Sindh,
The world resembles a shiny Rumi sword.
The brave Rostam, with his razor-sharp blade,
Has ignited in these regions the furnace of destruction.
He has dispatched to the king
The leader of Indians with his black banner.

"In Dahestan, Khaarazm, and the surrounding lands

Where the Turks once raised their heads,
They have been chased and have scattered on all sides.
Ashkesh showered a hail of shots on Shiddeh,
Practically killing him, and he has sent to Kay Khosrow
Prisoners and bounty of all sorts.

"Finally, on this border, you and I shall fight
To determine which of us will acquire fame and glory.
You have already yielded before me and these valiant lions.
If you agree, I shall dispense with these talks.
With the help of the strength given to me by Yazdan
And by the order of the king,
I shall make the battlefield run with blood.

"O illustrious hero, consider the turns of sun and moon.
The chains of fate have fallen from the sky,
And the head of the Tooranian fortune
Is placed beneath tactful, fatal shears.
Reflect on the retributions the Creator reserves for you.
Remove yourself from committing evil acts,
For then your fate will be a most dire one.
Ponder well, open your ears, and listen to reason.
Know that a vast army, innumerable such as mine,
Is made up of one hundred thousand sword-bearing riders.
They stand ardent to acquire glory in vengeance.
They will not divert from this battlefield
And will never waver or be swayed by cunning or sorcery.

"I now come upon the seventh point:
You certify your loyalty under oath,
But I wish not to discuss a treaty with you,
For your mind does not seek the path of reason.
Each time you agree to a peace accord,
You end up destroying the structure of good faith.
The life of Siaavoosh was wasted to the wind
Because he believed in and trusted your oath.
Since then, no one has relied on your word.
You did not save him on that fatal day,
Although he implored you often in his distress.

"In the eighth place, you say that you outshine me
With crown and throne, courage and good fortune.

I am now greater than you in army and treasure,
Though my heart suffers with vast pity.
You have sufficiently endured my strength in war.
You well witnessed my ability in combat.
Observe me well from head to toe,
For the possibility exists that my treasure,
Throne, crown, and courage bring me to your level.

"Finally, you ask me to select a few champions,
And you promise to bring on your side
A number of Turkish riders to spill blood
For the deep compassion you feel for your army.
I do not wish to act out of hate and hostility.
Though you speak kindly of benevolence,
Your impulses are of a different sort
And lead you to spiteful designs.
The king, world master, would be displeased with me
If I were to divide the army in such a way.

"Then you ask me to select just one brave man,
To measure himself against you on the battlefield,
But we are faced with an entire host charged with crimes
And filling with terror the population of Iran.
Kay Khosrow will not agree to such a proposition.
Our hosts must fight en masse.
We must form two lines of battle
To determine to whom victory belongs.
Otherwise we shall bring, each on his side,
A few renowned men to combat each other.

"Aside from these words, and no matter
How you retreat before the fulfillment of yours,
I shall never relinquish mine.
If your army appears to you unprepared,
Ask for reinforcements from your king.
Calculate deeply the stakes of this fight,
And expect our sons, relatives, and wounded allies
To fail to appear until they are cured by physicians.
It is in your interest right now to gain some time.
I shall grant you a delay, should you desire one.
Conversely, I shall grant you a battle,
Should such be your desire.

"I write to you so that you do not seek
Another pretext to evade a fight
And say that we have attacked you unexpectedly,
Though you have set a trap,
Raised an ambush, and refused to grant us a delay.
It does not matter for me if I execute vengeance
Right this very instant or in one hundred years.
However, I shall never renounce a fight,
No matter when or how, whether by day or night,
Or in times opportune or inopportune.
It is of no importance to me."

Once the reply to Piran's letter is complete,
The messenger appears, swift as a fairy,
Belt strapped tight, seated on his charger,
And surrounded by an escort of riders.
The brave Rooeen sets foot to the ground
And brings the noble warriors to the army leader.

Goodarz commands the sage men
And those renowned for their wisdom
To rush to his side.
They soon arrive, full of caution and serenity.
The hero asks for his reply to be read by a scribe
As the noblemen listen.

They understand Piran, how his acumen is vanquished,
And treat his advice with scorn.
They praise Goodarz, calling him world hero.
Then he affixes his seal on the letter
And hands it to Rooeen, son of Piran, son of Viseh.

At the moment the Tooranians rise to leave,
Goodarz asks for gifts to be prepared for them.
He gives Rooeen Taazian steeds of golden bridle,
Diadems, and golden sheathed swords.
To his companions, Goodarz bestows gold and silver,
And to those worthy of them, helmets and belts.

Rooeen takes leave of the hero's court with his escort
And strides in the direction of the Tooranian army.
Once at the side of Piran,
He presents himself respectfully to his father

And bows his head before his throne.
The wise Piran folds his arms around him.
Then Rooeen delivers the message from Goodarz
And recounts what he saw in the Iranian camp.

As soon as the reading is completed,
Piran's face turns as black as tar
As his heart fills with grief and anguish.
He realizes that his end is drawing near.
But he resolves to have patience
And to keep the letter's contents from his warriors.

Finally he says to his troops,
"Goodarz refuses to walk down a righteous path.
The desire to avenge the death of his seventy sons
Does not allow him a moment's rest.
He wishes to revive the ancient vengeance.
Why should I not avenge my brother?
Why should I leave unpunished
The deaths of nine hundred warriors
Whose heads were sliced off in the previous battle?
Never again will a man as brave as Hoomaan
Seize weapons in the land of Turks.
Never again will Nastihan, tall cypress tree,
Spread his shade upon the earth.
We must strap for battle, deprive the Iranians,
Bar them from possessing a parcel of the earth.
With the aid of the strength given to me by Yazdan
And with my sharp sword, I shall destroy these people."

He selects stallions suited for war from every corner.
He promotes each infantryman to the status of cavalier,
Handing each warrior two battle steeds.
He takes out his ancient treasure and distributes gold.

22 | Piran Asks Afraasiyaab for Help

Once this is done, at the hour of sleep,
Piran sends a messenger to Afraasiyaab,
An aging envoy, wise and of sound advice,
An eloquent and courageous rider.

He says to him,
"Tell the King of Tooran, 'O crown seeker,
        Since the first revolutions of the dome of sky over earth,
        Never has a ruler of your stature occupied the throne.
        Never has royal glory risen to bond with another.
        No other is worthy of throne, crown, belt, and royal fortune!
        The World Master will reduce to dust the heads
        Of those seeking to confront you on battle day.

        'I stand as a guilty slave before you.
        I broke away from your forestalling command.
        The king held it against me
        When I allowed Kay Khosrow to flee.
        But I do not think it was my fault,
        For it was the will of Yazdan.
        What occurred was meant to be.
        There is no point speaking further of it.
        If the king deems me innocent, he will unburden
        This load from my shoulders and come to my rescue.
        I must divulge to him the afflictions
        The rotating skies have brought down on his slave.

        'I led my army to Mount Konaabad,
        And we cut off the road to the Iranians.
        On the other side, a huge host advanced
        With Goodarz and other heroes at the lead.
        Never, since the time of Manoochehr,
        Has such a vast host entered Tooran-Zamin.
        They settled in Raibad, occupying the mountain.
        For three days and three nights,
        The two hosts faced each other like leopards.
        I did not wish to engage in battle on this spot.
        I expected the Iranians to descend from the mountain
        To the plain where we could easily approach them,
        Where the heads of their warriors would fall to the ground.

        'But the leader of Iran did not advance imprudently
        From mountain to plain as we wished and expected.
        Many of our warriors perished.
        My brother Hoomaan, world conqueror,
        Boiling with rage, accosted them defiantly.
        I do not know what thought propelled this lion man.

'Bijan, son of Giv, advanced to pit his strength
Against this brave one and engage him in a fight.
Hoomaan was killed at his hands, and the grief
I subsequently suffered deprived my head of reason.
Who would have thought a tall cypress tree
Could be uprooted by a blade of grass?
The hearts of our brave men were shattered
By this action, and our joy transformed to sorrow.

'Then the noble Nastihan left me at dawn
With ten thousand skilled riders.
The valiant Bijan smote him with his mace,
Showing him the path to death as well.
In my heart's distress, I ushered my men to the field,
Hollering cries of rage, and the troops led a fierce battle
Until night descended over the mountains.
Nine hundred of the king's famed heroes
Lay on the ground, heads cut off.
Two-thirds of our troops lost the ability to fight,
Hearts wounded by grief, bodies injured by sword.
The Iranians had the upper hand
And remained strapped for further vengeance.

'I fear that the revolving sky
Has rescinded its favors from us.
Furthermore, I have heard some nasty rumors
That leave me in a state of confusion:
I have heard that Kay Khosrow will soon arrive
With reinforcements for his leader.
If the news of his approach is true,
Then the king knows that I cannot engage in battle
Unless you yourself advance toward Iran
With an army eager for vengeance,
Unless you determine to turn this misfortune
Away from the fate of the Tooranians,
Unless you, the king, strap yourself to join the clash.
Otherwise, the army of Iran will destroy us,
And you will find yourself utterly unprotected
And dispossessed of defenders.'"

After listening to Piran's words, the messenger charges
As swift as wind to climb upon a fast stallion.

In one shot he rushes to Afraasiyaab's court
Without taking time to pause, rest, or sleep.
He enters the king's chambers like a flame,
Kisses the throne, and delivers the message.

Afraasiyaab listens to Piran's words relayed by the envoy.
Grief causes his heart to swell and his cheeks to pale.
This stone-hearted ruler sits in his anguish,
Afflicted by the fate of his fallen leaders,
By the destruction menacing his land,
And by the armies advancing on all sides
With the intention to spread terror across the world.

He reflects on Piran's message and on the fact
That his troops stand geared and ready.
As hope recaptures his heart,
He thanks the envoy in a show of satisfaction.
He asks that a dwelling be prepared for him
And spends the night in counsel.

At dawn, Afraasiyaab fits the crown on his head
And opens his door to the messenger.

23 | Afraasiyaab's Reply to Piran

Afraasiyaab orders the envoy to return
To the powerful Piran, of auspicious footprint,
And to report the following reply:
"O my loyal friend, virtuous and true,
Since the moment your chaste mother gave birth to you,
You expand your chest before me as a shield.
You have enjoyed more esteem from me than anyone.
You rank higher than any of my warrior heroes.
You surrendered your body as voucher,
Your life as ransom. Despite your wealth,
You ruthlessly subject yourself to the hazards of war,
Always in service of my kingdom.

"You led your host from Chin to Iran-Zamin.
You dimmed my enemies' hearts and their fortunes.
You are a prince and world hero.

May your life be exalted with a thousand blessings!
You granted me a friendship loyal to Toor and Pashang.
The sky ceased to give birth to heroes of your stature.
The army no longer sets eyes on leaders of your kind,
As devoted and wise as you have proved yourself to be.

"In the first place, you say you were guilty
When Kay Khosrow passed from Tooran
To the land of Iran and oppressed us with hatred.
But know that, as king, I never held it against you.
Never did my heart cling to such a thought.
You need not trouble yourself over this past matter.
You must not allow the rust of worry to distress your heart,
For this had to happen according to the Creator's will,
And no single person initiated this disorder and chaos.
Since Kay Khosrow bears little regard for me,
Do not call him my grandson; it would be a lie.
Never will I be a grandfather to him,
And I shall never profit from a union with him.
No one stands guilty in this quarrel.
My only dispute is with the Creator, who wished it so.
This was the unfolding of fate.
How could I hold it against you?

"Secondly, you speak to me of army
And the rotations of sun and moon.
It is written that the fortune of war
Is a dark dust that flies every which way.
At times it elevates a man all the way to the sun.
At times it plunges him down in a flash.
It brings in turn joy and in turn sadness,
In turn wine, music, and song,
In turn scorching pain and unbearable exhaustion.
May these worries never afflict your heart!
May your soul be free from bondage!
The way of war is such, destiny is such,
The revolving dome sways this way or that way,
At times with you, at times against you.
What remains of the dead is a dream, a memory.
Do not relinquish the thought of avenging your brothers.
A heart torn apart by a brother's murder
Cannot be quelled by a physician's remedies.

"In the third place, you tell me that Khosrow
Leaves his court with an army to engage in war.
But the news you have received is false.
Commander Tous is the one who takes the road
Toward Dahestan with his troops.
May none of us see the day when Khosrow
Will lead a campaign against us.
I am determined to march with my host
And travel to the opposite bank of the Jayhoon.
I shall allow to survive neither Goodarz nor Khosrow,
Neither host nor timpani, neither palace nor crown.
I shall flood Iran-Zamin with troops
And destroy the throne of the King of Kings!
I shall deprive Khosrow of world domination!
I shall assail him unexpectedly,
Cut off his head with my dagger.
Those who love him will shed bitter tears for him unless
The ever-changing firmament wills a different outcome!

"O proud and worldly man,
You are above all need by divine grace!
You possess men, treasure, and strength.
I have sent an army of thirty thousand riders your way,
Illustrious, brave, and cautious warriors,
So that your troubled heart may be appeased.
A single one of ours would count for more than ten Iranians.
Once this army arrives, do not delay!
Take action to pluck off Goodarz, his head and crown!
Destroy beneath the hooves of your chargers
The mountain that serves him as fort.
Once you have the upper hand,
Do not stop our troops from spilling copious blood!"

After hearing the message of the king,
The messenger returns to the army hero.

Piran listens to the reply, assembles his army,
And asks the messenger to recite
The king's words before his troops.
In this way, he revives the courage of his brave men,
Who banish worry from their hearts.

Secretly, Piran cannot shake a sense of gloom.
He cannot ignore his heart swelling with blood.
He covers his forehead with fistfuls of dust.
He sees the king's armies weakening on all fronts
And losing their spirits by the effects of battle.
He is in a state of escalating distress
By the thought of the King of Iran drawing near.

He addresses Yazdan and pleads,
"O Creator, there are so many surprising elements
In the sudden twists of fate!
The one you raised has now turned against you.
O World Master, stand unwavering.
Look at Khosrow: Who would have thought
That at this hour he would become a powerful king?
Look how inconsistent are the exploits of destiny.
The dried-up brambles of the favored one
Grow new rosebuds, and the fortune shining
On a man converts to musk the dust beneath his feet.

"Even more astonishing is the fate of a nobleman,
Whose heart is endlessly beleaguered by worry.
I do not know why a vengeful battlefield
Stretches in the space between two kings,
Between a grandfather and his grandson!
Why do two princes exist with two distinct lands
So earnest to destroy each other,
Along with two unforgiving hosts to defend each?
What shall I say of the end of this war?
If Afraasiyaab and the brave men of Tooran-Zamin
Succumb on this battlefield,
My fortune will perish with them!"

He continues to sigh before Yazdan and adds,
"O Creator, O Master of light and justice,
If Afraasiyaab enters this war and dies in battle,
Our fortunes will have turned.
If Kay Khosrow exits Iran in vengeance,
If the extent of the earth falls into his hands,
I wish for my armor to be pierced
And my soul to exit my body.
May my eyes never witness someone

Seize and alter my line of conduct!
When the turning wheel no longer spins in favor of a man,
He becomes indifferent to life and death."

24 | The Battle Between the Iranians and Tooranians

As the sun's yellow brocade spreads its light across the earth,
A billow of deep emotions stirs across the troops.
The two armies shout the cry of war,
And the earth shakes beneath the horses' hooves.
Two hosts advance en masse.
Armors of steel cover mountain and plain.
Two chiefs, fierce leopards, lead their troops to war.

A shower of arrows falls on the battlefield
Like a deluge from a dark cloud.
A thick fog hovers above like a pitch-black night.
What cloud sends a downpour of javelins and swords?

The earth is converted to steel from the horses' hooves.
The heroes' chests and hands, smeared with blood,
Shine like precious rubies.
The field is strewn with corpses, heads cut off,
Bodies tossed about with no space left for horses to pass.

The earth is the color of tulips, the air the color of indigo.
A sea of blood undulates across the ground.
Two leaders say, "If we do not separate the warriors
On this field of vengeance, there shall remain at nightfall
Only the rotating dome of sky and the Divine Creator."

Once Piran perceives the extent of the despair
And the sad state of affairs, he commands Lahaak
And Farshidvard to unite the remaining troops,
The riders still able to handle weapons, and
To distribute them in three corps to reestablish battle.

The rearguard is to be entrusted to the most cautious
Warriors, most able to defend the army against
The enemy while advancing on both sides.

He tells Lahaak to hold the mountainside with his garrison

And Farshidvard to maintain the riverbank,
Where he is to make the dust rise to the sun.
These two noble warriors of Tooran-Zamin
Set in motion their troops, eager for vengeance.

Goodarz's sentry, keeping an eye on the enemy host
From the tower, notices that Lahaak and Farshidvard
Have separated and are traveling in two different directions.
The sentry immediately sends a message to the hero.

The Iranian riders engage in a battle,
Mixing blood with dust.

Messengers arrive from every corner
Of the land to take news to Goodarz,
Who proceeds to assess his line of warriors.
He notices his noble son Hojir, fierce lion,
Armed with bow and sword.
He commands him to take the rearguard next to Giv,
Son of Goodarz, the army's shelter,
And to tell him to send two units to rescue the troops
Guarding the mountainside and the river's edge.
He further commands him to add that a valiant warrior
Is needed to take control of the rearguard
And to present himself before Goodarz.

As soon as the cautious Hojir, strapped for battle,
Hears the words of his noble father, he rushes
To his brother and relays to him the hero's words.

Giv leaps up at the news.
He examines his celebrated warriors,
And his choice falls on Farhaad.
He calls him to his side and entrusts him with troops.
Then he commands Zangueh, son of Shaavaran,
To take with him two hundred skilled men
To assault and take over Farshidvard
And agitate mountain dust and river spume.

In haste, he hands over to Gorgeen, son of Milaad,
Two hundred warriors and a banner.
He says to him, "Swing your horse's reins.
Prepare spears of gleaming steel and heavy maces.

The time is here to observe the enemy
And to present ourselves on the battlefield.
The troops that formed their rearguard have dispersed.
Their hearts are deeply troubled."

Then he says to Bijan, "O my valiant son,
You are a raging tiger on the day of battle.
The moment has come for your courage to serve you,
The moment you must engage the enemy in a fight.
On your shoulders rest the hopes of our host.
Display then your valor on this very field.
Do not fear the Tooranians, but rejoice,
For the day of retribution is upon us.
Advance toward their army core
And fight with Piran, who stands there.
The entire force of our host resides in his person.
As soon as he catches sight of you,
His skin will surely split in fear.

"If you are able to defeat him, all will end well.
Yazdan and your good star will be in your favor.
Our army will have cause to rest
From its weariness and the dangers of war.
The king, world master, will greatly rejoice,
You will obtain vast treasure and your heart's desires.
Your fortune will never cease to prosper.
Afraasiyaab's back will be shattered,
His heart swollen with blood,
And his two eyes flooding with tears."

In this way, the hero speaks to his son,
And the youth straps himself for war.
Immediately he launches his battle steed
And takes off like Aazargoshasp.
He summons riders from the right and the left wings.
Goraazeh and Gostaham rush over,
Along with the leader Hojir and the valiant Bijan.

Like lions on the day of hunt, the warriors
Are fixed on the heart of the Tooranian host.
They hurdle on stallions of winded feet
And craning necks, into the army core

To satisfy their desire for vengeance.

The entire field is obscured by the sparkle of steel.
Everyone scatters in every direction.
Many men are trampled beneath horses' hooves.
Their armor serves as their shrouds
And the mouths of lions as their graves.

25 | The Battle of Giv and Piran

Once Rooeen, son of Piran,
Spots from the back of his black stallion
The dust and motion of the army
And the oncoming force of the battling Giv,
He rises like a wolf and exits the ranks with his noblemen.
He pounces into the fight like a leopard,
Making vain efforts to penetrate the core of the melee.
His Indian sword falls from his hand,
And he takes off, despairing but gaining ground.

The leader Piran and a few of his men
Observe the fight from their posts,
Surprised by the developments.

At once Giv spots Piran, urges his horse
Toward him, and, with his spear,
Flings four of his warriors off their mounts.

Piran, son of Viseh, binds his bow
And sends a shower of shots at his enemy.
The valiant Giv protects his head with his shield
And advances like a wolf, spear in hand.
But at the moment he is within Piran's reach,
His charger stops short, refusing to take another step.

In his anger, the warrior strikes his horse with his whip.
He is boiling with rage and parts his lips
To curse this infamous deev, the cause of his demise.
Then he flings away his spear, grabs his bow,
And, guarding his head with a shield of rhinoceros skin,
He opens out his chest, extends his bowstring, and shoots,

Hoping to nail Piran's hand to his shield.
The arrow is made of four layers of poplar wood,
But it fails to wound the brave leader.
Giv shoots another one, this time of triple-layer wood,
Toward Piran's horse to pierce through its armor.
Neither the horse nor the bold rider is wounded in the least.

In this moment, Giv's companions approach.
Piran's rage increases at the sight of them.
He falls on Giv like a whirlwind of dust.
He knows that if he succeeds in wounding him,
His troops will scatter.
But Giv, as swift as smoke, removes Piran's helmet
With a single blow of his spear.
Nonetheless, Piran remains unharmed
While Giv finds himself deeply dismayed.

Bijan dashes to his father and says, "O illustrious father,
I have heard that Piran intends to engage in many more fights.
He is meant to escape many a dragon's claws.
In the end, he is fated to die at the hands of Goodarz.
Do not trouble yourself needlessly, dear father,
His time is not yet up.
Why pursue him with such passion, such perseverance?"

Giv's companions arrive, illustrious heroes
Whose hearts are filled with rage.

Witness to this, Piran turns his back on Giv
And retreats to his camp.
He approaches Lahaak and Farshidvard
With cries of anguish, his cheeks pale.
He says to them, "O my illustrious brothers and bold
Companions always ready to wield your swords,
It is for such a day that I have prepared you.
Our army is barely ready for battle.
The enemy renders black our world.
I see no one able to lead us in our search for fame and glory."

At Piran's words, the renowned heroes
Leap with a desire to fight. They rush over saying,
"If our hearts fall under the threat of dishonor,
Why should we fear a danger to our lives?

PART FIFTEEN

We have fastened the flaps of our coats of mail.
We shall maintain our waists cinched for as long
As this battle lasts, lest we succumb to humiliation."

Lahaak and Farshidvard advance toward Giv to assail him.
The intrepid Lahaak is first to approach the hero.
He strikes his midsection with his spear
In the hopes of dismounting him
And flinging him headfirst to the ground.
The blow is so powerful that it splits his armor,
But Giv's feet remain secure in the stirrups.

For his part, Giv strikes Lahaak's horse with his spear,
Making the animal plummet painfully to the ground.
The brave Lahaak finds himself on foot,
Deprived of mount. Farshidvard runs from afar,
Administers a blow of his sword, as swift as wind,
On Giv's spear, and cuts it in half effortlessly.

Astonished at the sight, Giv seizes his heavy steel mace.
He hollers like a dragon of blazing breath and hits
Farshidvard, whose sword escapes his grasp.
Right away, Giv strikes him again at the neck
As if he were making fire rain onto his body.
The blow causes a torrent of blood
To spill from Farshidvard's gaping mouth.
His body caves in, his head wobbles.

While Giv is busy with his adversary,
Lahaak, as swift as a darting flame, leaps on a horse
Of wind-like speed and lunges toward them.
The two heroes attack Giv anew with spear and mace,
Making many blows fall on him.

But Giv remains steady in the saddle of poplar wood,
The fight nothing more to him than entertainment.

Once Lahaak and Farshidvard realize the strength of their foe,
They say in anger, "The star of our fortune is turning.
It is as if this man's head and brains are made of steel
And that his body is made of lion skin."

On his side, Giv asks his escort for a new spear

And proceeds to turn right and left,
Unrelentingly assailing the two brothers.
Yet he is unable to pound down either one.

He reflects, "A strange thing occurs
With these two brave men eager to battle.
It is as if they are deevs from Mazandaran
And not chief leaders of the army of Tooran."

To the right of Giv arrives Goraazeh,
Like a whirl of dust, to fight Farshidvard,
A mace of Rumi steel, large as a column, in his hand.
He rides a charger as strong as a dromedary.
Presently he extends his hand on the Turk.
At the sight of him, Farshidvard secures himself in the saddle.
He strikes him at the waist, but his metal belt remains intact.

Bijan rushes like a lion to the rescue of the valiant Goraazeh
And strikes with his sword the top of Farshidvard's helmet.
The latter fights as if he wishes to split the earth.

Bijan is about to seize his helmet with his right hand,
But Farshidvard evades his grasp.
Gostaham runs behind Bijan with other Iranian warriors.
They approach the Tooranian troops,
Hearts wounded and avid for vengeance.

On the Tooranian side, Andariman rushes up,
Leaping on the ground swift as dust.
He deals Gostaham a blow of his mace,
Powerful enough to break his back.
The mace meets with the Iranian's sword, breaks it in two,
While Gostaham's heart fills with terror.

Hojir flies to the rescue making a shower
Of shots rain down on Andariman.
One of his arrows pierces the horse's saddle and strappings,
Forcing the animal to plunge to its death.

The valiant rider is flung to the ground
But quickly guards his head with his shield
And raises himself up though bruised.

A cry of pain rises from the Turkish ranks.
From end to end, they rush forth like deevs.
They succeed in pulling Andariman out of the melee,
To distance him from the front of the army.

From dawn to dusk, the Iranian cavaliers
Descend on the mountain and on the Tooranian host,
Making the dust of battle fly about fiercely,
Impregnating the earth with a flow of abundant blood.
Men and horses fall in defeat,
Their paralyzed mouths gaping from cries and hollers.

26 | Goodarz and Piran Agree on a Pact

Once the earth assumes shades of ebony,
One hears, rising from both camps,
The sound of clarions, timpani,
And musicians seated on elephants.

Leaders from both sides agree
To retreat from the battlefield at nightfall.
They select their most renowned, most eager
Warriors to march to the front in the morning.
These are men able to reduce to spume
The waters of the deep ocean.
In this way, they exempt the armies from engaging
In further battle, to avoid more innocent bloodshed.

Once this convention is set aside,
They return to their camps by way of a shorter route.
Two leaders leave the battlefield,
Hearts full of dismay about the earlier struggle.
One host takes the direction of Konaabad.
The other host drives toward Raibad.

Goodarz, leader of the king's army,
Instantly sends infantrymen on the road.
The noble warriors, heads raw from helmets,
Swords and hands drenched in blood,
Unfasten their armor and coats of mail
And remove their headgear.

After freeing themselves from the weight of
Their equipment, after eating and drinking bright wine,
Together, young and old, fully aware,
Take the direction of the leader Goodarz
To discuss matters of war with him.

Giv says to Goodarz, "O father,
A strange thing occurred today.
Once I attacked the Tooranian host,
I broke their ranks, and they opened the way for me.
But as soon as I came face to face with Piran,
My charger stopped and refused to take another step.
My ardor was such that I was about to chop off its head.
Then Bijan remembered the words of the king
And revealed to me the secret:
It is at your hand that Piran is to perish.
The king said it was dictated by the stars."

Goodarz replies, "O dear son,
Without a doubt his hour is in my hands.
I shall avenge the death of my seventy cherished sons
With the strength given to me by the World Creator."
Then he surveys the troops, witnessing the extent
Of their exhaustion from battle and carnage,
And from the relentless attacks of the enemy.

At the sight of the warriors' pallor,
The army's guide, master of good fortune, is moved.
He commands them to take their positions
So that their weary bodies may rest from their labors.

They depart and return in the early morning
With renewed fervor, armed for battle.
They greet their leader and say,
"Illustrious world warrior, how did you sleep last night?
In what state did you rise?
What did you decide on the battle with the Turks?"

The hero Goodarz replies, "O renowned soldiers,
You must give thanks day and night to the World Creator
For the fact that, until now, the events of war
Have turned according to our hearts' desires.
I have witnessed in my life many a wondrous thing,

But never have I viewed the world as a mere passage.
The turning skies create many men like us,
Reaping the fruits of what it pleases to sow.
First, let me remember Zahaak, the unjust,
Who seized the kingdom by way of wicked deeds.
After a few years, Yazdan threw this miserable one
Into the throes of misfortune.

"The Justice Giver did not approve of crimes
By a man who brought tyranny to the world.
Zahaak, who was made of wind, returned to wind
Because of his pride, greed, and unjust ways.
Fereydoon the fortunate, a just ruler,
Freed the world from oppression and tyranny,
And strapped his royal belt in kingship.
He seized weapons to conquer sovereignty,
Shattered Ahriman's spells,
And set the world just again, from end to end.
It is from Zahaak, a man of corrupt character,
With whom kings dwelled in quarrel,
From whom Afraasiyaab inherited his evil nature,
His hunger for plunder and murder,
And his interest in the arts of sorcery.
The evil Tooranian ruler spread war across the region
And abandoned the path of justice, faith, and grace.
He trampled beneath his feet the laws of religion.
In the end, he killed the noble Siaavoosh
And devastated the land of Iran.

"After these events, Giv left Iran-Zamin,
Wandering a long time through the land of Tooran,
Enduring vast deprivations:
Thorns served him as bed, stones as pillow,
Deer flesh as food, and leopard pelt as clothes.
He traveled in this manner from place to place,
Like a deranged person, searching for Kay Khosrow.
As soon as he found him, he approached him, praised him,
And together they took the road to Iran-Zamin.

"The hostile Piran heard the news
And rushed forth in haste with a vast host,
Hoping to make the two perish on the road.

He did all that he could to lose them,
And Yazdan alone came to their rescue.
Later we traveled to Kaasseh Rood,
Hoping to avenge Siaavoosh.
A vast army arrived in Laadan,
Attacked us by night in the battle of Pashan,
In which a great number of my sons
Perished right before my eyes,
Deeply troubling the hearts of our noblemen.

"Now, once again Piran appears, eager for battle,
At the head of innumerable troops.
If he does not feel strong enough to resist us,
He will utter many words in the hopes of a delay
To allow a second host from Tooran enough time to arrive.
We must immediately accept the challenge of war.
If we miss this opportunity, if we fail to strike the first blow,
He will find a pretext to refuse to fight
And renounce vengeance, fame, and glory.
Let us then reduce to dust these illustrious heroes
As soon as they ring the call to war.

"Furthermore, if Piran does not retreat
Before the fulfillment of his word,
If he awaits our attack, I shall present myself to fight.
Old as I am, I shall be the first to expose my body
To death on the battlefield before the Iranian troops.
The brave Piran and I, along with Giv and Rooeen,
We shall seize weapons like valiant warriors,
For no one lives forever on this earth,
And there will remain from us nothing but our honor.
The best course of action is to leave behind a good name.
Death straps its belt around each waist equally.
It does not matter whether our end is natural or violent.
One must harbor little faith in the turning skies.

"Any one of you able to engage in battle,
Must secure himself, seize spear and sword.
The domination of Tooran-Zamin reaches its end.
The time is here to rush to vengeance.
There never lived a rider as capable as Hoomaan,
Who tempted his strength in the battle against Bijan.

But his fortune dimmed.
He fell and his head was cut off,
His body rolling miserably in blood and dust.
There is no need to harbor fear.
There is no need to refrain from engaging in war.

"If Piran prefers an organized battle,
If he brings his army like a whirlwind of dust,
Then we must advance against him
And form a mass as large as a mountain,
For their minds are troubled, their hearts full of grief.
I think we shall have the upper hand.
We shall raise the black dust of destruction."

After the hero ends his speech
To the blessed and skilled warriors,
They shower him with praise: "O world leader,
O prince of pure faith, since Yazdan created the world,
No one has lain eyes on a hero of your grandeur.
Fereydoon, who brought the entire world to heel
Before his kingdom, from end to end,
Did not have a servant as prodigious as you.
You are the pillar of brave men, the glory of the king's host,
The support of crown, throne, and headdress!
You bestow on the king the sacrifice of your life,
The lives of your sons, and all your possessions.
What more could a monarch ask of his army leader?
All that Khosrow expected from Fariborz and Tous,
You will now have accomplished.

"If Piran brings his army leaders to engage in battle,
If we were ten against one thousand men,
You will never see a single one of us abandon the field.
If his entire host charges against us on mountain and plain,
We are ready, our hearts afire
With an intense craving for vengeance.
Our hips are belted for battle.
May our lives be the ransom for yours!
Such is our solemn agreement."

This reply fills Goodarz's heart with joy.
He utters blessings on the noblemen and says,

"O heroes of the world king,
You display the manner in which brave men act!
You are illustrious lions, valiant army chiefs!"

He commands his troops to mount their horses,
Seize weapons, and strap themselves for war.
His left wing has for its warrior the brave Rohaam
And for commander the sun-like Farhaad.
The right wing is under the command of Fariborz
And Ketmaareh, son of Ghaaran.

Goodarz relays his orders to Shiddush, saying,
"My dear son, be at the ready for any action.
No matter what danger you face,
Take the Kaaviani banner
And go to serve the army's rearguard."

Then he says to Gostaham,
"Place yourself at the head of troops.
Take the position of chief commander.
Remain attentive and cautious, and protect the army."

He enjoins his troops to maintain their ranks,
Prohibits them from taking a step forward.
He commands them to obey Gostaham
And maintain themselves on horseback day and night.

A great cry rises from the brave men as they lament
The challenge Goodarz is about to take.
They rush toward him, scatter dust on their heads,
And say, "O aging war hero,
May you be victorious on this battlefield!"

Goodarz summons Gostaham to give him advice:
"Watch over the army and protect it against the enemy.
Remain in armor day and night, keen on vengeance.
Maintain at all times your helmet on your head.
At the moment you cease to fight,
At the moment you recline to sleep,
Those awake will seize the moment to assail you.
Place a sentry on the mountaintop
To guard your army against a night attack.
Should the Tooranians surprise you with a strike,

You must fight like a brave man
And throw yourself in their midst to push them back.

"But if you hear from the Tooranian camp
Unfavorable news of the battle I am about to engage in,
If you hear that our troops have fallen
And that our headless bodies have been flung on the road,
Then refrain from engaging your unit for three days.
On the fourth day, the famed king will arrive with his throne,
With pomp and circumstance, to the aid of the army."

Gostaham's cheeks flood with tears.
He absorbs the advice of the army chief
And pledges to adhere to the requests.
He says, "I shall follow your instructions.
I stand here, strapped to serve, in the manner of a slave."

27 | Piran's Discourse With His Noblemen

After the war, the Turks feel humiliated by defeat.
Fathers mourn the deaths of sons,
Brothers bewail the deaths of brothers.
Everyone is in mourning from end to end.
Everyone is heartsick and worn out,
Greatly fearing the unlucky rotations of the skies.

As Piran takes in the sight, he realizes that his army
Resembles a herd savaged by a ravening wolf.
He summons his leaders and speaks to them at length:
"O skilled heroes, young and old, you have
Displayed power, dignity, and honor in battle.
Afraasiyaab has given you fame.
He has glorified your exploits and encouraged you
To exercise your influence over the world.
Though you have lost one battle,
You now renounce to fight?
Know that if a host deserts the battlefield,
The valiant Iranian leaders will pursue us
With heavy mace, and none of us, great or small,
Will have a chance to survive.

"You must free your hearts from such fears.
Determine to destroy those who have wounded you.
Wise men assure us that Yazdan is eternally victorious,
But the world is at times happy and at times aggrieved.
This is cause for concern.
The same army that fled in the past
Has now reclaimed the courage to attack us once again.
Anyone who cares for land, child, and home,
And for his oath of loyalty, must seize weapons
And vengefully advance against the Iranian army.
Goodarz and I agree to choose leaders
From our troops and to bring them together
While the two hosts cease their hostilities.

"We must not refuse battle.
Either Goodarz keeps his word and hands over leaders,
Or he engages in an organized fight.
It does not matter if we surrender our heads to the dagger,
For we are born one day and must die another.
If the vault of sky decides otherwise,
We shall hang our foes' heads on the gallows.
In either case, fate will take its course.
I shall behead any man who refuses to obey!"

The warriors rush to reply:
"O bold warrior of the noble Afraasiyaab,
You own an ancient throne and possess vast wealth,
Yet you expose yourself to the weariness of war
In the name of your affection for us.
You stand before us belted like a slave.
You have handed over to death son and brother.
How would we disobey you, so many we are?
Why should we stand as your loyal slaves
If not to fulfill your wishes and commands?"

After speaking, they rise to prepare for departure
And gear themselves for the battle ahead.
The entire night they repeat to each other
The words of truth spoken by their leader.

At the advent of dawn, the sound of clarions and trumpets
Echoes beneath Piran's pavilion.

The noblemen mount their chargers, bows on arms.
You would think the pounding of horses' hooves
Envelops the earth in a shroud of steel.

The leader says to Lahaak and Farshidvard,
"Illustrious heroes, take command of Tooran's army.
Place a sentinel at the mountaintop day and night.
If the revolving dome brings misfortune upon my head,
If it denies mercy and pity due me at last,
Rush to Tooran-Zamin, for our luck will have passed.
No one will then remain from the seed of Viseh.
Fate will disperse our family's remnants of dust.
What power do we have against fate,
Our guide and teacher from the beginning of time?"

They kiss each other in their sadness, shed bitter tears,
And then take their leave, lamenting all the while.
At this point, the vengeful leader of Tooran's army
Charges onto the battlefield with a loud cry of war.

28 | The Battle of the Eleven Heroes:
Goodarz and Piran Select Their Warriors

At the sight of Goodarz, son of Kashvaad,
Piran addresses him, then awaits his reply:
"O gifted warrior, you wear yourself out.
But what good will it do the soul of Siaavoosh?
What good will it do to stir the smoke of destruction
Above the land of Tooran?
He is now in the other world, in the sojourn
Of the righteous, yet you still refuse to rest?
Two armies destroyed each other like headless elephants.
Two hosts from two lands have been defeated.
The time has come to abandon the battlefield.
The world, from end to end, is depopulated of men,
And the excess of vengeance has turned cold.
Why then kill more innocent soldiers?

"Let us come into an agreement.
I propose two courses of action:
If you seek retribution, bring forth your host

From the foot of the mountain to where we stand.
Emerge out of the ranks,
For this is the only way to assuage your rage.
Let us fight, you and I, bravely in this arena,
And our warriors will follow suit.
The victor will be sovereign master and take the throne.
If I perish at your hands, you will no longer
Need to fight the Tooranian army.
It will appear at your side and submit to your rule.
It will turn over its chiefs as guarantee for the treaty.
Conversely, if you and your men succumb to our blows,
Your army will have nothing to fear from me."

Goodarz realizes that Piran's fate has dimmed.
He begins by giving thanks to Yazdan,
Then he prays for the famous King Khosrow.
Finally, he replies to Piran: "O glorious hero,
I listened to your discourse to the very end.
How did Afraasiyaab benefit
From spilling the blood of Siaavoosh?
His innocent head was cut off like a lamb,
His heart wounded, and his soul torn apart by grief.
Furthermore, Afraasiyaab provoked much pain
To people throughout the land of Iran
With his endless massacres, destructions, battles, and fury.

"Siaavoosh surrendered his head for an oath,
And you foolishly gave his life to the wind.
Later, when my son came to you,
You refused to listen to my advice.
You rushed to battle and flung yourself on us like a flame.
I have asked the Creator, in public and in secret,
For only one thing: That one day
You present yourself in the arena to fight me.
Now here you are!
Let us not waste time, and, despite our advanced age,
Let the two of us confront each other without our hosts.
Select from the army of Tooran skilled leaders
Armed with sword, spear, and heavy mace.
Bring them before my vengeful warriors.
They will fight and destroy each other."

The leader of the Turks begins preparations.
He selects ten cavaliers from his army,
Renowned lion men, braced with full armor,
Positioned on their chargers, and ready for battle.
They exit the ranks and advance on the field
To a spot out of range from sentry eyes,
According to the provisions they determined.

Every Tooranian rider stands opposite an Iranian warrior:
First Giv is placed before Garooy,
Both equally strong, both eager to fight.
Garooy, son of Zerreh, Tooranian leader,
The man most despised by Kay Khosrow,
For he seized Siaavoosh by the beard and viciously
Cut off his head to sever it from his pure body.

Fariborz, son of Kaavoos,
Rushes to oppose Kolbaad, son of Viseh.
Rohaam, son of Goodarz,
And Baarmaan confront each other.
Goraazeh opposes Siaamak,
Like a furious lion battles a whale.
Gorgeen, skilled warrior and a lion in the arena,
Appears against Andariman.
Bijan, son of Giv, proposes to fight against Rooeen,
A warrior able to extinguish the world's glimmer.
Zangueh, son of Shaavaran, is to fight Akhvaast.
Barteh is to confront Kohram.
Fooroohal opposes Zangaleh, who emerges from the crowd.
Hojir and Sepahram, akin to deevs,
Holler cries of rage on the battlefield.

Goodarz, son of Kashvaad, is pinned
Against Piran for the final face-off.
Armed for battle, wearing hostile expressions,
These two leaders are thirsty for blood
In their fight in the name of domination and faith.
They swear to each other that no one is to withdraw
Until it is decided to whom victory is granted.

Two hills stand between the two hosts,
Two hills with an encompassing view.

One is on the side of Iran, the other on the side of Tooran.
At the foot of these small mountains
Stretches an arid field where those who await
The will of fortune engage in battle.

Goodarz says to the noblemen, "O warriors full of pride,
The ones who overcome their adversaries
Will plant their banner on these heights."

Piran pitches his banner on the opposite hill
And gives his men similar instructions.

Then the Iranians descend on the field,
Armed and eager to spill blood.
They are ready to strike blows of all sorts
With sword and arrow, mace and noose.

The brave noblemen of Tooran arrive
Armed with mace, arrows, and Indian sabers.
If a mountain were to come to resist,
It would be flattened in an instant.
Their arms hang powerless,
Yazdan having closed to them the door of force.
They fling themselves in the lakes of misfortune,
For they shed abundant innocent blood.

The Tooranian battle steeds halt
As if an invisible hand has bound their legs.
All joy is gone, for their time has passed,
And their blood boils with grave trepidation.
Such is the will of the World Creator,
You would think the earth grabs the warriors.

So courageous are they that, despite adverse conditions,
The Tooranians fight for their king's throne.
They engage their heads for battle, in the name of royalty,
Surrendering their lives for fame and glory.

In this way the two parties rush to the staging ground
And take their places, face to face, eager to fight.
The leader Piran secretly senses
That misfortune is about to enfold him.
He says, "Keep tragedy at bay.

Until I can see my land once again,
I shall evade this time of suffering."
He gazes into the sky, realizing that he has lost favor.
Such is the way of the sublime dome,
At times giving you joy, at times exacting affliction.

Piran sees no way out of battle.
The time is near when the oppressor is to be oppressed.

29 | The Battle of Fariborz and Kolbaad

Goodarz and Piran come together
To discuss various matters.

Fariborz, son of Kaavoos, is first to exit the ranks.
Like a lion, bow in hand, the Iranian warrior
Throws himself on Kolbaad, son of Viseh.
Fariborz circles him. His arrow takes off
But fails to strike Kolbaad at the targeted spot.

With his right hand, he draws his sword,
Raises it, and deals such a blow
To the nape of Kolbaad's neck
That it splits him down to his waist.

Then he dismounts, unhooks his noose,
Unfastens the steel armor of the cadaver,
And ties Kolbaad's body to the saddle.
He climbs up the hill, triumphantly shouting,
"May our leader be victorious,
And may the hearts of the king's enemies shatter!"

30 | The Battle of Giv and Garooy of Zerreh

Next, Garooy of Zerreh, the warrior deev,
Advances against Giv, son of Goodarz.
They battle for a long time with spears,
Their blood mixing with dust.
The steel of spears snap in the riders' hands
In a terribly fierce battle.

They grab bows and arrows of poplar wood
And jump on each other without wasting time.

Giv is determined to remove his valiant adversary
From his saddle and to take him to Khosrow alive
As a gift of a different sort from the land of Tooran.

As Giv nears him, Garooy drops his bow in fear.
He reaches for his sword, but Giv falls on him,
A bull-headed mace in hand,
Roaring like a frenzied leopard.
He strikes him on the head, making blood
Flow from his skull down his cheeks.

Giv reaches to push the other from his saddle.
Garooy falls off his horse and loses consciousness.

The brave leopard sets foot to the ground,
Ties Garooy's two hands behind his back, tight as rock,
Bestrides his horse, places him before him,
And rushes in the direction of his companions.

Giv arrives at the hill, banner in hand,
Shouting cries fierce enough to flatten the mountain.
He invokes the sky on the head of the hero Goodarz,
Celebrating the victorious fortune of the world king.

31 | The Battle of Goraazeh and Siaamak

The third Tooranian to advance on the battlefield
Is Siaamak, who is to joust with Goraazeh.
They face each other, spear in hand,
The two shouting like mad elephants, their heads
Full of vengeance and a furious desire to fight.

They seize their heavy maces and leap like bold lions,
Hitting each other on the head.
Their tongues are fissured by thirst in a relentless battle.
They dismount and assail each other in a wrestling match,
Making the dust of battle fly about.

Goraazeh grabs Siaamak like a lion,

And swift as wind, turns him over beneath him.
He flings him to the ground so violently
That his bones shatter, and he instantly surrenders his soul.

Then Goraazeh ties him up on his horse
And mounts on the saddle like the flame of Aazargoshasp.
Hauling Siaamak's horse, he climbs to the hilltop
Proudly and exuberantly like a drunken man,
Brandishing his blessed banner in a sign of victory.

He dismounts, invokes blessings on Yazdan,
Justice Giver, and on the fortune of the world king.

32 | The Battle of Fooroohal and Zangaleh

The fourth battle finds Fooroohal against Zangaleh:
Two valiant men, two raging lions released from bondage.

In the entire Iranian army, no rider exists as bold
And no archer as skilled as Fooroohal.
At the sight of the fierce Turk from afar,
He binds his bow, stretches it, and sends a shower
Of shots over Zangaleh, assailing him on all sides.

One of the arrows made of poplar wood flies,
Swift as wind, and strikes the horse,
Penetrating right through the steed to the rider.
The charger comes down, falling with a shudder of pain.
Zangaleh's cheeks turn pale as he tumbles off his horse
Headfirst, his life and breath suspended forever.
Without a doubt, he was born on a most unfortunate day.

Fooroohal dismounts, lops off Zangaleh's head,
Removes his Rumi coat of mail, attaches the severed head
To his horse's strap, and seizes the dead man's steed.
He charges toward the hill like a leopard,
Chest, sword, and hand smeared in blood,
Holding his blessed banner, heart full of joy,
For he inflicted a deadly blow on the object of his quest.

33 | The Battle of Rohaam and Baarmaan

In the fifth battle, Rohaam, son of Goodarz,
Measures himself against Baarmaan.
Two brave riders grab their bows and arrows
Of poplar wood and loudly shout the cry of war.

Once their bows are splintered,
They reach for spear and sword.
These valiant men, two skilled riders full of caution,
Who witnessed many a battle, circle each other awhile.

Rohaam, eager to fight, begins to shake violently.
He pierces through Baarmaan's thigh with his spear,
Sending him off his horse, as was his intention.

Baarmaan runs off, swift as a whirlwind of dust,
But Rohaam chases after him on horseback,
Faster than the speed of wind.
He strikes the Turk once again with his spear,
Hitting him on the back and puncturing his liver.

Rohaam, driven by the vengeance due Siaavoosh,
Drags him on the ground, and, in his hatred,
Rubs his face in his adversary's blood.
Then he places him on his horse's saddle,
Ties him up as hard as stone,
Leaving his leopard's legs to dangle over.

As a last gesture, the hero mounts his eager horse
And gallops toward the banner.
He climbs up the hill, his heart free of worry.

By the victory of the king, his good fortune,
And the lofty throne, Rohaam completes his mission.
He summons divine blessings on the generous lineage
Of Kay Khosrow, glorious world master.

34 | The Battle of Bijan and Rooeen

In the sixth place, Bijan and Rooeen rush onto the battlefield.
They bind their bows and attack each other left and right,
One a furious lion, the other a war elephant.
But the arrows they send flying are ineffective.

The son of Giv falls on the brave Rooeen, mace in hand.
He takes advantage of a favorable moment,
Splits the earth in the momentum, and, faster than wind,
Strikes Rooeen on the head with his Rumi mace.
Brain and blood spurt out of Rooeen's skull.
He expires, still rooted on his charger,
Uttering the name of Piran, son of Viseh.
Then he falls off his horse, his body full of pain,
His mouth full of blood.

Though Rooeen departed to win, he loses everything
Without having enjoyed his youth for a single day.
Such is the world, full of misery and trouble.
Behind each climb there comes a steep decline.

Immediately, Bijan jumps off his horse and, like Ahriman,
Severs with his sword the head of Rooeen, whose body
Would fail to find the protection of a coffin or a shroud.
He ties up the head to his horse's saddle with his noose.
Not a soul stands witness to take pity on Rooeen.

Bijan ties Rooeen's body firmly to his charger,
Grabs the reins, shakes them hard, and rushes up the hill,
Gripping in his hand the banner with the image
Of purple circles on a background of silk.
He cries out, "May the king remain forever victorious!
May the head of the hero always sport a diadem!"

35 | The Battle of Hojir and Sepahram

The seventh hero to rush into battle is Hojir,
Glorious warrior and superior rider.
Sepahram, relative of Afraasiyaab,
Hero of high rank, blessed with honors,

Is to measure himself against the son of Goodarz,
Who has no equal among Iranian riders.

Both arrive on the battlefield stirring up
The black dust of war and brandishing swords.
They attack each other fiercely,
Provoking sparks to rise from their blades.

The brave Hojir falls on Sepahram like a lion,
Invoking the name of the World Creator
And the fortune of the young king, world master.
He strikes Sepahram's helm with his sword.
Sepahram dies forthwith, a miserable death,
As he tumbles off his horse to drown in his own blood.

The fortunate Hojir attaches the corpse to his charger,
Climbs on his mount, and grabs the other horse's reins,
Dashing off toward the hill.
All the while, he blesses the lucky star of his noble land,
For he has been granted fortune and power by the Creator,
Who watches over him and rewards him with victory.

36 | The Battle of Gorgeen and Andariman

Gorgeen, the eighth vengeful hero, and Andariman,
One of the champions of the Turkish army,
Two worldly men who have witnessed many a battle,
Take leave of their friends and advance onto the battlefield.

At first they come after each other with spears.
But once those break,
They arm themselves with bow and arrow.
They protect their faces with covers of rhinoceros skin.
They spill a shower of shots
That falls like hail on shield, helmet, and head.

In the end, one of Gorgeen's shots
Nails Andariman's Rumi helm to his head.
The powerful blow leaves the hero staggering in the saddle.

The famed Gorgeen shoots another arrow to strike him
On the side, making the Turk plummet off his horse.

The pain is so sharp it spurs blood to pour out of his eyes.

Gorgeen jumps off his horse like dust
And cuts off the head of Andariman.
He hitches it on the saddle's strap,
Climbs back on his horse,
Grabs the reins of his foe's charger,
And dashes toward the tall hill,
Bow hanging on his arm.

In this way, this brave hero returns from battle,
Triumphant through the strength
Given to him by the divine and by the influence
Of the victorious king, world master.
Once at the top, he plants the banner on the hill,
Bringing joy to a great number of hearts.

37 | The Battle of Barteh and Kohram

In ninth place, Barteh and Kohram appear
On the battlefield, two brave men,
Leaders of noblemen, ready to strike with sword.
They attack each other, enlivened by their leaders' hatred.
They make attempts with every sort of weapon,
And in the end they seize their Indian swords.

All at once, Kohram turns his back on Barteh,
And the latter deals him such a blow on the head
That it splits him in half down to his breast.

Even Barteh is moved by the fate of his opponent.
He dismounts and hooks up Kohram's body to the saddle.
Once again, he takes his place on his stallion
And rushes like a growling leopard up the hill,
Holding in one hand an Indian sword
And in the other his blessed banner,
Kohram's corpse bouncing against his horse's flank.

He cries out, "The king is triumphant!
May his crown rise all the way to the sun!"

38. | The Battle of Zangueh and Akhvaast

The tenth hero to fight, Zangueh, son of Shaavaran,
Advances toward his opponent, Akhvaast,
So bold and fearless that lions flee at the sight of him.

Akhvaast and Zangueh both grab their heavy maces.
They fight in excess, dealing each other such blows
That the two are soon beyond exhaustion.

Their battle steeds are rigid from fatigue.
It is as if their arteries no longer flow with blood.
The bright sun heats up the field, completing its course
Across the firmament as if warming a metal plaque.

The two combatants are stiff and worn out with fatigue.
They address each other and say,
"Heat is burning our livers. We must rest,
Catch our breaths. Then we shall resume battle."

They part ways, leaving their horses behind
And placing hindrances on their hooves.
After a time of rest, they rise
And once again prepare to resume battle.

Akhvaast, armed with a lance,
Charges as swift as flame to the center of the battlefield.

Zangueh takes advantage of the situation,
Directs his spear against him, and strikes him
At the belt, sending him headfirst off his horse.

Akhvaast cries out like a burst of thunder.
One would think the earth is splitting.

Zangueh dismounts, approaches him,
Drags his face through black dust,
Lifts him skillfully from the ground,
Tosses him over his horse's saddle,
And takes the direction of the hill.

O wonder of wonders,
How many ailments the sky inflicts on the Turks!

Zangueh travels from plain to hill, holding
In his hand his banner with the image of a wolf.
He plants it before his friends, invoking Yazdan's
Praise on the king and on the world hero.

39 | The Battle of Goodarz and Piran

Once nine hours of the day go by,
Not a single Turk remains on the vast plain,
Swords having separated heads from bodies.
It is as if the world holds no pity for them.
It raises a man with affection, helps him live,
Then it attacks in the middle of his joy
And assails him with all sorts of hardships.

We are born from wind, briefly given breath,
Ultimately to be returned to wind.
Death is a just end, though we view it as persecution.
The struggle brings adversity upon the Tooranians
And relentlessly persists on the battlefield.

At this time, Piran takes a look around and comes
To the realization that no warrior is left standing.

Leaders of Iran and Tooran advance in a combative
Manner, rolling beneath their feet the surface of the earth,
Hearts full of agony, heads resolute on vengeance.
The sun suspends its journey, so astonished it is
By the dust rising from the struggle.

They deploy all their resources:
Sword, spear, mace, and noose.
But Yazdan has long ago determined the outcome:
The Tooranians are to succumb to the Iranians.

Piran cannot resist the strength behind his charger.
He senses his end approaching
And accepts it as divine will.
Yet, in his courage, he fights on,
Struggling against the set revolutions of his destiny.

After having made use of their weapons,

Two leaders of two hosts,
Aging men full of caution, seize bow and arrow.
They send flying a shower of shots,
Like leaves gliding in an autumn wind.

Goodarz brings out an arrow of poplar wood,
Which neither steel nor stone can resist.
He shoots it and pierces the strappings of Piran's charger.
The stallion staggers, and as it tumbles to quickly expire,
It catapults Piran to the ground, rolls over him,
And crushes his right hand, splitting it in two.

Piran frees himself and rises once again,
Despite a sense that he will not survive this fatal day.
He attempts to save himself, fleeing before Goodarz
And taking the direction of the mountain,
Exhausted by pain and worn out by the race.
Still, he is able to reach the mountaintop,
All the while praying to outrun the hero.

Goodarz observes him, shedding bitter tears.
He fears that fate will change its course again.
He knows destiny can only be trusted to torment men.
He cries out, "Illustrious hero, what is happening to you?
Why do you run off on foot in this way?
You pass before me like hunted prey.
Where are your troops, O army leader?
Where is your strength? Where are your courage,
Your valor, your arms, your insight, your treasure?
Where is the wisdom of which you spoke?
O army pillar, defender of King Afraasiyaab,
Here the sun has eclipsed for your king.
Fate completely turns its back on you.
Now is not the time for tricks.
Forget your urge to escape.
Since you are reduced to it, ask for mercy,
So that I return you alive to the glorious king.
He will grant you pardon when he sees
Your head and your beard white as snow."

Piran replies, "May such a thing never come to be!
May this last misfortune not be reserved for me!

After all that's happened, I shall never ask for mercy.
I have come to this world to die
And, in battle, have offered you my head.
I have heard great men say that no matter
How long life may last in this joyous world,
In the end, death, inexorable, reaches out for you!"

Goodarz circles the mountain in vain.
He wearies himself trying to find a path.
Then he sets foot to the ground, grabs his shield,
And climbs the mountain like a huntsman,
Clutching a javelin, his eyes fixed upward.

The leader of the Tooranian host sees him from his post.
He leaps off a boulder, flings his dagger like one shoots
An arrow, and strikes the old leader in the upper arm.

Goodarz, tired and wounded by Piran,
Enters into a wild rage. Eager for revenge,
He sends off his javelin into Piran's chest,
Striking through his coat of mail
And piercing through the skin to his liver.

Piran hollers a mournful cry, his head troubled,
His mouth spewing his heart's blood.
Such is the way of the world.
He drops like a lion in fury,
Liver wounded by the blade of steel.
He writhes with convulsions for some time.
Then he is still, finally able to concede to eternal rest
And end the fatigues of battles and battlefields.
His soul departs to join his deceased companions.

Such is the rotation of time,
Unwilling to accept the teachings of any master.
When destiny dips its hand in bile,
It rips the heart of a lion and the skin of a leopard.

Once Goodarz reaches the mountain crest,
He spots Piran in such a state of distress,
Heart shattered, hand wounded, head full of dust,
Armor cracked open, belt ripped in two.

Goodarz says, "O valiant lion, O brave cavalier,
The world has seen many men like you and me
But grants neither one much time to rest."

He lifts a hand over Piran's body and dips it in blood.
He drinks it and rubs it on his face.
Then he hollers over the death of Siaavoosh.
He addresses prayers to the Creator,
Lamenting before the Justice Giver
Over the death of his seventy noble sons.

He wishes to cut off his enemy's head but cannot
Bring himself to perform this act of violence.
He plants Piran's banner to provide shade for his head.
He regains the road to catch up with his men
While blood trickles from his arm,
Drop by drop, like a fluid river.

40 | Goodarz Returns to the Leaders of Iran

The lion returns victorious from battle,
Bringing the shining banner up the hill.
Warriors, keen on vengeance,
March from hilltop to army camp.
Attached to their saddles are their victims' cadavers,
Handled in accordance with the ways of war.

With the prolonged absence of the world leader,
The Iranian troops, young and old, shout out and say,
"Is it possible that Goodarz, weak in his old age,
Has fallen into the hands of Piran?"
They shed bitter tears,
For they fail to see their flock's shepherd.

Finally, they spot a banner through thick dust.
Their laments turn into cries of joy
As they watch Goodarz appear through a veil of dust.
Their hearts shed all sense of distress.
The sound of timpani rises above the army,
And the dust lifts into the air to kiss the sky.

PART FIFTEEN

The noblemen run to the hero, joyful and laughing.
Soon they grow increasingly concerned.
Whispers travel through the troops:
"Without a body, one has to fear that Goodarz
Has been vanquished and humiliated by Piran.
Piran is a man of lion heart who spent his life in battle."

Goodarz addresses the crowd.
Young and old listen to him keenly.
He points to the place where he engaged in battle
And recounts to them what happened.
Then he commands Rohaam to climb on his horse
And go find Piran's corpse. He adds,
"Tie him to the saddle, return with his armor
And coat of mail attached with your noose,
And do not disfigure his face or body."

Rohaam takes off as commands the world leader,
Charging forward as swift as wind.
He flings Piran's corpse across his saddle,
Covered in armor and full of blood.
He ties it up and scampers back to the mountain.

At the sight of Piran's standard on the hill,
The Iranians invoke divine blessings on Goodarz:
"O famous support of Iranians, of the crown and throne,
You have surrendered, as ransom, your heart and soul."

Goodarz addresses his noble warriors:
"When I saw the weight of war bearing down
Heavily on us, I feared Afraasiyaab would
Send fresh troops across the Jayhoon.
Our host is weary and shattered.
With this foreknowledge, I have sent a message
Full of advice to our king, informing him
That if the King of Turks brings forth an army,
We would have a slim chance of holding out against it.
I think Kay Khosrow will soon come to our aid
And illuminate this battlefield with pomp and majesty.

"Let us then place on our horses' saddles the fallen men,
For their deaths free our weary hearts of worry
And allow us to rejoice for the soul of Siaavoosh.

If we take these cadavers to the king,
He will be pleased and shower us with honors.
We know that this hatred between the Turks
And the Iranians stems from Piran,
This evil man who has ceased to exist.
When Khosrow arrives, he will make sure,
By the power given to him by Yazdan the pure,
That we have nothing to fear from the Tooranians."

Everyone blesses Goodarz in unison and says,
"May earth and time never be robbed of your presence!
Every word you speak brings us good fortune.
The sun and moon shine by the mere sight of you."

They take off with the cadavers,
Making Garooy, son of Zerreh, run on foot,
Both hands tied to his shoulders with a yoke.

As they approach the army tents, Goodarz finds
Troops and leader awaiting him on foot.
Gostaham the lion, standing before the ranks,
Advances toward the brave hero,
Kisses the ground before him,
And invokes divine blessings upon him.
He says, "Look at all your troops.
You have freed them from worry.
I return them to you as you entrusted them to me."

While Goodarz and Gostaham speak with each other,
The voice of the sentry stationed on Mount Raibad
Strikes their ears with a shout:
"A dust as black as pitch covers the plain.
On every side, one hears the rising sound of cymbals.
The din of timpani and clarions shakes the ground.
A turquoise throne sits on the back of an elephant,
Shining like the River Nile.
The air appears like a colorful spread of purple silk,
So numerous are the floating banners of various colors.
From a distance, one can see a splendid standard,
Like a tall and slender cypress tree.
It is surrounded by riders wearing steel armor.
The earth from end to end is awash in shades of purple.

The eye can see banner after banner,
Sporting images of dragons, eagles, or the magical Homa.
If they continue at this pace, they will reach us in one day."

41 | Lahaak and Farshidvard Lament the Death of Piran

From atop Mount Konaabad,
The sentry observes the astonishing developments.
He dashes toward Lahaak and Farshidvard,
Heart throbbing with ache, exhaling deep sighs.
He says to them, "If my eyes are not dimmed,
If after all these concerns my sight is not troubled,
Yazdan has made the Turks perish
And rendered vain the labors they have endured.
I witnessed Iranian warriors
Climb down the mountain, shouting cries,
Each holding in his hand a banner.
I witnessed the banner of our leader Piran toppled,
His body drowning in blood.
I witnessed Piran's escort of ten brave men,
Disarmed, their heads brought down, spattered with blood.
The warriors of Iran triumphantly returned to Gostaham.

"On the other side of Raibad,
One can distinguish a black dust obscuring the plain.
In its midst billows the Kaaviani banner,
Ahead of a sea of swords.
Around it are the timpani and the clarions.
The earth appears as black as ebony."

Lahaak and Farshidvard climb up
The watchtower above the battleground.
They see with their own eyes the corpse
Of the aged leader, their brother and master,
Along with the bodies of the ten cavaliers,
Singled out among the most daring Tooranian warriors.

They stay frozen in the tower, moaning and crying,
Lamenting the death of their dear brother.
They say in their distress, "O valiant lion,

O leader Piran, rider full of courage,
Now your enemy's wishes are fulfilled.
The world no longer exists for you; it is all over!
Who will avenge you?
Who will follow your path, your example?
The time is here when the land of Tooran
Has fallen to ruins along with its king.
All that remains for us to do is cut off our heads,
Drown in blood our bodies, our blades, our hands!"

But they do not act in accordance with their words.
They recall Piran's last wishes after having provoked
Goodarz in battle, when he said to Farshidvard,
"If I fall on the field of vengeance and disappear,
The earth would constrict for our noble leaders,
And no man from the seed of Viseh with
The slightest sense of wisdom must linger there!
If we are killed in this battle,
Our bodiless heads will be taken to Iran.
Our warriors must beg Goodarz for protection,
And you must take, in secret, the desert road.
In this way you may save your life
From falling into enemy hands."

The two brothers return to their troops,
Sight full of blood, hearts failing.

The troops understand that this great flock
Has been deprived of its shepherd.
They burst into tears and mournful fits,
As if consumed by a most ardent flame.

They approach Lahaak and Farshidvard,
Hearts despairing and afflicted, and say,
"What shall we do here, now that the pillar
Of the Tooranian host has been snatched from us?
Who will be inspired to draw courage,
To strap himself, and cover his head with helm of steel?"

Lahaak and Farshidvard reply,
"What man is able to evade divine will?
Fate has written above Piran's head
That he is to perish on the field of vengeance;

That the double-edged sword
Is meant to part his soul from his body;
That his wounded, lifeless body would find
The comfort of neither shroud nor coffin;
That it would be dragged by his enemy,
Chest and coat of mail drenched in blood.
Now what was foreseen has ensued, and Piran is gone,
His labors and deeds fading in the wind.

"He was the army's pillar as long as he lived,
His heart full of affection for the troops.
He defended us against the enemy,
And son and brother were the same to him.
His joy and sorrow now belong to the other world,
And Yazdan will surely give him a seat among the just.
His consideration for us extended beyond his death,
And with Goodarz, he agreed on a treaty
According to which, if Piran succumbed,
Goodarz would renounce any fight against you
And would keep the road to Tooran open,
Refraining from an urge to destroy you.

"The Iranians will not break this treaty.
You have nothing to fear on this matter.
Listen, young and old, to our three options:
You could ask King Khosrow for mercy.
If so, take immediate resolution to do so.
Or, should you wish to return to your families,
Then take the road and risk exposure to danger.
Or perhaps you wish to resume battle,
Plunge your spears deep in Iranian blood.
Let us carefully examine each of these options.
But the end result will be no different from divine will.

"If you lean toward battle, then remain here.
Piran has asked Afraasiyaab for reinforcements.
The king has armed a host to arrive at any moment
So that you may execute revenge on the Iranians.
If you would rather return to your land and homes,
The Iranians may open the roads to allow passage.
Finally, if you decide to ask Khosrow for mercy,
You must prepare to leave this place.

If you wish to pass through the land of Iran,
You must do so, for the soul is the body's sovereign.
Do not rely on the two of us brothers.
Never will our hatred dissolve from our hearts!
Never has a man from the family of Viseh
Endured the belt the way ours have!
We shall honor Piran's last wishes and commands!
We shall return to the land of Tooran by way of the desert.
If the road is blocked, we shall fight until we win!"

The Turks listen to this speech and emit their reply:
"Our illustrious leader has been overthrown and killed,
Along with ten of our warriors.
Now Kay Khosrow is approaching by way of Raibad.
Who dares remain on this battlefield?
We have neither horse nor armor, neither feet nor wings,
Neither treasure nor leader, neither strength for battle
Nor land or road on which to flee.
Why should we bring further harm upon ourselves?
Besides, if we wished to fight in retreat,
Goodarz and Khosrow would send elephants and troops
To pursue us, in which case none of us would remain alive.
We would never again see our tents and relatives!
There is then no shame in asking for mercy,
For, although we form a huge army, we have no leader.
Why should we continue to fear the King of Tooran?
Afraasiyaab matters to us no more than a fistful of dust.
Why did he not act in the same manner as the King of Iran?
Why did he not take better care of his troops and host?"

42 | Lahaak and Farshidvard Take the Road to the Land of Tooran

After the army's reply, Lahaak and Farshidvard rise,
Aware that this is not the moment to fight or seek glory.
They know the army is right,
That a flock without its guard has little hope
For survival and is sure to perish.
The leaders bid farewell to their troops
And prepare to take the long desert road,

Banners in hand, hearts full of sadness, eyes full of blood.
They proceed with ten illustrious riders, brave and skillful,
But they find the road blocked by the Iranians.

The Turks launch their steeds
While the Iranian guards sit firm in the saddle.
A battle ensues, one not foreseen by either party.
The field blossoms with stains of blood,
Reminiscent of blooming tulips.

Eight men perish on the Iranian side, bold lions in battle.
Among the Turks, the two noble heroes
Are the only ones to escape uninjured.
They dash down the desert road
As the Iranian sentry warns from his tower,
"O valued men, two fierce warriors emerged
From the army of Turks, escorted by ten brave riders.
They fell on our patrols with fury, mixing dust with blood.
After killing eight Iranians, the two marched away."

Goodarz is certain and exclaims,
"These two must be Lahaak and Farshidvard!
They left with pride, not yet weary of battle.
If they travel from Iran to Tooran-Zamin,
Misfortune is sure to befall my army.
May the one who wishes to acquire glory
Dress his head with Rumi helm!
May he chase down Lahaak and Farshidvard
And destroy them both with his sword!"

The Iranians drained, their backs slouched by steel armor,
Do not reply except for Gostaham, a lion eager for battle.
He says to the leader, "O man worthy of throne,
When you left to fight the Tooranians,
You entrusted me with the protection of timpani and host,
And commanded me to stand at the head of troops.
Other heroes have acquired fame and glory, not me.
I have not yet played my part in battle.
The time has come for me to glorify my exploits.
I shall leave this instant and force these two warriors
To fall inside my noose's loop."

Gostaham's show of courage makes Goodarz rejoice.

His cheeks come to life and his back straightens
As grief is expelled from his heart. He says to him,
"You walk under a lucky star, and you resemble the sun!
You are a lion hunting down a deer.
May the Creator assist you in this venture.
May three hundred adversaries
Of the likes of Lahaak be your prey!"

43 | Gostaham Pursues Lahaak and Farshidvard

Gostaham dons his battle armor
And bids farewell to every warrior.
He exits the camp in haste,
On his way to fight the two proud Turks.
The entire army has qualms about Gostaham's victory
In a fight against two such mighty soldiers.

During this time, a host dispatched by Afraasiyaab
Boldly marches to the rescue, like a boat on water.

Once the troops arrive in the desert of Daghooy,
They learn of Piran's death and the outcome of his battle.
They return to Afraasiyaab with cries of anguish.

Meanwhile, Bijan is made aware that Gostaham
Has departed to fight Farshidvard and Lahaak.
Bijan thinks of the danger awaiting
Gostaham on the plains of Daghooy.
He cannot allow Lahaak and Farshidvard
To reduce his friend to dust.
Worried for Gostaham, he climbs on his stallion,
Finds his grandfather Goodarz, and says in a loud voice,
"O brave champion, wisdom does not approve
Of you delivering such a noble warrior to his death.
By doing so, you give the sky a reason to hurt us.
Two fierce Tooranian leaders
Have bravely taken the road like lions.
They are more valiant than Hoomaan or Piran.
They are by birth the noble leaders of their land.
Now Gostaham has gone to battle them.
We cannot allow them to gain the upper hand.

Our triumphs will turn to grief if this lion man
Were to disappear from the army ranks!"

Goodarz approves of the words of the glory-seeking hero.
After reflection, he decides to embrace Bijan's advice.
The chief leader of the king says to his warriors,
"Whoever wishes to acquire glory and honor
Must leave to follow Gostaham's trail
And assist him against the enemy."

No one in the gathering replies.
No one worries for Gostaham.
No man is sufficiently rested.

Bijan then says to Goodarz,
"No one besides me is able to save him.
These brave men are not yet weary of life.
They do not wish to rise and engage in conflict.
This venture is mine, for my heart is full of concern,
And my eyes are full of tears!"

Goodarz replies, "O lion-man,
You have not yet experienced life's ups and downs.
Do you not see that we are victorious?
Do not throw yourself so rashly into the conflict.
Gostaham will conquer these two Turks.
He will deprive them of their heads with his dagger.
Wait until I send after him a cavalier akin to a fierce lion
To assist him in battle and reduce them both to dust!"

Bijan replies, "O warrior hero, full of wisdom and sense,
It is during his life that a man needs a friend,
It will be too late after he has been slain.
When Gostaham falls in battle,
When his day passes and his fate ends,
Is that when you will command me to seize weapons
And to strap my belt to come to his aid?
If you forbid me to leave, I shall cut off my neck
With this very sharp and shiny dagger,
For I wish not to survive him!
Do not seek then a pretext to prevent me from acting!"

Goodarz retorts, "Go then, if you value your life so little.

Since you are not weary of battle, cinch your waist,
Seize your weapons, and do not waste a moment.
It seems that you have no pity for your father,
For you never cease to fill his heart with anguish.
If you have no fear of drowning your head in dust,
Why should I fear for you in this battle?"

At these words from his grandfather, Bijan bows down,
Kisses the ground, and immediately takes his leave.

44 | Bijan Follows Gostaham's Trail

Bijan secures himself for battle
And asks for his horse Shabrang to be saddled.

Giv learns of Bijan's intentions
And his earnestness to fight Farshidvard.
He rises in an instant, climbs on a Taazian steed,
And dashes on the road like a whirlwind of smoke.

He reaches Bijan, brusquely pulls on his reins,
And says, "I have recounted to you many a story,
But you never agree to come over to my side
So that I may be happy with you, if only once.
Why are you rushing off in this manner?
Do not seek to distress me at all times.
Tell me what new misfortune
You wish to afflict upon your poor, aging father.
I have no other son but you in the entire world,
And my heart is never at peace
For the constant anxiety I must endure.
You sit in the saddle for ten days and ten nights,
Holding above your enemy's head
The double-edged blade of vengeance.
Your body is used up by your coat of mail,
And yet you do not grow weary of bloodshed.
You never wish to confide in me.
Now that I am old, what more do you want from me?
When the Giver of good fortune grants us victory,
We must sit in joy, revel in feast, and rest!

"Why do you tempt fate?
Have you so much trust in your sword?
When one does not focus on the goal in life,
One does not always attain one's wish.
Do not tantalize providence so often.
It never stops to keep its eyes fixed on us.
Give up this venture for the sake of your father,
For it does not suit you to torment my heart."

Bijan replies, "O wise and sensible man,
People hold a different opinion of you.
You wish not to remember the past.
You foolishly turn your back on virtue.
But know, O father, that your words
Are not in harmony with justice!
Do you not remember the battle of Laadan
And Gostaham's great feats, all for my sake?
Do you not remember how he shared
With me both good and bad fortune?
The hardships brought on me by the dome of sky
Are unavoidable, and by abstaining from action,
One does not erase what has been written in the stars.
It is not necessary to speak at length of these matters.
Do not divert me from engaging in battle,
For I have devoted my life to this enterprise!"

Giv replies, "If you will not turn away from battle,
Then best for me to join you in these ups and downs,
And act as your companion in moments of danger."

Bijan says, "May such a thing never come to be,
That three great men of Kianian lineage make a journey
Stricken by terror for the sake of two Turks.
I implore you by the life and head of the noble king,
By the life of my grandfather, illustrious warrior,
By the blood of Siaavoosh to return
From this battleground and allow me to be on my way.
I shall obey your command to refrain from battle!"

At these words, Giv is determined to return.
He gives Bijan his blessing and says,
"May you be victorious and come back safe

And sound, with joy in your heart,
After having bound up the hand of evil!"

Bijan departs, charging forth on the trail of Gostaham
On whom he focuses his worries and his joys.
He chases after him on the road to save him
From any harm caused by Tooranian riders.

During this time, Lahaak and Farshidvard
Have crossed the battlefield and the river in haste.
In the space of one hour, they travel seven farsangs
And think they are safe from the Iranian troops.
They spot a forest with running streams,
Where travelers can find shelter from the sun.
There are birds, game, and lions, trees above their heads,
Greenery, shrubs, and water beneath their feet.
They stop to engage in the hunt
And approach the river to quench their thirst.
After drinking, they look to eat,
For neither grief nor joy can satisfy one's appetite.

They search through the forest
And bring down game of all sorts.
They light a fire, eat roasted meat,
And return to the stream to drink.

The fate of brave men is dreadful when misfortune looms.
Once dark night descends and the moonbeams shine,
Lahaak falls asleep while Farshidvard keeps watch.

45 | Gostaham Kills Lahaak and Farshidvard

Gostaham approaches the site where the Tooranians rest.
His stallion catches the scent of the two horses.
It whinnies and leaps around wildly.
In an instant, Lahaak's stallion responds
With a nicker, as if in a state of outrage.

Farshidvard runs to Lahaak and stirs him,
"Wake up from your sweet slumber.
We must bravely strike the head of misfortune.

A wise man once shared this profound notion:
    'When a lion runs off before a wolf's claws,
    The wolf must not chase after him,
    For he would cause his own demise.'
Come now, rise and hurry!
An army arrives from Iran to block our way!"

The two riders climb on their steeds
And gallop out of the forest.
They turn their sight to the plain,
Reflecting on how to proceed.

They recognize Gostaham in the distance,
Galloping toward them, unaccompanied.
The two brave men raise their heads
And say to each other,
"A lone man is coming our way without an escort:
Gostaham, with the banner of warriors in hand.
We must not run away but wait for him to arrive.
He has no chance of escaping us unless we face adversity."
They emerge from their shelter to take the sandy path.

Gostaham, avid for battle, rushes toward them.
Once near them, he cries out in fury
Like a mad lion and sends their way
A shower of shots with arrows of poplar wood.

Farshidvard charges to attack,
But Gostaham strikes his head with his blade
And mixes his blood with his brains.
Farshidvard, illustrious warrior, son of Viseh,
Instantly falls off his horse and dies.

At the sight of his brother's still face,
Lahaak understands his predicament.
Grief overtakes him, making him shake violently.
The world turns black before his eyes.
The excess of affliction renders his heart indifferent.
He binds his bow and stretches it.
He sends an arrow toward Gostaham
While his eyes spill a torrent of blood.
The two warriors assail each other in turn.
Not a single arrow touches the ground.

Wounded, they soon substitute sword for bow and arrow.

At once, Gostaham seizes the opportunity.
He tugs at his horse's bridle, falls on Lahaak,
Dealing him such a blow on the neck
That he tumbles to his death.
His head rolls beneath Gostaham's feet
Like a ball struck by a mallet.

Such is the way of the rotating dome of sky.
It deprives the very ones it once nurtured with affection.
When you seek a head, you fall on feet,
And when you seek feet, you find a head instead.

Gostaham remains on horseback,
But he is so deeply wounded
He feels as if he may fracture into small pieces.
He continues on horseback, slumped over the saddle,
Pushing his horse forth while shedding abundant blood.

In the end, he arrives at the edge of a spring
With running water and comforting shade.
He sets foot to the ground, ties his horse to a tree,
And succeeds in making his way to the water.
He drinks for a long time, expressing gratitude.
One would think he is nailed to the ground.
Then he begins to writhe and roll on the black earth,
His entire body torn apart by lesions.

He says, "O gracious World Master,
Send someone from our host to my aid.
May Bijan, son of Giv, or another valiant hero leave
Our famous host, driven by worry, and come to my side.
May he take me from this place, alive or dead,
To the Iranian camp so that they may be assured
That I have not died in vain, bereft of glory!
This is my one and only wish!"

He spends the entire night moaning and writhing
In pain, like a serpent slithering in the dust,
Until daylight, pure and bright, winks away the dark.

46 | Bijan Finds Gostaham Lying in the Meadow

As the vibrant shades of the sun's rays
Gradually spread their warm glow across the world,
Bijan arrives at the meadow.
He searches the grounds for a trail of his lost friend.
He spots in the distance a dun charger
Dashing across the prairie like a racing steed.
At times trotting, at times grazing,
Every so often, it leaps like a leopard,
Its saddle overturned, its bridle frayed,
Its covering dragging on the ground,
Stirrups, straps, and reins smeared in blood.

At such a sight, Bijan loses his mind.
He hollers like a lion: "My friend, full of affection,
O beloved companion, are you in this meadow?
The thought of you breaks my heart,
And my soul is about to leap out of my body!
What can I say? Where shall I find you now?
What trick has the sky played on you?"

He follows the horse's tracks to the spring,
Where he finds Gostaham's body sprawled on the field,
Where he fell headfirst, causing his wounds.
His armor and helm are grimy with dust and blood.

Bijan jumps off his mount Shabrang
And wraps Gostaham tightly in his arms.
He unfastens his Rumi mail, strips it off his chest,
Removes the helmet from his injured head.
He examines his wounds and realizes
That if they are not immediately dressed
He will be on the verge of death.
Gostaham's body expels a yellow mucus,
His soul grieves, and his heart aches.

Bijan places his face on Gostaham's lesions
And wails, "O my valiant companion,
I had no other friend but you in all the world.
You should have warned me from the beginning
And asked me to join you on the site of battle.

I would have been at your side at the time of peril
When you came face to face with Ahriman in a fight!
Now our enemies have attained their goal
And accomplished what they set out to do!"

In this way speaks Bijan while Gostaham trembles,
Exhales a deep sigh, and replies, "O dear friend,
Do not fret this way over my demise.
Your suffering is for me less endurable than my death.
Restore my helmet to my wounded head,
And find a way to lead me to the king.
I ask of providence only one thing:
That is to remain alive long enough
To gaze once again upon his majesty's face.
May death ensue! I have no fear of it,
For I know with certainty that ultimately
I shall have no other place of repose than the dust.

"Everyone who expires meets with his proper destiny.
The man who seeks only the fulfillment
Of his own dreams is not a compassionate man.
Take my two formidable foes who,
With the aid of Yazdan, perished at my hand.
Fling them, if you can, upon the saddle.
If you are unable to fulfill this task,
Then cut off their heads and carry them,
Along with their armor, to the Iranians
So that they may identify their features.
Tell the king, world master,
That I did not foolishly throw my life to the wind.
Tell him that I fought in every circumstance and never
Wavered when it came to acquiring fame and glory."

Then he indicates to Bijan the distant location
Of the pair of deceased Tooranians.
His strength is spent by his discourse.
Bijan too feels his head spin as he continues to weep.
Without delay he brings his friend's horse
And unfastens the tightly secured straps.
He places the cover of the horse beneath
The body of the injured man who moans painfully.

He tears off the hem of his shirt
And dresses all of Gostaham's wounds.
Then he climbs on some heights,
Mind troubled by grief, and, from an elevated spot,
He makes out scattered Turkish riders entering the desert.

He descends the hill in haste, shaking,
Disquieted about Gostaham's imminent death.
He falls on the fearful Tooranian riders
And assails two of them with his sword.
He removes from the saddle strap his rolled-up noose
And tosses it around the neck of one of the Turks,
Who falls off his horse and begs for mercy.
Bijan spares his life in return
For his assistance in the tasks ahead.

He then dashes, like a whirlwind of dust,
To the place where Lahaak and Farshidvard recline.
He finds them stretched out on the ground,
Drenched in blood, their chargers grazing in the prairie.

At the sight, Bijan utters blessings on Gostaham
For the execution of this bold act of vengeance.
He commands the Turk he released to lift the heroes
Off the ground, toss them on a horse,
And to assist him in tying their hands and feet.

Then he returns to Gostaham, bounding like a mad leopard.
He dismounts and, as swift as wind, places him gently
On the saddle, avoiding causing him unnecessary pain.
He commands the Turk to climb and hold the injured one
In his arms while maneuvering the charger to trot gently.

He implores Yazdan with passionate pleas
And departs, heart full of ache and worry
Over the condition of his friend Gostaham,
Anguished over the improbability of having him
Stay alive long enough to arrive at the king's court.

47 | Kay Khosrow Orders the Building of a Mausoleum for Piran

Nine hours pass in the day.
The sun moves across the dome of sky.
World master Khosrow arrives with pomp and glory
On the plain where his army camps.

Noble warriors and leaders march on foot to greet him.
Wise men invoke blessings upon him: "O King and leader,
Your body resembles that of a fierce elephant,
Your soul that of Gabriel.
Your hand lavishes affection like a winter cloud.
Your heart flows as plentiful as the River Nile."

The king bestrides his horse
So that the troops may perceive his features.
He salutes them and says,
"May the earth always flourish with brave warriors!"

Then Goodarz, the army's support,
Sets it into motion according to tradition.
The ten warriors, who reduced the Turks to dust,
Lead the procession, acclaiming the king.
Their weapons, bodies, and clothes are soaked in blood.
Tied to their mounts are the heads and corpses of their foes.

As soon as Goodarz sees the king in the distance,
He climbs off his horse and approaches Kay Khosrow,
Prostrating himself before him in reverence.
Goodarz displays the cadavers and heads,
And identifies those who fought one against the other.

Giv comes running with Garooy of Zerreh
Before the valiant ruler of Iran.
Khosrow sighs deeply at the sight of Garooy.
He immediately dismounts and asks for actions of mercy
From the Creator: "Glory be to Yazdan, who is my shelter
And who has given us dominion and victory!"

He remains standing in prayer,
Removes from his head his Kianian headdress,

And invokes the grace of the Justice Giver on hero and army:
"O illustrious men of fortunate paths,
You act as fire, deeming your enemy as brittle as reeds.
May the hearts of the leader Goodarz and his relatives,
Who have been consumed, be consecrated
For having sacrificed their lives.
From here on, my treasure and power belong to you.
I shall refuse you nothing that my right hand can dispense."

Then his eyes fall on the dead.
At the sight of Piran, he sheds bitter tears,
For he remembers his many good deeds.
His heart is consumed by pain, as if by a blazing fire.
He speaks of Piran's death, cheeks flooding with tears:
"Bad fortune is a fierce and horrific dragon
Whose breath devours the lion.
Courage does not give one strength to withstand it.
Here are the deeds of this sharp-clawed dragon.
For many long years, Piran watched over me,
Tending to my every wish like a father.
He deplored the murder of Siaavoosh,
And on this matter no one can reprimand him.
But then this man, once so gentle, became merciless
And filled the land of Iran with terror.
Ahriman perverted his heart,
And he diverged from the path he once followed.
I often gave him advice, but in vain.
He did not take my words to heart.
His downfall came from his loyalty to Afraasiyaab
And his refusal to defy the king.

"My mind nurtured other rewards for him.
I was prepared to offer him throne and diadem.
But the turn of events foiled my intentions
As the sky spun with a different purpose.
Cruelty supplanted benevolence to rule over his heart,
Thus exposing to us a new and unexpected face.
He charged at us with a huge army in a battle
In which so many Iranians succumbed and died.
He rejected the warnings of Goodarz,
As well as my commands and my warriors' strategies.
He altered the kindness within his virtuous heart

By blending poison into his nature.
He rushed from Tooran with weapons
To fight Goodarz, a leader of serene mind,
Only to fall victim to the point of the blade.
He sacrificed son, brother, headdress and belt,
Armor, troops, and an entire land.
He sacrificed everything for his affection for Afraasiyaab.
Fate did not idle away time
But devised a quick end to his life."

Kay Khosrow orders Piran's body
To be embalmed from head to toe with a mixture
Of musk, camphor, amber, and rosewater,
And to be dressed in Rumi brocade.
His head is to be filled with musk and camphor.
His place of burial is determined to be the mountain.
In his affection for the deceased, Khosrow orders
A mausoleum so tall its crest reaches the sphere of sky.
It is to hold massive thrones worthy of a prince.
They place the leader on one of the thrones,
Cover his waist with his belt
And his head with a proper headdress.

Such is the way of this deceitful world.
At times it elevates you; at times it casts you off.
The heart of a wise man remains confounded
By the promises and the withholdings of chance.

After Piran is set to rest,
Khosrow addresses the matter of Garooy of Zerreh.
A great sigh escapes his chest, and he curses him.
He observes this man of ill intentions, his hair in disarray,
His appearance reminiscent of a deev.
The king says, "O all-pervading World Creator,
It appears as if Kaavoos committed the gravest crimes
And deeply offended You,
For an evil deev slew his son, Siaavoosh.
I still do not know why Garooy held such hostility
Toward my father, a pure soul and an innocent man.
But I swear by Yazdan the One, Master of Victory,
Guide and Giver of all that is good,
That I shall, without delay, challenge Afraasiyaab

To account for the spillage of the blood of Siaavoosh!"

He calls for every joint of Garooy's body to be dislocated.
Once this is done, they cut off his head like that of a sheep.
Khosrow asks for his body to be flung into the water
And declares, "May I, one day,
Witness Afraasiyaab in a similar state!"

Such is the intention of the dome of sky:
To nurture one only to witness his collapse.

48 | The Tooranians Ask Kay Khosrow for Mercy

The king remains for some days camped on the battlefield
To help equip the troops for the impending campaign,
To proffer kingdoms to those who deserve them,
As well as robes of honor and diadems.
He offers Goodarz the land of Isfahan, a seat of power
And the residence of great men.
He gives others presents according to name, deed, and merit.

A messenger arrives from Tooran,
A man of sense, dispatched by Piran's men,
To communicate their hopes to Kay Khosrow:
"We are your slaves and your servants.
We trample the earth only at your will.
Man stands beneath Yazdan's hand,
Even when faced with a dragon's fiery jaws.
The world master knows why we have all,
As many as we are, strapped our waists for battle.
We did not take part in the murder of Siaavoosh.
Ahriman diverted our king's heart
Away from the right intention
And away from the right course of action,
Leaving him shameless and fearless before the divine.
Since that day, our suffering has been unrelenting,
And the anguish of our dim hearts
Has caused torrents of tears to flood our cheeks.

"The land of Tooran is filled with terror.
Our women and children are in a state of mourning.

We did not come voluntarily to engage in war,
Neither did we come to safeguard land and dwelling.
War brought us misfortune:
Fathers lost sons, and sons lost fathers.
If you wish to grant us mercy,
We shall stand before you bound as slaves.
We cast ourselves in the jaws of a whale in this host.
The highest ranked are those
Who make an oath of loyalty to the king.
If we seek a fight with you,
We are all guilty, and you are master.
You can do with us as you please.
We shall bring you our leaders, repentant for their deeds.
If your heart is unflinching in its hatred toward us,
Custom permits you to cut off our heads.
It may be to your advantage to opt for clemency.
Now, proceed in a way worthy of a world ruler."

The king of noble heart listens to their words
And pardons the Tooranians.
He orders them to appear before him.
They arrive, hoping to be spared.
They prostrate themselves low to the ground,
Eyes filled with blood tears and hearts with resentment.

Khosrow raises his head to the sky and says,
"O just Creator, you have blessed me
With throne, power, and courage.
Here is an army filled with animosity.
Once it wanted to turn the land of Iran into powder
And bathe the noblest heads with a caustic poison.
But divine justice reduced the Tooranians to a state
Where they no longer maintain either will or opinion.
I reach out my pleading hand toward Yazdan,
The Protector; I ask help of no one in the world.
The story told by a wise man is relevant in this instance.
He said as he climbed on his horse to go to war,
          'From here on, this charger will function
            As my shining throne, and the moment
            To act is here for my shining fortune.'

"I must either bring my throne and crown to this war

Or risk being placed in a narrow coffin of teakwood.
Else I shall find myself caught in the leopard's claws,
With my brains as a meal for vultures.
Your bad actions have turned against you.
Any man of sense will understand this.
I have not dipped my hands in your blood
And wish not to aggravate your misfortunes.
Your entire host will be under my protection,
No matter what ill intentions it harbored in the past.
Whoever among you wishes to leave is free to do so.
He will suffer neither good nor bad.
Anyone who longs to return to his king may do so.
The power given to me by Yazdan places me above
Glorification and diminution, above fatigues and greed."

At the king's words, the Turks remove their helmets,
Acclaiming Kay Khosrow and pronouncing him victorious.
These war leopards become as gentle as gazelles.
The world king commands them
To bring armor, sword, spear, and javelin.
The proud Turks stack a mountain-high heap
Of Rumi helmets and horse trappings around which
They pitch their yellow, red, and purple banners.
They solemnly swear to bind their hearts in devotion
To the king as his servants and slaves.

The wise Khosrow forgives them of their wrongs,
Commands them to scatter and populate his provinces.

49 | Bijan Returns With Gostaham

From the heights of his tower, the sentinel announces
That he makes out dust rising above the road
Through which emerges a single rider
With three horses and three bodies.

The renowned Iranian warriors look in the direction
In great astonishment, wondering,
"Who dares approach us from the border of Tooran?"

During this time, Bijan advances rapidly,

His bow bound and hanging on his arm.

Soon Lahaak and Farshidvard come into sight,
Their bloody, dusty bodies spread across their stallions.
On a third horse, a Turk holds in his arms
Gostaham, overcome with grief.

Once Bijan nears his king, the crown and lofty throne,
He bows low and kisses the ground.

Happy to see him, Kay Khosrow asks,
"O lion man, what did you find on the battlefield?"

Bijan recounts the fight between his friend
And the valiant Lahaak and Farshidvard.
He recounts the dangers that plagued Gostaham
And his fierce contest with the two riders.
He recounts everything in detail, then he adds,
"Gostaham has only one wish for the king to fulfill,
And that is to contemplate his majesty's face, if only once.
After that he is resigned to give way to death."

The generous and kind ruler summons Gostaham.
He is moved to no end at the sight of him,
A flood of tears rushing from his lashes.

Gostaham is so weakened by his wounds
That one would think he has no breath left in him.
As he smells the scent of the King of Kings,
He turns around and fixes his gaze on Khosrow.
Tears of blood and tenderness bathe his cheeks.

The noblemen weep and lament,
Consumed by a most ardent blaze of compassion.
The king is disconsolate to lose such a leader,
Whose head dressed in helmet is like battle anvil.

Now, in his possession he has a stone
He received in inheritance from his ancestors
Hooshang, Tahmures, and Jamsheed.
This stone, which he always wears on his right arm,
Is the hope of wounded men.
Wishing with all his heart to save Gostaham,

PART FIFTEEN

The king detaches the precious gem from his arm,
Fastens it to Gostaham's arm,
And rubs his wounds with his hand.

Kay Khosrow entertains physicians
From Rum, India, Chin, Iran, and Tooran-Zamin.
They travel with him for such occasions.
He asks them to sit at the side of Gostaham
And murmur all sorts of incantations.
Then the king secretly prays at the site of worship.

The injured one fights for his life for two weeks,
And in the end he recovers from his wounds.
They place him on a horse and bring him to the king,
Who takes one look at him and says to the Iranians,
"Be grateful and happy for Yazdan's deeds!
It is wonderful that my wish has been granted
And the compass of my fortune formed a circle so just.
In the spirit of victory,
My concern for Gostaham soured my joyous heart.
We owe our bounty to divine affection,
And we favor the conservation of lives
Over science and the solicitude of men."

Khosrow summons Bijan, son of Giv,
Places his hand in the hand of the brave Gostaham,
And says to Bijan, "You are a pious and fortunate man,
Do not ever fear death, for Yazdan spares lives,
And only Yazdan, everlasting, is able to take the hand
Of the one who falls into the throes of danger.
If ever the World Master revived a dead man,
It is this man here. It is Gostaham."

Then he turns to Gostaham: "Always watch over Bijan,
For no one has seen in our time a man of his stature.
He has endured such labors in friendship to you.
Had he not, we would not find ourselves
In a state of gratitude."

The king remains one more week in Raibad,
Distributing gold, silver, and all sorts of treasure.
In all directions, he sends envoys to warriors
And noblemen, calling them to his side

To help him in the forthcoming war
They are to wage on the ruler of Gang.
He summons them, equipped with weapons,
For they are to battle against the leopard.

Here, poet bard, you complete the tale of Piran's battle.
Introduce us now to the account of the great battle
Of Kay Khosrow with Afraasiyaab.
Formulate, in your exquisite mind,
Elegant words to convey to us how,
After infinite labors, the powerful king is able
To effectuate his revenge on the Tooranian ruler.

PART SIXTEEN

The Reign of Kay Khosrow:
The Great Battle Between
Kay Khosrow and Afraasiyaab

1 | In Praise of Sultan Mahmoud

May Yazdan's blessings grace the Shah,
Delight of crown, throne, and seal,
Whose treasure is derived from greatness,
Whose fame and glory ascend from his name.
O Creator of name and Creator of fortune,
Creator of sword, sorrow, and the timeless,
Bless the one whose treasury suffers from his generosity,
Though his power and his fortune expand from it.
His host extends from sea to sea to follow his directions.
The world lies beneath the splendor of his crown.

There is no gold left in the earth's mines
That is not to be distributed by him.
The king secures gold from his foes to dole out to friends.
The Creator, Donor of victory, is his support.
He lavishes wealth in times of feast.
But when the time of battle comes,
He easily defeats lion and elephant.
He captures borders with the tip of his sword,
And prepares the world for the day of resurrection.
He brings fruit to the tree of faith and wisdom.
Simple advice from him is more sound than the logic of others.

His foresight keeps evil at bay.
His refuge is the Creator's shelter.
When he attacks with his sharp blade of steel,
He turns the world upside down
And scatters precious gems all around.
He demands from the earth only the glory of deserving
The name of a generous sea in times of feast,
And from a lion, the sun's face when he engages in battle.

The earth, the sea, and the sun in the sky
Are witness that there never lived a king of his stature,
In courage, in generosity, and in passion for his work,
In glory, in fame, and in gentle power.
He frightens stars with his gaze.

His body is full of strength and his army so tight
That wind has no chance to pass between the troops.
Behind his host stand seven hundred war elephants.
His allies are the Creator and the angel Gabriel.

He demands tribute from world rulers and noblemen.
If they refuse, he seizes their land, wealth, and crowns.
Who would dare breach the terms of a royal treaty?
He makes the throne of earth shine with grandeur.
In battle he is a mountain braced in armor.

May the valiant and generous King Mahmoud,
The one able to free a deer from a lion's clutches
And lower to the dust the highest standing men,
Reign for as long as the world is the world!
May his banner shine as the moon's diadem!
He is the ornament of the revolving dome of sky.
Seated in times of feast, he is a rain-filled cloud.
He is a just, glorious, powerful and wise king.
May the world never be vacant of his head and crown!
He has an army and valor, treasury and advisor.
He is equally fond of battle, feast, and banquet.

A single carpet spreads across the world,
Its imprint never again to be erased.
On it are placed the pillow and the throne of Fazl,
Son of Ahmad,[21] leading source of wisdom,
On whom rests this empire's peace.
No ruler has ever boasted a minister like him,
So moderate, so generous, so faithful, so wise,
So eloquent, so sincere, so principled, so just,
So devoted to king and to the Divine Creator.
This learned minister has put an end to my grief.

I have framed in verse this book of customs,
Borrowed from an ancient collection,
Hoping that in my old age it would bear some fruit
And provide me with grandeur, gold, and diadem.

For many years, I did not see a generous king
Rule on the Kianian throne.

◇◇◇◇◇◇◇◇◇◇◇◇◇
21 Abbas Fazl bin Ahmad: Minister of Sultan Mahmoud during Ferdowsi's lifetime.

I kept my book to myself until a liberated man,
Full of splendor and a generous heart,
Acceded to the throne. He was a defender of the faith,
A guardian of the crown, powerful in battle,
Sound of judgment, and cognizant of life's mysteries.

In this way, I passed the age of sixty,
Living a life of poverty, labor, and misery.
Once five years added to my sixty,
I felt like a spring breeze completing
Its fluttering dash through fields and plains.

Once I turned sixty-six, I felt weary and intoxicated.
Instead of fortune, I came in possession of a cane.
My cheek that once was as bright as a tulip
Was growing sallow and as pale as hay.
My beard, black as musk, borrowed its hue from camphor.
Age was bending my stature, once erect,
And my eyes of narcissus were losing their youthful gleam.

At the age of fifty-eight, I still felt young,
Although my youth had already passed me by.
I heard a loud proclamation announcing to the world
To dissipate worries from hearts and danger from bodies.
It added that blessed Fereydoon had been resurrected,
That the era and the world were his slaves,
That he had conquered the earth with justice and giving,
That he held his head high as the King of Kings,
And that traces of his story shone with splendor and glory.

May the imprint of his foot
And the anchor of his roots be everlasting!
Since I heard this proclamation, I listen for no other sound.
I have composed this book in the name of our king.
May all greatness in the world be his share!

The master of sword, crown, and throne
Will be my support in my old age.
My only request from the all-powerful Creator
Is to entrust me with enough time and good health
To complete this book in the name of the world king.
I shall speak and conceal nothing.
After that, my body will belong to the dust

And my living soul to the holy face of paradise.

The generous world master, giver of justice,
Who has restored virtue to the earth,
Lord of India and Chin, Iran and Tooran-Zamin,
Master of splendor and supreme power,
Is the one beyond tragedy and blame.
World master Mahmoud, reminiscent of the sun,
A sword-bearing lion in battle,
Will assuage all my needs, fulfill all my desires
And offer me ranking among the nobility.
May his throne shine forever
And fortune prosper to his will!
At times of feast, dinars appear to him as dust,
Which he scatters fearlessly all around.
His voice splits mountains and boulders.
He is a whale in water and a leopard on land.

Valiant is the man who knows how to celebrate him
And who will appreciate the value of my praise.
He is a world ruler above imagination and power.
He is the diadem gracing the head of Jupiter.

I have slaved to create a work, O King,
Hoping to leave behind a memory of my being.
The palaces that we once erected with clay
Fall to ruins under the ravages of rain and sun.
With my verse, I have built a magnificent citadel
That cannot be weathered by either time or storm.
The years will pass over this book,
And men of sense and wisdom
Will continue to recite its rhymes.

May the King, world master, be blessed!
May his throne never be vacant!
His praises lie in his endeavors.
The world, from end to end, stands witness to his glory.
Alas, I find myself unable to praise him adequately,
Wishing to, at least, bless the dust beneath his feet!

May the world subsist in his grace!
May wisdom celebrate his good fortune!
His heart is as joyous as a sunny spring

In the midst of this ever-changing world.
He brings happiness to his people,
As he is victorious, and his word always inspires.

May the King of Kings live forever in joy and glory!
May the evil eye remain at bay!
May he be above all need for as long
As the revolving dome of sky spins
And the stars continue their course through it.

Beside the passage of time, I have no other call to duty
Other than to continue to set to verse this ancient book,
Composed from true and authentic traditions.
The time is here to resume the legends of yore
And the story of the battles of Kay Khosrow.

Listen to my tales of magical adventures.
I shall scatter pearls upon this story,
Sow seeds of tulips upon the stones.
I found the secret, long ago, of breathing life into word.
The theme of these stories is the very marrow of my verse,
As I weave this precious, sumptuous golden cloth.

O you, whose gaze is fixed on a bygone era,
You find yourself at times joyous, at times chagrined.
Cease to be surprised at this ever-changing spinning vault.
The soul is constantly burdened by new troubles.
One's share is nothing but honey and sugar,
A comfortable life, and good fortune,
While another faces grief and suffering,
His heart constricted by the fugitive nature of this world,
And yet a third person spends his life in deceit.

These are the dealings of providence:
The pain caused by the sharp thorn
Pricking the eager outreached hand
Is greater than the pleasure drawn
From viewing the vibrant hue of the blooming rose.

Any person entering his sixtieth year
Cannot count on what is beyond.
Few men surpass the age of seventy.
As for me, I have endured the rotations of the skies

And know that, if I cross that threshold,
My share will be nothing but misfortune and tears.

If the sixty nets of life were fishing nets,
The wise man would find an exit through them.
But we can escape neither the revolving dome
Nor the will of the Master of Sun and Moon.

No matter how much the world ruler
Struggles in his yearning for battles,
No matter how much he enjoys his wealth,
He must, one day, depart to the other world
And leave behind all that he labored for.

Take as example the fate of Kay Khosrow.
Accept as new these age-old stories.
Learn that, with the aid of sword, ruse, and strategy,
He punished his grandfather for the death of his father.
Though he killed his grandfather in vengeance,
He did not remain on the earth for long.
He departed soon after, and with his departure,
His people's ears ceased to listen to his command.

Such is the law of the fleeting world.
In your life, make every attempt to avoid hardship.

2 | Kay Khosrow Musters an Army Against Afraasiyaab

Once the fight between Goodarz and Piran ends,
The victorious king prepares for a new battle.
From every direction appear great and noble leaders
To reinforce the army with countless troops.

The sound of trumpets rises to the sky.
A camp with tent pavilions is spread across the plain.
The surface of the earth takes on a shade of indigo.

The king climbs upon a turquoise throne placed
On the back of an elephant and assumes the crown.
The plain and the royal court echo with cries.

PART SIXTEEN

No space is left to sleep in town or to walk in the country.

Once the king sounds the war signal
By dropping the balls into the cup and
Strapping for war, he calls everyone to his side.
The noble Kay Khosrow thus makes his mark.
He dispatches his instructions with his advice
To the borders where armed troops are stationed.

He summons his most powerful, eager warriors:
Lohraasp; the illustrious Rostam of sharp claws,
Able to draw the fiercest whale out of the sea;
Ashkesh, noble warlord of deep insight.
The king invites them into his audience hall.
He opens his treasury and pays the army.
He invokes his father's soul.

From court, he selects envoys from every province,
Eloquent and clear-minded advisors.
He writes a letter in Pahlavi to each renowned leader:
"O princes of good fortune, the prestige and honor
I grant you surpass anything anyone has dreamed.
Take the road in three different directions,
And safeguard my army from enemy blows.
I shall never cease to fight Afraasiyaab, by day or by night.
I have dispatched troops from every province,
Determined to put an end to this war and this hatred."

Once the letter is read by the empire's princes,
The warriors shout a cry that propels the earth
To surge like waves thrashing on the surface of the sea.
Noblemen from every province equip their troops for war
And drive their hosts in the direction of the royal court.

Kay Khosrow surveys every legion
And establishes camps for them on every side.
From among them, he selects thirty thousand riders,
Quick to strike with swords, and places them at his side
In the army core in anticipation of igniting the war.

He singles out three powerful and prudent men
Of brazen build, such as Rostam, the world warrior;
Goodarz, an aging, clear-sighted wolf; and Tous,

The hero of golden boots, bearer of the Kaaviani banner.
He assigns a place for Tous at his side,
For he is of blessed path and blessed counsel.
On the other flank, he places Manooshan and Khuzan,
Two fearless lions ready for war, bearers of golden helmets,
Wise advisors, and rulers of the land of Pars.

Beyond these stand Aarash, a blaze in battle;
The King of Guran,[22] impatient in conflict;
The King of Khuzan,[23] ally of good fortune in war;
The King of Kerman, [24] always dedicated to winning;
Sabbaah, wise King of Yemen; Iraj of lion heart,
Ruler of Kabol, world master, wise, and devoted;
Shammaakh, ruler of Syria, strapped for battle.
Further beyond is Ghaaran, always victorious,
Army destroyer, ruler of eastern lands,
World master, and a wise and commanding man.

To his left, the king stations descendants of Kay Ghobaad,
Distinguished princes by their birthright,
Who are to fall under the leadership of Delafrooz.
Next are leaders from the race of Goodarz,
Whose swords reach the clouds in the dark of night.
Among them are his noblest heroes:
Bijan, son of Giv, and Rohaam the brave; Gorgeen of Milaad;
And warriors from Rai, armed according to Kianian rank.
Finally, the son of Zarasp, worshipper of Aazargoshasp,
Takes his place with the others in the rearguard
With spears that reach to puncture the mercurial fog.

The king assigns the right wing to Rostam,
With troops unified in heart and body.
Leaders originating from Zabolestan,
Princes and relations of Zaal, prepare
To glorify their exploits and organize the army.

For the left wing, Khosrow selects troops
That shine as bright as the sun under the house of Aries:
The leader Goodarz, son of Kashvaad, Hojir, Farhaad,

◇◇◇◇◇◇◇◇◇◇◇◇◇◇
22 Guran: In today's Lorestan Province of Iran.
23 Khuzan: Small village in today's Alborz Province of Iran.
24 Kerman: A city southeast of Tehran.

And hero warriors from Bardah[25] and Ardabil.[26]
They form squadrons before the world master.
Under the leadership of Goodarz,
The left wing is thus established.

The monarch commands the center portion to be covered
With a line of war elephants bearing towers on their backs.
The earth, trembling beneath the weight,
Swells like the River Nile.
Within the towers are one thousand bold archers.
Each elephant is escorted
By three hundred keen and noble riders.

The warriors from Baghdad are led by Zangueh Shaavaran.
These troops, selected among men from Karkh,[27]
Are to be infantrymen armed with crossbows
And standing at the head of the elephants.
They are positioned to strike a mountain two miles deep
And pierce the hearts of boulders with their shots.
It is unimaginable that anyone could survive their assault.

Behind the elephants are additional foot soldiers
Brandishing spears nine cubits long, ready to pierce heads.
Blood simmers in their hearts.
Their hands clutch shields from Gilan.[28]
At their heels are brave warriors holding
Shafts and shields, followed by riders whose quivers
Are jam-packed with arrows of poplar wood.

The king forms a corps of troops from the west,
Fitted with shields, armor, and Rumi helmets:
Thirty thousand warriors under the guidance of Fariborz
And Tokhaar, ruler of Dahestan, who abhors the enemy
And comes from the noble race of Vashmeh,
A most powerful family.

By the side of Fariborz, the fearless,

<hr>

25 Barda: A city in present-day Azerbaijan that once was the capital of Caucasian
Albania.
26 Ardabil: An ancient city in northwestern Iran.
27 Karkh: Name of the ancient western section of Baghdad.
28 Gilan: Province in today's northwestern Iran bordering the Caspian Sea.

Stands a mass of seasoned, spear-wielding warriors
From the desert of the Taazian under the command
Of Zohir, a man able to snatch food from a lion's jaws.
Khosrow orders him to join Nastooh
To form the left wing of the host like a massive mountain.

More troops arrive from Rum and Barbarestan,
Thirty thousand riders and foot soldiers,
Who line up at the left of the king.
An additional host of eager, experienced men arrives
From Khorasan, driven by Manoochehr, son of Aarash,
A warrior eager to acquire fame and glory.

More warriors are stationed further to the rear:
A renowned man from the family of Garukhan;
A prince from the race of Kay Ghobaad,
Named King Firooz, a great leader,
Light of the troops, ruler of Gharchehgan.
He is a wild lion able to crush a war elephant.
The king places him at the side of Manoochehr
And assigns him the title of commanding officer.

Next come the highborn men of Mount Ghaaf.
They march proudly, armed with spear and mace,
Descendants of Fereydoon and Jamsheed,
Whose hearts rage for the race of Zaadsham.
Khosrow selects thirty thousand sword-wielding
World seekers from the royal family.
He entrusts these troops to Giv, son of Goodarz,
And by doing so sends a wave of joy through the borders.
Assisting Giv from the rear is Aaveh, son of Samkanan,
With troops and warriors full of caution and courage
Who march in single and double file.

Khosrow sends to their right ten thousand cavaliers
Expert with daggers and places ten thousand more
Behind Goodarz, son of Kashvaad.
Sword-brandishing Barteh advances in the army's midst
With proud and valiant mountain dwellers
Grouped in packs to assist the leader Giv.

Coming up are thirty thousand young and able
Battling cavaliers under the leadership of Zavaareh.

Next, the king elects ten thousand illustrious men
Armed with spears, under the command of
Ghaaran, the vengeful, head of the elite of warriors.
He directs him to lunge his horse
And occupy the space between the two hosts.

Khosrow commands Gostaham, son of Gojdaham,
To attend to Ghaaran, and Tous's son to go back and forth
With trumpet and timpani to inhibit evil,
Unfaithful men from committing unjust acts,
To assure that no one lacks in provisions,
And no one feels oppressed and fearful,
And to ask the king for anything they may be lacking.
Tous's son is to be, in all matters, the host's interpreter.

The world is covered with carts and livestock
Brought to serve as sustenance for the army.
Khosrow awakens those who have succumbed to sleep.
He asks to be informed of every detail.
He places sentries on every height
And keeps the troops from scattering.
He sends spies to gather information on all sides,
Through alleys and mountains, deserts and valleys,
As the reins of the illustrious steeds interweave.

Everyone feels secure with the knowledge
That the king is in possession of his wealth.
Once he has thus organized his host,
He raises his Kianian crown to the sky.
The dim hearts of men, good and bad,
Have no other longing but to fight.

3 | Afraasiyaab Learns of the Death of Piran and Mobilizes Troops

The Tooranian king sits peacefully on his ivory throne
On the other side of Chaadj.
He unites thousands and thousands of warriors,
A vast host equipped with fierce war apparatus.
They ravage everything on the mountainside:
Leaves on trees, crops and harvests, fruits and blossoms.

The world over despairs and covets death.

The Tooranian army leader sits in Paykand,[29]
Surrounded by a vast number of allies and kin,
Powerful men from Chin and Maachin.

The world fills with tents, great and small.
No empty space remains on earth.

World conqueror Afraasiyaab, full of knowledge,
Resides in Kondaz,[30] taking pleasure in life and rest.
He turns this city into his residence,
Since Fereydoon founded it, erecting there a fire temple.
On its walls is the complete *Zand Avesta*,[31]
Engraved in golden letters.

The name Kondaz is Pahlavi, as you may know
If you are familiar with the language.
Presently, the name has been changed to Paykand,
For our times are filled with imposture and fraud.

Afraasiyaab, descendant of Fereydoon,
Does not feel the rush to withdraw from Kondaz.
He remains settled on its plain with his close allies.
The troops are so numerous the sky looks down in awe.
The royal pavilion is ringed by an enclosure
Of Chini brocade, housing innumerable slaves.
Within this enclosure are tents of leopard skin,
As dictates the custom introduced by Pashang,
Tooranian king and Afraasiyaab's father.
In the principal tent is a throne inlaid in gold
And precious stones, where sits the Tooranian ruler,
A mace in one hand and a crown on his head.
At the entrance of the pavilion are many banners
Belonging to various men of honor,
Such as his brothers, his sons, a number of his leaders,

◇◇◇◇◇◇◇◇◇◇◇◇◇◇
29 Paykand: Or Baykand or Kondaz; city in Tooran-Zamin near today's Bukhara
(Uzbekistan).
30 Kondaz: Pahlavi name for the city of Paykand; city founded by Fereydoon and
holding a fire temple with a gold inscription of *Zand Avesta*.
31 *Zand Avesta*: *Avesta* is the Zoroastrian holy scripture; *Zand* is the interpretation of
it.

And the most distinguished foreign, visiting dignitaries.

The king's strategy is to depart in support of his host
And to join Piran on the battlefield.
But one morning a rider arrives as swift as wind
To report the last words of Piran.
Many wounded men file in, one after the other,
Weeping, their heads covered in dust.
Every man recounts what happened to him
And the wicked deeds of the Iranians.
They speak of Piran, Lahaak, and Farshidvard,
And all the others who appeared on the day of battle.
They recount the calamities that befell them
In the skirmish, at the vanguard and at the rear,
How the day Kay Khosrow appeared
Covering the land with his troops, from one mountain
To the other, the army fell at his mercy
Like a fearful herd of sheep having lost its shepherd.

At this account, Afraasiyaab's head is troubled.
His face is obscured and his heart dims.
He climbs down from his ivory throne hollering,
Flings his crown at the feet of his noblemen.
His troops' cheeks pale with grief
As they lament the fate of their beloved leaders.

The foreign dignitaries are dismissed from the audience hall.
The members of the royal family gather in counsel.
Afraasiyaab weeps in grief, pulls out his hair,
And sheds copious tears as he bitterly exclaims:
"O world keeper, highborn rider, my dear Piran!
O Hoomaan, Lahaak, and Farshidvard,
Riders and warring lions, leaders and army chiefs.
This battle has deprived me of son and brother!"

He moans and assumes a new resolution
As the pain and regret of his losses grow more intense.
In his distress and his heart's anguish, he vows:
"I swear by Yazdan that I no longer care for the ivory throne.
I swear my head is weary of the crown.
The armor will be my sole tunic, a horse will be my throne,
A helmet my headdress, a spear the tree sheltering me.

I no longer wish to enjoy the delights of this world,
Nor do I wish to live like a bearer of crown.
But first I must punish and condemn Kay Khosrow,
A man of evil race, for the blood of my noblemen,
My sword-bearing warriors, my cavaliers.
May the family of Siaavoosh vanish from this world!"

He continues to shout and cry until
He receives news from Kay Khosrow.
He learns that an army has approached the Jayhoon,
That the entire land is swarming with troops.
In his pain and despair, he gathers a host
And speaks at length of Piran, of his brother Farshidvard,
Of Rooeen and so many other lions fallen in battle.
He says, "I shall no longer think of rest or sleep.
The enemy mustered a host and sharpened its claws.
It is not the time to reflect and wait,
But the time to aim for revenge and bloodshed.
We must place our lives in the palms of our hands.
I give myself wholeheartedly to the affection
I have for Piran and my kin, and to the vengeance
I wish to wreak on Iran and its king."

The leaders of Tooran-Zamin respond,
Eyes full of tears, "We are the king's slaves.
We shall never forestall this revenge for as long as we live.
We lower our heads at the king's commands.
Never have mothers given birth to such sons
As Piran, Rooeen, and Farshidvard of Fereydoon's race.
Here we are before his majesty, all of us, great and small.
We shall not desert the battlefield until we have turned
Valleys and mountains into a vast sea of blood.
Even if the length of our host were the size of its width,
We should not crouch in fear when faced with war.
May the master of the sun act in our favor!"

These words renew the heart of the Tooranian king.
He smiles and takes new measures.
He opens the doors to his treasury, distributes wealth.
His heart longs for revenge; his head fills with pride.

He brings all the horses he owns from mountains

And fields, and offers them to his troops.
He selects thirty thousand sword-bearing skilled riders
And tells them to cross the Jayhoon on a vessel by night
So that no one would dare attack. On every side,
He sends troops, laying down all sorts of schemes.
No matter, for the will of Yazdan, the pure,
Is to bring the life of the unjust king to an end.

During the dark night, he sits in counsel
With his skilled wise men to see how to proceed.
They determine that the king must cross the Jayhoon.
He attempts to guard himself against harm.
He divides his troops into two parts.
He summons Karookhan, his eldest son.
When he arrives, it is as if he is Afraasiyaab himself,
So alike they are in stature, in mien,
In intelligence and prudence.
He entrusts him with half of the host,
Made up of renowned, brave, and skilled men.
He commands him to take the direction of Bukhara,
To form behind his father a rampart as strong as a mountain,
To continuously supply the troops with weapons and arms,
And to transport the provisions on camelback.

Afraasiyaab leads his army out of Paykand
And toward the River Jayhoon.
The riverbank is covered with troops, from end to end.
He gathers more than one thousand boats and rafts,
Viewing and reviewing them for one week.

Fields and mountain form a huge mass of armed warriors.
Throngs of elephants and lion men crowd the river fords.
The water disappears beneath the boats.
The army spreads across the plains of Amu.

Afraasiyaab tails his army on the water,
Spending the night occupied in various tactics of war.
On every side, he sends racing camels,
Each ridden by a prudent and wise man.
He says to them, "Look left and right.
Survey their host and observe its nature and its size."

These bold men return, and one of them reports,

"The sort of battle we are to engage in
Requires goods, fodder, and camping grounds.
On the edge of the Sea of Gilan, there is a road,
Pasture for the horses, and a suitable site to camp.
Karookhan will bring the provisions by way of the river.
Between the two hosts, there are sandy plains
Where we can set up our tent pavilions."

Afraasiyaab rejoices at this news.
He sits taller on the imperial throne.
As an experienced warrior, he rarely relies on others.
He organizes the army center and its wings.
He sends spies to observe the enemy host,
Fixes a site for the stocks and the baggage,
And assigns the placement of the two wings.

He takes measures worthy of a king for the order of battle,
Places at the core one hundred thousand sword-bearing men,
Reserving their leadership for his own person,
For he is at once chief and army coordinator.
To his left is the strong and valiant Pashang,[32] whom
His father calls Shiddeh the bright, for he shines like the sun.
He has no equal among leaders and warriors.
He is able to launch his horse, grab a leopard's tail,
And tear it off merely by the strength of his arm.
He wields an iron spear with which
He pierces a mountain's core.

The king puts him in charge of one hundred thousand men,
Distinguished warriors eager for battle.
Shiddeh has a brother named Jahn, younger than him
But his equal in valor, whose wandering foot
Has vastly trampled the surface of the earth.
His father takes him as advisor,
For there does not exist at court a wiser mind.

Afraasiyaab hands over to him one hundred thousand
Riders from Chagal,[33] worthy of delivering battle,
And positions him to protect Shiddeh's rearguard.
He is to remain strong and steady,

◇◇◇◇◇◇◇◇◇◇◇◇◇
32 Pashang: Son of Afraasiyaab who will be referred to as Shiddeh in the stories.
33 Chagal: A city in Turkestan.

Even in the advent of a shower of stones.

Next, he entrusts a corps of troops to Kehila
And another to the son of Illa, Afraasiyaab's grandson,
A youth able to tear the flesh from the backs of lions.
Kehila and Illa are two courageous Tooranian warriors
Whose dim hearts are as dense as boulders.

The right wing of the host has the power
To make the sun disappear from the world.
Karookhan, one of the ruler's sons,
Straps his waist and arrives at his father's side.
Riders armed with blade from Balkh, Khalkh,[34] and Tartar[35]
Are to be led by his fifth son, a noble world seeker,
Warrior destroyer, named Gurch.
In all, thirty thousand men are cinched for battle,
Armed with shining daggers.
Damoor and Jaranjas escort him, rushing to assist Jahn.
Nastooh is their chief, the bold Shiddeh their protector.

Behind them advance thirty thousand soldiers,
Turks armed with mace, sword, and bow,
Guided by the leader Aghriras,[36] burning for battle.
He sits on his horse, strong as a mountain.
Blood is, to him, like running water.

The king selects forty thousand more sword-bearing men,
Led by Garsivaz of elephant build, an ambitious soul.
The highborn king, leader of all, support of the army,
Gives him command of the elephants.
Then he selects ten thousand men who never tire of war
And orders them to stand, lips foaming, in the midst
Of two hosts to launch their stallions onto enemy troops
And spread terror among Iranians.

The fighters turn their backs on the west as night descends.
The road is blocked by the multitude of elephants.
The king, glory of the world, commands his army
To swing the reins toward the land of Sistan.

34 Khalkh: Region in present-day Mongolia.
35 Tartar: Situated in Tooran-Zamin and in today's Azerbaijan.
36 Aghriras: Different from Afraasiyaab's brother who was killed.

4 | Kay Khosrow Discovers
Afraasiyaab Is on His Way to Wage War

The moment Kay Khosrow receives the report
From his watchful patrols of the approach
Of King Afraasiyaab with his Tooranian troops,
Of his intention to traverse the River Jayhoon
And to make sand and rock disappear beneath his host,
He summons his leaders and relates to them the news.

He gathers a host consisting of Iranian warriors
Well suited to address the matter accordingly.
These men, who have endured tragedies
And the bitterness of the world, are to travel
To Balkh to assist Gostaham, son of Nozar.

He commands Ashkesh to drive troops, elephants,
Treasure, gold, and silver to Zam, to block the enemy
From attacking the rearguard and sabotaging their plans.

Next, he commands his warriors to straddle their steeds,
To beat the timpani and sound the call of departure.
He advances prudently, wisely, and leisurely,
For haste in warfare often leads to remorse.

Once on the plain, Khosrow inspects and shapes his troops.
On the right is the road leading to Khaarazm,
Where vast desolate fields enable easy battle.
On the left is Dahestan and a huge body of water.
In between are sandy fields beyond which stands Afraasiyaab.

Khosrow and his leaders, Rostam, Tous, Goodarz, Giv,
And a massive escort of illustrious warriors,
Survey the theater of battle from every possible angle.

After receiving news of his grandfather's host,
His heart grows troubled, and he seeks a solution,
For he did not expect so many men,
So many weapons, so many elephants.

To strengthen his position, he surrounds his camp
With a deep trench, dispatches scouts in various directions.

During the night, he asks for the moats to be filled
With water on the side where his grandfather awaits.
He scatters spiny caltrops around the plain
To inhibit the enemy's crossing.

Once the sun, shining in the house of Aries,
Casts its rays on the surface of the earth,
The leader of the Turks discerns the rival host.
He asks for timpani and the march of the forces.

The world fills with the sound of clarions
And the clamor of troops as they don their helmets of steel.
The face of earth feels as if it is made of metal,
The air as if it is dressed in an armor of spears.

For three days and three nights,
The two hosts maintain their positions.
No one speaks or stirs.
They remain with squadrons on each side
And footmen positioned before them.
It feels as if the world is a mountain of steel
And the dome of sky is armed with a coat of mail.

Astrologers sit before the two kings,
Deeply engaged in reflection before their charts,
Hoping to gaze into their astrolabes and to predict
For their leaders the secret spins of the heavens.
But the dome of sky continues to observe,
Leaving the observers at a loss to bear witness.

5 | Shiddeh Appears Before His Father, Afraasiyaab

On the fourth day, the time arrives to take action.
The brave Shiddeh presents himself before his father
And says, "O noble world master, there does not exist
Beneath the firmament a ruler of your grace and glory.
Neither the sun nor the moon contradict you.
Your name has the power to melt a mountain of steel.
The earth cannot resist your vast army.
The shining sun has no strength against your helmet.
No king comes forth to challenge you

Except Kay Khosrow, your relative,
A man of evil race with no father to claim.
You treated Siaavoosh as your own son.
You lavished him with a father's care and affection,
Barring the slightest gust of wind from affecting him.
Your love only turned to disgust once
You were assured that his sights were set
On depriving you of crown, throne, and host.
If the world king had spared his life,
He would have infringed upon your crown and seal.

"The man coming to fight you now
Does not have the luxury of a long life.
Anyone who forgets the affection of a father figure
Will suffer a fate as dire as that of Siaavoosh.
You raised this despicable Kay Khosrow
As a tender, caring father.
You did not allow his foot to touch the ground.
You nurtured him until he grew into a man,
Able to rule and able to wear the golden crown.
At that time, he flew from Tooran to Iran-Zamin
Like a bird, as if he had never known his grandfather.

"Remember all of Piran's actions executed out of
The kindness of his heart for this unworthy, thankless man.
Still, he rejected Piran's love, filling his heart with hatred
And his head with restlessness. In his ingratitude,
He proceeded to kill our most compassionate world hero.
Now he comes from Iran-Zamin with his sharp claws,
At the head of an army to lead an assault on his grandfather.
He is not satisfied with either dinars or diadems,
Either stallions or swords, either wealth or host.
He is after the blood of a close relative.
These are the only words that come out of his mouth.

"O father, you are a wise and virtuous king.
You will witness the truth of my words.
The Iranians are not worth so much discourse.
Do not then shatter the hearts of your troops.
What is the use of astrologers to them?
Brave warriors pursue honor and high deeds.
Cavaliers on the right wing are at one, ready for battle.

If the king permits, not a single Iranian will survive.
I shall nail down their helmets to their heads with shots,
Without concern for their trenches or their gutters."

Afraasiyaab listens to his son and replies,
"Do not act in haste and on impulse.
Everything you have said is true,
And one must honor the truth above all else.
But you know that the valiant Piran
Walked only down the road of merit.
His heart was unfamiliar with injustice and deceit.
He pursued only what was good and proper.
He was as strong as an elephant on the day of battle,
His heart as wide as a vast sea,
His cheek as bright as the brilliant sun.
He and his brother Hoomaan, leopard-like in war,
The valiant Lahaak, and Farshidvard,
Along with one hundred thousand Turkish riders,
Ambitious men, glory-seekers equipped for war,
Departed filled with simmering ardor,
While I secretly remained to bemoan our fate.

"This is how he perished on the field of vengeance.
This is how the ground became
A mix of blood and mud beneath corpses.
Every heart in Tooran-Zamin is shattered,
Souls stripped from immense grief.
Their dreams are invaded by visions of Piran's death.
No one invokes the name of Afraasiyaab.
Let us then wait until our leaders, warriors, and horsemen
Grow accustomed to observing the Iranians.
Then the weight of their sorrow and worry will lighten.
Let us wait until the Iranians, for their part,
Set their sights on this mighty army,
Its treasures, thrones, and crowns.
It would be a baneful strategy to deliver a broad battle.
A certain defeat would be ours,
And we shall be left clutching nothing but wind.
A better tactic is to set forth lone warriors
To disperse and drench the ground with Iranian blood."

Shiddeh replies, "O sire,

If this is the manner in which you wish to lead the battle,
Let me be the first warrior to step forward,
For I am a passion-filled rider able to launch my stallion.
I am strong. I am invincible.
I know of no one on the day of battle
Who dares scatter the wind's dust like me.
I long to contend with Kay Khosrow, the new world king.
If he accepts the challenge, as I'm sure he will,
There is no way he will escape my grasp alive.
At that time, the heart and soul of the Iranian army
Will be shattered and their strategies gone to waste.
Should another warrior come to battle,
I shall immediately bring down his head into the dust."

The king replies, "O inexperienced young man.
I am the one that Kay Khosrow seeks quarrel with.
Should he challenge me, I shall accept unwavering.
I shall trample beneath my feet his body and his glory.
Should he present himself on the battlefield,
Our troops will have a chance to rest from their labors."

Shiddeh says, "O skillful ruler, if Kay Khosrow
Comes to fight you, do not forget
That you have five sons who stand by you.
We shall not look on idly while you accept battle.
No one, neither army nor faithful man,
Will agree to allow you to risk your life."

6 | Afraasiyaab Sends a Message to Kay Khosrow

The world ruler says to Shiddeh,
"O my noble son, may misfortune deflect from you!
Do not distress; you will joust with Kay Khosrow.
Do not take this to heart. Go now to your host.
Find yourself a wise ally as escort.
May the Creator protect you,
And may the heads of your adversaries collapse!
Relay this message to Kay Khosrow:
        'Your actions go against this world's customs and laws.
        A grandson's head keen on fighting his grandfather
        Must be full of ill intention and deceit.

Is it the will of the Creator
To fill the world with war and strife?
Siaavoosh was not killed without reason,
For he turned away from his masters
And did not heed anyone's advice.

'If I am the one to blame, then what have Piran, Rooeen,
Lahaak, and Farshidvard done to have fallen to such fates,
Their bloody frames snarled to mad chargers?
Should you say to me that I am an evil man
With wicked thoughts, born of the seed of Ahriman,
Be wary for you originate from the same seed,
And such an insult would rebound on your person.

'Leave this vengeance to Goodarz and Kaavoos,
Who will soon rush to raise an army against me.
You are my relation, and they are my foes.
I am not telling you this out of fear
Or out of reticence in my old age.
My troops are as numerous as grains of sand in the sea.
They are brave warriors and lion men, who,
Upon my command and on the day of war,
Stir up Mount Gang like the raging waves of the sea.
Nevertheless, I fear the Creator, carnage, and misfortune,
As far too many innocent men will be deprived of heads.

'You are embracing war.
Have you no fear to be disgraced by humiliation?
If you wish to commit under oath to a peace treaty
And execute its terms earnestly,
I shall help you safeguard your troops and your treasure.
Once you forget the fate of Siaavoosh,
Your grandfather in Tooran-Zamin will rejoice.
Then two brothers, Jahn and the warring Shiddeh,
Who rattles Mount Gang like a turbulent sea,
Will envisage you as a brother and make
The Turks withdraw from the land of Iran.
All the wealth I possess from my ancestors,
Dinars, crowns, thrones, horses, and armaments,
All that I acquired from the inheritance of Zaadsham,
The assets of our noblemen, thrones, and diadems,
Anything you desire for your host, I shall send to you.

'My son is a warrior hero, his father is your kin.
The two hosts will rest from their labors,
And our worried hearts will turn to feast.
But if, on the other hand, Ahriman distorts
Your mind to wear the shroud of death,
If your only wish is to fight and spill blood,
If there is no room in your mind to heed sound advice,
Then move to the head of your troops
To see if this fight can assuage your desires.
We shall measure ourselves against each other,
You and I on this field, while our troops are at ease.
If I perish, the world will be yours, my warriors
Will be your slaves, my sons will be your relatives.
On the other hand, if my hand brings you down,
I shall do no harm to yours.
Your host will fall under my protection.
I will turn your warriors into my leaders and allies.

'If you dare not advance toward the skilled whale,
If you are unwilling to fight, then be prepared,
For Shiddeh will strap himself to challenge you.
Do not hesitate to accept his offer.
The father is aging, his alternate is young,
A glorious youth, strong and full of caution.
He will step onto the battlefield
With a fierce lion heart and leopard claws.
We shall then see which man is favored by fortune,
Which will bear the crown of affection.
Still, if you do not want him as an adversary,
If you wish to deliver battle under other conditions,
Wait until my troops can take a break tonight,
And tomorrow, once the mountains
Are girded with their golden diadems
And the dark night has withdrawn its skirt's hem
And concealed itself behind a veil of felt,
We shall select brave and noble mace-bearing warriors.
We shall tint the earth with blood like silk brocade.
We shall surrender to the ground your severed bodies.

'On the second day, at the call of the rooster,
We shall place timpani on elephant backs.
We shall send forward leaders to back us up

> And deflect the flow of spilled blood into wide rivers.
> On the third day, we shall lead to battle
> Hosts as large as mountains to execute vengeance.
> Let us discover which side the lofty dome rejects
> And which side it chooses to honor.'

"Such is the message I wish to relay.
If my wicked opponent repudiates it,
If he draws back and revokes my proposal,
Fight with him yourself in a single battle,
Somewhere far from our hosts."

Shiddeh selects four wise and experienced men.
He spends some time in praise of the king,
Then takes leave of his worried father,
Whose eyes are brimming with tears.
He marches off with an escort of one thousand warriors.

Iranian scouts spot Toor's shining banner in the distance
And the number of Turks at the lead.
The young and inexperienced riders
Fall on the Iranian sentries to shed blood,
Against Shiddeh's wishes and before his arrival.

A number of Iranian troops are injured,
And they are still fighting when Shiddeh joins them,
His heart aggrieved at the sight of them.
He calls his warriors and addresses the Iranians,
"Send a rider to Kay Khosrow,
According to custom and path, and say to him:
> 'A clear-sighted man has arrived named Shiddeh,
> Bearing a message from King Afraasiyaab,
> Master of Chin, father of Khosrow's mother.'"

A rider dashes from post to royal court.
He swiftly approaches the Iranian king and says,
"A messenger from the Tooranian ruler, a noble warrior
Named Shiddeh, holder of a black banner,
Bids permission to relay his missive."

The shah's heart is moved.
Warm tears streak his cheeks.
He says, "Shiddeh is my maternal uncle,

My peer in height and valor."
He scans the assembly and selects Ghaaran,
A highborn man from the lineage of Kaaveh.
He addresses him and says, "Go swiftly to Shiddeh,
Send him my greetings, and listen to his dispatch."

Ghaaran rushes off toward the shiny black banner.
He greets Shiddeh on behalf of the king and the Iranians.

The youth, in turn, answers in a gentle manner,
For his soul is serene and his mind is sharp.
He relates Afraasiyaab's words of peace and feast,
The hazards of war and of acting in haste.

Ghaaran listens to the kind words of the noble Turk.
Then he returns to the King of Iran,
Conveys to him the wise and sensible message.

7 | Kay Khosrow Listens to Afraasiyaab's Message

Ghaaran's words stir up old memories in Kay Khosrow.
He laughs at his grandfather's deeds,
At his calculations, and his cunning skills.
He exclaims, "Afraasiyaab regrets having crossed the river.
His eyes are dry of tears and his lips are full of discourse,
But my heart fills with the woes of ancient disputes.
He now seeks to make me tremble in fear
With the mention of his countless troops.
Yet he knows not which way the almighty skies,
Obedient to no other command,
Will face on the day of misfortune.
The only option left for me is to march toward him,
My heart full of animosity.
I shall measure my strength against his
Without seeking a delay at the time of fight."

The noblemen and army leaders speak in unison:
"This is not a reasonable course of action.
Afraasiyaab, experienced and knowledgeable,
Dreams of nothing but schemes and strategies.
He is familiar only with deception, malice, and black magic.

He has picked Shiddeh, considering him
The only leader able to untie the bonds of misfortune.
He challenges the King of Iran
Only to fill our days with distress.
Do not take his old age lightly.
Do not attempt to pit yourself against him,
And endanger your land and your throne.
Do not rush into action without proper reflection,
For we must avoid a life of grief and misery.
If Shiddeh is the one to contend with,
He will make us pale with concern.
If he is vanquished by you,
Their army will be reduced by just one nobleman.
But if you are the one to perish in some faraway field,
A dark cloud of dust will rise above the entire spread of land,
And none of us will survive such a dreadful blow.
No city, no province in all of Iran-Zamin will remain intact.
With you gone, no one will prevail from the Kianian lineage
To strap himself to avenge your death.

"Your grandfather is a worldly old man,
Well respected in the lands of Tooran and Chin.
He asks forgiveness for the wrongs he has committed
And wishes to fight only when left with no other recourse.
He is willing to transfer to you his riches, his steeds,
His coins and treasures, gathered by Toor for Zaadsham:
Golden thrones, crowns, golden belts, and heavy maces.
He hopes to compensate you for his past crimes.
In addition, he offers for the Turks
To evacuate the lands you claim belong to Iran.
Let us withdraw our troops
And erase bygones from our memory."

In this way young and old speak,
Except for the celebrated warrior Rostam,
Who turns his back on reconciliation
And whose heart continues to mourn the loss of Siaavoosh.

The king bites his lip and fixes his gaze on the speakers.
He says, "It would not be wise to desert the battlefield
And retreat to Iran-Zamin.
Where are the battles we are to fight?

Where are the promises, prisoners, and slaves?
Where is the counsel? Where is the wise advice?
If Afraasiyaab remains alive on his throne,
He will destroy the land of Iran.
What excuse am I to invent before Kaavoos?
How shall we dare look into his face?
Have you not heard how Toor treated the blessed Iraj
For the sake of crown and throne?
Have you not heard the sufferings
Afraasiyaab inflicted upon King Nozar?
Furthermore, Afraasiyaab killed Siaavoosh
In order to hold on to treasure, crown, and throne.
May he never find happiness, not even in dream!

"Now, a scheming Turk from his army
Presents himself at court to challenge me.
Why have you turned pale in fear?
I am surprised it affects you so, when it only urges
Me more keenly toward my goal of retribution.
Upon hearing Afraasiyaab's message you recoil in fear?
Never did I imagine the Iranians would retreat
When my yearning for vengeance has only intensified."

Upon hearing this speech, the Iranians turn to remorse:
"We stand before you as your slaves.
We spoke only out of our affection for his majesty.
The King of Kings seeks only glory and a just ending.
The World Master, whose will is supreme,
Would not wish to see blame directed at us
Or the rumor circulate that not a single Iranian rider
Appeared on the battlefield to face up to Shiddeh,
Or that with such a vast host standing by,
The king alone had the courage for the task.
Kay Khosrow, king of wise men,
Would not wish for us to be immersed in eternal shame."

The king replies, "O shrewd guides and advisors,
Know that this Shiddeh, on the day of battle,
Does not consider his father a worthy contender.
Afraasiyaab made his son's armor with the use of black magic,
In ways that are impious, scheming, and spiteful.
Your weapons will be powerless and unable

To pierce through his breastplate and steel helmet.
His horse is of the race of deevs, his heart of lion strength,
And his feet have the speed of wind.
Only those endowed with royal dignity by divine grace
Can resist Shiddeh and evade his grip.
Furthermore, he will not wish to fight against any of you,
For that would dishonor his stature and his birth.
The descendants of Fereydoon and Ghobaad
Are two warriors equal in courage and in rank.
By killing Shiddeh, I shall burn his father's dark soul
As he burned Kay Kaavoos's heart with his son's murder."

The lion warriors of the land of Iran acclaim the king.

8 | Kay Khosrow's Reply to Afraasiyaab

Khosrow then summons Ghaaran, his loyal leader,
And asks him to return to Shiddeh with his reply:
"Our debate is long and stubborn,
And we find ourselves at an impasse.
A man of honor and a bold warrior
Does not waste time with delays in times of war.
Let the Master of Sun and Moon determine
Who will be the victor on the battlefield.
I care neither for the land of Tooran nor for its treasure,
For this passing dwelling remains for no one.
But I swear by the might of the World Creator
And by the crown of Kaavoos who raised me
That I shall grant you no more time than roses
Have before the arrival of crisp autumn winds.

"Next you speak of a vast wealth,
Of horses and accumulated gold.
We have no use for riches amassed
Through acts of misconduct and oppression.
Fortune smiles on the one embraced by Yazdan.
Your land, your treasure, your army are mine,
As well as your throne, your cities, your headdress.
Shiddeh has come, girded in armor, inviting me to battle
With an escort, and with much pomp and pageantry.
Tomorrow at dawn, he will be my guest

To witness the efficacy of my blade.
No one, no Iranian warrior is to be present.
It will just be the two of us, Shiddeh and me,
The field between, and my cutting sword above,
With which I shall bring down his head.

"If I win this battle, I shall not sit on my laurels
And welcome your delays.
We shall raise the cry of war on both sides.
The field will shimmer with spilled blood.
Later, we shall bring forth troops in tight formation,
Like mountains, to launch the war.
You will then tell Shiddeh,
        'O celebrated leader full of sense and reason,
        You have come alone from Tooran-Zamin
        To fall captive to my nets.
        You thought you came in search of fame and glory,
        Or to relay your father's message,
        But sadly it is rather to cut short your wicked deeds.
        The Creator has singled you out
        To give you a shroud to serve you as tomb.
        The innocent prince who was slaughtered like a lamb
        Will bring you bad luck, and your father will weep,
        Just as Kaavoos wept inconsolably for his son.'"

Ghaaran leaves the king's side in haste
And approaches Shiddeh and his black banner.
He reveals the message from Khosrow,
Hiding neither the bad nor the good.

Shiddeh returns to Afraasiyaab,
His heart roasting like deer flesh on a stake.
The King of Turks is dismayed by the news.
In his anguish, he breathes a deep sigh,
Remembering the dream he had long ago,
Which he kept secret for so many years.
His head spins, his heart quavers
As he feels his downfall approaching.
He cries, "Tomorrow, so many corpses will fall
On the battlefield that ants will have no space
To carve a path to crawl through it."

Then he turns to his son: "From now on,
Allow two days to pass without talk of battle.
I feel as if I am shattered by thoughts of war.
I feel so miserable that I wish to pluck out my heart."

Shiddeh answers, "O ruler of Chin and Tooran-Zamin,
Once the sun raises his shining banner
To light up the dark dome of sky, you no longer need
To exert yourself on the day of vengeance.
I shall meet Khosrow on the battlefield
And reduce this king to a speck of dust!"

9 | Kay Khosrow Battles Shiddeh

The cobalt veil of sky lights up at dawn,
And the world resembles a golden gemstone.
The valiant Shiddeh, his head full of youthful wind
And breathing only battle, climbs on his war horse.
He secures his chain mail on his gleaming breast
And his royal helmet of steel on his head.
With a brave Turk carrying his war banner,
Shiddeh rides forth like a leopard toward the arena.

He soon reaches the Iranian host,
Where a nobleman rushes to the king to announce:
"A rider advances between the two army lines.
Of tall stature, he wields his sword and shouts,
        'Tell your king that Shiddeh has arrived.
        He is like a battling dragon wishing
        To devour the world with his breath.'"

The ruler laughs and asks for his coat of mail.
He raises the royal banner with the image of his might,
Places his Rumi helmet on his head,
And hands Rohaam, son of Goodarz, his banner.

His warriors are in a state of anguish and tears,
As if they are consumed by a fierce blaze.
In their midst, a great cry rises: "O King,
Do not tire yourself with this armor of steel.
The right place for a ruler is on the throne.

May this man, who forces you to wear battle gear,
Find no other dwelling than the dark dirt of earth!
May his designs swiftly be curtailed!"

The ruler, equipped with belt, mace, and helmet,
Sends the following address to his host:
"May no man move from his rank or leave the royal camp,
Whether on the left or on the right,
Whether in the center or on the wings.
Let no one try to join the fight or even stir.
You must follow the directions and command
Of Rohaam, son of Goodarz.
When the sun reaches the midday sky,
You will go and see which man has been downed.
If you find Shiddeh victor, Rostam will assume leadership.
Stand by him as obedient slaves
And listen to his instructions.
With such a man in charge of the army,
You will soon find an antidote to your pain.
The troubles of war and peace are easy to endure
When led by a commander of his stature.
Do not give in to anguish and dread.
Such is the start and the end of war.
At times we prevail, at times we fail, at times
We experience joy, at times we succumb to fear."

Kay Khosrow launches his horse Behzaad,
A charger the color of night, able to, in a gallop,
Roll the wind beneath its hooves.
He charges forth, outfitted with armor, spear, and helmet.
The dust raised by his steed rises to the clouds.

Meanwhile, Shiddeh, standing between the two lines,
Spots him approaching. He sighs deeply and says,
"O admirable man, are you the son of Siaavoosh?
Are you the wise, aware, and insightful
Grandson of Tooran's army leader,
Whose helmet grazes the sphere of the moon?
You do not act as one would expect of a worldly man,
Nourished by wisdom, reason, and prudence.
For if you did, you would not rush to war
To challenge your uncle, your mother's brother.

If you wish to fight, let us break away from our hosts.
Select an isolated field beyond the periphery
Of either Tooranian or Iranian army lines,
For we must not have anyone come to our aid."

The king replies, "O lion eager to fight, I am the son
Of the innocent Siaavoosh so brutally murdered by the king.
My blazing heart beats to the rhythm of rebellion.
I come for vengeance rather than glory, throne, and seal.
Since you have provoked this battle with your father,
I see no other opponent of high rank apt for the challenge.
So you may determine a field of battle far from our hosts."

The two men settle on the rules: Neither side will send
Warriors to assist them or to take part in battle.
Their standard bearers are to remain free from harm.

They take leave of their hosts, departing in joy
As if they are marching to banquet and feast.
They arrive on a suitable field, a barren, uneven,
Desolate wasteland on the border of Khaarazm,
Where neither lion nor leopard dares set foot,
Where neither eagle nor falcon dares fly across its skies.

They begin to joust: Two chargers and two riders
Akin to wolves or, better, two famished lions full of rage,
Circling and appraising each other on the day of hunt.
They lunge at each other with long razor-sharp spears.
As the sun sinks low, the steel strips away from blades.
Their horses' reins and armor are drenched in sweat.

They fight ruthlessly with Rumi mace, with bow
And arrow, with piercing sword, until the ground
Is black with blood and the air is dark with dust.
Still neither rider grows weary of the fight.

At the sight of Khosrow's courage and strength,
Tears stream down Shiddeh's cheeks.
He recognizes that his opponent's force is a divine gift
And that he might as well bemoan his undeniable end.
His horse is burdened by thirst.
He feels his own vigor slowly fading and reflects:
"If I propose to the Iranian king that we dismount

And fight on foot, with blood and sweat,
He would refuse such a battle that he would deem
Dishonorable and unfit for a monarch,
For his royalty would be at stake.
Yet if I do not save myself with a ploy,
I am as good as prey in the dragon's maw!"

He says to Kay Khosrow, "O King, most warriors
Are able to fight with the aid of sword and spear
While handling their horse's reins.
Better for us to assail each other on foot
And stretch out our hands like lions."

Khosrow, world ruler, reads his opponent's mind
And thinks, "If this powerful lion,
Descendant of Fereydoon and grandson of Pashang,
Is given the opportunity to catch his breath,
He will kill and scatter my head,
And be the source of my people's distress."

Rohaam then says to him, "O bearer of crown,
Do not disgrace your royal birth with such an act.
If Kay Khosrow is to fight on foot,
What good are the riders on the field?
If anyone is to dismount,
Let it be a descendent of Kashvaad,
For you are the blessed and illustrious world king!"

The shah replies to Rohaam,
"O kind and valiant warrior,
Shiddeh comes from the family of Pashang.
He will never accept a fight with you.
Besides, you cannot withstand his strength,
As the Turks have no comparable leader.
It is not a disgrace for me to challenge him on foot.
He comes from the lineage of Fereydoon,
And never has a mother given birth to a bolder son.
It is no shame, and we shall fight a fierce battle on foot."

On the other side, Shiddeh's interpreter nears him
And says, "You must retreat
Before allowing your foe to cause you further harm.
You cannot withstand Kay Khosrow.

It is better to lay off and flee before the enemy than
To submit to blows that would cause your demise!"

Shiddeh replies to his illustrious interpreter,
"It is not suitable for brave men to cower back.
Since I first strapped myself for battle,
I have held my head up, high as the sun.
Never in all this time have I witnessed
A warrior so powerful, so glorious, so valiant.
But I would rather lie in a grave than have to retreat.
Once I have committed to fight, I cannot withdraw.
Although I may exchange blows as a dragon,
One never knows the workings of heaven's rotation.
If I must die right here at his hand,
Neither friend nor enemy can rescue me.
I know where he draws his strength and courage.
This warrior has the favor of divine grace.
Still, I might be the stronger one on foot
And in the fight make him shed abundant blood.
Neither friend nor foe can keep me alive if I must die."

Then the world ruler says to Shiddeh, "O celebrated one,
Son of noble lineage, of all the men of Kianian race,
None ever agreed to fight dismounted.
Still, if such is your wish, I shall not oppose it."

10 | Kay Khosrow Kills Shiddeh

The king alights from his night-colored horse, Shabrang,
Removes his royal helmet, cedes the reins to Rohaam,
And marches like the flame of Aazargoshasp.

As Shiddeh, warring whale, spots Khosrow on foot,
He follows suit and dismounts.
The two warriors, two raging elephants, fall on each other,
Soaking the dusty ground with abundant blood.

On foot, Shiddeh can better assess the king's physique,
His strength and skills, his gift of divine grace.
He prays desperately for a way out, a way to retreat,
 Aware that his body will lose value once his head is crushed.

Khosrow has a sense of the other's wavering reflections.
He reaches out like a lion extending his paw on a deer and,
With the power bestowed upon him by the World Creator,
Grasps Shiddeh's neck with his left hand
And his back with his right hand.
He lifts him up, then flings him to the ground,
Shattering his legs and every vertebra in his back,
As if his spine were as fine and brittle as a reed.

Khosrow then draws out his blade of steel
And slices the chest of the illustrious prince in two.
Then he carves his breastplate into tiny pieces.
In his grief, he tosses dust on his head
And says to Rohaam, "This evil man without equal,
Valiant but hesitant, was my maternal uncle.
Show him compassion now that he is dead.
Raise for him a royal resting place.
Brush his head with honey, musk, and rosewater,
And his body with pure camphor.
Place a golden torque around his neck,
A helmet of ambergris upon his head."

Shiddeh's interpreter looks on from the road,
Perceives the corpse of the celebrated prince,
And, once it is lifted above the dusty sands
And taken to Khosrow's camp, he approaches and shouts,
"O glorious and just King, I was Shiddeh's weak servant.
I am neither a combating rider nor a warrior.
Show mercy, and may the heavens rejoice on your life!"

The king replies, "Return and recount to my grandfather
And the entire court my deeds and my actions."

The heart and eyes of the Tooranian warriors
Are fixed on the road, awaiting Shiddeh's return.
Soon a rider appears to them over the billowing sands,
His head bare, his eyes shedding warm tears of blood.
He reveals to them the hidden mystery,
Relating the account of the battle to the King of Turks.
Afraasiyaab, world master, despairs for his own life.
He plucks out his camphor-colored hair
And tosses dust over his head.

His army warriors draw closer.
Whoever witnesses the Turkish ruler's face
Finds himself heartbroken and tears to shreds his clothes.
A lament rises from the army's midst, so plaintive
That it makes sun and moon feel a deep sense of pity.

Afraasiyaab speaks as he weeps,
"From now on, I shall enjoy neither rest nor sleep.
Remain my companions in my grief.
Share the deep sorrow I feel for my son.
The tips of our swords will never again
Perceive the shadows of their sheaths.
Never again shall I surrender to joy and regaling.
Let us bind ourselves together in agreement
And leave no field untouched in Iran-Zamin.
Let us assume any man who does not feel our grief
Is as inhuman as a wild beast.
May no eye ever again shed tears of pity
For those whose eyes do not expel warm tears for us!
Our suffering on the loss of this valiant, moon-faced rider,
This cypress tree growing on the riverbank, devours us.
We are plagued by a condition incurable by leeches."

Afraasiyaab continues to weep painfully,
Tears of blood drenching his cheeks.

The noblemen part their lips to speak:
"May the Just Creator help you endure this tragedy!
May your enemies' hearts tremble with fear!
In our grief, none of us will occupy himself,
By day or night, with any other pursuit
Than that of avenging the death of Shiddeh.
We shall make the army core roar the cry of war,
Drive it to the battleground, and scatter heads all around!
Khosrow left no part of himself in Tooran-Zamin,
And now, starting with the slaying of Piran and Hoomaan,
He compiles hatred upon hatred."

The troops are grief-stricken, the king filled with despair.
The field resounds with clamor and screams.

11 | The General Battle of the Two Armies

As the sun ascends above the bull's back
And the lark's song rises over the land,
The beating of drums and timpani
And the din of clarions is heard
At the openings of both kings' pavilions.

Jahn leads ten thousand brave men,
Skilled in the handling of sword, to war.

At the sight of these preparations,
Khosrow commands Ghaaran, always eager for fight,
To emerge from the army center like a mountain,
With a corps of ten thousand expert troops.

On the right wing, Gostaham, son of Nozar, charges forth
Like a cloud of dust, waving his war banner in the air.

The world turns purple beneath the dust of riders.
Troops fill the land while banners cloud the sky.

Khosrow and Afraasiyaab train in the hearts of their hosts.
The battle is such that the world had never seen before.
So many Tooranians are slain that the field is a sea of blood.
The situation remains dire until dusk descends
And the warriors' vision dims.
The valiant Ghaaran corners Jahn and overcomes him.

Once the moon ascends on its throne of sky
And the warriors withdraw from the battlefield,
The king praises the Iranians for their victory.
Rather than indulge in feast and rest,
They prepare for a new skirmish through the night.

When the sun reaches the sign of Cancer,
The world plummets into chaos
With the clank of battle and the beat of war drums.
Two armies from two nations line up their troops,
Every mouth uttering wishes to assault and overcome.

Khosrow distances himself from the rearguard,
Aided by a loyal and humble friend.

He sets foot to ground to glorify the Creator at length.
He rubs his forehead in the dust in devotion
And says, "O holy Master of Justice,
As you know, I have been mistreated and oppressed,
Yet I have surrendered to your will,
Suffering patiently through long days of misfortune.
Punish the wrongdoers for their crimes.
You are Guide to the one who has endured."

From there he goes to the army center,
Shouting the cry of war, his soul deep in grief,
His heart full of fury for the descendants of Zaadsham.
He places on his head his blessed helmet.

The sound of trumpets, drums, and cymbals
Rises all the way to the sky.
The enemy host advances like a massive mountain,
Men upon men agitated like the ever-stirring sea.
Jahn and Afraasiyaab stand tall at the heart.

As the two armies line up to confront each other,
You would think plain and valley are set in motion.
The sun turns black with the dust of troops.
The air twinkles with the gleam of steel
And the flutter of flying eagle feathers.

Such is the trumpet blast, the cry of warriors,
And the clash of steel on steel across the battlefield
That metal, boulders, mountain, leopards,
And whales in the sea soften and melt in fear.
The earth buckles, the air roils with dust and cries,
The sound of timpani splits the ears of wild lions.
You would think the world belongs to Ahriman
Or that skirt and sleeve have declared war.

On all sides rise mountains of cadavers,
Iranian and Tooranian fallen soldiers.
Most of the plain of sand is soiled with blood
And strewn with remnants of heads, hands, and feet.
The heart of the world is shaken at its core.
Beneath the trampling of countless horses' hooves,
The field resembles a solid sheet soaked in blood.

Afraasiyaab's warriors rush forth like vessels on water.
They approach to assail the archers' elephant towers.
These form a sort of elevated fortification
Right before the Iranian host, barring the way.
A shower of shots falls from the towers,
And the sound of blows administered and received echoes.
Elephants and spear-waving riders advance.
A multitude of warriors emerges from the army core.

From a distance of two miles, Afraasiyaab observes
The fight, the towers, and the elephants.
He commands the march of his animals and host,
And the world dims as dark as night.
He shouts, "O famed warriors, why do you
Complicate the course of battle for yourselves?
You crowd before the towers and the elephants
While the Iranian host is vast and stretches for miles.
Disperse left and right; move away from the center."

He commands Jahn, a skilled warrior, to leave his post
With his army's strong men and lead ten thousand
Seasoned riders, skilled swordsmen to fight.

Kebord, valiant elephant, takes off like a wolf,
With heroes charging toward the left wing.

Witnessing this assault by the Turks
And the way the sun's light is obscured,
Kay Khosrow turns to two princes, avid lions,
Samkanan and his son, Aaveh,
And commands them to take the left wing.
Shining like the sun in the house of Aries,
They march off with ten thousand illustrious riders.
Braced in armor and eager for battle,
They wield bull-headed maces
And pierce everything in sight with their spears.

Next, the king says to Shammaakh, ruler of Syria,
"Select, among our noble warriors, ten thousand young
Fighters covered in mail, armed with bull-headed mace.
Draw out your sword in the space between the two lines,
And allow no one to lower his head with impunity."

The two hosts fall on each other
As if they were melding and merging together.
On every side rises the crashing sound of blows.
Torrents of blood flow on the scene of carnage.

The elephants, bearers of towers, are sent away.
The world resembles the River Nile.
Dust rises left and right.
World ruler Khosrow asks for his war armor.
He leads from the center accompanied by hero warriors:
Rostam, Manooshan, and Khuzan, the army's support,
Who march to the beat of trumpets and clarions.

On one side of Kay Khosrow is Commander Tous,
Carrier of the Kaaviani banner,
Along with his warriors of golden boots.
They advance with bitter hearts to form the left wing.

The combative Rostam and his brother Zavaareh
March on the right of the king.
The worldly Goodarz, son of Kashvaad,
With numerous noble leaders, stay close to Rostam,
Along with Zarasp and Manooshan, wise advisor.

The racket of war reverberates through the battlefield.
No one has ever witnessed or will ever witness such a contest.
The field is bestrewn with wounded soldiers and corpses,
With men who have ceased to exhale breath.
So numerous are they that there is no space to cut across.
The flood of blood makes the field appear like the Jayhoon.

One man's corpse is headless, another headlong.
The bellowing of horseman and horse
Echoes louder than the beat of drums.
It is as if the heart of the mountain splits in agony
And the earth takes flight with the riders.

There are bodies without trunks, necks without heads,
And all the while heavy mace collides against heavy mace.
Blows rebound and resound;
The clang of daggers resonates.
The sun seeks a path of retreat,
Fearful of the blaze of swords of steel.

You would say a dark cloud is drifting above,
Pouring a rain of blood over the battleground.

Fartoos is killed on the left wing
At the hands of Fariborz, son of Kaavoos.
Kehila, who alone compares to one hundred elephants,
Falls on the right to the blows of Manooshan.

At the noon hour, there is a thunderous storm.
A cloud veils the face of the world-illuminating sun.
The earth darkens, obscuring visibility.

As the sun begins its descent,
The Turkish ruler's heart is overwhelmed by fear.
He observes the whirlwind of riders advancing
From every nation, every border, every kingdom.
They are dressed in all sorts of armor,
Wave banners of various colors,
Sending hints of red, yellow, and purple across the land.

Garsivaz, commander of the king's reserves,
At the sight of the proceedings
Brings forth his troops into the melee.
On the right, he rushes illustrious warriors
United in body and heart.
On the left, he similarly deploys troops
To sustain the fight: Forty thousand brave, illustrious,
Dagger-brandishing riders singled out for battle.

From the rearguard, Garsivaz rushes to his brother,
Who, at the sight of him, is renewed in courage
And commands his troops to advance.
The bashes of blows, received and dispensed, echo.
The face of the sky is veiled by feathered shafts.

Once the sun disappears, the day dims into shades of night.
Garsivaz, the cunning warrior, runs to his brother once more,
Lamenting: "Which of our warriors will still wish to fight?
The earth is filled with blood, the sky with dust.
Call your troops off; cease your efforts.
Let us retreat now that night has arrived.
We will soon hear despairing cries of anguish.
You will find yourself in the middle of the fight.

Your host will resort to flight,
And your precious being will be exposed to danger."

Afraasiyaab's heart simmers with rage,
And in his outburst he has no ears to listen with.
He launches his charger from the army core to the vanguard,
Rushes to the field with his black banner,
And kills a number of the most illustrious Iranians.

Witness to this frenzy, Khosrow dashes to rescue his men.
Two warrior kings from two nations advance
Toward each other with ordinary fighters at their sides.

But Garsivaz and Jahn do not wish to see
Afraasiyaab challenge Kay Khosrow.
They snatch his horse's bridle, turn it around,
And rush him toward the sandy plains of Amu.

As soon as he departs, Ostaghila storms like a gust of smoke
To engage in battle with Khosrow with his allies Prince Illa,
A war leopard, and the renowned Borzvila,
Imposing figures, solid as granite, fierce and merciless in war.

Catching sight of them, the king launches his horse,
Charges at them like a mountain,
Strikes the brave Ostaghila with his spear,
Lifts him off the saddle and flings him to the ground.

Prince Illa dashes to the vanguard
And strikes Khosrow at the waist with his spear.
But he fails to pierce through his armor,
And Khosrow's royal heart clings to its audacity.

Noticing his enemy's power,
Khosrow reaches for his sharp sword,
Strikes him hard, cuts his spear in half.
The heart of Borzvila fills with terror as he takes
Note of the king's courage, strength, and skills.
He flees into the darkness as if his skin
Has come undone by the sheer force of fear.

At the sight of Khosrow's victorious feats,
The Turks swiftly withdraw, one and all.

Afraasiyaab considers a sentence of death
For his troops for exposing their backs to the Iranian king.
His hope evades him quickly.
It is as if his days have reached an end,
Yet, while they abandon the battlefield,
He yells to Khosrow: "Your lion valor does not weaken us.
The reason for our retreat is the advent of night.
Today, the wind has, for once, blown in your favor,
Showering you with joy and victory.
Be assured that at the first light of day,
You will witness us with our blessed banner,
Turn the surface of the field into a sea of blood,
And tarnish the bright sun into the Pleiades."

In this manner, two kings from two lands
Withdraw into their respective camps,
Planning to resume battle on the following day.

12 | Afraasiyaab Deserts the Field

Once half the night has passed, and the firmament
Makes a half turn over the mountains,
Afraasiyaab asks his troops to pack up the loads.
He hands out armor and helmets to the warriors
And asks for a patrol of ten thousand rider Turks,
Handling as many decorated stallions.
He addresses his host: "I shall cross the River Jayhoon.
Follow me in good order, corps by corps."

In the dark night, Afraasiyaab abandons Amu
With his host and crosses the river,
Leaving in his wake the surface of the land
Strewn with vacated tents and pavilions.

As the first light of day oscillates in the east,
The Iranian sentinels find the field empty of warriors.
They bring the happy news to Khosrow,
Saying that he is relieved from battle,
For, although the field is covered with tents,
One can find there neither horse nor horseman.

At the news, Khosrow bows down to the dust
To give thanks to the Master of Justice:
"O Supreme Being, resplendent with light,
You watch over everyone; you nurture everyone.
You have bestowed me with dignity, crown, and power.
You have rendered blind the hearts and eyes of my foes.
Drive away from the earth this tyrant and oppressor,
And cast misfortune on him for the rest of his days."

Once the sun dons its golden shield
And night waves its turquoise-colored mane,
The world ruler sits on his ivory throne
And places on his head the light-emanating crown.

His army arrives to sing his praises,
Wishing for this king, worthy of throne, to rule eternally.

The soldiers are now in possession
Of the vast spoils of war abandoned by the Chini army.
They consider most unfortunate Afraasiyaab's flight,
With his troops, clarions, and timpani, and the fact
That the illustrious prince escaped the Iranians
To go into hiding, taking shelter in the dark night.

Their wise king tells them, "O noble Iranian leaders,
It is a good day when the king's enemy is killed
But even better when he drifts off in flight.
Since the Giver of victory has awarded us
With glory, power, diadem, and royal grace,
Offer thanks, day and night, to the Creator,
And worship equally on the day of misfortune,
When an unskilled man, sitting on the throne,
Will cause the demise of another.
The most strenuous efforts, the most earnest
Scrutiny of the stars are powerless,
For human subjects cannot oppose divine will.
I shall remain on this battlefield for five days.
On the sixth day, on Ormazd day,[37] light of the earth,
We shall set forth to fight and retaliate, as Afraasiyaab
Has incited in me the deep craving for vengeance."

◇◇◇◇◇◇◇◇◇◇◇◇◇
37 Ormazd Day: First day of any month in the solar calendar. Ormazd is Avesta for
Ahura Mazda, Creator.

For five days, they search the land for fallen Iranians.
They find them, wash them, then the king builds
A mausoleum in order to honor each with a proper burial.

13 | Kay Khosrow Announces His Victory to Kay Kaavoos

Khosrow summons a scribe to his side,
Equipped with paper, musk, and spice.
He draws up a letter to Kay Kaavoos
As suits royal custom and reverence.
The letter begins in praise of the Creator,
Supreme Guide in good fortune and adversity.
Then Khosrow dictates, "O King and master,
Who fears for my life as would a father,
May your power last as long as mountain and hill!
May the hearts of your foes be shattered!
I have traveled from Iran to the plains of Farab[38]
To fight three great battles in three nights.

"Afraasiyaab's riders counted more in numbers
Than any sensible mind can bear to imagine.
I am sending to the king three hundred noble heads,
Which include the heads of Afraasiyaab's brother,
His son, his noblemen, and his relatives.
Next, I send two hundred captive distinguished men,
Each equal to one hundred lions in strength.
We fought these battles in the desert of Khaarazm.
In the great war, heaven was on our side.
Afraasiyaab escaped, and we are in hot pursuit of him.
We shall soon find out the will of the rotating sky."

The letter is affixed with a seal of musk.
Khosrow crosses the sandy field, saying,
"May this battlefield be blessed!
May each year be governed by a lucky star!"

◇◇◇◇◇◇◇◇◇◇◇◇◇
38 Farab: An ancient city located on the Silk Road in a region that is present-day
Kazakhstan.

14 | Afraasiyaab Arrives in Gang-Dej[39]

Afraasiyaab retreats, fast as a whirlwind,
Determined to cross the Jayhoon,
His host combined with the host of Karookhan.
Every man retells the course of events.
The Tooranian king and his surviving men shed bitter tears
On the deaths of his glorious son, his relatives, his allies.
The lamentations are such it is as if the clouds
Are extracting tears of blood from lion eyes.

He pauses in Bukhara a while longer
In the hopes of renewing the battle of lions.
He convenes the most valiant of his remaining leaders,
And once they arrive, the army elders declare to the king
That they despair of the war:
"Our boldest warriors have succumbed to execution,
Leaving our hearts deeply troubled.
Out of one hundred men, perhaps twenty survive.
We shed copious tears for the departed.
Along with a great number of our allies,
We have renounced treasure, children, and friends,
And delivered, on the other side of the Jayhoon,
A battle as fierce as the king ordered.
You know well the turn of events due to our foolishness,
As you are king and we are your subjects.

"If the king agrees to follow sensible counsel,
He will lead his host to Chaadj.
If Khosrow comes to fight,
The time will come to mobilize troops.
May it please the king to retreat to the Golzarioon
And remain at ease in his paradise of Gang,
As it is a site well suited for rest and war."

Since no other counsel is brought forth,
Everyone agrees to march to the River Golzarioon,
Eyes moist with tears, hearts full of sorrow.

◇◇◇◇◇◇◇◇◇◇◇◇◇
39 Gang-Dej: A city built by Siaavoosh where Afraasiyaab constructed palaces for
himself.

The King of Turks spends three days at the river's edge,
Hunting with falcon and cheetah.
From there, they travel without pause to Gang-Dej,
A town much like a paradise,
Where the ground is made of musk and the bricks of gold.
He rests there in joy and smiles as if immunity is his mate.

On every side, he calls for an army of noblemen
To join in regaling in drink amid blossoming groves,
Music from harp and lute, roses, hyacinth, and cups of wine.
In this way, he delights in life, awaiting the turns of fate
And the secrets hiding beneath the apparent.

He dispatches sentinels to every corner of the land
And feasts with his leaders day and night.
He remains there for some time, waiting to see
What the world will reveal from the hidden.

15 | Kay Khosrow Crosses the River Jayhoon

The moment Kay Khosrow crosses the river,
He sets aside feast, rest, and sleep.
The moment his troops have traversed,
He sends out messengers to noblemen,
To declare that they need not fear his host
And to pray to the pure Creator for him.
He distributes wealth to the poor,
Handing out more to those most loyal to him.

From there, he travels to the border of Sughd,
Where he finds a peaceful world, the dwelling of owls.
He brings forth treasure to this land to help it prosper.

At every station, an escort of riders arrives pleading for mercy.

News reaches Khosrow of Gang and of Afraasiyaab,
Of his vast host and of Kaakooleh, a descendant of Toor,
Full of hatred and resentment, impatient for battle.
He has arrived at Afraasiyaab's side with troops
As restless as leashed lions.
Afraasiyaab has sent armed forces to Chaadj

To prepare there the throne of Iran and its crown.
Under the command of Tuvarg, he expedited
A huge host to the desert, and all the princes there
Have accepted to engage in war against Khosrow
And promise to block the path for the Iranians.

Kay Khosrow is indifferent to the enemies' moves,
As wisdom drives his strategies.
He commands troops arriving from Barda and Ardabil
To advance, division by division, ahead of him,
In order to give him an account of the warriors,
Wise men, and governors, allies of Afraasiyaab.

This battalion departs under the leadership of Gostaham,
A man who never flinches before quarreling lions.

Next, he sends the troops from Nimrooz
To march off with Rostam, destroyer of warriors,
And to ride horses as strong as ardent race camels
While maintaining fresh horses on a leash
To surprise the Turks with a quick night advance.

These two leaders, the glory of their diadems,
Depart, one for the desert, the other for Chaadj.

The king remains in Sughd for one month,
A land well suited for him, its people devoted to him.
He distributes dinars to his troops,
Asks them to rest, as he assesses the time for battle.

He deploys all the units fit for war
And alert to the art and trickeries of a siege.
He makes friends and fills
The heads of evil men with fear.
Then he straps himself for war and exits the land
With a proud army from Sughd and Kushan,
Soldiers protected by mail and breastplate,
Strapped for battle and ready
To spread terror across the world.

News reaches the Turks that Kay Khosrow's army,
Longing to possess the world,
Is advancing in search of vengeance.

Everyone seeks shelter in fortresses.
The land resounds with noise and chaos.

Kay Khosrow addresses his army and says,
"At this time, we must lead a different sort of war.
Do not assail those among the Turks
Who obey us and repent from provoking us.
Do not needlessly shed their blood,
And do not allow others to cause them harm.
On the other hand, you may strike and overthrow
Anyone who attacks us, anyone whose vengeful heart
Has veered off the righteous path."

The Iranian warriors vow to obey the king's command.
They proceed to assail the fortresses.
Anywhere they find a man wishing to defend his place,
They make the walls disappear instantly.
They leave behind neither fort nor palace,
Neither slave nor man or woman,
Neither horse nor anything else, good or bad.

They travel across one hundred farsangs,
Destroying castle, mountain, and plain.
Soon they reach Golzarioon.
Kay Khosrow surveys the surroundings with a guide.
He finds the land akin to a spring garden,
Valleys and fields, plains and hills in full bloom and beauty.
The mountains are replete with wild beasts,
The fields covered with trees,
And the ground worthy of being settled
By those endowed with an auspicious fortune.

He dispatches sentinels and spies
To be mindful of any hidden danger.
They set up the camp and the royal pavilion by the river.
The king, world master, sits on his golden throne,
Surrounded by his leaders and servants.
He spends the night, until the first light of day, engaged
In a feast that would make the dead rise from their graves.

On the other side, Afraasiyaab, who is in Gang,
Speaks day and night to his wise and prudent council:
"Now that the enemy has reached our bedside,

How can we continue to reside in Gang peacefully?"

They answer, "Since our evil opponent is here,
There is no option for us but to fight.
Why should we surrender?"
They speak, then rise to leave the king's side,
And spend the night making preparations for war.

16 | The Second Battle of Kay Khosrow With Afraasiyaab

At the advent of dawn and at cockcrow,
The beat of timpani breaks the silence in Afraasiyaab's palace.
A host so vast it leaves little room for ants and flies to pass,
Departs from Gang and takes the direction of the desert.
As it approaches Golzarioon,
The earth becomes a mass as large as Mount Bisootoon.

A line of warriors stretching over seven farsangs
Advances for three days and three nights,
Filling the world with fear, noise, and clatter;
Troops more numerous than ants crawling on the ground.

On the fourth day, they form the ranks of battle,
Spume from the water's flow rising to the sky.

Afraasiyaab and his most noble and wise warriors
Occupy the center of the host. Jahn, Afraasiyaab's son,
Whose spear flies beyond the sun, takes the right wing.

At the head of the left wing is Kebord, war lion,
Similar to a wolf, surrounded by skilled riders.
The rearguard belongs to the vengeful Garsivaz,
The army's support against enemy shots.

On the other side, Kay Khosrow, a pillar of strength,
Occupies the very heart of his host.
Rising like a mountain, he is surrounded
By Goodarz and Tous, son of Nozar;
Manooshan and Khuzan, two victorious princes;
Gorgeen, son of Milaad, and Gostaham the lion;

Hojir and Shiddush the valiant.

Fariborz, son of Kaavoos, holds the right wing
With troops united in body and soul.
Manoochehr commands the left wing,
A warrior who never yields in battle.
Giv, son of Goodarz, protector of borders,
Commands the rearguard.

Horseshoes bind the land into an iron mass.
The blood-infused river gleams like a sea of rubies.
A dark cloud of dust looms above warrior heads.
The beat of drums shatters the hearts of boulders.
The air is a veil of ebony. The earth wavers
As if it could no longer support this mass of troops.
The sound of timpani ignites the stars with fear.

The battlefield is strewn with brains and limbs
To such abundance that no space is left on the ground.
Horses' hooves crush the heads of the deceased,
Making sparks flare into the air.

Wise men stand at a distance.
The two hosts agree that, should they remain long
On this field of vengeance and devastation,
No rider would survive and the sky itself would collapse.

Such is the clangor of axes crashing on helmets
That souls quickly bid farewell to bodies.

As Kay Khosrow witnesses the upheavals,
He feels the world weigh heavy on his heart.
He pulls away from the scene to address the Creator.
Asking for justice, he says,
"O World Master, you are above the grace of saints.
O King above all kings, had I not been unfairly treated,
Had I not been warped, bent like metal in the furnace
Of a blacksmith, I would not be asking now for victory.
I would not disturb your peace with my prayers."

He speaks in this manner, rubbing his face in the dust.
The world fills with his mournful lament.

Suddenly, a great storm rises that splits the limbs of trees.
A cloud of dust fiercely lifts off the battlefield
And blows in the direction of the Turkish king and army.

The Tooranians are shaken, many of theirs are wounded,
Many are dead, yet others have fallen captive.
The moment Afraasiyaab witnesses a Tooranian warrior
Deserting the battlefield, he would proceed to cut off his head,
Leaving him in the sand with a layer of dust as shroud.

The battle continues until sky and earth are dark,
And a vast number of Turks are taken prisoner.
Night descends with its musk-black robe,
Making it impossible for anyone to fight.

Both kings call off their troops
As the sky spreads out its cloak of darkness.
From mountain base to river's edge,
The plain is further obscured by armor, breastplate, and helmet.
Fires are lit all around while sentinels keep watch.

Afraasiyaab prepares for a new battle, wishing to wait
Until sunrise shines its fountain of light across the hills,
Turning the land into a ruby from Badakhshan.
He awaits further battle and the outcome of fate.

But the Creator would decide otherwise,
And everyone has no choice but to defer to divine will.

17 | Afraasiyaab Takes Shelter in Gang-Behesht[40]

Once night grows as dark as ebony,
An envoy sent by Gostaham, son of Nozar,
Arrives at the shah's side and says,
"May the world king reign eternally!
We return in joy and victory.
We led a surprise night attack on Afraasiyaab's warriors.
They had not the wits to build outposts for guards.
As soon as they awoke,

◇◇◇◇◇◇◇◇◇◇◇◇◇◇
40 Gang-Behesht: Same as Gang-Dej, or the city Siaavoosh built.

We reached for sword and heavy mace.
Once night made way for day, only the valiant Karookhan
And a small number of his troops survived.
The entire field was strewn with limbs and heads,
The earth serving as their resting pillow
And dust as their blanket."

A camel rider hurtles toward them at dawn
With good news of Rostam.
He says, "We received word on the field
Where the enemy host was stationed,
And we followed the lead in haste.
Rostam traveled day and night.
We reached the site at fist daylight,
When the sun, glow of the world,
Transmits its first rays over the mountains.
Rostam, who has no equal, strung his bow
And approached, with helmet on his head.
The entire army of Turks was annihilated
With the first arrow that left his hand.
Now he marches into Tooran-Zamin,
Pursuing his longing for vengeance,
And news of him will soon reach the king."

A great cry of joy fills the camp,
Piercing the Turkish leader's ears.
He commands anyone in support of him
To mount their steeds.

A cavalier approaches Afraasiyaab in haste,
Screaming and announcing that Karookhan,
The only one remaining alive from his host,
Is approaching with sixty warriors. In addition,
A mass of Iranian fighters enters the land of Tooran,
Their numbers so high streams and rivers disappear.

Afraasiyaab addresses his advisors:
"Fortune betrays us once again.
If Rostam seizes my palace, we will lose our way.
But at the moment, he believes we remain in the dark,
And we are occupied with a battle against Khosrow.
Let us attack him now, quick as fire.

At nightfall, let us turn the field into a torrent of blood,
Wide as the Jayhoon River.

The heroes and wise advisors agree to his counsel.
They leave the loads behind and depart as swift as fire.

Soon a patrol guard arrives on the field
To announce that the sky is murky
With the dust of decamping Turkish troops.
He sighted many of the attackers retreating
And was here to tell the people's king, Kay Khosrow,
That, though the field is littered with various tents,
Small and large, there is not a single Turk in sight.

Khosrow realizes that the King of Tooran and Chin
Left the battleground precipitously
After news of the approach of Gostaham and Rostam.

He immediately dispatches an envoy to travel
At high speeds to Rostam and relay a message:
"Afraasiyaab has renounced his fight with me.
Without a doubt, he is about to fall on you.
Hold your host at the ready, remain on guard,
Maintain bow and arrow at your side, day and night."

The envoy, a worldly man familiar with the roads
And off-roads, departs at once toward Rostam.
He finds the hero of lion heart equipped for fight,
Troops girded and armed, mace on their shoulders,
Ears straining to listen for a distant threat.
He relays the message to Rostam
With the goal of ensuring his safety.

On his side, Kay Khosrow, eager for vengeance,
Sits in peace and distributes the spoils of war to troops,
Possessions and goods abandoned by the Tooranians:
Tents and pavilions, thrones and headdresses.

He asks that the deceased Iranians
Be washed clean of blood and mud,
Placed in coffins in a royal mausoleum.

Once the dust and blood of war is removed,

He calls for the loads to be packed up
And the troops to mount their steeds.
They swiftly get away
In pursuit of the trail of the King of Tooran.

Afraasiyaab, having arrived in the city of Gang,
Believes Rostam to be asleep and says to his army leaders,
"Let us surprise him! Let us destroy him and his army!"

In the darkness, he perceives a patrol,
Hears in the field the neigh of chargers.
Confounded at Rostam's caution,
He pauses to reflect on his army's misfortunes,
Its decline and defeat, how his men held on to their lives.

Rostam, quick to strike, is now before him,
And behind him are positioned king and warriors.

Afraasiyaab calls his council and speaks to them
At length of his worries, asking for guidance.
One of the advisors says to the illustrious king,
"Why should we further endure the toils of war?
Here we are in Gang-Dej, the seat of the king's treasury.
It is a place of eight farsangs in height and four in width,
Full of women, children, men, and a vast host.
It is the seat of power, kingdom, throne, and crown.
No eagle may fly above its walls, no one has ever
Observed such tall ramparts, not even in dream.
One can find here provisions, palace, wealth,
Diadem, power, order, throne, and a host.
This is a land we refer to as paradise,
Where everything is joy, rest, and delights.
In every corner, there is a fountain
And a pool of water, deep and as long as an arrow.
Wise men have come from India and Rum.
It is a dwelling akin to paradise.
From its tower's height, one easily discerns
Men in the field as far as twenty farsangs.
Your share in this world has been to launch battles.
In the end, the world remains for no one."

The king listens to these words
And finds them suitable and pleasing to his ear

As they renew his confidence in fate.
He joyously enters Gang-Behesht with his host
And his war apparatus, makes the rounds of the city,
And does not find there any uncultivated land.

There is a palace with roofs reaching the clouds,
Built by the powerful king.
He enters its hall to hold an audience.
He hands gold and silver to his troops.
In every corner, he sends armies led by renowned princes.

In the tower stands a lookout. During the day,
A guardian is on watch, during the night, a sentinel.
To the right of the king sit noblemen and wise men.
Afraasiyaab beckons his scribe.

18 | Afraasiyaab Writes to the Faghfoor of Chin

The king dictates a letter to the Faghfoor of Chin,
After one hundred thousand greetings, he declares:
"The revolving dome of sky sends only battle my way.
I raised a man I should have killed long ago, and now
He disrupts my life, plunging me into anguish and misery.
I would be honored if a renowned prince like the Faghfoor
Came to my side, for I hold his friendship in high esteem.
Should his excellency be unable to travel himself,
May he dispatch an army our way, ready for war."

Afraasiyaab's envoy departs with the letter
And arrives at the Chini court at the hour of sleep.
The Faghfoor, a highborn man, receives him graciously
And assigns him a pleasant dwelling.

Meanwhile in Gang, Afraasiyaab loses his appetite,
He is unable to rest or sleep in his anguish.
He places catapults on the walls
And sets the towers into a state of siege.
He orders his sorcerers to lift heavy boulders
And position them on the ramparts.
He summons a great number of skilled Rumi men,
Scatters his troops on the battlements,

And a chief full of vigilance places on the towers
Beacons, catapults, crossbows,
And shields crafted out of rhinoceros skin.
Forts and bastions are crammed with men
Braced in helmets and coats of mail.
A great number of blacksmiths work hard
To mold sharp claws of steel attached to long spears
To either grasp those approaching the walls
Or to force them back into retreat.

The king distributes money to his troops,
Provides them with the necessary gear,
Giving each generous gifts of helmets and swords,
Caparisons and shields from Chin,
And an infinite number of bows and arrows.
He pays heed not to overlook a single able warrior.
Once this task is accomplished,
He sits in joy with his noblemen
And the servants who helped him prepare for war.

Every day, one hundred fairy-faced harpists
Assemble around the king's throne.
He holds court day and night, listening to songs,
Drinking wine, and thinking of neither today nor the morrow.
If thoughts of the future torment him, he reflects that fate
Would be kind to spare him, and he need not worry.

He lives thus in revelry for two weeks.
Who knows whose heart will live in joy tomorrow?

19 | Kay Khosrow Arrives in Gang-Dej

In the third week, Kay Khosrow arrives in Gang
To the sound of flute and harp.
He laughs and makes the rounds of the forts,
Surprised at the changes he discovers.
He reflects, "The one who built these walls
Did not do it to resist either enemy or misfortune,
But after having spilled the blood of the King of Iran.
Then he took refuge behind these walls."

PART SIXTEEN

The king observes the city in astonishment.
He finds it akin to the celestial sphere
That brings joy to human hearts.

He says to Rostam, "O brave hero, can your clear mind
Comprehend the extent of grace and victory
The World Master has bestowed upon us?
This evil man, more notorious than any other
For his anger, his perverse nature, and his insanity,
Has fled before us and sought shelter behind the walls
Of this fortress in the hope of avoiding battle.
This evil man, leader of the world's most evil men,
Is even more wicked today in old age than in his youth.
If I do not express gratitude to the Creator,
I shall not merit sleep at night.
Yazdan is Giver of victory and power,
Creator of Sun and Moon.
On one side, the town leans against a mountain,
Thus keeping it safe from an attack.
On the other side flows a river, the delight of human souls."

They pitch their tent enclosures across the field
And plant the Kaaviani banner in the ground.
The army occupies a space of seven farsangs,
And the entire world submits to it.

Rostam places his camp to the right, asking the king,
World master, the command of an army corps.
On the left is Fariborz, son of Kaavoos,
Along with Tous wielding the blessed Kaaviani banner
And commanding the sound of clarions and timpani.
His men join him there and pitch his tents.

Next, the son of Goodarz selects his camp.

Night falls. On every side one hears uproar.
The world fills with tumult and chaos.
The heart of the earth leaps from the sounding
Of so many clarions, trumpets, and flutes.

Once the sun transmits its rays from the dome of sky
And tears apart the black veil shrouding the world,
The king sits on his horse the color of night,

And makes the rounds to review his host.
He says to Rostam of elephantine stature,
"O my dear friend, army leader, I hope the world
Will never see Afraasiyaab again, not even in dream!
May he either perish in battle or fall prey to me!
Either way, he will feel the tip of the sword.
I think that from every corner, troops will come to his aid.
They will seek to rescue him out of fear
And out of duty, for his power is fierce,
Rather than from a sense of enmity toward us
Or from the eagerness to engage in battle.
But before he even gets a chance to gather his host,
We shall make every effort to prevent an escape.
We shall destroy the walls of his fort city,
Cast away rock and boulder into the rushing river.

"The most trying days are behind us,
And weariness will turn to peace and rest.
When a foe seeks refuge behind bulwarks,
A host need no longer fear struggle and war.
Afraasiyaab feels disheartened in this city,
Which will soon be reduced to brambles and weeds.
Let us remember Kaavoos's forewarning words,
Encouraging us to make every effort to execute justice:
        'This tree of hatred, along with its ramifications,
        Will never again be covered by the rust of time.
        It will be like a tree always growing green leaves.
        In this vengeance of kings, the heart will not fear death.
        One generation after another will perish
        Until a hundred times sixty years pass.
        The father will be gone while vengeance prevails,
        And son after son will hold the grief and pass it on.'"

The brave warriors pay tribute to Kay Khosrow,
Acclaiming him as king of holy faith, and saying,
"May you bring to realization your father's vengeance!
May you live forever in joy and victory!"

20 | Jahn Brings Afraasiyaab's Message to Kay Khosrow

The next morning, as the sun reveals its face
Over the mountain crest and burns its golden torch
In the dome of sky, a great clatter rises from the fortress,
Disquieting the heart of Kay Khosrow.

All at once, the castle gates spring open to expose the secret.
Jahn exits the fortress escorted by ten riders
Cautious, sensible, and full of knowledge.
He advances to the opening of the royal pavilion,
Where he dismounts with his illustrious retinue.

The great chamberlain enters the royal court
To announce Jahn's arrival with his ten cavaliers.
The King of Kings sits on his ivory throne,
His head sheltered in the crown, delight of dim hearts.
Then the brave Manooshan invites Jahn to enter.

At the sight of the newcomer, Khosrow's eyes flood with tears.
The brave Jahn halts in surprise.
He removes his royal helmet, sighs, approaches the throne,
Bowing low in worship and saying, "O celebrated King,
May you bring joy to the world eternally!
May the lands you conquered from us prosper!
May your enemies' hearts and eyes be snatched away!
May you always have good fortune
And live in service to the Creator!
May your departure and your return be blessed!
May you be inclined to speak kind and just words!
I come here with a message from Afraasiyaab
And will relay it should his majesty wish to hear it."

Khosrow calls for a golden seat for his guest.
Jahn sits and unburdens himself of his father's message:
"Afraasiyaab sits on his throne, eyes moist with tears.
In the first place, I bring greetings from the ruler
Of Tooran's army, whose heart is broken. He said to me,
        'May praise be to the Creator, who is our shelter,
        That my grandson has attained such high status,
        That he leads a vast host and governs the empire.

On his father's side, his ancestors have been kings
Since the reign of Kay Ghobaad.
On his mother's side, he is a descendant of Toor.
His head stretches higher than any world king.
His name is the crown rising above the imperial throne.

'O King, the eagle flying through clouds
And the whale deep in the sea guard your throne.
Wild beasts rejoice in your good fortune.
Princes, owners of crowns and jewels, are of lesser rank.
It is the machinations of the wicked Deev,
Whose only goal is to cause me harm.
How did my heart fail me so?
Despite my righteousness and my affections,
My hand reached out to kill the noble Siaavoosh,
Innocent son of Kay Kaavoos. Since that day,
My heart remains shattered by such an atrocious act,
And I sit in grief devoid of hunger and rest.
I am not the one who caused his death.
The blame lies with the impure deev who
Snatched from my heart fear of the Creator.
The world belonged to Siaavoosh.
I had against him only an excuse,
For all I had on my side was a lie in the fight.

'Now, you are a sensible and fair king
Who approves of compassionate men.
Observe for yourself the cities full of gardens,
Palaces, and homes devastated by this war,
A war that is an excuse for vengeance.
Think of the battles led by valiant cavaliers,
With bodies as strong as elephants and as powerful
As whales, whose shrouds became the jaws of lions,
Whose heads were brutally slashed from their trunks.
Reflect on the fact that there remains no place of rest
In these parts of the world, not even in the desert.
Everywhere, cities and towns have been depopulated.
Reflect on the fact that our name will be remembered
Only in relation to battles and blows of sharp swords.

'Yazdan, the Creator, cannot approve of this.
We shall end up writhing from the pain we inflict.

If you wish to fight, your heart will not tire of war.
Reflect on the revolutions of fate, seek lessons from it.
We are in a fortress; the open countryside is yours.
Your head is full of vengeance, your heart full of blood.
I named my city Gang.
It is a paradise created in my land,
Its bushes and trees planted by my hand.
It is the seat of my treasure, army, seal, and crown.
It is where I work and enjoy life,
And where my lion warriors reside.
Meanwhile, the fine weather and the heat are over.
Vividly hued roses and tulips have withered and died.
The winter chill will soon be here
To benumb your hands on the hilts of your spears.
Once clouds show their wrinkles on mountains' slopes,
The shifting sands of this land will turn to bedrock.
I will muster troops from every land on earth,
Leaving you no way to evade
The spinning motions of sun and moon.

'Suppose that the ever-changing fate abandons you.
At that moment, it will burden you beyond your fears
And another man will profit from your suffering.
If you contemplate such thought:
          "I shall seize the lands of Tooran and Chin.
          I shall make the sky collapse onto the earth.
          I shall exterminate this court with my sword,
          And Afraasiyaab will plummet from his seat."
Do not think that such a thing is likely to occur,
For he who is not meant to perish cannot be defeated.

'I am the grandson of Zaadsham, the greatest king of all.
I come from the race of Fereydoon and Jamsheed.
Mine are divine knowledge and grace,
Attributes given by the Creator to kings.
I possess the stature of Sooroosh.
Should misfortune strike me, I shall ask no one for help.
According to the will of the Creator, I shall disappear
At the hour of sleep, like a star vanishes before the sun.

'I shall cross the Sea of Kimaak,[41]
Surrender to you my army, kingdom, and crown.
Gang-dej will be your residence.
My land and people will never see me.
But once the day of vengeance is here,
Take care to equip your host accordingly,
For I shall, vengefully, reestablish my faith in the land.
Should you wish to dismiss thoughts of reprisals,
Should you wish to bring happiness all around
With a show of mercy and compassion,
I shall bring out my treasures of crowns and belts,
Silver, gold and gems, and you may take
What Fereydoon failed to bestow on Iraj.
Never again bring up the thought of vengeance.

'If you wish to possess the lands of Chin
And Maachin, you are welcome to them,
For one must go where the heart leads.
Khorasan and Mokran[42] stretch before you,
And I consent to all of your wishes.
I shall send as many troops as you demand
On the road taken by Kay Kaavoos.
I shall bring wealth to your army,
Give you a golden throne and a diadem.
I shall support you in your battles
And recognize you as king before my court.

'Express your wishes and desires.
Reflect on your past and your future.
But if you reject my counsel and contemplate
Executing vengeance against your grandfather,
Then you better prepare for war.
As soon as Jahn returns, I shall be ready
To leap like a leopard to engage in battle.'"

◇◇◇◇◇◇◇◇◇◇◇◇◇◇
41 Kimaak, Sea of: Kimaak was the name of a Turkic tribe; may refer to the Ural River, which discharges into the Caspian Sea.
42 Mokran: In Iran-Zamin and in the coastal region of today's Baluchistan.

21 | Kay Khosrow Replies to Jahn

The king listens to Jahn's message,
Smiles at him, and says, "O battle seeker,
I have listened to your words from beginning to end.
Firstly, in regards to your wishes for me,
May they come true as far as my throne, crown, and seal!
As for the greetings you relay from Afraasiyaab,
Whose eyes, according to your account,
Are filled with tears, I have heard them.
May they bring good fortune to my throne and crown!
May they always shower us with victory and joy!
Next, let me address the fact that he gives thanks
To the Creator to see his grandson devoted to Yazdan,
Happier than any other world king,
The most beloved and triumphant ruler.

    'My answer is that the Creator has bestowed
    Upon me all that Afraasiyaab insinuates.
    May my worth be above this benediction!
    Although your language is pleasing to the ear,
    You are neither pure of heart
    Nor a true servant of Yazdan.
    When one has a strong mind,
    Actions hold more value than speech.

    'Fereydoon, the benevolent, did not become a star,
    And his body did not abandon the dark earth.
    You claim that I rise above the firmament.
    Have you renounced all sense of decency?
    Your mind depends only on sham and deceit,
    And a word out of your mouth is just an adornment.
    Your lips are full of speech, your heart is full of lies
    That have not the power to dazzle a wise man.
    Do not call me king of the earth,
    For you are my father's murderer,
    And now Siaavoosh's remains have vanished.
    In a similar show of hate, you dragged my mother
    From the women's chambers out into the public.
    As for me, who was not yet born,
    You proceeded to pour fire over my head.

    'Anyone who stands before your throne

Curses your vicious heart,
For no one in the world acted in this manner,
Neither king nor hero, neither warrior nor ordinary man.
You are a prince who dragged a woman,
His own daughter, shamefully before men
And handed her over to the executioner to be whipped.
You wished to force her to suffer a miscarriage!
The wise Piran intervened and witnessed a sight
That he had never seen or heard of before.
Ultimately, Yazdan willed
That I was to raise my head above the multitude.
Fate designed a secret stratagem,
Where it turned the hand of hardship away from me,
Disabling you from causing me further affliction.
Later, once my mother gave birth to me, you exiled me,
Sent me off to live with shepherds, like a worthless child,
Surrendering me to the lions' pasture.
Goats served me as milkmaids, buffalos as guards.
I enjoyed no peace during the day
And little sleep in the dark of night.

'Thus passed time. In the end,
Piran fetched me and brought me back to you.
You took one look at me and instantly nurtured
The fear that I would snatch your royal throne.
You wished to bring down on me the same fate
As Siaavoosh, to savagely cut off my head.
Yet you did not consider granting me a shroud.
But the holy Creator tied my tongue.
I showed myself confounded in my seat.
You found me a being devoid of heart and wisdom,
So you cast aside your evil designs.

'Now think of Siaavoosh's deeds, his righteous ways,
And how much he suffered in deprivation and pain.
Like a wise man, he selected you as his shelter.
He abandoned for you the throne and crown of Iran.
He came and hailed you as world king, all the while
Acting in good faith, sending away his procession,
So that you might not accuse him of betrayal.
Once you set your sights on his chest and his waist,
His power, his valor, his ways, your ill nature stirred,

And you proceeded to slay this man of pure heart.
You cut off a most noble head, holder of crown,
As if it were a lowly sheep's head.

'Since the time of Manoochehr,
You have been nothing but mean and malevolent.
Misfortune was brought down by Toor,
Who acted in wicked ways before his father.
This is how, from generation to generation,
There was neither royal behavior, nor order, nor faith.
You struck the head of the illustrious Nozar,
The king's father, born of royal race.
You killed your own brother, Aghriras,
A gentle man who sought only to acquire a good name.
Since the day you were born,
You have acted spitefully and with ill intent,
And you have followed the ways of Ahriman.

'If one were to enumerate your transgressions,
One would surpass the rotations of sky.
You are a reject sent from hell!
Do not pretend to have incurred a human birth.
Furthermore, you contend that the evil deev
Has bent your will and heart to recur to misdoing.
Long ago, Zahaak and Jamsheed blamed Eblis
For provoking their hearts to diverge from virtue,
Rendering them powerless to act with integrity.
But adversity stayed with them because of
Their ill nature and the advice of their master deev.
Whoever turns away from the righteous path
Will end up weak, bent over against his will.
Again, in the battle of Pashan,
Where Piran killed so many riders, the earth
Stained in red by the blood of Goodarz's sons,
You seek only to inflict pain.
You hunt only for an evil way.

'Now you show yourself here with one thousand
Times one thousand Turkish riders ready for war.
You bring your army to Amu to fight me.
You sent Shiddeh to cut off my head
So that you might abscond to destroy my land.

But Yazdan, the World Master, came to my aid
And impaired my contender's fortune.
Tell me now, how could your heart rejoice
In my happiness and seeing me on the throne?
Tell me, with all the memories I have of your deeds,
How can I believe you? How can you be sincere?
From here on and until the day of resurrection,
I shall communicate with you only with my sharp sword.

'I shall fight against you with the power
Of my treasures and armies,
With the help of my guiding star
And the rotations of the sun and moon.
I shall stand humbly before Yazdan,
Wanting, needing no other guide,
In the hope of plucking weeds out of the garden,
To renew the world with justice and generosity,
To destroy my enemy,
To remove the diadem from evil hands.'
"Now go and relay my words to my grandfather,
So that he no longer seeks an excuse to avoid battle."

He gives Jahn a crown inlaid with gems,
A golden torque and two earrings.
Jahn returns to his father and relates the exchange.

Afraasiyaab is stirred by Khosrow's reply.
His heart fills with grief and his head with impatience.
He distributes gold and silver to his troops,
Mace, sword, helmet, and headdress.

22 | Kay Khosrow Attacks Afraasiyaab and Captures Gang-Dej

All night and until the rising sun saddles the horizon
To paint the mountain in the colors of a white elephant,
Afraasiyaab spends his time setting order to his troops.
Not a single rider surrenders to sleep.
At the sound of kettledrums over the city,
The earth is covered in steel and the air fills with black dust.

At sunrise, Khosrow, benevolent king, chief wise man,
Climbs on his horse to make the rounds
And to finalize his plan of battle.
He orders Rostam to march to one side of the city
With an army corps as large as a mountain.
On the other side, the king sends Gostaham, son of Nozar.
In yet another direction, he dispatches Goodarz,
The hero of opportune advice.
Finally, the king takes position on the fourth side,
Establishing his will with timpani, elephants, and troops.
After distributing necessary equipment to his host,
He returns to sit on his throne.

The king commands the troops to dig a trench
To run the circumference of the ramparts.
Those suited for the job and able to attack the fort,
Whether from Chin or the land of Rum,
Whether a wise man or a skilled hero,
Surround the king to offer their skills and services.

After the trench is dug to measure in depth the length
Of two spears, Khosrow mobilizes his troops into
A blockade so that the Turks may not escape by night
Or draw out their swords to rise threateningly.

Before every gate he places two hundred catapults.
Behind the troops, he positions two hundred
Large, stone-throwing siege engines
To be deployed by two hundred men.
Further back are one hundred archers
Armed with crossbows.
They would assail approaching enemy troops
With a deluge of shots and catapulted rocks.
Behind the mangonels are Rumi soldiers,
Strapped and ready for war.
Finally, the king commands two hundred elephants
To be placed around the city's battlements.

Wooden columns made of tree trunks
Are planted inside the ditch to lean
Against the city wall and support it.
The wood is then covered

With a layer of black crude oil,
A shrewd stratagem conceived by the king.
If these columns were to collapse,
The entire structure would come crashing down.

The stones launched by catapults and the shots of archers
Render pale the cheeks of warriors who encounter
Fire, oil, and wood below, and fierce blows of mace above.
Having thus prepared the attack on four sides,
As it suits a proper siege,
The king of the earth takes leave of his troops
And marches to the site of prayer
To secretly invoke the World Master.

In his yearning for vengeance, Kay Khosrow
Thrashes in the dust like a serpent and pleads,
"You are the One who fulfills our wishes.
You are the One who assigns power.
In times of danger, you provide shelter.
If you deem my request just,
Then do not force us into retreat.
Remove these sorcerers from their seats of power.
Satisfy my yearning heart.
May fortune favor our cause."

After his prayer, Kay Khosrow raises his head
And shelters his shining chest in a thick coat of mail.
He seizes his weapons and charges into battle like smoke.
He commands every gate to be fiercely attacked,
The wood coated in oil to be set aflame
And rocks to be heaved on the head of the besieged.

At the sound of the archers,
The smoke obscures the sun's radiant face.
The earth turns a shade of blue, the sky lapis lazuli
From the dust raised by catapults and mangonels.
Cries of elephants and warriors rise over the fort.
The flash of steel on steel and of mace on steel
Makes it appear as if sun and moon are jousting.
Such is the shower of blows and the darkening dust
That the firmament disappears in the obscurity.

The black oil sets the trees on fire as they ignite

Like kindling wood, as if by divine intervention.
The wall appears to rise, then crash down like a mountain.
A great number of bold Turks are hurled off the walls
Like lions falling unexpectedly into a ditch.
The lives of these men, thus abandoned by fortune,
Slip into a precipitous end.

A great cry of victory echoes through the king's divisions.
All eyes turn to the breach of the fortress.
Rostam surges, eager to join the battle.

Afraasiyaab, immediately made aware
Of the collapsed city wall, rushes forth,
As swift as dust, shouting to Jahn and Garsivaz,
"What do we care about the wall!
An army must build walls with swords
To safeguard land, children, treasure, and family.
Strap together the hems of your coats,
And do not allow the enemy to remain standing!"

A host of Tooranians, as massive as a mountain,
Forms tight battalions to defend the fort.
They fight like lions, and a huge clamor rises on both sides.
Turkish riders quiver like leaves on a willow tree.
They despair and begin to doubt a recovery.

At this moment, the king orders Rostam
To have all the men, holders of spears, dismount
And advance on foot toward the collapsed wall.
A great number of renowned warriors, avid for battle
And armed with quiver, sword, arrow, and weapons,
Sit on horseback behind the glorious Rostam.

The valiant king instructs them as they charge into the fray.
The riders and sentinels of both armies
Fling themselves en masse into the battle, like mountains.

Rostam, avid for vengeance, brings his troops to the ruins.
Like a furious lion, he advances on foot, as swift as dust,
Brings down Afraasiyaab's black banner, and plants
Over the walls the purple banner of the King of Iran,
Illustrated with the drawing of a valiant lion.

The winning cry of the Iranian host resounds on the field,
For many Tooranians are killed as their fortunes dim.

At the point where the battle is most fierce,
Rostam seizes two men and flings them to the ground:
Garsivaz and the valiant Jahn,
The support of the Tooranian throne.
One is the brother of Afraasiyaab and the other his son.
In this way captured, they succumb to their downfall.

The Iranian army enters the city, troops nursing
An ulcerated heart eager to execute vengeance.
They proceed to loot and pillage.
The sounds of clamor and laments rise.
Women and children holler cries
And abandon their homes to the Iranians.
Many women and young children disappear,
Trampled beneath elephant feet.

Throughout the city, the inhabitants flee like wind,
Everyone forsaking thoughts of land and belongings.
Eyes are filled with the blood of distress
For the vanquished fortune of Tooranian warriors.
Their women and children are captured,
Their treasures seized, their hearts wounded by fate,
And their bodies punctured and pained by arrows.

23 | Afraasiyaab Flees From Gang

Heart swelling with fear, eyes brimming with tears,
Afraasiyaab takes shelter in his palace.
He climbs the tower and takes a look at his city.
He notices two-thirds of his warriors are dead,
And the remaining ones have absconded from battle.
He hears the holler of riders and the beat
Of kettledrums from the backs of elephants.

He sees elephants trampling men and crushing them.
He sees the city overtaken by smoke,
Lament, fire, pillage, and storm.
He finds some people joyous,

PART SIXTEEN

While others are burdened by grief and fatigue.
Such is the way of this passing world.

Once Afraasiyaab assesses the state of affairs,
The awful massacre and the way fate abandoned him,
Once he is fully aware that he has lost Jahn, his brother,
His lands, his crown, his kingdom, his throne and belt,
Everything gone, heart wrenched with sadness,
He says to himself, "Look how many calamities
The celestial dome of sky sends down upon my head.
When I consider the days ahead,
Dying no longer appears a hardship to me."

He climbs down from the tower, full of sorrow and woe.
He bids farewell to the royal throne, lamenting,
"When shall I ever lay eyes again on joy, rest, and delights?"

He takes leave of this site in great distress and disappears.
Reason exits his mind, like a bird taking flight.
Some time ago, he had built
An underground passageway leading out of his palace.
No one in his army is aware of its existence.
He selects two hundred of his noblemen
And departs by way of this secret path.
From there, he leaves his land through the desert.
His subjects remain confounded by his absence.
No one in all the world knows of his whereabouts,
So speedy is his escape.

Kay Khosrow enters his palace
And tramples over his predecessor's star.
He sits on the golden throne
With heroes of golden headdress
And asks for Afraasiyaab's whereabouts.

The search goes on for a long time,
But no trace of the illustrious leader is found.
The king asks again after Garsivaz and Jahn,
And the leader of the Tooranian army,
How he left and where he could have taken shelter.
Despite a thorough search, no one can find him.

The blessed king says to the Iranians,

"My enemy has fled like a coward.
But since his glory and power have faded,
It is quite irrelevant whether he is dead or alive."

24   Kay Khosrow Pardons Afraasiyaab's Family

Next, Khosrow selects a number of wise warriors,
Noble, skilled and worldly, and says to them,
"May your bodies remain strong and healthy!
May your hearts fill with justice!
I entrust you to secure the treasury
Of this Turk whose fortune has dimmed.
Do all you can to defend it, for no one and nothing,
Not even the sun from high above,
Must find access to Afraasiyaab's palace.
Furthermore, I do not wish to hear the wail
Of his veiled women outside of the bastion walls."

He sends guardians to care for the horses
Grazing peacefully around the border of Gang.
As suits kingship, he assures that no harm is directed
At members of the Tooranian royal family.

When the Iranian host witnesses the king's actions,
Murmurs erupt from one end to the other:
"Kay Khosrow acts as if he is a guest in the paternal home.
He does not remember the spilled blood of his father,
Whose head was unjustly severed in a moment of madness!
He forgets his mother, plucked off her royal sanctuary
To be dragged by the hair uncovered through the streets.
This king is incapable of harming anyone because
He was raised by shepherds and nursed with sheep milk.
Why does he not attack Afraasiyaab's dwelling
Like a leopard with sharp claws?
Why does he not tear down palace and audience hall,
And consume in flames the royal relatives?"

Someone relates these words to the king,
Who sends an envoy to convene the wise men.
Kay Khosrow addresses them at length:
"One must never exhibit anger,

Nor give praise to those who act unwisely.
Despite my longing for vengeance, a wiser course of action
Is to act justly, to think of glorifying my exploits,
For good deeds are the only memories we leave on earth.
The world remains for no one forever.
The rotation of the vault of sky can spread all sorts
Of hardships for anyone, at any time, if it so wishes."

Next, the world king summons in secret
The veiled wives and daughters of King Afraasiyaab,
None of whom has ever stepped outside
Of the women's chambers and into the street.

Once the Iranians learn of this, they rush to the palace,
Full of a desire for vengeance, for these heroes believe
That Khosrow should sentence the women to death.
The soldiers wish to treat them with disrespect,
Prepared and eager to destroy them and kill them.

From inside the palace walls, voices and laments rise:
"O wise king, justice giver, we are defenseless,
Yet we do not deserve to be treated
With such degradation and dishonor!"

The head queen, escorted by her daughters,
Appears shaking before the king.
Each woman wears a dress embroidered in gold and jewels,
And a ruby diadem on her head, a slave standing by her.

The young women's hearts beat wildly
With terror for the King of Kings
As they approach, their heads lowered in shame.
Each holds in one hand a golden cup filled
With pearls, rubies, musk, and precious gems,
In the other hand a censer burning amber and sandalwood.
It is as if Saturn, from high above,
Scatters a shower of stars down on earth.

The noble queen advances toward the throne.
She renders homage to the king, and all the idols
Raised with such care begin to worship him as well,
Each shedding bitter tears, restless in her disgrace.

They praise him in their sorrow.
The queen tells him, "O noble King of blessed race,
On the day of need, be generous toward those
Who have known only comfort and luxury.
What peace we would enjoy if the land of Tooran
Had not filled your heart with grief
And with the longing for vengeance!
You would come here happy and ready to be celebrated.
You would become the ally and friend of princes.
As king and master of this land,
You would sit on your grandfather's throne.
Siaavoosh would be alive; he would not
Have perished by Afraasiyaab's foolish deeds.
Yet such are the actions of the rotating sun and moon.
The deed was accomplished by Afraasiyaab,
Descendant of an evil race, who must not count,
Not even in dream, on the possibility of pardon.
I have given him constant advice,
But he did not take advantage of it,
Foolishly turning away from my counsel.
The Creator is my witness:
My eyes have shed copious tears of blood.

"Furthermore, Jahn, your relative,
Who only unfastens his bonds to you with great pain,
Observed the anguish I felt in my heart and soul
For the departed Siaavoosh when he was with me.
How many warnings Afraasiyaab, the wicked,
Refused to heed until the day fortune abandoned him.
His kingdom was overthrown, his crown and belt pillaged,
The light of his day obscured, his being humiliated,
And his miserable life worse than death itself.
It is surprising that his skin is still attached to his body.

"Now look at us with your royal eye. We are innocent.
We are Kay Khosrow's devoted relatives and subjects.
We hear no other name but his in the world.
He would not wish to punish his innocent women
For the wicked deeds of Afraasiyaab, the sorcerer.
He would not wish to attack them, shed their blood,
And injure them without first reflecting on the fact
That they have done nothing wrong.

It is not dignified for a king to hang a guiltless head.
You, O King, have other intentions.
No one remains eternally in this fleeting world.
Act in a way that you have no regrets
For your actions on the day of judgment."

Khosrow is touched by these words
And by these fair-faced women abandoned by fortune.
Their veiled cheeks shine like lamps in their grief,
And the hearts of sensible men shake with emotion,
For each one thinks of his own wife and children.

Army leaders and valiant princes praise the glorious king,
Beseeching him in the name of the Creator
To abstain from exacting vengeance on the women.

The wise Khosrow replies, "Despite the suffering and grief
I was subjected to, I shall not hurt anyone,
Although my heart is avid for vengeance.
I worry about the conduct of this powerful prince,
But the misfortune of his women deeply saddens me.
Although he acted with malice toward my virtuous mother,
I do not wish to act in the same manner with his ladies."

The world master, son of holy parents,
Orders Afraasiyaab's women to return to their dwellings.
He says to them, "Surrender yourselves to trust.
Do not believe idle rumors.
From here on, you have nothing to fear from me.
I am not deceitful like a wicked person.
From here on, no one will dare cause you harm.
Anyone who attempts to will be dealt a short life.
Remain in your palace with confidence.
Devote yourselves to Yazdan, body and soul."

25 | Kay Khosrow Gives Advice to the Iranians

The victorious king says to the Iranians,
"May throne and crown endure forever!
All the cities of Tooran-Zamin have been conquered
And now belong to the people of Iran-Zamin.

Cast aside all thoughts of vengeance;
Bring joy to this land with your clemency.
The inhabitants' hearts are filled with fear,
As everywhere the soil is kneaded with blood.
I give you all the wealth of Tooran-Zamin
And address to you only one wish:
Make every effort to act with good intentions.
Wherever you encounter winter cold, transform it to spring.
Soon I will lavish the army with dinars and treasures.
You must abstain from bloodshed
And cutting off the heads of innocent people.

"It is not noble for a man to strike, in his restlessness,
Those who have been vanquished.
Turn your gaze away from the women
And away from anyone veiled coming out into the street.
Respect the virtues of others as they turn enemy into friend.
Harming the innocent does not find grace in Yazdan's eyes.
Whoever wishes to gratify me
Will abstain from destroying my empire.
May we call unjust the one
Who turns my land into a barren desert!"

Next, the king orders his army to open the doors
To Tooran's treasury, with the exception
Of the private royal wealth, to which no one has access.
He distributes most of it to his troops:
Silver, arms, thrones, and crowns.

On every side, numerous Turkish soldiers,
Scattered throughout, return to join forces with Khosrow.
The latter grants them pardon, treats them with kindness,
And quickly arranges their affairs.

He divides Tooran-Zamin to allocate various parcels
To his army leaders, giving a city to each renowned warrior.
Anyone in the land who refuses to obey Kay Khosrow
Has no power to prevent his head from falling.

As soon as the letters to noblemen make their way
To the provinces, the entire land surrenders to the king.
Envoys rush in to bow before him, bearers of gifts and letters.
Each local ruler proclaims loyal submission to Kay Khosrow.

26 | Kay Khosrow's Letter of Victory to Kaavoos

Khosrow summons his scribe,
Who arrives with paper, musk, and amber.
He relates to him all necessary information
And composes a letter to Kay Kaavoos
About the events and the outcome
Of the fight with the Turks in Tooran-Zamin.
At the start of the letter, he praises Yazdan,
"Who heals the world from its ailments,
Who awakens the latent celestial star of our empire
To shine brightly and curtails sorcerers' heads,
Who brings happiness to the oppressed,
The One from Whom we draw power, wisdom, justice."

Then he adds, "By the shining light of Kay Kaavoos,
Powerful, skilled, and prosperous king,
Afraasiyaab's town of Gang has been seized,
And the fortune of the Tooranian has plunged.
In a single battle, forty thousand brave, noble,
Mace-wielding warriors have been killed
On the field on the edge of the Golzarioon River.
A great thunderstorm has soared,
Plucking roots and branches off the tree.
A great number of his troops rebelling against us
Have been cast into the river's waters.
Afraasiyaab himself fled from Gang-Behesht,
A stronghold full of men and easy to defend.
We attacked the fortress, killed thirty thousand men.
Because of his unjust nature,
Neither his skills nor his fortune could save him.
His army dispersed on the surface of the land
While he fled, disappearing from the world.
I shall send further news to the king at a later time,
Once I receive additional favors from providence."

Khosrow applies his golden seal to the letter
And sends the envoy joyously to King Kaavoos.
Then the young shah settles happily with a goblet of wine,
Surrounded by cupbearers and fairy faces.
He takes some time to rest until spring renders the world
As beautiful as paradise, filled with color and scent.

Desert fields are draped in sprinkles of flowers,
To appear like an expansive spread of embroidered silk.
The air, speckled with clouds,
Resembles a leopard's hide.
Deer and gazelles dash through the plains.
In this way Khosrow spends some time in joy,
Hunting with cheetahs and winged falcons,
Drinking musk-scented wine and in the company
Of women as beautiful as idols from Taraaz.

They collect the wild horses who cross the desert,
Galloping full speed like deer, necks as strong as lions,
Ears pricked up and heads as fine as the heads of stags.
The king dispatches sentries to all corners
To search throughout the world for the unjust Afraasiyaab.

27 | Khosrow Learns of Afraasiyaab's Advance With the Faghfoor's Army

News reaches King Khosrow from Chin and Khotan
That Afraasiyaab has received shelter
From the Faghfoor of Chin, his ally.
The land of Chin fills with the clatter of war.
The stretch from Chin to Golzarioon is occupied
By a vast host under the command of Afraasiyaab.
No one knows the value of the presents
Or the number of the slaves and horses in coverings
Given to him by the Faghfoor of Chin.
He is respected there, retaining the title of king,
And in possession of Piran's wealth.
He has one hundred and sixty camels weighed heavy
With loads of gold that they hauled to Khotan,
Where he is mustering a formidable army.

Once Afraasiyaab's troops,
On whom Khosrow showed mercy,
Are made aware of their king's whereabouts,
They desert the Iranians and gear up for revenge
Once again, allowing Afraasiyaab to exit Khotan
With an army so vast the earth buckles beneath its weight,
Rivaling the stars to match its size in numbers.

PART SIXTEEN

He departs from Chin, heading straight to Khosrow,
Deeply irritated and escorted by an army hungry for war.

Aware of the approach of king and army,
Kay Khosrow sends scouts on the road.
He commands Goodarz, son of Kashvaad,
Gorgeen, and Farhaad to remain cautious in Gang,
With guards making the rounds day and night.

He says to Goodarz, "These troops are at your command.
Should there be a threat of danger, they will be faithful.
If you find a Turk speaking favorably about our foe,
Take him to the stakes to hang, feet above and head below.
But cause no harm to those who do not provoke you.
Take care of the army. Protect the troops and the treasure."

The echo of drums and the din of bells, camels,
And elephants rebound against the palace walls.
An army exits Gang, as if the sun itself
Appears to be cast in the throes of battle.

As soon as his troops are outside the city,
Khosrow forms the ranks and advances at the lead,
Charging toward Afraasiyaab.

The distance between the two hosts closes to two farsangs.
The world master calls his noble heroes and says to them,
"Remain quiet and vigilant at the hour of sleep.
Stay awake, your weapons in close reach."

He sends patrols to cross the desert
And keep vigil on the camp throughout the night.
He remains in this manner for one week,
Using the time to prepare for battle.

On the eighth day, a top player returns and announces
To Kay Khosrow that a host is advancing toward them.
The king places his troops in rank of battle,
In a way as to tickle the curiosity of sun and moon.

Once Afraasiyaab sees the Iranian army, he forms
The line at the vanguard and says to his advisors,
"This battlefield is for me a stroll and a feast,

Which I receive with pleasure, even at the hour of sleep.
If war had not presented itself, I would incite it myself.
I have fled for a long time, my head full of vengeance,
My heart buzzing with the passion for combat.
I do not know if this is a sign of Kay Khosrow's fortune
Or a good omen for me, but I have decided to fight
With him in person and to find in it either the fulfillment
Of my desires or the prospect of suffering and death."

His wise advisors, relatives, and strangers reply,
"If the king is to fight himself,
Why then such an army and such pomp of war?
In Chin and in Tooran, everyone stands at his command,
Whether of his race or of a foreign race.
May your life be your ransom!
Such has been our oath of loyalty since the beginning.
Whether one hundred of us fall or one thousand,
What is the difference? Do not risk your life.
We are devoted to you at heart,
For we live only by the grace of your diadem."

A great uproar billows through the crowd.
The world fills with the tumult of war.
Stars appear in the dark firmament,
And the sun's face darkens.

28 | Afraasiyaab's Letter to Kay Khosrow

The leader of the Turks selects from his gathering
Two skilled and worldly men,
And sends a message through them to Khosrow:
"You have traveled far to come after me.
There are, O King, one thousand farsangs
From the land of Iran to the city of Gang.
Two vast hosts with troops like ants and grasshoppers
Have crossed mountain and plain, field and marshland.
The ground from Gang to Chin all the way to Iran
Has converted into a massive sea of vengeful blood.
If the pure Creator commanded to condense
In one valley the blood of the deceased,

It would form a sea as immense as the Sea of Gholzom,[43]
Into which every single warrior would drown and disappear.

"Should you seek treasure or army, the land of Tooran,
My throne and crown, I shall surrender it all and withdraw.
But as far as my life, it will be yours
Only at the tip of your sword.
Since I am your mother's father and of the race
Of Fereydoon, the prophet, do not try to take my life.
Although your heart is keen to avenge your father,
Although the respect due me is tainted
By the death of Siaavoosh, who, after all, was guilty,
Still, it filled my heart with grief and worry.

"Furthermore, reflect on the spinning of the powerful stars
As they bring at times security and at times great loss.
Sixty years have passed over my head
Since my first campaign at the lead of noblemen.
You are my son and King of Iran-Zamin.
You have lion claws in war.
Select a battlefield away from divine worshippers,
And we shall fight there, you and I, away from hosts.
If I am defeated by you, your net will pull
The whale out of the deep waters.
But do not attempt to strike at either
Your mother's family or my allies.
Forgive them and do not give way to the fury of vengeance.
If, on the other hand, I kill you,
I swear by divine protection that I shall not
Allow a single one of your relations to suffer
Or to hear the sound of the weapons of war."

Khosrow listens to the message,
Then he turns to Zaal's son, offspring of Saam,
And says, "This duplicitous Turk will never
Distinguish between the rise and fall of fortune!
Through guile, he escaped the hardships meant for him.
Who wants to wait until he climbs back on the throne?
He has wagered his bets on one battle.
Does he seek the tomb of Shiddeh?

◇◇◇◇◇◇◇◇◇◇◇◇◇
43 Sea of Gholzom: Perhaps a reference to the Persian Gulf or Red Sea.

He is Fereydoon's grandson and the son of Pashang,
Yet I shall not feel shame in contending with him."

Rostam replies, "O king,
Do not thrust fuel to set ablaze your chest!
It would be a shame for you to fight him in person,
Even if it were a leopard confronting you.
He asks that you refrain
From attacking his army, his family, and his land.
Yet your army fills the earth from sea to sea,
With troops of a different opinion.
To execute a proper peace treaty with your grandfather,
There must be no deceit in our hearts.
Lead your army to war, and despise and disregard
His vain and misleading words."

29 | The Battle Between the Iranians and the Tooranians

Khosrow is pleased to hear Rostam's words of wisdom.
He says to his messenger, "This evil man provokes a fight.
He once gave Siaavoosh even more solemn assurances,
But his tongue is full of lies and his heart full of injustice.
Tell Afraasiyaab to abstain
From seeking glory through perversity.
His soul is dimly confused,
And his heart drowns in falsehoods.
If he is determined to fight, he can find warriors
Other than me to measure himself against.
Here stand the great Rostam and the brave Giv,
Both seekers of fame and glory.
If king were to fight against another king,
Then what purpose serve armies and war apparatus?
From now on, I shall not have to fight you,
For you are to witness a day of darkness and misfortune."

The messenger departs as swift as wind
And relays the dispatch to King Afraasiyaab, whose heart
Fills with worry, for he did not wish to engage in battle.
With Khosrow launching his army,
He has no choice but to set his Turkish forces in motion.

One advances in haste, the other with uncertainty,
And the earth rouses and shifts like the ocean tide.
A shower of arrows falls on armor,
Mail and helm from a lion's jaws,
Like a fierce hail descending from clouds.
From dawn until dusk, the earth, a glorious ruby,
Is soaked in blood and trampled by horses' hooves.
At nightfall, the troops retreat as their vision dims.

Kay Khosrow arrives at camp in grace and glory.
He says to Tous, "The son of Pashang cannot be pleased
With the battle he led today, and I believe
He will attempt to surprise us with a night attack."

He asks his soldiers to dig a trench across the road,
On the side where the Tooranian cavalry would arrive.
He restricts lighting fires and placing bells on horses.
Khosrow selects the most valiant army riders
And gives their command to Rostam.
Then he makes a second selection of Iranians,
Orders them to dress in battle garb,
And entrusts Commander Tous with their charge,
Telling him to march toward the mountains.

In this way, Rostam is to lead his troops to the battlefield
While Tous takes his to the mountain heights.

The king orders them to advance in great strides,
But both groups are to maintain themselves in the desert,
One on the right and the other on the left, without scouts
And without making a show of either light or torch.
That way Afraasiyaab, if indeed he is planning
A night assault, would then be trapped
And captured between two groups
Like a young falcon caught in a cage,
Before him the ditch, behind him the army corps,
And, behind the ditch, the king with elephants and host.

30 | Afraasiyaab Leads a Night Assault and Is Vanquished

As soon as night invades the sky,
The leader of Turks outfits himself in battle gear.
He calls for his most skilled and experienced warriors,
And speaks to them at length of past deeds.
Then he adds, "This vile man and traitor
Has foolishly marched against his grandfather.
At this hour, without a doubt, his troops are asleep,
Scattered throughout mountain and plain.
Let us cast fear away from our hearts.
Let us surprise the Iranians before sunrise.
If we succeed and vanquish them at night,
You will see me climb back on my throne.
But if our fortune does not regain its glory,
It is that all is nothing but wind and deception,
And courage is nothing but a farce."

The great leaders approve of this plan.
They rise to prepare for a night assault.

Afraasiyaab selects fifty thousand riders,
Skilled men from his army, quick with dagger.
He asks for scouts to precede him,
Aging soldiers restless with the ardor of war.

The head of the scouts goes to Khosrow's camp
In search of a night guard,
But nowhere does he hear the sound of a voice.
He finds everyone at rest, perceives neither patrol
Nor fire, feeling not even the breath of the wind,
As if no one lends a thought to the enemy.

Witness to this, he rushes back to the Tooranian camp
And says, "No one there seems to be in a state of lucidity.
They are all sleeping the sleep of the dead.
Either that or they spent the day engaged in drink.
In all the desert, there is no sign of a single patrol.
I could only discern the bush standing tall."

Afraasiyaab's heart fills with joy.

He commands his army to depart, climbs on his horse,
And, along with his warriors, seizes weapons of war.
The Turks take off in waves, like the ocean tide,
Eager to charge at the enemy.
They set out gradually, without a sound,
Not even the din of clarion or the bellow of a shout.

As they close in on the Iranian pavilions,
The blare of trumpets at once rings out
And the drum of timpani hanging on horses' pommels.
The black banner rises swiftly, high into the sky.

The Tooranian vanguard launches its cavalry
With loud shouts, but some riders plummet into the ditch,
While others shy away from battle and abscond.

On one side advances Rostam, returning from the desert.
The air fills with the dust of horsemen.
On the other side advance Giv, son Goodarz,
And Tous, preceded by clarions and timpani.
Finally, Kay Khosrow emerges with the Kaaviani banner.
The air turns a shade of violet
From the spark of countless brandished swords.

Blows are received; blows are administered.
Men fall, either dead or into the snare of captivity.
Horses are at a loss for breath; men are at a loss for reason.
The motions of two hosts are two oceans of blood.
Waves color the ground in varying shades of crimson.
Armor-bearing men turn into fierce army destroyers,
And the mountains tremble in fear.
Out of one hundred Tooranians, not even ten remain alive.
Those who survive are unable to find a path to flee
In this moment of daunting adversity.

Once the King of Tooran receives news of the battlefield,
He grows so afflicted and distressed
That even the wounded men moan in pity for his grief.
He says, "All the knowledge in the world
Cannot help one escape the rotations of the skies.
It does not matter that the enemy seizes our lives.
Let us continue to strike!
We must either perish or regain Iraj's crown!"

The cry of combatants rises above both camps.
The world fills with the sound of brazen trumpets,
And the two armies, lined up for three farsangs,
Grab their swords and javelins.
The battlefield becomes a sea.
One can no longer distinguish either sun or moon.

The troops advance, army corps by army corps,
Like waves picked up and raised by a tempest.
Valley and desert vanish beneath abundant floods of blood,
And the sun disappears from the celestial dome.
No warrior pities himself or his own body,
And the face of the sky is covered in tar.

At this moment, a great wind stirs
And rises, the likes of which no one has ever seen.
It crashes against the Tooranian troops,
Filling their eyes with dust, plucking off their helmets,
Leaving the King of Turks in a state of astonishment.

The entire desert is bestrewn with blood and brains,
And the sand takes on the color of jujube.

The Turkish horsemen, who on their day of leisure
View the hunt for leopard as an effortless task,
Realize that they cannot resist against the sky
Stirring up the dusty desert sands.

Kay Khosrow, noticing this restless storm
And the courage and good fortune of the Iranians,
Advances to the army core, preceded by timpani
And accompanied by Rostam, Giv, Goodarz, and Tous.

The entire army center stirs.
On one side marches the king; on the other, Rostam.
The air full of dust is like fog, but a fog generating
A shower of blows of mace and sword.

Everywhere lie mountainous heaps of body parts.
On both sides fountains of blood gush copiously.
The air becomes a blue veil, the earth a sea of blood.
So many arrows crisscross the sky
It takes the appearance of an eagle's wing.

PART SIXTEEN

Afraasiyaab looks on in dismay.
He notices the dim glow of Khosrow's shiny banner
And hides his own in the center of his host.
He abandons his troops, sending them to battle
Escorted by their leaders.
He absconds with one thousand brave warriors
From among his allies, men suited for battle.
He leads a tiresome search in the countryside
For a hidden path to the desert to save his own life.

Khosrow pursues his grandfather into the army ranks.
He charges at the center of the Turks, guiding his horse,
Pressing on the stirrups, but is left with no signs of him,
Failing to perceive his black banner.

The Turks beseech the Kianian king to grant them mercy,
And they pledge to cast aside arms and weapons.
Khosrow receives them with kindness,
Assigns them a place away from his troops.
He asks for a golden throne and for the interior
Of a tent to be decked with ornaments from Chin.
He summons wine and musicians,
Calls a great number of army leaders,
And spends the night engaged in a feast the likes of which
Plucks the dead from the breast of the dark earth.

As soon as the sun extends its reach on the celestial vault
And shreds the shadowy cheeks of night,
The King of Kings, ruler of Iran, washes head and body,
And searches for a secluded place to pray
Where no wild beast could hear his voice.

From early morning until the rising moon
Dons its illuminating crown in the indigo firmament,
The king remains in a stance of worship to the Creator,
Expressing gratitude for the fortunate turn of events,
Rubbing at length his forehead in the dust
And flooding his cheeks with two streams of tears.
From there, he returns to his throne and crown,
Walking proudly, heart joyous and perfectly happy.

They remove the fallen Iranians sprawled in the dust,
Whether dead or alive, but enemy corpses are cast aside

With scorn, and the battlefield is freed from them
To make room for graves for their own.

Khosrow abandons the spoils of war to his army
And returns to Gang-Behesht with his troops
Equipped with all the necessary gear for war.

31 | The Tarkhan of Chin Sends an Ambassador to Kay Khosrow

Once news of the outcome of battle
Between Iran and Tooran reaches Chin and Maachin,
The Faghfoor and the Tarkhan, Emperor of Chin,
Writhe in anguish. No other word is uttered
But those relevant to the powerful throne of Iran.

They regret having helped Afraasiyaab
And, in their concern, seek a remedy.
The Faghfoor says, "From now on, Afraasiyaab
Will not see his fortune rise, not even in dream.
Without a doubt we shall be punished
For having offered him troops and treasure.
Our fate is repentance, and our land is sure to be destroyed."

They gather presents made in Chin and Khotan,
Amass a vast treasure.
The Faghfoor summons a kindhearted envoy,
Entrusting him to deliver fitting words to Kay Khosrow.
All that Chin produces in terms of pure and rare jewels,
Gold and pearls, he sends to the king to make peace.
The messengers load up and take the road.

These noblemen from Chin travel without rest
And arrive in Gang in seven days.
The victorious world master receives them graciously,
Assigns them a suitable dwelling, and accepts the gifts,
The rarities, the chests filled with gold, and the slaves.

Khosrow says to the envoy, "Tell the Faghfoor:
          'Do not incur disgrace.
          Afraasiyaab must not come to you,

> Even in the dark night at the hour of sleep.'

The envoy departs, as swift as wind,
And relates the message to the Faghfoor.

The Faghfoor listens to it and sends a nightly message
To Afraasiyaab: "Maintain your distance
From the borders of Chin and Khotan.
You must endure the consequences of your actions.
The evil man who wanders adrift
Always suffers punishments for his misdeeds."

32 | Afraasiyaab Crosses the Sea of Zerreh[44]

Afraasiyaab is now remorseful
And wishes to atone for his past deeds.
He renounces the advantages of power in order
To save himself and takes the road of the desert,
Navigating his way across his kingdom.

Every new day only adds to his fear, fatigue, and grief.
In this manner, he arrives at Mount Asprooz,
Keeping watch day and night, tormented by thoughts
Of the enemy, and living only on the product of his hunt.
He continues his journey until he reaches the Sea of Zerreh,
Hips shattered by fatigue, by the strain of the stirrups,
And by the weight of his armor of steel.

Once he arrives at the edge of the deep lake,
He can distinguish neither middle nor bank.
He demands a boatman to prepare a vessel
That would carry him across the sea.
The weathered mariner replies,
"O noble man from Chin and Khotan,
You cannot cross these deep waters.
I am seventy-eight years old, and I have never seen
A vessel traverse successfully across."

The powerful Afraasiyaab retorts,

◇◇◇◇◇◇◇◇◇◇◇◇◇
44 Sea of Zerreh: Situated in southwestern Afghanistan.

"Blessed is the one who dies in the water!
Since the enemy sword did not succeed in killing me,
I shall not allow myself to be taken captive."

He commands his men to place boats on the water
And to sail toward Gang-Dej.
This is a man who holds his head high,
Whether in joy or in misfortune.

Once he is settled back in Gang-Dej, safe and secure,
He spends time in rest and feast.
He says, "Let us remain here in joy, free from worry,
And let us cease to dwell on the past.
Once my dim star regains its luster,
I shall cross the Sea of Zerreh in my boats again.
I shall avenge myself on my enemy,
And I shall elevate my path and my kingship."

As Kay Khosrow grows aware of Afraasiyaab's
Movements and actions, and how the old man
Is strategizing a different plan, he says to Rostam,
"Afraasiyaab has crossed the water
And has returned to Gang-Dej.
This occurrence confirms what he had said:
That the brilliant sky continues to safeguard him.
He crossed the Sea of Zerreh on vessels.
All our troubles have been in vain.
The only instrument I shall employ to communicate
With my grandfather will be my sharp blade.
I shall not give him the chance
To allow the ancient vengeance to wane.
With the strength given to me by the victorious Yazdan,
I shall strap myself to avenge Siaavoosh.
I shall spread my troops across Chin and Mokran,
Navigate through the Sea of Keemaak,[45]
And once the lands of Chin and Maachin surrender,
I shall no longer need the aid of Mokran-Zamin.
I shall travel across the Sea of Zerreh with troops,
Should the revolving dome of sky dictate in my favor.
No matter how long the delays, one must hope that

◇◇◇◇◇◇◇◇◇◇◇◇◇
45 Sea of Keemaak: Most likely refers to the Caspian Sea.

This bloodthirsty man will ultimately fall into our hands.

"O world warrior, you have borne many a fatigue.
You have left behind your cultivated lands in our behalf.
Take upon yourself one more challenge, a choice that
Would far outweigh conceding the world to the enemy.
We shall celebrate your victory,
Along with Afraasiyaab's defeat,
And aggrandize our name until the day of resurrection."

This discourse irritates the Iranian warriors.
Their mouths fill with vain words;
Their eyebrows furrow as they say,
"This sea is turbulent with a navigation of six months
And troops too numerous to fling into the wind.
Who knows what consequences await us?
Afraasiyaab brings constant misfortune upon the army.
On the ground, we confront endless battles.
On the sea, we face the terrible jaws of the whale."

Each warrior holds various speeches,
And the clamor among them increases.
Rostam says, "O great men of the kingdom,
Skilled leaders and warriors, you are tested in battle.
We must not allow our labor to have been in vain
And drift away in the winds of inaction.
Furthermore, the victorious king
Must pluck the fruit of his good fortune.
We traveled from the land of Iran to Gang
Only to chance upon outstretched hands eager to fight.
Khosrow must take joy in the work he created.
That is the reason he has come, and for that
He will go far and ultimately reach his goal."

Hearing Rostam's words, the wise and powerful men
Rise and shout a unanimous response:
"We stand as the king's loyal subjects and friends.
Authority and command are yours,
Whether on the ground or on the sea."

33 | Kay Khosrow Sends Prisoners and Treasures to Kay Kaavoos

Kay Khosrow kindly receives his warriors,
Assigning each one a seat to suit his rank.
He opens the doors to his grandfather's treasures,
And, without mention of his relation and duties
As grandson, he orders strong camels to be loaded
With gold and brocade inlaid with pearls,
Ten thousand buffalos with war equipment,
And, finally, one thousand camels
Laden with vast silver treasures.

The king asks for all of Afraasiyaab's family and staff,
Whether royalty or slave, to be transported in carriages
From the palace to the royal court.
He summons one hundred noblemen and princes,
Renowned for their courage, Afraasiyaab's friends
And relatives, shedding tears of pity for their master.
Jahn and Garsivaz are to be loaded, feet bound.
One thousand Turkish and Chini prisoners,
Taken hostage by Khosrow, reply by abandoning their cities.

Then he picks out ten thousand Iranian soldiers,
Hands over their command to Giv, and says,
"O blessed man of auspicious path,
Travel with this army corps to Kay Kaavoos,
And tell him what has transpired here."

He calls for a scribe to compose a letter on Chini silk
With black smoke, musk, and rosewater.
The scribe's reed dips in musk and black ink,
And begins in praise of the Justice Giver:
"The One who resolves what is to be preserved
As well as what is to be destroyed,
The One who molds and forms the universe,
Creator of ant, elephant, all things and all beings,
From the insignificant blade of grass
To the flowing waters of the River Nile,
Everything is created at the will of divine supremacy
And the Master of life and nonlife.
Should the celestial dome nurture you with affection,

You will be immune to hardship and suffering.

"May benedictions grace the head of the king,
Creator of the interlaced matrix of harmony and security.
I arrived in Gang-Dej, a city built by Afraasiyaab
To serve him as a refuge for rest and peace.
It is the seat of his throne and crown,
Of his power, treasure, diadem, and army.
For forty days, we led interminable battles
Constricting the world for our foes.
In the end, he eluded us while his relatives have either
Escaped or their hearts have been consumed by grief.
In your worship to Yazdan, pray for me, night and day.
I led the army to Chin and Maachin, and from there
I shall direct it toward the land of Mokran.
Then we shall pass the Sea of Zerreh,
If the pure Creator wishes to act in our favor."

Giv takes leave of the King of Kings
With instructions to recount to Kay Kaavoos,
Point by point, the events of the struggle.
He marches as swift as wind with a vast host
And numerous valiant warriors toward the royal court.

At the approach of the auspicious hero,
Kaavoos sends an escort to stand at the ready
In the city, like a field of lions.

The brave Giv nears the king, his gaze falls
On the monarch, and he bends low
To kiss the ground at the foot of the throne.

Kaavoos observes him, rises smiling,
And brushes his hand against his cheeks.
He asks after the king and the army,
After the rotations of the sun and shining moon.

The valiant Giv recounts all that he knows
Of the fate of the warriors and the powerful Khosrow.
The aging king regains his youth with this account.
Then Kaavoos hands over Khosrow's letter
To his scribe to read, to the surprise of the congregation.

Kaavoos Shah descends from the throne,
Removes the Kianian crown from his head,
Rolls in the dark earth, and engages in prayer.
From there, he returns to his palace,
Orders a royal feast in the joy of his heart.
Kaavoos calls for wine and musicians.
He convenes army leaders from Iran
And spends the night engaged in conversation.

The dark night dissipates, and his guests
Joyfully retire to their residences,
Guided by the light of flaming torches.

As the sun climbs to the heights of the sky
To reveal its brilliant beams of rays,
As night swings its chargers' gathered reins,
The sound of drums is heard at the palace gates,
And the noblemen assemble at court.

The world ruler asks for Giv to sit on his illustrious throne.
Giv displays Khosrow's presents
And summons the noble and brave captive leaders,
As well as the innocent veiled women kept in tyranny
By Afraasiyaab within his palace walls.
Jahn and Garsivaz are also brought forth,
Feet bound, the former of sinister intentions,
The latter responsible for the fall of Siaavoosh.

At the sight of the wicked Garsivaz,
Kaavoos curses this man deserving of maledictions.
He asks for Jahn in iron chains to approach his throne.
He assigns separate instructions for the fate
Of each prisoner and member of Tooran's elite.
One is handed over to the Iranians as a watch guard,
Another to be cast to chains of steel.
One is hopeful; the other is aggrieved.
Ultimately they all leave the king's audience hall.

Then Kaavoos's lashes moisten with tears as he peers
Into the faces of the daughters of Afraasiyaab.
He grants them shelter in his female chambers
And assigns them attendants and servants.

Next, he distributes all sorts of treasures to the Iranians:
Dinars, gold, and untouched pearls.
Everyone acclaims and praises the king of the earth.
He hands over the slaves to his noblemen
And sends no one to his palace, no matter how qualified.
Then he determines a dwelling for Jahn
And selects his servants and his guard.
Garsivaz is flung into an underground passage
Beneath the castle, a gloomy, dismal, tomblike place.

Such is the way of the everchanging providence.
Fortunate is the man who is king
If he is generous of hand and pure of heart.
He knows that this world is transitory
And will avoid interaction with foolish men.
But if his wisdom is weak and his desire impure,
Physicians will consider him a demented person.

Once the king has determined everyone's fate,
He dismisses the visitors from his hall.
A scribe prepares paper, sharpens
The point of his reed as fine as a diamond,
And letters are written to every province,
To every renowned man and every prince,
To announce that the lands of Turks and Chin
Have conceded to the Iranian king and that
The leopard and the lamb unite at the drinking trough.

For two weeks, Kaavoos distributes
Dinars, gold, and silver to the poor,
Whether they are his subjects or his people.
The crowd pressing close to receive his gifts is so vast
One could no longer distinguish the palace floors.

On the third week, he sits on the throne of power
In peace and in all his grace and majesty.
The music of flute and song resounds.
Hearts are cheered with cups of wine.
During seven days, the crimson liquid
Pours abundantly into King Kaavoos's goblet.

At the start of the month, he prepares presents for Giv,
Among which shine gold and turquoise,

Golden trays and cups inlaid with turquoise,
Golden belts and golden bridles,
Slaves decked in golden torques, earrings, and bracelets,
Crowns inlaid with precious gems, cloaks and thrones,
Carpets of glorious colors, and many other fineries.

Then he summons Giv, invites him to take a golden seat
As these presents are placed at his feet.
Giv bows in reverence at the foot of the kingly throne.

34 | Kaavoos's Reply to Kay Khosrow's Letter

A scribe enters, with paper, musk, and amber.
He composes the king's reply:
"The Creator has bestowed joy upon us.
Fortune showers us with honors, for our son is triumphant,
Worthy of power, crown, and throne. The wicked man
Who confined the world to a state of anguish,
Who looted vastly and slaughtered innocent men,
Has fled before you and gone astray.
No one utters his name except in secret.
His entire life was spent shedding blood,
Committing base and evil acts in his wrath,
Stirring up disputes. He struck King Nozar at the neck,
Destroying our crowned prince, our ancestors' royal heir.
He is his brother's assassin and a king's murderer.
He is a wicked man whose intentions are evil,
With a dishonored name and a pernicious intellect.

"Prohibit him from entering Mokran and Tooran-Zamin,
The entire region to the edge of the Sea of Chin.
Let us hope that the universe will soon be free of him,
Cleansed from the defilement of evil ones,
So that the earth may heal from its ailments,
From the words and acts of foolish men.
Rejoice in the will of the Just Yazdan.
Create a new era, a new order of happiness.
I hope that I shall see you again in joy after you have
Successfully filled the hearts of our rivals with grief.

"I shall remain in the presence of the Creator,

From Whom originate hope and fear,
Until you return victorious and joyous.
May your head remain young, your heart full of justice!
May the Divine Creator be your guide!
May the throne never be deprived of your being!"

He affixes the royal seal on the letter,
Hands it to Giv, who immediately takes the road,
Traveling without a moment's pause,
Making his way to Gang and to Kay Khosrow.
At the court, he offers homage to the king,
Turns over the letter, and relays Kay Kaavoos's message.

Kay Khosrow is delighted with his grandfather's words.
He summons wine and singers, and spends
Three days in feast, celebrating his victories.
On the fourth day, once the sun reveals its illumining rays
To the world, the king distributes helm and armor
To his troops in the custom of just rulers.

He gives Gostaham, son of Nozar,
The command of a large, glorious, and brave army.
The king sets off from Chin toward the city of Gang,
Subjecting people everywhere to the sword.

Not a day goes by without battle,
Not even the dark night.
During the day patrols are dispatched.
During the night sentinels are placed.

In this way, Khosrow continues his march,
Heart consumed with grief and full of blood,
Until he arrives at the city founded by his father.
He wanders in Siaavoosh's gardens
And finds the urn containing his overflowing blood.
He secretly addresses the Supreme Judge:
"If the Creator, the One who distributes justice,
Wishes to be my Guide, I shall shed here,
And in a similar manner, Afraasiyaab's blood
And make it pour in overflowing torrents."

Khosrow returns to his throne,
Continuing his discourse with the Creator.

35 | Kay Khosrow Sends a Message
to the Faghfoor of Chin and the King of Mokran

Kay Khosrow singles out his team of envoys,
Skilled in the art of speaking and listening,
And sends them to the Chini Tarkhan,
The Faghfoor, and the King of Mokran.

He bids them to say, "If you wish to turn your hearts
In the direction of justice and to obey me,
If you repent for your evil actions,
Send provisions ahead of the army
That you will infallibly force to set upon the road.
But whoever disobeys me,
Even if he abstains from attacking,
Whoever does not receive me with great pomp,
May he prepare to face my sword,
For I shall cut off his head with my sharp blade,
And destroy his palace and his land."
A messenger travels to the provinces ruled by a prince.

The Faghfoor of Chin and the noblemen grow fearful.
They address the messengers warmly,
Pronounce sweet words in sweet voices, saying,
"We are the king's subjects.
We rule only by his command.
We shall inspect the sites where warriors pass,
And if there are difficult paths,
We shall smooth them out before the border.
We shall carry along provisions and gifts."

The men of wisdom say, "If the king wishes
To travel through our land without causing harm,
We shall vastly donate to the poor.
We shall prepare, for his majesty, provisions and gifts."

The messenger receives many presents
And returns happily to the royal court.

But the renowned envoy who travels to Mokran
Finds its ruler in a different sort of disposition.
He appears before the throne, hands over the letter,

And communicates the message he memorized.

The ruler has a sudden outburst that sends tremors
Of fear through the hearts of those assembled.
In his foolishness, he curses the emissary and cries out:
"Return to the King of Iran and tell him
Not to attempt to exert his authority over me.
The era gives in to my fortune.
The world is brilliant because of my throne and crown.
The rising sun casts its first rays tenderly over my land.
I hold wisdom and a full treasure,
An army of brave warriors and a valiant hand.
If you wish passage for yourself, that is good and well,
For every creature is a ruler on the earth.
I shall allow you entry provided you are without a host.
But if you march into this land with troops, know
That you have no right to trespass into my kingdom.
I shall forbid you to traverse it, cross its borders,
Or trample upon any part of my nation.
You will not enjoy victory,
No matter how auspicious your star of good fortune."

As soon as Kay Khosrow receives the reply,
He sets forth, proudly entering
The land of Khotan with his glorious army.

The Faghfoor and the Tarkhan of Chin
Approach the king to offer greetings and praise.
They march toward him for three days, traveling
Beyond the border of Chin with their noble leaders.
The road is as clear as a hand, and the valleys and deserts
Come into view, decked like royal dwellings.
Across the pathways are gifts of clothing and food,
Banquets are prepared, and carpets are spread.

In the town, the army is received with feasts.
Chini brocade hangs on walls,
And musk and amber are scattered about.

The Faghfoor, at ease with the king, precedes him,
And together they take the direction of the palace.
There, the ruler says to Kay Khosrow,
"Though we may be unworthy of him,

We are his majesty's subjects.
The world is happy by the effect of your fortune.
The hearts of your friends rejoice because of you.
If our palace is not worthy of the king,
At least it is preferable to being on the road."

The renowned king enters the palace
And sits in the magnificent audience hall.
The Faghfoor of Chin asks for one hundred
Thousand Chini dinars as a welcome gift.
He remains standing before Kay Khosrow
With governors of the provinces and wise counselors.

Khosrow resides in Chin for three months
In the company of the leaders of the Iranian host.
Every morning, the Faghfoor pays him tribute
And showers him with new gifts.
At the start of the fourth month,
The King of Iran departs from the land of Chin
In the direction of Mokran,
Leaving Rostam stationed behind in Chin.

36 | The Battle Between Kay Khosrow and the King of Mokran

Kay Khosrow marches forth to the land of Mokran.
He singles out one of his skilled and worldly warriors
To dispatch to the King of Mokran and to say to him,
"Wisdom must be the ally of a monarch!
Look and see where I come from.
I am not inebriated. I do not fall asleep on my projects.
My crown and good fortune brighten the world.
The heads of noblemen are at the foot of my throne.
Prepare food, supplies, and the road for my troops,
And deck a royal residence for my arrival.
When an army lacks provisions, you know what ensues,
For no one wishes to surrender to distress.
Unless each has his own portion, unless I am present,
Hands will reach out to steal the other's share.
If my men fail to find sustenance,
They will bring the war upon you, constrict your space.

If you choose to disregard my words,
Your feet will step in the blood of many men.
If you attack my lion warriors,
Against whom you harbor no thought of vengeance,
You will destroy the land of Mokran."

The envoy departs to carry out the command.
But advice and justice lack access to the soul
Of the King Mokran, whose foolish head boils with rage
And whose brains are permeated with evil thoughts.
He gathers his scattered troops
And prepares to engage in battle in the desert.
He replies to the envoy: "Return to my wicked enemy,
And tell him that the rotations of the uncertain skies
Have given him delusory joy and power.
Tell him that he will feel our strength when he advances.
He will distinguish between the brave and the weak."

As soon as the envoy departs,
The entire land of Mokran fills with clamor.
The army occupies the territory and the desert
From one mountain chain to another,
And from one border to another.

The king asks for two hundred war elephants.
It is as if there is no space left on earth.
The whinny of horses and the cry of warriors
Are such that the moon drifts astray in the sky.

A patrol informs Kay Khosrow that the land of Mokran
Is obscured by the dust of troops and
That the region is covered in banners and elephants,
Distinguishable for a distance of two miles.
The king orders troops to form ranks,
To seize mace and sword.

A rider from Mokran advances onto the field
And spends the night appraising the Iranian army.
Tokhaar, the guardian of the Iranian army,
Never fearful of combat, falls upon him like a wild lion,
Attacking an elephant full of pride.
He strikes him with his blade, cutting him in half,
And the heart of the King of Mokran fills with terror.

The two hosts form two lines facing each other.
The sky disappears beneath the dust.
They advance toward each other like mountains
And assail one another in all their mass.

The leader Tous proceeds to the center,
And the world fills with the sound of timpani.
Tous is heralded by the Kaaviani banner
And followed by warriors of golden boots.
The air fills with shots and the ground with elephants.
The world resembles the River Nile in turbulence.

Tous strikes the King of Mokran in the army core,
And the soul of the king flies away with the wound.

A warrior says to Khosrow, "O King, let us cut off his head!"

But the king replies, "Let us hold back acts of cruelty.
One should never sever the head of a king or else
He will be deemed inferior to the lineage of Ahriman.
One must not cause further harm to this man,
Who has been struck thus through his armor.
Prepare a coffin for him, pour musk and rosewater
Over him, bury him in a peaceful resting place.
His body must not remain bare.
Shield it as a wound is shielded by a coat of mail.
Cover his face with Chini brocade,
For he died the death of a valiant man."

Ten thousand army men are killed,
Brave riders and sword-wielding warriors.
One thousand one hundred and forty fall captive.
The heads of the surviving men fill with terror.

Elephants and treasures, tents and thrones are looted.
The Iranian warriors, full of ardor for battle,
Devastate, destroy, and plunder the land.
They gain tremendous wealth, crowns, and thrones.

In towns and countryside, the wail of women swells.
The entire land of Mokran trembles with fear.
The forts and cities are set on fire.
It is as if the sky is about to tumble to the ground.

Many men are wounded, bodies punctured by arrows.
Many women and small children are captured.
In the end, the anger of the king for these people
Is appeased, and he commands his army to retreat.

Khosrow orders Ashkesh of quick wit
To end pillage, battle, and ardor.
No one is allowed to further commit violent acts.
The innocent are to be spared from needless suffering.

The land's righteous noblemen come to the king,
Seeking forgiveness and saying,
"We are innocent and reduced to despair.
We are continuously oppressed by tyrants.
If his majesty honors innocence,
He is worthy of exercising mercy."

The king makes a proclamation to the army,
Declared loudly over the entrance of the royal pavilion:
"O warrior heroes, men of sound counsel,
If from now on one hears a single cry ushered
By acts of injustice, I shall cut in two the culpable,
For they do not tremble before the Justice Giver."

The world king remains in Mokran for one year.
He brings ship builders forward from every corner.
Once spring arrives and the earth turns green,
The mountains are covered in anemones and tulips,
The pastures with roaming horses,
And the hunting preserves dress in flowers
And blossoming fruit trees.
The king requests for Ashkesh to remain stationed
With a host in Mokran, to maintain his authority
And to act only out of righteousness and duty.

As for Kay Khosrow, he marches out of the city,
Takes the road to the desert,
Determined to endure further hardships.

Yazdan's will removes the dust from the desert.
The air fills with rain, the earth with greenery.
The entire world blossoms with tulips and fenugreek.

Men bring provisions for the army
To load on wagons lugged by buffalos.
The green fields offer plenty of space to camp.
The sky is replete with clouds,
And the earth is soaked with rain.

37 | Kay Khosrow Crosses the Sea of Zerreh

Once Kay Khosrow reaches the Sea of Zerreh,
The warriors unfasten the knots of their belts.
The king gathers seamen from Chin and Mokran,
Making every attempt to sail across the sea.
He asks for one year's supply of provisions,
And preparations are made for the passage.

The world master, king of auspicious star,
Seeker of the divine path, his face resplendent with tears,
Drifts away from the water's edge.
He prays humbly in worship to the World Creator,
Asking for a safe passage to the opposite bank
With his leaders and troops, court and war apparatus.
He whispers, "O World Creator, you have
Knowledge of the revealed and the mysterious.
You are Guardian of land and sea.
You rule over the firmament and the Pleiades.
Protect my life, protect my army,
My throne, crown, and treasure."

The turbulent waters make everyone seasick.
For six months, the vessels navigate the sea
As each person seeks a place of comfort.

In the seventh month, after half the year has elapsed,
The north wind thrusts the king to the other shore.
The sails make a turnabout, the ships traverse,
The sterns cannot be governed,
And they get off the desired path.
They sweep in the direction of a place called the lion's jaw.
Still, Yazdan acts in a way that the sky's winds
Do not oppose the king's lucky star.

The army is in awe of what they see in the water,
And each warrior points out to Kay Khosrow.
They see lions and bulls, and bulls contending with lions.
They see men with noose-like hair and sheep-like woolskin.
They see one with the form of a fish and the head of a leopard.
They see one with the head of a deer on the bulk of a whale.
They see men with buffalo heads,
Two hands in the rear and two feet in front.
They see men with boar heads and the figures of lambs.

The sea is filled with these peculiar creatures.
Each person points them out to the others,
Invoking the divine and Just Creator of the sky,
By whose grace the air calms and the storm dissipates.

They are able to cross the sea in seven months
Without another tempest holding them hostage.
Once Kay Khosrow disembarks on firm ground,
Once he sees the fields and inhabitable lands,
He presents himself to the World Creator
And lowers his face to the ground.

He asks for the vessels to be drawn out of the water.
He feels the urge to rush and hasten toward his goal.
Before him is a vast field with desert and plain,
But he passes the shifting sands easily, his body free.
He finds cities reminiscent of Chin,
But the spoken language resembles that of Mokran.
He rests in these cities and calls for provisions for his troops.

Entrusting this land to Giv, he says,
"Fortune has always acted in your favor.
Do not behave harshly, not even with the culpable,
For this land and all things hold no value in my eyes.
I no longer feel any attachment to anyone.
I only wish to maintain myself in a state of prayer."

Kay Khosrow selects a warrior with knowledge of languages.
He sends through him a message to various rulers:
"Whoever wishes to rest and fulfill their desires
Must joyously and trustingly appear at my court,
Arms stretched out in friendship and with good intentions.
On the other hand, whoever disobeys my command

Will suffer punishment for his unsolicited disposition."

The envoy relays the king's missive.
Not a single one of the border guards and rulers
Challenges the order, and they arrive at the court bearing gifts.
Khosrow greets them with benevolence,
Raising their heads to the sun.

Next, the king asks for news of Gang-Dej,
Afraasiyaab, and the throne of power.
Among the group of princes, one of them steps forward
To speak: "You will come across neither river nor mountain.
Counting both safe and treacherous roads, there is
No more than one hundred farsangs from here to Gang.
Due to the wicked Tooranian king, very few men remain.
He took the direction of Gang with his companions,
After having crossed the Sea of Zerreh."

The king delights in these words.
His future undertakings appear less laborious.

They prepare gifts and presents for the princes,
Then they ask for the horses of these skilled men.
The king orders them to return, and he, in turn,
Takes the road to Gang-Dej with his army.

38 | Kay Khosrow Arrives in Gang-Dej

Khosrow brings order to his troops
And distributes the balance.
He remembers the divine presence, Source of all things.
He says to his men, "Whoever seeks evil deeds will,
Inevitably, have cause to recoil and face divine retribution.
You must not enter the town of Gang en masse.
You must not attempt to harm anyone, not even an ant."

Once the world ruler's sight falls on Gang-Dej,
His cheeks disappear beneath the tears.
He dismounts and offers homage to the Creator.
His head in the dust, he says, "O Supreme, Holy Judge,
I am your slave; my heart festers with fear and worry.

You have bestowed upon me glory and royal grandeur,
A brave army, an auspicious star, fame, and power,
So that one day I may set my sights on the walls
Of the city my father erected as high as the sun.
Siaavoosh, who, by the power given to him by Yazdan,
Raised such a structure from a ditch,
Met a dismal fate when the tyrant extended his hand
And tore apart troubled hearts by his murder."

The army sheds abundant tears over these walls,
With painful thoughts of the innocent Siaavoosh,
Viciously slain, his murder sowing
The fertile seed of vengeance across the world.

Afraasiyaab receives the news that the Iranian king
Has crossed the sea and reached the city.
Without sharing this secret with anyone,
He departs in the middle of the dark night.
He abandons his worldly leaders
And absconds alone, heart throbbing with fear.

Kay Khosrow enters Gang,
Head full of sadness, heart rushing with blood.
He sees the enchanting gardens, the delight of many,
With their fruit trees planted by the noble Siaavoosh,
Their lawns akin to the lights of paradise.
Everywhere are freshwater springs and groves of roses.
The earth is covered with fenugreek,
And the lark finds shelter in the limbs of verdant trees.

Each person exclaims, "Here is a beautiful dwelling.
We could live here in joy for the rest of our days."

Then the prudent Kay Khosrow orders the Iranians
To assess the whereabouts of the King of Tooran.
They leave in a flurry to search for him in desert, gardens,
And palaces, taking guides with them everywhere.
In their fervent search, they discover many noble relatives
And are forced to kill many innocent ones.
But they find no signs of the unjust and cruel ruler.

The king remains in Gang-Dej for one year,
Engaged in banquet and feast.

The world is like an enchanting paradise,
Full of rose bushes, orchards, parks, and gardens.
Unable to resign himself to part ways with Gang,
He sits there, victorious and happy.

His army leaders gather at his side to say,
"If his highness's heart is not moved,
It is because it no longer cares for the throne of Iran.
Your grandfather Afraasiyaab
Must have crossed the waters by now.
Furthermore, the aging King Kaavoos,
Though he sits on the throne, holds neither power
Nor majesty, neither treasure nor army.
Your empire's chiefs and elite warriors are with you.
If Afraasiyaab, full of hatred, is on his way to Iran,
Who is there to protect our land?
If he were to capture the throne and crown,
All our work would have been in vain."

The king replies, "Your advice is sound and wise."
He gathers all the brave heroes of the city,
Speaks at length to them of the great ills he suffered.
He selects the noblest, most respected, most able man,
And dresses him in a robe of honor.

In this way, he singles out in Gang-Dej a friend as governor
And offers gifts of horses brought from the fields.
He says to him, "Stay here in joy.
Remain watchful of the enemy."

Khosrow distributes all that he holds precious:
Horses and amassed treasures.
The entire city is rendered wealthy
With his gifts of torques, thrones, and diadems.

39 | Kay Khosrow Travels From Gang-Dej to Siaavoosh-Guerd

At the moment when the rooster awakens
And the sound of timpani is heard at the palace gate,
An army hastens to depart on the desert road.

PART SIXTEEN

Noblemen rush over from various districts.
Provisions are handed out to the king and his host.
The valleys and plains resemble a marketplace
On the roads traveled by the troops.

No one wishes to raise a hand to the Iranians,
Neither in the mountains nor in the valleys,
Whether they are in motion or at rest.

The noblemen stand on the road with presents
And offerings of silver, waiting for Kay Khosrow.
They bow low to venerate his grace and glory.
In turn, the king distributes items to them
From his treasury, which they dismiss,
Preferring to accompany him to war.

Giv advances to meet the king with his army
And the powerful leaders of the land.
Once he spots the majestic, crown-bearing head,
He dismounts to properly express his devotion.

The world master receives everyone graciously
And prepares a dwelling full of Kianian splendor for them.

Khosrow notices the ships are ready.
He remains two weeks on the water's edge,
Engaged in conversation with Giv:
"Anyone who has not visited Gang and has not experienced
Its wonders must make the trip and see for himself."

Then he asks for the preparation of two ships.
He commands those with knowledge of navigation
And those fearless of the deep sea
To deploy the sails and advance on the water.
Behind them drift one thousand more ships.

The winds blow with such force that the crossing,
For which one must dedicate at least one year,
Is completed in seven months by king and army,
Without being troubled by an adverse wind.

The king commands for the ships to drop anchor
And the troops to disembark.

He observes the field before him, advances,
And rubs his face against the ground's dust,
Addressing the Creator, pure and perfect.

He draws coins and presents from his treasury,
Distributes provisions and clothing to the sailors,
To those responsible for the rudder
And anyone who labored during the voyage.
Then he turns his back on the shores and makes headway
Toward the plain as men watch him admiringly.

Ashkesh receives news of the king and pushes ahead
With a well-equipped army to greet him.
He climbs off his horse, kisses the ground,
And pays proper tribute to Kay Khosrow.

The land of Mokran is decorated.
Singers and musicians are summoned.
Everywhere, on the roads and in the most distant corners,
Rings the sound of instruments.
It is a beautiful dance of the warp and woof
Of the strings converging with the air.

Brocade hangs on the walls, coins and sugar
Are scattered beneath the hooves of the king's charger.

Princes of the land of Mokran, illustrious men and warriors,
Arrive with presents and offerings for the king.
Ashkesh brings the most precious things the land produces.

Approving of the way Ashkesh has governed this land,
The king names him ruler of Mokran-Zamin,
Showering him with presents and saluting him as monarch.

Kay Khosrow and his Iranian army leaders
Then travel from Mokran to the border of Chin.
Rostam, son of Zaal, arrives with his host to greet him.
Everyone cheers in joy at the sight of the world ruler.

The moment his eyes fall on Khosrow's parasol,
The hero warrior dismounts to pay proper tribute.
The king, full of pride, embraces him
And recounts to him the marvels of the sea

PART SIXTEEN

And how Afraasiyaab, the sorcerer, vanished.

Khosrow remains Rostam's guest in Chin.
After one week, he departs, entrusting the land of Chin
To the Faghfoor, who highly praises the king.
The king banishes trouble from the Faghfoor's heart
With gifts and sound advice.

Kay Khosrow takes the direction of Siaavoosh-Guerd
On the twenty-fifth day of the month of Esfand.[46]
He enters his father's city.
Heartbroken and cheeks flooding with tears,
He approaches the sight of the vicious beheading
Executed by the evil Garsivaz and the cursed Garooy.
He grabs a fistful of the dirt to sprinkle over his head.
He claws at his cheeks and at his chest.
Rostam follows suit while cursing the wicked Garooy.

Kay Khosrow says, "O King Siaavoosh,
You left me as a memory of you in this world.
I shall allow nothing to remain in my search for vengeance.
My suffering will endure as long as this world endures.
I have destroyed Afraasiyaab's throne,
And from now on I shall enjoy neither rest nor sleep
As long as I nurse the hope of catching him myself
And rendering the world dark and constricted to him."

Then the king goes to his father's treasury,
Its whereabouts revealed to him by his mother.
He opens its door to distribute the contents to his troops.
For two weeks, he remains in his father's city.
He gives Rostam two hundred purses of dinars
And offers Giv many presents and gifts.

At the news of the king's visit to his father's town,
Gostaham, son of Nozar, departs with a vast host.
Once he spots the crowned head, he climbs down
His charger and travels the rest of the way on foot.

The entire army unites to pay tribute to the just king,
Who commands Gostaham to mount his horse.

◇◇◇◇◇◇◇◇◇◇◇◇◇
46 Esfand: Twelfth month of the year.

They depart together, happy and holding hands.

They go to Gang-Behesht, where the king honors his troops,
For his loyalty to them exceeds the trust one has
For a fruit tree to bear new fruit every season.

The king and his able riders engage in banquet and hunt.
Khosrow acts with benevolence toward the noble Turks.
Day and night he relentlessly inquires after Afraasiyaab,
But not one of them is able to lead him to his whereabouts.
Not one of them is even willing to utter his name.

One night, the world master washes his head and body,
And walks a far distance with the book of *Zand Avesta*.
He stands all night before the Creator sobbing,
Forehead to the ground: "Your feeble servant
Remains in a constant state of suffering.
He cannot find any indication of Afraasiyaab,
Neither on mountain nor on plain,
Neither in desert nor in the sea.
O Justice Giver, this man does not walk in your light.
He respects no one in the entire world.
You know that he keeps distant from the righteous path
And sheds abundant innocent blood.
Could Yazdan, the just, the inimitable,
Guide me in my search for this evil man?
While I am an unworthy slave,
At the very least, I worship the divine Creator.
Afraasiyaab's name has vanished from the world.
No one hears his voice; his location is a mystery to me.
But for you it is not a secret. For you nothing is hidden.
If you are satisfied with him, O Giver of justice,
Then turn my head away from the desire to fight him.
Extinguish from my heart the blaze of vengeance,
And may your will be mine."

The proud young prince, on whom fortune shines,
Leaves the site of prayer and ascends the throne.
He remains one year in Gang-Behesht,
Resting from his emotions and the labors of war.

40 | Kay Khosrow Returns to Iran-Zamin

After his long stay in Gang,
Khosrow yearns to see Kaavoos again.
He entrusts the command of the territory,
From Ghabchaagh[47] to the Sea of Chin,
To Gostaham, son of Nozar.
Giving him charge of a vast host, he says,
"Be happy and always stand vigilant.
Extend your reach to Chin and Mokran-Zamin.
Send letter carriers to every prince and province.
Seek news of Afraasiyaab's whereabouts
So that we may finally free the surface
Of the earth from his presence."

He takes with him goods: Dinars and valuable things;
Musk, camphor, golden bridles, bracelets,
Thrones, horses, and slaves; Chinese carpets and silks,
And all sorts of precious objects from Mokran-Zamin.
The king sends ahead of him
Forty thousand oxen pulling loaded wagons.
Everyone speaks of the fact that the world
Has never seen such considerable wealth.

Khosrow's troops are so numerous that for ten days
And nights they cover the mountain and plain.
The moment the vanguard reaches one station,
The rearguard loads the beasts of burden
At the previous station and readies to depart.

In this way he reaches Chaadj
And hangs his crown over the ivory throne.
For more than one week, he remains in Sughd,
Where Taliman and Khuzan, two allies, come to his side.
From there he rides to the city of Bukhara,
Where the ground disappears beneath the army's dust.
In Bukhara, he gives in to feast and rest for one week.
At the start of the second week, he enters the fire temple
Dressed in new garb, shouting and lamenting for lost time,
His face rubbed with dust, for at this site is the temple

◇◇◇◇◇◇◇◇◇◇◇◇◇◇
47 Ghabchaagh: Must be in Tooran-Zamin.

Founded and built by Toor, son of Fereydoon.

Praying, he rubs dust over his face,
Tosses gold and silver over the heads of wise men,
And flings precious gems into the fire.
He resigns to leaving the land
And departs happy to have satisfied his heart's desires.

He crosses the Jayhoon on the side of Balkh,
After having suffered the struggles and bitterness of life.
He remains one week in Balkh, then takes the road again.
Every city he passes is decorated with color and scent.
He is greeted by noblemen and invited to banquet and feast.

Kay Khosrow arrives in Taleghan by the River Marv.[48]
He finds the entire city decked out.
Musicians and singers are summoned.
People sprinkle saffron, gold, and musk over him.

From there he rides in the direction of Nishabur,
With elephants, treasury, and army.
He distributes dinars and gold to the poor of the city
And thus depletes fifty-five bags of coins.

He travels to Damghan,[49] further handing out dinars.
At the end of one week, he takes the road to Rai,
Encountering on his way music, song, and wine.

For two weeks, he dwells in this city,
Occupied with good deeds.
At the start of the third week, he departs for Baghdad
After having sent from Rey a few messengers
On camelback to Kaavoos, who resides in the land of Pars.

◇◇◇◇◇◇◇◇◇◇◇◇◇
48 River Marv: May be a reference to the Murghab River, which is not too far from
the city of Marv.
49 Damghan: A city and province in northern Iran.

41 | Kay Khosrow Returns to His Grandfather

Word of his grandson's return renews the heart
Of the aging king, which feels as if it is expanding.
He asks for golden seats in the throne room
And lines his palace walls with Chini ornaments.

In the countryside and on the roads, feasts are prepared.
Houses, streets, and markets are dressed up
With streams of colorful banners.

The powerful men and city governors
Travel to greet Khosrow on the road.
Everywhere, triumphal arches are erected,
And the world resembles golden brocade.
Everywhere, people blend musk with fine stones
Sprinkled from the arches over the heads of noblemen.

Kay Kaavoos exits the city with his blessed warriors.
The young king discerns his grandfather in the distance.
He launches his blazing horse, dismounts, and they embrace.
Kaavoos kisses him many times on the head and cheeks.
Both shed copious tears for having lived so long apart.

Kay Kaavoos sings the praises of the blessed prince,
Whose path is fortunate and prosperous.
He says, "May the world, the throne of power,
And the royal dwelling never be deprived of your being!
Never has the sun witnessed a prince of your stature,
With armor, horse, and helm the likes of yours.
The sky and the earth have never seen more refined royalty,
Not since the era when power was transmitted
From King Jamsheed to King Fereydoon.
No prince has suffered such hardships.
None has seen the known and the unknown
On the earth as you have.
May you bring happiness to the shining world!
May the hearts and souls of your enemies perish!
May Siaavoosh return, if only for one day!
Your glory would complete his wishes!"

The king replies, "Everything is a result of your good fortune.

A branch of your tree is bearing an abundance of fruit.
Anyone with you as grandfather has the ability
To grow herbage on the surface of stone."

The grandfather kisses Khosrow and says,
"May you never again leave my sight, by day or night!"
He takes a handful of emeralds, rubies, and gold,
And sprinkles the gems over the youth's head,
So much that the heaps rise high enough
To conceal the legs of the bejeweled throne.

Kaavoos opens his audience hall,
Where banquets are spread in the golden hall,
In the company of wealthy, blessed noblemen.

The young king recounts the marvels
Of his aquatic travels, and the unheard,
Unseen stories his warriors related.
He speaks of the sea and of Gang-Dej.
The noblemen sigh longingly for the city,
For its verdant valleys and plains,
Its fields and gardens as bright as shining lamps.

Kay Kaavoos remains in awe of his grandson
And begins to comprehend the scope of his deeds.
He says to him, "The youthful words of a youthful king
Render even the new day and new moon young again.
No one has seen in the world a ruler like you.
No ear has ever heard such magnificent tales.
Now let us celebrate this lucky star.
Let us, cup in hand, honor Kay Khosrow."
He asks for the banquet hall to be decorated,
Wine be brought by cupbearers of ruby lips.

For one week, wine flows freely in Kaavoos's palace.
On the eighth day, the king opens his treasury
And rewards his lead warriors,
According to rank, for their efforts.
They depart in the direction of their respective provinces,
Each holding his head high and escorted by a glorious host.

Then the king tends to the troops
And distributes the balance of one year.

Grandfather and king, two world seekers, sit in counsel.
Kay Khosrow says to Kay Kaavoos,
"Whom shall we consult for direction, if not the Creator?
With wounded hearts, my troops and I
Have traveled through desert, mountain, and sea.
The latter requires an entire year to cross.
But nowhere did I find a sign of Afraasiyaab.
If he is able, for one moment, to return to Gang,
An army will immediately surround him on every side.
We shall have before us the same hard work,
Even if Yazdan were to grant us a triumphant victory."

Kay Kaavoos replies to his grandson
With the sage advice of a wise old man,
"Let us both ride together on separate mounts
To the temple of Aazargoshasp.
We shall wash our heads and bodies, hands and feet,
As is the custom for divine worshippers.
We shall secretly offer homage to the World Creator.
We shall stand before the fire and whisper our prayers
In the hopes that the pure Yazdan will be our Guide,
In the hopes that the One who shows us
The path of justice will point out
The road leading to Afraasiyaab's hideaway."

They agree to this plan and execute it carefully.
In haste, they ride swiftly to the temple.
They enter, dressed in white robes,
Hearts aquiver yet hopeful.
As they catch sight of the fire, they shed tears.
They approach and scatter precious stones over the flames.

The two kings lament and mourn,
In a state of pain and humility as borne by supplicants.
They address prayers to the Creator of Sun and Moon
Toss precious stones over the wise men.
Khosrow, cheeks flooding with his lashes' tears,
Covers the *Zand Avesta* with golden coins.

They maintain their stance before Yazdan for one week.
But do not think that they worship fire,
For fire, in this temple, is only the object

Toward which one turns at the moment of prayer.
The eyes of the worshippers are full of tears.
No matter how deep your thoughts,
You will always need the pure Yazdan.

The king and his noblemen pass one month
In the temple of Aazargoshasp.

42 | Afraasiyaab Is Captured by Hoom, Descendant of Fereydoon

During this time, Afraasiyaab roams the land
In search of food and rest.
His mind is in turmoil with worry, his body weary,
Always in a state of fear for looming danger.

He searches for a place where his heart
May enjoy peace and his body be in good health.
Near Barda, he finds a cavern on the rocky
Mountainside, so high it grazes the clouds.
No falcon dares fly above, no lion imprint
Is visible below, and boars are kept at bay.
The Tooranian ruler takes provisions to this site
And turns it into his dwelling for fear of death.
He carves within the cavern's walls a room.
This remote place, close to a running spring,
May be referred to as the den of Afraasiyaab.
The miserable king remains there for some time,
His heart festering as he repents of his deeds.

A prince who becomes bloodthirsty
Does not stay on the throne for long.
Here is a king, master of throne, world ruler,
Born under a good star and fortune's favorite,
Who spilled blood, accumulating enemies.
Happy is the king who never sets sights on royal blood.

At this time, there lives a man of good deeds,
A wise man from the family of Fereydoon.
With all the splendor and glory of a Kianian,
He is a humble worshipper of Yazdan.

His waist is cinched, always ready to serve the king.
The entire mountain is for him a place of worship,
For he dwells far from worldly pleasures and crowds.
The name of this virtuous man is Hoom.

On the mountaintop, right next to his dwelling,
There is a fissure in the rocks. One day, the hermit,
Dressed in a simple frock, prays there when at once
His ear is struck by a whimper coming through the crack.

He hears a man sobbing and moaning:
"O Creator higher than all, you know my inner thoughts.
If I have acted in evil ways without reason,
Causing you to suffer, I bow low as your slave,
Full of sin, in misery beneath your shelter.
Return to me my crown and throne, my treasure and host.
Otherwise sever my soul from my body.
Without crown, treasure, noblemen, and warriors,
I wish not to continue this life of pain and suffering.
Where is your power and worth, courage and strength?
Alas, kingdom and land! Alas, gold, jewels, and glory!
Alas, golden crown and throne!
Alas, bracelets, torques, and diadems!
Alas, sword and heavy mace! Alas, horsemen holding reins!
Alas, my brother and my son!
Look at the calamities that have befallen me.

"O leader above all noble and powerful men,
The lands of Tooran and Chin are under your command.
Your words and your pledges find their way
To the most remote corners of the world.
Where are your provinces and your vast hosts,
O you who are now confined to this constricted lair,
This rocky fortress, your place of refuge?
What has happened to your wisdom, your throne and crown,
Your power, your courage, your discernment,
Your treasures, your fortune, your land and troops,
Your arm's muscle, your shoulders and hands?
You have nothing left.
Where is your ruby seal that governed half of the world?
Where is the host that you guided to war day and night?
Where are your wise advisors and brave noblemen?

Where are your lofty palaces, peaceful sanctuaries?
Where are your wise men and your warriors
Lining up in support of you on the day of war?
Now here you are in a narrow, stone-walled cave."

Hoom hears this complaint in the Turkish language.
He quits his prayers and exits the place, saying,
"Such lamentations in the middle of the night
Can only be the crying sobs of Afraasiyaab."

This thought solidifies in him.
He spends some time searching for an entrance,
Climbing the mountain during the time for sleep.
He discovers the opening of Afraasiyaab's den,
Enters like an enraged lion, takes off his frock,
Grabs the noose that he wears like a drawstring,
Which assures him divine protection,
Wields it, and breaks into the cavern.

At the sight of him, Afraasiyaab rises and pounces on him.
The two men struggle for a long time.
In the end, Hoom brings the king beneath him,
Strikes him down, and, once on the floor, ties up his arms.
Then he leaves, dragging Afraasiyaab with him,
And despite his resistance, he runs like a mad person.

It is normal to be surprised of such a turn in the story.
But when one is world king,
One must wish only for the glory of generosity
And not give surrender to worldly pleasures.

Afraasiyaab selected a cavern for his dwelling.
How could he know that it would entrap him
And ultimately cause his demise?

43 | Afraasiyaab Escapes Hoom

Hoom ties up Afraasiyaab's arms
And drags him out of his hiding place.

Afraasiyaab says to him, "O wise and pious man,
O Yazdan worshipper, what do you want with me?

Who am I in the world but a simple merchant,
Minding his business in this narrow cavern?
I have lost all my money and sit to reflect on my story."

Hoom replies, "Your rightful place of rest is not here.
Echoes of your name resound throughout the world.
It is the name of a king who killed his own brother,
And by doing so, gravely offended the Creator.
Besides the noble Aghriras, you proceeded to kill
The famous Nozar and, later, the blessed Siaavoosh,
Son of Kay Kaavoos and heir to the Kianian throne.
You never thought you would end up here.
Spilling royal blood has prompted you
To trade a shiny palace for a dark, rocky cavern."

Afraasiyaab hears him out
And feels as if he is losing his sense of reason.
He retorts, "O powerful man,
Is there anyone in the world who is innocent?
The rotation of the mighty firmament has turned me
Into an instrument of suffering, weariness, and ruin.
No one can evade Yazdan's commands,
Even in the event of a male lion breaking his neck.
Have mercy on me, for I am a pitiful man.
Even though I have committed some crimes.
I am the grandson of the blessed Fereydoon.
Ease off the knots of your noose.
Where do you wish to take me thus bound up
And in a state of utter disgrace?
Do you not fear Yazdan?
Do you not fear the day of retribution?"

Hoom answers, "O malevolent, evil man,
You most likely don't have much time left.
Your words are weeds sprouting in the rose garden,
But your fate is in the hands of Kay Khosrow."

Still, his heart feels pity
For the other's downhearted state,
And he relaxes the knots of his royal noose.

Afraasiyaab, seeing this holy man moved by his lament,
Frees himself from his grip with a brusque motion

And dives into the lake, disappearing into its depths.

It so happens that Goodarz, son of Kashvaad,
Enjoying a run through the king's palace grounds,
Approaches the lake with his procession,
Consisting of a select group of noblemen
And, most notably, his son Giv.
He recognizes Hoom holding his noose,
Hand on his waist, running on the water's edge
Like a mad person, a lost look on his face.
At the sight of Hoom and of the surface of the lake
Rippling with waves, he thinks,
"Could this holy man be fishing in these waters?
Why is he so distressed?
Might a whale have snatched his fishhook?"

Goodarz calls out, "O holy man, tell me your secret.
What are you looking for in the waters of this lake?
Do you wish to wash your grimy body in it?"

Hoom replies, "O renowned leader,
Pay attention to what is happening to me.
I have a dwelling on the mountaintop,
A place where the Creator's servant
Can worship in peace away from crowds.
I was standing, expressing devotion in the dark night,
When, at the hour when the birds sing their songs,
The sound of human cries reached my ear.
At that moment, my clear mind gave me the idea
That I would succeed in plucking from the earth
The root of vengeance, for I deduced
That such laments, at that hour,
Could only be from the mean-spirited Afraasiyaab.
I rose to search the mountain and the caverns.
I discovered the entrance to the den
Of the mournful, miserable ruler.
I entered and found him in such a state,
Shedding bitter tears for his crown and throne.

"Upon my arrival, he rose quickly and stiffened,
With two feet against the boulder.
I bound his hands as tight as a rock,

So tight blood dripped from his fingernails.
I dragged him running out of the mountain
As he whimpered and howled like a woman.
He wept for so long and vowed so many oaths
That, in the end, I loosened his bonds.
That is when he escaped,
Breaking my heart with his getaway.
He is hiding in this very Lake of Urmia.[50]
Now I have related to you the tale in all its truth."

Goodarz is reminded of the ancient prophecies.
He returns to the fire temple, deep in thought,
Like a man who has lost sense and reason.

He begins by worshiping the flame
And addressing prayers to the World Creator.
Once his devotion is completed,
He reveals to the two kings what he has seen and heard.
The two Kianian rulers immediately mount their steeds
And leave the palace adjacent to the temple of Aazargoshasp.

44 | Kay Kaavoos and Kay Khosrow Approach Hoom

As they make their way to Hoom the hermit,
World ruler Kaavoos reflects on the events.

Hoom recognizes the faces and the crowns of kings,
He pays them a tribute worthy of their stature.
The kings invoke the graces of the Just Creator.

Kaavoos says to Hoom, "May Yazdan be praised,
For I see the face of a pious man, strong, wise, and valiant!"

Hoom, the servant, replies,
"May the earth enjoy the fruits of your justice!
May the life of this young king prosper!
May the hearts of his enemies perish!
I was worshiping Yazdan in this mountain
When Kay Khosrow passed on his way to Gang-Dej.

◇◇◇◇◇◇◇◇◇◇◇◇◇
50 Urmia: Saltwater lake in the northwest part of Iran.

I was praying for peace on earth.
When his majesty returned,
I was happy once again and returned to my prayers.
One night, blessed Sooroosh revealed to me fate's secrets:
Shouts arose from the deepest cavern.
I heard them and listened carefully to the voice.
Someone was bitterly moaning over the loss
Of crown and treasury, army, land, and ivory throne.

"I climbed down the mountain crest to a narrow cave,
Holding my noose in my hand, for it serves me as a rope.
I distinguished the head and shoulders of Afraasiyaab,
Who settled in the cavern hoping to make it a place of rest.
I lunged at him, tied him up securely with my noose,
And dragged him out of his narrow den.
He wept and wept, overwhelming my heart with pity.
At his insistence, I loosened the knots of his bonds.
Once at the side of the lake, he was able to free himself.
Ultimately, he plunged into the waters of the lake,
Where he has taken shelter and where he hides.
We must find him and cut off his feet.
If we fail to capture him and kill him, if so is his fate,
Garsivaz's heart will boil with tenderness and affection.
If the king allows the brother to be brought here,
Feet tied up and sewn in cow skin until he passes out,
Then Afraasiyaab will, without a doubt,
Emerge from the water at the sound of his brother's shouts."

The king commands his executioners to take off
With sword and Gilani shield.
The wretched Garsivaz, a man who has caused
His share of trouble, is transported to the water's edge.

Kaavoos tells the executioner to drag him before him,
To pluck off the veil covering his face and his shame,
To sew around his neck a fresh piece of cow skin
In a way that drains him of all his strength.

Garsivaz's skin tears to bits in fear.
He begs for mercy and summons the Creator.

At the sound of his brother's cries,
Afraasiyaab emerges to the surface of the water.

Moved and in tears, he swims in the lake
All the way to the shallow shore.
Death appears to him a state preferable
To the sight of his brother's torment.

In turn, Garsivaz sees him in the water.
Eyes full of blood, heart full of fear, he shouts,
"O world king, leader of warriors, crown of emperors,
Where are your pomp and your royal court?
Where are your crown, treasure, and army?
Where are your bow, noose, and snare
With which you entrapped deevs and sorcerers?
Where are your mallet and balls? Where are your field
And your horsemanship so celebrated in games of polo?
Where are your night attacks, when you lunged
Like a lion able to vanquish a leaping wild creature?
Where are your wisdom, knowledge, and power?
Where are your renowned and devoted men?
Where are your glory and your fame in battle?
Where is your opulent, majestic palace?
Where is your celebratory cup in times of feasts?
For now you feel the need to cowardly hide in the water.
This is the fate the deev's star of misfortune devised for you!"

Afraasiyaab cries bitterly and,
Dropping blood tears in the lake, he replies,
"I have wandered throughout the world,
Openly and secretly, wishing to alter my dismal destiny.
But now my woes have taken a turn for the worse.
Life to me is made abominable,
And your fate, my brother, fills my heart with grief.
How can a descendant of Fereydoon, a son of Pashang,
Have fallen entangled in the web of the whale?"

45 | The Second Capture of Afraasiyaab and His Sentence to Death With Garsivaz

As these two fallen royals speak in this way,
The mind of the devout Hoom strategizes a plot.
He advances toward Afraasiyaab,
Enough to distinguish him from a distance.

He unties his Kianian noose that serves him as a rope,
Crawls like a lion, flings his rolled-up noose in the air,
And captures in it the Tooranian king's head.

Hoom drags Afraasiyaab from the water to the shore,
Where he loses consciousness.
The holy man grabs his arms and feet,
Hauls him out of the water like a vile load.
He ties him up, hands him over to the kings,
And departs as if the wind were his companion.

Khosrow approaches, wielding his sharp sword,
Head full of hatred, heart full of aversion.

The witless Afraasiyaab says to him,
"I dreamt of this day, your day of triumph.
The revolving dome of sky turned for a long time,
And, in the end, it tears open the veil of secrets."
Then he adds in a louder voice,
"O malevolent vengeance-seeker,
Tell me why do you want to kill your grandfather?"

Khosrow replies, "O evildoer,
You are worthy of reproof and ignominy.
I shall first mention the murder of your brother,
Who never hurt anyone, let alone anyone of royal blood;
Secondly, the murder of Nozar, the illustrious king,
Iraj's descendant and heir.
You slit his neck with your double-edged sword
And sent the world spinning into a state of chaos.
Thirdly, I will cite the case of Siaavoosh,
The most valiant equestrian the world has ever seen.
You cut off his head like a lamb,
A deed that surpassed the vault of sky.
Why did you kill my father?
Did you not foresee this day of misery?
You rushed to commit crimes,
And today you stand to face the consequences."

Afraasiyaab replies, "The past is as you recount.
What occurred, occurred. Now listen to me,
But allow me to lay eyes on your mother's face.
Then you can tell me your stories."

Khosrow says to him, "As to your wish to see my mother,
Remember the misfortunes you brought upon my head.
My father was innocent. I was not even born,
Yet so many calamities did you burden us with!
You cut off the head of a king
For whom crown and throne shed bitter tears!
I cannot restrain you as one cannot restrain a blaze.
When the shepherd captures the wolf,
He has no choice but to kill him.
When the valiant warrior captures a lion,
He must not nurse him back to life.
If he finds himself drawn in affection to the lion,
The latter will overcome and kill him.
Today is the day of divine retribution.
The divine sentence for evil-doers is misfortune."

Khosrow strikes a blow at Afraasiyaab's neck
With his Indian sword and covers his dark body with dust.
Ruby-colored blood creeps onto his face and white beard.
Meanwhile his brother despairs of life.
In this manner, the throne of kings becomes vacant,
And Afraasiyaab's fortunes come to an end.
His evil deeds caused him his own demise.

My son, do not search for the key that unlocks evil.
If you do, be aware that the crime
Will always drive the criminal to his ruin.

A king bestowed majesty by the Creator must,
In a moment of anger, only make use of chains and prison.
If he elects bloodshed, he will remain abhorred,
And the sublime dome of sky will punish him.
If you desire to keep your crown on your head,
Proceed with benevolence, prudence, and patience.

Look and see what the crown says to your head:
"May wisdom always be your mind's ally!"

Kay Khosrow approaches Garsivaz,
Whose cheeks pale and heart troubles.
The executioners drag him away,
Weighed down by heavy chains, overcome by grief,
Surrounded by guards and slayers, as suits evil-doers.

Once he stands before Kay Khosrow,
Blood tears streak his indigo face.
The King of Kings, ruler of Iran, reminds him
Of the dagger and vase with which he killed Siaavoosh.
He speaks to him of Toor, son of Fereydoon,
Of the wild Salm and of Iraj, a just and powerful prince.

Then he gives the order to the executioner,
Who draws out his sharp-edged sword,
Approaches, heart full of resolve,
And splits the leader in two at the hips.

The hearts of the men in the king's escort quiver with fear.
The remains of the two brothers are collected into a pile,
And the crowd gathers around in a large circle.

Kay Khosrow observes the two corpses
As he enumerates the evil acts of two evil men.
Then he commands his minister to wash their bodies
Clean of dust and blood, dress them in Chini brocade,
And wrap them in silken shrouds.
In the grave, they place Afraasiyaab on a golden throne
And fill his head with amber.
They put him to rest as the Iranian king weeps for him.
Garsivaz's body is washed over the ditch.

Khosrow says, "We have avenged my father's death
And have thus snuffed out the blaze of fury.
I hope that my grandfather will be forgiven.
It is time for me to return to court and rest at peace.
I must prepare a new order, show mercy to prisoners.
My grandfather was the perpetrator of much bloodshed.
Now that he is gone, I have no use for captive men.
Do not act with injustice, for you will be the one
To suffer the consequences,
As your name will wallow in shame and dishonor.
Look at the revolving dome of sky. It hides nothing other
Than the distinction between hot and cold, love and hate.
Pay heed and pray to the pure Yazdan,
Our Source of victory and defeat, in joy and suffering.

46 | Kay Kaavoos and Kay Khosrow Return to Pars

Once Kay Khosrow receives the fulfillment of his prayers,
He returns from the lake to the fire temple.
He and his grandfather pour gold over the fire.
They murmur long invocations and remain standing
For one day and one night before the Supreme Guide.

Upon the arrival of Zarasp, Kay Khosrow's treasurer,
The king donates a fortune to Aazargoshasp,
Along with robes of honor to wise men,
And abundant gold and silver.
He distributes riches to the city's poor
And to those who labor with their hands.
In this way, with justice and generosity,
He renders the world young again.

Then he climbs back on the Kianian throne,
Opens the doors to the audience hall in a state of silence.

A letter is sent to each province and to each
Lord and governor, from east to west,
In every place ruled by a renowned prince,
To announce that the earth has finally been freed
Of the dragon's oppression by the sword of Kay Khosrow,
With the strength and power given to him by Yazdan,
Master of victory, the king tireless with armor and war gear
Cleansed the world of evil men and evil deeds,
And banished fear from the hearts of men.
The spirit of Siaavoosh is renewed by him.
Everyone in every nation is his subject.

Then the world king says,
"O illustrious men, fortunate and powerful,
Allow your women and children to leave the city,
And take provisions and music to the fields."

He donates generous wealth to the poor,
To servants of the divine, and to men of war.
He executes his plan and prepares a grand feast.
Members of the royal family and of the seed of Zarasp
Present themselves to the temple of Aazargoshasp.

Kay Khosrow spends forty days in feast with Kaavoos,
Reveling with music, song, and wine.

Once the new moon shines in the sky, as bright as the sun,
A golden crown on the head of a young king,
The noblemen take the road to the land of Pars,
Content to be free of battle.

In every city they come across,
Crowds squeeze up against the king.
Golden crates are brought to render good men rich.

47 | The Death of Kay Kaavoos

Once Kay Kaavoos returns to safety,
He confesses his heart's deepest secret to Yazdan,
"O Creator above fate, instruct us on what is good and fair.
From You I have received majesty, glory, and fortune,
Power, diadem, merit, treasure, and throne.
I am the only recipient of these royal attributes and fame.
I prayed to you so that a noble man, strapped for battle,
Might successfully avenge the death of Siaavoosh.
I have witnessed my grandson, the joy of my sight,
Brilliantly carry out my quest for vengeance.
He is ambitious, full of dignity, strength, and wisdom.
In every way, he surpasses all the earth's rulers.
One hundred and fifty years have passed over me,
And my head and beard, once black as musk,
Have turned white as camphor.
My stature, once tall as a cypress tree,
Has now curved in the shape of a bow.
I do not envisage an end to my life as a calamity."

Not long after he says this, he passes on,
Leaving behind only the memory of his name.

Kay Khosrow climbs down the throne on the floor.
Renowned and noble Iranians arrive on foot,
Lips full of words, clothed in black and blue robes.
For two weeks, they maintain a state of mourning.

They erect a tall structure for Kaavoos Shah's tomb,
Measuring ten nooses in height.
The court's servants bring a piece
Of black Rumi silk embroidered with gold.
In it they pour aloeswood, camphor, and musk,
And wrap the king's dried up body with it.
They place him on an ivory throne
With a crown of camphor and musk on his head.

Once Kay Khosrow leaves the place of burial,
They close its doors, and Kay Kaavoos,
Never to be seen again, may finally renounce
Reflections on war and vengeance.

Such is the law of this passing world:
You do not remain with enduring hardships forever.
Even the wisest man or the bravest man
Is incapable of evading the grips of death,
Even if protected by helmet and coat of mail.
Even if you were a king, even if you were Zartosht,[51]
Your resting place would still be the dirt of earth
And your pillow a block of brick.

Try to remain joyous. Pursue the object of your desire,
And once you obtain it, yearn for a good name.
But know that the world is your enemy,
The earth will serve you ultimately as a bed,
And your shroud will be one woven out of dust.

For forty days, the king wears his grandfather's mourning,
Detached from delights and from the crown and throne.
On the forty-first day,
He places himself on the ivory throne
And lowers on his head the shining royal crown.

The army gathers at the palace gates.
Noblemen and dignitaries salute Khosrow as king
And toss precious stones over his crown with joy.
The entire world celebrates his victory with feasts.

◇◇◇◇◇◇◇◇◇◇◇◇◇◇
51 Zartosht: Spiritual leader Zoroaster, founder of Zoroastrianism, who brought the
Avesta to the people sometime between 1500 and 500 BC.

In this way, the earth obeys Kay Khosrow,
And sixty years pass over the world.

48 | Kay Khosrow Frees Jahn
and Gives Him the Kingship of Tooran-Zamin[52]

The king summons Jahn, son of Afraasiyaab, with respect.
The servants approach him and notice his feet are bound.
They break the chains without hurting him
And lead him to the king.
The noble prince arrives at the celebrated court.
At the sight of the king, Jahn humbly kisses the ground
And approaches, tears of blood flowing from his eyes.

Kay Khosrow sighs deeply as he watches Jahn step forward.
He feels as if the blood on his mother's side simmers,
And his face turns the color of fire.
Then he sheds tears at the memory of Afraasiyaab's deeds.
"If he had not dipped his hands in blood," he says,
"And breached the ways of custom, faith, and order,
If he had not drenched his white beard with crimson,
He would not have despaired of losing his kingdom.
I would still be a son by his side hailing him as world king.
But such is the unfortunate rotation of the vault of sky,
A tree that bears leaves of poison and fruit of snake."

The words of the king appease Jahn's heart.
He sings the praises of the mighty Iranian ruler
For having revealed to him his mind's reflections:
"May you be victorious and retain throne and crown!
The noblest men gain their glory in service to you.
I am and will always be your most humble, devoted servant.
I shall not walk on any path without your permission.
My sole purpose in life is to obey your commands."

The king rises, happy with Jahn's speech,
And offers him a seat to his right. He says,
"How are you? What have you learned from this era?

◇◇◇◇◇◇◇◇◇◇◇◇◇
52 This section consists of 114 couplets that are not in other editions of *The Shahnameh*.
In the Florence Edition, there are only nine lines on the subject of Jahn.

Rest at ease and be happy,
For I wish to bestow upon you crown and throne.
Since you descend from the lineage of Toor,
I wish to offer you governance of the land of Tooran.
You are the grandson of Pashang, of the seed of Fereydoon.
Maintain yourself on the path of honor.
You and I are bound by blood and affection.
You must always follow my counsel.
Do not take the world so seriously.
Do not divert from the path of righteousness,
Or else I will cut off your head,
Like I cut off your father's head.

"Afraasiyaab brought evil upon himself,
And for that reason he left the world
To find a dwelling in hell in the dragon's jaws.
Like deevs, he strayed off Yazdan's path
With the murder of the innocent Siaavoosh.
That is the reason I had to go after Afraasiyaab.
I executed vengeance with courage and decency.
I cleaved his head like the head of a lark
And let it writhe and roll in the dust,
His hair and beard tinted red with blood.
He lost any hope he may have clung to for this world.
No one wept for him because of his wicked ways.
Look at the fate of Zahaak and Toor,
Who acted so viciously and nourished
Themselves on the blood of others:
Zahaak killed Jamsheed in hatred,
And Toor cut off the head of the pure Iraj.
Do you know how Yazdan dealt with these two evil kings?
With courage and divine power, Fereydoon flung
His warrior noose to capture the criminal, impure Zahaak,
Obliging him to topple off his throne.
He then hauled him before a crowd to a mountainous cave,
Thus liberating the people from his reign of terror.

"Furthermore, consider King Manoochehr, who,
In justice, cinched his waist to avenge the death of Iraj.
He went from the land of Iran to the land of Chin,
His head vengeful and his heart restless.
With divine power, he acceded to victory

And severed Toor's unlawful head.
Such are the workings of divine will and justice:
Anyone who cuts off the head of an innocent man
May expect his head to be similarly severed
And his impure heart to be entombed.
Pay heed to avoid acting like these evil men,
For no one will come to your rescue,
And you will end up meeting a similar fate."

Jahn replies, "O just King,
I fasten my belt to your command.
I drop my head to the dust at the foot of your throne.
I am lower than your lowest slave,
Devoid of throne and crown.
If you send me to Tooran-Zamin,
I shall pray for you for the rest of my life.
Every year, I shall pay tribute,
As much as my wealth allows.
Every now and then, I shall come to visit you,
Set my sights on your crown-bearing face.
I shall kiss the ground beneath your seat,
Praise your fortune and your throne.
I shall bring you offerings of amber, myrrh, and musk.
I shall cover the floors with Chini brocade.
May I make one request from your majesty as his slave?
I long for the veiled women, the children,
My sisters and my relatives to be forgiven, and
To be allowed to travel with me back to Tooran-Zamin.
Should I so deserve it, this is my most fervent wish."

At this exchange, the king summons a scribe to bring
Paper, musk, amber, and a reed, and they write on silk
The command of the king in line with Kianian custom,
In the same manner as Fereydoon gave the land to Toor
And told him, "This is your land; do not wish for more.
Act with justice, and care for the needy."

The king commands the treasurer to select a royal attire
And a crown, which they place on the prince's head.
Gratified, Jahn is pleased with the knowledge
That he will be free from the fear of execution.
At the same time, after giving each a royal robe

And crown according to rank and status,
The king releases the women and relatives
To allow them to reunite with Jahn.

Kay Khosrow tells them, "Travel back to your home
And homeland with Jahn in joy and happiness."

The king once again summons his scribe to write
A missive with musk and amber upon a sheet of silk
To Gostaham: "Transfer all the Tooranian lands to Jahn,
And return to Iran-Zamin without wasting time."

In the early morning hour, timpani beat at the court of Jahn.
Jahn sits on his horse and takes the road to Tooran-Zamin,
Traveling in joy with his escort and his kin.

The king tells an envoy, "Go straight to Gostaham,
And recount to him all that transpired here."

The messenger departs like wind toward Tooran-Zamin.
At the side of Gostaham, he tells him
That Jahn is on his way at the king's command.

Gostaham marches off to greet Jahn on the road.
They deck out the towns, celebrate with music and song.

Jahn arrives in Tooran-Zamin in royal pomp.
Silken spreads are everywhere;
Dinars are tossed over his head.
He climbs upon Afraasiyaab's throne,
And all those who had fallen asleep are awakened.

For two weeks Jahn remains in the presence of Gostaham,
Handing out royal gifts to him in joy.
Then he opens the doors to his treasury
And prepares to send Gostaham back to Iran.
He hands him the gifts and says, "O wise warrior,
Take these valuables to the king and tell him
That the World Creator is our support and shelter.
You are king, and we are your slaves.
Wherever you may be, we shall worship you."

Gostaham accepts the presents and tells him,

"May you always live and rule in happiness!"

They spend the night in revelry with women from Taraaz.
As the revolving dome grows white with light
And parts the cloak of night, Gostaham,
A prince from the lineage of Nozar,
Regally mounts on his stallion and returns
To Iran-Zamin and to the king of brave men.

At the news of his return, leaders and warriors
Swiftly march off to receive him.
They surround him, praising his crown and bearing.
Gostaham dismounts and greets
Tous with a brotherly embrace.
The warriors line up to salute the newcomer.

After the greetings, they straddle their horses
And gallop away, swift as Aazargoshasp.
Once in town, they march to the king's court, where
Gostaham dismounts to approach the throne on foot.
As soon as his eyes fall on Kay Khosrow,
He bends down to kiss the ground in veneration.

At the sight of him strong and well,
The king holds him close for some time.
Then he sits him near his throne and asks
For news of Jahn and the Tooranian army.

Gostaham responds, "O King, Jahn sends salutations.
He thinks of you always and is cinched in service to you."

Kay Khosrow commands his chamberlain to bring wine
And to prepare the banquet for the feast.
After the meal, musicians and singers entertain them.
They revel through the night to the sounds of flute and harp.
Everyone sits in reverence and in praise of the king.

Once the sun reveals its golden face
And blends the darkness into its loving light,
Gostaham lays down Jahn's offerings at the king's feet.

49 | The Reign of Kay Khosrow: Kay Khosrow's Hopelessness for Life

Kay Khosrow's mind fills with thoughts of the passing days
And the power given to him by the divine Creator.
He thinks, "I have crushed the enemy everywhere,
In populated lands from India to Chin,
From Iran to Rum, from western borders to eastern ones,
In mountains and deserts, on water and firm land.
Everywhere, I stand as master and king,
And the world no longer is inclined to fear evil.

"Many days have passed over my head.
Yazdan bestowed upon me my heart's desires.
I no longer dedicate thoughts to vengeance.
At this time, I cannot succumb to my own passions,
To self-indulgence, to evil or to the faith of Ahriman,
Else I shall become egotistical and spiteful
Like Zahaak and Jamsheed, fall under a spell
And transform into Toor and Salm.
On one hand, I am a descendant of Kay Kaavoos,
On the other hand, I am a son of Tooran-Zamin,
Full of pride and impatience.
I shall one day turn away from Yazdan,
Divine grace will abandon me.
Fear will invade my peaceful mind, like it did
The minds of Kaavoos and Afraasiyaab, the sorcerer,
Who, even in dream, dwelt on deception and bloodshed.
I shall surrender to injustice and folly.
I shall press forward into the darkness
Until my crowned head falls into the dust,
And nothing will remain of me in the world
But a bad name and a miserable end.

"This flesh and these colored cheeks will perish.
My remains will be scattered across the earth.
My crowned head will tumble and roll in the dust.
All my virtues will be wiped out,
To be replaced by ingratitude for the divine.
My name will be sullied in this world.
My soul will be dim in the other world.
Once another will seize my crown and throne,

My fortune will further dim.
My name will be cursed for all eternity.
The blossoming rose of my past deeds
Will be transformed into dried-up thorns.

"Now that I have avenged the blood of my father,
Now that I have put order into the world,
Sent to death those who deserved to die,
Vicious men and rebels of the divine path,
There remains no one, whether in the desert
Or populated land, who does not salute my rulership.
I hold titles, splendor, and stateliness.
No matter how vast their wealth, how countless their jewels,
The world's most powerful men are my subjects.
Now that I still am thankful to the divine
For giving me kingship, grace, and majesty,
A favorable rotation of stars, and abundant power,
I hurry to appear before Yazdan at the height of my glory,
Wishing that the Creator may enfold my heart
And lift it toward a peaceful sojourn,
Since this crown and throne of power must perish.

"No one can acquire a greater name
Or better satisfy his wishes, enjoy more power,
More happiness, more rest and dignity than I have.
I have seen and heard the secrets of the world:
Its joy and misfortune, things hidden and revealed.
I have seen that man, whether he cultivates land
Or whether he sits on a throne and bears a crown,
Will end up crossing the threshold from life to death."

The king orders his chamberlain to dismiss visitors
From his audience hall, politely and with consideration.
He shuts the Kianian court and rushes to the garden,
His clothes in disorder, to wash his head and body, sighing.
He searches for the divine path with the candle of wisdom.

Then he dresses in a new white robe
To worship Yazdan, his heart full of hope.
At the site of worship, he murmurs secret thoughts:
"O Creator, you are above the most holy souls.
You have created fire, wind, and dust.

Guide me and give me wisdom.
Preserve my mind from error.
I shall adore you for as long as I live.
I shall perform great deeds from now on.
Forgive me of my past offenses and trespasses.
Allow me to discern between good and evil.
Distance from my life the misfortunes of fate
As well as the plots of the wicked, alluring deev.
Guide me so that greed may not dominate my heart,
As it did the hearts of Kaavoos, Zahaak, and Jamsheed.
Once the deev covers the door of virtue with his lies,
Safeguard my soul from his wicked machinations.
Send it on a journey of pure men,
And shield my path and my honor."

He remains standing day and night for one week.
His body firmly planted there, his soul is elsewhere.
At the end of one week, he becomes so weak
He can barely hold himself up anymore.
On the eighth day, he leaves the site of worship
And climbs swiftly on the throne of the King of Kings.

50 | The Noblemen Question the Closure of Court

The warriors of the Iranian army
Are surprised at the actions of the king.
These men, renowned in battle, are of a different opinion.

Once the glorious king sits back on the throne,
The chamberlain appears at the audience hall.
He commands the curtains be raised
To allow the heroes to enter.

Great warriors, skilled equestrians, elephant vanquishers,
Men with lion faces, such as Tous, Goodarz,
The brave Giv, Gorgeen, Bijan, and Rohaam the lion,
Shiddush, Zangueh of Shaavaran, Fariborz, Gostaham,
And other noblemen enter, arms crossed respectfully.

In the presence of Khosrow, they revere him,
Then reveal to him their most secret thoughts:

"O King, O brave warrior, O judge and world master,
So mighty among the most powerful men,
From the moment Yazdan created the world and the earth,
Never has a ruler of your stature sat on the ivory throne!
The sun and crown borrow their splendor from you.
You are the one to give strength to armor, sword, and steed.
You ignite the blaze of the blessed Aazargoshasp.
You hold no fear for the labors of war.
Wealth has not the power to soften you.
Your treasures are below the fatigues you have endured.

"As for us great warriors, we are your subjects and slaves.
Our lives revolve around your being.
You have flung your enemies into the dust.
You have eradicated fear from the world.
The hosts and treasures of all the lands belong to you.
Evidence of your labors are everywhere.
We do not know why his majesty's thoughts
Have turned somber in the midst of his good fortune.
The time for enjoyment is upon us in this world,
And not the time for wasting away with worry.
If we are to blame for the king's melancholy, may he say so,
And we shall return joy to his heart by repenting
With blood tears in our eyes and fire in our hearts.
If rather he has a secret enemy, may he tell us as well.
Rulers everywhere, owners of crowns,
Place the honor of their throne and diadem
Either on vanquishing your enemy
Or on expiring their helmet on their head.
May the king reveal to us his secret,
And may he allow us to seek a remedy to his ailment."

The illustrious king replies, "O great heroes,
Seekers of the path, I have neither enemy nor
A member of my army who gives me cause for concern.
No part of my treasure has been dispensed,
And none of you has done anything wrong in my eyes.
Since I have avenged my father,
I have spread everywhere justice and faith.
There remains not even a fistful of dust
That fails to succumb to the imprint of my seal.
You might as well place your swords within their sheaths,

Allow the cup to prevail over the gladiator's blade.
Instead of the hum of arrows shooting through the air,
Make resound the sound of flutes and string instruments,
Accompanied by a grand banquet full of tasty delicacies.

"For seven days I stood before Yazdan with pious thoughts.
I have a secret wish, which I submitted to the Creator.
I shall reveal it to you once it has been addressed
And I have received divine orders leading to my happiness.
You as well worship Yazdan. Pray that my wish be granted,
For Yazdan is the One to give power to the pious.
Give in to joy and delights, and do not consider evil in me.
Rest assured that the continuous rotations of the sky
Make the distinction between neither king nor subject.
All that happens to us, whether fair or unfair,
Comes only from the divine firmament.
It nourishes young and old alike."

The great warriors leave the king, full of doubt and worry.
Khosrow commands his chamberlain
To sit behind the audience hall and to prohibit
Entry to all visitors, whether relative or stranger.

At the advent of night, he goes to the site of prayer,
Opens his lips before the just Yazdan, and says,
"O Creator, most magnificent of all beings,
You favor those who are virtuous and pure,
Be my guide toward heaven, so that I may leave
This transitory life without my heart turning to deceit.
Be my guide in such a way that my soul finds
A home in the resting place of the blessed."

51 | The Iranians Summon Zaal and Rostam

One week passes without the appearance of the king.
Words of confusion are uttered as to his whereabouts.
Wise and sensible heroes and noblemen,
Such as Goodarz and Tous, son of Nozar,
Convene to speak at length of justice and injustice,
Of the past exploits of powerful kings,
Whether they were divine worshippers or not.

After having recalled the deeds of kings of long ago,
Goodarz says to Giv, "O son favored by fortune,
You have always revered the throne and crown.
You have endured many hardships for the sake of Iran.
You exiled yourself from land and family for many years.
We face a sad affair, which is not to be taken lightly.
You must travel to Zabolestan and send an envoy to Kabol.
You must relay this message to Zaal and Rostam:
      'The king strays off the divine path.
      He has closed his court's audience hall.
      We fear that he nurtures an alliance with deevs.
      We have expressed our regrets and our prayers.
      We have implored him to act with justice.
      He listened to us at length but did not reply.
      His soul appears troubled and his heart full of pride.
      We fear that with the deev leading him astray,
      He will be pressed to transgress like Kay Kaavoos.
      You are valuable heroes, wise and powerful men.
      Gather men of sound counsel
      From Ghennooj to Dambar and from Margh to Mai,
      As well as wise men and mystics from Kabol and Zabol.
      Bring them with you to the land of Iran, for this kingdom
      Is full of rumor since King Khosrow rejects our counsel.
      We have consulted one another and feel our only hope
      For a solution resides in the person of Zaal.'"

Having heard Goodarz's speech, Giv selects
A number of brave men, and, urged by worry,
He rushes to take off in the direction of Sistan.
In the presence of Zaal and Rostam,
He relates the strange incidents he observed at court.

Preoccupied, Zaal replies to the noble Giv,
"What grave misfortune has befallen us!"
He turns to Rostam: "Summon wise men
And seers from Zabol and Kabol to accompany us."

Noblemen assemble around Zaal,
And together they take the road from Zabol to Iran.

World ruler Khosrow, meanwhile, remains one week
Standing in worship before Yazdan.

On the eighth day, once the world-illuminating sun rises,
He climbs on his golden throne
As his chamberlain parts the curtains of his audience hall.

World heroes and wise men appear before the king,
Who receives them graciously and assigns them seats,
As is called for by Kianian custom.

The noblemen, full of wisdom and sound advice,
Remain standing before him, arms crossed on their chests.
Not one among these illustrious royal servants takes a seat.
In the end, they open their lips to speak:
"O illustrious King of wise men, you are pure and just.
Power and majesty belong to you.
Everything from the earth and the sun
To fish swimming at the bottom of the sea is yours.
We stand before you as your slaves, your warriors,
Your wise advisors, awaiting your command.
May it please the king to tell us what is our crime
And why he has banished us from his presence.
Our dim hearts have plunged into a state of affliction.
May the king reveal his secret to us, keepers of his borders,
For we have lost our sense of direction.
We can no longer discern which path is ours to follow.
If it is the sea that distresses him, we shall dry up its waters.
We shall cover it in a blanket of dust and musk.
If it is a mountain, we shall uproot it from its foundations.
We shall pierce his opponents' hearts with daggers.
If treasures have the power to cure his majesty's ailment,
He need not ever trouble himself about a lack of wealth,
For we declare ourselves the guardians of his assets.
Filled with sadness, we bitterly weep for his suffering."

The world master replies,
"I shall never cease to have use for my unrivaled warriors.
My heart is afflicted neither by the waning of my strength
Nor by the fear of men, and certainly not by a lack of wealth.
No enemy has appeared in any of my provinces,
And I hold no prospect of war, therefore no trepidation.
The seed of a desire has been conceived within my heart,
One that will continue to consume me.
From the dark night to the first light of day,

I spend time in the hope of completing this goal.
Once I sense the time is right, I shall share my secret
And reveal the mysterious longings of my soul.
Return to your homes, contented by your victories,
And do not hole up with grim thoughts."

The noble world leaders and warriors pay the king tribute,
Unable to shake the sadness lodged in their hearts.

52 | Kay Khosrow Dreams of Sooroosh

Once they leave, the prudent king asks
For the curtains to be closed on the audience hall.
The chamberlain follows the order, hopeless for the king.

The world owner appears before Yazdan, Supreme Master,
Prays for guidance, and says, "O Creator of the sky,
O Source of all good, justice, and affection,
Kingship has lost its worth and purpose for me
If the Supreme King is not satisfied with me.
I have committed much good and much evil.
Still, do grant me a seat in paradise."

He remains thus standing for five weeks,
Imploring the Master of the universe.
During the dark night, his aching allows him no rest.
Only when the moon returns to the sky does he sleep.
During wakeful hours, wisdom remains his mind's mate.

He sees the blessed Sooroosh in dream,
Who whispers to him secret words:
"O King of prosperous star, favorite of fortune,
You have made use of many a torque, crown, and throne.
Now that you have achieved all that you hoped for,
If you were to be abruptly plucked from this world,
You would have a seat in the dwelling of the Supreme Judge.
Do not then remain on this obscure earth.
Distribute your goods, donate wealth to the destitute.
Bestow to others this passing dwelling.
Enrich the poor and bring joy to those loyal to you.
This world and that world are one and the same

In the eye of the unjust man.
Whoever escapes the dragon's jaws
Must find shelter from misfortune's claws.
Whoever has endured weariness as you have
Understands that hardships are borne
In the hopes of ultimately gaining wealth and glory.

"Give generously to the poor,
For you will not remain on earth much longer.
Select a benevolent king to succeed you on the throne,
One who would protect the earth's creatures, even the ant.
Once you have organized the world, do not rest,
For the time of your departure will arrive.
Lohraasp is worthy of receiving your throne and crown.
Just as you expressed your wishes to Yazdan,
You may now prepare to travel beyond mortal life."

Sooroosh shares with him secret confidences,
To the delight of Kay Khosrow.
When he awakens, weary of life,
He observes the site of prayer is wet with sweat.
Weeping, he presses his forehead to the ground
In worship to the Creator, saying,
"Were I to suddenly die, I would have obtained
From the Creator my heart's most burning desire."

He climbs on the throne, the cradle of royalty,
Dresses in new attire, and fills the ivory seat,
Divested of torque, bracelet, and crown.

53 | Zaal Appeals to Kay Khosrow

At the end of the sixth week, Zaal and Rostam
And their escort of wise, virtuous men,
Members of Zarasp's family, finally present
Themselves at court, hearts full of sadness.

At the news of their arrival, the distressed Iranians
Prepare their steeds and rush to receive them,
With Tous, carrier of the Kaaviani banner,
And noblemen of golden boots.

Goodarz reaches Rostam, tears of blood flooding his cheeks.
Warriors and troops advance, faces pale, their bleak,
Sorrowful hearts troubled for the plight of Kay Khosrow.

The Iranians say to Zaal and Rostam, "The king has
Fallen prey to the lessons of Eblis, who has led him astray.
His court is black, and no one has seen him day or night.
After one week, the audience hall opened once
And we entered, but O, world heroes, Khosrow is no longer
The king that we once knew, content, his mind at peace.
His cypress stature is no longer lofty. He is hunched over,
And the bright-colored rose of his joy has been plucked.
We do not know what evil eye has fallen upon him
And how this young flower has withered away.
Could it be that the fortune of the Iranians has dimmed
Or that the stars wish to crush our king?
Perhaps it is the workings of the wicked Deev,
Whose sole design is to destroy the entire world."

The brave Zaal replies, "It appears
That his majesty has grown weary of the throne.
Sometimes life unfolds in tranquil flows.
Sometimes it swings to take an adverse turn.
At times we dwell in happiness, at times in misfortune.
But do not abandon thus your heart to worry,
For worry gravely troubles a soul at peace.
We shall attempt to thoroughly counsel the king,
And our advice will return the stars' favors to him."

The newly arrived warriors promptly appear at court,
Draw the curtains open, and are admitted in joy.
Each is received graciously and assigned a place
In accordance to rank and in Kianian courtly tradition:
First Zaal, then Rostam of elephant stature,
Then Tous and Goodarz, their companions,
Then Gorgeen, Bijan, Gostaham, and their escort.

At the sight of Zaal's face and at the sound of Rostam's voice,
The King of Kings rises from his throne full of wonder.
He extends his hand and questions them on their journey.
One after the other, he addresses the wise men
Who have traveled from Zabol, Ghennooj, Dambar, and Kabol.

Once they each have a seat of honor,
Zaal pays homage to Kay Khosrow: "O just King,
May you live happy as long as there are months in the year!
From the time of Manoochehr to the time of Kay Ghobaad,
From the reign of these illustrious kings we remember,
Powerful rulers of blessed paths,
From Zu, son of Tahmasp, to Kay Kaavoos,
From the time of Siaavoosh, who was like a son to me,
A prince full of majesty, splendor, and glory,
We have not witnessed a wiser, more distinguished king,
One so favored by divine grace as you!
May your magnificence be everlasting,
For it is a result of your victories and courage,
Your wisdom, generosity, and integrity!

"You have wandered through the world
With the only intent to spread justice.
Now upon your return, enjoy your triumphs.
What king is not like dust beneath your feet?
What poison exists that your name cannot negate?
I have received some unfortunate news,
And I have subsequently rushed to your court.
A man came to me from Iran-Zamin to tell me
That the victorious king has commanded the chamberlain
To maintain the audience hall inaccessible
And to conceal from everyone the blessed royal face.
At the sound of the cries of the Iranians,
I rushed, like an eagle in the air or a vessel on water,
To ask the world king what secret troubles him.

"Astrologers and governors of provinces,
Leaders of all the lands that I know,
From Ghennooj, Dambar, Margh, and Mai,
Have come with their Indian astrolabes
To search into the mysteries of the firmament,
To determine what has provoked the King of Iran
To scorn his rule and sovereignty.
Three things are essential to bring a matter to closure
And to bring the throne to flourish:
Wealth, hard work, and valiant warriors.
Besides these, there can be neither honor nor war.

"Then there is a fourth requirement:
To worship Yazdan and engage in prayer day and night.
The divine creator comes to the aid of those who serve
And rejects those who wish to cause harm.
We shall give generous gifts to the poor,
Donate what we hold as most precious,
So that Yazdan lightens your heart,
So that wisdom may be your mind's shield."

54 | Kay Khosrow Replies to Zaal

Khosrow replies to Zaal wisely: "O aging, lucid man,
Your words and counsel are thoughtful and kind.
Since the time of Manoochehr until this very moment,
You have refrained from tormenting anyone
And have always nurtured virtuous thoughts.
The illustrious Rostam of elephant stature,
The support of Kianians and the army's delight,
Raised and taught Siaavoosh glory and righteousness.
Often troops have fled at the sight of his warrior helmet,
His lion head, his horse's mane, and his mighty arm.
In their haste to retreat, they abandoned their weapons,
Leaving the field strewn with bows and arrows.
Rostam walked tall, at the head of my ancestors,
Leading them steadfastly into battle,
Like a fortune-bearing minister pointing the way to victory.

"If I were to remind you of your name and glorious feats,
I would have tales to tell for one hundred generations.
Yet if one were to compare my praise to your high deeds,
They would appear merely as blame and condemnation.
As for the question you directed to me regarding my actions,
My discomfort, and the fact that my audience hall is closed,
I shall tell you everything so that you know, O great hero.
I have a single final wish, and that is to turn to Yazdan.
I have renounced this passing world with contempt.
I held myself in a stance of prayer for five weeks,
Beseeching the Supreme Judge, my Guide,
To forgive my past sins and to shine a light on my path.
May this temporary dwelling be snatched from me!
May pain and fatigues no longer be my legacy!

May the divine grant me a happy sojourn in paradise,
And may I be guided toward virtue and transcendence!

"Such is my most earnest wish for fear
That I may not renounce the righteous path,
For fear that my head would lose its way,
As in the case of certain former rulers.
I have asked and obtained a great deal from the world,
But I must now prepare for feast.
Yesterday morning, when my eyes surrendered to sleep,
Blessed Sooroosh, sent by Yazdan,
Came to whisper in my ear,
          'Prepare yourself. Your death is imminent.
          The time for trials and tribulations
          As cause for insomnia must end.'

My reign and my concerns for the empire and the army,
For crown, throne, and royal belt have come to a close."

The hearts of the warriors fill with distress
And with a deep sense of loss.
Zaal cannot shake his dismay at the king's words.
He exhales a great sigh and turns to the Iranians:
"This is not the way. Reason has vacated his mind.
From the moment I have cinched my waist,
I have stood in service to the Kianian throne.
But never have I witnessed a king speak this way
And speak so frankly. We cannot remain still.
We must not give our approval to him.
I fear that the deev has inspired him
And that he is turning away from the divine path.
Fereydoon and Hooshang, Yazdan worshippers,
Never extended their arms to reach this limb of the tree.
I shall tell him the truth, even at the risk of my life."

The Iranians exclaim,
"Never did a Kianian utter words of surrender.
We shall support you in regard to Kay Khosrow.
May he never abandon the customs and the path of kings!"

55 | Zaal Reprimands Kay Khosrow

After this exchange, Zaal rises and says,
"O noble and just Khosrow,
Listen to the words of an old and knowing man.
If his advice is erroneous, do not follow it.
But if it feels bitter and true to you, if it closes the door
To ruin and wickedness, do not hold it against me,
For I speak frankly before this assembly.

"Your mother gave birth to you in the land of Tooran.
Where was your cradle? Where was your dwelling?
On one hand, you are the grandson of Afraasiyaab,
Who set his sight only on sorcery, even in dreams.
On the other hand, you are the grandson of Kaavoos,
The wicked one, of wrinkled face and fraudulent heart.
His power, his throne, his crown and belt
Were revered from east to west.
But he wished to rise above the skies
And count the circles through which drift stars.
I gave him many suggestions on this subject,
Spoke to him with bitterness and counseled him.
He listened to my words but refused to follow my advice.
I turned away from him, pained and saddened.
He rose to fly through the air. Then his flight
Was abruptly shortened as he plunged into the dust.
Yet the Creator allowed him to survive the fall.
The ungrateful one returned to the throne,
His head full of dust, his heart full of fear."

"You journeyed into Iran-Zamin.
You organized one hundred thousand men
Armed with swords, dressed in coats of mail,
Wielding bull-headed mace, and ready for battle,
Like fierce lions in the desert of Khaarazm.
Then you rushed out of the vanguard to engage in war,
On foot, in a fight against the brave Shiddeh, even though
The world was not deprived of mace-bearing warriors.
If Shiddeh had defeated you,
Your demise would have opened access
To Iran-Zamin for the powerful Afraasiyaab to enter.
Iranian women and children would have been captured,

And no one could have resisted him.

"Yazdan took pity on you, granting you victory
Over the deadly grip of Shiddeh.
You sent to his death anyone who inspired fear
And did not worship the Just Creator.
And now that we claim it is a time of rest,
Of wearing the attire of feast,
And reveling with gifts and drink,
You burden the Iranians with renewed hardship,
Causing their ailments to be even more severe
And their hearts more aggrieved than during the war.

"You are now abandoning the divine path,
Walking down the tortuous trail of evil, a trail that
Will neither benefit you nor please the world Creator.
If such is your intention, O King, your court will empty.
No one will remain to obey your command.
You will have cause to deeply regret your affairs.
Think hard and do not act according to the will of deevs.
Were you to do so, the master of the universe
Would pluck off your royal majesty.
You would remain overburdened with suffering
And no longer be deemed or called a king.
Yazdan, Dispenser of good and bad fortune,
Is your shelter. You must go there.
By rejecting my advice entirely,
By placing your faith in the hands of the evil Ahriman,
No one will wish to greet you or praise you.
You will be left with neither fortune nor homage,
Neither crown and throne nor kingship.
May wisdom guide your heart!
May holy thoughts preserve your mind from drifting astray!"

Once Zaal completes his speech,
The heroes say in a common voice,
"We approve the words of the aged warrior!
One must not conceal the door of truth."

56 | Kay Khosrow's Reply to Zaal

Zaal's address angers Kay Khosrow,
But he holds himself together for some time, stifling tears.
Then he solemnly reflects: "O Zaal, wise and skillful hero,
You have lived many years exhibiting nothing but virtue.
If I spoke to you harshly before the gathering,
The World Master would not approve.
Rostam would be aggrieved,
And Iran-Zamin would have to endure his torment.
If I were to enumerate Rostam's exploits,
They would surpass the world's wealth.
He has defended me with his body as shield
And allowed my enemy neither sleep nor joy.
Furthermore, I shall answer you gently
And not break your heart with punitive words."

The king raises his voice: "O victorious warriors,
I have listened to Zaal's arguments before my subjects.
I swear by the World Master that I keep myself
At a wide distance from the devious path of deevs.
My entire being reaches for the divine,
Where I find the remedy to my worries.
I have observed this world with a peaceful mind,
And wisdom has been my protective shield."

Then Khosrow turns to Zaal and adds,
"Do not rush to anger. Measure your words.
In the first place, you first declared
That there never existed a man of sense and reason,
Descendant of the Tooranian race.
I am world master, son of Siaavoosh, a descendant
Of intelligent Kianian kings, and yet, I am not a foolish man.
I am the grandson of world master Kay Kaavoos,
Blessed king full of wisdom, the delight of men.
On my mother's side, I belong to the family of Afraasiyaab,
Whose fury deprives one of hunger and rest:
He is the grandson of Fereydoon, son of Pashang.
I have no reason to blush for my race,
For lions from Iran-Zamin, in fear of Afraasiyaab,
Refuse to enter the sea to wash.

"Next, you reminded me that Kaavoos
Prepared a crate hitched up by eagles
And that he wanted to rise above the rank of king.
Know that even the most powerful men
Do not fly into a fit to blame a king.
As for me, since I have avenged my father,
Bent the world to my will with my victories,
Sent to death the one deserving punishment,
The one who enforced injustice and tyranny,
I have nothing left in the world to accomplish,
For the authority of evil men has dissolved.

"Every time I reflect deeply on kingship
And this domination that lasts a long time,
I am gripped by the fear I may transform
Into a king like Jamsheed or Kaavoos,
And like them lose my sense of reason.
Or perhaps I shall take the example
Of the impure Zahaak and valiant Toor.
Both rulers plagued the world with their oppression.
I fear that time, handing over to me the snows of old age,
May precipitate me, like them, to hell.

"Next, you accuse me of having battled Shiddeh
Like a whale full of courage.
Well, I did so because I looked around and failed
To discern a cavalier able to charge with his horse,
Able to measure himself against him alone
And without hesitation. Any man not graced
By divine dignity or on whom the stars do not shine
Would have been crushed in the hands of Shiddeh
And turned into a fistful of dust.
Thus I chose to fight him myself.

"For the past five weeks,
I have opened my lips by day or night,
With the sole purpose of worshipping Yazdan
So that the World Master frees me from my worries
And steals me from this transient sojourn on earth.
I am weary of army, throne, and crown.
I am impatient to depart and have packed my bags.
O you, old and wise Zaal, son of Saam,

You say that the deev set a trap for me.
But I have not gone astray in the darkness.
I have not deviated into the detours of the path,
For if I did, most of my troops would have perished.
Everyone would have suffered greatly from my actions.
I would have captured seeds from farmers.
I would have never sought to fight greed and corruption.
You would then have seen the flame of *Zand* burning in me,
And you would be unable to provide me with sound advice.
Had I been enticed by deevs,
I would have stifled the blaze with water.
I would have caused injury to the warriors.
Since my character was pure and not wicked,
I am privy to entry into paradise.
Understand that my wish comes from divine intervention
And not by command of deevs.
I know not what misfortune will befall you
For the words you have addressed me.
I know not how the Creator will respond to your fate."

At these words, Zaal finds himself perplexed.
His eyes dim. He stands up, shouts a cry,
And says, "O King, Yazdan worshipper,
I spoke in haste like a foolish man!
Your majesty is a saint and a wise ruler.
May you forgive an error thrust upon me by a deev!
I had never heard similar words emitted by anyone,
Whether great or small. Now I realize that your thoughts
Are aligned with Yazdan's way and not the deev's.

"For innumerable years, I have stood before kings,
Cinched at the waist in loyal service to them.
Never did I see a king, in search of a path,
Address the Creator of the Sun and Moon.
Khosrow is our guide.
May misfortune be cast away!
I wish not to part from you.
Wisdom is witness to my troubled heart,
Yet your resolution to leave us must prevail in Iran,
And it will bring grief to many a good man.
We wish not to be separated from Khosrow,

Our just and benevolent master!
May you never witness evil in the world,
For you are our guide and teacher!"

Kay Khosrow approves of Zaal's excuses.
He extends his hand to seize his friend's hand
And directs him to a seat next to him.
He understands that Zaal spoke only
Out of the affection he beholds for the sun-faced king.

57 | Kay Khosrow Relates His Last Wishes to the Iranians

Kay Khosrow says to Zaal, "The time has come for you,
Rostam, Tous, Goodarz, and Giv, and any other warrior
And nobleman to cinch their waists.
Transport tents and royal banner out of the city,
And set up in joy a delightful camp on the plain.
Take the banners of the nobility, take elephants and army."

Rostam obeys the king's command.
The troops strap themselves and load up the tents,
And the Iranians take the direction of the desert.
From one mountain to another, the ground is covered
With a mantle of white, black, purple, and blue tents.
In the middle of the camp towers the Kaaviani banner,
Sending reflections of red, yellow, and purple into the world.

Zaal's tent enclosure is next to the royal pavilion,
Before the troops on the plain.
To his left is world hero Rostam with noblemen from Kabol.
In front of the king's enclosure are the camps of leaders:
Tous, Goodarz, Giv, Bijan, and warrior Gorgeen.
Behind are those of Shahpoor, Gostaham, and their escort.

The King of Kings sits on the golden throne,
Holding in his hand a bull-headed mace.
On one side stands Zaal, and next to him, Rostam,
One bears the stature of a noble elephant,
The other, a ferocious lion.
On the opposite side are Tous, Goodarz, Giv, Gorgeen,

Farhaad, and Shahpoor the brave.
Their eyes fasten on the king in anticipation
Of his verdict and the disclosure of their fate.

The king speaks loudly to them, "O illustrious men,
Favorites of fortune, whoever has sense and wisdom
Knows that good and evil will push on.
We are born into a fleeting world only to die.
Why then such sadness, such worries, such pain?
One day, one's only wish will be to shorten one's existence.
When your back is bent, your fists hold nothing but wind,
Your hearing fails, your body and your mind weaken,
Your eyesight dims, your legs buckle beneath the weight,
You will loudly lament,
          'O Creator, take me! I wish not to linger here.
          I am weary of this dark earth.
          Take me now while I hold on to army and kingship.
          Take me before I lose everything: Glory and dignity.'
I am not yet prepared for the journey, for the consequences
Of of my actions will be revealed in the other world.
Remain in a state of awe before the pure Yazdan.
Do not succumb to a life of comfort on this grim earth.
This day will come and go, as time counts every heartbeat.

"From Hooshang, the world hero, to Kaavoos Shah,
Many have enjoyed royal honors, throne, and crown.
Yet nothing more than their names remains in the world.
No one gets to read the prescription of the deceased,
Many of whom failed to express gratitude to the Creator.
In the end, they had to face their deeds in trepidation.
I am, like them, a slave who stands before the divine.
Although I have spent my life in struggles,
Having worked hard and borne many pains,
I shall die, for I see that no one remains here.
I have detached my heart from this passing sojourn.
Having attained my goals,
I have reached the end of my worries and labors.
I may now turn my eyes away from the Kianian throne.

"I shall access my treasury and bestow gifts
Upon those who have borne hardships in my service.
I shall recount their deeds in gratitude to Yazdan,

Who knows what is just and right.
I shall give to the Iranians what I hold as most precious:
My weapons, my gold, my amassed treasures.
I shall bestow a province to the most powerful.
I shall bequeath my gold, my slaves, and my steeds.
I shall bring a list and distribute the lot,
For I am ready to depart, and my heart
Has severed itself from the darkness of life.
Revel in joy, in banquet, and feast for one week.
Pray to Yazdan that I may be released
From this passing dwelling and that
I may find some peace from my laborious deeds."

The Iranians are confused by Khosrow's statement.
One of them says, "This king has gone mad.
Wisdom has become a stranger to his mind.
I do not know what he is thinking
Nor how he will command the army."

Another says, "His words are inspired by the divine,
Not from a deviating source or path.
No prior king has ever spoken in this manner.
Any man of wisdom would not share such reflections."

The leaders are deeply chagrined.
Joy vacates their hearts, and they survey each other,
Unable to find the key to this grave mystery.
They stand before the king, heads low.
It is as if they are losing their minds.

Zaal addresses the assembly:
"I do not know what will transpire.
What is to be the fate of this throne and crown?"

They disperse in groups.
The desert, valley, and mountain swarm with men.
The sound of flutes and the neigh of horses is such
That you would think they are about to pierce the sky.
In this way they engage in feast for one week,
And everyone forgets their grief and their exhaustions.

58 | Kay Khosrow Relates His Last Wishes to Goodarz

On the eighth day, the king sits on his throne
With his bracelet, his mace, and his Rumi helmet.

As the time of his departure approaches,
He opens the door of one of his noble treasures.
As soon as he does so, he relates instructions
To his executor, Goodarz of Kashvaad:
"Observe what is happening in the world,
Both the evident and the indiscernible.
There is a time when one must amass wealth
And a time when one must dispose of it.
Pay heed to fortified posts, bridges, and reservoirs
That have fallen to ruins near Iran's borders
During our wars against Afraasiyaab.
Seek children without mothers, widows without shelter,
And anyone in need who conceals his misery.
Open for them the treasury.
Be generous, and remain fearful of misfortune.
Observe cities that are now leopard and lion's dens.
Light the fire in any temple
Where the flame is short of an overseer.
Use the riches to rescue injured and disabled men
Who spent their fortunes in the days of their youth.
Finally, you will rebuild, with the aid of this treasure,
The wells that have dried up for a number of years.
Treat the money like a vile thing, and reflect on death."

Then Kay Khosrow commands Goodarz to take
The riches called Aroos, wealth amassed in the city of Tous,
And give it to Zaal, Giv, and to the master of Rakhsh.

He counts the robes and presents them to Rostam.
He gives torques and chains worthy of heroes,
Armor and heavy mace to the deserving Gostaham.
The herds of horses grazing freely in pastures
And their saddles he gives to Commander Tous.
He presents parks, gardens, and palaces to Goodarz.

He turns over to Giv the artillery and precious weapons
With which they suffered the labors of war.

He gives Fariborz, son of Kaavoos, the remaining palaces,
The tents and tent enclosures, great and small,
The stables and the creatures contained within.

Then he takes armor, a helmet, a golden crown,
A torque brighter than Jupiter, and two glittering ruby rings
On which the name of the world king is engraved,
And gives the lot to Bijan, to whom he says,
"Take these as souvenir, and sow only seeds of virtue."

Finally, he says to the Iranians,
"My time has come; my wishes are fulfilled.
May you each ask of me what your heart desires,
For this is the moment for the court to disperse."

The great and noble men shed tears in their distress.
They are consumed by grief, for they are about to lose
The King of Kings, and each one wonders,
"Who will be the heir to the legacy of the royal throne?"

59 | Zaal Asks Kay Khosrow for Rostam's Order of Leadership

Saddened by King Khosrow's words,
His devoted servant Zaal bends to kiss the ground,
Rises, and says, "O world master,
I find myself unable to conceal my wish.
You know Rostam's sacrifices in defense of Iran-Zamin,
In battle, in labor, in danger, and in wars.
When Kay Kaavoos journeyed to Mazandaran,
He followed him on a long and perilous road.
You know how the deevs chained up Kaavoos,
Along with Tous and the renowned Goodarz.
Rostam departed as soon as he heard the news.
Alone, he rode off in the direction of Mazandaran.
In his passage through the dark desert,
He fought and faced trials and obstacles
Involving deev, lion, witch, and mighty dragon.
Still he forged ahead on the shorter path
And finally arrived in Mazandaran.

"He tore apart the side of the White Deev,
And the ribs of Poolaad of Ghondi, and Beed.
He cut off with one stroke the head of Sanjeh,
And his cries of triumph climbed to the clouds.
Later, when Kaavoos voyaged to Haamaavaran
And he was taken captive, burdened by heavy manacles,
Along with Tous, Goodarz, and Giv, his valiant warriors,
Rostam once again sped on the road with a vast host,
With select leaders from Iran and Zabolestan.
He successfully liberated Kaavoos, Goodarz, Giv, and Tous.

"Let us not forget how, during subsequent wars
In favor of Kaavoos, he killed his own son, Sohraab,
A death that left him grieving for months and years.
Let us not forget how, in the battle of Kaamoos,
He reduced the land to dust with his courage.
He wrestled and killed the violent Poolaad.
He seized Afraasiyaab by the belt
And forcefully flung him to the ground.
After that, Akvan Deev advanced like a wild boar,
Filling the land with his strident screams.
Rostam traveled alone to fight
Both the evil Deev and the King of Tooran-Zamin.
Once he fell asleep from exhaustion,
Akvan came and hurled him into the sea.
Rostam swam to the opposite shore
And proceeded to kill the deev.
At your command, he crawled into the dragon's jaws
To free and rescue the warrior Bijan.
Yet, no matter how long I praise his high deeds,
I would never succeed in enumerating them all.
If the king is weary of his throne and crown,
What will remain for this friend of lion heart?"

The king replies, "His exploits, his labors,
The dangers he submitted himself to on my account,
Who can know the extent of it all
But the Creator of sky, Master of justice, peace, and love?
Rostam's life did not unfold in a concealed way.
He has no equal in any part of the world."

Kay Khosrow calls a scribe, and, with the aid

Of paper, amber, and musk, he draws a certificate
In favor of the warlord, hero of elephantine stature,
Feted at court for his courage,
Champion of troops the world over,
World master, vigilant and victorious army leader.
Rostam, the army's glory, is handed the territory
Of Nimrooz, from Zabolestan to the Sea of Sindh.

A golden seal is affixed to the certificate,
According to Kay Khosrow's tradition.
The king hands it to the hero with many blessings:
"May the world flourish in the care of Rostam!"

The noblemen, holders of astrolabes, who escort Zaal
Receive from Kay Khosrow robes, gold and silver,
And each a cup replete with a variety of gems.

60 | Kay Khosrow Composes Giv's Order of Leadership

Zaal praises the victorious, vigilant ruler and takes his seat.

The wise Goodarz rises and addresses the king,
"O King of blessed fortune, never have I witnessed
A world master of your stature climb on the throne,
From the time of Manoochehr to the time of Kay Ghobaad,
From Kay Kaavoos until the reign of this glorious king,
We have stood with arms in service to monarchs,
At the head of noblemen, never taking time to rest.
I had seventy-eight sons and grandsons.
Now I am left with eight, as all the others have been slain.
The cautious Giv spent seven years in the land of Tooran,
Greatly challenged in his search for food and a place to rest.
In the desert, he made meals out of deer meat
And clothing out of the pelts of wild beasts.
In the end, he led the king to Iran-Zamin, a witness
To all that occurred, and how Giv suffered for him.
Now the world master is weary of throne and crown,
And Giv counts on an act of generosity."

Khosrow replies, "Giv has done much more than that.

May he be blessed a thousand times!
May he receive divine protection!
May his enemies' hearts fill with thorns!
All that I have belongs to you.
May your soul rest in peace and your body be safe!"

He commands the scribe to write with musk and amber
On a sheet of silk a decree in the name of the king
Containing a certificate for Ghom and Isfahan,[53]
The residences of great men and the dwellings of princes.

A golden seal is affixed to it,
And the king pronounces blessings over it:
"May Yazdan be pleased with Goodarz!
May his enemies' hearts be full of anguish!"

Then he says to the Iranians,
"May Goodarz never grow weary of high deeds!
Know that he is a memory of me I leave behind.
He is the defender that I place in my seat.
Obey him, all of you, never deviate from Goodarz's path."

The warriors from Goodarz's family shower the king
With blessings and words of praise.

61 | Khosrow Drafts Tous's Order of Leadership

As Goodarz sits, Tous rises, kisses the ground,
And says, "O King, may your life be eternal!
May the hand of misfortune remain at bay!
I am the only descendant of Fereydoon here.
From the time Kay Ghobaad climbed down Mount Alborz,
I have borne weapons in the first rank of Iranians
And have not unfastened my belt since.
On Mount Hamaavan, my body was wounded in my armor,
The only attire I have ever sported.
In the war to avenge the death of Siaavoosh,
The army was under my guardianship day and night.

◇◇◇◇◇◇◇◇◇◇◇◇◇◇
53 Ghom and Isfahan: Two cities in Iran.

"In Laadan, I was unable to save the troops
And found myself trapped in the dragon's jaws.
In Haamaavaran, Kaavoos was taken prisoner,
And Tous had to bear the chain around his neck.
In Mazandaran, I was captive again with the king,
Who caused me to always be in a state of anguish.
Whether good or bad, I have always led his host.
Never did I abandon the troops.
Never did anyone have cause to complain about me.
Now the king is weary of crown and treasure.
He wishes to leave this fleeting dwelling.
What command does he address to me?
What power does he assign to me?
For his majesty knows my faults as well as my high deeds."

The king replies, "Your labors exceed the call of fortune.
Remain the guardian of the Kaaviani banner.
As leader, retain the right to wear the golden boots.
Your part in the world is Khorasan.
The great men of the land will seek your protection."

A decree is drawn up to secure the ownership,
And a golden seal is attached to it.
Kay Khosrow gives Tous a golden torque and a golden belt,
Utters many a blessing on him, and says,
"Never did I have any cause to think poorly of you!"

62 | Kay Khosrow Hands Kingship to Lohraasp

Once the affairs of the noblemen are settled,
The King of Kings takes his seat on the throne.
Among illustrious names on the list of royal decrees
Remains a single one, not mentioned yet,
The name of Lohraasp, whom he summons.

The world king rises abruptly at the sight of Lohraasp,
Blesses him, and extends his hand toward him.
He climbs down the illustrious ivory throne,
Removes from his head the shining crown, relegates it
To Lohraasp, and salutes him as King of Iran-Zamin.

Bidding farewell to the ivory throne,
Kay Khosrow says to Lohraasp,
"May your new throne bring you good fortune!
May the entire world be subject to your dominion!
I hand over to you kingship and treasure
After having suffered much grief.
From here on, use words founded in truth and justice.
Only by way of justice will you obtain victory.
If you wish to maintain good fortune,
Prohibit the deev access to your heart.
Be wise, and do not submit to bouts of anger,
Be watchful of the words you speak."

Then he turns to the Iranians to say,
"May you live in joy in the shadow of this throne
And by the influence of the king's good fortune!"

The Iranians are stunned by these words.
They blush like wild lions, bewildered that
They are to consider Lohraasp their king.

Zaal rises in their midst and speaks frankly
And from the heart to the magnificent king,
"O distinguished monarch, it may please you
To give honor to what is only vile dust.
May the head of anyone
Who calls Lohraasp king be covered in dust!
May the remedy turn to poison!
You advise Lohraasp to rule with justice.
We shall never consent to this wrongful accession.
When Lohraasp arrived in Iran-Zamin to see Zarasp,
He was poor and possessed only one horse.
You sent him to the war of Alaanan.
You gave him army, banner, and belt.
I am unfamiliar with his origins and his skills,
But this sort of king is not in line with Kianian tradition.
In selecting him, his majesty must have overlooked
The highborn men, descendants of monarchs."

The assembly expresses agreement with Zaal's words.
The voice of Iranians rises, saying,
"From now on, O King, we no longer serve you!

We refuse to engage in wars to protect the crown
And throne if the king is to be Lohraasp!"

Khosrow listens and addresses Zaal,
"Do not speak so hastily and so irritably.
Whoever addresses others with unjust words
Retrieves only smoke from the fire.
I wish for you to approve of my decision.
Light is always more beneficial than darkness.
The Creator does not endorse evil in us, and evil men
Have cause to tremble before the rotations of fate.
Yazdan gives one good fortune, the ornament
Of the throne, rendering him worthy of kingship.
Lohraasp enjoys modesty, piety, and a noble birth.
He will be an upright, decent king,
Triumphant and an ally of justice.
The World Creator is my witness when I assure you
That Lohraasp possesses all these virtues.

"He is a pure descendant of Hooshang, world master.
He boasts prudence, wisdom, and integrity.
He is of the race of Pashang and Kay Ghobaad.
His heart is full of wisdom, his head full of justice.
He will wipe out sorcerers, turn them into dust,
And bring to light the path of Yazdan.
His era will be renewed by his counsel, and his son
Of pure faith will rule in the same just manner.
This election is sanctioned by divine command.
Praise him as king for the affection you have for me.
Whoever disobeys my last wishes will lose
The price of the labors he suffered on my account,
He will be regarded as a rebel before the divine,
And on every side his heart will be invaded by fear."

At these saintly words, Zaal extends his arms
And presses his fingers against the ground.
He sullies his lips by bending down to kiss the dust.
He recognizes Lohraasp as king in a loud voice,
And says to Khosrow, world king,
"May you remain forever happy!
May your being ward off the hand of misfortune!
Aside from the victorious king, not one of us

Had knowledge that Lohraasp is of royal race.
By swearing an oath to him, by staining my lips
Against the dark dust, I pledge obedience to him.
Do not ascribe this as my fault."

The noblemen toss precious gems over Lohraasp
And celebrate him as their new king.

After having determined the fate of Lohraasp,
Kay Khosrow turns to his army and its future.
Finally, the blessed king says to the Iranians,
"Farewell, O imperial throne, delight of hearts!
Farewell my faithful warriors!
After I have left this vile earth, I beseech Yazdan,
So that we may be reunited once again."

He kisses the court's leaders on the cheek
And prepares to take his leave, shedding copious tears.
He cries loudly and says, "Oh how I wish
I could take this noble assembly with me!"

The Iranian troops cry in such a way
That the sun in the sky is led astray.
Children and women in their quarters,
The crowds and assemblies in the streets,
Everyone grieves in a state of confusion and awe,
Laments echoing in every intersection.
Noblemen scatter dust over their heads
And tear their robes to shreds.
The earth trembles beneath the woe.

The king says to the Iranians,
"Remember my counsel, point by point.
May anyone who possesses grace and glory
Live joyously in the will of the Creator.
I shall now ready my mind for death.
I shall depart leaving behind a good reputation.
I did not attach my heart to this passing dwelling
Or else Sooroosh would have ceased to be my guide."

After speaking thus, he asks for his stallion,
Shabrang of Behzaad, to be brought from the vestibule.
The troops shout in sorrow as he rides to his royal palace,

His face saddened, his cypress figure stooped.

63 | Kay Khosrow Says Goodbye to His Favorites

Kay Khosrow has four women, fair and as bright as the sun.
No one has ever seen such beauties, not even in dream.
He summons them from their chambers to his side
And reveals his heart's secret to them:
"I am about to leave this fleeting world.
Do not surrender your hearts to grief and worry.
You will not have the chance to lay eyes on me again.
I am weary of this world full of injustice,
And, in my wish to join the pure Creator,
I fail to find a reason to prolong my stay on earth."

Sense and reason abandon the sun-faced beauties.
They wail shouts of pain and affliction.
They tear at their cheeks, tug at their hair,
And shred to bits their musky fineries.

As they regain their bearings, they plead with him:
"Take us away from this fleeting life!
Take us with you and be our guide to happiness!"

The noble king replies,
"You will one day walk down this road,
Just like the sisters of world owner Jamsheed,
Just like prior noblemen and crowned heads of state,
Just like my mother, daughter of Afraasiyaab,
Who crossed so bravely the waters of the Jayhoon.
Where is Maah Aafareed, Iraj's wife,
A woman the likes of which has not been seen?
They all have found their cradles of dust and bricks,
And I know not if they are in heaven or in hell.

"If the earth recounts its secrets, its past and future,
Numerous warriors, crown-bearers,
And the blood of riders abound over
And beneath the surface of the ground.
Whether you wear a crown or a helmet,
The claws and fangs of death will open for you one day.

One must dress in garments of virtue,
An attribute you cannot gain from another.
Do not seek to frighten me with your fear of death,
For the road I see before me is a painless one."

He shouts a cry, calls for Lohraasp,
To whom he speaks at length of his women, and says,
"Here are the beauties and flowers of my garden.
Here are the ones who have shone in my bed chambers.
Allow them to remain in the same residence
And the same palace for as long as you live.
When you are called before Yazdan,
Your deeds must not foster a sense of shame,
Or you will have cause to blush before two kings
When you find me with Siaavoosh."

Lohraasp consents to Khosrow's wishes
And allows the women to live in their palace,
Where they are to remain untouched and unseen.

Then Khosrow cinches his belt
And returns to the side of the Iranians.
He says to them, "Retire to your palaces.
Do not fill your hearts with wounds and anguish.
Avoid getting familiar with this world, a secret enemy.
Always remain happy, and act in charitable ways.
Remember me fondly.
Be happy, trust Yazdan, and depart in joy."

The warriors of the Iranian host press their heads
Against the ground before the king and cry,
"The words of the king are as valuable as our lives,
And we shall heed them for as long as we live!"

64 | Kay Khosrow Travels to the Mountain and Disappears in the Snow

Kay Khosrow commands Lohraasp to take his seat:
"My days on earth have passed.
It is your turn to occupy the royal throne,
In line with our customs and traditions,

Sow only seeds of good deeds in the world.
If you find yourself exempt from worry,
Refrain from feeling pride in the throne and treasury.
Remember that before long your day will dim,
And you will find yourself treading closer
To the end of the road to Yazdan.
Always exercise justice; it will ennoble you
And free your body from this illusory world."

Lohraasp climbs down his horse swiftly,
Kisses the ground,
And maintains himself absorbed in grief.
Khosrow bids him farewell, adding,
"In weaving the framework of justice,
You must act as both the warp and the woof."

A number of elite army leaders, prudent warriors,
Depart to accompany Kay Khosrow.
They are Zaal, Rostam, Goodarz, and Giv,
Bijan the valiant, and Gostaham the courageous.
In seventh place is Fariborz, son of Kaavoos,
And in eighth place is the renowned Commander Tous.

Their procession takes the road, troop by troop.
The king climbs from desert to mountain crest.
They remain positioned there for one week to rest,
Moistening their parched lips and lamenting all the while,
Plunged in a state of despair for the king's intentions.
No one could imagine how this painful affair would end.
Every wise man secretly reflects on the fact
That such a tale has never been heard
Or even imagined in the history of the world.

As the sun peeks its head over the mountain crest,
A crowd of people gathers,
Travelers from all over the world.
One hundred thousand Iranians, men and women,
Come to surround the king with cries and lamentations
That echo through the mountain and shake the boulders.
They howl, "O King, what happened to trouble you
And ignite your serene mind with soot and smoke?
If you have a complaint against the army,

If you have reached a point where you despise this throne,
Tell us the cause, but do not abandon your land of Iran.
Do not surrender this ancient world to a new master.

"We shall be the dust beneath your horse's hooves.
We are worshippers of your Aazargoshasp.
What happened to your knowledge,
Your wisdom, your insight?
What is the meaning of your actions?
You are a rare person to have set eyes on Sooroosh,
A being who never materialized before other kings.
We pray in the fire temple to the Creator to show us
Mercy and shine a favorable light on your sage heart."

An astonished king says to his illustrious men,
"One must not shed tears on what is well and right.
Be grateful to Yazdan, be pious and joyous,
And learn how to appreciate the Creator.
Do not trouble yourselves; we shall soon be reunited."

Then he addresses his company of hero warriors:
The road before me is long and tenuous.
There is neither water nor blades of grass,
Neither greenery nor foliage.
Spare yourselves this road.
Turn your minds toward divine light.
No one can travel through these sands
Without the gift of vast strength and glory."

Three of the famed warriors hear him out,
Obey the king, and march off to return to court:
They are Zaal, Rostam, and the aged Goodarz,
The one full of ambition and wisdom.
But Tous, Giv, Fariborz, and Bijan refuse to part with him.
They accompany him one day and one night
But find themselves exhausted
By the heat of the desert and by the drought.

They observe on the road a source of water,
And Khosrow, world master, goes to it.
They pause by the freshwater spring,
Drink their fill and rest.

The king says to his border patrols,
"Today we shall not go beyond this point.
We shall speak at length of the past,
For after a while you will cease to perceive me.
Once the sun raises its shiny banner of liquid gold
Above the dark surface of the earth,
The time will come for me to part with you.
I hope to then be in the company of Sooroosh.
If my heart rebels against this resolution,
I shall pluck from my body this troubling organ!"

After part of the night passes in darkness,
The renowned king prostrates himself before Yazdan.
He washes his head and body with the fresh water
And recites verses from the *Zand Avesta*.

He says to the noble heroes full of caution,
"I bid you eternal farewells.
The sun is about to reveal its glorious rays,
And from then on you will see me only in your dreams.
Do not linger in these desert sands.
Musk is about the fall down from the clouds.
A great storm will come from the mountain,
To pluck off branches and leaves from trees.
The sky will force down a snowfall so fierce
You will never find your way back to Iran-Zamin."

65 | The Heroes Are Buried in the Snow

The heads of the hero warriors grow troubled,
And they fall asleep sorrowfully.

As the sun raises its face over the mountains,
The king is nowhere to be found.
They disperse to look for him, crossing sand and desert.
They find no trace of Khosrow.
They return like men who have lost their minds,
Hearts heavy and tormented
For having been deprived of their king.

They return to the spring of water,

Full of grief and anguish, lamenting.
They soon give up on ever seeing the world king
Again and bid him one last farewell.

Fariborz declares, "As far as what Khosrow said to us,
May reason always be his heart's companion!"

The others reply, "We are not in agreement.
We shall remain by this source of water tonight,
For the earth is warm and humid, and the sky is calm.
Once we have eaten, we shall sleep by the spring.
We cannot find a reason why we would leave this site."

They take their seats near the spring
And speak at length of Khosrow, saying,
"No one will ever see a more astonishing thing.
Never have we heard such a tale:
For a king to vanish and disappear.
Alas, what happened to his auspicious star,
His wisdom, power, valor, and high stature?
Alas, this King of Kings of incomparable splendor,
More glorious and powerful than any earthly ruler!
Men of good sense will laugh to hear
That he vanished alive to emerge at Yazdan's side.
What shall we recount of this adventure?
For ears will refuse to hear the truth."

Giv says to the noble warriors,
"Never has the world witnessed a greater man
In valor, generosity, justice, and virtue,
In beauty, fame, and high birth.
He presented himself as a mighty elephant
At the head of his army in times of battle.
He shone resplendent, a crowned moon, in times of feast."

After that, they eat what they have and hurry to sleep.
But at that moment a great wind brings dense clouds,
And the sky takes on the appearance of a lion's hide.
Snow falls down like an expanding
White sail on a ship, so deep and so heavy,
It spreads an even covering on the ground,
Making the spears of heroes disappear beneath.

The brave leaders Tous, Bijan, Fariborz, and Giv
Have no idea how to survive the storm,
And they find themselves engulfed by snow.
For some time they stamp around
To pound down the snow.
They manage to form only steep ditches on every side.
But their strength is spent by the effort,
And in the end they lose their sweet lives to the blizzard.

Meanwhile, Rostam remains on the mountain
With Zaal, Goodarz, and a number of cavaliers.
They spend three days shedding copious tears.
On the fourth day, as the shining sun rises, they say,
"This matter is dragging on far too long.
We have spent a long time among these boulders.
If the king has disappeared from the earth like the sky's
Unleashed wind, where are the other world heroes?
I fear they may not have heeded the king's advice."

They spend one week on the mountaintop
And are completely discouraged by the seventh day.
They wander here and there, lamenting and sobbing,
And being consumed by the blaze of grief.

Goodarz, son of Kashvaad, pulls his hair out, sobs,
Tears at his cheeks, and says, "Never has anyone
Endured what I have endured for the race of Kaavoos.
I had an army of sons and grandsons, hero warriors,
Bearers of diadem, who died in the wars to avenge Siaavoosh.
This bitter vengeance destroyed my family.
Now I face the death of another one of my sons,
Who disappeared right before my eyes!
Who has ever endured such astonishing calamities?"

Zaal speaks to him at length and says,
"Reason must reconcile with divine acts.
Unless they find their way back themselves,
How are we going to detect their footprints in the snow?
We must not remain on this mountain where there is no food.
We must return, send men on foot here to search.
They will one day find traces of the king's retinue."

They leave the mountain sobbing with grief,

Each one speaking in remembrance of a son or a parent,
Either a friend or the king,
Once a tall cypress tree, now vanished.

The men leave on foot, find the deceased,
Remove their bodies from the mountain
And carry them to the city. This is the state in which
Their families find these mighty heroes again.
Each one builds their loved one a tomb and wears
The garb of mourning for an extended period of time.

Such is the custom and the state of the world.
We do not remain eternally, not even the best of us.
The world raises one, seizing him from the dark dust,
Plucks the other off the Kianian throne,
Without delighting in one or grieving over the other:
Such is the nature of this fleeting sojourn.

Where are they now, these kings and heroes?
Dismiss from your heart worry for as long as you can.

66 | Lohraasp Learns of the Disappearance of Khosrow

Lohraasp is made aware of the fate of the king
As the army reaches his side and his court.
He sits on the throne with the golden crown on his head,
And the heroes arrive strapped with golden belts.
The most important men, the most illustrious
Among the elite, sit before the new king in counsel.

Lohraasp looks at them, rises, and addresses them
In a high voice with true, benevolent words:
"O army chiefs, you have heard the king's last wishes.
Anyone who does not acclaim me as this era's monarch
Will be contradicting Kay Khosrow's last wishes.
I shall implement every one of his directives.
I shall devote myself to kind deeds
And in every way uphold his commands.
Follow my example and obey his last wishes.
Do not attempt to hide any secret from me.

Anyone who does not submit to the recommendations
Of a king will appear as a criminal in the Creator's eyes.
Reveal to me what you know, good and bad."

Zaal replies, "Khosrow gave you the title of king.
I have surrendered to his will and shall not deflect from it.
You are the king, and we are your subjects.
We shall obey your wishes and your commands.
Rostam and I, and the residents of Zabol,
Vow to remain loyal and committed to you.
Anyone who does not walk down this path
Will be deprived of joy and happiness."

Lohraasp hears Zaal out, thanks him,
And, breathing more freely, he says,
"May your justice and your righteousness
Preserve you from evil and a fall of fortune!
Yazdan has created you
To be a stranger to worry and hardship.
The World Master whose star is blessed
Has given you governance of Nimrooz.
Now I add to it any additional lands you wish to rule.
You will always have a share of my treasures,
For my family, my empire, and myself belong to you."

Then he turns to Goodarz and says,
"O world warrior, reveal to me your heart's secrets."

Goodarz replies, "I am a lonely man,
For I have lost Giv, Bahraam, and Bijan."
He says this and tears to bits his robe of Chini silk
And his tunic of Rumi brocade.
Then the aged Goodarz turns to the noblemen and adds,
"Happy the one whose companion is his coffin!"

The memory of the loss of his relatives troubles him so
That he moans and cries, "Alas, Giv, hero of brazen stature!
Alas, Bijan, sword-brandishing world conqueror!
Alas, my pure-hearted children, my loved ones!
I approve of Zaal's words, conceal no secret from him.
You are king, and we are your subjects.
We shall abide by the treaty that binds us to you
And by our duty of obedience to you."

The great and noble men hail the king and exalt him
By placing their foreheads humbly on the ground.

The heart of Lohraasp is made young again,
His stature rises, and his height grows taller.
He selects an auspicious day to crown himself,
Like Fereydoon of illustrious birth, who did so
On the blessed day of Mehr in the month of Mehr,[54]
At the time when the sun shines on a straight path.
Lohraasp adorns the audience hall with kings
And makes Iran-Zamin shine with new splendor.

Such is the world: At times it guides one to ascend in joy,
And at times it plunges another into a fearful fall.
It allows no one the right to impose his actions,
Neither in manner nor in duration.

Now that I have completed the story of King Khosrow
And his life, I shall turn to the rule of Lohraasp Shah.
I shall address his crown and his kingship.
I shall place him on his throne, by the permission
Of the great victorious king, from whom depend
Hope, fear, and ruin, who fills his friends' hearts
With happiness and who destroys evil men.
The king harbors benevolence for life
And a deep gratitude for the Creator.

Such are the customs, such is the nature of this world.
It turns from this one with scorn,
Then toward another and then toward yet another.

When a heart is ruined by calamities,
The ripened wine removes the rust.
When old age surprises a man,
The ripened wine reintroduces him to youth.
The wine renders evident men's virtues and their mischief.
When a coward drinks, his head reaches Saturn,
And he believes himself to be a hero,
Like a fox who imagines himself to be a devouring lion.
When an unhappy man drinks, he appears joyous,

◇◇◇◇◇◇◇◇◇◇◇◇◇
54 Mehr: The sixteenth day of the month of Mehr and the celebration of Mehregan,
corresponding to the autumnal equinox.

And his cheeks gleam as bright as pomegranate seeds.
The one who holds a cup of wine
Longs only for feast, music, and song.

But you urge me to present you with ancient stories
About the words and the high deeds of good men.
Listen then, and hear the tale of an old peasant bard,
And try to commit to memory his words of wisdom.

PART SEVENTEEN

The One-Hundred-Twenty-Year Reign of Lohraasp

1 | Lohraasp Founds the Fire Temple of Balkh

Once Lohraasp takes the throne of justice,
Once he places on his head the crown of the King of Kings,
He celebrates the Creator by giving thanks.
He says, "Remain full of hope, fear, and respect
For the Supreme Judge, pure and perfect,
Designer of the revolving firmament,
Giver of the glory to his earthly servants.
After creating sea, mountain, and earth,
A palette of sky to spread above, revolving swiftly,
In its midst, the earth, a sphere lacking feet to move around.
Here we are, us humans, living in a state of distress,
Worrying about the capricious fluctuations of our wealth.

"While your heart rejoices, the sharp claws of death await,
Like a fierce lion bearing a grudge.
Let us abandon the urge to greedily aggrandize ourselves.
Let us confess our ignorance.
Let us make use of royal crown and lofty throne
With the sole purpose of exercising justice,
Bestowing peace, and acquiring guidance,
So that our part in this fleeting world
Be not vengeance, curse, and hardship.
I shall exceed Kay Khosrow's commands.
I shall dismiss from my heart hate and greed.
Be just, and justice will bring you happiness.
Enjoy rest, and forget old hostilities."

The noblemen of various lands pay him homage
And call him king of the world.
The blessed Lohraasp continues to enjoy peace
While remaining wise, wealthy, and prosperous.

After this, he sends men to Rum and India,
To Chin and all the world's inhabited lands.
Anyone who is learned, anyone who is a land surveyor
Takes the road and travels quickly to the king's court.

The king himself, who tasted the bitterness of science,

Immediately departs for Balkh, where he establishes
A city with intersections, streets, and marketplaces.
At every junction, he places a fire shrine
To celebrate the feast of Saddeh.
He founds a vast and magnificent fire temple,
Which he names Aazar Borzeen.

2 | Goshtaasp Leaves Lohraasp in Anger

Lohraasp has two sons, as striking as two moons,
Worthy of kingship, throne, and headdress.
One is called Goshtaasp and the other Zarir.
Both have the ability to conquer lions.
Holding first rank in the army in courage and valor,
They surpass their father in every science.
These are two proud princes of blessed lineage,
Grandsons of Kay Kaavoos, world master.

The two sons are the pride and joy of King Lohraasp.
But the king worries about Goshtaasp,
A prince full of vanity, whose head,
After some time, turns against his father.

One day, in the land of Pars, the royal throne
Is placed under a tree that scatters flower blossoms.
Lohraasp invites a number of army leaders.
He asks for a banquet with delicacies, wine, and cups,
And the men spread good humor into the king's heart.

After drinking his wine, Goshtaasp stands and says,
"O just and righteous King, may your reign be joyous
And your name be forever hailed!
The Creator and Kay Khosrow, the just king,
Have bestowed diadem and royal belt on you.
I stand before you as your slave,
The humble servant of your star and crown.
I know of no one among the bravest men
Who would dare appear before me on the day of battle
Except for Rostam, the son of Zaal, of Saam the rider,
Against whom no one can measure himself.
When Kay Khosrow's head filled with worry,

He relinquished the crown to you and departed.
If now you view me as worthy of rule and wish
To bestow upon me the Kianian throne and crown,
I shall remain your slave, as I stand at this very moment,
And I shall acclaim you and declare you as king."

Lohraasp replies, "O my cautious son,
Violence does not suit a royal prince.
If I remind you of the last words of Kay Khosrow,
Listen to me. Do not turn your head from what is right.
This king, giver of justice, said to me,
        'If a weed grows in your spring garden
          And a stream of water feeds it, it will grow strong
          And multiply, devastating the entire patch.'
You are still young. Reflect before you speak!"

Goshtaasp pales at these words and replies,
"You show benevolence to strangers
And treat your own children poorly."

Goshtaasp gathers a procession of three hundred men, brave
And ready for battle, to whom he reveals his secrets,
Then adds, "Prepare yourselves to leave this very night.
Unfasten your hearts and your gaze from this court."

One of them says to him,
"Where will you go? What road will you take?
If you leave, what place of rest will you find?"

He replies, "In India, I shall be received well and with joy.
I have a letter from the King of India, written on silk
With black musk, in which he tells me that if I traveled to him,
He would consider himself my subject and would in no way
Distance himself from my wishes and my commands."

As soon as night falls, he climbs on his horse with his host
And charges away, mace in hand and boiling with rage.

In the early morning hours, Lohraasp receives the news,
Which torments him greatly, forcing his joy to dissipate.
He calls his army's wise men to his side and explains
To them the state of affairs: "Look at Goshtaasp's deeds.
He fills my heart with worry, covers my head with dust.

I raised him to be a hero without equal in the world.
But at the moment I thought he would bear fruit,
He vanished from my garden."

He says this and remains a long time absorbed in thought.
In the end, he summons Zarir and speaks to him thus,
"Select one thousand brave and warring riders,
And march in haste toward the land of India.
Take care to avoid the land of sorcerers."

Gostaham, son of Nozar, takes the road to Rum,
While Goraazeh quickly marches toward Chin.

3 | Goshtaasp Returns With Zarir

Meanwhile, Goshtaasp continues on the road to Kabol,
Heart full of anger and passion.
He comes upon a field with a spring of water,
Where trees overflow with roses.
In this pleasant spot, he stops to rest for one day.
The entire mountain offers him the delights of hunting,
And the river swells with water as tasty as milk.
In the dark night, he summons cupbearer and wine,
And asks for torches to light the water's edge.

Once the world-illuminating sun shines over the mountains,
He and his troops leave the grove with cheetahs and falcons.
Meanwhile, Zarir launches his horse on Goshtaasp's trail,
Galloping for a long time without pause or rest.

At the sound of horses on the road,
Goshtaasp's companions emerge from camp.
Their prince listens attentively and says to his warriors,
"This can only be the sound of my brother Zarir
Approaching, for I hear the lion-roar neigh of his horse.
If indeed it is he, he is not alone
But attended by a war-seeking host."

At this moment, a fierce dust storm rises over the road,
Out of which emerges a banner exhibiting an elephant.
At the head of troops, one can make out the stocky figure

Of the leader Zarir rushing forth, as swift as wind.

Teary eyes fixed on his brother, he runs to him,
On foot and alone, expressing words of gratitude
To the World Creator as he greets his brother.
They embrace and sit in joy on the field.

Goshtaasp, valiant prince, calls his army leaders.
They surround him and discuss all sorts of subjects.
One of the most renowned chiefs says to Goshtaasp,
"O hero of golden belt, the Iranian astrologers,
Able to give depth to knowledge
And to decipher your horoscope,
Say that you will attain kingship just as Kay Khosrow,
That you will be seated on the throne of power.
But now that you wish to become the subject
Of the king of India, we do not approve.
His people do not count as Yazdan worshippers.
They do not align with their ruler.
Mind that your wishes are in accordance
With sense and reason.
A king need not obey a rajah.
Your father has always treated you with kindness,
And I do not perceive any action on his part
That may have caused you the slightest affliction."

Goshtaasp weeps bitter tears and says, "O name-seeker,
You must know that my father shows me no respect.
He wishes to bless the dynasty of Kay Kaavoos,
To whom he seeks to bestow power and royal crown.
Neither you nor I have a place at his side,
As he plans to continuously reduce us to servitude.
I shall return because of you,
But my heart swells at the thought of Lohraasp.
If he gives me the throne of Iran-Zamin,
I shall worship him like a shaman worships idols.
Otherwise, I shall not remain in his court.
My heart will not calm beneath the moon's rays.
I shall hide somewhere far from reach
And surrender the empire and everything in it to Lohraasp."
He says this and abandons the field to go to the exalted king.

News of his approach reaches Lohraasp and the noblemen,
Who set on the road with a procession to greet him.
At the sight of his father, the ambitious young man
Dismounts and walks over to him to honor him.

Lohraasp holds Goshtaasp close to his chest,
And his son's repentance returns his mind's serenity.
He says, "May the crown remain as brilliant as the moon!
May you vanquish the evil Deev,
For he would continuously guide you on a wicked path,
Like a wicked vizier may do to a wicked king.
I am master of crown and throne in name only.
To you belong love of subjects, authority, treaties, and riches."

Goshtaasp replies, "O King and father,
I stand before your gate as your lowly servant.
If you were to diminish my joy and status,
My life would remain the gauge of my loyalty."

The noblemen depart with him, marching with pomp
And strutting all the way to the king's palace.
The king asks for the hall to be decorated with jewels,
For spreads be placed, and healthy wine brought.

A dazzling banquet is celebrated as if the stars
Circling the moon cascade down on the hall.
The great leaders reach such a state of inebriation
That each places a crown of roses on his own head.

The festivities complete, some time passes.
Goshtaasp fails to receive a fatherly show of kindness.
Lohraasp fondly remembers the family of Kaavoos
And does not cease to speak of Kay Khosrow.
Goshtaasp spills spiteful blood tears
And holds with his confidant lengthy talks:
"No matter how hard I wrestle with my mind,
I cannot find a way to support this behavior.
If I leave with cavaliers, as it suits a prince,
My father will send someone with an army
To bring me back by any means.
He will burden me with demands and counsel.
If I leave alone, I shall do so in shame
And will hold it against Lohraasp.

His heart is devoted to Kaavoos's family,
And his affection is never for his own sons.
Well then, if I leave by myself,
How will people be assured that I am a noble prince?"

4 | Goshtaasp Departs for Rum

In the dark night, Goshtaasp places his saddle
On a black horse belonging to Lohraasp.
He dresses in a tunic of Rumi brocade,
Attaches an eagle feather to his diadem,
And loads up as many dinars
And precious gems as he can.
He leaves Iran and takes the road to Rum,
His heart eager to capture the throne,
His mind anxious to find the correct path.

Upon learning of his undertaking,
His father squirms in anguish and his joy vanishes.
He calls Zarir and wise men to his side and speaks
To them at length on the subject of Goshtaasp:
"This man of lion heart lowers royal heads to the dust.
What do you think? What remedy do you propose?
Do not take this matter lightly."

One of the sages replies, "O King of fortunate path,
May men revere your throne and crown!
No one has ever seen a son like Goshtaasp.
Never has a warrior heard of anyone comparable.
He blesses and glorifies your kingdom.
Your rivals bow before you in fear of him.
Send noblemen full of heart in every direction,
And if he returns, do not show him bitterness.
Prove your virtue and do not follow the path of greed,
For though the sky has seen many crowned Kianians,
It does not grant favors to anyone endlessly.
Entrust an army to Goshtaasp.
Place a glorious diadem upon his head.
I do not see in all the world a hero of his strength
And standing, only Rostam, illustrious warrior.
Never has the world heard of a prince

With his stature, his beauty, his prudence and wisdom."

Lohraasp sends for a number of his noble warriors
And asks them to search the world for his son.
They take the road but return hopeless,
For they left under a latent star.

Lohraasp shoulders the blame of this adventure,
While Goshtaasp has his share of worries and fatigues.

5 | Goshtaasp Arrives in Rum

Approaching the sea, Goshtaasp dismounts.
He greets the guardian of the shores, a generous
And cautious old man named Heshoo, and says,
"May wisdom always be your pure soul's mate!
I am a scribe from the land of Iran,
Wise, insightful, and eager to learn.
If you allow me to cross the water on a boat,
I shall be eternally grateful."

Heshoo replies, "You are worthy of crown,
Or at least of sword and armor.
You are able to obliterate an entire nation.
Reveal to me your secret, trust me with it,
But do not try to cross the sea in this way.
You must either give me a gift or tell me the truth,
For you have neither the manner nor the air of a scribe."

Goshtaasp listens to Heshoo and says,
"I withhold no secret, and I shall gladly do as you wish:
Take my diadem, my seal, my gold, or my sword."

He brings joy to his heart by handing him a fistful of dinars.
Heshoo immediately deploys a sailboat
To take the young man to the opposite shore.
There is a city built by the mighty Salm in the land of Rum,
The seat of noble Caesars. It extends over three farsangs.

Goshtaasp enters this wealthy city in search of work and home.
He roams its streets for one week, feeling unhappy
And regretting having spent his possessions.

He comes across the palace and the offices of the Caesar.
He says to the chamberlain, "O honorable man,
I am a scribe from the land of Iran
Who wishes to acquire name and glory.
I wish to help you in your labors
And would be happy to work in your offices."

The palace scribes signal each other and murmur,
"This man would make a rosebush of steel shed tears,
And his hand would have the power to burn paper.
He must climb on a powerful charger,
Hang a bow on his arm and a noose on the saddle."

Out loud they declare, "O clever man,
We have more scribes than we need.
There is no work here for you. You may go."

Goshtaasp exits the office, heart aggrieved,
Cheeks pale, and heaving a deep sigh.
He goes to Nastaar, the guardian of the king's horses,
A generous man, brave, prudent, and just.
The young prince humbly salutes Nastaar.

The guardian receives him in friendship,
Invites him to sit next to him, and says to him,
"Tell me who you are, for you have
The dignity and the aspect of a royal prince."

Goshtaasp replies, "O illustrious man,
I know how to ride a young steed
Bravely and as it suits a horseman.
If you wish to keep me, I shall make myself useful.
I shall help you with any challenge
Or hardship you may have."

Nastaar says to him, "Do not speak in this way.
You are a newcomer, and there is
No one to testify as to your character.
Here is the plain where horses roam free.
How can I entrust a herd to an outsider?"

Goshtaasp departs deeply troubled.
He says to himself, "Whoever causes his father grief

Is expected to endure even greater travails."
Then he dashes to the Caesar's caravan of camels.
He greets its chief driver and says,
"May your mind always be awake and serene!"

When this sensible man sees Goshtaasp,
He advances toward him and assigns him a place of honor.
He spreads a carpet and offers him something to eat.

Goshtaasp addresses the driver again:
"O blessed friend of peaceful soul, give me a caravan
Of camels and, should you wish, assign a land to me."

The chief driver replies,
"O lion man, this job will never suit you.
Why are you asking for it? We make little income.
You may wish to entreat the Caesar,
Who will place you above all need.
If the road is lengthy, I shall give you a strong camel
And a man to serve you as guide."

Goshtaasp praises him and takes the city road in distress.
His worries weigh heavy on him
As he arrives at the blacksmiths' market.
He finds a notable man named Booraab, a gifted
And happy blacksmith who shoes the king's horses,
A man well esteemed by the Caesar.
He has thirty-five workers and apprentices
Who work hard to mold and shape wrought iron.

Goshtaasp remains at length in the workshop, and,
In the end, the artisan, tired of his presence, asks,
"O benevolent man, what do you want in my shop?"

Goshtaasp replies, "O auspicious man,
I do not fear hard work and would like to help you,
Should you wish to keep me.
I shall work bravely with hammer, anvil, and chisel."

Booraab consents to have him assist in the workshop.
He heats up a mass of iron in the fire
And drags it to the anvil.
He gives Goshtaasp a heavy mallet,

And the blacksmiths form a circle around him.
Goshtaasp hammers such a blow that
He shatters the anvil and the mass of metal.
The market resounds with exclamations of awe.

Mortified, Booraab says, "O young man, neither anvil
Nor hammer, neither iron nor stone will resist your blows!"

A despairing Goshtaasp tosses aside the hammer
And departs, overcome with hunger,
For he has no means of acquiring food or dwelling.
But neither misery nor wealth,
Neither joy nor rest remains for anyone.
The good and the bad pass equally over us,
And whoever has some common sense
Will not allow himself to be knocked down.

6 | A Notable Man Welcomes Goshtaasp Into His Home

Goshtaasp departs, his heart full of worry.
He cries and curses the sublime sky
For dealing out a fate that is poison to him.
Approaching the city, he spots a neighborhood
With blooming trees and running water.
It is a happy place for valiant youths.
He observes, on the water's edge, a tree casting
A long shadow to shelter travelers from the sun.

The young man sits beneath the tree's canopy
In great distress, his soul dim, his heart full of concern.
He says, "O almighty Judge,
This life has given me nothing but grief!
My star is one of misfortune, and I do not know
Why so many calamities must fall upon my head!"

A notable man in these lands, passing by,
Finds Goshtaasp with his eyes full of blood tears
And his chin resting on the column of his fisted hand.
He says to him, "O noble young man, why are you upset?
Why such a somber expression?

If you wish, you can come with me to my home,
Enjoy my hospitality for some time.
Maybe your heart's distress will dissipate
And your eyes will dry out."

Goshtaasp says to him, "O name-seeker,
Tell me, what is your lineage?
From which family do you originate?"

The leader of the borough replies,
"Why do you ask me such a question?
I am from the race of the valiant Fereydoon,
And with such kinship, how can I be despised?"

Hearing these words, Goshtaasp takes the road
At the side of this illustrious one, who leads him
To his home and prepares to receive him as his guest.
He treats Goshtaasp like a brother,
And for some time satisfies all his desires.

In this way many months pass.

7 | The Story of Katayoon, the Caesar's Daughter

It so happens that the Caesar has a daughter
Who has come of age and for whom he seeks a husband.
He holds in his palace a gathering
Of noble, wise, and sensible men, in other words,
All the men equal to him in power and in name.
He proposes that his moon-faced daughter wander
Through them and take her pick among those convened.
She would remain surrounded by her slaves in a way
As to allow no man to discern even the tip of her diadem.

In the women's chambers,
The Caesar boasts three spring flowers,
Three daughters celebrated in the world for their stature,
Their beauty, their grace, their virtue, and their modesty.
The eldest one, named Katayoon, has a sharp spirit
And a serene yet joyous character.

One night, she dreams her nation is lit up by the sun.

She sees a crowd of men appear like the cluster of Pleiades.
At the head of this gathering is a stranger whose heart
Is full of worry and his head full of knowledge.
He is as tall as a cypress tree, as handsome as the moon,
And bears the posture of a king upon the throne.
Katayoon hands him a bouquet of flowers.
She receives one from him full of beauty and fragrance.

In the morning, as the sun begins to shine
And sleep exits the heads of noblemen,
The Caesar convenes a number of brave heroes,
Who merrily take their seats in the assembly hall.
Then he summons moon-faced Katayoon.

She leaves her room surrounded by sixty women slaves
And holding in her hand a bouquet of narcissi.
She travels through the crowd in the audience hall
Until she tires, but no one seems to suit her.
She walks proudly back to the women's chambers
But secretly weeps, for her heart longs for a husband.

The earth is as black as the plumage of a crow.
Once the sun's torch ascends above the mountains,
The Caesar commands the gathering in the royal palace
Of wealthy men of inferior rank living in the land of Rum.
He hopes that one of them would please Katayoon.
The news spreads, and renowned men as well as
Men of lesser rank take the direction of the Caesar's palace.

The leader of the borough says to Goshtaasp,
"How much longer will you remain hidden in this house?
Go to the palace, where you may find crown and throne,
Where your heart will be free of worry."

Goshtaasp hears him out, and the two quickly depart.
He enters the palace, places himself in a corner,
Away from noblemen, and sits wistfully, heart aggrieved.

Clever slaves arrive followed by Katayoon,
Surrounded by rose-colored servants.
She makes the rounds of her father's audience hall.
Behind her are her wise men, and before her are her slaves.
Once her gaze falls on Goshtaasp, she says to herself,

"I see my dream coming to light."
Immediately she decks the head of the happy prince
With her rich and noble diadem.

The vizier runs to the Caesar and cries,
"She has selected among the assembly
A man whose stature is as tall as a cypress tree.
His cheeks are like a rose garden,
And his arms and shoulders astonish witnesses.
We do not know who he is, but he appears
To personify divine majesty."

The Caesar replies, "I shall never have a daughter
Who will taint the women's chambers with disgrace!
Were I to unite my daughter with this man,
It would cover my head in shame.
The only option is to cut off her head
As well as the head of her chosen one."

The bishop replies, "This is not such a serious matter.
In prior times, many princes were selected this way.
Still, you told your daughter to pick a spouse.
You did not insist for her to wed an illustrious prince.
She has selected the one who suits her.
Do not avert your mind from the divine path.
This custom dates back to your ancestors,
Your fathers full of pride, devotion, and virtue,
And through it, Rum has gained its strength.
Do not introduce new paths in this flourishing land;
It wouldn't be worthy of a king.
Do not utter such words,
And do not walk down an unfamiliar path
A path that is unknown to you."

8 | The Caesar Gives Katayoon's Hand to Goshtaasp

The Caesar agrees to give his daughter
In marriage to the illustrious Goshtaasp.
He says to her, "Leave with him,
But do not expect from me either
Treasury or seal, crown or throne."

PART SEVENTEEN

Goshtaasp remains confounded
And addresses lengthy prayers to the world Creator.
Then he turns to the celebrated young lady
And says to her, "O fair woman, you have lived
Surrounded by delicacy and abundance.
What made you select me from among so many princes,
Among so many men, bearers of glorious diadems?
You opted for a stranger unable to give you wealth
And with whom you will live poorly.
Select one who is your equal among noblemen
So that you do not dishonor yourself before your father."

Katayoon replies, "O man of little faith,
Do not be afflicted for what the sky offers you.
If I content myself with my fate,
Why ask for diadem, throne, and crown?"

Katayoon and Goshtaasp exit the Caesar's palace
With sorrow in their hearts and sighing deeply.
By the time they reach the chief of the borough,
They are in a state of utter distress.
He prepares a dwelling for them,
And summons provisions and luxurious carpets.
He says to them, "Live in happiness and joy!"

Goshtaasp gives thanks and praises the glorious lord.
Katayoon possesses innumerable fineries and gems.
Among them she selects a stone of incomparable beauty,
The likes of which no one had ever seen.
They take it to a man, expert in precious stones.

He observes it with infinite admiration and gives them
Six thousand dinars for it, a sum worthy of a king.
They purchase necessary items suitable for a life of poverty.
They subsist for some time with this small amount,
At times joyous, at times somber.

Goshtaasp occupies himself with the hunt,
Spending all day with quiver and arrow.
One day, returning with his catch of various game,
His quiver still loaded with arrows,
His path leads him to Heshoo.

When the latter sees him, he runs happily to him,
Spreads a carpet for him to sit upon, and fetches a meal.
Goshtaasp eats and rests for a short time,
Then he returns to Katayoon as swift as dust.

As Goshtaasp befriends Heshoo, their bond deepens.
He feels him like a second skin because of his vast wisdom.
Any day he spends hunting,
He brings two parts of the game to Heshoo,
As the third part is for the borough chief
Or for one of the eminent inhabitants of the city.

In this way, Goshtaasp lives in friendship with
The borough chief, enjoying the peaceful life of a sage.

9 | Mirin Asks to Marry the Caesar's Second Daughter

In Rum lives an illustrious, wealthy man named Mirin.
He sends a message to the Caesar saying,
"I am a man of high rank, rich and powerful.
The glory of my courage reaches the sky.
Allow me to wed your noble daughter
And thus renew your crown and name."

The Caesar replies, "I shall no longer admit
Any son-in-law as I have in the past.
Katayoon and this common spouse of hers
Took me away from my customary path.
From now on, anyone who wishes to form an alliance
With my family, even if he is of a higher rank than mine,
Must accomplish a high deed so that mighty men
May recognize his power, so that he is celebrated
In the world and may serve me as support.

"May Mirin go to the entrance of the forest of Fasghoon,
Where he will dip his heart, hand, and brain in blood.
He will encounter a wolf as large as an elephant,
With the body of a dragon and the strength of a whale.
It is spiked by horns and bears tusks like a boar.
No warrior, lion, tiger, or elephant,
No matter how valiant, is able to kill the beast.

Anyone who can capture and skin it will be given
The title of my support, my friend, my son-in-law."

Mirin thinks, "Ever since Yazdan created Rum,
My ancestors defended it loyally with their heavy mace.
What is it that the Caesar is asking for now?
Is it with hatred that he speaks to me thus?
I must find a way to complete this mission
And reach the goal in the best way possible."

This man, a favorite of all,
Returns to his palace and reflects at length.
He brings books, places them before him
With constellation boards and his horoscope.
He sees that in some time, an illustrious man is to come
From Iran, a man who would carry out three great deeds
Surpassing any accomplished by noble Rumi men.
First, he would be the son-in-law of the Caesar
And would shine like the crown on the imperial head.
Then there would appear in the land of Rum
Two wild beasts who would harm and destroy people.
Both will be slain by this fearless, powerful hero.

When he learns the story of Katayoon joining her fate
To the valiant Goshtaasp and the friendship uniting
The latter with Heshoo, illustrious chief,
He rushes to Heshoo, relates to him all that occurred,
And explains to him the constellation which,
According to the Rumi wise men,
Forecasts the marvels that would fall upon their land.

Heshoo says to him,
"Remain in my home in friendship and justice.
The man you speak of is an illustrious one.
He spends the entire day in hunt,
Never lending a thought to the Rumi throne.
Yesterday he did not visit my home.
He did not bring joy to my heart by his presence.
But without a doubt, his steps will lead here today,
As soon as he completes the hunt."

He brings wine, and they drink, seated in the midst
Of color, scent, and musicians, golden cup in hand.

After draining four cups of wine, Heshoo and Mirin
Spot the brave cavalier emerging on the plain.
They run toward him on the field.

Mirin takes one look at him and says to Heshoo,
"He has no equal in the world.
This famous hero with his stature, his arms,
And his winsome appearance must be of royal blood
And noble birth, for he appears endowed
With divine majesty and a blessed fortune."

Heshoo replies, "This generous man is a lion
On the battlefield, and his courage, his humility,
And his nobility are even greater than one may presume."

At Goshtaasp's approach, they walk to the water's edge,
Where Heshoo orders a spread with wine and song,
A new sort of banquet with his new young friends.

Soon the ruby-tinted wine colors the men's cheeks.
Heshoo says to Goshtaasp, "O noble hero,
You call me your best friend on the earth.
You are not acquainted with anyone but me.
Meanwhile, Mirin has taken shelter at my side.
He is a renowned, wealthy man, able to write,
A learned man who calculates the motions of the sky.
He can forecast, like the wise Rumi men,
The prosperity or the downfall of the empire.
He traces his ancestry to the family of Salm,
Of whom he remembers the name from father to son.
He is in possession of Salm's sword,
Which he has never parted with.
He is a rider, a hero, a brave lion
Whose arrow scores an eagle high in the sky.

"Now he wishes to be even greater
And to form an alliance with the Rumi Caesar.
He has declared his intentions to him.
But the reply he has obtained makes him tremble,
For the Caesar said to him,
            'There lives in the forest of Fasghoon
            A wolf as large as a camel.
            You must go there, find it, and kill it.

      Once this deed is complete, I shall greet you
      In my palace in Rum as my honored guest,
      As my son-in-law and a powerful prince.
      The world will grant you what is my right.'
Now if you wish to help Mirin, I will be your slave,
And this renowned man will be your relative."

Goshtaasp replies, "I find this matter agreeable.
Now where is this forest?
How can a wild beast cause such chaos
And such fear among men great and small?"

Heshoo says, "This old wolf is taller than a strong camel.
His two tusks are as solid as those of an elephant.
His eyes are red like the blossoms of the fruit of jujube.
His skin is indigo, his horns are like beams of ebony,
And when he is angry,
He pierces through two horses with one thrust.
The many illustrious princes who traveled to the forest
With heavy mace returned either dead or defeated,
Covered in shame, their hearts splitting with fear.
I call this creature a dragon and not a wolf,
For you must know that no wolf is the size of a camel.
If you can successfully defeat this beast,
Your name and reputation will rise above valiant men."

Goshtaasp says, "I shall require Salm's sword
And a blazing and proud charger."

Mirin rushes to his home,
Selects a black stallion from his stables,
A magnificent coat of mail, and a Rumi helmet.
He grasps his rich sword of steel, sharp as diamond,
Once dipped in poison and bloodied by Salm.
He takes from his treasury many presents, rubies,
And five varied, precious stones.

Once the sun tears apart its soot-colored shirt
And reveals itself from beneath the veil of night,
World seeker Mirin leaves his palace and runs to Heshoo.

Goshtaasp, on his side, returns from the hunt to join them.
Heshoo observes him and make his way to him with Mirin,

Stunned at the strength of his horse and the size of his sword.

Goshtaasp observes Mirin's presents,
Selects the horse and the sword, and gives the rest
To the ambitious Heshoo, who is overjoyed.

Goshtaasp dresses quickly in the coat of mail,
Climbs on the battle steed, binds his bow,
Hangs the noose on the saddle's hook,
And thus is settled on his lofty horse.
He feels disposed for the challenge.

Heshoo and Mirin accompany the noble rider
To the edge of the ominous forest,
Trembling for him, hearts swelling with blood.

10 | Goshtaasp Kills the Wolf of Fasghoon

Once they arrive near the forest and the wolf's den,
Mirin trembles at the thought of the horrific creature
And points out to Goshtaasp the location of the dragon.
He and Heshoo return, hearts full of terror, eyes full of tears.

As he parts with the distinguished man,
Heshoo says with certainty to his companion,
"We shall never set our sights on him again.
Alas, his stature, his arm, his face!
Alas, his strength, his mace!"

Goshtaasp approaches the forest,
His fretting heart set on battle.
He climbs down from his proud horse to pray:
 "O Creator, pure and perfect, you nurture all beings.
You dictate the rotations of fate.
Come to my aid in this dangerous feat.
Have pity for the soul of the aging Lohraasp.
If this powerful dragon, called a wolf by foolish men,
Succeeds in vanquishing me,
My father, when he learns of my defeat,
Will weep bitterly and lose sleep for the rest of his days.
He will remain in the throes of grief like a madman,

Wandering here and there, shouting, looking for my trail.
If I run away, afraid of the evil beast,
I will have to hide in shame before the world."

At the end of his address, he climbs on his charger,
Shouting and boiling with ardor, sword in hand,
Girded with bow and arrow hanging on his arm.
In this way he advances prudently, heart pumping wildly.

Once he arrives at the den, he makes his voice explode,
Like thunder emerging from a spring cloud.

The wolf spots him at the entrance of the forest,
Shouts a cry that rises to the dark clouds.
He rips apart the surface of the ground with his claws,
Like a lion or a brave leopard.

Goshtaasp sees the dragon, rubs his bow, and extends it.
As swift as wind, he sends a shower of shots at the wolf.
His bow is for him like a spring cloud casting lightning.

The ferocious beast is wounded by the arrows,
His courage awakened by the pain, and he's seized by fury.
He wavers and falls. Then he rises like a large dromedary,
Charges at Goshtaasp, horns pointing forward like a stag,
Body suffering from wounds, and heart swollen with blood.
Once he reaches the rider, he strikes the backside of the horse
With his tusks and splits its skin from testicles to navel.

Goshtaasp draws his sword, drops to the ground,
Strikes the wolf at the center of his head and cracks
His shoulders, back, and chest by cutting him in half.
He bows low before the Master of wild beasts,
Master of knowledge, Master of good and bad fortune
To give homage: "O World Creator,
Guide to those who have gone astray,
You are a Supreme Master and Giver of justice.
The fulfillment of our wishes and victory
Depend on your will and your glory.
Royalty and knowledge bear your name."

After his prayer, he rises, removes the tusks of the wolf,
And exits the forest on foot, marching all the way to the sea.

Heshoo and Mirin sit on the shore, full of worry,
Speaking only of what happened, of Goshtaasp and the wolf.
They say, "Alas, this brave and valiant cavalier has engaged
In a great battle only to be torn apart by the wolf!"

Soon they spot Goshtaasp arriving on foot,
Cheeks covered in blood
And yellow like the flower of fenugreek.
They rise abruptly and shout cries of distress.

They embrace him, sobbing, their cheeks pale,
Lashes flooding with tears like a spring shower,
Asking what happened in the battle against the wolf
And telling him how much their hearts worried.

Goshtaasp says to Heshoo, "O man of sound counsel,
Is there in Rum no fear of the divine to allow such
A fierce dragon to dwell for so long in this land?
This was a beast able to kill anyone in its path
And for whom the Caesar was a mere fistful of dust.
I cut him in half with Salm's sword
And have freed you from such terror.
Go and hurry to see this marvel, look at
The corpse of the evil monster I skinned.
It has the appearance of an enormous elephant
And fills the forest with its width and length."

The two men hurry to the forest,
Happy to hear the news, their hearts at peace.
They find there a wolf as large as an elephant,
With the claws of a lion and the color of a whale,
Split in two in one blow, from head to waist,
As if one had cut out two lions in one skin.

They break out in praise of the illustrious hero,
Who appears to them like the sun to the earth.
They return gaily from the forest
And dismount at the side of the warring lion.
Mirin offers him presents worthy of a brave hero,
But he accepts only one horse and returns home.

At the edge of the sea and near his dwelling,
He is greeted by the clear-sighted Katayoon, who says,

"You left to hunt, and you return wearing a coat of mail
And an embossed sword that can split anvil?"

He replies, "Listen to me, O moon-faced beauty.
A company of wealthy men arrived from my land.
A number of my relatives gave to me this coat of mail,
This sword, and this helmet before taking their leave."

Katayoon brings wine as fragrant as rosewater
And drinks some with her spouse until the time to retire.
These two young people, who observe the stars, lie to rest,
But Goshtaasp is repeatedly startled in his sleep,
For he dreams of the battle with the dragon-like wolf.

Katayoon says to him, "What is making you tremble so
And jump so while no one is threatening you?"

He replies, "I was dreaming of my fortune and my throne."

At this moment, Katayoon understands that by birth
He is of royal blood, a great nobleman, who wishes
Neither to tell her nor to ask for power from the Caesar.

Goshtaasp adds, "O moon-faced wife,
O cypress tree of silver breast and musk-scented hair,
Prepare everything for us to travel.
We are going to Iran, land of the brave.
You will find there a kingdom full of splendor,
And a just and benevolent king."

Katayoon says, "Do not speak so foolishly!
Do not act on impulse!
If you intend to leave our nation, confer with Heshoo.
Perhaps he will help you cross the sea in his boat.
When he brought you here, the world was renewed.
As for me, I shall be resigned to a long period of mourning,
For I do not know when I shall set eyes on you again."

They both weep for their future and the blaze of grief.
But once the sun's rotation brings light in the dome of sky,
The young couple, full of foresight and hope, rises
To make preparations and to speak on various subjects.
They say, "We shall see whether the sky above

Revolves over us with affection or with resentment."

On his side, Mirin swiftly appears at the Caesar's court
And says to the ruler, "O powerful and renowned master,
The wolf can no longer cause chaos and devastation.
His dragon corpse fills the entire spread of the forest.
You must go there to witness this wonder.
He came upon me to attack me, but my arm dealt him
A blow that cut him in half from head to waist.
You should have seen the deev's heart tremble."

The Caesar sits up. His pale cheeks gain color.
He commands buffaloes, wagons, tents be pulled
From the city to the forest to haul the wolf back.

Once there, they catch sight of the once furious wolf,
His corpse cracked open by a bash of the sword.
They attach him to strong buffaloes, and,
Causing the mountains to shake,
They drag him to the field where they display him
For the world to observe this old and terrible wolf
With the appearance of a massive deev.

At the sight, the Caesar rubs his hands in joy
And on that very day calls his chamberlain.
He agrees for his daughter to wed Mirin
And asks for a letter to be written to every nobleman,
Every bishop, patrician, and ruler of every land,
Relating how Mirin, the proudest son of Rum,
Freed the realm of the formidable wolf.

11 | Ahran Asks for the Hand
of the Caesar's Third Daughter

There is a man younger than Mirin,
Whose waist surpasses all the noblemen of Rum,
A brave hero full of dignity, named Ahran.
Of brazen stature, he descends from a powerful lineage.

This prince sends a message to the Caesar and says,
"May this land prosper forever under your rule!

I am superior to Mirin in every aspect:
In wealth, in the power of my sword, and in courage.
Give me the hand of your youngest daughter,
And I shall renew your domain and your diadem."

The Caesar replies, "You have perhaps heard
The promise I made to the Creator.
I swore that my daughter will not select her spouse
And that I will deflect my ancestors' customs.
You must perform a high deed, as did Mirin.
Only after being tested will you be my counterpart.
There is in Mount Saghilaa[55] a dragon bent on destruction.
If you free Rum of his presence, I shall give you
My daughter, my treasure, and a province.
It is the match of the wolf who struck down lions,
And its poisonous breath is a trap set by Ahriman."

Ahran replies, "I shall do as you command.
May my life be the assurance of my good will."

He leaves the Caesar's side, heart simmering with blood.
He says to his friends, "This deathly blow of the wolf
Could only be from the sword of a powerful warrior.
It is doubtful that Mirin was capable of such a deed.
The Caesar cannot distinguish one man from another.
I shall find Mirin and ask him a few questions.
He will perhaps point to someone who has a solution."

He rushes to Mirin's palace
And sends a servant to announce his visit.
Mirin has a hall so magnificent
Not even the moon in its orbit has the likes of it.
He is an ambitious man, haughty and brave,
Bearer of a diadem akin to the Caesar's crown.

A servant announces Ahran of elephant stature.
Mirin decks his hall with even greater magnificence,
And his main servants exit to receive Ahran and his escort.

Mirin embraces Ahran, asks after his health,
Then dismisses everyone from the audience hall.

◇◇◇◇◇◇◇◇◇◇◇◇◇◇
55 Mount Saghilaa: Appears to be a fictional mountain in Rum.

The two princes sit alone on the throne.

Ahran says to him, "Answer my questions truthfully,
Without attempting to deceive me.
I wish to marry the daughter of the Caesar,
The greatest lady in all of Rum.
I expressed my intentions to her father,
And he demands that I fight the mountain dragon.
Tell me about your battle with the wolf.
Serve me as guide and mentor in this mission."

Mirin grows troubled, fearing that it would be useless to lie
To Ahran about the lengths Goshtaasp went to on his behalf.
He thinks that a man should, above all,
Behave with dignity and speak the truth,
As tortuous, dark paths can only lead to tears.
Perhaps the brave Goshtaasp could strike the dragon's head,
And then he and Ahran would be friends,
Their enemies left with nothing but wind.
Later, they could kill the rider Goshtaasp,
And their secrets would be safe.

He says to Ahran, "I shall tell you what happened
With the wolf after you swear an oath
Never to speak of this secret to anyone,
Never to open your lips on this matter."

Ahran immediately utters a solemn pledge
In acceptance of every point of the agreement.
Then Mirin takes up reed and paper
And writes a letter to Heshoo in which he says,
"Ahran, descendant of the Caesar's family,
Is an ambitious prince, wealthy and just.
He asks to marry the Caesar's youngest daughter.
But the dragon will set a trap and attempt to kill him.
He requests your help in finding a way out.
I have revealed to him our past adventure,
Relating in detail the story of the wolf and the rider.
The one who came to my rescue will be happy
To do the same for Ahran, giving in this way power
To two youths in this land like two crown-bearing suns."

Ahran takes the letter and marches to the seashore.

PART SEVENTEEN

The ambitious Heshoo spots him, greets him humbly,
Receives the letter, breaks the seal, and says,
"You never know. Your blooming garden
May one day be damaged by your friends!
A young, glorious stranger gave Mirin his life as pledge,
And now he may perish when he battles the fierce dragon.
Be content tonight of this dwelling.
Settle yourself here and enjoy the sight of the sea.
The illustrious hero will come tomorrow,
And I shall relate to him what you want me to say."

They place torches at the seaside and engage in eating
And drinking wine until the first ray of sunshine spreads
Across the green surface of earth and the blue dome of sky.

At this time, from his spot on the water's edge,
The renowned Ahran discerns a valiant horseman nearing.
He says to Heshoo, "The glorious man approaches!
Look, the sky clouds with the dust stirred by his horse."

As he gets closer, the two lighthearted men run to him.
The valiant rider dismounts
And asks Heshoo for wine and provisions.

Heshoo rushes to address him, "O distinguished man,
May you be joyful day and night!
Look at this descendant of the Caesar
Who brings joy to the revolving dome of sky.
Not only is he from a noble lineage, but he possesses power,
A celebrated name, treasure, and all that one may need.
He wishes to become the Caesar's son-in-law
And seeks someone to guide him in this endeavor.
He is equal to the Caesar himself in birth and rank.
He is young, glorious, brave, powerful, and tall of stature.
He has requested the hand of the Caesar's daughter,
But the answer was a new demand by the father, who said,
        'Don't think of it unless you can vanquish the dragon.
        If you are of my lineage, leave the mark of a Caesar.'

"Before noblemen, he speaks only of Mirin day and night,
Emphasizing to everyone that any man who wishes
To become the ornament of the throne
Must emulate Mirin's feats, fame, and fortune.

Now there is, not far from here, a tall mountain,
Offering adequate sites for feast and banquet.
But a dragon dwells on its crest, and the entire land of Rum
Is mortified by the devastation the beast creates.
It sucks the vulture from the breast of air,
Plucks out a whale from the depths of the sea.
Its breath and its poison consume the earth.
Never has anyone witnessed such a thing.
If you succeed in killing it, you will astonish the world.
If the pure Creator comes to your aid in this venture,
The sun will only revolve to fulfill your wishes.
With your stature and your arm's power,
You will successfully defeat the dragon."

Goshtaasp replies, "Go and prepare a long dagger,
One with a strong handle and a tip in the shape of claws.
It must have on both edges sharp teeth like a snake.
Its point must be like a thorn dipped in poison and blood.
It must be sharp and well polished.
Equip me with a charger with covering,
A mace, a sword, and a royal robe.
With the help of Yazdan and my good fortune,
I shall make the dragon plunge from the height of its tree."

12 | Goshtaasp Slays the Dragon, and the Caesar Offers His Daughter to Ahran

Ahran leaves and returns with the requested objects.
Once everything is set at the shore, Goshtaasp mounts
His horse and takes off with his two friends.

At the time when the sun reaches the tip of its spear,
Heshoo points to Mount Saghilaa.
He and Ahran retreat
As the world seeker nears the mountain
That serves as the dwelling of the vicious viper.

The youth places his helmet on the saddle.
He imagines the ease with which he will defeat the dragon.
He approaches the mountain hollering,
Sending a shiver of fright through the beast,

Who attempts to capture him with its breath.
But the young man hooks his quiver on the saddle
And sends a hail of shots toward the dragon, like
A shower of petals tumbling from a pomegranate tree.

The dragon draws closer.
The hero gathers his strength, evades its reach,
And shoves the dagger in the dragon's jaw,
Invoking the name of the Giver of virtue.

The dragon closes its sharp teeth on the dagger,
And the weapon pierces through its palate.
The dragon expels venom until the point of exhaustion,
Flooding the mountain with poison and blood.

At that moment, Goshtaasp, the lion, seizes his sword
And strikes a blow at the head of the brave dragon,
Making its brains gush out over the entire boulder.

The hero, favored by fortune, climbs down from his horse,
Plucks out two teeth from the dragon's jaws,
Then proceeds to wash his head and body.

He brings his forehead to the ground
And gives thanks to the Creator, Master of victory,
For granting him triumph over dragon and wolf.
He cries out, "Lohraasp and the noble Zarir
Grew weary of Goshtaasp, body and soul.
Whether in times of war or in times of feast,
Neither of them ever has dreams of me.
Fate hands me nothing but anguish and misery,
And nourishes me only with bitter poison.
Yet my brilliant mind, my pure heart, and my strength
Availed to bring down a massive dragon.
May Yazdan grant me life, long enough
For me to set my eyes, if only once,
On the king's face so that I may say to him,
'What purpose did it serve to seek the throne?
Look at me who went after it
While fortune left my side.'"

Then he climbs on his charger, cheeks flooding with tears,
His shining dagger in his hand.

He nears Heshoo and Ahran, and recounts his exploits.

He says to Ahran,
"This sharp dagger destroyed the dragon.
You were fearful of its powerful breath
As well as the fight against the wolf.
I fear an even greater, more challenging fight
With proud leaders armed with heavy mace
Over a battle with a whale emerging
From the water's depths and armed with claws.
I have seen many a dragon like this one,
And never have I declined to fight against them."

Heshoo and Ahran listen to the young hero,
Whose words and knowledge are worthy of an old man.
These two highborn youths humbly pay tribute to him:
"O fearless lion, never has a mother
Given birth to a warrior of your worth and power!"

Ahran offers him many precious things
And magnificent horses dressed in fineries.
But he accepts only one sword, one golden horse,
A noose, and ten arrows of triple-layer wood.
He gives Heshoo the rest, the dinars, and the new attire.

Goshtaasp says then to his two influential friends,
"No one must ever hear a word of this,
Neither the matter of the dragon
Nor the fact that I heard the howl of the wolf."

Then he departs, happy and satisfied,
And swiftly takes the road leading to Katayoon.

Ahran leaves with buffaloes and wagons,
And gives the dragon's body to his servants, saying,
"Take it to the Caesar's palace,
And place it before the eyes of his noble leaders."

Then he rushes ahead of the buffaloes to the royal court.

All of Rum echoes with the tale of the dragon's slaying.
Worldly men rush to see the powerful beast.
As the buffaloes emerge from the mountain

And begin their march across the plain,
The crowd shouts in awe at the sight of the dragon,
A heavy load for the buffaloes and the wagons.
The voice of the multitude rises to the sky,
Blending with the song of the lark.
One would think that the buffaloes
Are about to yield beneath the weight.

Any witness to the wound caused by the blade
Or the sound of buffaloes and wagons says,
"This blow can only be the workings of Ahriman
And not the striking blade of Ahran."

Meanwhile, the Caesar exits his palace,
Convenes sages and noblemen, and from dawn to dusk
Celebrates the death of the dragon with a grand feast.

As soon as the sun places the crown over its head
And the leaves of the plane trees turn golden,
The Caesar summons the bishop, inquires after his health,
And asks him to sit next to him on the golden throne.

Priests and clerics and the town's men of name
Gather before the bishop with the Caesar and his advisors.
Ahran receives the ruler's daughter in marriage
With the full consent of her caring mother.

As soon as the crowd leaves the audience hall,
The heart of the illustrious Caesar blooms as he says,
"This day is a most auspicious one
As the glorious sky fills my heart with joy.
No one in the world among an assembly of men,
Great and small, has ever seenwo more glorious sons-in-law!"

He asks for a letter to be written to all the princes
Who possess throne and diadem to inform them
That the valiant dragon and the proud wolf
Have fallen prey to the blows of the two famed heroes.

13 | Goshtaasp Proves Himself in the Arena

The Caesar asks for the construction of a forum
Next to his palace, one to resemble a shining throne.
His two sons-in-law present themselves in the arena
And bring joy to his enchanted heart
By casting arrows, playing polo, and throwing spears.

They lurch left and right, guiding their horses
To turn in a perfect art form. One would think
That horsemanship was created only for them.

Some time passes in this manner when
The wise Katayoon approaches Goshtaasp and says,
"O dear one, why do you sit here despondently?
Why do you trouble your heart with worry?
There live in Rum two most powerful men,
Who possess crown, treasure, and diadem.
One of them is the one who killed the fearless dragon,
Having faced many a danger without turning his back.
The other is the one who slit the wolf's skin.
Now all of Rum is full of their names and glory.
They are at the Caesar's arena collecting honors,
Fighting and making dust rise to the sky.
You should attend these events, watch the spectacles.
Perhaps they will relieve your heart's sorrow."

Goshtaasp replies, "O beautiful wife, your father,
Chief of this nation, has no affection for me.
He has banished you and me from the city.
How can he act in a suitable manner at the sight of me?
Yet, if you wish, I shall follow your advice,
For you are my spouse and my guide."

He asks for a speedy, powerful horse to be saddled,
And he departs, soon reaching the Caesar's showground.
He arrives at the time of the polo match.
He asks the players for a mallet and ball, and,
Charging his horse, he sends a ball straight into the riders.

The heroes feel their hands and feet grow feeble.
No one will ever find Goshtaasp's ball in the arena.

PART SEVENTEEN

It completely disappears at the strike of his mallet.
The Rumi riders turn pale.
Spectators and players are in a state of confusion;
The field is in a state of chaos.

A number of brave warriors decide to seize
Bow and arrow of poplar wood and advance.
Observing the tumult, Goshtaasp thinks,
"Here comes the time to exhibit my skills.
He casts aside ball and mallet, seizes his bow,
And the Rumis raise their hands above their heads,
Positively stunned at his skills.

The Caesar glances at his hands, arms, and long stirrups,
And asks, "Where does this skilled horseman come from?
I have seen many highborn riders,
But never have I witnessed one so talented.
Call him so that I may ask him who he is,
Whether he is an angel or a seeker of name."

They call Goshtaasp to the side of the Caesar,
Whose suspicious heart trembles at the discovery.
He lavishes Goshtaasp with the name of brave warrior,
Leader of heroes, diadem of powerful rulers,
And questions him on his land, his name, and his family.

The young man ignores these questions but says to him,
"I am that vile stranger the Caesar cast away.
When I became his son-in-law, he chased me from the city,
And no one had the chance to read my name at court.
Katayoon has been unjustly treated by her father
Because she selected a stranger for a husband.
She has done nothing but conform to the land's customs,
And this righteous act cost her an unfair treatment.
I am the one who brought down the ill-intentioned wolf
In the forest and the terrible dragon in the mountain.
Heshoo has been my guide in these matters.
I have in my possession the teeth of these beasts,
And the edge of my sword is the proof.
May the Caesar interrogate Heshoo on this affair,
For this is a recent happening and not an ancient one."

Later, Heshoo arrives with the teeth in question.

He recounts the two adventures to the Caesar,
Who asks forgiveness from Goshtaasp and says to him,
"O young man, the time of this injustice has ended.
Where is the noble Katayoon?
You have every reason to consider me a tyrant."

He grows angry toward Mirin and Ahran,
Commenting that nothing remains secret forever.
Then he climbs on his swift horse and charges
To the woman of pure habits to beg forgiveness.
He calls for forty beautiful slaves from Chegel[56]
To escort her back to court.
He praises her for holding on to her pledge.
He admires the beauty of her silvery stature
And the depth of her wisdom.
He says, "O my dear moon-faced daughter,
You have selected a husband worthy of you.
As such, you have increased your family's status!"

At the sight of her father in a state of humility,
Katayoon approaches him, arms crossed at her chest,
And pays homage to him, speaking softly into the dust.

Then the ruler says to his daughter,
"With your engagement to him,
You have improved your future.
You are my right eye in the world.
I had no other wish than to see you.
Ask your mate for his origins.
Perhaps he will reveal to you his secret.
Ask him what is his ancestry, his lineage, and his land.
If I were to ask him, he would resort to lying."

She replies, "I have often questioned him,
But never did he come near to revealing the truth.
He does not want to expose his secret to me.
He conceals his home, his land, and his birth to everyone.
He says his name is Farrokhzaad.
My opinion is that he comes from a glorious race,
For he is a brave hero eager to fight."

◇◇◇◇◇◇◇◇◇◇◇◇◇
56 Chegel: Name of a Turkish tribe famous for the beauty of its members.

On this note, the Caesar returns to his palace,
And the sky turns in this way for some time.

One morning, Goshtaasp, full of wisdom,
Rises and presents himself at court.
The Caesar is mystified by the sight of him.
He asks him to sit on a golden throne
And calls for riches from the treasury:
A belt, a ring, and a magnificent royal diadem.
Then he kisses him, places the crown over his head,
And speaks about the events that took place.

He addresses the assembly:
"Remain vigilant, young and old, and obey Farrokhzaad.
Follow closely his command and his example."

The same advice is propagated throughout the empire,
To every king and every prince.

14 | The Caesar's Letter to Elias Asking for Tribute

The closest neighbors to the Caesar are the Khazars,[57]
Who always manage to dim the light of his days.
The prince of Khazaria[58] is Elias, son of the aging Mehraas.

The Caesar writes a letter to Elias,
As if he dips the end of a reed in blood:
"The people of Khazaria exploited us for a long time.
Your happy days end here.
You must immediately send us tribute, heavy fees due
My court, as well as a few of your noblemen as hostages.
Otherwise, Farrokhzaad will come like a furious elephant
And raze your land, converting it to dust."

Elias reads the letter, dips his reed in poison, and replies,
"Long ago, there was nothing of value in the land of Rum.
If I do not ask you for tribute, you should rest at ease.
The courage you rely upon belongs to a single rider,

◇◇◇◇◇◇◇◇◇◇◇◇◇◇
57 Khazars: Semi-nomadic people.
58 Khazaria: Or Khazar, land northwest of the Caspian Sea, which occupies today's
Ukraine.

A man who sought shelter in your midst.
But know that this is a trap set by Ahriman
And that Farrokhzaad, even if he were as strong
As a mountain of steel, is but a single man.
Do not burden him with such a war,
For I shall not allow this matter to last long."

The messenger returns as swift as wind
And delivers the message to the Caesar,
Who grows troubled, his regard for Elias waning.

Mirin and Ahran hear word of Elias and his ruse.
Mirin sends a message to the Caesar, saying,
"Elias is not a dragon that will fall into a trap,
Nor is he a wolf that we can kill with cunning ways,
Who will writhe as we inject him with poison.
Once Elias, in his wrath, attacks,
Farrokhzaad, world owner, will shed tears of blood.
Be prepared that this man, full of pride,
Squirms with fear on the battlefield."

These words further worry the Caesar,
And he pales as he commits himself to obscure strategies.
He says to Farrokhzaad, "You are a noble man.
You are the ornament on the forehead of our land.
Know that Elias is a lion, a horse vanquisher.
When he is irate, he turns into a brazen elephant.
Tell me if you have the power to overcome him,
But do not seek to aggrandize yourself by deceiving me.
If you think you are unable to stand up to him,
I shall come to an amicable agreement with him.
I shall make him come around with gentleness.
I shall shower him with kind words and with fortune."

Goshtaasp replies, "Why such lengthy discourse?
Why such hesitation? Once I climb on my charger,
Whose hooves leave their imprint on the earth,
I am fearless, even before the land of Khazar.
But on the day of battle,
Let there be no mention of Mirin and Ahran,
For they would carry to battle their hatred of me.
Their falsehood and their dispositions are worthy of Ahriman.

When the Khazar army exits its land,
Take my troops' command with one of your sons.
Then, by the strength given to me by the one and only,
The victorious Creator, I shall advance with brave warriors,
And neither Elias nor his army will have a chance of survival.
I shall destroy his power, his throne, and crown.
I shall seize him by the belt, remove him from his horse,
Raise him to the clouds, and smash him into the ground."

The next day, as the sun makes its appearance,
Reflecting its golden shield on the surface of the water,
The sound of trumpets resounds on the side of Khazar,
And the dust rises all the way to the sky.

The illustrious Caesar says to Goshtaasp,
"Now bring out your troops!"

Goshtaasp exits Rum with warriors and heads to the plain.
He advances on the water's edge,
Holding a bull-headed mace like a lithe cypress tree.
He selects his field of battle on the plain
And makes the dust rise to the clouds.

Elias witnesses the man's chest and stature,
The way his hand manipulates his mace.
He sends a rider to him to deceive his subtle mind.

The messenger advances and says,
"O proud man, do not deploy such valor for the Caesar.
You are a lone cavalier without an army.
You are his spring; you are his hero.
Distance yourself from the two hosts.
Why do you maintain this stance, lips foaming?
Elias is a lion on the day of battle.
He will come to you faster than a cloud of dust.
If you wish gifts, he is wealthy.
There is no need to make use of your hand
To tire yourself to obtain the objects of your desire.
Select a portion of the earth to rule over,
And your name will be sung across the world.
Elias will remain your friend and your subject.
He will never cut off the ties of the alliance."

Goshtaasp replies, "It is too late!
There is no point in uttering words that carry no weight.
You are the one who instigated the quarrel,
And now you wish to go back on your word.
But speeches are useless when it is time to fight."

The messenger swiftly returns to Elias with the reply.

As the sun pales on the mountain crests,
It is too late to engage in war.
Night descends and envelops the red visage
Of the sun with a veil as dark as ebony.

15 | The Battle of Goshtaasp and Elias, and the Capture of Elias

The next morning, the sun finds its light
And climbs on the throne in the house of Sagittarius.
The land of Rum glows in a shade of sandarac red,
And everywhere resound clarions and timpani.
On both sides echoes the clatter of weapons,
And the battlefield quickly transforms into a sea of blood.

The Caesar advances quickly on the right wing,
Leading with kettledrums and elephants,
Having left his two sons-in-law near the supplies.
On the left wing, he positioned his son Saghil.
The two armies advance, one squadron at a time.
It is as if the sun and moon are about to wrestle each other.

Goshtaasp bolts to the head of the ranks
On his whale-like charger, clutching a dragon-like mace.

Elias says to his brave warriors,
"The Caesar, secure with a son-in-law as mighty
As Farrokhzaad, demands tribute from me.
The time has come to exhibit our valor!"

The two leading cavaliers urge their horses forward.
They are armed with spear and arrow
So sharp they can pierce through armor of steel.

Elias makes an arrow fly out of his hand,
Hoping to strike and wound Goshtaasp.
But the latter injures the enemy first,
Bringing down a blow with his spear
That sends him crashing down from his horse
Like an oscillating, drunken man.
Then extending his arm, he grabs Elias
To drag him away from his riders
And fling him at the feet of the Caesar.

Next, Goshtaasp charges against the Khazar host,
Dashing across the way like a vicious tornado,
Killing and taking so many prisoners
That the world remains in awe of his exploits.

The entire Rumi army shouts with joy.
Goshtaasp stops to observe it and then retreats.
After having charged his troops,
He returns to the Caesar, head high and victorious.

The Caesar observes him on the road leading the army.
He joyously advances toward him with his warriors.
He kisses the head and the eyes of the nobleman
And falls into a state of grace toward the World Creator.

Then they return gaily to court.
The army chief places a diadem on Goshtaasp's head,
And Rum receives the prince with presents and offerings.
The earth is decked for feast,
Wine is brought along with music and song.
Such is the custom of ever-changing fate:
At times it feeds you honey and at times poison.

16 | The Caesar Requests Tribute From Lohraasp

In this way, the dome of sky turns for some time,
Hiding its designs within its heart.

One day, the Caesar says to Goshtaasp,
"O name-seeker, ask me for a portion of the world.
Think in your mind of my words,

For reflection brings expansion and joy.
I shall send a messenger to Iran, a man of experience,
Wise and noble, and ask him to tell King Lohraasp,
          'You are happy to possess half of the world
          And to own the treasure of illustrious men.
          If you wish to send tribute to me from your land,
          You will continue to enjoy your wealth and splendor.
          Otherwise, I shall send troops from Rum
          That will make the ground disappear
          Beneath their horses' hooves.'"

Goshtaasp replies, "This is your path,
And the era is at the mercy of your foot's sole."

There is a renowned man named Ghaaloos,
A cautious man, wise and of good counsel,
Successful in all his ventures.
The Caesar calls him to his side and says,
"Depart and travel to Iran's royal court
With this message to its king:
          'If you wish to pay tribute to Rum,
          If you wish to obey my command and bow your head,
          You may retain the throne and crown of Iran
          And remain world master of blessed fortune.
          Otherwise, I have numerous troops drawn from Rum,
          As well as from the desert of spear-riders.[59]
          The plain will resound with the crash of weapons.
          I shall destroy your entire nation,
          Transform it into the den of lions and crocodiles.
          We shall surely be triumphant, for Farrokhzaad
          Charges forth at the head of my troops.'"

The messenger takes off, as swift as wind,
Head full of wisdom, heart full of justice.
Once he reaches the powerful king's residence,
He perceives the sublime gate and the tall palace.

The great chamberlain, cognizant of his arrival,
Rushes to the king and says,
"There stands a worldly old man at the gate,

◇◇◇◇◇◇◇◇◇◇◇◇◇
59 Desert of spear-riders: Arabian desert.

Without a doubt an envoy of the Caesar.
He brings with him many famed spear-waving riders
And asks for an audience with his highness."

Lohraasp takes his seat on the ivory throne
And places on his head the luminous crown.
The noblemen of Iran, men of prosperous fortune,
Sit some levels below at his feet.

He commands the curtains be drawn at the entrance
And signals the envoy to be admitted.
Ghaaloos greets the king humbly,
Expressing his deference, then he relays
The message of the powerful Caesar
While maintaining a wise and modest posture.

The king feels wounded by the missive,
A bit astounded by the turn of fate.
He prepares a magnificent apartment,
Asks for wine, music, and musicians,
Sends the messenger carpets of brocade, clothing, and food.
But after feasting, he retires, writhing with worry,
Taking grief and sorrow as his bed companions.

Once the sun climbs on its golden throne
And claws away at the dark night,
Lohraasp summons Zarir and speaks to him at length.

At daybreak, Lohraasp calls for Ghaaloos,
Dismisses the court's visitors and says,
"O sensible man, may insight only nourish wise thoughts!
I shall pose you a question and expect an honest reply.
If you are a man of logic, you would not resort to guile.
Long ago, the land of Rum was not so brave,
And the Caesar appeared humble before kings.
Now he dispatches messengers to all the lands
To claim taxes, or the crown and throne of rulers.
In this way, Elias, a renowned leader in the land of Khazar,
Has been taken by him, and he and his army
Have been reduced to a state of slavery.
Who showed the Caesar this path of ambition?"

The envoy replies, "O cautious king,

I was sent to Khazaria to demand tribute.
I have had to endure much in this attempt,
And no one has questioned me as you have.
But since his majesty received me so courteously,
It would not be right for me to betray him.
A cavalier approached the Caesar,
A man able to vanquish lions with his hands.
He laughs at the most valiant men on the day of battle
And at cups of wine on the day of feast.
Never has your eye seen a rider like him,
Whether in times of war, banquet or hunt.
The Caesar gave him his beautiful daughter,
Who is his most precious diadem.
He is the subject of all the Rumi tales,
For he killed the terribly fierce dragon.
Then there was a wolf, as large as an elephant, in the plain.
No one, not even the Caesar,
Dared pass through the region.
The audacious young man brought the beast down,
Plucking its teeth and liberating the land of Rum."

Lohraasp asks, "O trustworthy man,
Does he resemble anyone, this battle-seeking hero,
Before whom succumbed the fierce dragon
And who has become the object of Rumi legend?"

Ghaaloos replies, "It appears, at first glance,
That he bears a close resemblance to Zarir,
And one would presume that he is
The valiant Zarir himself in stature and mien,
In wisdom and in sound counsel."

At these words, Lohraasp's face blossoms,
And he spreads his grace on the Rumi envoy.
He gives him a great number of slaves and cases of gold,
And lets him leave the court happy and content.
He says, "Communicate to the Caesar
That I am on my way with an army, eager for battle."

17 | Zarir Takes a Message From Lohraasp to the Caesar

Lohraasp remains seated at length, absorbed in thought.
Then he summons Zarir and says to him,
"This man who threatens us has to be your brother.
Find a way to quickly take care of the matter.
Do not waste a moment. A delay would ruin us.
Take with you a vivacious horse, a throne, a crown,
Golden boots, and the Kaaviani banner.
I shall give your brother the kingship of Iran,
And will not demand gratitude in return.
Go to Halab,[60] ready to engage in battle,
And address your army no other words but those of war."

The shrewd Zarir replies, "We shall uncover the secret.
If he is my brother, he is master and king,
And the noblest men are his subjects."

He says this and begins to prepare and mobilize
An illustrious host consisting of illustrious leaders:
The grandsons of powerful and noble men such as Kaavoos;
Goodarz from the family of Kashvaad;
From the seed of Zarasp, Bahraam, lion vanquisher,
And Rivniz; two grandsons of Giv,
Shiruye, world seeker, and Ardeshir;
Two sons of Bijan, two noble lions,
Two heroes of pure race.

These leaders arrive with two stallions each,
Shining like the flame of Aazargoshasp.
They halt only when they reach the land of Halab.
The world fills with battle and the clatter of weapons.

The imperial standard is planted, tent enclosures are drawn.
The leader Zarir places the troops
Under the command of the proud Bahraam.
He himself takes off, disguised as a man
About to bring good news to the king,
And escorted by five brave and prudent friends.

◇◇◇◇◇◇◇◇◇◇◇◇◇
60 Halab: The city of Aleppo in today's Syria.

At the Caesar's palace, he is received by the chamberlain.
The Caesar himself is in the palace, his humor somber,
With Goshtaasp present at his side.

When the Caesar hears the announcement
Of the envoy's arrival, he commands him to enter,
And Goshtaasp is quite content with his presence.

Zarir enters like a tall cypress tree
And sits before the throne and the noble assembly.
He asks for news of the Caesar's health, bids forgiveness,
And expresses polite words to the Rumi men.

The Caesar says to him,
"You have not addressed Farrokhzaad.
Is justice foreign to your heart?"

The noble Zarir replies to the Caesar,
"He is a slave weary of servitude.
He has run away from the king's palace,
And now I find him here enjoying a high rank."

Goshtaasp listens to him without replying,
As he is without a doubt thinking of Iran.

The Caesar, hearing the words of the young man,
Feels his heart's peace troubled by doubt and reflects
That this speech must be an expression of the truth.
Then he continues, "O messenger, relate to us your news.
Let us assess whether it is surly or amicable."

Zarir conveys to the Caesar the message from Lohraasp:
"When the one who is to give justice strays away from it,
He will never find a place where he can rest peacefully.
If you distance yourself from ancient customs and say,
          'I shall from here on establish
          The siege of my empire in Rum
          And not allow many people to remain in Iran.'
You must then leave and prepare for battle without delay.
You have heard my words. Make your decision,
For Iran is not the country of Khazars, and I am not Elias,
Whose power and whose court's power you have crushed."

The Caesar replies, "I am always ready for conquest.
Today I am an ambassador; return then in security.
All we have left is to prepare the battlefield."

Zarir is deeply wounded by the response of the Caesar
And immediately prepares to head off.

18 | Goshtaasp Returns to Iran with Zarir, and Lohraasp Surrenders the Throne to Him

Zarir having risen to leave,
The Caesar turns to Goshtaasp and asks,
"Why did you not raise your voice to speak?"

Goshtaasp says to him,
"Long ago, I served the King of Iran-Zamin.
The army and the royal court are aware of my high deeds.
It is best for me to speak with them and listen to them.
I shall extract from them what is to your advantage.
I shall make your name shine the world over."

The Caesar replies, "You are the wisest,
Most trustworthy man able to grant me
The fulfillment of my wishes."

Goshtaasp, hearing these words,
Climbs on his ardent horse
And goes to Zarir's camp, diadem on head
And wind-footed charger beneath his saddle.

Once the troops spot Goshtaasp, the proud son of Lohraasp,
They march to him on foot, hearts full of grief,
Faces flooding with tears. They bow low at his feet,
Pleased that their enduring suffering is to be curtailed.

As soon as Goshtaasp reaches Zarir,
He dismounts, weary of fight.
He embraces his brother as the latter expresses regret.
They sit on the throne with the nobles,
Surrounded by the powerful men of Iran.

The blessed Zarir says to Goshtaasp,
"May your throne be your life's companion!
Our father is old, and you are young at heart!
Why do you avoid his glance?
Fate makes a laughing matter of his advancing years.
Ill at ease on the throne,
He turns his face toward faith and devotion,
And toward the Creator, pure and perfect.
He bestows on you throne and treasure.
You have no need to expose your body to hardship.
He says that the entire land of Iran belongs to you.
Yours are throne, crown, and army.
A small corner of the world is enough for us
While another man occupies the throne of power."

Goshtaasp asks for the imperial crown,
For bracelets, torque, and ivory throne.
He climbs on his father's throne, his heart blissful,
And places the royal crown on his head.

The grandsons of Kay Kaavoos, world master,
The blessed descendants of Goodarz, such as Bahraam,
Shahpoor, and Rivniz, all those with some merit,
Their army leader, the valiant Ardeshir, son of Bijan
And lion vanquisher, pay homage to Goshtaasp
As ruler and call him world king. The warriors stand
Before him, belts strapped and in full armor.

When Goshtaasp sees the good measures taken,
The determination and the realization of his wishes,
He sends the Caesar a message saying,
"All that you desired from Iran has been fulfilled,
And the words that I hear surpass your hopes.
Zarir and the army rely on your arrival here with pomp.
We shall form an alliance with you by treaty.
We shall forfeit our lives in loyalty to you.
If the desert crossing is not too exerting on you,
Make the voyage to this land.
The affairs of this world progress in your favor."

At the Caesar's court, the envoy recounts
What he has seen and heard in the land of Iran

And relays the message, revealing Goshtaasp's rank
As the eldest and noblest son of King Lohraasp.

The Caesar's cheeks blossom like flowers with joy.
He climbs on his horse and takes off like an autumn wind.
He gallops to the Iranian camp and to the lion warriors.
He sees Goshtaasp on the ivory throne
With a turquoise crown on his head.
They embrace and speak at length.

At this moment, the Caesar comes to the realization
That Farrokhzaad is Goshtaasp,
The one to bestow luster to Lohraasp's throne.
He showers him with praise and adoration.
Then they return to the hall and the throne,
Where the Caesar excuses himself for his past deeds,
Trembling before this astonishing fortune.

The king accepts his apologies, holds him close and says,
"When night descends, we must light some torches.
Send me the woman who selected me for mate,
For she shared with me my pains and my worries."

The Caesar moves away, suffering from fatigue and shame,
And counting in his wicked heart many wrongdoings.
He sends Katayoon assets, a red diadem and five rubies,
One thousand Rumi slaves and servants,
A torque adorned with gems worthy of a queen,
Five camel-loads of Rumi brocade,
And a wise man as guardian of this fortune.

An envoy transfers the lot over to Goshtaasp's treasurer,
Counting the items before him, one at a time:
Arabian stallions in trappings, coats of mail,
Robes of Indian cloth, gold, brocade, crowns, seals,
And all that one is accustomed to from Rum and Chin.

The king distributes weapons and dinars to the Iranian host
And sends many presents to the land's noblemen,
To any descendant of noble lineage, to any skilled archer.
He wants each man to have his share,
And he accompanies his gifts and actions
With addresses to the Creator of time and space.

Katayoon makes her entrance at the royal court
To the bursting beat of timpani.
The army takes the direction of Iran-Zamin,
And the dust raised by the horses invades the air.

The Caesar escorts him for two days,
But then Goshtaasp turns his horse's reins away.
He sends him off back to Rum, swearing friendship,
Showering him with good wishes and promising:
"As long as I live, I shall not ask tribute from Rum,
For my sojourn in your land was a happy one."
He travels in haste to the royal court of Iran,
Land of heroes and land of the brave.

When Lohraasp learns that Zarir, great warrior,
And the valiant lion Goshtaasp are on their way,
He marches off to meet them, escorted
By his land's distinguished princes and powerful men.

Goshtaasp quickly dismounts,
Kisses the ground and expresses his joy,
While Lohraasp rises to embrace his son
And laments about the evil turns of fate.

At the royal palace, they shine as bright as the sun
In the sign of Pisces. Lohraasp says to his son,
"Do not resent me, for it was the will of the World Creator.
It was written above that you must leave your land."
He kisses him, places the crown on his head,
Praises him, and is happy to set eyes on him again.

Goshtaasp says to him, "O King,
May the world never be deprived of your presence!
You are emperor, and I am of lower rank.
I force myself to walk in the dust of your footsteps.
I shall trample the heads of my enemies beneath my feet.
May your fate remain fortunate!
May we never be deprived of your glorious name!"

The world does not belong to anyone for long
Or else it burdens you with fatigue.
Such is this unstable world!
Attempt to refrain from sowing seeds of evil.

One day a man finds himself in search of a loaf of bread;
The next he is bestowed an empire and a throne.

I pray to the Just Creator to give me enough time on earth
To complete this book of ancient kings in my flowery verse.
Then my body, once full of life, will belong to the dust
While my eloquent soul will ascend
To the blissful dwelling of the pure and righteous.

PART EIGHTEEN

The One-Hundred-and-Twenty-Year Reign of Goshtaasp

1 | Ferdowsi Dreams of Daghighi[61]

One night, the poet dreams of holding a goblet
Filled with rosewater-scented wine.
All at once, Daghighi appears to him
And speaks to him of the cup of wine:
"Drink wine in the manner of Kaavoos the Kianian,
For you have chosen as world master
The one to whom fate has tossed crown and throne:
King of Kings Mahmoud, conqueror of lands,
Who shares his royal fortune with everyone,
Whose treasures will never diminish,
Whose pains will not increase for another eighty-five years,
Who will lead his army to the land of Chin,
Where princes will clear the road for him.
He need never speak harshly, for the crowns of kings
Will effortlessly fall into his hands.

"You have made fast progress on this book,
And you will soon attain all of your goals.
I, too, have done my part by having started this epic poem.
If you come across my verses, show me kindness,
As I once composed, before my life came to an abrupt end,
One thousand couplets on the reigns of Goshtaasp and Arjaasp.
If this vast fortune and my labor are handed over
To the Shah of Shahs, Mahmoud the Magnificent,
My soul will rise from the lowly dust up to the moon."

I accepted his words in my dream
And replied to him with gentle speech:
"I shall one day arrive at your side.
I shall one day drink the syrup of death."

I shall now include the words that he poeticized,
For I am alive, while he is the companion of dust.

◇◇◇◇◇◇◇◇◇◇◇◇◇◇

61 Approximately one thousand verses from this section are attributed to the poet
Abu Mansur Daghighi (932-977).

2 | Lohraasp Retreats to Balkh, and Goshtaasp Rises to the Throne

Once Lohraasp hands over his crown to Goshtaasp,
He climbs down the throne and prepares to leave.
He travels to Balkh and the site of Nohbahaar,[62]
A temple built for worshippers of Yazdan, a site
Of pilgrimage similar to today's Mecca for Arabs.

This man full of devotion settles at the temple
And straps himself for prayer.
He bans entry to anyone of a different faith
And closes the door to the glorious temple.
He dons a robe of linen as worn by clerics,
A suitable way to worship supreme wisdom.
He strips himself of bracelets, frees his straight hair,
And turns his face toward the Giver of Justice.
For thirty years he remains before Yazdan,
Engaged in endless prayers to the Sun,
As was the custom of King Jamsheed.

Meanwhile, Goshtaasp climbs on his father's throne,
Inherits Lohraasp's power, his fortune, and his crown.
May a crown serve well the head of a nobleman!

He says, "I am king, worshipper of Yazdan,
Who gave me the powerful diadem
So that I may chase wolves away from herds of sheep.
My hand will not weigh down on those who help me.
As I apply the rules of the king's conduct,
I shall not constrict the world for noblemen
But convert evildoers to the cult of Yazdan."
His just ways spread far and wide, allowing
Sheep and wolf to drink at the same source.

Later, Katayoon, the Caesar's illustrious daughter,
Gives birth to two sons, bright as moons.
One of them is the blessed Esfandiar,
Warrior prince and valiant rider.
The other is Pashootan, sword-striking fighter,

◇◇◇◇◇◇◇◇◇◇◇◇◇
62 Nohbahaar: Buddhist temple.

Illustrious prince, and army-destroyer.

Once the king conquers the world,
He wishes to be another Fereydoon.
World rulers pay tribute to him.
He binds the dim hearts of those loyal to him.

Only King Arjaasp, ruler of Tooran-Zamin,
Before whom the deevs stand as slaves,
Withholds due payment and rejects his advice.
Should he refuse counsel, he would be burdened by chains.
Furthermore, Arjaasp expects tribute from Iran.
But why should one pay tribute to one's equal?

3 | Zartosht Appears, and Goshtaasp Adopts His Religion

Some time passes as a tree takes root in the earth,
A tree growing in Goshtaasp's palace,
Rising above the rooftop with abundant branches.
Its leaves are for guidance; its fruits are for wisdom.
How could anyone fed on such a tree perish and die?
Of blessed trail, Zartosht appears to the world king
And says, "I am the one who killed the evil Ahriman.
I am the prophet and your guide before Yazdan."

Then he brings a pail of fire, adding,
"I bring this blaze from paradise.
The world Creator says to you,
        'Accept the faith. Look at this sky and this earth,
        Which I shaped without the use of clay or water.
        Observe and see how they have been molded.
        Think of who could produce such things,
        If not me who is the One, World Giver.
        If you recognize that I have created this world,
        You must call me Creator.
        Accept from my messenger his good faith.
        Learn from him the path and the worship.
        Take care to do as he says. Allow yourself
        To be guided by wisdom and despise the world.
        Learn true faith and true religion,

For royalty is worth nothing without belief.'"

Once the excellent king hears this doctrine,
He accepts the path of the true faith.
Others follow suit: his valiant brother, the blessed Zarir,
Able to assail the most formidable elephants;
The aging King of Kings retired in Balkh,
Because his wounded heart found the world bitter;
Finally, powerful leaders, learned men,
Physicians, sages, and warriors from around the world.
They visit the royal court wearing the Kushti[63]
And ready to convert to the new faith.

At that time, the grace of Yazdan is revealed.
Evil disappears from hearts. The cult of idols perishes.
Tombs fill with divine light as the cult of fire spreads
And the sown seeds are free of impurity.

The noble Goshtaasp climbs on the throne
And sends armies to all the corners of the world
To establish fire temples according to the rules.
The first fire temple houses the brilliant fire of Mehr Borzeen.[64]
Look at all the cults he establishes in all the lands!

There is a noble cypress tree from paradise.
Zartosht plants it before the door of the fire temple,
Writes on the tree that Goshtaasp adopts the good faith.
He takes this noble cypress as witness to his intention
Of spreading wisdom with justice.

Some years pass.
The cypress tree grows taller than the sky,
So large, its branches proliferating, making it
Impossible to reach around it with a noose.
There, the king raises the foundation for a palace,
Forty cubits tall and forty cubits wide,
A palace built with neither water nor clay,
The interior structure covered in pure gold,

◇◇◇◇◇◇◇◇◇◇◇◇◇

63 *Kushti*: A sacred belt or girdle worn by Zoroastrians around their waists; it has 72
interwoven white strands of sheep's wool representing 72 chapters of a part of the
Avesta.
64 Mehr Borzeen: Iranian fire temple.

With walls of silver and floors of amber.
A statue of Jamsheed is in the hall,
Worshipping Sun and Moon;
Another of Fereydoon with his bull-headed mace,
And numerous figures of prominent men.
Look and see who has ever exhibited such power!

Once this golden palace is completed in all its beauty,
The world king inlays the walls with precious gems,
Surrounds the edifice with an iron enclosure,
And turns it into his royal residence.

Then he sends messages everywhere:
"Where in the world does there exist anything
That resembles the cypress of Kashmir?
Yazdan has sent it to me from paradise,
And through it I may access paradise.
Now all those who heed my advice,
Travel on foot and come to the cypress of Kashmir.
Adopt the faith of Zartosht;
Turn your backs on idols of Chin.
Fasten the sacred girdle of Kushti
In the name and the grace of the Iranian king.
Cast aside your ancient customs,
Rest in the shade of this cypress tree,
And take the direction of the fire temple
As decreed by the true and pure prophet."

His orders are spread throughout the world,
Handed out to noblemen, princes, and crown-bearers
Who arrive to gather around the cypress of Kashmir.
In this way this site of worship becomes a paradise,
And Zartosht binds the deev there.

If you are unaware of its name: The cypress of Kashmir,
You may refer to it as the tree of paradise,
Is the first of its kind to be planted into the earth.

4 | Goshtaasp Refuses to Pay Tribute to Arjaasp

Some time passes.
The stars align in favor of the world master.
The old Zartosht says to him,
"It is not right for you to pay tribute to the ruler of Chin.
It is not worthy of our faith, and I cannot consent to it.
Our ancient kings never paid tribute to Tooranians,
A people without religion, power, and strength."

Goshtaasp welcomes this speech and replies,
"I shall no longer pay these unfair fees."

A brave deev gets wind of this and instantly
Marches to the King of Chin, to whom he says,
"O King of the earth, everyone in the world,
Great and small, obeys your orders.
No one dares refuse your treaties
Except for the son of Lohraasp, Goshtaasp Shah,
Who wishes to direct an army against the Turks.
Furthermore, he has founded a new religion
And renounces the path of idol worship.
He openly exhibits his enmity
And pretends to be independent from you.
I can muster more than one hundred thousand riders,
If you wish, so that we may examine his actions.
Beware of fear that may overwhelm you to battle him."

At the words of the deev, Arjaasp, ruler of the Turks,
Climbs down the throne.
Concern over Goshtaasp makes him weak and ill,
As he has qualms about an attack.

He summons all the wise men
And repeats to them what is happening, saying,
"Goshtaasp has abandoned the ancient cult and faith.
Wisdom and holy greatness have deserted him.
An old, foolish man has come to him in Iran,
Pretending to be a prophet, and said to him,
          'I come from the firmament and from the World Master.
          I have seen the Creator in paradise,
          Who composed the *Zand Avesta*.

> I have seen Ahriman in hell,
> But I could not bear to be near him.
> The Creator sends me to the world king,
> To teach him this religion.'

"The leader of the great people of Iran,
The powerful son of King Lohraasp,
The one Iranians call Goshtaasp,
Secured with girdle of Kusthi.
Then his brother Zarir, brave rider, leader of Iran,
A father figure among warriors and an eye to scribes,
Examined the doctrine, fearing the old sorcerer.
They all have adopted this code of worship,
And the world now scorns our ways.
The old man succeeded in instituting himself
As prophet with lies and foolishness.
He commanded the king to plant a cypress tree
And closed the door to the ancient path with his doctrine.
He showed this man a basin full of fire and a book,
And said to the oppressor king,
> 'This is the *Zand Avesta*.
> Your prayers must be addressed to the blaze.'

"Now we must write a letter to the ruler
So that he may submit to my command.
We must present him many gifts,
For gifts not requested are well received.
We must tell him to leave the road to perdition,
To fear the master of paradise,
To cast away this impious old man,
And to celebrate a feast in line with our ancient tradition.
If he follows our advice, his feet will remain free of bondage.
But if he refuses, if he insists on worshipping the new faith,
We shall renew the ancient hatred and seek vengeance.
We shall unite our scattered troops and lead a vast host.
We shall enter Iran-Zamin to destroy his work.
We shall not fear animosity or resistance,
And we shall drive him before us, abase him,
Tie him up, and hang him at the gallows alive."

5 | Arjaasp's Letter to Goshtaasp

The warriors of Chin agree with him.
They select two of their men: the powerful Biderafsh,
An older, valiant, belligerent sorcerer, a relentless wolf;
And a sorcerer named Namkhaast,
Whose heart is intent on destruction.

Arjaasp writes an embellished letter, full of dignity,
To the illustrious Goshtaasp of new faith.
He begins by invoking the World Master:
"The One able to identify the hidden and the revealed,
Arjaasp, leader of the Chini army,
A brave rider, master of the earth, selected hero,
Wishes to address a well-meaning letter to the world king:
The courageous Goshtaasp, leader of Iran-Zamin,
Illustrious Kianian, worthy of throne, guardian of kingship,
Oldest son of King Lohraasp and favorite."

In this royal letter, full of praise and written
In characters from the language of the Turks,
He further adds, "O illustrious world ruler,
You bestow glory on the crown of the King of Kings!
May your head, soul, and body be forever healthy!
May the back of Kianians never relent!
I have heard that you have selected a perverse path
And that you have dimmed the light of day.
An old man has come, a powerful, deceitful man,
Who filled your heart with fear and doubt.
He spoke to you of heaven and hell,
And has erased all joy from your heart.
You have welcomed him and his doctrine.
You have smoothed the way out for him,
And you have celebrated his worship,
Rejecting the customs of your forefathers,
The noble world kings who preceded you.
You have destroyed the Pahlavi faith of world heroes.
Why did you not look before and beyond yourself?
You are the heir of the benevolent king, Kay Khosrow,
Selected from among the troops and his kin
To bequeath the crown and grant you royalty
Greater than that of the sons of Jamsheed.

PART EIGHTEEN

"Kay Khosrow, the avenging man, and you
Have enjoyed greater honors than any Kianian.
O proud King, power, royalty, fortune,
Force, majesty, grace, shining banners,
Elephants in trappings, a vast host, and
An inexhaustible fortune have been granted to you.
All the noblemen have surrendered to your rule.
You have shone upon the world like the sun
In the month of Farvardin[65] under the ram.
Yazdan presented you sovereignty over the entire world,
And all the princes stand at your feet as slaves.

"But you do not worship the World Creator.
Yours is not the proper path to follow!
When Yazdan made you king,
An old sorcerer led you astray.
When the news reached me,
I saw stars in the midst of day,[66]
And I write this letter in friendship as we continue
To support one another as friends and allies.
Once you complete reading this missive,
Take time to wash your head and body.
Never lay eyes again on the imposter.
Remove the Kushti from around your waist,
And begin to celebrate with cup of shining wine.
Do not reject the customs of your ancestor kings,
Powerful world masters who preceded you!
If you heed this advice, no harm
Will come to you from the Turks,
And the lands of Kushan, Chin, and Tooran
Will be yours in addition to Iran-Zamin.

"I give you innumerable treasures accumulated
With hardships: Chargers of auspicious color,
With golden and silver trappings,
And bridles ornate with precious gems.
I shall send you slaves loaded with presents,
Beautiful women whose curly manes are bejeweled.
But should you reject my counsel, it will be

◇◇◇◇◇◇◇◇◇◇◇◇◇
65 Farvardin: Spans the months of March and April under the sign of the Ram.
66 Reference to ill luck and the dimming of one's day.

As if you are abrading the iron bonds of our friendship.
I shall depart one or two months after this letter,
With an army comprised of Turks and Chinis,
And we shall devastate your entire nation.
We shall bring tents too numerous for the earth to bear.
I shall fill the bed of the River Jayhoon with musk
And drain the waters of the sea with goatskins.
I shall burn your palace and your sculptures
And completely destroy you, from root to limb,
Consume your land with fire from one end to the other,
And sew your shrouds with multiple arrows.
I shall proceed to decapitate all the men of Iran-Zamin
Who are too old to be slaves and are worth little.
I shall take the women and children as slaves.
Your nation will be a desert as I will uproot all its trees.
I have spoken from beginning to end.
Now reflect deeply on this letter of appeal."

6 | Arjaasp Sends Messengers to Goshtaasp

As soon as the king's scribe finishes the letter
In the presence of the noble army warriors,
Arjaasp folds it, affixes his stamp, and hands it over
To wizened old men from the land of sorcerers.

He summons Namkhaast and name-seeker Biderafsh.
He gives them his command, saying,
"Go to Goshtaasp, and say to him,
        'Why do you cover your family with shame?
        If you refuse to listen to his command,
        If you refuse to accept his evil faith,
        You must bring him to your side and burn him
        In order to renew your family's religion.
        If you see that he is Ahriman and refuses to listen,
        You will tell your minister to send him to me.
        Tell all the noblemen to come
        And prepare a magnificent feast.
        Have a scribe read my letter before the assembly.
        Tell Zartosht to give me a quick answer,
        To bring a reason for his faith as a prophet,
        So that I do not show you further hostility.

> If he has a good enough reason, I shall accept his faith.
> Otherwise, I shall refuse to listen to him.
> Guard your heart from falling for his lies.
> Listen to my righteous and proper words.
> You will see that he is not truthful and has no honor.
> Tell Zartosht that he cannot rule over a king.
> You will see that he holds
> Only spells and deceit in his hand.
> Do not believe him when he claims to be Zartosht.
> Hang him alive at the gallows, head below
> And feet above, and refrain from telling anyone.'"

Arjaasp tells his two envoys to travel as swift as smoke,
Escorted by three hundred dagger-wielding riders.
He says, "Be vigilant and go together to the royal palace.
When you find the king on his seat of honor,
Stoop low to the ground.
Extend a greeting worthy of shahs, without
Casting a look at his crown and Kianian throne.
Once the two of you are seated before him,
Then you may set your eyes on his shining crown.
Relay my missive, carrier of good fortune,
And listen carefully to his response.
Once you have heard it to the very end,
Kiss the ground and take your leave."

Biderafsh, eager for vengeance, leaves Arjaasp
And points his banner in the direction
Of the celebrated city of Balkh.
He is escorted by his friend Namkhaast,
The depraved, someone you must avoid at all cost
If you are seeking a good name.

They travel from Tooran-Zamin to Balkh,
Dismount at the king's palace,
March on foot to the threshold of the audience hall.

At the sight of him seated on his throne,
Shining in his place of honor
Like the sun next to the moon, they bow low
Like slaves before the Kianian monarch,
Ruler of a blissful people, and they hand over to him

The royal letter written in the script of Turks.

The world king unfolds the letter and, confounded by it,
Trembles uncontrollably with fury.
He calls to his side the illustrious Jaamaasp, his guide,
And all the representatives of Iran-Zamin,
Leaders, skilled men, and sages.
He asks for the Book of *Avesta*, which they place before him.

He calls for Zartosht and his own brother,
Army leader Zarir, as Esfandiar the rider
Is still too young for such a rank.
Zarir is the shelter of the world and the support
Of the troops, commanding them as the king himself.
He frees the world of evil men.
In every battle, his spear towers over the others.

Goshtaasp says to the assembled wise and noble warriors,
"Arjaasp, chief of Tooran and Chin, has sent a letter."

He shows them the rude words of the Tooranian king,
Adding, "What do you make of this?
What do you say? When and where
Shall we reach the conclusion of this matter?
What misfortune to have befriended a foolish man!
I originate from the seed of Iraj, the pure,
While he comes from the race of Toor, the sorcerer.
How can there be peace between us,
Though I deluded myself into considering him my ally?
Whoever has sound advice may confer with everyone!"

7 | Zarir Replies to Arjaasp

As the king utters these words,
Zarir and Esfandiar draw their swords and cry,
"If there is a person in the entire world
Who refuses to recognize Zartosht as a prophet,
Who refuses to surrender to his word,
He is not welcome at the court of the blessed king.
Should he not stand, strapped as servant, before the throne,
Should he reject the right path and the right doctrine,

We shall make him surrender his soul with our swords
And ultimately hang his head at the gallows."

Zarir, the leader of Iran, valiant cavalier
And leaping lion, says to the world king,
"O illustrious one, if you give me permission,
I shall reply to Arjaasp the sorcerer."

King Goshtaasp consents and says,
"Well then, go and immediately compose your response!
Do it in such a manner as to torture the Turks of Khalokh."

Zarir, the noble Esfandiar, and Jaamaasp,
Happy in all things, together take leave of him,
Frowning and hearts dim with fury.
They address a harsh letter to Arjaasp,
A response worthy to contest with his dispatch.

Zarir takes it in hand to carry unfolded and unsealed,
And reads it to the king.
Goshtaasp, world master, is in awe of the leader,
As well as of Jaamaasp and Esfandiar, son of the king.
He seals the letter and writes his name on it,
Then he summons the envoys and says to them,
"Take my reply to Arjaasp and never return here.
If the *Zand Avesta* does not protect couriers from trouble,
I would have awakened you from sleep
And hung you alive at the gallows
So that Arjaasp, in his rapacity, dares not
Raise his head above this king!"

He flings the letter at them and adds,
"Leave and take this to the Tooranian sorcerer.
Tell him that his end is approaching, that the time
Has come for him to merge with blood and dust.
May his neck be struck and his waist broken!
May his bones be shattered
And scattered beneath the ground!
The Creator willing,
I shall don my armor of steel this very month
And lead my host into the land of Tooran.
I shall obliterate the land of Gorgsaran."

8 | Arjaasp's Envoys Return

After his speech, the king summons his army leader,
Puts him in charge of the envoys, and says,
"March them out of Iran and out of our borders."

The Chini envoys take leave of the world master,
Having been humiliated, rejected,
And treated with contempt.
They abandon the blessed land of Iran
And take the direction of Khalokh.
As they approach, they feel trepidation.
As soon as they discern the royal palace from afar,
Before which is planted the black banner,
They descend from their leaping mounts,
Heartbroken and eyes blinded by tears.

In this way, they march on foot to the king,
Dressed in black and pale of visage,
To deliver Zarir's reply to Arjaasp.

Arjaasp convenes scribes and men, young and old,
And commands them to unseal the letter
And read the contents from beginning to end.

The king, support of Iran-Zamin, brave horseman,
Goshtaasp, son of Lohraasp, worthy world guardian,
Had written: "The Creator sent a prophet to me
Before whom noblemen must stand as slaves
And who says to you,
        'O evil, audacious man, whose face resembles a lion
            And whose body is that of an old wolf,
            You have rejected the true and holy path.'
Your heart is full of obduracy and falsehoods.
Your contemptible letter to me has arrived,
And we have heard words unbecoming of you,
Words that are best left unspoken,
Words that no one must ever write, read, or hear.

"You say that in a few months
You will lead a host into this beautiful land of ours.
You may not need to wait two or four months,

As we shall be the first to drive our lions to battle.
Refrain from straining yourself too much.
We have opened the doors to our treasures.
We shall direct thousands and thousands of troops,
Lion-men from the lineage of Iraj, skilled with spear,
With no relation to the race of Afraasiyaab or to the Turks,
Slender cypress trees always leaning on the truth,
All bearing moon faces and royal statures.
They are worthy of kingship and throne,
Worthy of treasury, crown, and command,
Spear-bearing, lion-vanquishing, army-destroying men,
Worthy of brace and earring, clutching spear and rein,
Each cradling my name engraved on his ring.

"Once they discover that I have strapped timpani
To the backs of elephants, they will flatten
Mountains with their horses' hooves.
Their nature is free of greed and grief.
Once they dress in armor on the day of battle,
They will make dust fly beyond the dome of sky.
Seated on their chargers, solid as rocks,
They will smash mountaintops with their swords.
Two men among them, two brave riders,
The leader Zarir and the noble Esfandiar,
Do not hesitate to attack the firmament
Once they are braced in their iron coats of mail.

"Glory and power gush from their maces
When they raise them above their shoulders.
Beware. You will see them at the head of their army,
Resembling the sun with their thrones and crowns
And their faces radiating majesty and bliss.
They are heroes, chosen leaders,
Men praised by all, agreeable to all, and true sages.
Do not pour musk into the Jayhoon, for I shall myself
Fling open the doors of your miserly treasure.
If the gleam of my sword reaches the river
Or if the wind of my mace reaches your field,
Elephants will weep and the river flows will churn.
The Creator willing, I shall fight you on the day of battle,
And crush your head beneath my feet."

After reading the letter, the Tooranian king
Climbs down his throne, quite perplexed.
He commands his leader to call at dawn
Troops from all corners of the kingdom.

The army warriors, defenders of Chin,
Travel to Tooran-Zamin and unite the hosts
And the leaders of the kingdom's borders.

Arjaasp has two Ahrimans as brothers,
One named Kohram and the other Andariman.
They seize timpani and elephants,
Red, yellow, and violet banners.
The Tooranian ruler entrusts his brothers
With three hundred thousand men,
Singled out as the most valiant cavaliers.

He opens the door to his treasury.
He asks for the blare of trumpets and the packing of loads.
Then he hands command of one of the army wings
To his brother Kohram while giving the other to Andariman,
Keeping for himself the charge of the army center.

Arjaasp gives the leadership of the troops
To a Turk by the name of Gorgsaar, advanced in age,
Who appears to be acquainted only with evil.
Wielding an axe, his nature is worse than Ahriman.
He spends his time, night and day, engaged
In burning and destroying anything on his path.
It is as if he saves his evil ways for himself.

Arjaasp hands his brother Biderafsh
A banner with the figure of a wolf.
He nominates another Tooranian, a man feared by lions,
Named Khashaash, as leader of the scouts
And commander of the army vanguard.
Designated to speak before the king,
He is offered a banner.

Then Arjaasp sends a message to one of his men,
The malicious Hooshdeev: "Maintain the rearguard.
If one of ours attempts to retreat, kill him instantly.
Carry out your mission with vigilance and intelligence."

Arjaasp charges a warrior named Tabah
With the leadership of the army core.

In this way, the Tooranian king is swept by a wave of fury.
Heart swollen with blood, eyes full of tears,
He occupies himself in destroying
And burning homes, trees, branches, and roots.
In this way, the leader of infidels, heart full of hatred,
Leads his troops into Iran-Zamin.

9 Goshtaasp Gathers His Army

Once King Goshtaasp learns of the preparations
For war initiated by the King of Tooran and Chin,
He and his host leave his place of residence,
Sending ahead of him the fierce Khashaash.

The moment he learns of Arjaasp's departure
Toward Iran-Zamin, he directs his army commander
To load up the elephants and equip the troops.
He writes a letter to the leader of his borders:
"The Tarkhan diverged from the path of good men.
Bring your troops to my court,
For my enemy has crossed our nation's limits."

As soon as the border patrols receive the letter
Announcing the approach of the world-seeking enemy,
A great host appears at the royal court with troops
More numerous than blades of wheat on the earth.

The warriors of the entire world arm themselves
To serve the world master, Kianian leader.
The border commandants take the direction
Of the royal court, and before long
Thousands and thousands of men arrive and set up camp
In the vicinity of the illustrious and benevolent ruler.

The blessed king inspects the army at camp
And selects those best suited for battle,
Happy, his mind in awe of the competition.

The next day, Goshtaasp, along with his wise and

Noble leaders, opens the door to Jamsheed's treasury
And accords the army the balance of two years' pay.

Having distributed armor to the troops,
He asks for the sound of trumpets and timpani
And the loading of the baggage.
He commands the imperial banner at the vanguard.
Then he leads his troops to war against Arjaasp.
These are troops such as the world has never seen.

The dust rising from horses and men is so black
That neither the shiny day nor the moon is visible.
The neigh of horses and the clatter of the multitude
Are such that the sound of timpani fails to reach human ears.

Numerous banners are deployed.
The tips of spears pierce through the clouds,
Like trees growing on mountains,
Or like fields of reed in springtime.

In this way, by the order of king Goshtaasp,
The army crosses one province after another.

10 | Jaamaasp Reveals to Goshtaasp the Outcome of Battle

The king and his army exit the glorious city of Balkh
And arrive at the Jayhoon, where they stop.
Goshtaasp dismounts and climbs on the throne.
He calls the illustrious Jaamaasp, his spiritual guide,
Leader of wise men, king of nobles, torch of leaders,
A man of such pure body and soul,
Such clear insight that he can forecast the future.
He is a skilled astrologer, having attained
The first rank in wisdom and knowledge.

The king questions him: "Yazdan bestowed
Upon you the true creed and a lucid mind.
There is no one in the world who compares to you,
As the World Master has granted you all knowledge.
You must calculate the stars and tell me my fate.

What is the beginning and end of this battle?
Who will be struck by misfortune on this field?"

The questions trouble the aging Jaamaasp,
And he answers Goshtaasp with an aggrieved expression,
"I wished that Izad, the Justice Giver, had not qualified me
With these faculties, for then the king would not ask me
To divine what is to come. I shall disclose the future
Or else the King of Kings would sentence me to death."

The king replies, "I vow in the name of the pure Creator,
On the life of Zarir, brave cavalier, on the soul of Esfandiar
That I shall never cause you any harm,
That I shall never order anyone to hurt you,
And that you will never have reason to fear me.
Say what you have to say, and may you discern
A way to save us, as I shall be in need of assistance."

The sage one replies, "O noble King,
May your crown continuously be renewed!
Know, O valiant and illustrious Kianian,
That at the time when enemy warriors face each other,
At the time when they shout cries in the clamor of war,
You will feel like boulders plucked from their bases.
The bravest men will advance.
The air will darken with the dust of fight.
You will see the skies turning gray,
The earth full of fire, the air full of smoke.
Amid the clatter of swords and blows of mace
Tumbling down like the steel hammers of blacksmiths,
The shrill sound of bowstrings will pierce through brains.
The world will fill with the burning breath
Of warriors and horses in the throes of battle,
And loads, vaults, and wheels will shatter.
The flowing waters will be sullied by human blood,
And the world will be fought by sons deprived
Of fathers, as well as by fathers deprived of sons.

"Ardeshir, the famed Kianian son, princely leader,
Will be the first to launch his Taazian steed,
Assailing and slaying anyone opposing him.
He will bring down so many rider Turks

That we shall never be able to assess their numbers.
But in the end he will perish,
And his great name will disappear.
Shiddasp, another royal son, will charge his black stallion
On the trail of Ardeshir to avenge his brother's death.
He will draw his sword in a bout of fury.
He will kill many men in battle,
But his misfortune will be his loss in the end,
And his head, once bearing crown, will be deprived of it.

"At that time, my son, strapped in my belt,
Will dash like Rostam to the center of the battlefield
To avenge Shiddasp, royal son and prince.
Many are the brave and heroic men of Chin
Who will be flung to the dust by this lion man.
He will endure many strains in this struggle,
But dare I reveal to his majesty how, my son Gueraami,
Spotting from atop his horse the blessed Kaaviani banner
Fallen and cast to blood and muck,
Will jump off his steed, grab the standard,
And bravely carry it away, brandishing it in one hand
While wielding his sword in the other.
He will bring down many a foe
And pluck the life out of Ahrimans.
But the time will come when a relentless adversary
Will knock him down and wound him with his sharp sword,
Making the hero seize the purple standard
With his teeth and carry it thus as he continues to fight,
Obliterating many with one hand.
What a strange phenomenon! But not for long.
A Turk will shoot an arrow through his waist,
Bringing his crowned head into the dust,
And making him fade away forever.

"That is when the noble Nastoor, son of Zarir,
Will exit the ranks on horseback, like a brave lion.
He will make many a foe disappear.
No one will ever see a more glorious battle than his.
In the end, he will be victorious,
Having made the enemy feel the strength of his arm.
Nivezaar, son of world master Goshtaasp,
Elite rider, will advance, pouncing on these Ahrimans,

Bringing down sixty of them,
Deploying valor worthy of a great world hero.
Still, the Turks will end up striking him on the head
And flinging to the ground his heroic body.

"The valiant lion, the rider eager for battle named Zarir,
Will in turn advance, armed with noose,
Seated on a dun-colored Taazian charger,
Shining like the moon in his golden armor,
And making the entire army retreat in awe of him.
He will seize one thousand enemy warriors,
Tie them up, and send them to the king.
Whenever and wherever he displays his royal face,
The blood of our enemies will flow in torrents.
No one will dare contend with him, and the king
Of the people who dwell in tents will tremble.

"Zarir will perceive the body of the powerful Ardeshir,
Whose face will be black and his limbs yellow.
He will cry bitter tears, his anger stoked.
He will stir up his Taazian steed of dun,
Take the direction of the Tarkhan,
Full of rage and desire for vengeance,
As if he were going to tear him off his horse.
At the sight of Arjaasp in the middle of his army,
He will sing the praises of King Goshtaasp,
Destroy entire ranks of enemy troops,
And will worry about no one else on earth.
He will recite from the *Zand Avesta* of Zartosht
And place his trust in the divine Creator.
But in the end, his fortune will dim as well,
And this once chosen tree will be brought down.

"A Turk by the name of Biderafsh
Will advance toward this hero armed with a spear
And carrying the purple banner, but he will not risk
Coming face to face. He will set up an ambush,
Awaiting there like a mad elephant,
A poison-dipped sword in one hand.
When the world king returns from battle
As if he is emerging from a feast,
Armor torn and hammer broken,

This Turk, without daring to reveal himself,
Will cast a shot, and the Iranian ruler will perish
At the hands of the vile Biderafsh, who will take
Away to his people Zarir's charger and saddle.

"Who will be the first one to avenge him?
Our entire glorious and powerful army
Will fall on the enemy like lions and wolves.
A formidable melee will ensue,
And the earth will redden with blood.
The faces of the men will pale
As they stagger and fall on one another.
A black dust will fly all the way to the sun,
A dust so thick no one will distinguish the moon.
The tips of spears, arrows, and swords will shine
Like stars bursting through the fog.

"Then the vile and violent Biderafsh will advance
Wolf-like, brandishing a sword dipped in poison,
And riding a leaping charger as fierce as a war elephant.
A great number of renowned heroes
From the royal army will fall under his blows
Until the fortunate Esfandiar, protected by the divine
And followed by devoted troops,
Launches his ardent horse against him,
Eyes full of blood, heart full of animosity.
He will strike him with his Indian saber, and half
Of his body will fall from the heights of his horse.
Esfandiar will seize his mace of steel,
And make his strength and tall stature shine.

"In a single assault, he will shake up the Turks.
When he breaks up the ranks,
Why should he allow them to live?
He will harvest them with the tip of his spear,
Destroy them completely and disperse them.
In the end, the Emperor of Chin
Will flee before the glorious Esfandiar.
He will retreat to Tooran, his shield shattered,
His spear lost, his eyes spilling blood tears.
He will cross the desert with a small escort.
The King of Iran will be victorious

PART EIGHTEEN

And his enemy badly defeated.

"Know, O King of Kings, chosen by the divine,
That I have told you everything that is meant to occur.
You will not hear from me another word.
Cease to cast my way these wrathful glances.
I have spoken only upon your insistence,
O triumphant King! As for the other questions
Posed by his blessed majesty in regards
To the bottomless sea and the obscure path of destiny,
I have seen nothing that I conceal from him.
If it were otherwise, why would I take the pains
To divulge the secrets that I have revealed?"

The world master sits back to ponder the projections,
Sagging in the corner of his throne.
His golden mace slips out of his hands.
You would think that his glory, his grace,
And all his power have abandoned him.
He leans against his face as he falls and faints.

Once he regains consciousness,
He climbs down the throne and weeps bitterly, saying,
"What good are throne and kingship if my days are dim
And my sons, handsome as moons,
Valiant cavaliers and princes, are meant to perish?
What good are empire, fortune, power,
Army, crown, and throne when those dearest to me,
The most renowned warriors, will disappear,
Making my heart leap out of my chest?"

Then he says to Jaamaasp, "Since it is so,
I shall abstain from summoning my brother
When the time comes to march onto the battlefield.
I shall not distress the heart of my aging mother.
I shall forbid Zarir to take part in war
And entrust the army command to the blessed Gorazm.
I shall summon my young and noble sons,
Who are as dear to me as my body and my life,
Forbid them from donning armor
And leading at the head of troops.
How will the tip of an arrow of poplar wood

Reach this mountain and these lofty boulders?"

The wise man replies to the world master,
"O gracious king, if these men do not lead the troops,
Kianian helmets on their heads,
Who will dare advance against the heroes of Chin?
Who will bring back the splendor of our pure faith,
Rise above this dust, and climb on the throne?
Do not allow majesty of royalty to be lost,
For this is the secret of Yazdan. There is no remedy,
And the actions of the Creator are not unjust.
There is no point in you giving in to grief,
As what is meant to be is an accomplished deed.
Do not allow your heart to get you down.
The best way to proceed is to respect divine justice."

In this way, Jaamaasp continues to advise him.
The king listens, returns to shine bright as the sun,
And climbs back on his throne
To reflect on the pending battle.
Anguish robs him of sleep and the fervor to strike war.

11 | Goshtaasp and Arjaasp Prepare Their Hosts

In accordance with the counsel of Jaamaasp,
The king takes off for camp at daybreak,
Just as stars evanesce from the firmament.
He positions the selected troops in a place
Where the early morning wind carries
The scent of roses from gardens to homes.

In accordance with custom,
He dispatches sentinels throughout the land.
One of the riders returns and says to Goshtaasp,
"O King, the army of Turks is drawing near,
Such an army as one has never witnessed before,
Marching from the land of Tooran and Chin.
It halted not far from here, covering mountain,
Valley, and plain with warrior tents.
The leader of the Turks has singled out scouts,
Who have rushed forth to collide with ours."

Goshtaasp, noble, courageous king,
Calls to his side his leader, the blessed Zarir.
He hands him a banner and commands him to make haste,
Gear up the elephants, and equip the troops.

Zarir immediately departs to ready the army,
Whose only wish is to battle with the leader of Turks.

The world king places fifty thousand riders
Under the command of Esfandiar,
Entrusting him with one of the army wings,
For he has a lion's heart and an elephant's chest.

On the other wing, the king positions
An elite corps under the leadership
Of his son and his equal, Shiddasp, noble warrior.

Then he gives fifty thousand brave cavaliers
And the command of the army center to Zarir,
A wild lion who battles like the king himself.

Finally, he puts Nastoor of blessed birth,
Royal light of his father, Zarir,
In full command of the rearguard.

After having settled the troops, he climbs the mountain,
Heart full of grief and body weary with stress.
He sits on his resplendent throne
And observes the host from his post.

King Arjaasp, on his side, similarly mobilizes troops.
He separates one hundred thousand men from Khalokh,
Brave and skilled riders, and sends them to Biderafsh,
Who has the grand timpani and the golden banner,
Entrusting him with one of the army wings,
For this brave lion dares not fight him.

He gives the leadership of the other wing to Gorgsaar
And the command of one hundred thousand elite troops.
Then he selects special warriors for the army corps,
Led by Namkhaast, inflexible and self-seeking sorcerer.
He keeps as reserve one hundred thousand more riders
Who have already displayed their exploits to the world,

Placing them strategically to aid the rear division of troops.

Finally, the king appoints Kohram as leading commander.
Son of Arjaasp, a glorious rider, expert in the skills of war,
Kohram is worldly and mature and an able army guardian.

12 | The Beginning of the Battle

Once night passes and day reveals its first ray of sunshine,
King Goshtaasp, from the mountaintop, observes warriors
From the two armies as they straddle their steeds.

The celebrated ruler asks for Behzaad, his black stallion.
You would think it is Mount Bisootoon.
The charger is prepared with trappings,
And the valiant world hero climbs on him.

The two hosts approach one another.
Brazen clarions are sounded on the backs of elephants.
The ranks are formed, and the heroes challenge
Those who are worthy to dare contend with them.

A shower of shots flies through the air like a spring hail
And the sun disappears from the world.
Anyone who has never witnessed such a marvel
Has a hard time believing that it is possible.
The surface of the sun is hidden by the tips of arrows,
A rushing downpour like a deluge of water.
You would think that the air carries a heavy cloud
That rains down diamonds.

The mass of cavaliers armed with mace and spear falling
On each other makes the air disappear from the world
As it adopts the color of night,
And the entire surface of the earth is soaked in blood.

The first to advance is a cavalier full of dignity,
Ardeshir, son of the world king.
He enters the battlefield like a drunken elephant.
You might take him for Commander Tous.

He dashes from one end of his host to the other,

PART EIGHTEEN

Without doubting for a moment
The fate that the moon and sun reserve for him.
But an arrow strikes him mid-waist,
Piercing through his armor.
The prince plummets from his horse,
And his royal body is drenched in blood and dust.
Alas, the king would never again lay eyes
On this fair-faced hero, dazzling as the moon!

After him advances Shiroo, as swift as wind,
A warrior who instructs in the ways of war.
He speeds forth, grasping a dagger dipped in poison.
He roars like a lion about to assail a deer
And kills one thousand enemy warriors
To avenge the hero prince, son of the king.
But at the moment when he is about to leave the battle,
After having tinted the surface of the earth with blood,
A shot pierces through the back of his coat of mail,
And this prince, son of the king, succumbs to his wounds.
Alas, this noble warrior dies
Before his father sets his sight on him again!

Next Shiddasp, who resembles the king
And shines like the moon, quickens the pace.
He is seated on a charger like a fierce whale,
Swift as wind and strong as an elephant.
He sprints to the battlefield waving his spear
And turning it like a baton while directing his horse.
He cries, "Where is the valiant Kohram, tiger and wolf?"

A deev emerges from the ranks saying, "I am the one
Able to seize with my teeth a famished lion!"

They fence about with their spears, as swift as wind,
But the king's son strikes the Turk with his weapon,
Removes him from the saddle, cuts off his head,
And flings his golden belt-bearing body into the dust.

Then Shiddasp advances to the front of the Chini warriors.
He saddles his horse and appears as strong as a boulder.
Never has anyone caught sight of such a man.
He is so fine-looking that eyes follow him everywhere.

But then a warrior Turk launches an arrow toward him,
And this son of a monarch instantly perishes.
Alas, this prince raised by the king with gentle affection!
Alas, his father will never see his son again!

13 | The Deaths of Gueraami, Son of Jaamaasp, and Nivezaar, Son of Goshtaasp

A rider emerges from the army ranks,
The noble son of Jaamaasp, the king's commander,
A valiant cavalier whose name is Gueraami
And who resembles Rostam, son of Zaal.

He saddles a huge dun charger of elegant stride.
He stops before the line of Chini warriors
And invokes Yazdan, Giver of justice.
Then he shouts, "Is there among you a man of lion heart
Who dares defy a life-destroying spear?
Where is the magician who acts according to his own will,
The seeker of fame whose name is Namkhaast?"

Namkhaast sprints up to him, a mountain on his horse.
The two nimble cavaliers wrestle
With mace and spear, sword and arrow.
Gueraami is a hero as powerful as a lion.
The valiant Namkhaast could not resist him.
This warrior flees at the sight of the Kianian's
Strength and double-edged sword.

Gueraami charges, burning with fury,
Heart full of blood and the desire for vengeance,
Soul full of ardor for battle.
He falls in the midst of enemy troops.

The wind rises on the side of the mountains.
The two armies fall on each other.
A most dreadful and sweeping gale blows.
In the midst of the jolts of swords
And the black dust, the shining Kaaviani banner
Evades the hands of the Iranians.

Gueraami spots the blue standard fallen on the ground.
He dismounts, shakes it to blow off the dust, and wipes it.

The brave warriors of Chin perceive him
Leaning the banner's post against his horse's saddle
And wiping it clean of dust.
The boldest ones surround him, attack him on all sides,
And cut off one of his arms with a slash of sword.

At that point, Gueraami grips Fereydoon's banner in his teeth.
What a marvel to watch him strike with his mace-holding hand!
But in the end, they kill him miserably, as if a vile thing,
Casting him to the ground, warm with spilled blood.

Alas, this valiant rider, full of heart,
The aged man never will set eyes on him again!
Nastoor, the lion, the valiant Kianian, son of Zarir,
Immediately advances to avenge the fallen Gueraami.
With abilities acquired from his father, he skillfully
Makes use of weapons to kill a great number of foes.
In the end he is victorious
And takes his place once again alongside his father.

Then the selected horseman Nivezaar, son of a world king,
Charges forward and climbs on his swift horse
In a way that has no equal in all the land.

In this manner, he storms onto the battlefield,
Where he cries in a very loud voice,
"O elite warriors, is there among you an illustrious man
Full of experience, brave and skilled with spear,
Who wishes to contend with me in the arena?
For here stands a man of lion heart!"

The selected Chini cavaliers rush toward him
In an attempt to overthrow him,
But the courageous Nivezaar, illustrious rider,
Crosses this mass of warriors in every direction,
Like a furious elephant or a ferocious lion.
You would think that he is
Rolling the ground beneath his feet.
He kills one hundred and sixty warrior heroes,
All raised in the midst of fights and battles.

But in the end, a crossbow bolt strikes him,
An arrow tossed as if lightning from the sky.
He falls off his colorful charger of speed and expires.
Such is the fate of battles! Alas, another noble cavalier
Falls before having fulfilled his destiny!
He resembles his father and is his equal.
Alas, his fine features, alas, his tall stature!

Once the hero of strong features dies,
Thousands and thousands of riders surround him,
Rush to all corners of the battlefield,
And raise the dust above the surface of the earth.

In this way, two weeks pass in relentless battle,
During which time no single cavalier sleeps.
The ground is encumbered with corpses and wounded bodies.
The dust is so thick it prevents the wind from passing.
The valleys and plains turn the color of tulips.
Blood floods the countryside and the desert.

14 | Biderafsh Kills Zarir, Goshtaasp's Brother

Two weeks pass in this manner,
And every instant the battle becomes more brisk.
The brave Zarir appears and climbs on a powerful steed.
Like a flame ushered by wind and devouring grass,
He falls onto the enemy camp,
Killing some, overthrowing many.
At the sight of him charging, everyone flees.

When Arjaasp recognizes that this son of a king
Is about to wipe out his army, he cries out to his troops,
"Do you wish to surrender the land of Khalokh to the wind?
We are in battle for two weeks,
And I do not see the end approaching.
The heroes of King Goshtaasp have already
Killed a great number of our illustrious warriors,
And now comes Zarir, like a mad wolf
Or a lion, tearing everything in his path.
He is slaying my pure and noble Tooranian warriors!

"We must either find a way of salvation
Or retreat back to Tooran-Zamin.
If Zarir is allowed to carry on for some time,
He will obliterate both the lands of Tooran and Chin.
Is there anyone among you desirous of glory,
Who dares emerge from the army ranks?
Is there anyone who will stand before him like a man
And acquire name and grandeur in this world?
The soldier who charges his horse out of the army line
And who flings Zarir into the dust before the sky
Will be rewarded with my daughter's hand
As well as my host and banner."

The troops remain unresponsive to Arjaasp's speech,
As they are transfixed by fear of this wild boar.

At that moment, the world hero Zarir
Appears like a wolf and falls on the Turks like a lion,
Killing some and disarming others.

Arjaasp is further troubled by the sight,
The light of his day dimming before his eyes.
He reiterates, "O brave warriors from Chin and Tooran,
Do you not see the attacks on your relatives and allies?
Do you not hear the laments of wounded men
At the feet of this madman who strikes with mace
Like Saam the rider and casts his shots like Aarash,
This bold warrior whose breath consumes my entire host
And will soon consume my entire land?
Where is the skillful, worldly man among you,
Ready to face this drunken elephant?
Whoever seizes this warrior destroyer and makes him
Tumble off his charger will be given a treasure of gold,
And I shall raise his headgear to the firmament."

Arjaasp, astounded at the lack of reaction, grows pale.
Thrice he repeats his appeal. Thrice he is met with silence.
In the end, Biderafsh, the angry, the vile, the dog,
A sorcerer and aging wolf, says to Arjaasp,
"O powerful sun, you are from root to stem
The very image of Afraasiyaab. I place my life at your feet.
If the king wishes to give me command of this vast host,

I shall advance like a drunken elephant to vanquish him
And hurl his body to the ground, once and for all."

The king, thrilled to hear these words, sings his praises.
He gives him his own charger and saddle, a javelin
Dipped in poison able to pierce a mountain of steel.

The impure sorcerer, full of hatred,
Advances toward the valiant and cautious cavalier.
But when he sees him from afar, so strong and so vibrant,
Face covered in dust, eyes full of tears, holding
In his hand a mace in the manner of Saam the hero,
When he sees before him a mountain of corpses,
He dares not confront Zarir face to face.

He slips unseen behind him and tosses
His poisonous javelin toward the princely cavalier,
Who does not expect it and is surprised by the blow.
The weapon pierces through his armor, his royal body
Floods with blood as he plummets off his horse.
Alas, this valiant prince, son of a king!

Biderafsh the vile sets foot to the ground,
Robs him entirely of his coat of mail, brings
Zarir's horse to Arjaasp King, along with his belt,
His beautiful banner, and his gem-encrusted diadem.

The Tooranian host cheers in jubilation,
And the banner is placed on the back of an elephant.

Goshtaasp, observing from the mountaintop,
Fails to see his brother charging in the dust.
He says, "I fear that this twirling moon,
Whose light ceaselessly shone on the army,
My valiant brother, the blessed Zarir,
Skilled in the conquest of fierce lions,
Has been overthrown from his horse.
The warriors have ceased their attack.
I no longer hear the sobs of sons of brave warriors.
Could it be that the leader of nobles has been killed?"

He sends cavaliers to the battlefield
Where the black banner is planted and says to them,

"Go and see what happened to my royal brother,
For the grips of worry have stifled my heart."

The king of the earth is in such a state
When the envoys return shedding blood tears.
They say, "The guardian of your crown and host,
The world hero, the valiant Zarir, your moon,
Has been killed miserably by one of the Turkish warriors!
Biderafsh, chief of world sorcerers, has flung him
To the ground and taken his Kaaviani banner."

At the news of Zarir's execution,
The world king feels as if death knocks at his door.
He tears his clothes to shreds, down to his feet,
Pours dust over his royal crown,
And says to the wise Jaamaasp,
"What shall I report to King Lohraasp?
How shall I dare send a messenger to his court?
How shall I explain the son's demise to an aging father?
Alas, this princely hero, son of a king!
Alas, his loss is like a shining moon shrouded by fog!
Bring me Golgoon, Lohraasp's charger,
And place on him the saddle of Goshtaasp.
I shall depart to avenge my brother,
Else I shall perish from the grief caused by his death.
I long to avenge him and to spread my faith and religion."

His worldly minister, Jaamaasp, says to him,
"Remain here; your duty is not to avenge him."

Goshtaasp obeys the orders of the wise man
Who can foretell the secrets of the future.
He dismounts, sits back down, and says to his troops,
"Who among you is the lion
Who will avenge the noble Zarir?
Who will launch his charger for this fight
And bring back my brother's steed and saddle?
I promise before the World Master,
An honest promise of a man and a king,
That such a feat will be rewarded
With the hand of my daughter Homay."

No one steps forward to volunteer.

15 | Esfandiar Learns of Zarir's Death

Esfandiar learns that the prince has been killed,
That his father is withering with grief,
And that he wishes to avenge this death himself.

The illustrious hero wrings his hands together and says,
"What does misfortune hold in store for us?
Every day I have watched Zarir in the midst of battle,
I have trembled at the affairs of providence.
Alas, this rider and hero, this prince,
Whose crown has been robbed by fate!
Who is responsible for the slaying of this war elephant?
Who is the one who dared uproot
This mountain of steel from the ground?"

Esfandiar hands his brother his banner, his troops,
And his post, and marches forward to the army core.
He steps into battle armor and grabs the imperial banner.
He has five brothers, worthy of throne,
All illustrious counterparts of the king,
Who stand before Esfandiar, for he is an army destroyer.

Like a brave lion, he takes Zarir's post at the center.
Then this army protector says to the noble troops,
"O renowned Iranians and sons of the king, listen to me.
Have trust in the faith of the World Master!
Know, O rulers, that the day has come for us
To distinguish between the pure and the bad doctrine.
Refrain from fearing death, or anything else for that matter,
For no one dies except at the time assigned for him to die.
If a man's fortune has to change,
What better death than one on the battlefield?
Do not pay attention to the corpses.
Do not seek salvation or count the fallen heads.
Refrain from placing hope on a retreat or fearing fight.
Lower the tips of your spears to battle,
And wrestle long, hard, and with courage.
If you act according to my command,
My soul will continue to dwell in my body,
Your name and glory will prosper in the world,
And the entire army of Arjaasp will perish."

At this point in Esfandiar's speech, his father's voice
Is heard from the mountain, "O my great noble heroes,
As dear to me as my own body and soul,
Do not fear spear, arrow, and sword,
For not one of us can escape our determined fate.
I swear by our holy faith, by the life of Esfandiar,
And by the soul of Zarir, generous rider,
Who has just been admitted into paradise,
That Shah Lohraasp has written a letter to me.
I have accepted and made a promise to the old king
That if fortune grants me victory,
I shall pass down to Esfandiar the crown and throne,
Just as my father handed kingship down to me.
I shall hand over the troops to Pashootan
And place on Esfandiar's head the imperial crown."

16 | Esfandiar Attacks Arjaasp

When Esfandiar, hero of elephantine build, prudent man,
Endowed with astounding force,
Hears his father's cries echo from the mountain,
He drops his head, overcome by grief.
He advances, spear in hand,
Head hanging low out of shame for his father.
He climbs on a powerful charger the color of ash,
Fuming like a deev escaping its bonds,
And charges at the enemy host like a hurricane,
Pounding on and pulverizing rose-colored leaves.
He kills many Turks, cuts off many heads,
So many that men retreat in terror at the sight of him.

Nastoor, Zarir's son, exits from his tent,
Takes the direction of the guardian of his father's horses,
And asks for a bounding charger, well rested and well fed.
On the back of the horse, he places a golden saddle
And attaches his Kianian noose to the saddle's knob.
He dons his armor and climbs on the horse,
Advancing on the field, spear in hand.
He strides in this manner to the battlefield,
Surveys the terrain for a path to reach his father's corpse.

Quickening the pace, he arrives and surrenders
To vengeance, killing many enemy troops.
He asks the whereabouts of the army warrior
To every Iranian he meets on the way:
"Where has my father fallen, the brave Zarir?"

There is a generous rider named Ardeshir, a lion hero.
The young prince asks him for directions
To his father's corpse, and the hero points to it, saying,
"He fell in the center of the army, near this black banner.
Go there without delay, for he is lying on the ground,
And you could possibly see him one more time."

Nastoor launches his steed, kills many Turks,
Shouting cries of mourning as he dashes on his father's trail.
Once he perceives Zarir's corpse in the dust
And he is close enough to discern his face,
His eyes dim and his heart fails him as he loses sense.
He flings himself from high on the saddle to the ground
And on top of his father's body, hollering,
"O my shining moon, torch of my heart, my eyes and soul,
You raised me with much effort and attention.
Now you are gone. To whom will you hand over my care?
Since the time King Lohraasp gave you the army's command
And to Goshtaasp the throne and headdress,
You have led troops and governed provinces.
You have called for war with all your wishes.
The world has celebrated your name according to your will,
But you died before having accomplished your goals.
I shall go to your brother, the blessed king, and say to him,
          'Come down from your glorious throne.
           My father does not deserve this indifference.
           Go and draw vengeance from your enemy!'"

Nastoor holds a stance of grief for a long time.
Then he climbs back on his charger
And takes the direction of court,
All the while sobbing and bellowing his sorrow.

The king sits high on his throne and says to Nastoor,
"O dear child, why do you weep so?"

Nastoor says to the king, "O benevolent ruler,

Avenge the death of my fallen father.
His black, musk-scented beard rests in the dry dust."

Nastoor's words dim the king's sight.
His lofty stature shrinking, he cries out,
"Bring my black steed, my coat of mail and helmet,
For on this very day, I shall make the blood of heroes
Flow in torrents in retaliation for my dear brother's death.
I shall destroy the world with a blaze,
Make smoke rise all the way to Saturn!"

When the noble warriors see Shah Goshtaasp
Gearing up to avenge his brother, they say,
"O leader of faith, you must not speak thus!
You, the king, must not fight,
For Arjaasp would jump on you!
We shall not suffer that the world master,
King of Kings, goes to battle to avenge his brother.
Why should he command the troops himself?"

Jaamaasp, the noble leader, says to him,
"You must not show yourself on the battlefield.
Hand the charger you wished to mount over to Nastoor,
And send him to fight the enemy, for he can better
Avenge his father's death than you could."

17 | Nastoor and Esfandiar Kill Biderafsh

Goshtaasp gives his horse Behzaad to Nastoor,
Along with his armor and helmet of steel.
The son, deprived of his father, dons the armor,
Mounts Behzaad, the deeply-hued black stallion,
Takes position before enemy lines, sighs a cold sigh,
And cries out, "I am Nastoor, son of Zarir,
Before whom the lion dares not appear.
Which one of you is the culprit Biderafsh,
Who seized the Kaaviani banner?"

As no one responds to the noble Nastoor,
And no one advances to accept his challenge,
He lurches with Behzaad, a stallion the color of night,

And kills a great number of warriors.

On the other side,
Esfandiar brings down a multitude of riders.

When the King of Chin spots Nastoor,
Offshoot of Kianian race, offspring of a world hero,
He says to his troops,
"Who could be this man able to strike such blows?
He has killed an infinite number of my warriors.
Could it be that the horseman Zarir is still alive?
When he first charged at me,
He launched his steed in a similar manner.
Where is Biderafsh, selected warrior and world hero?
Send him immediately to my side."

Biderafsh takes off, wielding the Kaaviani banner.
He sits upon Zarir's royal charger
And dons the armor of the world hero.
He advances toward Prince Nastoor, torch of the army,
The king's brother's son. Biderafsh raises
The lethal blade with which he killed Zarir.

The two of them fight fiercely with sword and arrow,
One Turk, leader of sorcerers, and the other Zarir's son.

The blessed Esfandiar, son of the king,
Hears of this battle and rushes to the warriors' side.

At the sight of him, Biderafsh, chief of magicians,
Urges his horse to quickly withdraw.
He tosses his poisoned sword toward Esfandiar's head,
Hoping to render pale his brilliant face,
But the weapon dipped in venom misses the warrior hero.

Esfandiar takes hold of it and strikes
Biderafsh in the rib such a heroic blow
That the tip pierces through to the other side.
Biderafsh falls off his horse and instantly dies,
Vanquished by the son of a Kianian.

Esfandiar dismounts, strips the vile sorcerer of Zarir's armor,
And separates his head from his body.

He seizes Zarir's deeply colored horse and his banner,
And carries off the head of Biderafsh.

Acclamations of joy rise from the army to the dome of sky,
Announcing the prince's triumphant victory,
Having killed the enemy and returning
With the blessed banner and the dun charger of Zarir.

Prince Esfandiar approaches Goshtaasp on horseback
And places before him the head of the aged sorcerer.
Such is the will of custom and law.

18 | Arjaasp Flees the Battlefield

Having thus led in good faith this noble act of vengeance,
Esfandiar asks for a saddle to be placed on Zarir's horse,
Returns to the battlefield to divide his host into three corps.
He gives the first corps to Nastoor, the hero,
The honor of the army, and prince of blessed birth.
He entrusts the second corps to his brother,
A force comprised of Iran's bravest men.
He reserves the third corps for himself
As the troops holler shouts like a thunder bursting cloud.

Nastoor, of tall neck and pure body, and Nooshaazar,
The victorious, take their positions before Esfandiar,
Destroyer of armies. They commit to a solemn oath:
They refuse to return from battle and to withdraw
Until they bring on the demise of the evil Arjaasp,
Even if their enemy's double-edged
Swords were to split the earth.

The three horsemen, thus invested, take off for war.
As they charge in the midst of troops,
The warriors of Iran move together,
Dazzling the world with the gleam of their armor.

They kill so many Tooranians
That there is no room left to fight.
Blood floods through valleys and plains,
Turning rivers crimson and making mills spin.

Arjaasp, witness to this, advances, escorted by warriors.

Esfandiar, destroyer of heroes, brings down his spear
On the brave deevs of Tooranian race.
He pins their chests to their backs and continues
In this manner until he crushes their proudest leaders.

The Tarkhan understands that from here on,
No one will dare pit himself against Esfandiar,
That the army is shaken to its core, the battle lost.
He remains in the midst of the tumult until dusk.
Then he departs and takes the direction of the desert.

The Iranians continue to assail the Tooranian host.
They kill on every side and in great numbers.
But, O marvel of marvels, one man shows clemency!

19 | Esfandiar Grants the Tooranians Mercy

As the Tooranians become aware of Arjaasp's departure,
As they see that they are assailed
On all sides by scorching swords,
The chief leaders dismount and approach Esfandiar.
They strip off their coats of mail, cast aside their bows,
And cry in their distress: "O king, have mercy on our lives!
We shall accept your faith. We shall learn from it.
We shall worship only the holy blaze."

The Iranians do not pay heed to them.
They strike with their swords and kill so many
That blood tints the world in shades of red
Until Goshtaasp Shah ultimately agrees to pardon them.

Esfandiar hears their cries and decides
To show mercy for their bodies and their lives.
The mighty warrior hero, prince and son of a king,
Asks to be announced among his victorious troops:
"O illustrious Iranians, halt your killings!
Now that enemy troops have been vanquished,
Stop your carnage, for they are distressed, debased,
And left without recourse. Let these dogs live.

Abstain from taking additional prisoners.
Do not spill any more blood. Do not run anymore.
Refrain from trampling corpses beneath your feet.
Make the rounds of the battlefield and count the wounded.
For the love of Zarir's soul, do not take more captives.
The time has come to climb down from your war stallions."

When the troops hear this declaration,
They all go to the valiant hero, return to their camps,
And beat the drum to celebrate their victory,
A victory worthy of the invincible Rostam.

As dark night passes, blood flows in desert and plain.
The renowned Kianian, escorted by his army's brave men,
Marches off to inspect the battlefield.
He wanders through the maze of corpses.
When he is able to identify one, he weeps,
Continues on until he finds his brother,
Killed miserably and lying in the dust like a vile thing.
At the sight of him in such a state, King Goshtaasp
Tears off his royal garment,
Climbs down from his dun charger,
And grabs his beard with his two hands, crying,
"O King of Balkhian heroes, my life has turned bitter.
Alas, this prince and leader, this king and flaming torch!
Alas, this diadem of the world empire!"

Esfandiar bends low and picks him up off the ground.
He wipes his deathly face with his own hands
And places him in a golden coffin.
You would think that Zarir was never born.

Then he places the Kianian and his young sons in coffins
And commands the dead to be counted
And the wounded to be hauled away.

The entire space of battle is searched,
Its heights and lowlands, its plain and roads.
Thirty thousand fallen Iranians are gathered,
Among them one thousand one hundred and sixty noblemen.
One thousand and forty illustrious warriors are wounded,
Having avoided being trampled beneath elephant feet.

On the side of the Turks,
There are one hundred thousand dead,
Of which eight hundred are noteworthy
And three thousand two hundred wounded.

Do not linger in such a place if you can avoid it.

20 | Goshtaasp Returns to Balkh

The illustrious Kianian, the brave King Goshtaasp,
Makes his way back to the battlefield in Balkh
And commands his leader Nastoor to prepare the army
To send off the next day for the glorious land of Iran.

In the early morning hours, the renowned chief
Sounds the brazen trumpets and loads up the gear.
Leaving nothing behind,
The troops turn in the direction of Iran-Zamin.
Dim hearts stand proud, eagerly desiring new battles.
Every single wounded man is lifted and carried
To the land of Iran to be treated by learned medicine men.

Once the world king returns, he unites his eldest son
To his daughter Homay the fortunate.
He weds another daughter to Nastoor.
Such is the custom and the law of the Iranians.[67]

He entrusts Nastoor with the care
Of ten thousand brave, spear-wielding horsemen.
He gives him the command, saying,
"O skilled warrior, retrace your steps.
Fall on the King of Turks. Penetrate the land of Khalokh.
Kill everyone you find there to avenge your father's blood."

He equips Nastoor with the needed gear for his enterprise.
The latter immediately departs with troops,
And the king, seated upon the throne
And bearing the Kianian crown, opens access
To his treasury to distribute jewels to his warriors.

◇◇◇◇◇◇◇◇◇◇◇◇◇
67 Marriage between cousins was favored in pre-Islamic times, but here we have a
union between siblings.

Then he gives the leaders the command of cities,
Gifting every single warrior with something of value.

King Goshtaasp bestows land to those worthy of governing.
He raises the ranks of those worthy of honor.
Having thus rewarded the deserving,
He sends them to their respective homes.
He sits on the imperial throne and asks for a fire temple
To be built in which Indian aloeswood could be burned.
The structure is completed with a paved floor of pure gold.
The blaze consumes the aloeswood,
And a sprinkling of ambergris is spread across the floors.

Everything is to be executed according to the rules.
The king names this temple the House of Goshtaasp,
As the sign above the sanctuary door reads.
Jaamaasp is to protect the site as a wise man.

Then the king addresses a letter to his governors:
"The Divine Creator did not allow us to be degraded,
For our obscured night was converted to day,
And victory was granted to Kianians everywhere.
Defeated and cursed, Arjaasp has fled,
While we have been showered with blessings.
Who else could do such a thing but the World Creator?
Upon receipt of news of your master's victory,
Send your tributes to the fire temple."

The Caesar, ruler of Rum, hearing of the king's triumph
And Arjaasp's plunge into the depths of misfortune,
Dispatches messengers with gifts of slaves and horses in frills.
The King of Barbarestan, along with princes from India
And Sindh, similarly pay their taxes and tributes.

21 | Goshtaasp Dispatches Esfandiar to Promulgate the Religion of Zartosht

The illustrious hero Goshtaasp sits on his royal throne.
He offers access to his empire's brave warriors,
Powerful men, and princes of royal birth.

The valiant Esfandiar presents himself at court,
Clutching his bull-headed mace
And wearing the Kianian headdress,
His face shining beneath it like the moon.
He assumes the position of a slave before the king.
He braces himself, head hanging low.

The world shah observes him,
Favoring his being over everyone else's, even his own.
He smiles and says to him, "O brave Esfandiar,
Do you not end the fight and discord?"

The skilled swordsman replies, "The command is yours,
For you are king, and Iran belongs to you."

The illustrious Kianian hands him a golden diadem
And opens before him the door to his treasury.
He entrusts him with the power over Iran,
For he has the strength of a true world hero.
He gives him banner, treasure, and an army, adding,
"The time is not yet here for you to sit upon the throne.
You must climb on the saddle, travel,
And convert all the lands of earth to the true faith."

The proud son of the king, sword-bearing hero,
Departs to make the rounds of the lands with his army.
He crosses the territories from Rum to India,
Travels across seas and much darkness,
Interpreting everywhere the mysteries of the religion,
According to the command of the Creator of living beings.

Upon hearing him deliverva the precepts,
The people are quick to adopt his path and his cult,
Receive the good religion, and demand clarifications.
In the temples, they burn down idols
And ignite the holy blaze.
They write letters to the king in which they say,
"We have received the faith from Esfandiar.
We have strapped ourselves with the Kushti,
Quietly pronounced the prayer.
You must then not demand tribute from us,
For we have entered in the order of the true religion.
You may send us the *Zand Avesta*

PART EIGHTEEN

Handed to you by Zartosht."

Goshtaasp, having read the letter of the rulers,
Sits on his throne and gathers his friends around him.
He sends one book of the *Zand Avesta*
To each nation and each prince.
He further commands the illustrious world hero,
Esfandiar, to travel to the four corners of the world.

Everywhere this prince presents himself,
Everyone submits to his wishes, and evildoers
Throughout the world take shelter and hide.

Once he subjects the entire earth to his father's will,
He divests himself of his golden belt, sits on the throne
Like a Kianian, and rests for some time with his troops.

Then he calls his brother Farshidvard and gives him
The command of an army of bold warriors,
Entrusts him with abundant coins and jewels
And the governorship of Khorasan, sending him on his way.

Some time passes.
The world is purified and under the will of the holy faith.
Warriors protect the world; farmers plant the seeds.

One day, Esfandiar sends a horseman to his father
To say to him: "O illustrious and victorious King,
I have purified the world by the grace of the Creator.
The shadow of the kingly eagle stretches over many lands.
No one has reason to fear anymore.
No man in the entire world lacks either gold or silver.
The earth is resplendent like paradise,
Cultivated and layered with harvest.
Horsemen protect, while ploughmen
Are busy with the labor of the land.
The world is thus at rest, and evil men have dispersed."

22 | Gorazm Slanders Esfandiar

There lives a proud man named Gorazm,
A renowned hero having led many a battle.
He nourishes in his heart great animosity for Esfandiar.
I do not know the origin of such hatred.
I simply heard a tale that he came from
The family of Goshtaasp and that everywhere
He wishes ill to the son of the king.
Every time the name of Esfandiar is uttered,
He speaks maliciously of him,
Making every effort to bring him down.

One day at dawn, the illustrious king
Sits in joy on his throne in the company
Of his valued, highborn chiefs and noble princes,
Reveling in music and song.

Gorazm assumes his place before the blessed king,
His face pale and his heart dim with thoughts of vengeance,
He seeks a pretext to talk about the king's son
And to harm the aging branch of the royal tree.
Watch how the ill-intentioned man arrives at his end.
He begins by wringing his hands and saying,
"We have been told by a wise man of pure faith:
When a bad son becomes powerful, like a foe,
The fate of the father is all the more miserable.
When a slave submits solemnly to the obedience
Due a master, his head must be chopped off.
When I first heard this from the man of secrets,
It did not appear right to me."

The world king cries out, "What is the meaning of this?
Who is the master of secrets, and what is the secret?"

The Kianian replies, "O most sincere man,
This is not the time to reveal the mystery."

The King of Kings descends from his throne
And says to the deceitful one, "Approach,
And tell me everything, from beginning to end.
Tell me the secret my dragon son is hiding from me."

The wicked Gorazm replies,
"An evil man must only do what is right.
The king has placed me above all need.
I must not withhold a secret from his highness.
I shall not refuse the king's advice.
I shall hide nothing, even if he were to disapprove.
It is better for me to speak without being heard
Than to keep the secret a mystery.
Know then, O world master,
That Esfandiar plans to fight against you.
Numerous troops have approached him,
Their gazes turned and fixed on you.
Their intention is to throw you into bondage,
And once he seizes you and binds you,
He will capture the rest of the world.
You know that Esfandiar is a warrior without equal.
When he is in shape, the knot of his noose whips circles.
The sun itself would not dare oppose him.
This is what I have heard and have told you in truth.
Now you know how to proceed, for command is yours."

Confounded, the illustrious King of Iran asks,
"Who has ever heard such a thing?"
He turns somber, and aversion for his son grows in his heart.
He refrains from drinking wine and giving in to joy,
And sits at some distance from the feast, sighing deeply.
He finds himself unable to sleep during the night,
So great is his outrage for Esfandiar.

At the first and faintest light of day over the mountains,
Banishing the glimmer of stars,
King Goshtaasp calls the aging Jaamaasp and says,
"Summon Esfandiar to court without delay.
This is a matter of great importance.
He is the most powerful prince of the land.
Tell him that the world belongs to him
And that I cannot act without him."

He writes an urgent letter to his son in these terms,
"O noble and fortunate Esfandiar,
I send the old Jaamaasp, who was acquainted with Lohraasp.
As soon as you see him, strap your waist,

Climb on your speedy horse, and present yourself to me.
If he finds you sleeping, rise immediately.
Remain up; do not delay for a moment!"

The wise man departs, taking the king's letter.
In great haste, he clears mountains and plains.

23 | Jaamaasp Arrives at the Side of Esfandiar

Esfandiar is on the plain, busy with the hunt,
When he hears that the king has dispatched Jaamaasp.
He is surprised, moved, and laughs.
Esfandiar has four great sons,
Avid for battle and skilled horsemen:
Bahman; Mehrnoosh; Aazarafrooz, the discerning hero;
And Nooshaazar, the one who builds the fire temples.

The son Bahman says to the world ruler,
"May your head remain green forevermore!"

Esfandiar smiles at length and says,
"I don't think such will be the case."

He continues to his son, "In this moment,
Someone arrives from my father's court.
The king is infuriated with me.
His heart has turned away from his humble servant."

The noble son asks him, "Why is that?
What have you done to the master of the empire?"

The princely leader replies, "O my son,
I am not aware of any crime against my father
Unless it has been in the aim of teaching the true faith.
Everywhere in the world I have ignited the sacred fire
And purified the earth with my sharp sword.
How could the king's heart hold it against me?
It appears he has been misled by a wicked deev,
To have this foolish desire to throw me in prison."

As he thus reflects, a cloud of dust rises in the distance.
Esfandiar realizes that Jaamaasp is on his way

And takes off to advance toward him in greeting.
They dismount from their leaping chargers,
And the hero and aging man reach each other on foot.
The blessed Esfandiar asks after the king's well-being.

The wise Jaamaasp replies,
"He is in good health and happy."
He kisses the prince's head, hands him his father's letter,
And informs him on the state of things,
And how the deev has led the king astray.

Esfandiar says to the prudent Jaamaasp,
"What is your advice to me?
If I go to court with you, my father will mistreat me,
And if I refuse to appear before my master,
I deviate from the obedience I owe him.
Find me a way out, O wise old man,
For I cannot remain in this state of uncertainty."

The sage replies to him, "O prince, guardian of borders,
You are aged in knowledge and young in body.
You know that even the anger of a father for his son
Is more tender than the gentlest filial affection.
You must leave. Such is my counsel,
For no matter what happens, your father is king."

The two agree and return together to Esfandiar's palace.
The prince prepares for Jaamaasp a beautiful residence.
Then they engage in feast and drinking.

Aloeswood is burned before Jaamaasp
As if they are celebrating a joyous festival.

The next day, Esfandiar sits on his throne,
And a great number of warriors assemble around him.
The noble prince gives army command to Bahman,
Leaves with a number of leaders, arrives at the royal court,
His belt cinched and his helmet on head.

24 | Goshtaasp Sends Esfandiar to Prison

As soon as the king learns of his son's arrival
And of the fact that he wears the Kianian headdress,
He unites leaders, great and small,
And places the book of *Zand Avesta* before him.
He assigns seats to each wise man.
Then the sword-wielding prince is summoned.

The hero enters, hands extended out.
He approaches his father and pays homage to him,
Standing before the king like a slave, head low,
Arms crossed respectfully.

The King of Kings says to the wise men and army leaders,
"Imagine a noble man raising a son with great needs,
Entrusting his care to a nurse to feed him with milk,
Placing the royal crown on his head,
Caring for him until he grows strong,
Teaching him how to drink wine and mount a horse,
Taking great pains to train him as a skilled horseman.
The son turns into a man shining
As bright as gold excavated from a mine.
Ambitious men search for him, poets celebrate him.
He is a winning horseman in war, an intrepid hero in feats,
Trampling beneath his feet the entire world,
Becoming worthy of the imperial diadem.
The father retains only his throne and crown,
And remains in the palace, as guardian of the family goods.
The son becomes world conqueror with banner and host,
While the father is reduced to golden crown and throne.

"Have you heard of a son who would cut off
His father's head just for the throne and diadem,
And conspires with his army against him,
His heart consumed with the desire to overcome him?
What man would approve of such a thing?
Have you ever heard of such an astonishing tale?
What do you say, aging wise men, of this son,
And what should the father do?"

The others reply, "O King, it is inconceivable!

A son seeking the throne while his father is alive
Is a most dreadful, shameful thing."

The world owner says to them,
"Well, here is this son who wishes to take his father's life.
I shall strike him with a stick to make an example of him.
I shall send him to prison as he deserves and
Chain him up like no one has been chained before."

The son replies, "O my dear father of noble heart,
Why should I ever aspire to see you bereft of life?
I am not aware of a single crime I committed
Against your person for as long as I remember.
Never have I entertained such evil thoughts.
But you are king and master.
I belong to you, and chains and prison are yours.
Command me to be tied up, and if you wish my death,
My heart is at peace and my spirit is calm."

The King of Kings asks for chains to be brought
And summons blacksmiths who come
With handcuffs, neck braces, and heavy chains.
In the presence of the king, world master,
They tie up the hero's hands and feet so tight
That all those witnessing this sight shed tears of pity.

Once an iron ring is looped around Esfandiar's neck,
The king commands him
To be locked up in the Fortress of Gombadan:
"Bring a male elephant able to run like a bird in flight
To carry him away to his cell."

A great strong elephant is brought.
Esfandiar is placed on its back.
He is taken from his illustrious father,
With a wounded heart and tearful eyes.
He is led, guarded and surrounded by army leaders,
To a fortress at the top of a mountain,
Where he is bound to four metal columns.

In this way, he is plunged off the throne,
And providence turns its back on him.
The king assigns him a number of guardians.

Esfandiar's heart fills with grief and worry.
In this confined way he continues to live, tied up,
And, every once in a while, shedding bitter tears.

25 | Goshtaasp Travels to Sistan, and Arjaasp Reunites His Army

Much time passes. At some point,
The illustrious king travels to Sistan to introduce
The *Zand Avesta* and takes wise men as witnesses.

Upon his arrival, Rostam, governor of Nimrooz,
A skilled horseman equal to the valiant Saam,
Comes to greet him with his father, the aged Zaal,
And with noblemen and army leaders.

From one border to another, they position
Musicians on the road to play music for the journey.
A procession advances to meet the blessed king,
Who is pleased with the sights and sounds.
They direct him to Zabol, where troops line up,
Standing in devotion as his slaves.
They learn the doctrine of *Zand Avesta*
And light the sacred fire.

The visit lasts for two years, during which time
Goshtaasp and the son of Zaal
Enjoy each other and life immensely.

But soon rulers from various lands,
No matter where they are, learn of Goshtaasp's deeds,
How he submitted the heroic body of his son
To the confinement of heavy chains
And how he traveled to Zabolestan
To spread his religion and curse the powerful idols.
They rebel against Goshtaasp
And break their treaties with him.

Once Bahman learns that his illustrious
And innocent father is enchained by order of the king,
He and his brothers desert the army

And take the road to Esfandiar like lions.
The Kianian sons reach their father.
They stay with him to distract and entertain him,
Not wishing to leave him alone in his confinement.

Meanwhile, Arjaasp, King of Tooran and Chin,
Is informed that the moon has disappeared
From the house of Sagittarius,
That Goshtaasp has grown furious with Esfandiar
And has appallingly chained him up in Gombadan Castle,
And that he himself traveled from Balkh to Zabolestan,
Across a vast desert, across the Jayhoon River,
That he has settled in Zabol as Zaal's host,
And that two years have passed in such a way.
The King of Chin learns that Iranians have deserted Balkh,
And from the army, only King Lohraasp,
With his seven hundred fire worshippers,
Uniquely occupied to pray at the altar,
Are alone in the city, without the support of troops.

The Tooranian ruler calls his brave men
And prepares to attack Lohraasp.
He tells them, "Know that King Goshtaasp
Has traveled to Sistan with his army.
He has settled in Zabol and there remains
In all his kingdom, not a single horseman.
This is an opportune moment to execute our revenge.
We must gather a host.
His noble son Esfandiar is no longer a threat,
For he is in prison, restrained with shackles.
Where is the man able to deepen the secrets,
The one who wishes to explore this lengthy road,
Journey through it with its twists and turns,
Avoiding the well-traveled paths
To observe the situation of the Iranians?"

A man by the name of Sootooh volunteers.
He is a sorcerer able to infiltrate roads and secrets.
He says, "I am flexible and always ready for travel.
What is your command?
Tell me everything I need to know."

The King of Chin replies to him,
"Go to Iran-Zamin. Observe with wisdom
Where the border guards are stationed,
And make your way to various locations."

The spy travels the length of the road and arrives
In the glorious city of Balkh to search for the king's palace.
Unable to find Goshtaasp, he comes across Lohraasp
And a few men engaged in worship.
He reports his discovery to the Tooranian king.

Arjaasp is pleased and relieved by the news.
He calls army chiefs to his side and commands them
To depart and to collect the dispersed troops.

The warriors take the road through mountains and plains
And through various pastures to gather the empire's
Bravest warriors and bring them to the king.[68]

26 | End of Daghighi's Contribution
and Return to Ferdowsi's Verses:
In Praise of Sultan Mahmoud Ghaznavid

O insightful poet bard, return to your own words.
Daghighi, before his life ended and before his soul
Was freed from this illusory world, suffered greatly.
But for these insubstantial verses,
There remains no memory of him on earth.
He was robbed of his life before he could finish his work.

Learn from Ferdowsi's pure, enchanting writings.
This book fell into my hands,
Like a fish caught on a fish hook.
I examined these verses, and they appeared weak to me.
Many of the couplets felt poorly constructed,
But I copied them here anyway,
So that the king might witness a tale devoid of art.

The jeweler brings here two gems:

◇◇◇◇◇◇◇◇◇◇◇◇◇
68 Here ends the section of 1,040 verses borrowed from the poet Daghighi.

May the king pay heed to these words.
If one is reduced to telling a tale in this manner,
One should maintain silence and not wear out one's mind.
When one thinks of the mental
And physical strain one places upon oneself,
Better not to dig up a mine empty of precious stones.
When talent does not equate inspiration,
It is unwise to undertake a treatise on the life of kings.
Better a mouth remain unfilled with nourishment
Than to stuff it with unworthy sustenance.

I encountered a book full of stories,
With serious and truthful words,
A book of ancient traditions written in prose,
As skilled men had no thought of converting them to verse.
My delighted heart contemplated such a venture.

Should the inquiry be reliable,
Two thousand years passed on this book.
I therefore acclaim the blessed scribe,
From whom we inherit this glorious book.
Though he did so with a mere one thousand verses,
He constructed a tale of feasts and battles.
Nevertheless, he carved the road for later poets
To place upon the throne this royal jewel.

He received honor and wealth from princes,
And it was only his ill passions that drew him suffering.
He celebrated kings and adorned the forehead
Of famed men with a diadem of praise.
But his lyrical word was weak,
And he did not succeed in renewing the ancient times.

With great joy, I took hold of this book as a good omen
And dedicated many years to such labor.
Yet I did not discern an eminent man, generous and bright,
Seated upon the imperial throne of Iran.

My poem became for me a source of concern
For which I had no other remedy than silence.
I saw a garden lined with numerous trees,
A place worthy of serving as residence to a fortunate man,
But nowhere could one find an entrance.

It wore no other garment than the name of royalty.
I needed an entrance worthy of this garden.
If it were too narrow, it would not suit me.

I withheld my poem for twenty years,
Until I found someone worthy of this treasure.

In the end, Abul Ghassem, world master,
The one who renewed the crown of the King of Kings,
The powerful Mahmoud, the majestic, the gracious,
To whom the Moon and Saturn pay homage,
Appeared and sat on the throne of justice.
Who can remember a world master of his stature?
His name is the crown gracing the head of my work,
And his glory has brought light into my dim heart,
Purifying it like ivory.
Never, since the beginning of time, has there lived
A prince as generous, wise, glorious, and brave.
He surpasses the ancient kings,
And not a breath of blame ever rises against his deeds.

In his eyes, dinars are nothing but specks of dust.
He fears neither banquet nor battle.
In times of feast, he distributes gold;
In times of war, blows of his sword.
And never does he refuse to give to those in need.

May his throne always be resplendent!
May the Iranians live forever in happiness!

27 | The March of Arjaasp's Army

I shall now renew the tale of the fight with Arjaasp,
And, with my skills, pluck weeds out of the garden.

Arjaasp, aware of the Iranian king's presence in Sistan,
Commands Kohram, his sword-brandishing eldest son,
Whose head rises above the shining sun, to come to court.
He says to him, "Select riders from the army,
Heroes worthy of battle, and march in haste to Balkh,
For this city is the source of our dim and bitter misfortune.

PART EIGHTEEN

Cut heads off our enemies, fire-worshippers,
And any Ahriman who crosses your path.
Burn their homes; turn their bright day into dark night.

"May the smoke lifting from the flames
At Goshtaasp's castle rise as high as the dome of sky.
If you find Esfandiar, feet bound, promptly end his life,
Cut off his head and fill the world with your deed's glory.
The entire land of Iran is yours.
You are the sword while the enemy is your sheath.
In a short while, I shall in turn leave Khalokh
And swiftly follow the trail of your stages.
I shall bring together the dispersed troops
And spend a portion of my amassed wealth."

Kohram assures him, "I shall obey you, father!
May my life comply to the fulfillment of your wishes!"

Once the sun unsheathes its resplendent sword
And the dark night withdraws its mantle's folds,
Kohram drives one hundred thousand
Dagger-wielding troops to Iran,
And the earth turns as black as the dark face of night.

As soon as he invades the border,
Kohram releases the hands of idol worshipers,
Unleashing their vengeful hearts deprived of virtue
As they engage in destruction, devastation, and slaughter.

At the news of Kohram's hateful actions
And the Turks' vengeful approach to Balkh,
Goshtaasp ushers in grief as his companion
And says to Yazdan, "O Creator,
You are above the rotations of fate.
You are almighty, eternal, all-knowing,
Master of the shining sun, Protector of faith,
Of my body and mind, my spirit and strength.
Do not let me fall into the hands of these men.
You are the support of those who implore you.
Safeguard my name from being obliterated
And my life from capitulating to the point of a dagger."

Noblemen and horsemen have evacuated Balkh.

Only one thousand artisans come from the bazaar,
Men little suited and equipped for battle.

At the approach of the army of Turks,
Lohraasp dons his armor and Kianian helmet,
And strides from temple to battlefield.
Despite his advancing years,
He bellows a cry like a war elephant.
Brandishing a bull-headed mace,
He assails and knocks down many Turkish fighters.

Everyone says that his strokes of mace are reminiscent
Of the ones administered by the bold Esfandiar.
No matter which direction he spurs his horse,
He kneads together blood and dust.
Whoever hears Lohraasp's voice feels himself wilting.

Kohram says to the Turks,
"Do not attack him alone. Use a combined force.
Surround him, roaring at him like furious lions."

At that moment rises the sound of hammers
Breaking through armor and the tumult of vengeful riders.

Lohraasp remains alone in the midst of enemy troops.
He invokes the name of Yazdan in his distress.
He feels overwhelmed by the weight of years
And by the heat of the sun as his fortune wanes.

A Turkish arrow finds its way to pierce the old man,
And this valiant Yazdan worshipper is toppled.
His crowned head falls into the dust,
And a crowd of enemy riders fall upon him.

They break his Kianian armor
And slash his body with their swords.
They had assumed he was a young warrior.
But once they remove his helmet from his kingly head,
They notice his camphor white hair and his celestial face,
Reddened by the steely weight of his headress.

They remain confounded at his side and exclaim,
"O how this old man skillfully brandished his sword!

If Esfandiar had been present, our host would have perished.
Why did we come in such small numbers?
We advanced like a herd going to pasture."

Kohram replies to his companions,
"This battle is the goal of our labor.
We were meant to execute it and succeed.
This crowned prince is King Lohraasp,
The father of world ruler Goshtaasp.
He was once King of Kings,
Drenched in majesty and divine grace.
His life was divided between feastly hall and battlefield.
But in his declining years, he committed himself to Yazdan,
His heart rejecting the crown and throne.
Now that Goshtaasp has lost his support,
He will tremble fiercely for his royal diadem."

The Turks enter Balkh, and the world plunges into ruins
From their relentless murders and massacres.
They take the direction of the fire temple,
Toward the palace and the golden room of the king.
They burn the entire *Zand Avesta*
And consume in flames palace, temple, and valued assets.

Eighty men of faith, worshipping in the shrine,
Whose tongues ceaselessly utter Yazdan's name,
Are slain, their deaths ending their lives of devotion,
Their blood extinguishing the sacred blaze of Zartosht.
I do not know what purpose there was
In killing innocent men of faith.

28 | Goshtaasp Learns of the Death of Lohraasp

Goshtaasp has a wife full of sense and reason,
One endowed with powerful wisdom.
She selects a charger from the stables,
Mounts it, and, dressed in the fashion of Turks,
She exits the palace and takes the road to Sistan.

Moved by the events that transpired,
She does not rest when she arrives at a station

But travels the distance of two days in one.
She continues in this manner until she reaches Goshtaasp
To communicate to him the news of the loss of Lohraasp.

She says, "What is taking you so long?
Why have you left the illustrious city of Balkh?
A vast host has come from the land of Tooran,
Rendering the day bitter to the city dwellers.
The entire region is plagued with pillage and murder.
You must instantly make your way back."

Goshtaasp replies, "Why fret so? Why worry so?
Is this grief, this lamenting for a single assault?
When I take the road with an army,
The entire land of Chin will bend to my will."

She retorts, "Do not speak foolish words,
For a terrible thing has happened to you.
Lohraasp, King of Kings, has been killed in Balkh,
And our days have dimmed and turned bitter.
Then the Turks entered the temple of Nooshaazar,
And they cut off the head of the venerable Zartosht.
The brilliant flame was consumed by the blood
Spilled when they beheaded the religious men.
One must not take such matters lightly!
Next, they took your daughters captive.
Do not belittle such dour calamities!
If it were only the distress of your daughter Homay,
The heart of a sensible man would be broken.
They removed Behaafarid, your child, from her seat,
Who had never been seen by the slightest breeze.
They plucked off her crown and bracelets!"

These words engulf Goshtaasp with a sense of grief,
And blood tears flow from his lashes.
He convenes the noblemen of Iran-Zamin
And relates to them the latest news.

Everyone sheds copious tears.
Each feels as if he is consumed by a terrible blaze.
"May thousands of blessings fall upon the dust
At the feet of the one who succeeds in ridding
Lohraasp's throne of the presence of the spiteful Turks!

May paradise rejoice in pride to welcome his pure soul!"

The king summons a scribe.
He takes off his crown and steps down from his throne.
He sends horsemen to distribute his missive
To every leader at every border, with the command:
"Do not even take a moment to wash your hands!
Pay attention to neither mountain nor valley.
Rush to my court dressed in coats of mail,
And equipped with mace and Rumi helmets."

Every powerful prince of the empire receives the message.
Soon armies of vengeful horsemen, from every corner
And every province, take the direction of the royal court.

Goshtaasp distributes tribute, leaves Sistan,
And sets off for the glorious city of Balkh.
Rostam travels the distance of one day with him.
Mournful, the warrior hero says, "O world King,
Such is the end of life in the world
When there remains neither father nor offspring.
Do not distress. We have no choice but to accept our fate.
You are king, and I am merely your humble servant."
Rostam says this and kisses the royal face.
He remains stationary while the king marches off to war.

Once Arjaasp learns that Goshtaasp,
Master of throne and crown, has dispatched an army,
He, in turn, musters such a vast host
That the circles of sun and moon dim
And no part of the ground can be distinguished
On the surface of the earth, from sea to sea.

Soon, the dust from the two hosts blend,
The earth turns black, the air the color of lapis lazuli.
The armies spread their lines on both sides,
Steeled with sword, spear, and javelin.

On the right wing of the Iranian host is Farshidvard,
Son of a king, eager to battle ferocious lions.
On the left wing, the brave Nastoor, son of Zarir,
From whom the revolving dome of sky borrows its light.
World owner Goshtaasp stands at the center,

Keenly observing his troops.

On the side of the Tooranians, Kondor commands
The right wing, followed by infantrymen and supplies.
On the left wing is the skilled swordsman Kohram
And at the center, Arjaasp, with his entourage.

The sound of timpani is heard on both sides.
The earth is covered in a mantle of steel.
The sky is the color of ebony.
It is as if the firmament itself has taken flight
And the earth would shatter beneath the weight of hosts.
Boulders conceal their peaks, so struck with fear are they
By the neigh of horses and the clash of weapons and axes.
The field is covered with headless corpses,
Lying in the dust and broken by heavy mace.
The blades of swords are ablaze; arrows rain down like hail.
Heroes scream as they strike and are struck.
The stars seek to flee. Troops prepare to surrender their lives.
Arrows descend from the skies like morning dew upon grass.
The plain resonates with the lament of the wounded.

Many warriors are trampled beneath horses' hooves.
The maw of lions serves as shroud, their blood as casket.
Everywhere are headless, limbless bodies.
The riders' mouths foam in the manner of elephants.
Fathers have not the time to feel sorry for sons.

In this way turns the vault of sky,
With the battle lasting three days and three nights,
Galvanized by hatred and rage, fervor, and much clamor.

The battlefield is in such a state that the abundant
Flow of blood turns the face of the moon crimson.
In the midst, Farshidvard pounces lion-like on Kohram.
The latter strikes him with his sword.
Farshidvard finds himself wounded so deeply
That his soul swiftly exits his graceful body.

Many Iranians are killed, and the earth
Is covered with the blood of brave warriors.

Goshtaasp has thirty-eight brave sons on the mountain

And many a warrior on the plain.
Every one of them falls on the battlefield,
And the king, abandoned by fortune, begins to despair.

29 | Goshtaasp Runs Away From Arjaasp

The thought of his fallen sons
Deeply wounds Goshtaasp's heart,
Rendering his body weak and powerless.
He must contend with the death of a father
As well as the deaths of many sons.
He is stranded on an island of sadness and sorrow.
His hand, paralyzed, can no longer reach for his sword.
The world and kingship have lost their worth to him.

In the end, fate condemns, so that the king is forced to flee.
The Turks pursue him for two stations,
Hoping to seize him, but a mountain appears before him,
Covered in green and on which
There are rushing springs able to spin windmills.
Goshtaasp has secret knowledge of the only path out.

Heartbroken, he climbs the slope with his troops,
Leaving a number of them to camp on the way.

As Arjaasp arrives in this place with his army,
He goes around the mountain, unable to find access.
He occupies the surrounding land, hoping to find a path.

Goshtaasp, the king of noble character,
Finds himself without resources.
Fires are lit on the mountain,
And weeds and bushes are burned.
Each man kills a charger to feed on,
And they begin to reflect on their grim fate.

The compassionate king, seeing himself surrounded
By the enemy, takes his head in his hands in despair,
Calls the wise Jaamaasp, speaks to him about the stars,
And adds, "Tell me what you know of the sky's rotation.
Hurry. Question the stars and reveal your discoveries.

Tell me who can save me from such calamity."

At these words, Jaamaasp rises and cries,
"O just King, if you wish to listen to me,
If you wish to have faith in the rotation of the stars,
I shall tell his majesty all that I know,
As long as he considers me an honest man."

The king replies, "Reveal to me the secrets of the sky,
And do not hide anything from me.
Even if my head were to reach the clouds,
I would not escape the rotations of fate."

Jaamaasp says to him, "O King, lend me your ear.
At your command, Esfandiar is bound by chains,
The cause of his grave misfortune.
If you wish to return his freedom to him,
You will no longer be locked up in this mountain."

Goshtaasp relies, "O honest man, you speak the truth.
You show me the path to a resolution.
On the word of a cunning adversary,
I burdened with bonds my innocent son.
Since then, I have deeply regretted it.
My wounded heart has searched for a remedy.
If I see Esfandiar appear on the battlefield,
I shall give him my throne and crown.
But who dares travel to my noble son?
Who will free his innocent body from the bonds?"

Jaamaasp replies, "O King,
I shall go, for this is a serious affair."

Goshtaasp says, "May reason always be your mate!
Go in the dark of night to find this ally
Whom we afflicted so sternly despite his innocence.
Take my blessings to him, talk to him, be kind to him.
Tell him that the man who committed this injustice
Has left the world, anger lodged in his heart,
And that I have struggled with grief
Ever since I committed these unjust actions.
I listened to a subject devoid of knowledge.
I am now willing to atone for my deeds.

If my son wishes to dispel
Thoughts of vengeance from his heart,
He will help lower to the dust the heads of our foes.
Otherwise, both kingdom and throne are lost,
And the Kianian tree will be uprooted.
If he comes, I shall give him my throne
And the treasures I have amassed with great labor.
I shall engage in the worship of Yazdan, like my father.
The Creator is my witness, and Jaamaasp is my guide."

Jaamaasp dons the Tooranian armor,
Descends the mountain to the plain without a guide.
He carefully traverses the Tooranian camp in the dark.
Then he sends his steed of wind on a high-speed gallop,
All the way to the princely son.

Once he approaches the Castle of Gombadan,
He senses that he is protected by fate.

30 | Jaamaasp Visits Esfandiar

Nooshaazar, one of Esfandiar's noble sons,
Stands at the top of the castle ramparts,
Guarding the road, waiting for Iranian troops
In the hopes of reporting back to his father.
Once he discerns Jaamaasp astride on the road,
A handsome Tooranian helmet on his head,
He thinks, "I must tell my father
About this rider coming from Tooran."

He climbs quickly down the rampart and cries out,
"O illustrious world hero, I have spotted from afar
A horseman wearing a black helmet.
I shall return to see whether he is a subject of Goshtaasp
Or an adversary, perhaps a man sent by Arjaasp.
If he is a Turk, I shall swiftly cut off his head
And fling his cursed body into the dust."

The noble Esfandiar replies, "Who could be
This man traveling on the road without an escort?
He is most likely someone from the Iranian host

With a message from my father, who, fearful of the enemy,
Must have placed this Turkish helmet on his head."

At these words, Nooshaazar rushes back
To the castle ramparts, and once Jaamaasp is close to him,
The prince recognizes him, descends, and announces
To his father that the blessed Jaamaasp stands at his door.

Esfandiar asks for the gates to be opened.
The wise Jaamaasp enters, pays homage to him,
And repeats to him, from beginning to end,
His father's message and the blessings sent from end to end.

Esfandiar responds to him, "O heir of great heroes,
O wise, powerful, and proud man,
How can you pay tribute to a bound man?
When one is clamped hand and foot in manacles,
One is no longer a child of men but of Ahriman.
You bring me blessings from the Iranian king;
Is your heart then deprived of true sense?
It is Arjaasp who sends me blessings,
Since he has flooded the desert with Iranian blood.
I have been burdened by chains, innocent as I am,
Because, without a doubt, Gorazm is son of the king.
He is a prince, while I needed to be restrained in chains.
But I take my bonds as witness before Yazdan
That Goshtaasp executed grave injustice
And that Ahriman rejoiced at the words of Gorazm.
Here is the reward for my suffering!
The treasures reserved for me are these shackles!
May I never forget my father's most wrongful act!
May I never lose my mind as a result of your words!"

Jaamaasp says, "O prince, you speak the truth.
You are world conqueror, hero vanquisher, name-seeker.
If you turn your heart away from your father in loathing,
Know that the kingly throne has been snatched from him.
May your heart be sensitive to the plight of King Lohraasp,
A pious man viciously killed by the Turks in battle!
May you take on the aging Yazdan worshippers,
Standing quietly before the altar with the *Zand Avesta*.
Eighty wise men of faith have been slain,

Sages of pure heart devoted to the cult,
Whose blood extinguished the sanctuary blaze.
One must not treat lightly such grave felonies.
May your anger unfurl and your cheeks grow pale!
May your heart take pity then on your grandfather,
And may you dash away to avenge him,
Or else Yazdan our Guide will disapprove!"

Esfandiar responds, "O famed warrior of auspicious star,
Reflect a bit on the fact that the devoted Lohraasp,
Goshtaasp's father, is better avenged by his son,
Who robbed him of his throne and royal honor!
Why should I be the one to go to his rescue?"

Jaamaasp replies,
"If you refuse to avenge your grandfather,
If you harbor no concern in your heart, learn that
Your sisters, Homay the prudent and Behaafarid,
Whose faces have never been glanced upon,
Not even by a breath of air, have been captured
By Tooranians and are afflicted and miserable,
Forced to walk barefoot, their cheeks pale."

Esfandiar retorts, "Did Homay ever lend a thought
To my condition as I lay here bound up?
As for the noble Behaafarid,
It is as if she has never seen me before.
Why should I endure hardships
When neither one enquired after my condition?
It is better for the father to attempt to assist them."

Jaamaasp further pleads, "O brave hero,
Your father's mind is troubled by his fate.
He is now on the mountain, surrounded by his leaders.
His eyes are full of tears, his lips in need of sustenance.
He is encircled by Turkish troops, and never again
Will you set eyes on him or on his diadem.
Yazdan, the Creator, would not approve of you
Turning your heart away from warmth and faith.
How you have endured relentless hostility from your father!
A better course is affection to supplant his aversion.
Do you not feel pity for the fate of your two sisters?

No one has experienced such deep feelings of vengeance.
Even the heart of black stone weeps for them,
For the names of the noble maidens have been ruined.
What will people say? They are your royal sisters.
Contemplate the matter without giving thought to yourself.
Allow wisdom to be your guide.
You had thirty-eight brothers,
Each as fierce as mountain leopards and desert lions.
They all rest on beds of mud and brick,
For our enemies have not allowed a single one to survive."

Esfandiar replies, "I had so many illustrious brothers
Who spent their years in feast
While I sat in confinement, restrained by shackles.
Not once did they remember me in my misery.
Not one of them had the compassion to ask about me.
Not one of them doubted my father
For his decision to imprison me.
If I were to engage now in battle,
What good would it do them, since they are gone?"

Jaamaasp's heart filled with anguish, he rises,
Heart in a fury, tears of despair streaking his cheeks.
He says, "O world warrior, no matter how troubled you feel,
What will you say of the fate of Farshidvard,
Endlessly afflicted with misfortune?
Whether in battle or in feast, no matter where,
He was filled with anger and cursed the wicked Gorazm.
I witnessed him pierced and wounded by a sword,
With helmet and armor splintered over his lifeless body.
My soul breaks from the extent of my wish to bend you.
Have pity for his weeping, shining eyes.
He is surrendering his life on the battlefield.
Forgive the past deeds if only for his pure soul.
He suffers many wounds, yet he prays for your release:
        'Do not take my life, until I can set my sight,
            If only once, on the person of Esfandiar.'"

At this account on the subject of Farshidvard,
Esfandiar's cheeks flood with blood tears, his heart clamps,
He cries out, "Alas, my valiant brother, brave hero,
Prince of lion heart, I feel the agony of your wounds!

My cheeks flood with my heart's blood!
Your heart has always been united with mine.
I shall cinch my waist to avenge you."

He utters these words, loses his mind,
Falls back, and begins to holler.
As he calms down a bit, he says to Jaamaasp,
"Why did you hide this matter from me?
I would have forgiven it all for the sake of Farshidvard
Without causing you further grief.
Now quickly bring blacksmiths to file down my chains."

Upon Jaamaasp's order,
Blacksmiths arrive with hammer and anvil of steel.
They grind at chains, nails, neck ring, and a Rumi steel post.
But all these objects could only be crushed at a slow rate,
And the prisoner grows restless and impatient.

He says to the blacksmith, "O clumsy one,
You are the one who forged these irons,
And you cannot break them fast enough!"
He removes his hand, stands up,
And, in his fury, extends his shackled limbs.
He straightens his legs, bends his hands,
And breaks in one strike all of the chains.
Once freed, he is so drained that he collapses
From exhaustion and loses consciousness.

The astrologer witnesses this marvelous feat.
He invokes Yazdan's grace on the illustrious prince.
The hero, endowed with such astonishing strength,
Regains consciousness, places all the chains
In front of him, and says, "These gifts from Gorazm
Have obstructed my path to battle and feast!"

He collects the chains and heads toward the plain.
He says, "I lament to the World Creator about my father,
Who is the source of these iron bonds and nails.
I was bound to the will of Yazdan and not to these chains.
Zartosht dictated ups and downs in the *Zand Avesta*.
Anyone who refrains from obeying his father's order
Will adopt the name of sorcerer son.
The act of imprisoning the son by a father

Is a more valued one than scattering flowers on your foes.
I never dismissed my father's command.
I never spoke back to him.
Anyone who acts wrongfully will suffer consequences."

Next, he takes an escort to the baths.
He dips his aching body into the water,
For his limbs are creased and rusty from the chains
And his chest by a heavy iron brace.

Once he is cleaned of rust,
He demands royal armor, a warrior coat of mail,
A fervent charger, a helmet, and a sword.

Jaamaasp collects the required items.
Esfandiar suits up and rises.
As his eyes rest on the horse,
He invokes the name of the Creator and cries,
"If I have committed a sin, I have atoned with bonds.
But what crime has this poor, stiff horse committed,
A creature who once walked so proudly
And now has been rendered so thin and sickly?
Wash it, and wash every stain on its hide.
Feed it, so that it may regain its vigor."

Then he summons skilled blacksmiths and orders them
To forge coats of mail and repair his bulky armor.

31 | Esfandiar Sees His Brother Farshidvard

Night emerges, as black as a malicious Ahriman,
And the ringing of bells rises in the palace.
A number of horsemen gather around Esfandiar,
Who climbs on his charger in the dark,
Holding in his hand an Indian saber.
He departs for a long voyage with Bahman
And Nooshaazar, preceded by their guide, Jaamaasp,
As instructed by the blessed Goshtaasp.

They exit through the palace gates and march to the desert.
Esfandiar turns his face toward the sky and says,

"O true Supreme Judge, you are the almighty Creator,
You have filled with joy Esfandiar's heart.
If I am victorious in battle, if I succeed in constricting
The world for Arjaasp and cast on him the vengeance
Due Lohraasp and my thirty-eight innocent brothers,
Who have colored the desert sand red with blood,
I vow before you, Just Master, that I hold no resentment
For the shackles that my father confined me with.
I shall establish one hundred fire temples in the world.
I shall free and purify the earth from tyrants.
No one will witness my foot touch a carpet
Before I have the chance to build
One hundred caravansaries in the desert.
I shall excavate wells and plant ten thousand trees
Around them in barren lands where no wild beast
Ventures and where deer and vulture steer clear.
I shall distribute one hundred thousand coins
From my treasury to the poor and the needy.
I shall guide the faithless to the true faith,
Overturn the heads of sorcerers,
And stand in worship before Yazdan.
No one will ever see me surrender to rest."

He says this and launches his charger.
He finds Farshidvard resting on a bed of dust,
Asleep, wounded, and disheveled.
His eyes spill such torrents of tears
That the medicine man is touched by his grief.

Esfandiar says to his brother, "O battle-seeker,
Who has caused you such grave injuries?
Tell me so that I may avenge you in fight,
Whether your enemy is a valiant lion or a whale."

Farshidvard replies, "O brave warrior,
Goshtaasp is the one to inflict these mortal wounds.
If he had not dismissed you and cast you to chains,
The Turks would never have treated me so wickedly.
In the same way, our father is to blame
For Lohraasp's death and the destruction of Balkh.
No one has ever endured fiercer troubles
Than the ones caused by Gorazm's malicious words.

But do not fall into a fit of anger.
Surrender to divine justice.
Remain in the world as a tree bearing abundant fruit.
As for me, I leave for another dwelling
While you remain here eternally.
Once I abandon the earth, maintain a memory of me,
And bring joy by spreading good deeds.
Let me just say that my wounds were inflicted by Kohram.
Farewell, O world warrior!
May you be happy and your life everlasting!"
Farshidvard, glorious lion, says this with pallid cheeks.
He pants feebly and soon expels his last breath.

Esfandiar strikes his armor with his hand.
He tears his silk clothes to shreds and cries,
"O pure Creator, guide me as I avenge Farshidvard,
And convert stones and water into dust!
I shall spill Arjaasp's blood and calm Lohraasp's soul!"

He places his deceased brother on his horse's saddle,
Heart full of hatred, head full of impatience.
He carries him away from plain to mountain
On his dun charger, saying to his brother,
"Now what can I do for you?
How can I raise a proper resting place?
I possess neither gold nor gems, neither brick nor water,
And there are no masons around these parts.
I must find some trees to provide shade for you."

In the end, the noble prince buries his brother's corpse
At the foot of a tree to shield it from the scorching sun.
He divests himself of his war armor and creates a shroud for him
Out of his tunic and out of the cloth protecting his head.
Once this task is complete, he takes off toward Goshtaasp,
A king who has gone astray from the just and true path.

Esfandiar finds so many Iranian corpses on the ground
That they make dust and sand disappear.
He weeps bitterly for the dead,
These poor men whose days have vanished.

In a place where the battle was fierce,
His eye is struck by the pallid face of Gorazm,

Next to whom a horse is sprawled
And on whom dust has been tossed.

Esfandiar addresses the deceased: "O foolish one,
Reflect on the words of an insightful man from Iran,
Uttered when he revealed the most profound secret:
That a wise adversary is more valuable than a friend.
Wisdom is as favorable in friendship as in enmity.
The sage says that one must think of his actions
And not strain himself to search
For something beyond his power.
You wished to seize my seat in Iran, and by doing so,
You gave rise to so much misery in the world.
With your ruse and your lies,
You smeared the empire's splendor.
You will have to answer in the other world
For the blood you have spilled in this battle."

Then, sobbing, he turns away from the dead
And approaches the Tooranian army.
He sees a camp stretching seven farsangs across the plain,
The size of which propels the sky into a state of stupor.
A ditch runs around its circumference,
Wider than the length of an arrow.

He crosses this gap with a thousand strains
And spurs his horse into the desert.
At this moment, a patrol of eighty Tooranians
Gallops across the field, charging toward him in chaos,
Screaming, and showering him with questions.
Someone asks Esfandiar, "O lion man,
What are you doing on the battlefield?"

He replies, "You think only of rest and feast in the arena.
When Kohram received news that you allowed
Esfandiar to pass through, he commanded me to seize
My double-edged sword and to destroy you all."

He draws his blade and falls on them,
Invoking the memory of the battle they launched.
He overthrows a great number of them on the road
And takes off in the direction of King Goshtaasp.

32 | Esfandiar Arrives at the Mountain

Esfandiar nears the rocky mountain,
Spots his father, and pays homage to him.

The father, with a remorseful heart, rises, kisses him,
And touches his face with his hand, exclaiming,
"Praise be the Creator, O young man.
I set my eyes on you, my heart full of joy!
Do not hold it against me, do not be upset at me,
And do not use your strength in retaliation.
Gorazm, this wicked, ill-natured man,
Blinded my heart, turning it against my son.
His evil words cast misfortune
Upon his own vicious person,
And his sinful deeds propelled him to his end.
I swear by the World Creator,
Who is aware of the revealed and unrevealed,
That as soon as I am once again happy and victorious,
I shall surrender to you the empire, throne and crown.
My last wish is to retire from court
And spend my declining years in a temple.
I wish to lavish you with the hidden treasures I possess."

Esfandiar replies, "May the king be pleased with me!
His approval is the crown and throne that I long for.
May the world master know
That once I saw Gorazm lying on the battlefield,
I could only weep over this man who cursed me.
I thought with anguish of the king's suffering.
The bitterness of our days is now over.
I regard past events as nothing more than wind.
Now, when I draw my sword of vengeance,
When I exit this mountain of granite, I shall allow
To survive neither Arjaasp nor Aayaas of Chin,
Neither Kohram nor Khalokh, nor the land of Tooran."

When the warriors learn that Esfandiar has been freed
Of his heavy chains and of his state of misfortune,
They arrive on the mountaintop, division by division.
Noblemen, relative or stranger,
Press their foreheads at his feet in reverence.

PART EIGHTEEN

They acclaim him as a vengeance-seeking king.

Esfandiar of fortunate star says to them,
"O illustrious dagger-wielding men,
Draw your double-edged blades dipped in poison,
Engage in battle, and destroy the enemy!"

The noblemen praise him and cry,
"You are our diadem!
You are the blade of vengeance!
We wager our lives as a solemn pledge to you.
Our weapons express joy at the mere sight of you."

They spend the night preparing the army,
Polishing armor and swords.

Once again Goshtaasp speaks with sorrow
To the blessed Esfandiar of the adversities of fate.
Torrents of tears flood his cheeks
As he expresses his grief for the death of his young sons,
Princes full of zeal for war, killed on the battlefield,
Whose royal heads have, ultimately,
Been garlanded by a crown of blood.

That very night, Arjaasp learns that Goshtaasp
Has been joined by his son, a mighty warrior
Who slew many enemy troops on the road
And forced many others into flight.

The King of Tooran grows anxious,
Convenes his leaders, and discusses at length,
Addressing Kohram: "We counted
On a different outcome when we initiated war.
At the time we set the army into motion,
I believed the world was out of danger,
Since this deev Esfandiar was bound in chains.
I envisioned myself master of Iran and Chin.
Holding dominion over the world,
I envisioned all nations paying homage to us.
But today, this son of a deev has been freed.
We are left to worry with the prospect of battle.
Not one Tooranian equals him in strength,
Not one can stand up to him in combat.

It is better for us then to return to Tooran-Zamin,
Content in the security of our crowns and thrones."

He orders the gathering of all that is precious:
Horses in trappings, dazzling golden brocade,
Golden jewels, dinars, rubies, crown, and belts.
All the loot from Balkh he hands over to Kohram.
His four younger sons are charged
With piling the loads onto camels
And departing in every direction, each son leading
One hundred camels, each escorted by a guide.

Arjaasp's heart fills with fear, his head with impatience
As hunger, rest, and sleep evade him.

Now there is a Turkman named Gorgsaar
Who emerges from the army line and approaches the king.
He says, "O master of Tooran and Chin,
Do not allow your glory to be crushed by a single man.
Observe the Iranian army, defeated and in flight.
Their fortune has been shaken, the royal sons are dead,
And the king himself is in the throes of despair.
The only man to come to his aid is Esfandiar.
You would shatter your army's courage,
You would allow them to feel overcome by your words
Without having engaged in battle?
A wise king does not reside in the dwelling of fear.
No helmet has yet been shattered by mace or blade.
No barding has yet been pierced by arrows.
I am Esfandiar's counterpart in fight,
And I shall fling to the dust his heroic corpse!"

Arjaasp listens to the valiant and prudent man,
And replies, "O warlord eager for battle,
You have name, birth, and prominence.
If you are able to fulfill your promise,
If your courage extends the length of your tongue,
I shall give you lands from Khargaah to the Sea of Chin.
I shall give you treasures amassed in Iran-Zamin.
You will be appointed army chief,
And I shall obey your command."
Right away, he places him at the head of the troops

And promises him the governance of two-thirds of the world.

Once the sun raises its golden shield,
The dark night clasps its head in its despair
And discards its musk-colored robe.
At the moment the face of the world shines
As bright as a ruby, a vast host exits the mountain,
Steered by Esfandiar, world master.
The world dims like a sea of tar with the army's motion.

Nastoor, son of Zarir, before whom fierce lions flee,
Commands the right wing, head full of thoughts.
Esfandiar sits on his horse at the head of troops,
A bull-headed mace hanging on his saddle.
King Goshtaasp is positioned at the center,
His heart full of vengeful fervor for Arjaasp.
Finally, Gargooy the brave leads the left wing,
Shining like the sun in the house of the ram.

On the other side, Arjaasp forms the ranks.
Stars can no longer glimpse the ground.
Numerous are the spears and dimmed swords.
The earth billows softly with the movement
Of colorful silk-embroidered standards.

The center, where Arjaasp stands, is as black as ebony.
Kohram leads the right wing, with clarions and timpani.
The left wing belongs to the King of Chegel,
From whom lions borrows courage on the day of battle.

Arjaasp, at the sight of this mass of brave cavaliers
Armed with spear, cries the call of departure.
He selects a raised hill, a good surveillance spot
To observe the troops on every sides.
His heart fills with fear of the enemy.
The world darkens before his eyes.

He asks the camel driver to bring one hundred beasts
And says in secret to his noblemen,
"If battle lasts too long,
If the outcome appears contrary to a victory,
I shall retreat with my entourage on speedy camels."

Esfandiar, in the midst of the two hosts,
Begins to move like a ferocious lion, mouth foaming,
Bull-headed mace in hand, like the revolving dome.
You would think that his being pervades the field
And his skin is about to crack, so intense is his fury.

The clatter of battle rings with the blowing of trumpets;
The army warriors are set in motion.
The desert ground appears like a sea of blood,
And swords shine in the air like the Pleiades in the sky.

Esfandiar kicks the stirrups, hollering thunderous cries
And striking with his bull-headed mace.
Clutching it tight in his hand of steel,
He kills three hundred warring Turks in the army core.
He yells, "Today I shall reduce the sea to dust
To avenge the death of Farshidvard."

Then he lurches on the right wing,
Releases the reins of his keen horse,
And kills one hundred and sixty soldiers.

Kohram chooses to flee as Esfandiar cries out,
"This is how I avenge my grandfather,
Whose death has consumed the king's heart with grief!"
He pivots, swinging the reins to the left,
And the entire ground becomes a sea of blood.

He kills one hundred and sixty-five valiant men,
Powerful warriors, possessors of crown and treasure.
He shouts, "This is how I avenge
My thirty-eight noble, deceased brothers!"

At the sight of him, Arjaasp says to Gorgsaar,
"Our innumerable host is already destroyed.
There remains no one, not a single warrior in the ranks.
I do not understand why you remain quiet
And why you have told me all these tales."

These words awaken Gorgsaar's courage,
And he advances toward the vanguard,
Brandishing a royal bow in one hand
And a steel-tipped arrow in the other.

Drawing close enough, he affixes the arrow to the bow
And sends a shot into the hero's chest.
Esfandiar collapses on the saddle,
Pretending that the arrow has pierced through his armor
And wounded his glistening, Kianian breast.

Gorgsaar draws a shiny steel blade
And prepares to sever Esfandiar's head.
But the latter, fearing an injury,
Reaches for his rolled-up noose
And flings it around Gorgsaar's neck,
Uttering the name of the World Creator.
With Gorgsaar's head and neck captured in the knot,
Esfandiar hurls to the ground his trembling body.
Then he ties his two hands behind his back,
Clamps the ends of the string at the nape of his neck,
Removes Gorgsaar from the army ranks,
And drags him to the Iranian camp, mouth spewing blood.

He sends his enemy to the auspicious Goshtaasp,
Surrendering him to the king of golden helmet,
And says, "Let us tie him to your tent enclosure
And abstain from killing him for the moment
Until we can evaluate the turns of fortune.
We shall soon find out which side will be victorious
And which side is to be vanquished."

Esfandiar returns to the field with his host
To rekindle the blaze of battle.
The earth dims from the dust of riders.

Arjaasp says to his brave men, "Where is Kohram?
One can no longer mark his banner on the right wing.
Where is lion-vanquisher Kondor,
Who boldly strikes with sword and pierces through
Mountains with his spear and arrows?"

They tell Arjaasp that Esfandiar has engaged in a fight
With the lion Gorgsaar and has captured him,
That the air gleams in shades of violet
From the reflection of warrior blades,
And that the banner with a wolf's face has vanished.

Such an account fills Arjaasp's heart with anguish.
He demands a camel and heads toward the plain.
His close men trail him on camelback,
Leading their horses by the reins.
He deserts his host on the battlefield
And takes the road to Khalokh.

Esfandiar hollers to the Iranians, causing
The mountain to tremble at the boom of his voice:
"Do not brandish your swords of war without using them!
Pierce into your adversaries' hearts.
Make them function as sheaths for your blades.
Convert the land of Tooran into Mount Ghaaran."[69]

The brave warriors, eager for vengeance, hold tight
To their chargers as the two hosts fall on each other.
The earth disappears beneath torrents of blood that rush
With enough speed to set windmills into motion.

The entire field is scattered with legs, heads,
Trunks with split chests, and hands still gripping swords.
Rider warriors charge onto the battlefield,
Unable to collect all the finery scattered upon it.

When the Turks learn that Arjaasp has fled,
They feel their skin crawl off their bodies with grief.
Those on horseback take the road and gallop away.
Others cast aside their armor and helmets,
And rush to Esfandiar, shouting cries of distress.
Their eyes spill tears like rain falling from spring clouds.

The mighty hero grants them mercy,
And from that day on, he refrains from further killing.
He imposes silence to his heart
On the subject of his grandfather's murder
And charges a warrior with the guard of the Turks.

Esfandiar and his host go to the royal court,
Their chests, swords, and golden helmets drenched in blood.
His dagger is wedged in blood in the palm of his hand.

◇◇◇◇◇◇◇◇◇◇◇◇◇
69 Mount Ghaaran: Perhaps a fictional mountain; convert the land into a heap of
corpses.

His chest and shoulders are deeply creased by his armor.

They dip his hand and blade in milk to pull them apart.
They wrench the arrows from his coat of mail.
Then this hero, wishing to possess the world,
Lowers his body into water, washes his head and limbs
With a light heart and a healthy body.

Esfandiar demands garments of worship
And presents himself before the true and just Master.
For one week, he and his father, Goshtaasp,
Stand in reverence before Yazdan, pure and perfect.
On the eighth day, Esfandiar returns to court.

Gorgsaar approaches the throne, despairing of life,
His body quivering with fright
Like a willow branch fluttering in the wind.
He kisses the ground at the foot of the throne.
His face as yellow as sandarac with fear, he says,
"O King, this gathering will not welcome my death.
Allow me to stand behind you as your loyal slave,
To serve you as your guide to good fortune,
To lessen hardships that may befall you,
To lead you to the bronze castle."

Esfandiar orders him to be dragged, bound, to his tents.
Then he marches over to the camp of his enemy, Arjaasp,
The one culpable for the spillage of Lohraasp's blood.
He adorns his leaders, his horsemen, and foot soldiers
With precious objects found in the arena.
He executes all the Tooranian prisoners who caused harm.

33 | Goshtaasp Sends Esfandiar to Battle Arjaasp Once More

Next, Esfandiar finds the king in his royal pavilion
And speaks to him on various subjects: Lohraasp,
Farshidvard, his glorious sons on the day of battle
And the manner in which they avenged him.

Goshtaasp says to him, "O powerful man,

You rejoice while your sisters are enslaved!
Happy are the ones who fall on battlefields!
The survivors bow their heads in shame.
What will my subjects say
When they see me on the throne?
This dishonor will cause me
To cry bitterly for the rest of my days.
My head is consumed by a most intense blaze.
I have promised the Creator that, if you successfully
Invade the land of Tooran and remain unscathed,
If you defy the dragon's breath in a manly manner
And free your sisters from the captor's grasp,
I shall offer you the imperial crown, the throne of power,
And my treasure, although you have not labored for it.
I am devoting my remaining days to prayer and worship.
The wealth I have carefully amassed is meant for others."

Esfandiar replies, "O dear father,
May the world never be deprived of your presence!
I stand as a slave before you, not seeking kingship.
May my body and soul vouch for my integrity and loyalty,
For I desire neither throne nor power.
I shall depart, take revenge on Arjaasp once again.
I shall destroy the land of Tooran.
I shall release my sisters from captivity,
Return them to the throne,
Thanks to the fortune of the noble world master."

Goshtaasp praises him and says,
"May wisdom always be your companion!
May you journey on, shielded by divine protection!
May the throne be your seat upon your return!"

Goshtaasp summons troops from all sides,
Any place ruled by a wise man or a lord.
He singles out twelve thousand skilled riders.
He distributes treasure and coins to them,
And leaves no one displeased with his gifts.
He presents Esfandiar with a throne
And a crown inlaid with gems worthy of a king.

Two hundred camels are loaded

With equipment of war and feast.
Voices call in the royal courtyard,
Demanding suitable chargers for the princes.
Tents are lugged to the plain,
Where they raise the banner depicting a royal eagle.
The army is set in motion, and dust dims the shining sun.

Pashootan, the king's counselor,
Is appointed Esfandiar's vizier.
Three thousand camels bear loads of provisions and dinars.
The road is arduous and long,
A road never traveled leading from Iran to Tooran.
The world seeker dismounts to bid farewell to the king.

Father takes son in his arms and speaks to him wisely:
"May you return victorious to assume crown and throne!
May Yazdan be your traveling companion!
At the sight of you in good health,
I shall surrender throne, crown, and treasure."

Esfandiar kisses his father's hand in affection
And returns, his face resplendent.
In the palace, he seeks his mother behind the drapes.
He asks after her well-being and bids her farewell,
Just as the wise man had instructed him.

PART NINETEEN

The Seven Stages of Esfandiar's Quest

The Battle of Esfandiar and Rostam

The Adventure of Rostam and Shaghaad

The Seven Stages
of Esfandiar's Quest

1 | In Praise of King Mahmoud Ghaznavid

Now I shall recount the adventures of the seven stages.
I shall weave a new, flowery tale full of scuffles and schemes,
Full of dissention and resolution,
Full of acts of vengeance and justice, fights and feasts.
If fortune wishes, for once, to come to my aid
And to give free rein to my talent, I shall recount
An astonishing tale that will mystify even wise men.
I shall speak under the auspices of King Mahmoud,
His glorious reign, and his royal crown.
May the world king live forever!
May the earth's great men stand as his devoted slaves!

Once the shining sun reveals its face as it adorns the earth
And places on its head the crown under the sign of the ram,
East and west are both pleased.
Mountains are filled with the rolling din of thunder,
The edges of streams are blanketed with tulips and narcissus.
Narcissus provide delights, tulips restore patience,
The flower of the spikenard causes anguish,
And the pomegranate tree blesses one with fineries.

The hearts of clouds swell with flares, their eyes with tears.
It is the sound of a melody full of rage and fury.
When the thunder is silenced and torrents shower down,
Heads fall asleep beneath the drumming beat.
But when you awaken, look at the earth,
Beautiful as the satin painted by Mani[70] in Chin.

◇◇◇◇◇◇◇◇◇◇◇◇◇◇

70 Mani: Iranian prophet who wrote the holy books of Manichaeism entitled *Arjang*
and also known as the *Book of Pictures;* he preached throughout the land of Persia in
the 3rd century CE.

When the earth shines beneath the sun,
It seeds the cheeks of narcissus and tulip with dew.
It smiles and says, "O pretty ones, it is for the love of you
That I weep, and not out of grief or anger.
In fact, the earth only smiles when the sky sheds tears.
Furthermore, I shall not compare the king's hand to the sky,
For the sky brings down rain only in spring
And does not resemble the unending generosity of rulers.
The king's hand is akin to the sun under the house of Aries.

Whether his treasure comes from the earth
Or from the waters of the sea, whether it is pearl or musk,
Never does he hide his splendor,
Neither from the poor nor from a proud prince.

The hand of King Abul Ghassem, the noble prince,
Is equally plentiful, whether it extends
Before the righteous or before evil men.
Never does he recoil when faced with an act of kindness.
Never does he rest on the day of action.
When he must battle, he fights and seizes the heads of kings.
He openhandedly draws from his wealth
To lavish on anyone who serves him,
Without dwelling on the pains he endured.

May Mahmoud remain world master,
Spread his good deeds, and distribute justice!
If Jamsheed, Kay Khosrow or Kay Ghobaad,
Fereydoon or Eskandar of noble lineage
Were to raise their crowned heads out of the dust,
They would purify this world from injustice.
Still, they rank lower than our glorious king,
Whose mate is the Supreme Creator.

I dedicate this book to the renowned King of Kings.
I do not wish to aggrandize my name.
I only wish to remain alive long enough
To see the realization of my dream.
With these stories, I shall revive the glory
Of highborn warriors who died long ago.
My task is analogous to that of Jesus:
I seek to resurrect their heroic names

While their souls dwell in paradise.
My most fervent hope is for this book
To remain in the world until the end of time.

Now pay attention to the old man full of wisdom
As he relates what comes to pass at the impregnable castle.[71]
Commit the tales to memory, and learn from them.

2 | The First Stage: Esfandiar Kills the Two Wolves

The wise poet bard, gifted storyteller,
Takes his seat to recount the legend of the seven stages.
He raises a golden goblet and begins to speak of Goshtaasp,
Of the impregnable castle, of the high deeds of Esfandiar,
His road, and the instructions given to him by Gorgsaar.

Esfandiar departs from Balkh,
His mouth and heart full of bitter words.
He bids farewell to his father and takes the road
To Tooran in the company of Gorgsaar.
He continues until he reaches a place with a fork in the road.
He asks his men to set up camp, erect the tents,
Organize the spreads, and summon wine and music.
The army heroes join the king.

Esfandiar calls Gorgsaar of sickened heart to his side
And asks that his cup be filled four consecutive times.
Then he says, "O ill-fated man,
I shall help you accede to throne and crown.
If you answer truthfully to all my questions,
Tooran-Zamin will belong to you.
I shall turn it over to you when I am victorious
And raise your head above the shining sun.
I shall not hurt any of your allies or any of your relatives.
But if you forge a lie, it will have no power over me.
I shall cut you in half with my dagger
And fill this gathering with terror."

◇◇◇◇◇◇◇◇◇◇◇◇◇◇
71 Impregnable castle: Arjaasp's fortified castle "roeen dej" meaning unconquerable,
unassailable, or even better: shielded.

Gorgsaar replies, "O illustrious and blessed Esfandiar,
You shall hear from me nothing but truthful words.
Do your part, and act in the manner of kings."

Esfandiar asks, "Where is the impregnable castle?
Is it situated away from the border of Iran-Zamin?
Which road leading to it is the most direct,
The easiest to access, and the least dangerous?
How many troops stand there at any given time?
How high are the ramparts?
Tell me all that you know on the subject."

Gorgsaar replies, "O Esfandiar, O King of blessed trail,
Three roads lead from here to Arjaasp's court,
To which he gives the name of his fortress.
One demands a journey of three months,
The second one will take two months,
And an army can be led there by either road.
On the first one, there is plenty of water,
Fodder, and cities, and it crosses the domains
Of two-thirds of the noblemen of Tooran-Zamin.
On the second road, which requires two months,
You will face challenges in finding sustenance.
There is neither greenery nor water tanks for animals,
And there is no place to stop and rest.

"The third road takes only one week to cross.
The army will reach the invincible castle on the eighth day,
But it is full of lions, wolves, and bold dragons
Who easily capture men in their claws.
Besides, a witch dwells there whose chicanery
Is far more dangerous than the wolves and the lions,
And even worse than the powerful dragons.
She takes one man and ejects him from the sea to the moon
While tossing another into a deep, dark abyss.
On this road, one finds deserts, simorghs,
And a cold so penetrating that it makes trees explode
Into small fragments at the slightest gust of wind.

"Once at the fortified castle, you will be astounded,
For it is such that no one has seen or heard of before.
Its ramparts' crest rises above black clouds.

It is filled with troops and weapons.
It is encircled by a river of running water,
The sight of which stuns the soul.
On his way to hunt, the king crosses this river in a boat.
Were Arjaasp besieged for one hundred years in this fort,
He would need to draw nothing from the countryside,
For there are planted fields and meadows,
Fruit trees and windmills."

Esfandiar shakes his head for some time and sighs deeply.
In the end he speaks: "The third road is the only road for us.
Nothing is better in the world than a short journey."

Gorgsaar replies, "O king, never has anyone tackled
A passage through the road of the seven stages,
Neither by force nor by uproar,
Unless such a person has given up all hope for life."

The hero replies, "If you are with me,
You will witness my courage and my strength.
Tell me, what must I contend with
To find a resolution to the dilemma?"

Gorgsaar replies, "O blessed King and elected rider,
Two wolves will attack you first, a male and a female,
Each one akin to a formidable elephant.
They bear antlers on their heads like stags
And display the fervor of warring lions.
They have tusks like furious elephants.
Their chests and limbs are wide and bulky;
Their hips are thin."

Esfandiar dismisses the vile man to his tent,
Bound up in chains. He asks for a feast
And places the Kianian diadem on his head.

Once the sun's crown climbs down to graze the horizon
And the sky reveals its secrets to the earth,
The sound of timpani rises above the gates.
The earth is covered with steel; the sky is tinged in ebony.

Esfandiar happily takes the road of the seven stages
And departs for Tooran-Zamin with his host.

They march toward the first stage.
He selects an illustrious man from his troops,
Pashootan, a cautious man
Able to safeguard the army from enemy traps.

He says to him, "Keep the troops in order.
Gorgsaar's words have worried me.
I am the leader, and if something happens to me,
Misfortune must not come down on the others."

Then Esfandiar dons his battle armor.
He tightens his black charger's strap,
And he advances toward the wolves,
Clamping his thighs with the strength of a mighty elephant.

The wolves see his chest and his arms,
His belt, his hand, and his mace.
They charge at him across the field
Like two formidable elephants ready to fight.

The hero bends his bow and shouts a terrible cry,
Similar to a howling lion.
He sends a shower of shots toward the Ahrimans
And charges toward a threat so dreadful
It is avoided by many.

The wolves suffer wounds from the arrows' tips.
Neither one finds a path to the hero without being stricken.

Esfandiar observes them with a still heart,
Noticing that the beasts are weakened and in distress.
He draws out a sword dipped in poison,
Launches his horse, and charges wildly.
He splits their heads, tears open their chests,
And plants mud in the dust from their blood.

He dismounts his celebrated charger,
Acknowledging Yazdan for his body's strength.
He wipes out traces of the wolves' blood from his limbs
And his weapons, selects a spot clean of blood,
And turns his flushed face toward the sun.
Heart still full of worry and head covered in dust,
He says, "O Justice Giver, you are the one

Who bestowed strength, glory, and virtue on me.
You have lain these wild beasts in the dust.
You will be my guide in all good deeds."

When Pashootan's troops arrive,
They find the hero engaged in prayer.
In awe of his exploits, they reflect and say,
"Are these creatures wolves or mad elephants?
May Esfandiar's heart, sword, and hand endure forever!
May the royal throne of power, feasts, and army
Never be deprived of his company!"

The leaders, full of wisdom, establish their tents
Next to Esfandiar's pavilion.
They prepare a golden spread,
Eat copiously, and drink abundant wine.

3 | The Second Stage: Esfandiar Kills the Lions

Esfandiar summons the prisoner who comes trembling,
Eyes filled with tears. He cannot help but feel
Deep sorrow for the good fortune of Esfandiar,
Who offers him three cups of wine
And asks, "What do you say now?
What marvels will I be confronted with?"

Gorgsaar replies, "O master of crown, king of lion heart,
At the next stage you will be attacked by lions
With claws so sharp no whale can escape them.
The brave eagle, no matter how valiant he may be,
Dares not soar above their lion's den."

Esfandiar, with a still heart, smiles and says,
"O ill-fated Turk, tomorrow you will witness
How brave I can be in the battle with lions."

At dusk, the king commands the troops to set forth,
And they march off in the dark, singing his praises.
The king's eyes are full of blood and his heart full of worry.

As the sun transforms the dim veils of night
Into swathes of golden brocade,

The leader leaves the encampment
And marches into the field where he is to wrestle the lions.

He calls Pashootan, gives him countless advice,
And says to him, "I entrust this noble army to you
As I depart to engage in a fierce and terrible clash."

He takes off to approach the beasts.
The world dims before the lions' souls.
One is a male lion and the other a lioness.
They crouch boldly in a menacing stance before him.

As the male threateningly approaches him,
Esfandiar strikes him hard with his sword,
So hard the face of the wild beast turns a shade of coral,
And its body splits in half from head to waist.
The heart of the lioness fills with dread,
But she bounds toward him as boldly as her mate.
The hero hits her with a blow of his sword,
Making her head roll in the dust.

The chest and hands of the warrior are stained with blood.
He jumps into the water to wash his face and body.
He solicits the assistance of the Supreme Master:
"You are the One who killed these wild beasts."

During this time, troops appear.
Pashootan observes the chest and limbs of the lions,
And the entire army pays homage to Esfandiar,
Acclaiming him as the most illustrious prince on earth.

Then the hero who serves them as guide returns to his tent.
Spreads are dressed, and the pure King of Kings
Asks for delicate and sumptuous dishes to be served.

4 | The Third Stage: Esfandiar Kills the Dragon

Once again, Esfandiar summons the wicked Gorgsaar.
He gives him three cups of ruby-colored wine,
And, as the syrupy liquid brightens this Ahriman,
The prince says to him, "O miserable man,
Reveal to me what I am to face tomorrow."

Gorgsaar replies, "O King, whose fame exceeds
His splendor, may you never fall to misfortune's sting!
You flung yourself at once, like fire, into peril,
And in this way you outstripped danger.
You have no idea what awaits you tomorrow.
Have pity on the fortune that watches over you.
When you arrive at the third stage,
You will find before you a much graver menace:
A terrible, formidable dragon will come at you,
One that attracts, with its jaws, fish in the sea;
One whose burning breath sets ablaze everything in its path;
Its body is as dense as a mountain of stone.
You should retreat and return to where you came from.
My soul can attest as my witness to this sound advice.
Although you have little care for your well-being,
At least think and take care of this army that surrounds."

Esfandiar replies, "O ill-natured man, I shall drag you
With me thus chained up, and you will see that in battle
The dragon will not escape my double-edged sword!"

He asks for carpenters and solid wood stakes,
And has them build a sturdy wooden chariot,
Adorned with swords, a fearsome sight,
Topped with a cabin designed to conquer.

The ingenious carpenters build the object.
The ambitious Esfandiar, holder of crown,
Is to sit in the cabin to test it out.
He asks to be pulled around by two horses,
Dressed in his coat of mail, holding in his hand
A Kaboli sword, his head clad with a warrior helmet.

Once the prince's preparations are complete,
The world turns black like the face of tar
And the moon shines on its throne under the sign of the ram.

Esfandiar sits on his charger and departs,
Followed by his illustrious army.
The next morning, the world is awash in light,
And the banner of dark night lifts.
The warrior hero, world master, dresses in his coat of mail
And entrusts the army leadership to the blessed Pashootan.

This man of lion heart brings the chariot and the cabin,
And the brave king sits in it.
Noble horses are hitched up to it,
And he takes the direction of the dragon.

The creature hears the distant sound of wheels
And sees the leaping horses full of ardor.
He bounds forth like a massive black mountain.
It feels as if it obscures the sun and moon.
His two eyes are like two fountains of shining blood,
And wicked flames flow from his jaws.

He opens his mouth to reveal a black cave
And glares furiously in the direction of Esfandiar,
Who, at the sight of the monster,
Asks for divine protection and holds his breath.

The horses yearn to find a way to retreat,
But the dragon swiftly inhales them in one breath,
Swallowing them up along with the chariot.

The hero on the box grows concerned,
But the swords pierce the dragon's mouth,
Forcing him to vomit a torrent of blood.
He is unable to release himself as the swords
Are the blades while his mouth is their sheath.

Encumbered by the chariot and the swords,
His strength begins to wane.
The hero exits the cabin, brandishing a sharp sword,
And with it he slashes the dragon's skull.
The exhalations of venomous fumes
Rise on the earth, making Esfandiar dizzy.
He falls like a mountain and loses consciousness.

Meanwhile, Pashootan arrives on his trail with his vast host.
He grows fearful of the misadventure of the prince.
His heart swells with blood, and tears inundate his face.
The troops burst into laments,
Set foot on the ground, and abandon their steeds.

Pashootan rushes over and pours rosewater
Over the head of the world-seeking prince.

Esfandiar opens his eyes and says to the noble warriors,
"Inhaling the poison caused me to faint,
But my body is free of injury."

He rises and approaches the water
Like a drunken man waking up from sleep.
He asks his treasurer for new clothes
And immerses himself in the water to wash.

He addresses the pure Creator,
Quivering, rolling in the dust, and crying,
"Who could have destroyed the dragon
Without the support of the Divine Master?"

The troops bow low to pay homage
To Yazdan, the Justice Giver.
But Gorgsaar is filled with grief to see that Esfandiar,
Whom he thought would surely be dead by now,
Is still standing and breathing with life.

5 | The Fourth Stage: Esfandiar Kills the Witch

The king asks for his tent pavilion to be set up
By the water's edge and surrounded by other tents.
He summons wine and invites guests.
Standing, he drinks to the health of world master Goshtaasp.
Then he calls Gorgsaar to his side,
A man wounded at the heart and walking shakily.
He gives him three cups of royal wine,
Smiles, and talks to him of the dragon:
"O worthless, wicked man, look at this brave dragon
Whose lethal breath once killed everyone.
Reveal to me what I am to face in the next stage
And what new adversities I must contend with."

Gorgsaar replies, "O victorious King,
May your good star serve you well!
Tomorrow, when you arrive at the fourth stage,
You will be greeted by a witch who has seen many a host,
Yet her heart has never trembled before anyone.
When she desires, she converts desert into sea

And brings the sun from its zenith down to the horizon.
She is given the name of Ghool.
Do not allow her to drag you into her clutches
By the ardor of your youth. Return to Iran-Zamin,
Satisfied to have vanquished the dragon,
For you must not put your glory in peril."

Esfandiar says to him, "O impudent man,
You will witness my feats tomorrow.
I shall treat this witch in a way as to shatter
The backs and hearts of every sorcerer,
Crush each head beneath my feet,
By the victory granted to me by the Justice Giver."

As the day dons its pale tunic of night
And the shining sun descends toward its setting,
Esfandiar mobilizes his army, loads the baggage,
And addresses a prayer to the giving Creator.

The king marches with his troops throughout the night,
And when the sun raises its golden helmet
Like a ruby under the sign of the ram,
The surface of the earth appears to smile.
Esfandiar hands over the army's command to Pashootan.
He takes a golden cup, asks for a jeweled tambur,[72]
And prepares for a feast, though he intends to go to war.

He perceives a forest, as lush and verdant as paradise.
You would think that the sky has sown tulips,
As one could not distinguish it through the trees.
Abundant springs gurgle with rosewater.

Esfandiar dismounts, as the site calls for it,
Selects a fountain in the forest,
Holding in his hand the golden goblet.
When he is joyful with drink,
He plucks the strings of his tambur,
Leaning it against his chest, and sings with all his soul:
"The wretched Esfandiar who never sees wine
Has no mate or companion to share in drink.
His only encounters are with lions and bold dragons,

◇◇◇◇◇◇◇◇◇◇◇◇◇◇
72 Tambur: A long-necked string instrument.

Never evading the clutches of misfortune,
Never enjoying worldly pleasure,
Or the sight of a fair-faced maiden.
His heart's dearest longing would be fulfilled
If the Creator could provide him just one
Of the women whose beauty delights the soul,
Whose stature matches that of a cypress tree,
Whose face shines like the golden sun,
Whose hair of musk drapes down to her feet."

The witch hears Esfandiar's words of longing.
She blossoms like a rose in spring and reflects,
"Here comes a lion falling into my trap.
He is decked, he sings, and holds a full cup of wine."

The impure creature, horrid, craggy, and wrinkled,
Begins to write her magic formula in the dark.
She transforms herself into a beautiful Turkish lady,
With cheeks like brocade of Chin and hair as black as musk.
Thus beautified, tall as a cypress tree,
She approaches Esfandiar,
Her musk-like hair cascading to her ankles,
Cheeks like a rose garden, and flowers at her side.

When the prince spots her, he sings louder,
Plays with more gaiety, and downs his drink.
He says, "O Justice Giver, you are my Guide
In the mountain as well as in the desert.
I have found a young, fairy-faced beauty
To be at my side and to please me in this forest.
My wish is granted, for my heart and soul adore her!"

He gives her a cup brimming with musk-scented wine,
And her cheeks color a deep shade of ruby.

Esfandiar possesses a beautiful chain of steel brought
From paradise and presented to Goshtaasp by Zartosht.
He holds it at the ready, though hidden from sight.
The prince quickly reaches for it
And wraps it around the witch's neck,
In a way as to drain her of her strength.

She transforms into a lion,

But Esfandiar draws out his sword and says to her,
"You cannot hurt me, even if you were a mountain of steel.
Return to your true shape,
Or I shall respond to you with my sword."

At that moment, trapped in the chains,
Appears an old, foul-stinking witch,
Whose hair is white and face as black as tar.
Esfandiar strikes her a blow of his piercing sword.
The witch's head and body tumble to the ground.

At the instant when the witch expires,
The sky dims so that eyes can no longer see.
A storm rises along with a dust, so dark
That it renders the sun and moon imperceptible.

Esfandiar climbs on heights to shout a thunderous cry.
Pashootan rushes to him with the troops and says,
"O glorious King, neither whales nor witches or sorcerers,
Neither lions nor wolves can withstand your blows.
May you always remain here, holding your head up high,
For the world needs your protection!"

Meanwhile, Esfandiar's victories set Gorgsaar's head ablaze.

6 | The Fifth Stage: Esfandiar Kills Simorgh

The world-seeker brings his forehead to the ground
For a long time in veneration to the World Creator.
Then they set up tents in the forest,
And a spread is arrayed with the necessary fare.
Esfandiar commands the executor of high deeds
To fetch the wretched Gorgsaar,
And he offers him three cups of royal wine.
Gorgsaar revels in the ruby-colored drink.

The prince says to him, "O miserable Turk,
Look at the head of the old witch on the gallows.
You told me she was able to cast an army into the sea
And raise her head to the cluster of the Pleiades.
Now tell me what awaits me at the next stage,

Since we have witnessed the value of the witch."

Gorgsaar replies, "You are indeed a war elephant.
A most hostile threat awaits you at the next stage.
Reflect well, and be on guard more than ever.
You will see a mountain so tall its crest reaches the clouds.
On it is the residence of the powerful bird
Travelers call Simorgh, a winged mountain eager for battle.
It is able to seize an elephant in its talons and lift it into the air.
It plucks a whale right out of the sea, a leopard right off
The ground, and effortlessly carries them off in flight.
One cannot compare this bird to the wolves or to the witch.
It has two young ones just as large; the three act in concert.
When it darts into the air and spreads its wings,
The earth loses its strength and the sun its majesty.
Should you retreat now, you would return victorious.
You cannot overcome Simorgh on this high mountain."

The powerful warlord smiles and says, "O marvel!
I shall nail the bird's two wings together with my arrow.
I shall split its chest with my Indian saber,
And fling its head off to roll in the dust."

Once the shining sun lowers to turn its back,
The heart of the east deepens in shades of ebony.
The leader of warriors sets his army in motion
While reflecting on the attributes of Simorgh.
He escorts his army during the night,
Until the sun's rays spill over the mountains
And the torch lighting the world renews the earth
To transform valleys and plains.

Esfandiar hands over leadership of the troops
To Pashootan and departs with horse, chariot, and cabin.
He gallops as swift as wind to the mountain.
He finds its crest rising to the sky.
He places the horses and the chariot in the mountain's shade.
His mind surrenders to thoughts as he prays to the Creator,
By whose order the world is born.

From its crest, Simorgh spots Esfandiar's box.
He hears the clang of the host and the blowing of clarions.
The bird darts from its boulder like a black cloud,

Making sun and moon wane.

Simorgh hopes to grab the chariot in its talons,
Like a leopard seizes its prey.
In the attempt, swords bore deep into wings and feet,
Depleting the bird's strength and majesty.
For some time, it strikes with beak and claws.
In the end, exhausted and spent, Simorgh stays still.

When the young birds see their parent
Shedding blood tears, they swoop down
To the land, their shadow blinding human eyes.

Simorgh is weakened by its wounds.
Its blood floods horses, chariot, and box.
Esfandiar leaves the cabin shouting thunderous cries.
Armed for battle and dressed in a coat of mail,
He brandishes his Indian saber.
How could a bird resist a massive whale?
He strikes Simorgh with his sword, cuts it into bits.
And this is how the majestic bird meets its end.

Esfandiar addresses the Master of Moon with gratitude
For giving him the strength to vanquish every peril:
"O Supreme Justice Giver,
You endowed me with intelligence, might, and virtue.
You are the One who overthrew the sorcerers.
You are my Guide in my righteous exploits!"

At this moment, trumpets resound,
And Pashootan arrives with tents, weapons,
Brothers, army, sons, and noblemen of Iran-Zamin,
Bearers of crowns and royal belts.

The field disappears beneath the body
And the bloody talons of the deceased Simorgh.
From mountain to mountain, the land swells with blood.
The bird's wings are so massive
That one might question the existence of a field beneath.

The Iranians find the king covered in blood,
A sight to frighten even the moon.
The leaders and brave riders acclaim him:

"May this world warrior live forever,
With wisdom, vigilance, and insight."

Gorgsaar learns that the illustrious king is victorious.
His body shakes, his face dims, he bursts into tears,
And his heart fills with grief.

The young king bids for the tents to be raised.
The brave heroes camp all around him.
Carpets of brocade are spread on the ground,
And they sit to feast and drink wine.

7 | The Sixth Stage: Esfandiar Crosses Over the Snow

Esfandiar summons Gorgsaar,
Gives him three cups of wine in quick succession,
And watches his cheeks color like the flower of fenugreek.

Esfandiar says to him, "O man of ill body and soul,
Observe the turnings of the world.
One can see neither Simorgh nor the lion,
Neither the wolf nor the powerful, sharp-clawed dragon.
Who will spread terror on the next stage?
Will there be water and grass for our chargers?"

Gorgsaar replies loudly, "O illustrious, blessed Esfandiar,
Nothing will be surprising if you return now.
You must take the measure of your fortune.
O favorite of chance, you have enjoyed divine favors
Until now, and this royal tree bears fruit.
But tomorrow, an even greater danger awaits you,
Before which a valiant man would weigh nothing
On the day of battle.
You will have no chance to resort to mace or sword.
You will find neither door for battle nor path for flight.
You will face an invincible, formidable enemy:
There will be so much snow its depth will reach
As high as a spear, and you and your glorious host
Will be stuck in the snow, O noble Esfandiar!

"No one will be surprised if you give up at this point.

Do not think my words are driven by vengeful thoughts,
Especially since such a fierce storm
Will undoubtedly lead your men to collapse.
But you still have use of your feet.
You still may trudge down the road of return.
I know that a blustery wind will pluck out trees
And unravel the ground through which no bird,
Ant, or serpent dares venture.
The ground boils beneath the ardent sun,
And nowhere will there be a drop of water.
No lion can cross this land, no swift-winged eagle its skies.
In this sterile desert, there is not even a blade of grass,
And the earth is nothing but burning, shifting sands.

"You will have to traverse forty farsangs thus,
Incapable of carrying the loads atop your mounts,
And with an army of weak and exhausted men.
From there you will reach the impregnable castle,
Where you will find shaded shelter.
It is a land that has everything
And a fort where the crenels converse in secret with the sun.
Outside its walls, there is no food for animals,
And not one soldier will arrive there on a mount.
If one hundred thousand sword-wielding warriors
Were to arrive from Iran and Tooran,
To camp by the castle for one hundred years
And send a shower of shots on the fort, it would be in vain.
Their numbers, small or vast, would mean nothing,
For the enemy cannot hurt this castle or the ring on its door."

Hearing this forecast, the Iranians are troubled.
They say, "O King of free men, do not approach this danger.
If Gorgsaar speaks the truth and this will soon be evident,
We would have made the journey here only to perish
Rather than succeed in castigating the Tooranians.
You have crossed this difficult road.
You have upheld the assault of wild beasts.
No man or king of the bravest sort can boast to have borne
Such hardships as you have in the stations.
Give thanks to the divine Creator,
And when you return victorious from your travels,
Appear happy with a joyous heart before your father.

When you engage in war by taking another route,
You will see the land of Tooran submit to your will.
After these words from Gorgsaar,
You must not despise your life.
Do not provoke the death of your troops.
This ancient wheel of sky has new games in store for you.
After your victories,
You must not lose your head to the wind."

Esfandiar's expression dims. He says to the leaders,
"Why are you opening the door of fear?
Have you come from Iran-Zamin
To give me advice or to gain fame?
If you wished to speak of retreat,
Why then cinch your waists to assist me on the road?
The words of the vile Turk send shivers down your spines.
Where are the king's presents?
What happened to his counsel?
Where are the golden belts and the golden diadems?
Where are your promises, your oaths and testimonies
Before the Creator and before the fortune-giving stars?
Have your feet grown weary?
Have your resolutions vanished?
Return happy and victorious.
As for me, I seek nothing but battle.

"Since your hearts are discouraged of war
Because of the words of an evil deev,
I neither require nor desire any of you as companion.
The triumphant World Master is my support,
And I hold in my heart my shining star.
I swear by my courage that none of you will escort me.
Whether I kill or am killed, I shall show the enemy
My bravery, my skills, and the power of my hands.
You will without a doubt receive news of my royal glory,
Of the fate of this castle by the force of my arms,
All in the name of the Creator of Saturn and Sun."

When the Iranians cast their eyes on him,
They see his face full of fury.
They advance toward the king to beg for pardon:
"May it please his majesty to forgive our trespasses!

May our bodies and souls be ransom!
Such will always be our engagement to you.
We are concerned for the king's life,
But we are not disheartened of battle and war.
As long as even one of the noblemen is alive,
No one will even consider to engage in flight.
Our heads are flung at your feet's dust.
We shall devotedly follow your commands."

The brave leader listens to the Iranians, blesses them,
And, his anger calmed, he says,
"High deeds never remain obscure.
We shall return victorious, enjoy the fruits of our labors.
Your troubles will never be forgotten.
Your treasuries will never be depleted."

He continues to consult with his noble leaders
Until the air turns cold and a wind blows their way.
At that time, the blare of trumpets is heard
Beneath the door of the royal camp,
And the troops are set in motion, as swift as fire,
All the while invoking the name of the divine Creator.

As dawn sheds it tapering light on the mountaintops
And night envelops its head in its dark veil
To conceal the sun, this vast host,
Armed with mace and javelin, reaches the station.

It is a beautiful spring day,
A day to bring joy to hearts, a day to deck the earth.
The Kianian commands tents and enclosures to rise.
He asks for spread, feast, and wine.

At this moment, a violent wind rushes
From the mountain, so violent
It bring fright to the heart of the illustrious prince.
It renders the world as black as a crow's wing.
One no longer distinguishes the plain from the valley.
The mountain darkens with the snowfall.
The earth is soon blanketed in white.
For three days and three nights,
A fierce and terrible wind sweeps across the plain.
The tents and tent enclosures are steeped in humidity,

PART NINETEEN

And the cold drains everyone of vigor.

The air is like a chain and the snow like a screen,
And the powerful Esfandiar, left unable to act,
Consults with Pashootan: "Our position is worrisome.
I have bravely appeared before the dragon's breath,
But in this situation, a warrior's might is of no use.
Let us pray and celebrate Yazdan,
And then perhaps these challenges will dissipate,
Or else none of us will remain to trample the earth.
We must all unite in this effort."

Pashootan appears before the divine Creator,
Guide in joy and misfortune.
The entire army raises supplicant hands,
Uttering infinite words of prayer.

Right away, a gentle breeze chases away the clouds.
The air is at once more serene.
The Iranians regain courage and praise Yazdan.
They remain for three days, but on the fourth day,
As the illuminating sun ascends, the prince convenes
His warriors, to whom he speaks words of wisdom:
"Keep your loads here, and take only weapons with you.
Men of sense and owners of one hundred beasts of burden,
Load up fifty of them with water and provisions,
And the others with household supplies.
Leave here the rest of the loads.
The door of battle opens for us.
Whoever ceases to place hope in Yazdan
Cannot expect to be granted good and victorious fortune.
The man who commits evil deeds and worships idols
Can only be vanquished by the gift of divine force.
You will all become wealthy in this castle,
And have treasures and diadems."

Once the sun places the pale veil of night on its head
And the skies turn as pale as a flower of fenugreek,
The warriors load up the baggage and depart with the king.

As part of the night passes, Esfandiar hears, with surprise,
The squawking call of a crane.
Worried, he sends a message to Gorgsaar:

"You said that there is no water in this station
And that we shall find no place to rest or sleep.
Now we hear in the sky the squealing voice of a crane:
Why did you make us worry for the lack of water?"

Gorgsaar replies, "From here on,
The horses will not have access to sources of fresh water.
You will find springs with salty water, bitter like poison,
And the birds and wild beasts will have no other."

The king bemoans, "I have selected
A guide who wishes to lose us."

Following Gorgsaar's words,
Esfandiar sets his army in motion,
Addressing prayers to Yazdan, Giver of all that is good.

8 | The Seventh Stage: Esfandiar Crosses the River and Kills Gorgsaar

Once a fraction of the dark night elapses,
One hears the sound of cymbals on the plain.

The young king smiles, climbs on his charger,
And travels from army center to the vanguard.
After passing the troops,
He spots a vast body of water with no end in sight.

A camel from the caravan leading the way
Is immersed in the water, unable to pull itself out.
The leader rushes to the rescue, grabs its leg
And liberates the beast from the mud.
The malevolent Gorgsaar trembles in fear.

Esfandiar summons the enchained Gorgsaar,
Who is humiliated and wounded at the heart,
And says to him, "Evil impostor,
You act in deceitful ways like a snake.
Did you not tell me that there is no water here
And that the sun's heat would consume me?
Why did you convert water to ground

And predict the end of our host?"

Gorgsaar replies, "The army's ruin
Would bring great joy to my heart,
Brighter than the sun and moon.
What have I received from you but iron chains?
What else could I wish for you but misery and pain?"

Esfandiar smiles and observes him.
Though this Turk surprises him, he does not exhibit anger.
He says to him, "O foolish Gorgsaar, once I reach victory,
I shall make you the master of the impregnable castle.
I shall never cause you any harm!
The empire will be yours if you tell the truth.
I shall harm neither your children nor your people."

Gorgsaar's heart fills with hope.
Astonished, he kisses the ground and begs forgiveness.

Esfandiar replies, "I shall pardon what you said.
Your empty words cannot convert the land into water.
But where is the path through this vast sea?
Show me the right way. Lead me to it."

Gorgsaar replies, "A winged arrow
Cannot travel through the water burdened by chains.
If you liberate me of these bonds, the sea will open for you."

Surprised, the leader immediately frees him of his cuffs.

Gorgsaar enters the water, holding a camel by the reins,
And walks into a shallow part allowing for easy passage.
The army follows him in succession.

The leader quickly asks for goatskins to be filled with air.
Thus lightened, they serve as a mode of transport
Over the water, allowing the troops to cross.

The host reaches dry land with the loads and
Forms into ranks with the left and right wings as one line.
They advance toward the impregnable castle,
Positioned ten farsangs away. The army chief sits to eat
While his servants stand by him, cups in hand.

The lion asks for his coat of mail, armor, sword, and helmet.
Happy with his victory, he summons Gorgsaar
And says to him, "Now that you are unbound and safe,
You must act accordingly and speak the truth:
Once I separate Arjaasp's head from his body
And brighten the soul of Lohraasp;
Once I avenge Farshidvard by beheading Kohram,
Who filled with grief and blood the army's heart;
Once I cast the same fate to Andariman, who killed
Thirty-eight of our brave men in a moment of success;
Once I have cut off the guilty heads in order
To avenge the murder of my grandfather
And satisfy my grudge in every way possible,
Turning this land into prey for lions
And allowing the Iranians to live in joy;
Once I have pierced the Tooranians' hearts with my shots
And taken captive their women and children,
Then will you be happy or displeased?
Tell me all that you hold in your heart."

Gorgsaar's heart constricts with blood.
His tongue and his mind overflow with fury.
He replies, "May you be cursed!
Until when will you continue your diatribe?
May the stars of misfortune conspire against your life!
May your side be stripped by sword,
Your bleeding limbs cast to the ground!
May the earth serve as your pillow and shroud!"

Angered, the king leaps on the miserable Gorgsaar,
Strikes him on the head with his Indian saber,
And splits him in half, from skull to chest.
The body of this hateful man is then dumped
Into the deep water to become a target for fish.

Esfandiar mounts on his charger, dons his armor,
Still in a fury, and climbs to observe the castle.
From the heights, he notices a splendid wall of iron
Enclosing a space three farsangs wide
And forty farsangs high.
No part of it is built with mud or water.
The depth of the wall is the length of four riders.

Watching this marvel, a deep sigh escapes his chest.
Esfandiar says, "This place is surely impregnable.
The path I have opted for is one of misfortune.
Alas, all my struggles! I shall have cause for deep regret."

He glances around the desert
And notices two Turkish riders galloping
On the plain, preceded by four retriever dogs.

Esfandiar climbs down the hill, clutching his battle spear,
With which he removes the two men off their steeds
And swiftly brings them on foot to the heights.
He asks them about this renowned fortress
And how many cavaliers are in it.

They speak at length to him of Arjaasp
And give him a description of the castle:
"Look at the fort, how deep and large it is.
One of its doors opens on the land of Iran
And the other on the land of Chin.
It houses one hundred thousand sword-striking men,
Proud, illustrious warriors, devoted to Arjaasp as slaves.
Their heads bow to his every wish and command.
One can find endless food and goods
Of the freshest sort, and wheat conserved as corn.
Should the king keep the doors closed for ten years,
There would be enough food to sustain the army.
Should he demand riders from Chin and Maachin,
There would arrive one hundred thousand famous troops.
He lacks for nothing and asks for no one.
They have enough for the men to defend the walls."

Esfandiar seizes his Indian sword
And quickly beheads the two simple-hearted men.

9 | Esfandiar Enters the Impregnable Castle Disguised as a Merchant

From there, Esfandiar marches to his camp
And dismisses foreign visitors from his tent.

Pashootan enters, and they discuss all manner of battle.
The princely warrior says to him,
"This castle will not fall into our hands by force,
No matter how long and for how many years we try.
I must then risk my life and invade by way of ruse.
You stand guard here day and night,
And protect the army against a surprise assault.
A man is worthy of honor, empire, and throne of power
Only when he fears not a battle against an advancing host,
When he fears neither the leopard in the mountain
Nor the whale in the deep sea.
At times he makes use of force, at times of ploy.
At times he is high, at times he is low.

"I shall enter this castle disguised as a merchant
And reveal to no one my identity as a great warrior.
I shall use this scheme and all sorts of tricks.
Maintain sentinels on guard at all times.
Send scouts and spies to every corner.
Never cease to lift the safety measures.
If your sentinels spot smoke by day or night,
Or a fire that lights up the world like the sun,
Know that it is my doing and not a plot of our adversary.
When you see the blaze, you must mobilize the troops.
Send them out, equipped with armor, mace, and helmet.
Immediately deploy my banner,
Take your place at the army center, and advance rapidly,
Bull-headed mace in hand, pretending to be Esfandiar."

Then he summons the leader of the camel drivers,
Asks him to kneel before Pashootan, and says to him,
"Prepare one hundred red-furred camels,
Strong, superb, and noble beasts."

Ten of them he loads up with dinars, five with Chini brocade,
And five more with a variety of gems,
A golden throne, and a very sizeable crown.
He asks for eighty pairs of chests with invisible locks.
He singles out one hundred and sixty discreet warriors,
Secure in the knowledge that they will not betray his secret.

He places these heroes inside the crates,

Asks for the baggage to be loaded, and he takes the road.
He selects twenty of his bravest men,
Noble and quick with sword, and commands them
To march before the caravan like camel drivers.

The prince swiftly takes the direction of the fort, and,
Disguised as a merchant wearing boots and a woolen robe,
He carries bundles of jewels, gold, and silver.
He travels thus with his magnificent caravan,
Preceded by the camel drivers toward the castle.

Once there, he presents himself with insight.
The residents hear the bells of the convoy
And spot at its head the merchant.
The fortress guardians relay the news to the noblemen:
"Here comes a merchant
Who will sell for a dirham what is valued at a dinar."

The noblemen, wishing to buy some goods,
Walk out to meet him, each inquiring after the bundles
And praising the magnificence of the merchandise.
They ask the caravan leader:
"What useful items might you have?"

Esfandiar replies, "Before anything, I must see the king
And make sure that he is safe and well.
After that, I shall show my goods, should his majesty permit."
He asks that his camels' loads be brought down
And reflects as to how to attract the buyers.
He takes his horse, ten robes of Chini brocade
With shining sleeves, stones of ruby and turquoise,
A cup full of royal gems worthy of a king,
Dinars, and a piece of silk to cover the cup,
Beneath which is musk and ambergris.
He dresses in magnificent brocade, with scent and color,
And in this manner, the traveler nears Arjaasp.

Once he sees the king, he showers him with dinars and says,
"O King, may wisdom be the companion of rulers!
I am a merchant born of a Turkish father and a Persian mother.
I buy merchandise from the Turks
And take it to Iran or to the desert of brave men.
I have brought a caravan of camels.

I sell and buy cloth for robes, rugs for spreading, horses,
Precious gems, diadems, and all sorts of fineries.
I have left my goods outside the castle gates,
For I deem that the world is under your command.
If the king allows my camel drivers to reach the castle gates,
I shall be free of ill-will by the grace of his fortune,
And I shall rest in the shade of his loving protection."

The king replies, "May your heart rejoice!
May your body be exempt from injury!
No one will bother you in the lands of Tooran,
Chin, and Maachin if you wish to travel through them."

He assigns him a grand building,
A shop in the vicinity of the castle,
And commands his merchandise to be taken to it
So that he can create a place to sell in trust.

Esfandiar's companions load the boxes on their backs
And lead the camels by the bridle.
A sensible man asks one of the porters,
"What is hidden in these boxes?"

The other replies, "We place our deaths on our shoulders."

Esfandiar organizes the store and decks it like a spring rose.
He welcomes in throngs of buyers.

Night passes, and at dawn,
Esfandiar approaches the king in the audience hall,
Bearing gifts of dinars, musk, and three bolts of fabric.
He kisses the ground, blesses Arjaasp at length, and says,
"I have brought this merchandise and this caravan
In haste with the help of camel drivers.
We bring dinars, bracelets, and diadems,
Musk and ambergris, and many items worthy of the king.
Command your treasurer to come to the store
And appraise our merchandise,
As long as it is not too much trouble.
He may take anything worthy of your treasure.
It is my pleasure for the world king
To accept these gifts from a humble merchant."

Arjaasp smiles and treats him graciously.
He bids him to take an honorable seat
And asks him for his name.

The other replies, "My name is Khorraad.
I am a traveler, a merchant, a happy man."

The king says, "O youth, you make my heart rejoice.
There is no need for you to express sorrow.
From now on, you need not ask for permission.
You may have an audience with me any time you desire."
Then he asks him some questions on his travels,
On Iran, its king, and its army.

Esfandiar replies, "For five months,
I have endured troubles and worries on the road."

Arjaasp asks him what they say in Iran
On the subject of Esfandiar and Gorgsaar.

He replies, "O benevolent prince,
Each speaks according to his wishes.
Some say that Esfandiar was mistreated by his father
And that he is rebelling against him.
Others claim that he is on the road of the seven stages,
With the intention to engage in war in Tooran-Zamin,
To bravely avenge his family against Arjaasp."

Arjaasp laughs and says,
"No man with age and experience will say that,
For if an eagle crosses seven stages,
Call me an Ahriman and not a man."

The hero listens to these words, bends down to kiss the ground,
And leaves Arjaasp's palace full of joy.
He opens the door of his renowned store,
And the fortress echoes with the sound of his footsteps.

He remains at length occupied in buying and selling.
Everyone's eye is twisted to deceive him,
As he receives only dirhams instead of dinars,
And he exchanges items for items.

10 | Esfandiar's Sisters Recognize Him

As the shining sun withdraws from the dome of sky
And the buyers desert the marketplace,
Esfandiar's two sisters emerge from the palace,
Sobbing and carrying pitchers of water on their shoulders.

At the sight of them, Esfandiar covers his face to hide,
Shielding it with his robe's woolen sleeves.
He fears for what they are about to do.

They near Esfandiar in a state of distress and humility.
Cheeks flooding with blood tears, they appeal to him:
"May your days and nights be blissful!
May the sky devotedly obey your commands!
O illustrious hero, what news have you
Of Goshtaasp and Esfandiar?
We are two royal daughters held captive by impure hands.
Our heads and feet are bare,
Our shoulders burdened with pitchers of water!
Our father lives in joy during the day
And peacefully sleeps at night.
We run around unclothed, exposed to the world.
Happy is the one whose body is dressed in a shroud!
This is how we shed tears of blood.
But you can heal our wounds with news from our land.
Here, even the opium is poison to us."

Esfandiar yelps out beneath his robe,
A shriek that evokes great fear in the sisters:
"I wish Esfandiar never lived!
I wish those who speak his name never existed!
Damn Goshtaasp, wicked, unjust king!
May the likes of him never possess crown and belt.
Do you not see that I come here for trade,
Exerting myself to win my keep?"

The noble Homay's heart sinks
At the recognition of the voice.
Still, she keeps the secret to herself,
And stands before him with a wounded heart,
Tears running down her cheeks,

Her clothing frayed and tattered,
Her two bare feet caked with dust and mud,
And her heart full of fear of Arjaasp.

Realizing that Homay recognized him,
The hero of pure heart reveals his sun-like face,
Eyes full of tears, heart swelling with blood.
Perplexed at the outcome of fate,
He turns pensive and bites his lips.
In the end, he says to his sisters,
"You must remain quiet for a few days.
I have endured great pains to come here,
To engage in battle, and gain fame and glory.
If there exists a father whose daughters are reduced
To fetching water and whose son's life is in danger
While he sleeps a sweet slumber, one is better off
With the sky as father and the earth as mother,
For such a fate would be unendurable."

The generous prince leaves his store,
Runs to Arjaasp, and says to him,
"O King, may you live in happiness!
May you remain forevermore world master!
On the road, I came across an unfamiliar deep sea.
From the sea rose a whirlwind so violent, prompting
The skipper to remark on the peculiar phenomenon.
All of us on the ship sobbed in distress,
Wishing to surrender our lives.
At that moment, I prayed to the Creator,
Justice Giver, and pleaded that if I could debark alive,
I would give a feast in every land governed by a prince,
That I would grant everything to my guests,
Shower the poor with favors and gifts,
Overlooking my own needs.
Now if today the king may honor me,
He would magnify my glory by granting me my wish.
I shall prepare a feast where I shall be the host
Of all your noble army warriors holding seats of honor.
The fulfillment of this wish will settle my heart in peace."

Arjaasp agrees with great joy,
And the head of this ignorant man fills with folly.

He allows those he respects the most, renowned leaders
And warriors, to go to Khorraad's palace as his guests
And to become inebriated upon being offered wine.

Esfandiar says to Arjaasp, "O illustrious king,
Wise warrior, world master, ruler of holy men,
My dwelling is too narrow and its terrace is too high.
But we will be fine on the rampart of the interior castle.
We are entering the month of Teer.[73]
We shall light a fire outdoors,
Render joyful the hearts of noblemen with wine."

Arjaasp replies, "Go anywhere your heart desires.
He who gives the feast is king of the dwelling."

The hero rushes off in joy.
He puts together piles of wood on the rooftop.
He kills horses and a number of lambs to take to the ridge.
Soon, a great smoke rises from the amassed wood,
A smoke that renders the sky invisible.
He calls for wine, and when all of it is gone,
The guests appear to be Esfandiar's slaves.

In the end, all the noblemen depart drunk,
Each holding a stem of narcissus in his hand.

11 | Pashootan Attacks the Impregnable Castle

At nightfall, Esfandiar lights a huge fire,
It's blaze consuming the sky.
The Iranian sentinel, observing from his tower,
Watches the air dim with flames and fumes.
He leaves his surveillance post and rushes, as swift as wind,
To Pashootan to inform him of the fire and smoke.

Pashootan remarks, "In his use of deceit,
Esfandiar assumes a place above the lion and the elephant.
May the evil eye keep at bay, and may his life be full of joy!"
He asks for the sound of brazen clarions and timpani,

◇◇◇◇◇◇◇◇◇◇◇◇◇◇
73 Teer: Fourth month of the solar year.

And the blare of trumpets rises from his tent opening.
The army advances on the plain toward the fort,
And the dust it stirs obscures the shining moon.
Everyone is secured in coat of mail and helmet,
And each dim heart sheds torrents of blood.

The occupants of the fort learn of the army's approach.
They see the world disappear beneath a dust of ebony.
The name of Esfandiar echoes through the castle,
And the tree of misfortune begins to bear bitter fruit.

Arjaasp dons his coat of mail and wrings his hands.
He commands Kohram, lion vanquisher,
To seize mace, sword, and arrow,
And to take the lead at the head of the army.

He says to Tarkhan, "O renowned hero,
Leave at once and prepare for battle.
Take with you ten thousand illustrious warriors,
Eager to fight and ready to strike with sword.
Determine who is attacking us
And what they seek in this invasion."

The proud Tarkhan departs at once to the front of the fort,
Accompanied by an interpreter.
He sees troops covered in armor, equipped for war,
And a black banner with the image of a leopard.
He sees army leader Pashootan standing at the center
Of troops who have washed their hands in blood.
Mounted on a famed charger,
Pashootan brandishes Esfandiar's mace.
His demeanor recalls the hero himself,
And no one addresses him
Other than with the title of his majesty, King of Iran.
He spreads out the two wings of his army
To make the brilliant day disappear.
Spears with tips of steel strike in such a way
It is as if a shower of blood tumbled down from the sky.

On both sides, battling warriors
Fling themselves into the brawl.
Nooshaazar takes the lead, ready to strike with sword
And incite the enemy into a fight.

The bold Tarkhan charges at him,
Hoping to make his head roll in the dust,
But Nooshaazar, spotting him on the field,
Quickly draws his sword and cuts his body in half.
Seized by fear, Kohram charges into the army core,
Killing aimlessly, without discrimination for great or small.

The two hosts fight in such a way
That the dust forms a dense cloud in the air.

The highborn Kohram dashes toward the castle
And says to his father, "O famed King, glorious as the sun,
A vast host has arrived from Iran, led by a celebrated hero
Who, by the aspect of his stature, can only be Esfandiar.
Never has an equal warrior dared show his face at this fort.
He bears in his hand the spear of battle
That you once saw in the fort of Gombadan."

The revival of the ancient vengeance afflicts Arjaasp's heart.
He says to the leaders of his troops, "March off!
All of you, leave the fortress and go to the plain.
Take with you the army.
Lead a siege on the enemy, and be fierce as lions.
Do not allow a single Iranian warrior to survive."

The vast Tooranian army exits the fortress
With wounded hearts and vindictive drive.

12 | Esfandiar Kills Arjaasp

As the dark night descends, Esfandiar dons battle armor.
He uncovers the boxes to allow fresh air to reach his men.
He brings them grilled meats and wine,
War equipment and coats of mail.

Once they have eaten their fill,
He gives each three cups of wine, and, as they rejoice,
He says to them, "This night is a night full of danger.
This field is where we are to glorify our exploits.
Take great pains, battle as bold men,
And seek shelter against misfortune in Yazdan."

He divides the fame-seeking warriors into three sections:
The first section is to attack the interior of the fort
And kill anyone obstructing the way.
A second section is to march on the gate,
And never cease to combat and shed blood.
To the third division, he says, "We must not leave a trace
Of the leaders who drank with me and were intoxicated.
Cut off all their heads with your swords!"

He leaves with twenty fearless men
And entrusts the remaining warriors to the third section.
He marches bravely on the gate of Arjaasp's palace,
Dressed in a coat of mail and shouting the cry of a fierce lion.

As the clatter of this tumult echoes in the palace,
Homay and her sister Behaafarid
Run to the noble prince, cheeks flooding with tears.

Esfandiar nears his two veiled sisters, alike to spring:
"Run like smoke from here to where I hold my march.
There is plenty of gold and silver, and I shall lead to it.
Remain there until the outcome of this battle is determined.
We shall see whether we must surrender our heads
Or acquire the diadem of victory."

He says this, casts his eyes away from them,
And vengefully marches on Arjaasp's palace.
Brandishing an Indian saber in one hand,
He kills anyone who crosses his path.

The entire palace court is in such a state
That it is impossible to pass through it.
There are so many wounded, so many dead,
And so many men trampled beneath the warriors
That the floors resemble a turbulent sea.

Arjaasp is shaken awake by the uproar.
Heart aquiver, he dashes out of his bed chamber,
Dons his coat of mail, and dresses in a Rumi helmet.
His hand holds a shining sword,
His mouth shouts the cry of war,
And his heart swells with blood.

Esfandiar bounds across the threshold,
A glittering sword in hand, and says to him,
"You will receive your death from this merchant at no cost.
I bring you a present from Lohraasp,
Saddled with the seal of Goshtaasp.
When you receive it, you heart will surge with blood,
As black dust will enfold you in its embrace."

Arjaasp and Esfandiar attack each other
And fight with immeasurable fury.
They strike blow upon blow of sword and dagger,
At times on hips, at times on heads.
But in the end, Arjaasp is thwarted,
His elephant body pierced and wounded.
Esfandiar promptly cuts off Arjaasp's head.

Upon Arjaasp's death,
A cry of anguish rises from the women's quarters.

This is the way fortune turns,
At times offering honey, at times poison.
Why would you attach yourself to this passing dwelling,
Since you hold the certainty that it is transitory?
Do not be distressed when you must depart.
Whether you are king or warrior,
One day the world will overpower you.

After killing Arjaasp, Esfandiar destroys the palace,
Provoking smoke to whirl upward to Saturn.
He asks for flames to be ignited everywhere.
He surrenders the night quarters to eunuchs,
Taking with him all that once gave it glamor and beauty.
He places his seal on the treasury doors in gold,
For there is no one left in the castle to contend with.

At the stables, he climbs on a steed,
Brandishing an Indian saber.
He selects Taazian stallions to be saddled
And mounts them with his sisters,
Thus departing from Arjaasp's residence
Escorted by one hundred sixty men,
Elite riders on the day of battle.
He entrusts a number of illustrious Iranians

To the noble Saaveh, to whom he says,
"Once I leave the fort, once I reach the plain,
You will close the castle gates to the Turks.
I hope that fortune will be my support.
Once you assume that I have reached my noble host,
Then your sentinel must call out from his tower:
        'May the head and crown of Shah Goshtaasp be blessed!'
If the Turkish army, in flight, returns from the battlefield
And pounces en masse on the palace, then you must,
From this tower, toss the head of Arjaasp into their midst.
A watch guard must announce from the ramparts
That King Esfandiar is victorious
And has severed the head of the King of Turks,
That he has made it roll in the dust
And glorified the name of King Goshtaasp."

In this way, the hero leaves the castle
With one hundred and sixty men,
Shouting and bouncing on the battlefield.
He rushes forward, killing any unfortunate
Turk who crosses his path.

Once he nears Pashootan's army,
This illustrious man showers him with praise.
The entire host is astonished
At this young hero's impressive display of valor.

13 | Esfandiar Kills Kohram

As the moon takes its seat on its silvery throne
And one-third of the dark night vanishes,
The watch guard from his post calls in a loud voice:
"Goshtaasp is king! His fortune is victorious!
May Esfandiar remain forever young!
May the sky, moon, and fortune protect him,
For he has cut off Arjaasp's head to avenge Lohraasp,
And he has restored glory and majesty to the throne!"

The Turks, hearing this call, hearken as one.
Kohram's heart dims at the sentinel's words.
His mind confounded, he says to Andariman,

"In the dark, no sound is lost.
What do you think will happen tonight?
We must hold counsel.
Who dares cry out in this way during the night
And at the very bedside of a king like Arjaasp?
We must send this man to the castle,
No matter who he is, and cut off his head.
If sentinels, on the day of battle, play games,
Our army will be in grave danger.
Let us send someone to pierce with his dagger
The skull of the man who shouts such fateful cries.
If our enemy is among us, we must consider him a stranger.
Because of the evil words he utters and our ill omen,
We shall club his head with our mace."

As the cries continue, Kohram's heart
Grows more wary of the sentinel's voice.
Everywhere the ear of brave men is full of boisterous chatter.
The Turks say, "So much clamor
Beyond what is allowed a sentinel.
Let us chase the enemy from the palace.
Then we shall destroy the army."

Kohram's heart is constricted even more by the voice.
He squirms, and his forehead wrinkles with alarm.
He says to his troops, "This host before us
Has filled me with concern for the fate of the king.
But now we must enter the palace,
And I know not what to do after that."

The Chini leaders leave the battlefield at night.
Esfandiar follows them, covered in mail
And holding his bull-headed mace.

Kohram, reaching the palace gate,
Spots the Iranians behind him.
He says, "Now we have no option
But to go to war with the valiant Esfandiar.
Draw your swords from their sheaths,
And charge your daggers with a reply."

But fortune wrinkled his forehead,
And fate is harsh with this noble man.

The two armies battle with great fury.
They riddle each other with blows until daybreak,
When the defeat of the Chini warriors is clear.

The men Esfandiar had left in the kingly court
Come with the severed head of Arjaasp, the ambitious,
The one who shed the blood of Lohraasp.
At the sight of their king's head, the Turks cease to fight.

A great cry rises from the Tooranian ranks.
The heroes divest themselves of their helmets.
Arjaasp's two sons burst into tears, consumed by grief.
Their troops recognize the perpetrator
And for whom they must weep on this day of misfortune.
They lament, "Alas, our leader, our hero, our valiant King!
Who killed you on the field of vengeance?
May he disappear! May his hour pass to never return!
To whom shall we entrust our existence now?
To whom shall we present the banner of our right wing,
Since the center position is no longer occupied by the king?
May the army perish! May the diadem perish!
We no longer have need for any of it, only for death.
From Khalokh all the way to Taraaz,
Everything is mourning and woe."

They press on in search of death, armed with heavy mace
And covered in coats of mail and helmets.

The clatter of blows administered and received echoes.
The air turns into a black cloud.
Everywhere tumble body parts
Belonging to men whose days have passed.
The entire plain is strewn with heads, limbs, and weapons.
Floods of blood thrash at the palace gates,
And no one can distinguish between right and left.

Esfandiar advances, emerging out of his troops.
The leader Kohram strengthens his position in the stirrups.
The two warriors fall on each other
In such a way that one would think their bodies are one.

Esfandiar grabs Kohram by the belt.
He lifts him, bending his back unnaturally,

And flings him to the ground.
The troops burst out to acclaim the king.

They tie Kohram's hands and carry him as a vile thing.
His noble army scatters and flees.
Blows of mace fall on heads like a fierce hail.
The earth is covered with helmets, and the sky breathes death.
Heads fall off bodies like leaves falling from trees.
Some lose everything they have; others acquire thrones.
Blood swamps the battlefield in waves.
The head of one man is crushed beneath horses' hooves,
While the head of another is adorned with a diadem.

No one knows the secrets of this sterile world,
For it never reveals what it conceals.

Any man with a horse makes haste and flees.
Any man trapped in the maws of the dragon
Has no chance of escape, no matter how hard he battles.
Very few Turks and Chini warriors survive,
And those who remain are unrecognizable.

They cast off their helmets and armor,
And their eyes drown with blood tears.
They come rushing to Esfandiar,
Eyes glimmering tearfully like spring.
But the leader is bloodthirsty and ruthless,
And his army delights in his cruel nature.
Unwilling to pardon anyone,
He orders the killing of all the wounded men.
No Chini warrior survives.
No Tooranian prince remains alive.

The Iranians withdraw to their tents and tent enclosures,
Abandoning the dead on the battlefield.
Esfandiar, having witnessed the good and the bad,
Travels to the other side of the fort, where they dress his tents.

He demands gallows be set from the palace doors,
From which they tie rolled-up lassos.
He hangs there the head of Andariman
While his brother is attached alive on the other side.

He sends out his troops to every corner of the land,
Anywhere there are signs of Turk or Chini warriors.
He commands the execution of everyone
And the burning of every province.

The entire land of Tooran-Zamin is thus set ablaze.
You would think a black cloud has traveled across,
Sending a firestorm on the battlefield.

Witness to this, the prince who seeks world dominion
Assembles his army leaders and calls for wine.

14 | Esfandiar's Letter to Goshtaasp and the King's Reply

Esfandiar summons a scribe and speaks to him at length
Of the strategies of deceit he applied and the battles he led.
The noble scribe takes a seat of honor
And asks a slave for a reed and a piece of Chinese silk.
As soon as he dips the tip of the reed in black ink,
He writes, singing the praises
Of the Master of Moon, Saturn, Venus, and Sun:
"Creator of ant, elephant, victory,
Glory, crown, soul and wisdom,
Preeminent Benefactor and Guide:
May King Goshtaasp's wishes always be granted!
May paradise shine in the glory of King Lohraasp!
I arrived in the land of Tooran by way of a road
That I shall never place blessings upon.
If I were to describe the heartache I have endured,
The head of a young man would bleach with grief.
If the king permits, I shall relate my schemes and scuffles.
I shall be happy to see him, and I shall bless him.
I shall be liberated from the burden of ancient worries.

"The means I utilized to satisfy my hunger for vengeance
Were so extreme that both Arjaasp and Kohram perished.
Nothing remained of the impregnable castle
But shrieks, suffering, and death.
I granted mercy to no one.
Even blades of grass bowed their heads in fear.

Lions and wolves devoured the brains,
And fierce leopards desired only dim hearts.
May the sky shine with the glimmer of Goshtaasp's crown!
May the earth be a rose garden by the grace of Lohraasp!"

The letter is affixed with Esfandiar's seal.
A number of equestrians are to ride to Iran-Zamin
On race camels with foaming mouths.
Esfandiar remains to await the letter's response,
Occupied in extinguishing the fire of his fury.

Before long, a reply arrives containing the key of the doubts
That occupied his mind when he was enchained:
"May the one who seeks a prosperous and long life,
A man of wisdom who comprehends the Creator,
Learn to worship by the kind favors he receives.
I ask the divine Justice Giver to be your Guide.
I have planted a tree in the garden of paradise,
More glorious than any planted by Fereydoon.
Its fruits grow into gems of ruby inlaid in gold.
Its branches and leaves spread to out,
Majestic in their reach for the revolving dome.
Its roots are more precious than anything.
May this tree forever flourish!
My dim soul brightened upon receipt of your letter,
Its contents relating your exploits and feats.
You left to avenge your grandfather,
A vengeance you pursued fiercely and relentlessly.
Then I shall turn to the blood that you have spilled
And the battles you have waged in person.
Rulers must hold reverence for the body.
It is not through fight and war that one acquires glory.
Take care of your body. Cultivate your intelligence,
For its wisdom will nourish your heart.

"You say that you have granted mercy to no one
Among a few thousand cavaliers.
But your heart should always be lenient and generous,
Full of humility, and your mouth emitting gentle words.
Your occupation must be neither spilling blood
Nor fighting rashly with noblemen.
You had thirty-eight brothers to avenge,

But you have spilled blood above and beyond measure.
Finally, this old man, your grandfather,
Had banished hatred from his heart,
Yet you killed in the same way his blood was spilled.
You flung yourself into battle like a warring lion.
May you always remain happy and content!
May your wisdom always serve you as guide!
I feel the need to see you again, my son
Whose soul is awakened and full of virtue.
Once you complete the reading of this letter,
Command your troops to climb on horseback
And come to my court with your noblemen."

The speedy camels depart.
The entire land of Iran fills with noise,
And once the messengers have returned,
They descend to the door of the world hero.

15 | Esfandiar Returns to Goshtaasp's Side

Esfandiar reads, then puts away the letter,
Completes his tasks, and distributes dinars.
Once he exhausts Arjaasp's treasure,
He draws his donations from the family wealth.
He renders his troops rich,
And their affairs prosper beyond measure.

There are camels and horses in plain and mountain,
Bearing the mark of the master of Tooran.
Esfandiar requests ten thousand camels,
From every corner of desert and mountain.
Treasurers open Arjaasp's coffers to assess their contents.
Esfandiar loads one thousand camels with valuables and dinars,
Three hundred with brocade, thrones, and headdresses,
One hundred with musk, ambergris, and precious gems,
One hundred with noble crowns,
One thousand with carpets of brocade,
And, finally, three hundred with clothing from Chin,
As many made of chamois leather as of painted silk.

They proceed to prepare two litters with brocade coverings

To transport Esfandiar's two sisters,
Along with two groups of maidens from Chin,
Whose cheeks resemble spring
And who bear the statures of cypress trees,
Their waists as slim as reeds and their strides as tall as pheasants;
All in all, one hundred illustrious, beautiful young ladies.
Following them are five veiled women from Arjaasp's harem,
Full of tears of grief: two sisters, two daughters, and one mother.
The five exhibit expressions of deep sorrow.

After committing the impregnable castle to flames,
Its blaze rising to the lofty dome of sky,
Esfandiar razes the fortress ramparts to the ground
And makes the dust of destruction fly over the land of Chin.

He entrusts the army command to his three young sons,
To whom he says, "Remain vigilant, and may joy be your ally!
You will take the road through the desert
And hold the tips of your spears shining as bright as the sun.
If on the road you encounter someone with his back to justice,
You may instantly cut off his head with your blade.
Go now. Do not linger or delay.
As for me, I shall remain on the side of the seven stages,
Engaged in the hunt of lions.
I shall take my time to travel to the end of the road,
Where I shall catch up with you in one month."

Esfandiar follows the path of the seven stages,
Where he chases prey attended by a noble escort.
When the hero arrives at the site
Where he experienced the intense cold,
He finds the loads where he left them.
He finds the air agreeable and the ground a carpet of flowers.
It is as if spring just arrived to meet up with summer.

He resumes his march, transporting all his wealth,
Surprising even himself with his good fortune.

At the border of Iran, the land of heroes and lions,
He spends two weeks in the hunt of leopards and falcons.
Then he grows weary from his long journey,
Restless and impatient to see his three noble sons.

PART NINETEEN

In the end, the army and his sons appear,
And the hero worthy of crown smiles at each of them.
He says, "I have endured a strenuous journey.
I was impatient to set my sight on you."

His three sons kiss the ground and exclaim,
"There exists no one in the world with a father like ours!"

They head toward Iran, the land of brave men,
Dragging along loot and treasure.
All the cities of Iran are adorned,
And with plenty of wine, music, and song to go around.
Fabrics hang on the walls of dwellings and residences.
From above, people sprinkle a mixture of musk
And ambergris to usher Esfandiar back.
The air is full of song and music.
The earth is covered with armed spear-riders.

Once Goshtaasp learns of Esfandiar's approach,
He surrenders to his joy and asks for cups of wine
While listening to the woven tales of his exploits.
He commands his army and the powerful men of the land
To assemble at court with drums.
Then Goshtaasp, the father, takes the road
With an escort of illustrious wise, noble, and learned men
To meet Esfandiar, son of fresh face.
The entire city fills with the sound of voices.

At the sight of his father,
The young king's heart rejoices and grows serene.
He urges his night-colored horse to leap.
Goshtaasp nears Esfandiar and takes him in his arms.
The latter, surprised at his action,
Showers him with blessings and says,
"May time and space never be robbed of your presence!"

From there, they depart for the king's palace,
And everyone comes to offer them their good wishes.
Goshtaasp has the audience hall and throne bedecked,
His heart rejoices at the sight of his son, a favorite of fortune.
Spreads are displayed in the festival hall.
The king commands the chamberlain to call the noblemen.
From every palace, a guest takes off for the king's court.

Cupbearers, shining as bright as the sun,
Pour royal wine in crystal cups.
The faces of the guests blossom with color
While enemy hearts dim and burn with despair.

Esfandiar drinks modestly to his father's health,
And the latter similarly drinks to his son's health.
Goshtaasp asks him to tell the noblemen of Iran
What happened to him on the road of the seven stages.

Esfandiar replies to Goshtaasp,
"Do not ask me this question at the banquet.
I shall recount to you everything tomorrow, O wise King.
My lips will utter true words of these long tales.
Once you have listened to them with your wise mind,
You will come to worship the justice
Bestowed by Yazdan, Giver of victory."

At the end of the night,
The guests return to their homes inebriated,
Each escorted by a moon-faced page.

The adventures of the seven stages are now complete
In the name of the World Creator, Giver of justice and power,
Master of Sun and shining Moon.
If my tale pleases the triumphant King,
I shall straddle the sphere of the revolving sky.
Praise be to his magnificence!
May his heart never dwell in worry!
May Yazdan's praise echo mine!
May the victorious Creator be his ally!
May the star of his majesty's good fortune always shine!

The Battle of Esfandiar and Rostam

1 | Introduction

We must enjoy the delightful wine
As the scent of musk drifts to us from the mountainside.
The air fills with clamor and the earth with tumult.
Happy is the one who entertains his heart with drink,
Who owns silver, gold, bread, and delectable fare,
Who has the ability to cut off a sheep's head.
Happy is the one who possesses these!
May he donate some to those in need.
As for me, I fail to possess any of them.

The garden is dotted with rose petals.
The mountain is bestrewn with tulips and hyacinths.
The nightingale grumbles in the grove,
And the rose blooms beneath its whimpers.
In the dark night, the nightingale fails to sleep,
And the rose slumps with the force of wind and rain.

I see wind and rain emerge from clouds.
I know not why the narcissus is disheartened.
The nightingale laughs at both wind and rain,
And sings every time it perches on the rose.
I know not which is in love, the cloud or the rose.
When I hear the cloud rumble like a lion,
When I see it tear apart the front of its tunic
To thrust fire from its breast in the form of lightning,
Then great tears fall from the sky to the ground,
Thus proving its great love before the powerful sun.

But who knows the meaning of the nightingale's song
And what it searches for beneath the rosebush?
If you pay attention, at the crack of dawn, you will hear
The nightingale's heroic laments for the death of Esfandiar,
And its songs are the only vestiges left of the world hero.
During the dark night, the clouds split open
With echoes of Rostam's cries,

Piercing the elephant's heart and the lion's claws.

2 | The Beginning of the Story

My ear hearkened to the nightingale's song
And a story drawn from ancient traditions.
Listen as I recount this painful tale.

Esfandiar returns from the king's palace, drunk and upset.
His mother, Katayoon, the daughter of the Caesar,
Takes him in her arms in the dark of night.
He awakens before dusk, asks for a cup of wine,
And speaks to his mother: "The king treats me unfairly:
He promised that once I exhibit courage
And reprove Arjaasp Shah for the death of Lohraasp,
Once I free my sisters from captivity and glorify our name,
Once I wipe out the race of evildoers
And renew the world by my efforts and my deeds,
Then the army and empire would be mine,
As well as throne, diadem, and royal treasure.
Now, as soon as the sphere's rotation brings sunlight
And the king awakens from his slumber,
I shall remind him of his words,
And he will not dare deny me what is rightly mine.
If he were to bestow on me the imperial crown,
I would worship him like shamans worship their idols.
If he shows a sign of hesitation,
I swear, by the Creator of the revolving dome,
That I shall place the crown on my head with courage
And distribute the empire and treasure to the Iranians.
I shall make you queen of the land of Iran
And, by my force, undertake lion-like feats."

These words deeply distress Esfandiar's mother,
And her silken dress rubs against her skin like thorns.
She knows that the illustrious king
Would not surrender the crown, throne, and diadem.
She says, "O my son, do not trouble yourself.
What does the heart of a great man desire in the world
If not treasure, power, the right to counsel, and army control?
Well, you possess them all. Do not make claims to more.

O son, your father bears the crown on his head,
But army and empire are yours.
What more could you want than to be a powerful lion,
Standing at his father's side, always strapped for battle?
As soon as he passes on, his crown and throne will be yours.
His might, his dignity, and the favor of fate are yours."

Esfandiar replies to his mother,
"Let us remember these wise words once spoken:
  'Do not confide your secret to a woman.
  Should you do so,
  You will find your words scattered in the street.
  Do not ever act upon the guidance of a woman.
  You will never find one who knows how to give advice.'"

The heat of shame rises on Katayoon's face,
And she regrets having spoken to her son.

Esfandiar does not appear again before the king.
He remains in his chambers, engaged
For two days and two nights
In reveling and drinking a pure liquid.
He appeases his heart with moon-faced women.

On the third day, the king is notified that his son
Covets the possession of the throne,
That his heart is obsessed with worry,
And that he longs only for Kianian sovereignty.
Immediately, the king summons Jaamaasp
And Lohraasp's astrologers, who arrive with their astrolabes.

Goshtaasp asks them questions on the subject of Esfandiar:
Will his days be long?
Will he live a virtuous, peaceful, and gentle life?
Will he place on his head the imperial crown?
And, if so, will the royal crown be his for long?

Jaamaasp, the Iranian sage, consults his ancient tablets,
His eyes filling with tears of grief.
The future he sees causes his brow to furrow.
He cries out, "Cursed be the day and cursed my star!
My knowledge burdens my head with sorrow!
May it please Yazdan that my fate delivered me

To the lion's claws before the noble Zarir and that
I was not overthrown in battle, covered in dust and blood.
O, how I wish my own father would kill me
So that Jaamaasp might escape his ill fortune!
Alas, a man like Esfandiar, before whom lions' hearts rupture,
Who purifies the earth of our enemies,
Who, in battle, knows neither fear nor weakness,
Who splits in two the body of the dragon!
Alas, we have to mourn this world hero.
His fate will sentence us to misfortune and acrimony."

The king says, "O loved one, tell me what you have to say,
And do not deviate from the path of wisdom.
If Esfandiar must end up like the leader Zarir,
My life will then be nothing but misery.
Hurry and tell me everything,
For your science floods me with bitterness.
Who, in the world, holds my son's fate in his hands?
I must know so that I may shed tears on such a great loss."

Jaamaasp replies, "O King, I am not accountable
For the misfortunes brought on by providence.
It is in Zabolestan that death will strike Esfandiar,
At the hands of the noble hero Rostam, son of Zaal."

The king says to Jaamaasp,
"Do not treat with indifference what happens today.
If I give him the imperial throne, treasure, and royal crown,
Then he will not travel to Zabolestan,
And no one will set eyes on him in Kabolestan.
He could brave the ways of fate,
Allow his good star to work to his favor."

The astronomer replies,
"Who can evade the will of the revolving dome?
What man can escape through bravery or science,
The sharp-clawed dragon lurking above us?
Whatever is meant to be will be without fail.
The wise man does not have the clarity
To foresee the precise moment of his downfall.
Esfandiar will die at the hands of a powerful man,
Even if Sooroosh were to sleep at the foot of the throne."

This projected adversity fills the king with worry.
His mind is misled by his reflections,
As if he were trapped in a forest with no outlet.
His deceptive thoughts, combined with the thrust of fate,
Irrevocably lead him down a deviating path.

3 | Esfandiar Asks His Father for Kingship

As night passes and dawn gathers its charger's reins,
Unveiling the sun's brilliant, spear-like rays,
The king takes a seat upon his golden throne.

Esfandiar presents himself to him, mind full of worry,
Arms crossed in humility in the manner of a servant.
A congregation of warriors, wise men, and leaders
Gathers and forms a line before the king.

Esfandiar, the hero of elephant build, driven by his concerns,
Speaks to Shah Goshtaasp: "O King, may you live forever!
Your being shines divine majesty upon the earth.
You are the one who teaches justice and clemency.
You are the adornment of crown and throne.
O father, I stand before you as your loyal subject.
I walk and act in accordance with your will.
You know that Arjaasp was on his way,
With riders from Chin, to destroy our religion.
You know that I, having fulfilled sacred wishes,
Had solemnly sworn that I would split in two
With my sword anyone who would attack our faith,
Anyone who would turn his heart toward idols.
I pledged that I would fear no one and tremble before no one.

"Next, when Arjaasp arrived to challenge us,
I did not cease to battle against lions and leopards.
I turned the field of vengeance into a sea of corpses.
I flung every rider off his horse's saddle.
Yet, with all that, you treated me with contempt,
Preferring to listen to Gorazm's words of slander.
The day of the feast, when you drank from the royal cup,
You placed heavy chains on me
And sent me to the dungeon in the palace of Gombadan.

Even worse, you surrendered me to the guard of strangers.
You left for Zabol, abandoning Balkh.
You imagined that feasts had replaced wars.
You did not set eyes on Arjaasp's sword and permitted
The evil Tooranian ruler to spill Lohraasp's blood.

"When Jaamaasp came to Gombadan,
He found me chained up, my body wounded by shackles.
He promised me kingdom and throne,
And did all he could for me to accept them.
I answered him that on the Day of Judgment,
I would expose my bondage to the Creator.
I would show him the heavy iron chains
And blacksmiths' spikes, and I would complain
About the man who slandered me.
He asked me if I was not struck at the heart
By the blood spilled by so many noble leaders,
By the body of my noble brother Farshidvard,
Wounded and lying on the battlefield,
By my sisters having been shamed into captivity,
By the king having taken flight before the Turks
And now repenting for having cast me to bonds,
By so much adversity, suffering, grief, and offense.
He spoke to me further on many more subjects,
His words full of concern and pain.
He called upon the blacksmiths to grind down my chains.

"The work of the blacksmiths took too long.
I nurtured the intention to wrestle the enemy with my sword.
In my impatience, I shattered my neckpiece and chains.
I came rushing to the people's ruler, killing innumerable foes.
I shall not utter before the king a single falsehood.
But if I wished to tell him all that happened to me
In the seven stages, my tale would be endless.
I cut off the head of the wicked Arjaasp,
And by doing so, elevated Goshtaasp's name.
I brought back to this palace the women and children
Of the princes and rulers of Tooran-Zamin,
Along with their treasures, thrones, and crowns.
All this wealth you placed in your treasury
While I suffered hardships and spilled my blood,
Intense weariness as my only reward.

"Your promises, your oaths, and your engagements
Rendered my heart more eager to execute your wishes.
You said to me that if you would see me again,
You would cherish me more than life itself,
You would give me diadem and ivory throne,
Because my courage makes me worthy.
I blush before the court's noblemen
When they ask me about my treasure and army.
Why have you not kept your word?
Where do I stand? Will I accede to the throne?
For what purpose have I exerted myself so?
Kings always stand by their words and their pledges.
Now the time has come for you to place
The crown upon my head, just as your father
Made this gesture for you to ascend to kingship."

4 | Goshtaasp's Reply to His Son

The king addresses Esfandiar,
"Anyone who distances himself from justice
Wanders off the true path.
You have done more than you tell us.
May the World Creator be your support!
The world is free of our enemies.
Not a single one remains, neither visible nor invisible.
Anyone who hears your name shudders in fear.
Why do I say shudders? It is more like expires in fear.
I know no one equal to you, perhaps only Rostam,
The skillful son of Zaal,
To whom belong Zabol, Bost, Ghaznein, and Kabol.
His courage surpasses the sky,
And he deems himself no one's subject.
He turns away from my ways and my commands,
And refrains from securing an agreement with me.
He stood by Kaavoos, the Kianian, like a slave
And remained so until the end of Kay Khosrow's reign.
But he speaks lowly of the kingdom of Goshtaasp,
Saying that the royal crown is renewed
While his crown is an ancient one.
There is no one in the world who can resist you:
No one among free men of Iran, of Tooran, or of Rum.

"You have heard how, when Kay Khosrow
Bestowed his crown and throne to Lohraasp,
Everyone scattered gold about the throne
Except for Rostam who chose to scatter dust.
He spoke loudly and said,
            'This evil man succeeds the highborn king.
            We must scatter dust upon the head
            Of any man who accepts Lohraasp as king.'

"Since Rostam speaks thus and refuses to obey me,
He harbors resentment toward us in his heart,
Proclaiming himself ruler of his domain.
Have you not seen how Arjaasp arrived in Balkh
And turned our lives upside down?
Rostam did all he could to avoid engaging in war.
It was as if he were ashamed to do so.
Besides the words I have spoken,
What more could be said about the enemy?
You must leave for Sistan and call for war.
Make use of ruse, strength, and strategy.
Draw your sword, brandish your mace.
Bring back as prisoners Rostam, son of Zaal,
Along with Zavaareh and Faraamarz,
And do not allow any of them to sit in the saddle.
I swear by the World Master, Giver of power,
The One able to ignite stars, Sun and Moon;
I swear by the *Zand Avesta* and the faith of Zoroaster,
By Nooshaazar, divine fire and divine glory,
That when you have accomplished this deed,
I shall refuse you nothing that you may yearn for.
I shall bestow upon you treasury, throne, and army,
And place you on the royal seat, crown on your head."

Esfandiar replies, "O valiant and illustrious King,
You distance yourself from ancient customs.
You should maintain measure in your words.
Engage in war with the King of Chin,
Destroy and obliterate his land.
But what do you hold against the aging hero,
Whom Kaavoos referred to as lion vanquisher?
Since the time of Manoochehr to Kay Ghobaad,
He protected the land of Iran and spread joy all around.

He is the master of Rakhsh.
He is a world conqueror and a giver of crowns.
He is not a young, ambitious man
But a powerful one, who drew a treaty with Kay Khosrow.
Now if royal treaties are not observed,
We must not ask Goshtaasp for an investiture."

The king says to Esfandiar, "O prince of lion heart,
Any man who forgets divine faith,
The faith due him converts to wind.
You have heard without a doubt how Kaavoos Shah
Strayed off the right path at Eblis's instigations,
That he climbed to the sky carried away by eagles
Only to be miserably pitched into the water.
Next, he brought into his female chambers,
From Haamaavaran, Sudaabeh, the daughter of a deev.
She destroyed Siaavoosh with her persecutions
And provoked his entire family to perish.

"When a man forgets his duty toward the Creator,
One must safeguard himself from passing before his door.
If you desire throne as well as crown,
Take the road to Sistan with your host.
Once there, tie Rostam's hands and bring him enchained.
Do not allow Zavaareh, Faraamarz, and his father, Zaal,
To deceive you or set a trap for you.
Bring them on foot to my court, O illustrious prince.
After that, no one will turn against us,
No matter how wealthy and how powerful he may be."

The leader furrows his brow and says to the world king,
"Do not stray from the path of faith.
It is not a question of Zaal and Rostam for you.
You only seek to find a way to get rid of Esfandiar.
You cannot resolve to abandon the royal throne to me,
And you wish to rid the world of my presence.
May the crown and throne of kings remain yours!
I shall find myself a corner of the world.
I am merely one of your devoted slaves,
Ready to submit to your wish and command.
I shall immediately ride off in the direction of Sistan
To comply with your desire for vengeance.

If the venture I step into is not a righteous one,
You will have to face the Creator with an answer
On the day of Resurrection."

Goshtaasp replies, "Do not act carelessly.
If you seek to acquire power, do not act timidly.
Select many horsemen, experienced and skilled in battle.
My weapons and troops are entirely yours,
And your enemy's soul must tremble in fear.
Without you, what good would be treasure and army,
Royal throne, and golden crown?
Why fret so much? Try not to worry excessively.
Take the road in the direction of Zabol, and once there,
Burn everything down to the ground.
Turn their bright day into the darkest night."

Esfandiar replies, "I do not need troops,
For when the time of death arrives,
The most powerful king cannot deter it,
Not even with the vastest army."

He withdraws from his father's presence,
Inflamed by his words and the desire to acquire the throne.
He enters his palace, torn by contrary feelings,
Lips uttering foolish words, heart full of worry.

5 | Katayoon Gives Advice to Esfandiar

The sun-like Katayoon visits her son, heart full of anger,
Eyes full of tears, and says to the noble Esfandiar,
"O heir of heroes, I learned from your son Bahman
That you wish to leave the rose garden
To travel to Zabolestan, to capture and enchain
Rostam, son of Zaal, master of sword and mace.
Listen to a mother's sound advice:
Do not fling yourself mindlessly into misfortune,
And do not attempt to harm another.

"Rostam is a powerful equestrian, as strong as an elephant,
Whose force eclipses the flows of the River Nile in battle.
He is capable of tearing apart the hips of the White Deev.

The sun itself retreats before his sword.
He killed the King of Haamaavaran,
And no one ever dared speak to him rudely.
He slew Sohraab, his indomitable, powerful son.
He flung Poolaadvand into the center of the arena,
A warrior able to capture riders in his noose.
You have heard of the earsplitting shouts of distress
Cried by Akvan Deev during his fight with Rostam.
He captured Kaamoos in his noose,
Tied him up and led him away on foot.
You have heard how, on the battlefield,
He vanquished Shangal with his dagger?
He converted the earth into a sea of blood
In his attempts to avenge the murder of Siaavoosh.

"His exploits and feats are so numerous
That tales of them are endless.
Do not consider battle with Rostam as a game.
Do not provoke your head and body
To surrender to the wind for the royal crown.
Kings are not born from their mothers bearing the crown.
Cursed be diadem and throne!
Cursed be murders, struggles, and theft!
Your father is now old while you are still young.
Your power stems from your courage and your strength.
The troops devotedly obey your command.
Make sure you do not cause them to fall in battle.
There are many other places in the world besides Sistan.
Do not act foolishly, for you would make me
The most miserable person in this world and in the other.
Listen to the words of your loving mother."

Esfandiar replies,
"O my compassionate mother, remember my words!
Rostam is indeed as you describe.
Your tale of his high deeds is as true as the *Zand Avesta*.
Search all you want, you will never find anyone
In all of Iran who has done more or better than he.
It is not right for me to capture him.
It would be an evil act, one unfit for a king.
But on the other hand, you must not break my heart.
Should you do so, I shall pluck it out of my body.

How can I disobey the king and resolve to lose the throne?
Even if I must perish in Zabolestan, I have no choice.
The sky will force me to travel there, no matter what.
But if Rostam wishes to obey my command,
Never will he hear a cold word come out of my mouth."

Blood tears flow from his mother's lashes.
She tears out her hair, clutches her heart,
And says, "O young and brave elephant,
In your passion you make little of life.
You alone cannot vanquish Rostam.
Do not then leave without a host.
Do not risk your precious life for this fierce elephant,
Exposing yourself without defense to his blows.
He will never agree to a pact with you.
He will never obey your commands.
His status higher than anyone, he evades blame.
His essence is from the lineage of Jamsheed.
There is no one he deems his equal in strength.
I have heard that when he was at Kaavoos's court,
He departed without honoring the king properly.
With the back of his hand,
He struck Tous and made him collapse to the ground.
He proudly told Kaavoos,
          'I am the one who found Kay Ghobaad
          And sat him on the royal throne.
          I fear neither your justice nor your vengeance.'

"His youthful age made him shun Kaavoos's commands.
How do you expect him to give up his name and fame?
You think that with advice and deceit you can fool him,
And tie up his hands and feet?
Anyone who came into this world,
Even one day before you, is wiser than you are.
Listen to your mother and refrain from this mission.
Listen to my counsel with your mind's wisdom.
If you are determined to assume this undertaking,
It is precisely what Ahriman the malevolent wishes for.
But at least do not take your sons to hell,
For no man of sense would approve of it."

The hero, eager for battle, says to his mother,

"It would be wrong to leave my sons behind.
If a young man is accustomed to staying put,
His soul becomes lowly and his mind tarnishes.
Men must employ muscle, mace, and force
To aggrandize their standing and their name.
I shall make use of them on every battlefield.
O wise mother, I shall not need a vast host
Outside of family, allies, and a few choice warriors."

6 | Esfandiar Leads an Army Into Zabolestan

Early the next morning, at the cry of the rooster,
Kettledrums resound at the palace gate.
Esfandiar of elephantine stature leaps on his horse,
And sprints away with his army.
He marches on until he reaches a fork in the road,
Where the prince and his host come to a halt.

One of the roads leads to Gombadan, the other to Zabol.
The camel at the head of the procession lies on the ground,
As if he is at one with the earth, refusing to budge.
The camel leader strikes him on the head with his stick
To no avail, and the caravan cannot proceed.

Esfandiar exclaims, "This must be a bad omen."
He orders his driver to cut off the head of the camel
So that misfortune falls back on the beast
And the divine splendor of the king remains untarnished.
The warriors obey and cut off the head of the creature,
An act that only propels the course of his destiny.

After this misadventure, Esfandiar grows concerned.
Still, not wishing to take it as a bad omen,
He says, "The one who is victorious
And whose throne shines on the world
Must receive all things equally, with smiling lips.
He must accept the auspicious as well as the distressing,
As both are handed to us by Yazdan."

Still shaking and fearing a calamity,
He travels to the edge of the River Hirmand,

Where his army camp is set up according to custom.

Esfandiar asks for tent pavilions, draperies, and throne.
All those favored by fortune gather around him.
He summons wine, song, and musicians,
With Pashootan at his side.
The music delights the prince's heart, and the hearts
Of the noblemen fill with a sense of pride.

The cheeks of the assembly and of the valiant prince
Blossom like roses under the influence of wine.
Esfandiar says to his companions,
"I am digressing from fulfilling the king's wishes.
He commanded me to take on Rostam,
To capture, enchain, and humiliate him.
I have yet to obey his command.
I have been reluctant to follow my father's path,
For this man of lion heart, always ready to fight,
Has spared the kings of Iran much pain in the past,
Maintaining order in the world with his heavy mace.
All the people of Iran, from kings to slaves, have survived
Because of him and his efforts against the enemy.
I now need a brave envoy, a prudent, wise,
And mindful rider, with glory and grace.
One whom Rostam will not be tempted to deceive.
This courier will communicate the king's wishes to the warlord:
        'If Rostam wished to draw near me,
        He would bring joy to my somber heart.
        If he would peacefully surrender his hands to chains,
        He would bind with his wisdom the harm I may cause him.
        I only wish him well, as long as he feels no hostility for me.'"

Pashootan says, "You are right in your decision.
Carry on as mediator to spare people from suffering."

7 | Esfandiar Sends Bahman to Rostam

Esfandiar asks for Bahman and speaks to him at length:
"Deck yourself in Chini brocade and mount your black stallion.
Place on your head the royal crown inlaid with precious gems
So that those who lay eyes on you appreciate your royal race

And invoke upon you the Creator's grace.
Take with you five horses of golden harnesses
And ten renowned wise men.
March to Rostam's palace without growing weary.

"Greet him on my part. Be good to him,
And select your words carefully.
Be perfectly polite, respectful, and say,
        'The one who grows powerful
        And rises above the threat of misfortune
        Must show gratitude to Yazdan,
        Who is omnipresent and benevolent for all eternity.
        If a man strains to be righteous
        And abstains from greed and ill wishes,
        The Creator increases his power and wealth.
        He will be happy in this passing sojourn on earth
        And rewarded with the gift of paradise,
        Since he refrained from committing wicked acts.
        The wise man knows that good and evil pass over us
        And that, in the end, our bed is the dark earth
        While our soul flies away to the pure divine.
        Anyone in the world who has recognized Yazdan
        Takes great pain to conform to the kings' wishes.
        We are recompensed according to our deeds
        And receive a response compliant to our speeches.

        'Now we wish to measure your acts,
        And you must neither diminish nor embellish them.
        You have lived for countless years,
        Having witnessed many a king rule the world.
        You know it is not worthy of you
        To stray off the sensible path.
        You received from my ancestors so much power,
        So much treasure, weapons, stallions, crowns, and thrones.
        Assets you obtained in return for your service to the realm.

        'During all the years Lohraasp was world master,
        You did not once present yourself at his court.
        When he turned over the crown to Goshtaasp,
        You no longer paid attention to the royal throne.
        Never did you write a letter to him.
        You extricated yourself from any duty

Expected of a loyal subject.
You did not appear before him respectfully,
Honoring him for bearing the title of king.

'But since the time of Hooshang, Jamsheed,
And the bold Fereydoon, who seized the empire
From the race of Zahaak, going down to Kay Ghobaad,
On whose head you placed the Kianian crown,
The throne has not been occupied
By a more capable ruler than King Goshtaasp,
Whether in times of battle or feast, counsel or hunt.
He has adopted the pure faith,
Annihilated injustice and lawlessness.
The path of the world master has become,
Under his rule, as bright as the sun.
Wicked doctrines and the ways of deevs have disappeared.
Then when Arjaasp came to fight with countless troops,
As fierce as leopards and as powerful as whales,
The illustrious king boldly greeted him.
He turned the battlefield into a cemetery,
Leaving no sliver of the ground visible.
Until the day of resurrection, the memory of it
Will not grow old in the minds of noblemen.

'Now everything belongs to him, from east to west,
As he breaks the backs of valiant lions.
Go from Tooran to the borders of Sindh and Rum.
You will find the world, in his hand, as malleable as wax.
Spear-riders from the desert stand at his court,
Regularly paying tributes and fees,
For they can neither resist him nor fight against him.
O world hero, you have offended the king
By your absence at his illustrious court.
You have failed to meet
The highborn men who surround him.
You have decided to hide behind a distant border.
How could noblemen forget you,
Unless they have lost their minds?
You always lived in pursuit of justice.
You always bent to the will of kings.
If one were to enumerate the struggles you have endured,
The list would be longer than that of your vast treasures.

But there is a king who does not approve
Of the tales and rumors spreading on your account.
He told me that, after having your fill of skills,
Land, and wealth, you have become arrogant,
Locking yourself away in Zabolestan,
In a constant state of drunkenness, afraid to engage in war.
If the king requires your aid, you are powerless.
As for me, you will never find me in banquet halls.

'One day, in a bout of fury, he swore,
By the bright day and the dark night, that no one
In his vast host will ever see you again at court
Unless you were captured and enchained.
Now, I have come from Iran without a moment's rest
To take you at my king's request.
Surrender yourself to appease his fury.
Do you not know what gaze of rage his eyes cast?
But if you come with me, if you promise to obey,
If you repent to have remained so isolated and distant,
I swear by the sun, by the glorious soul of Zarir,
And by the soul of my father, world master and lion,
That I shall make the king repent for his harshness.
I shall make the dimmed moon of his grace shine again.

'Intelligence and wisdom are my guides.
Pashootan has witnessed my attempts to calm the shah,
Though I have seen the crimes you have committed.
But my father is king, and I am his loyal subject.
Never shall I distance myself from his command.
Now your entire family must consult on this matter:
Zavaareh, Faraamarz, Zaal, and the glorious Rudaabeh.
Weigh my advice. I hope you will yield to my wise words.
We must not allow your palace to be deserted
And become the prey of wild beasts.
If I lead you, tied up, to the king,
If I expose your many sins to him,
I shall hold myself humbly before his majesty,
And appease his anger and desire for vengeance.
I shall not allow a blow of wind to affect you,
As suits a man of my birth.'"

8 | Bahman Meets With Zaal

As soon as Bahman hears the prince's words,
He takes the road,
Fit in a golden royal robe and a princely helmet.
He exits the tent enclosure proudly,
Followed by his dazzling banner.

The moment this ambitious man of cypress stature
Crosses the River Hirmand, a sentinel spots him
And hollers out toward Zabolestan announcing
That a valiant cavalier, riding a black steed of golden straps,
Is on his way, galloping swiftly toward Zabol,
Trailed by a number of ordinary horsemen,
As they have nimbly crossed the river.

Zaal immediately climbs on his horse, hangs his noose
On the saddle knob, and brandishes his mace.
He advances, and, as soon as he discerns Bahman,
A great sigh escapes his chest as he says,
"This is an illustrious prince and hero dressed in royal garb.
Without a doubt he belongs to the family of Lohraasp.
May his footsteps bring good fortune to our land!"
He returns from the sentinel's tower to his palace gate
And remains bent over his horse, absorbed in thought.

Bahman appears with the Kianian banner deployed.
This young man, unfamiliar to Zaal, extends his noble neck.
Drawing close, he raises his voice:
"O man, son of a peasant bard, where is your leader?
Where is the son of Zaal, the support of the era?
Esfandiar, the hero, is on his way to Zabolestan.
He has pitched his tent pavilion on the river's edge."

Zaal replies, "O impetuous young man, climb off your horse.
Let us drink some wine and rest.
Rostam will soon return from the hunt
With Zavaareh, Faraamarz, and his retinue.
Come with your horsemen, O noble warrior,
And delight your heart with a few cups of wine."

Bahman replies, "Esfandiar does not allow me

To revel in feast, wine, and playful companions.
Select a man who knows the way,
So that he may guide me to the hunting grounds."

Zaal says, "What is your name? What is your wish?
I think that you are from the family of Lohraasp
Or one of King Goshtaasp's glorious sons."

The other replies, "I am Bahman, son of Esfandiar."

Zaal dismounts to pay homage to the eminent prince.
Affection and attention always come to a man's aid,
Whether it is extended from an old man or a young one.

Bahman also dismounts, laughing,
And questions Zaal on his health and well-being.

Zaal implores him to take some time to rest,
Saying that it is not reasonable to rush off like that.
But Bahman insists, for he cannot neglect
Or delay a message given to him by Esfandiar.
Zaal selects a brave man, familiar with the roads,
And sends him with Bahman toward Rostam's hunt.

The guide marches before the prince.
He is an experienced man by the name of Shirkhoon.
He points with his finger in the direction of the hunt,
While he turns back to retrace his steps.

9 | Bahman Delivers the Message to Rostam

The young man finds himself in front of a mountain
Onto which he launches his warrior stallion.
From the crest, he examines the hunting grounds
And homes in on Rostam, renowned warrior hero,
A man akin to Mount Bisootoon.
In one hand, he clutches a tree trunk with a skewered deer.
In the other hand, he holds a cup of wine.
His mace and his war attire are spread out at his side.
Slaves line up in a row in front of him,
With another row behind him.
Rakhsh dashes about the field in pastures abounding

With trees, greenery, and freshwater springs.

Bahman reflects, "This is either Rostam or the rising sun.
No one has ever lain eyes on a man like him
Nor heard of anyone, not even among our illustrious ancestry,
To equal his glorious exploits.
I fear that he may resist Esfandiar and refuse to fight with him.
But I shall take on the task, kill him with a massive rock,
And shake with dread the hearts of Zaal and Rudaabeh."

He picks up a boulder
And makes it roll down the mountainside.
Zavaareh discerns it and hears it from below.
He cries out, "O famed hero and skilled horseman, beware!
Here comes a boulder bounding down the mountainside!"

Rostam smiles and, without letting go of the deer,
And to Zavaareh's great fear, waits for the rock to reach him.
The mountain disappears behind a cloud of dust.
Then Rostam strikes it with the heel of his boot
And catapults it into the air.

Zavaareh and Faraamarz rejoice.
They shower him with blessings.

Such a feat leaves Bahman dismayed,
As it clearly displays Rostam's strength and nobility.
He thinks, "If the blessed Esfandiar engages in a joust
With this renowned warrior, he will be slighted.
Better for him to make a show of courtesy.
If Rostam vanquishes my father,
He will proceed to capture all of Iran."

Bahman climbs back on his charger of fleet hooves
And descends the mountain deeply troubled.
He recounts to the wise men the marvel he observed
And slowly makes his way back to the road.

Once he arrives at the hunting site, Rostam, noticing him,
Says to his sage, "Who is this man marching toward us?
He appears to be a member of Goshtaasp's family."

Rostam greets Bahman, and Zavaareh follows suit,

Along with their hunting companions, great and small.

At the sight of Rostam, Bahman dismounts, as swift as smoke,
And addresses him with polite and kind questions.

Rostam replies, "I shall not answer your questions
Until you reveal to me your name."

The prince says, "My name is Bahman.
I am the son of Esfandiar, leader of righteous men."

Immediately, the famed hero takes him in his arms
And asks forgiveness for having held him up."

The two march off to Rostam's camp,
With the prince's noble servants in tow.

Bahman sits and conveys at length the salutations
From the king and from the Iranians.
Then he says, "Esfandiar left King Goshtaasp, as swift as a blaze.
He pitched his tents on the edge of the River Hirmand,
According to the command of the victorious king.
I have been tasked to transmit to the brave warrior leader
A message from my father, if he wishes to listen."

Rostam replies, "The son of a prince has had a long,
Tiresome journey and must be quite weary.
Let us feast on this repast,
Then the world will be at your command."

They set up the spread according to custom,
Presenting soft bread and roasted, warm venison.
Maidens serve Bahman
As Rostam recounts his ancient adventures.

He asks Zavaareh to sit next to the prince,
But he refrains from asking any
Of the noblemen present to join them.
Then he places before himself another deer,
For he requires an entire beast for nourishment.
He sprinkles salt over the meat,
Dismembers it, and indulges in it.

The noble Bahman observes the world hero,
Then takes a bite of the deer that is
Less than a hundredth of Rostam's portion.

The latter smiles and says,
"The king sits on the throne in joy.
But if this is the way you eat, how were you able
To pass the furnace of the seven stages?
How can you strike with your spear in battle
If your dinner consists of this measly portion?"

Bahman replies, "A king's son must speak and eat soberly.
But if his meal is required, his efforts must be bold in fight.
He has no choice
But to always carry his life in the palm of his hand."

Rostam bursts into a fit of laughter and speaks loudly,
"One must not hide one's valor before courageous men."
He fills a golden goblet
And drinks to the health of intrepid men.
Then he places another cup in Bahman's hand and says,
"Drink to the health of anyone you wish."

Bahman, dreading the wine, watches Zavaareh
Take the cup from him, empty it, and exclaim,
"O prince, may wine and companions cheer you up!"

Bahman takes the cup from Zavaareh, his heart appeased.
But this nervous young man is a weak drinker.
Everything confounds him about Rostam:
His appetite, his stature, his arms, and his shoulders.

At the end of the meal, they rise and call for their horses.
The two cavaliers climb on their steeds.
Riding beside the illustrious hero,
Bahman discloses to Rostam Esfandiar's message.

10 | Rostam Replies to Bahman

Hearing Bahman's discourse,
The mind of the aged Rostam fills with concern.
He says, "Well then, I have heard your message.

I have rejoiced at your sight and your company.
Convey my answer to Esfandiar as follows:
    'O illustrious prince of lion heart,
    Any sensible man ponders every matter carefully.
    When one is valiant and victorious,
    When one possesses all that one desires,
    Amassed treasures, power, courage, and a noble name,
    When one is honored by the most formidable men,
    When one has in the world the position you hold,
    One must cast aside any wicked thought.
    Let us worship divine justice
    And dismiss the hand of ill-will.
    A meaningless word is as good as a fruitless tree.
    If your soul concedes to greed,
    You prepare yourself for a life lacking reward.
    When a prince speaks, he must weigh his words,
    For it is better that his lips abstain from villainous speech.

    'Your servant has always been gladdened by the words
    Of those who said that never did a mother give life
    To a son such as yourself, that you surpass your ancestors
    In courage and wisdom, intelligence and prudence.
    Such is your reputation in the lands of India, Chin, Rum,
    And all the nations of sorcerers.
    These bonds that tie you to us fill me with gratitude,
    And I pray for you three times, day and night.
    I asked Yazdan, whose deeds bring joy to my heart,
    To set my sight on your dear face so that I may witness
    A man so powerful, so heroic, and so righteous,
    To allow us to sit together in joy, and to empty
    Our cups of wine to the health of the King of Kings.

    'I have obtained my heart's desires and rush to enjoy them.
    I shall present myself before you without a host.
    I shall hear from your lips the orders of the king.
    I shall bring you the settlements granted to me by just rulers,
    Starting with Kay Khosrow and going back to Kay Ghobaad.
    But now that you take care of me, O valiant man,
    Remind yourself of my high deeds, the justice I spread,
    The fatigues and the grief I have endured,
    From ancient times to the present, in my service to the kings.
    Now if chains are the reward for my torments,

If the King of Iran wishes to end my days,
I deem a better fate to have never been born
Or, even if born, at least to avert these troubling times.

'I shall come, and I shall tell you my secrets.
My voice will rise above the surface of this earth.
If my head must be severed because I am guilty of sin,
I shall then tie a leash of leopard skin to my upper arm
And travel on foot. Since I broke the elephant's neck
And plunged him into the blue waters of the Nile,
Since I am innocent of any crime deserving decapitation,
Spare me your harsh, unjust words.
Reserve your insolence for the deev.
Do not attempt to entrap the wind in a cage.

'No matter how powerful one is,
One may not pass through fire without burning
Or cross the sea without swimming.
One may not hide the moonlight
Or place the fox on equal footing with the lion.
Do not attempt to obstruct my path with quarrels,
For I can easily engage in the fiercest disputes.
Never has anyone caught sight of me in shackles
Or seen me retreat before an unchained, warring lion.
Act in a manner worthy of a prince.
In your passion, do not take council from a deev.
Have the courage to cast fury and vengeance aside.
Do not perceive the world with the eyes of youth.
If you allow your heart to calm and pass the river,
You will receive blessings from the pure Yazdan.
Honor my home with your presence in feast.
Do not keep a distance from those who venerate you,
And, just as I stood humbly before Kay Ghobaad,
I shall receive you in the joy of my heart.

'Come to us with your host,
And stay happily for two months.
Men and horse will enjoy a respite from their fatigues,
And jealousy will blind the hearts of our enemy.
The plain is full of wild beasts.
The waterways are full of birds.
No matter how long you stay, they will not run away.

I shall see you deploy your heroic force
When, with your sword, you strike down lions or leopards.
Whenever you wish to return your host to Iran
And revisit the king of brave men,
I shall open the doors to my ancient treasury,
Accumulated at the point of my sword.
I shall display before you all my possessions,
Gathered laboriously by the strength of my arms.
You will be welcome to my wealth.
You may take what you wish and distribute the rest.
But refrain from afflicting our hearts on such a day.
Hand out dirhams to your troops and remain patient.
When you find happiness, banish remnants of sadness.

'When the time of departure arrives,
When you feel the need to revisit the king,
The reins of my horse will link to yours on the road.
I shall present myself before the king in joy.
My excuses will wipe away his anger.
I shall kiss his head, his feet, and eyes.
I shall ask the illustrious king, in person,
Why he demands for me to be tied up in chains.'
O Bahman, remember well what I have said.
Go and repeat my words to the mighty Esfandiar."

11 | Bahman Returns to Esfandiar

Having heard Rostam's reply, Bahman departs,
Galloping away with his virtuous, wise men.

Rostam remains on the road for some time.
Then he calls Zavaareh and Faraamarz, and says to them,
"Go to Zaal and to Rudaabeh, the moon of Zabol,
And tell them that Esfandiar will arrive,
Like a man who seeks world ownership.
We must place a golden throne,
Prepare royal robes in the audience hall.
We must decorate the palace more magnificently than
In the time of Kay Kaavoos and prepare a regal feast.
Every one of his needs and desires must be met,
Even though he comes bitter and intent on battle.

Nevertheless, we must receive the king's son,
An illustrious hero and a bold, powerful prince,
Who fears not an entire field full of lions.

"I shall advance to meet him, and if he accepts our feast,
We can all expect a favorable outcome to this affair.
If I find kindness and compassion in him,
I shall bring him the diadem of gold and ruby.
I shall lavish him with my wealth,
With gems, strappings, swords, and mace.
But if he sends me away without the hope for peace,
I shall not spend a bright day with him.
You know what my rolled-up noose is able to do
And how it can capture the head of a mad elephant."

Zavaareh replies, "Do not concern yourself.
No one ever seeks a battle without provocation.
There is no king in the world who compares to Esfandiar
In strength, in nobility, and in courage.
A sensible man will not wish to cause anyone harm.
Esfandiar has nothing with which to reproach us."

Zavaareh approaches Zaal as Rostam stands up
And rushes to the River Hirmand,
His head spinning with the premonition of danger.
He halts with his horse at the riverbank
And awaits Bahman to bring him greetings from Esfandiar.

Bahman presents himself at his father's tent pavilion.
The blessed Esfandiar asks him for the hero's response.
Bahman sits before his father and tells him,
From beginning to end, all that was said.
He relates Rostam's greetings, his message, and the reply.
He gives an account of all that he observed in open or in secret.

Bahman adds, "One can find in the gathering
Of great men no one equal to Rostam.
He has a lion's heart and the figure of an elephant.
He draws out crocodiles from the blue waters of the river.
He comes now to the banks of the Hirmand
Without armor, noose, mace, or helmet.
He wishes to see the king,
And I know not what mysteries he will reveal."

Esfandiar grows furious with Bahman
And treats him unkindly before the assembly:
"It does not suit a nobleman to sit in secret with women.
If he makes use of children for vital matters,
He is not a valiant man.
Where did you ever see the deeds of warriors?
You have not even heard the voice of the fox.
By making Rostam a war elephant,
You bring distress to this illustrious gathering."

Then Esfandiar turns to Pashootan and says,
"This passionate lion, always eager for battle,
Behaves like a young man.
You will see that the years have been kind to him,
And his face does not display a single wrinkle."

12 | Rostam and Esfandiar Meet

Esfandiar orders a golden saddle for his black stallion,
Then departs with a procession of one hundred horsemen.
He rushes to the edge of the River Hirmand,
Noose wrapped around his saddle horn.
Rakhsh nickers on one end of the river
While on the other, Esfandiar's charger whinnies.
The world warrior dismounts and greets the world king.

After offering homage, Rostam addresses Esfandiar,
"I prayed for divine guidance, O illustrious prince,
For you to come to me in good health with your retinue.
Now let us resolve our problems in a way
As to bring joy to both of us.
May the Creator be my witness,
I am guided here only by the dictates of reason.
I have no need for pretense.
My goals and desires are never spurred by deceit.
The sight of your young face makes me happier
Than if I were to lay eyes on the features of Siaavoosh.
You very much resemble the giver of crowns.
Happy is the king who has a son like you,
A son whose stature and majesty exalt his father!
Happy the land of Iran, where the people

Venerate your throne and your good fortune!
May calamity befall the one who wishes to fight you,
For he will be toppled off the throne and into the dust!
May your enemies live in constant fear of you!
May their hearts split in two!
May your good fortune always be victorious!
May your dark nights convert into bright days of Nowruz!"

After Rostam's discourse,
Esfandiar climbs down from his charger.
He takes the elephantine body into his arms
And blesses him with joy:
"Mercy to the Creator, O world hero,
For I find you in good health and in peace!
It is a duty to celebrate your glory.
Warriors must turn to dust beneath your feet.
Happy is the one who has a son like you,
For he sees a branch bearing fruit.
Happy is the one supported by you,
For he is sheltered from the callousness of fate.
When I saw you, I was reminded of the leader Zarir,
Who brought down elephants like a brave lion."

Rostam replies, "O illustrious warlord full of wisdom,
Caution, and peace, I have a prayer and a wish
That I hope you will willingly grant me.
May you agree to come to my home
And cheer my heart with your presence.
If anything worthy of you is lacking,
We shall make every effort to procure it."

Esfandiar replies, "O warrior heir,
When one bears a name like yours,
One makes joy of the entire land of Iran.
No one can refuse any of your requests.
One must not pass your land or your dwelling
Without accepting your invitation and company.
But I shall never deviate, neither secretly nor openly,
From the orders of the world king.
He prohibited me from spending time in Zabol
And engaging in war with the noblemen of this land.
Do all you can to benefit from your impending fate.

Go as the king commands to where the king commands.
Without delay, place your feet in shackles,
For the bonds of the King of Kings do not bear dishonor.
Once I present you captive to his majesty,
All the accountability will fall back on him.
I myself feel disheartened to have to enchain you.
I stand before you, waist cinched in service to you.
I shall not allow your bonds to remain until night.
I shall not allow any harm to touch or affect you.

"O brave hero, you suspect treachery on the part of the king.
You cannot believe that he may wish to cause you harm,
But rest assured that you will incur no harm from his majesty.
He promised me ivory throne, treasure, and crown.
Once I lower the royal diadem onto my head,
I shall offer you command of the entire world.
What I ask of you is not deemed a sin by the Justice Giver,
Nor will it cause me to feel shame before the king.
Upon your return to Zabolestan,
At the time when the gardens are in bloom,
You will receive from me so many precious things
That your entire nation will be embellished by it."

Rostam replies, "O illustrious prince, I prayed to the Creator,
Ultimate Judge, that my heart would rejoice at the sight of you
And at the sound of your speech.
We are two noble, renowned men, one old, one young.
We are sensible and prudent. We are bold world warriors.
But I fear that the evil eye is directed at us
And that my head awakens from a happy dream.
I fear that the malevolent deev stands between us
And perverts your heart by the desire for crown and throne.
Such a thing is for me a deep source of shame
That, until the end of the world, can never be washed away:
The fact that a leader, a chief, a prince, a lion full of pride,
A powerful man like you would refuse to enter my home
And to be my guest in my land.

"If you repel this hatred from your heart, if you could
Make an effort and resist the temptation of the deev,
My heart would rejoice at your words,
And I shall obey all that you ask of me, although

I shall never agree to submit to the shame of shackles.
It would be a most wicked thing,
A thing that would surely rush me to my demise.
No one will ever see me alive wearing bondage!
My life and my labors are worth so much more.
A death where my head would be buried beneath stones
Is a better end than having my name denigrated."

Esfandiar replies, "O heir of renowned heroes,
You have spoken only the truth from beginning to end.
May men never find glory on tortuous paths!
Pashootan is well aware of the king's orders:
I must prepare to encounter Rostam,
With whom I shall either fight or trap in shackles.
If I accept your invitation and go to your palace
As your guest, happy and victorious,
I would then refuse to obey my king's command,
And the splendor of my day would be tarnished.
There is no doubt that if I attack you,
Fight you with the fury of a wild leopard,
I shall forget the rights of bread and salt.
You will have to question the virtue of my race.
On the other hand, if I defy the king and disobey him,
My place in the other world will be in the heart of fire.
If you wish, let us devote this day to wine.
Who knows what tomorrow will bring?
But it is useless to speak of the future."

Rostam says, "I shall act thus:
I shall go and change into my travel gear,
Feeding myself venison instead of lamb.
At the hour of supper, join my spread with your family."

He climbs back on Rakhsh,
Enclosing his worries in his fatigued, wounded heart,
And gallops away in haste to his castle.
He finds Zaal, son of Saam, and says to him,
"O illustrious prince, I have gone to Esfandiar.
I have found in him a skilled rider, a man as tall
As a cypress tree, full of sense, grace, and dignity.
It is as if the brave king Fereydoon
Had bequeathed to him his power and wisdom.

When one observes him,
One finds him grander than his fame.
He shines with the majesty of the King of Kings."

13 | Esfandiar Fails to Invite Rostam to Feast

After Rostam rides away, the powerful king
Remains at the edge of the Hirmand, full of worry.
At that moment, Pashootan, the king's advisor,
Enters the tent enclosure, and Esfandiar says to him,
"We have taken too lightly a complicated matter.
It is not my place to visit Rostam's palace,
And he, in turn, has no reason to visit me.
If he does not return on his own, I shall not summon him,
For if one of us must perish at the hand of the other,
The heart of the surviving one would bleed for the other,
And the friendship contracted would result in tears."

Pashootan replies, "O illustrious prince,
Who else is blessed with a brother like Esfandiar?
I swear by Yazdan that, when I first saw you together,
When I realized you did not seek to fight, I was appeased
By the friendship of Esfandiar and Rostam,
And my heart became fresh as a blooming spring.
Now that I have a chance to reflect on this,
I see that the deev has dimmed your wisdom.
You have a sense of this man's value.
You are aware of Yazdan's will as well as your father's wishes.
Abstain from placing your life in harm's way,
And listen to your brother's sensible words.

"I have heard all that Rostam said.
I have witnessed his power, which equals his humanity.
Your bonds will not bind his feet,
For he will not accept shackles.
The world conqueror Rostam, son of Zaal, son of Saam,
Will not easily fall into this trap.
I fear that this quarrel, between two proud men,
Will only grow more intense in duration and cruelty.
You are a noble prince and wiser than the king,
More powerful in strength and valor.

One chases after feasts
While the other yearns for fight and vengeance.
Reflect on which of the two merits validation."

The renowned Esfandiar replies, "If I disobey the king,
I will be cursed and condemned in this world.
In the other world, I shall have to answer to the Creator.
I do not wish to sacrifice myself in both realms for Rostam.
One cannot stitch the heart's eye with a needle."

Pashootan says, "I have shared with you wise advice
To safeguard your body and your soul.
It is now your turn to determine how to settle the matter.
Remember, the heart of a king must not incline toward hate."

The leader commands the cooks to set up a spread,
Refraining from sending someone to summon Rostam.
Once the meal is completed, he asks for a cup of wine.
He speaks of the impregnable castle, of his courage,
And then drinks to the health of the King of Kings.

During this time, Rostam awaits in his palace,
Looking out on the road,
Not forgetting his engagement for supper.
But no one arrives to fetch him.
Once the hour of dinner is long gone, the hero's mind
Is overcome by unfulfilled expectations.
He smiles and says to Zavaareh, "O dear brother,
Set up the spread, and call the noblemen.
If this is Esfandiar's way of showing common courtesy
By making light of our presence,
We might as well give up hope on him."

He calls for spread and meal, then he rises and asks
Faraamarz to saddle up Rakhsh with Chini strappings.
He says, "I shall ride to Esfandiar to tell him
That as a prince he must have integrity,
For dishonoring his word undermines his rank and stature."

14 | Esfandiar Makes Excuses for Not Inviting Rostam

Rostam climbs on his horse like an elephant.
Rakhsh's whinny is heard for two miles.
The world hero gallops swiftly to the water's edge.

At the sight of him approaching,
The Iranian troops rush to him.
Each man immediately nurtures in his heart
A sense of fondness and friendship with him.

They say to themselves, "This illustrious hero
So resembles Saam, the horseman.
He sits on his stallion like a mountain of steel.
It is as if Rakhsh is as resilient as Ahriman.
If a terrible elephant were to fight him,
One could only despair for the creature's life.
The king is foolish to send to his death a glorious hero
Like Esfandiar, a prince as handsome as the moon,
Who would expand the glory of his crown and throne.
The more Goshtaasp ages,
The more greedy he becomes for wealth and treasure,
The more attached he grows to seal and diadem."

Upon Rostam's approach,
Esfandiar exits his tent to greet him.

Rostam is first to speak: "O blessed young man
Who introduces the world to new forms and customs,
Do you not think your guest deserved a message?
Is this your way of keeping your word?
Such was indeed the agreement we had.
Pay heed to what I have to say.
Do not foolishly turn your anger toward an old man.
You have a high opinion of yourself and act rudely
Toward us, who come from an illustrious breed of men.
You view as insignificant my courage and valor,
And you hold me as weak of mind and will.
But know that the world acclaims me as Rostam.
I am the one who shed light on the seed of Nariman.
Because of me, the black deev bites his own hand.
I can fling leaders and wizards off their seats.

"Noblemen have seen my armor of leopard skin
And the roaring lion on which I climbed.
They all fled without engaging in fight,
Filling the plain with castoff bows and arrows.
Such men as Kaamoos, the fighter, and the Tarkhan of Chin,
Valiant horsemen and powerful warriors
Whom I captured in the knot of my noose,
Were plucked off their steeds and tied up from head to toe.
I am the protector of the kings of Iran
And the support of brave men everywhere.
My humble prayer exalts you,
But do not deem yourself as more powerful than the sky.
It is because of your royal dignity and your crown
That I seek to conform to your wishes and remain loyal to you.
It would be calamitous for a prince like Esfandiar
To perish at my hands on the day of battle.

"True, Saam the hero, before whom lions fled into the forest,
Was a brave man, and now I remind the world of him.
No lion dares stand audaciously before me.
I have been world warrior for a long time.
Never did I spend a single day harming anyone
Who was not opposed to our cause and our kingship.
I have purified the world of our enemies
And, in the process, endured interminable fatigues.
I am grateful to Yazdan that, in my old age,
I see the blessed fruit grow on the branch of the royal tree,
A man who is my equal,
Who will fight against men of impure faith,
And to whom the universe will pay homage."

Esfandiar smiles at Rostam and says,
"O grandson of Saam the horseman,
You are pained by my lack of communication.
It is what I intended, and I am glorified by this act.
The day is so hot and the road so long
That I did not wish to exert you.
Do not take it the wrong way and blame me.
I have been thinking that tomorrow, at dawn,
I shall travel the path to you and ask forgiveness,
To celebrate the sight of Zaal, and to give in to joy.
Now that you have taken this burden upon yourself,

Left your palace, and arrived in the desert,
Rest and sit down, take this cup,
And do not give yourself a reputation of wrath and fury."

He assigns him a place of honor on his left.
But the worldly Rostam says,
"This is not a suitable place for my rank.
I wish to take the seat due me on your right."

The prince commands Bahman to rise
And make way for Rostam.
Bahman obeys, his face twisted in a hostile frown.

Rostam, witness to his deportment, says in anger,
"Look at my stature and open your eyes.
Think of my high deeds and my illustrious birth,
For I come from the race of the powerful Saam,
The same man from the lineage of Jamsheed,
A man as bright as the moon and the sun.
One must expect courage from a royal prince,
A generous hand and a heart full of justice.
But if you do not have a proper seat for me,
I still have my victories, my name, and my rights."

Then the prince asks his son to fetch a golden seat
To be placed before the throne, and he tells Rostam,
"Sit here in peace and joy.
Your place will always be upon this golden seat."

Rostam takes his seat, still full of rage
But holding in his hand a scented citron.

15 | Esfandiar Belittles Rostam's Lineage

Esfandiar says to Rostam,
"O benevolent and powerful warrior,
I have heard from pure-hearted wise men
That Zaal, the wicked, is the descendant of a deev
And that this fact was concealed from Saam,
Who deemed it would cause the ruin of the world.
His body was black, his face and hair white,

And when Saam laid eyes on him, his heart despaired.
He asked for him to be carried to the sea
In the hope that birds and fish would devour him as prey.
Simorgh spread its wings and flew down to him.
Unable to find in the child a hint of glory or majesty,
She carried him away to her nest to make a meal of him.
She presented the baby to her young ones who,
Although they were famished, did not dare consume him,
For his body was bare and miserable.
No one could rejoice at the sight of Zaal.
The naked child subsisted on scraps of dead creatures
As Simorgh, feeling pity for him, grew fond of him.
In this way the skies turned over him for some time.

"After sucking at length on Simorgh's leftovers,
The bird carried him naked to Sistan, and Saam,
A man of little sense, by then old and despondent,
Took him back, having no other children.
The blessed noblemen, kings, and my caring ancestors
Made him rich and prosperous.
In this way many years passed.
He flourished into a cypress tree rising high,
And once he grew branches, the tree bore Rostam as fruit.
The warrior hero was elevated to the sky by his courage,
His stature, his majesty, and his mien,
Holding fast to royal dignity, becoming powerful,
And deserting the path of righteousness.
Now he refuses to listen to the king's command.
Do not speak of bird and animal carcass.
I am ashamed to even mention the name of your god."

16 | Rostam Defends His Lineage and His High Deeds

Rostam replies, "Hold on for a moment.
Why do you utter such insulting words?
Your heart must sigh in the face of perversity,
But your wisdom is distracted by deevs.
Speak as suits a king, for a king must only speak the truth.
The world master knows that Zaal, son of Saam,
Is a prevailing leader, a wise holder of a prominent name.
Saam was the son of Nariman, a noble-minded warrior,

Who spread justice and good deeds all around.
On one side we are descendants of Garshaasp
And on the other of Shah Jamsheed.
Meanwhile, kingship was handed to Lohraasp
By our forefathers. Without this occurrence,
Your family's name would not be recognizable.
I am the one who brought Kay Ghobaad
Down from Mount Alborz to rule the empire.
He was a divine worshipper who, until then,
Did not possess army, treasure, and glory.

"You have, without a doubt, heard of Saam's fame.
He was the most celebrated nobleman in all the world.
There lived in Tous[74] a fierce dragon,
Whom no one could overcome.
He was a whale in water and a leopard on land,
Able to convert mountains to pebbles and dust with his tail.
In the sea, he burned the heads of fishes,
And in the air, the wings of vultures.
He drew in elephants with his mighty tail,
And joyous hearts trembled at the mention of it.
This dragon fit in the vast waters,
Which turned into a dark sea of tar from his poison.
Saam, the hero, slew the dragon with his mace,
Ridding the world of the evil presence
And bringing onto his name fame and glory.

"Then there lived a ferocious deev
Whose body was sprawled over the earth,
only half immersed in the Sea of Chin
While its head stretched to the firmament.
This was a beast who obscured the light of day.
It drew fish from the sea to roast in the sun,
Raised its head above the dome of sky,
And made the turning sphere weep with fear.
Saam slashed this deev at the waist and split him in two.
He freed the world from the fear of him.
These two redoubtable monsters quivered
And perished from Saam's blade and courage.

◇◇◇◇◇◇◇◇◇◇◇◇◇◇
74 Tous: An ancient city in the province of Khorasan in Iran; also the site of Ferdow-
si's residence.

"Furthermore, my mother was Mehraab's daughter,
A woman who made the land of Sindh flourish.
Zahaak was her fifth-removed ancestor,
Who held his head higher than many world kings.
Where can one find a more illustrious family?
A sensible man never repudiates the truth.
My merit is such in the entire world
That warriors learn and borrow from me.
I am in possession of a treaty with Kaavoos
That must never be disputed.
Besides, I had one with Kay Khosrow, the just, as well,
Who was the most valiant of all the Kianian kings.

"I have crossed the entire world, from end to end,
Killed many unjust rulers.
Once I had crossed the waters of the Jayhoon,
Afraasiyaab fled from Tooran-Zamin to Chin.
When Kay Kaavoos traveled to Mazandaran,
Zaal spoke at length on the subject.
Have you heard what calamities befell the king,
How he suffered having been blinded by the deev?
I journeyed alone, in the dark night, for countless farsangs.
In the end, I eradicated Arjang, the White Deev,
Sanjeh, Poolaad of Ghondi, and Beed.

"Finally, I killed, unknowingly and to the king's advantage,
My own son, the valiant and cautious Sohraab,
A hero who had no equal in strength, courage, and skill.
Over six hundred years, I was given life by Zaal.
During all this time, I have been a world warrior,
My being consistent in every way,
My words and actions reflecting my heart's purity.
I resemble Fereydoon of blessed race,
Who placed the crown of noblemen on his head,
Who cast Zahaak off his throne
And trampled his head and crown in the dust.
In my exploits, I resemble Saam, my grandfather,
Surpassing the entire world in wisdom and ruse.
Thirdly, from the time I cinched my waist,
The noble king had a chance to calmly rest free of worry.
Never has the land seen happier, more glorious days.
The peace is such that the foot of a wandering man

Has never needed to seek refuge in a fortress.
My will gave order to a world of chaos and dispute,
And my joy came from my sword and heavy mace.

"I tell you all this so that you know the truth.
You are king, and the finest men are your subjects.
But you are new to the world,
And although the majesty of Kay Khosrow is your heritage,
You see only yourself in the universe. You are not
Acquainted with actions that have fallen into oblivion.
But I converse excessively. Let us drink
And cast aside our hearts' anguish with wine."

17 | Esfandiar Sings the Praises of His Lineage

Esfandiar's heart blossoms at Rostam's speech.
He smiles and says to him, "I have heard you speak
Of the grief and worries you have endured in battle.
Listen now to the tale of my deeds. You will see
How I have glorified my name through my feats,
My stature rising above everyone in the world.
In the first instance, I bore arms to defend the faith.
I freed the world of idol worshippers
In fierce campaigns that made the face of the earth
Completely vanish beneath a mass of cadavers.
I am from the race of Goshtaasp, son of Lohraasp,
Son of Arvand Shah, who, in his time,
Possessed a glorious throne and a noble name.
Arvand was a descendant of Kay Pashin,
To whom his own father paid homage.
Pashin was from the race of the wise and just Kay Ghobaad.
As you see, you can trace my lineage back to King Fereydoon,
Founder of the Kianian dynasty and ornament of the throne.

"My mother was the daughter of the Caesar
And the diadem on the head of the Rumi society.
The Caesar was born of the illustrious seed of Salm,
The celebrated son of Fereydoon,
The most glorious and just hero among the kings.
I say, and no one can deny it,
That men who stray are plentiful, while those

Who follow the righteous path are rather scarce.
You and your grandfather have always been loyal servants
To my forefathers, although today you rush here as a rebel.
Remain in your place until I tell you everything.
If any of it appears to be a falsehood,
You may call attention to it.
You have gained your grandeur from my ancestors
Because you have stood at the ready to serve them devotedly.

"Since Lohraasp handed the throne to Goshtaasp,
I am armed and powerful
By the strength awarded me by fortune.
I executed all those in the lands of Tooran and Chin
Who strayed from the path of faith.
Later, once my father, at Gorazm's instigation,
Imprisoned me, constricting me with shackles,
I was distanced from feasts and revelry.
But my chains brought misfortune to Lohraasp
As the Turks assembled massive armies,
Advancing on our lands to take advantage of a weak ruler.
Jaamaasp delivered a message to me from Fort Gombadan.
When he saw me chained up and despondent,
My heart, mind, and soul wounded,
He brought me blacksmiths to remove my heavy cuffs.
But their labor made me impatient
And forced my heart to swell with the need for a sword.
I shouted with rage at the blacksmiths, rejected them,
Rose, and shattered the chains with my bare hands.

"From there, I rushed to the battlefield,
Just as fortune was abandoning Goshtaasp.
At the sight of me advancing toward him,
Arjaasp fled with his illustrious entourage.
I strapped myself and chased them like a ferocious lion.
Moreover, you have heard how, at the seven stages,
I overcame Ahriman and the lions,
How I entered the impregnable castle, destroyed the world,
Avenged the Iranians, and seized weapons to spill blood.
My deeds in the lands of Tooran and Chin,
My labors and the dangers I faced
Far surpass anything a deer might have suffered from a lion,
Or the jaws of a whale captured in the fisherman's net.

"There was a castle on a mountain crest,
Placed by its elevation above the crowd.
When I arrived there, I found idol worshippers,
Men confounded and resembling drunken men.
From the time of Toor, son of Fereydoon,
No one had ever taken this impenetrable castle.
By my courage, I seized its walls and tossed aside its idols.
In a plate, I lit the fire Zartosht had brought from paradise.
Thanks to Yazdan, Justice Giver, I returned to Iran-Zamin.
Nowhere did I leave a single adversary
Nor any worshippers in the temples of idols.
I have always engaged in battle alone,
And no one has suffered as much as I have.
Now that we have spoken at length about ourselves,
If you are thirsty, take this cup of wine."

18 | Rostam Extols His High Deeds

Rostam replies to Esfandiar,
"Our actions will endure as a memorial of us
Long after we are gone. Treat me with fairness.
Listen to an old man drenched in glory.
If I had not, heavy mace on my shoulder,
Made the journey to Mazandaran,
Where Giv, Goodarz, Tous, and the king
Were held blind, captive, and in grave distress,
Who would have plucked out the liver of the White Deev?
Who would have split and splattered its brains?
Who would have freed Kay Kaavoos from his bonds
And returned him to the noble throne, as I did,
With the mere force of my arm?
I freed the king from heavy chains, restored him to his seat.
Iran was happy under his rule; fortune favored him.
I cut off the heads of sorcerers,
Granting them the protection of neither shroud nor coffin.

"In all my battles, my constant companions
Were my sword and the loyal and powerful Rakhsh,
World giver by the power of his hooves.
Then, when Kaavoos went to Haamaavaran
And once again was bound with heavy chains,

I led an army of Iranian warriors,
Drawn from every bastion with a leader or a prince.
I killed the King of Haamaavaran
And rendered vacant his illustrious throne.
Kaavoos, world master, was imprisoned, dejected,
And plagued by trouble and worry.
Afraasiyaab, during this time,
Invaded Iran with an army full of noblemen.
The world spun with evil and grief.
I liberated Kaavoos, Giv, Goodarz, and Tous.
I led them toward the land of Iran.

"In the middle of the night, I advanced alone,
In search of toils and glory.
Afraasiyaab spotted my shiny banner,
Heard Rakhsh's whinny, and fled from Iran to Chin.
Justice reigned supreme in a world full of blessings.
If blood had gushed from the limbs of Kay Kaavoos,
How could Siaavoosh have come into the world?
And subsequently, how would Kay Khosrow
Have been borne from his holy mother,
He, the blessed ruler who placed
The crown on Lohraasp's head?

"My father's lips filled with dust at the time
When Kay Khosrow awarded Lohraasp with kingship.
He acted in a way that Lohraasp's name prevails.
Hear me out, O valiant Esfandiar.
Do not rest at peace, for the world has ups and downs.
Do not depend on your youth. Listen to this old man.
Do not heed Goshtaasp's words, for they are unreasonable.
He usurped the throne from his father with his evil character.
May he be cursed! May his crown and fortune be cursed!
Once the father, Lohraasp, observed his son's vengeful behavior,
He retired to a remote corner of the world
And to a fire temple to pray, eyes brimming with tears.
Then, deserting his father in Balkh, he came to Zabol.
In the end, warriors arrived from Chin
And put an end to your grandfather's life.

"Do you really think that the one who brought misery
To his father would have the heart to worry about his son?

Goshtaasp is making use of deceit with you,
Failing you as a father, and treating you in wicked ways,
For he secretly hopes to pitch you to your end.
That is why he sent you to fight with Rostam.
He is fearful of you. It is as if his foot is stuck in the mud.
He does not envisage, not even in his dreams,
That you could effectively capture me,
Tie me up, and cause me the slightest harm.

"Listen to me, son. I am not an adversary; Goshtaasp is.
He does not wish to confer the throne to you,
And that is why he sent you to fight with me.
You must not obey his commands
Until he carries this crown, throne, and diadem
With him to hell or to a dark cloud.
A father who does not relinquish kingship to his son
Must be decapitated with the blade.
A father who guides his son down the wrong path
Can be compared to a vicious wolf.

"Take paternal affection from Zaal
And mace and power from Rostam.
We shall make you King of Iran as well as Tooran.
We shall cut short the hands of your foes.
But you will gain nothing by tying me up in chains.
On the day of vengeance,
I shall stitch the earth to the sky with my noose.
Name, glory, and nobility belonged to me,
With no attachment to Lohraasp, who went to Shaam.
Treasure and land belonged to me
When Goshtaasp was a mere blacksmith in Rum.
Why fret over Goshtaasp's crown, bracelet, and throne?
How dare he tell you to enchain me
When not even the lofty sky has the ability to bind me?
From my childhood to my declining years,
I have never been submitted to such degradation.
I shall neither act in shame nor beg for mercy.
For me to ask forgiveness would be humiliating.
Not even the subject of our discussion is worthy of my status."

Esfandiar smiles and reaches over to exchange
A handclasp with Rostam, to whom he says,

"O Rostam of elephantine build,
You are just as I have been told by noblemen.
Your arm is as strong as the burly leg of a lion.
Your chest and limbs are those of a valiant dragon.
Your waist is as thin and supple as a leopard's.
What man would dare confront you on the day of battle?"

As he speaks, he grips Rostam's hand harder,
But the old man smiles at the youth.
Though blood drips from his fingers,
He does not show a hint of pain.

In turn, Rostam presses the prince's hand, saying,
"O King, Yazdan worshipper, blessed is Goshtaasp,
Triumphant Shah, to boast a son as eminent as Esfandiar,
Who will be the glory of the world."

During this dialogue, he crushes the prince's hand
To the point of making the leader's face turn crimson.
His fingers are red with blood,
And his eyebrows are arched in a frown.

Yet the blessed Esfandiar smiles and says,
"O noble Rostam, drink wine today, for tomorrow
You will retreat in battle, and no one will ever wish
To drink to your health again in feast.
Once I hoist the golden saddle on my black charger,
Once I cover my head in my royal helmet,
I shall toss you off your horse with my spear
And hurl you onto the dusty ground.
After that, I shall no longer fight with you.
I shall no longer bear you a grudge.
Your hands secured, I shall take you to the king
And tell him that I have found no fault in you.
I shall appear before his majesty as supplicant,
To plead your cause in such a way
As to free you from grief, pain, and sorrow,
And reward you with immeasurable treasure."

Rostam smiles and retorts,
"You will have enough of the struggle.
Where did you ever see the strike of a heavy mace?
Where did you ever hear the whistle of its swing?

If the revolving dome turns in such a way,
If it erases feelings of affection between two men,
Then, instead of engaging in drinking red wine,
Let us surrender to vengeance.
Let us make use of bow, arrow, noose, and weaponry.
Let us make timpani resound instead of music.
Let us greet each other with sword and mace.
Then, O blessed Esfandiar, you will witness real struggles
And how chance determines the outcome of battle.

"When I appear tomorrow on the battlefield,
We shall fight man to man.
I shall take you off your horse with my bare arms
And carry you before Zaal,
To seat you on his famed ivory throne.
I shall place on your head the crown,
The delight of dim hearts,
Which I received from Kay Ghobaad,
May his soul rest in peace!
I shall open the doors to my treasury,
Display before you its magnificence.
I shall give you all that I possess of value,
Place your army above all need,
Raise your helmet above the clouds.

"Then we shall depart in the direction of the king's court,
Surrounded by all the pomp and circumstance of our stations,
Playing and marching on the road in a state of joy.
I shall bravely place the crown on your head,
And, in this way, give thanks to Goshtaasp.
Then I shall stand before you as a slave
As I did before the Kianian kings,
Plucking weeds from my heart's garden.
My body will renew with joy.
Once you are king and I your world hero,
Not one of our adversaries will have a chance to survive."

19 | Rostam Drinks Wine With Esfandiar

Esfandiar replies, "Your words are meaningless.
The noon hour has passed,
And we have not feasted upon the spreads,
Though we have spoken of war at length.
Bring out the fare, and let us not invite loquacious guests."

Once they are served and the meal begins,
The company is astonished by Rostam's appetite.
Esfandiar and his leaders summon roasted lambs
From near and far, and Rostam eats everything.

Then the prince orders cups of red wine:
"We shall see what Rostam asks for under the influence
Of drink, and how he speaks of Kay Kaavoos."

The cupbearer brings an enormous cup of aged wine,
So large that one would think Rostam would never drain it.
Rostam drinks to the health of the King of Kings
And empties his cup of crimson liquid.

The young cupbearer once again fills his cup.
Rostam whispers to Pashootan,
"The wine will lose its effect with water.
Why do you weaken the drink with it?"

Pashootan says to the cupbearer,
"Bring a new cup of wine without water."
Then he summons the singers,
And Rostam ceases to be the subject of wonder.

At the time of departure,
Rostam's noble face is colored by drink.
Esfandiar says to him,
"May you live in joy to the end of your days!
May the wine and the fare be to your liking!
May righteousness be nourishment for your soul!"

Rostam replies, "O illustrious prince,
May reason always be your guide!
The wine that I drink with you always does me good
And gives strength to my prudent mind.

PART NINETEEN

If you wish to distance your heart from this struggle,
Your power and your wisdom will only increase by it.
Leave the desert and come to my house.
Remain there for some time as my guest.
Honor my dwelling with your presence.
Do not distance yourself from your loyal servant.
I shall do as you wish. Allow wisdom to be your guide.
Rest for some time; do not exert yourself to cause harm.
Lean on clemency and return to reason."

Esfandiar replies, "Do not sow a seed
That will never have the chance to mature.
You will witness tomorrow the power of my valor
When I seize my weapons for battle.
Do not take too much pride in yourself.
Return to your palace and prepare for tomorrow.
You will see that on the battlefield
I am the same as before cupbearers and cups of wine.
You have not the power to defeat me,
So listen to the advice I offer you.
My skills are far beyond anything I have alluded to.
Do not be the cause of my distress.
Allow yourself to be chained as the king ordered,
For a pious man accepts the king's command
As devotedly as divine order.
Once we travel from Zabol to Iran,
Once we appear before the king of brave men,
He will have a great opinion of you from my tales.
Do not then cause me the grief of refusing me."

Rostam's heart is deeply afflicted.
The world appears to him like a forest so thick
He no longer can discern his own path.
He thinks, "Whether I allow him to enchain me
Or I defeat him and send him to his end,
These two fates are equally cursed.
Both options offer me two pernicious alternatives:
One is unthinkable; the other is calamitous.
The chains will extinguish my glory.
My splendor will drown in the waters of shame,
And nothing would remain in the world of my fame.

"On the other hand, if I kill Esfandiar on the battlefield,
My face will pale with embarrassment before the kings.
People will point at me and accuse me of killing a prince
Because he addressed me with some rude words.
What am I to do? How shall I proceed?
If I accept, I shall have cause to weep.
If I refuse, I shall have cause to weep.
I would be cursed even after my death to the end of days,
And I will be called an impious, old man.
Finally, if I were to accept the chains,
Everyone would lament that a young man
Arrived in Zabol and bound Rostam.
And if I were killed at his hand,
All of Zabolestan would perish and the name of Zaal
And the lineage of Saam would be dishonored.
No one in all of our land would acquire glory.
But at least people would repeat my good words.
I must do all that is necessary to maintain peace
Or my wisdom would push me to undo my life."

Rostam says to the proud youth, "Thinking makes me pale.
You always speak of these chains, but I fear your chains
And your intentions will be the cause of your downfall
Unless the decree of the sky dictates otherwise,
For no one can guess the actions of the revolving dome.
You have aligned yourself with the deev,
Taking his advice over words of wisdom.
You are pure-hearted and do not know the ways of the world.
Let me tell you that Goshtaasp is set upon your death.
He is not yet weary of throne and crown
As long as fortune smiles down at him.
He sends you hurtling through all the lands,
Placing you in harm's way.
The entire world appears suspect to him.
His wisdom is a hatchet, his mind is an axe.
As long as there is a warrior who fears you not,
As long as this warrior puts your life in danger,
Goshtaasp may cling to the throne and crown of power.

"Must I then curse the throne, and, for these reasons
Turn the earth into a bed of repose for you?
Why do you wish to dishonor my life?

Why does your mind avert reflection?
By your own hand, you sow ill wishes for me,
But your malice will only attract trials upon yourself.
Do not commit a rash, youthful act that would be criminal.
Do not afflict your heart, O King,
And put your life and mine in harm's way.
What need have you to assail me?
Fate urges you and your army to perish at my hand,
Rendering my name infamous in the world.
May this wicked end remain reserved for Goshtaasp!"

The proud Esfandiar responds, "O renowned Rostam,
Reflect on the words of a wise man
From a time when his mind was at its prime:
         'An old man who deceives dwells in foolishness,
            No matter how valiant and how astute he may be.
Is this how you wish to fool me,
To free yourself of the ring of servitude?
You wish people to believe your deceptive words,
To treat me, a righteous man, like one
Of impure intentions and you like a virtuous sage.
You wish them to say that you arrive bearing
Good news and kind words, and make me hope
We have no choice but to battle.
         'Anything Rostam wants from him,
            Esfandiar wishes not to act upon.
            His tongue is full of bitter words.'

"Know that I shall never disobey the king,
Even if it were for the throne and crown.
The world depends on him for its joy and grief.
In him reside my hell and my paradise.
May your meal bring peace to you
And misfortune to your enemy!
Now return in amity to Zaal's palace,
And repeat to him all that you have heard.
Prepare your war armor and cease to speak to me.
Come at dawn, fight loyally,
And let us not drag out this affair.
You will see, tomorrow on the battlefield,
The entire world turn black before your eyes.
You will know the true meaning of a battle

Between valiant men on the day of honor and fight."

Rostam says to him, "O man of lion heart,
Since this is your wish, the next time I see you,
It will be from atop Rakhsh, my passionate charger,
When I shall reconcile your head to my mace.
In your land, you have heard the credible stories
Of how the sword of brave men is powerless against you.
Tomorrow, you will witness for yourself the tip of my blade
And the reins of Rakhsh rolled up around my hand.
You will never again wish to fight with a renowned warrior."

The lips of the young prince curve in a smile.
Rostam deems himself inferior to this noble man.

Esfandiar replies, "O seeker of glory,
Why do you grow angry in speech?
When you come tomorrow on the battlefield,
You will witness a battle among brave warriors.
I am not a boulder, and the horse I ride is not a mountain.
I am a single man who will arrive without an escort.
Yazdan's name is my shelter
And will protect me from the blade's wound.
But either your head will be shattered by my mace
Or your mother will weep in the grief of her heart.
If you do not perish in battle, I shall tie you up
To the saddle and take you to Goshtaasp
So that a slave like you never seeks to fight against the king."

20 | Rostam Returns to His Palace

Before exiting Esfandiar's pavilion,
Rostam stands at the entrance for a moment,
Addressing its frame: "O dwelling of hope,
What magnificent days you witnessed
During the rule of Shah Jamsheed!
How celebrated you were in the eras
Of Fereydoon and Manoochehr,
So glorious in the time of Kay Ghobaad,
When the world filled with justice,
So auspicious in the time of Kay Kaavoos,

And so prosperous during the reign of Kay Khosrow,
Whose footprints left a most blessed trail.
But now the despicable prince who seized your throne
Is shutting tight and bolting the doors of glory."

The valiant Esfandiar overhears Rostam
And advances on foot toward the illustrious hero.
He says, "O sensible man,
Why do you direct your resentment at this pavilion?
Must we refer to the land of Zabolestan
As the land of struggles?
Once a guest is weary of his host,
He curses the gardener in his rage."

He adds, "This tent pavilion has seen
A time when it housed Jamsheed, who,
After abandoning the divine path,
Never enjoyed a happy day, not even in paradise.
The same occurred during the time of Fereydoon,
When a dark cloud descended to loom over the throne.
From the reign of Manoochehr to that of Kay Ghobaad,
No one gave a thought to Yazdan's faith.
Furthermore, there was a time when this enclosure
Served Kay Kaavoos as a retreat and as a shelter to his host.
Kaavoos wished to access Yazdan's secret
And observe the stars up close.
Yet he filled the world with looting, daggers, and clubs.
But now this pavilion's master is Goshtaasp,
By whose side stands the wise Jaamaasp.
On one side of the king sits Zartosht,
Who descended from heaven with the *Zand Avesta*.
On the other side sits Pashootan, the virtuous hero,
Who seeks both prosperity and adversity in the world.
Before him stands the blessed Esfandiar,
Who instilled joy into the revolving dome.
He returned life to the hearts of brave warriors,
Subjugating corrupt men into servitude with his sword."

Esfandiar watches Rostam turn around and leave.
He says to Pashootan,
"One must not deny the courage and value of others.
Never have I seen either a horse or a man of his worth.

I do not know how he emerges from battle.
When he comes to fight, shielded in armor,
He is a mighty elephant, seated on Mount Gang.
He is even greater in nobility and grace than in stature.
Yet I fear that tomorrow he will be defeated.
My heart is touched by the majesty of his features.
But I shall not deviate from the orders of the Justice Giver.
When I meet him tomorrow on the battlefield,
I shall dim the light of his brilliant day.
Or perhaps he will be the one to execute me.
No one can foresee the outcome of this fight."

Pashootan replies, "Listen to me, my brother,
When I beseech you to abstain from such a thing.
I have already told you, and I say it again,
For I cannot strip my heart from its righteousness:
Do not bring down and debase another man.
A liberated man will not submit to humiliation.
Spend this night in sleep, and tomorrow at dawn,
Go without an escort to his palace.
There we shall be happy for a day;
We shall answer all his questions.
Rostam has made the world prosper for people.
He will surrender to your command.
I see that his heart is full of loyalty toward you.
Why do you fight him with vengeance and fury?
Rinse hate from your heart and anger from your eyes!"

Esfandiar replies,
"A sharp thorn grows in my rose garden."
It does not suit a true believer to speak thus.
You are a world leader, the king's minister,
Who boasts a warrior's heart, ear, and eye.
You know well what is the proper path to follow
And how to guard ourselves from troubling the king.
All my pains and worry would turn to wind,
And Zartosht's religion would lose its truth,
For it proclaims that anyone who defies the king
Is sure to find a place in hell.
You continuously urge me to commit a sin,
To despise and disobey Goshtaasp's orders.
You insist, but how can I ever go back on my word?

Why would I resist his advice and his command?
If you fear for my life, I shall immediately reassure you.
No one dies in the world without the will of destiny.
The holder of fame and glory never perishes.
Tomorrow you will witness my deeds
Against the dragon's claws on the battlefield."

Pashootan replies, "O noble man,
You ceaselessly speak of battle.
Before you came here with your bow and mace,
Eblis did not have so much power over you.
But now you have surrendered your soul to the deev,
And you no longer wish to listen to your guide's advice.
I shred the clothes on my back at the sight
Of your head and heart foolishly attached to combat.
How could you suddenly free my heart from these fears?
You and Rostam are two brave men, two lions, two warriors.
How do I know which of the two will be vanquished?"

The prince refrains from answering him,
His heart wounded, his head full of wind.

21 | Zaal Gives Advice to Rostam

Rostam returns to his palace, convinced that he must go to war.
Finding him pallid and with an unsettled heart,
Zavaareh asks after his well-being.

Rostam says to him, "I shall need my Indian blade,
Bow and arrows, horse strapping, spear, and battle helmet.
I shall need my noose, my heavy mace,
And my Babreh Bayan, my armor of leopard skin."
Zavaareh commands the treasurer to draw these items.

Once Rostam's eyes fall on his battle gear,
He lowers his head and sighs deeply, saying,
"O warring armor, you have spent a long time at ease.
Now that you must engage in battle, be strong.
Function as a tunic of joy for me at all times,
For this is a battlefield where two heroes
Will wrestle like two roaring lions.

We shall soon assess Esfandiar's skills and strength,
And witness his maneuvers in the game of contention."

At the sound of Rostam's words,
The aging Zaal feels a pang in his heart.
He says, "O illustrious hero, what are you saying?
Your speech deeply troubles my soul.
From the moment you climbed on a battle steed,
You have maintained a pure heart.
You have gained glory by obeying the kings.
You have patiently braved unendurable ordeals
And have displayed utmost courage
When affronted by lions and dragons.
No deev could evade the blows of your heavy mace.
I fear that the light of your day is dimming,
That your auspicious star is about to abate.
If such is the case, then our family
Will be crushed down to its roots,
Our women and children flung into dust.
If you were to die at the hands of this young Esfandiar,
There will remain in Zabolestan neither water nor ground.
Everything that was once high in this land
Will be plunged into a lowly state.

"On the other hand, if Esfandiar is the one to perish,
So will your glory, and those who relate the story
Will come to persecute and decry your illustrious name.
You will be blamed for the murder of the young King of Iran,
A valiant cavalier, a lion of Kianian race.
Go instead on foot to him, and if you do not wish to do so,
Leave this land, go into exile in some corner of the world,
Far from everyone and from powerful men.
In this way, no one will ever hear a mention of your name,
For this misfortune will greatly trouble your mind.
Avoid this young king. Appease this affair with treasure,
And do not take an axe to Chini brocade.
Distribute presents to his troops, and, no matter what the price,
Buy your life back from him.
Once he leaves the banks of the Hirmand River,
Climb on Rakhsh, your powerful horse.
Travel out of Esfandiar's reach. Travel to court
And set your eyes on the face of the blessed king,

In whose presence no one can hurt you.
You will be untouchable. Never have you
Witnessed Iranian kings commit lowly acts."

Rostam replies, "O old man,
Do not speak lightly on this subject.
Many years have passed since I reached manhood,
And from that time
I have experienced both fortune and misfortune:
I trekked to fight the deevs of Mazandaran;
I fought armies of horsemen in Haamaavaran;
I contended with Kaamoos and the Tarkhan of Chin,
Beneath whose horse the earth trembles.
If I were to flee before Esfandiar,
You might as well abandon the palaces
And gardens of our nation of Sistan.
With the power of Yazdan,
I shall fear neither Goshtaasp nor Esfandiar.
When I cover myself with my Babreh Bayan,
I lower to the dust the sphere of the moon.
There is no difference for me, whether I go up against
One hundred elephants or a field full of formidable men.
I have desperately attempted to appeal as you suggest.
I have offered myself as vassal, but he scorned my words,
And chose to turn his back on the just and sensible path.
If he wished to hold his head away from Saturn,
If his pride opened the way for him to greet me,
I would gladly lavish on him all my wealth,
Mace, coat of mail, swords, and gems.
I expressed all this at length,
But he did not weaken in his stance.
My words left me holding nothing but wind.

"But do not fear for his life.
If he comes tomorrow to fight me, I shall not make use
Of a sharp blade, for I do not wish to harm his noble head.
In the fight, I shall handle my horse skillfully,
But neither my mace nor my spear's tip will touch him.
I shall force him into retreat.
I shall seize his belt with all my strength,
Fling him off the saddle, press him against my heart,
And recognize him as reigning king,

Thus repudiating the sovereignty of Goshtaasp.
I shall bring Esfandiar here to my dwelling,
Seat him on this noble throne,
And open the doors to my treasury.
He will remain our welcomed guest for three days.

"As soon as the fourth day retracts the dark veils of night
And the ruby cup presents itself, we shall don our belts
And travel together to Goshtaasp's palace.
There, I shall place him on the illustrious ivory throne.
I shall lower the glorious crown over his head,
Stand before him as his slave, and never leave his side.
You remember my acts of valor
When it came to the throne and the rule of Kay Ghobaad.
Yet you ask me to either cower in hiding
Or give myself up to be enchained on the king's order."

Zaal smiles at his son's discourse.
He shakes his head briefly, thinking, then speaks:
"O my dear son, what you say has little meaning.
Perhaps mad men may give credence
To your absurd statements.
Ghobaad sat in distress on a mountain,
Devoid of throne, crown, treasury, and dinar.
But do not approach the king,
Who has good sense, army, long-amassed wealth,
Before a man of the noblest ranking as Esfandiar,
Whose name is engraved on the seal of the Faghfoor of Chin.
You insist that you will merely remove him from his saddle,
To carry him in your arms to Zaal's palace,
But an old man would not bet on this feat.
Do not chase the star of your inauspicious fortune.
Such is my recommendation.
Now, O noble leader, you are well aware of how I feel."

After discussing the matter for some time,
Zaal bows low to the ground, imploring the Creator:
"O Supreme Judge and Master, keep misfortune at bay!"

His tongue ceaselessly utters laments
Until the sun appears above the mountain crests.

22 | The Battle of Rostam and Esfandiar

At the break of day, Rostam dons his armor, over which
He slips his Babreh Bayan as additional protection.
He attaches his noose to the saddle's knob
At the palace gates.

Then he summons Zavaareh,
Speaks to him at length of his army, and adds,
"Organize the troops into the lines of battle,
And position them on this sandy hill."

Zavaareh musters the troops
And directs them onto the battlefield.

Rostam departs, advancing spear in hand,
Followed by Zavaareh, the support of his grandeur,
And an army that receives him with great acclaim:
"May you never fail to your mace, horse, and saddle!"

They travel in this manner to the edge of the Hirmand River,
Mouths full of unease, hearts full of trepidation.

Before his march to the Iranian king's camp,
Rostam takes leave of his brother and his troops,
Confiding mournfully to Zavaareh:
"I shall attempt to change the mind of this wicked,
Hateful man and return peace to my heart.
But I fear that we cannot avoid the blows,
And I do not know what the future holds.
Maintain the troops here
While I depart to see what fate has in store for me.
If I find Esfandiar in a fury, like before,
I shall not call the leaders of Zabolestan
But fight in person and alone.
If he confronts us with an army, I shall summon you,
In which case you must not delay.
I do not wish for a single warrior to suffer.
The one whose heart enfolds justice
Can count peacefully on victory."

Rostam swiftly crosses the river and climbs on some heights,
Where he remains for some time,

Absorbed in reflections on the world.
In the end he cries out,
"O blessed Esfandiar, prepare yourself!
The one who is to fight against you has arrived!"

Esfandiar hears the roar of an old lion full of passion.
He laughs and says, "Here I am!
I have been ready and waiting since the moment I rose."
He asks for his chain mail, helmet, mace, and spear.
He shelters his glistening breast in war armor,
Places on his head the Kianian helmet,
And asks for his black horse to be saddled.

When the princely hero discerns his charger,
He inserts the shaft of his spear into the ground
And leaps from the dark earth lithely into the saddle
With the effort due his power and valor,
Like a leopard bounding on a terrified prey.

His troops watch him depart in awe and burst into praise.
Esfandiar nears Rostam and finds him alone on the hill.
From atop his horse, he says to Pashootan,
"I shall require neither help nor companion.
Since he is alone, I shall hike this steep incline on my own."
Pashootan, noble warrior, withdraws with his host.

Rostam notices a lofty mountain
Charging toward him in the distance.
The way these two men engage in battle
Makes one assume that never again in the world
Would men revel in feast.

One old, one young, two world warriors,
Lions full of pride, creep up on each other.
Their steeds emit an ear-piercing neigh.
You would think the battlefield is about to split open.

Rostam says in a loud voice,
"O King of joyous heart, favorite of fortune,
Do not be obstinate! Do not get carried away!
Open your heart to the words of a wise man.
If you yearn for battle and bloodshed,
Allow me to call on my Zaboli horsemen,

Dressed in mail and armed with Kaboli swords.
On your side, command the Iranians to advance
So that we can distinguish between real and fake coins.
We shall bring them onto the battlefield
And remain quiet and at rest for some time.
There will be blood spilled as you require,
And you will witness much tumult and chaos."

Esfandiar replies, "This is a most foolish speech.
You have left your palace with your sword.
You have summoned me to this mountaintop.
Why do you seek to deceive me?
Are you sensing your imminent defeat?
What good will serve me a war against Zabolestan,
Or one between Iran and Kabolestan?
By the Creator, may I never act in such a way,
For it is not agreeable to my faith to plunge Iranians
To their deaths while I place the crown upon my head.
When I engage in battle, I take the lead,
Even when defied by a leopard's claws.
If you need a protector, bring him.
As for me, I have no need for such a person.
Yazdan is my shield and shelter in times of battle,
And fortune smiles on my missions.
You are a battle-seeker, and I yearn for battle.
Let us fight without our hosts, and we shall see
If Esfandiar's horse will return to the stables riderless
Or if Rostam's Rakhsh will appear
At the gates of Zaal's palace without his master."

The two heroes agree to fight alone and unassisted.
They attack each other many times with their spears,
Causing the links of their armor to snap open.
In the end, the tips of their spears break,
And they are forced to seize their swords.
They brandish the sharp blades, assail left and right,
But the strength of the heroes and their blows
Succeeds only in shattering their swords.

They straighten up, reach for their heavy maces,
And strike each other jolts that resemble
The parting of large boulders from a mountaintop.

They struggle with great fury, like fierce lions,
Attack each other's limbs, their hands halting their motions
Only when the handles of their maces splinter.

At this point, they seize each other by the belt,
And the two fervent horses dash as if with wings.
One belt is in Esfandiar's hand, one belt in Rostam's.

These two brave men, full of pride, two heroes
Of elephantine stature, drag each other with all their might.
They exert themselves against each other,
But neither one is shaken off the saddle.

The two riders are spent, their steeds exhausted,
Their mouths foaming with a spume of blood and dust,
Their coats of mail and horse strappings in shreds.

23 | Esfandiar's Sons Are Killed
at the Hands of Zavaareh and Faraamarz

After rest from a long period of battle,
Rostam, son of Zaal, delays his arrival.
Zavaareh drives his army to the river's bank,
Troops with wounded hearts, eager for vengeance.

He says to Iranians, "Where is Rostam?
Why should we stay behind and rest on such a day?
You have come to fight the whale,
To attack Rostam and enchain him.
How can you remain inactive on the battlefield?"
Zavaareh further speaks, cursing the troops.

Esfandiar's son, a young prince named Nooshaazar,
A noble horseman, able and illustrious,
Who stands tall, eager for battle and of happy disposition,
Grows angry with the man from Sistan.
He proceeds to curse Zavaareh and his host,
Blurting out insult upon insult,
Something quite unworthy of the offspring of Esfandiar.
He shouts, "Only a vile person would disobey the king!
The brave Esfandiar has not allowed us to engage in fight

Against dogs[75] who submit to his command.
Who dares rebel against his sovereignty?
If you attack us against all rights,
If you foolishly come to the aid of an evil man,
You will succumb beneath our strength,
Beneath our blows of sword, spear, and mace."

Zavaareh commands his men to march ahead,
To assail and to strike the Iranian leaders,
To place a crown of blood on their heads.
He advances along as army support.
His soldiers leave their ranks, ten at a time,
And kill innumerable Iranian men.

Nooshaazar, observing the carnage, prepares for battle,
Climbs on his dun charger full of pride,
And arrives, brandishing his Indian saber.

Now there is a renowned hero by the name of Alvaah,
A proud man and skilled horseman of happy disposition,
Who holds Rostam's spear and always stands behind him.

Nooshaazar spots him from afar and draws out his sword.
With one strike on the illustrious warrior's head,
He flings him off his charger.

Zavaareh launches his war horse and shouts out in fury,
"You have killed this man. Now defend your own life,
For I do not include Alvaah in the rank of riders."
Zavaareh strikes the princely chest with his spear,
And he immediately tumbles down into the dust.
The army's fortune perishes with the illustrious Nooshaazar.

His brother Mehrnoosh, a young man ready to strike,
Is overwhelmed by grief.
He hurtles forth on his powerful horse and advances
To the army core and the enemy line, fuming with rage.

On the other side, Faraamarz, like a drunken elephant,
Exits the ranks, Indian blade in hand.

◇◇◇◇◇◇◇◇◇◇◇◇◇
75 Dogs: May have a double meaning, referring to the animal or referring to Sistan,
also known as Sagestan (sag=dog)

He attacks the illustrious Mehrnoosh.
The two hosts cry out at the sight
Of the two combative, noble young men,
One a king's son, the other a world warrior's son.
They leap like fierce lions and assault each other with swords.

Mehrnoosh falls into the scuffle with great ardor,
But he cannot withstand the force of Faraamarz.
He strikes him a blow to make his head roll in the dust,
But instead his sword falls on Faraamarz's horse's neck
And strikes down its head.
Faraamarz, though on foot, is able to kill his enemy,
And the blood of Mehrnoosh colors the battlefield crimson.

Once Bahman realizes his brother is dead
And the ground beneath him is soaked in blood and mud,
He rushes to Esfandiar, in the midst of his fight with Rostam.
He says, "O fierce lion, a host from Sistan has attacked us.
Your two sons, Nooshaazar and Mehrnoosh, have sadly
Perished beneath the blows of the warriors of Sistan.
While you fight here, we are burdened by grief.
These two young Kianian princes lie lifeless in the dust,
And the crimes of foolish men
Have covered our family in eternal shame."

The heart of the cautious Esfandiar fills with wrath,
His lips with pride, and his eyes with tears.
He says to Rostam, "O wretched man,
Is this the way world warriors abide by treaties?
You told me you would not lead your army to battle.
But you care for neither name nor honor!
Do you not feel shame before me or the Creator?
Do you not fear the questions on the day of judgment?
Do you not know that those who violate a treaty
Are cursed and hated in every elite congregation?
Two Sistani warriors from your land have killed my two sons,
And they continue to pursue their malevolent work."

Rostam, dismayed by these words,
Shakes like leaves on a willow tree.
He says, "I swear by my life and on the king's head,
By the sun and by my sword, by this battlefield,

That I did not call for fight
And that I shall disown those who have stirred it.
I shall fasten the hands of my brother,
If indeed he is the one who instigated this misdemeanor.
I shall bring Faraamarz, two hands tied behind his back,
Before the king, Yazdan worshipper.
You will have the chance to execute him to avenge your sons.
But do not lose reason over such a senseless act."

Esfandiar replies, "To spill the blood of a serpent
To avenge the death of a peacock
Is neither useful nor agreeable
And would not be concurring with the rules of monarchy.
O wretched one, seek to save your neck,
For you are about to expel your last breath.
I shall pin your thighs against Rakhsh with arrows,
And you will become one with your horse,
Like water mixed with milk,
So that never again will a servant dare fight against a lord.
If you survive, I shall tie up your hands and take you,
Without delay, to the king, and if you die by my shots,
Think that it is to expiate the blood of my noble sons."

Rostam says, "These quarrels can only diminish our glory.
Turn to Yazdan, invoke divine grace,
For the Creator is Guide to noble matters."
The warrior, crown-giver, says this and launches
His dazzling Rakhsh, bellowing with vengeance.

24 | Rostam Flees to the Mountaintop

They seize bows and arrows of poplar wood,
Making sunlight fade while flares flash from arrows' tips.
They nail their coats of mail to their chests.
Esfandiar's heart constricts with sorrow,
His brow and face deeply knitted in frown.
When he reaches for bow and arrow, no one can escape alive.
He clutches a bow and shoots an arrow.
Its point, as sharp as a diamond,
Can puncture coats of mail as if through thin paper.
He shoots, injuring Rostam and the valiant Rakhsh,

While he circles them, taking care to remain out of reach.

While the shots strike Rostam,
Those fired by Rostam fall out of reach.
The mighty hero finds himself weak in the fight.
In the end, he cries, "Esfandiar must indeed be invincible!"

Rakhsh's body weakens under so many wounds.
Neither charger nor horseman can sustain much more.
Both are about to flee from the battleground
When Rostam, feeling defeated, reflects on a way out.

He leaps off Rakhsh, as swift as wind,
And turns his noble head toward the mountaintop.
During this time, separated from his master,
Rakhsh returns to the palace.

Blood flows out of Rostam's body, and this hero,
With the stature of Mount Bisootoon, is weak and shaky.

Esfandiar laughs at the sight of him and says,
"O noble Rostam, how did the strength
Of a drunken elephant ever come to fail you?
How could this mountain of steel be pierced with one arrow?
What happened to your courage, your mace,
Your strength, and your majestic stance in battle?
Why do you retreat to the mountaintop
When you have heard the voice of the fierce lion?
How did the warrior lion turn into a fox,
Cowering away from the scuffle?
Are you the one who made the deev weep?
Are you the one who once burned wild beasts
With the flares of your blade?"

As the injured Rakhsh dashes toward his stables,
And, despite his wounds, crosses the river,
Zavaareh spots the trail of the blessed charger.
The world dims before his eyes from excess worry,
And he rushes to the place of battle, shouting vehemently.
He finds his brother gravely injured,
His wounds unattended to.
He says to Rostam, "Rise, climb on my horse.
Allow me to don your armor to avenge you."

Rostam replies, "Go to Zaal and tell him
That the glory of the seed of Saam has perished.
Ask him to see if he can find a remedy to this calamity,
A secret healing solution for my wounds.
If I survive this time the gashes Esfandiar inflicted upon me,
It would be as if I were reborn from my mother on this day.
When you arrive, attempt to save Rakhsh.
I shall follow you, but it will be sluggishly."

Zavaareh leaves his brother and rushes away,
Pursuing Rakhsh's journey with his eyes.

Esfandiar, who remained below, cries out,
"O famed Rostam, you remain up there for a long time!
Who is to come to your aid?
Toss aside your bow and quiver.
Strip off your armor of leopard skin.
Unfasten your belt, repent, and allow your hands to be tied.
I shall no longer cause you any harm.
Wounded as you are, I shall lead you to the king
And make him pardon all your deeds.
But if you long to fight, you might as well
Express your last wishes, appoint your land's governor,
Beg the Creator to forgive your sins.
You may be granted mercy if you are penitent,
And I hope that the Just Creator will be your guide,
For you are about to part with this passing dwelling."

Rostam replies, "It is late. We cannot fight at this hour.
Since you are so happy tonight, return to your home.
Who wishes to fight in the dark night?
As for me, I shall return to my palace to rest,
To catch my breath, and to dress my wounds,
Call my relatives of glorious name around me,
Zavaareh, Faraamarz, Zaal, son of Saam,
And I shall prepare to do as you command,
For loyalty reigns when convened with you."

The powerful Esfandiar says, "O eminent old man,
You are a mighty hero able to live by your wits.
You can make use of trickery and artifice to escape fight.
I detect your ruse. You do not wish for me to see

In what sad state you find yourself in.
I shall grant you mercy for this night.
Do not be tempted to go down tortuous paths.
Act in accordance to your pledge,
And do not speak in vain."

Rostam replies, "I shall listen to your instructions.
I shall find a balm for my wounds."

Esfandiar follows him by sight as the hero walks away.
Rostam crosses the river like a vessel,
Invokes on himself divine blessings,
And addresses the Supreme Judge with these words:
"O pure and just Creator, if I die of my wounds,
Who among the great heroes will avenge me?
Who will mimic my courage, wisdom, and comportment?"

Esfandiar, still following him with his eyes,
Sees that he has reached the other bank and says,
"One must not call Rostam a man.
He is a mad elephant and holder of mighty strength."
He has crossed the waters despite his lesions.
The terrible wounds caused by my shots
Have only quickened his stride."

Esfandiar remains for some time in astonishment,
Then he addresses the Supreme Judge, pure and perfect,
"You have created him as you wished him to be.
You have created and put order into time and space.
You have granted me victory in this war!"

Upon his return, Esfandiar hears cries rising from his tent.
Pashootan comes forward.
The deaths of the valiant Nooshaazar and Mehrnoosh
Have filled him with grief and fury.
The king's pavilion is sprinkled with dust,
And everyone's clothes are in shreds.

Esfandiar dismounts and holds close to his chest
The heads of the deceased, crying in his grief:
"O my two valiant sons,
The breath of life has abandoned you!"

Then he turns to Pashootan: "Rise,
And do not shed blood tears on these corpses.
I do not see what good will do tears,
For one must not be attached to this life.
Everyone, old and young, belongs to death.
May reason help us die as it suits us!"

Esfandiar sends his sons to his father, master of crown,
In golden coffins carried on stretchers of ebony.
With them is a message:
"Here are the fruits of your conspiracies!
You have launched a vessel beneath the water's surface.
You have demanded an act of servitude from Rostam.
But when you perceive Nooshaazar and Mehrnoosh's caskets,
You will cease to listen to Jaamaasp's counsel.
Esfandiar is still alive, but I know not if he will remain so.
You are seated on the throne of pleasures
While he is consumed by grief.
But throne and pleasure will not be yours for long."

Esfandiar sits on his royal seat in his grief and suffering,
And remembers Rostam's words, saying to Pashootan,
"The lion retreats before the hand of the valiant man.
I have seen Rostam today, observed the force
And frame of this man of elephantine stature.
I have praised the pure Yazdan, donor of hope and fear.
One must worship the One who created
The mighty Rostam and who created the world!
Today, I have grievously wounded the warrior
Whose hands have performed incomparable high deeds:
Who cast his net in the Sea of Chin to fish out whales,
Who was able to seize on the plain the tail of leopards.
My arrows so deeply pierced him
That his blood turned the ground into a lake.
He climbed down the mountain on foot
After having convened with me, rushing toward
The River Hirmand, burdened by armor and sword.
He crossed the waters despite his wounds,
Despite his body being riddled by the steel of my shots.
I think that by the time he reaches his palace,
His soul will have risen to Saturn."

25 | Rostam Holds Counsel With His Family

On his side, Rostam arrives at his palace,
Where Zaal finds him in a dreadful state.
Zavaareh and Faraamarz weep,
Consumed by grief at the sight of his deep wounds.
Rudaabeh pulls out her hair and scratches her face
At the sound of their cries.

Zavaareh approaches him to unbuckle his belt.
They undo and remove his armor and Babreh Bayan,
And all the wise men of the land sit around him.

Rostam commands those who have the skills
To heal Rakhsh, to fetch the horse
And find a remedy for his injuries.

The illustrious Zaal tears out his hair.
He rubs his cheeks on his son's wounds and says,
"What a calamity for me in my old age,
To witness my noble son in such a predicament!"

Rostam replies, "What good are laments?
The celestial dome has called for these occurrences.
But I have before me an even more taxing mission,
Which overwhelms me with far more concern
Than these minor though dreadful injuries.
Never have I encountered a more indomitable warrior.
I have traveled the length of the world.
I have attained knowledge on things known and unknown.
I have seized the White Deev by the belt,
And, as he trembled like the branch of a willow tree,
I fiercely flung him to the ground.
I shall have to surrender before the mighty Esfandiar!
My arrows, once able to pierce through an anvil,
Once finding the strongest shields as thin as paper,
Were powerless against Esfandiar's armor.
I felt as if I were striking a boulder with thorns.
No matter what excuses I make to sway his heart of stone,
Esfandiar will only seek to humiliate me with his words
And with actions motivated by pride and arrogance.

"Long ago, my hand could crush a rock
As if it were a mere cucumber.
Now I seized Esfandiar's belt,
But the force of my hand fell feebly.
Long ago, a leopard would abscond at the sight
Of my sword, but this same blade is ineffective
Against Esfandiar's chest plate,
Powerless against his silk head covering.
Even if I pleaded for forgiveness,
I would never succeed in drawing his heart of stone
Out of the darkness and into the light.
His words and his actions seek only to incite me.
I am grateful to the Creator for the advent of night
And for the darkness that weakened his eye.
I have escaped the dragon's claws for now,
But I know not if this release will shield me.
Upon reflection, I see no other way out
But to climb on Rakhsh in the morning and never dismount.
If Esfandiar engages in cutting off heads in Zabolestan,
He will eventually tire of doing so,
Even if the longing to commit evil acts remains with him."

Zaal says to him, "O son, be reasonable.
Every impasse reached has a path of resolve
Except for the door of death,
Which is an altogether different exit.
I bear a deep fondness for you, which you must accept.
I shall ask Simorgh to come to our aid,
And if she agrees to be my guide,
My land and kingdom will remain untouched.
Otherwise our nation will be ruined by Esfandiar,
This evil man who likes all things wicked."

26 | Simorgh Shows Rostam a Way Out

The two heroes having settled on this audacious plan,
The leader Zaal climbs the lofty mountain to its crest.
He brings from his palace three dishes set aflame
And an escort of three men full of caution.

When the magician arrives on the mountaintop,

He draws out a feather from a piece of brocade,
Pokes the fire on one of the dishes,
And burns a bit of the feather over it.
After some time, at dusk,
A dark cloud appears over the mountain crest.

Zaal looks up and discerns
The bird's beautiful frame gliding across the skies.
Simorgh's eyes sweep the land below from high in the air,
Sees the light of the ardent fire
And Zaal seated by it, deeply aggrieved.

She swoops down in circles to the ground.
Zaal rises before the three men burning the incense
And blesses Simorgh a few times in worship.
He fills the three dishes with fragrance
And floods his cheeks with his heart's blood.

Simorgh says to him, "O King,
What has happened that you find the need to call me?"

Zaal replies, "May the misfortune brought down on me
By evil men strike instead my enemy!
Rostam, my son of lion heart, is injured,
And my foot is paralyzed by worry.
I fear for his life because of wounds so deep,
Such as no one in the world has witnessed before.
Similarly, Rakhsh appears lifeless,
Writhing day and night in pain, his body riddled by shots.
Esfandiar arrived in our land with the breath of battle.
He is not satisfied with my kingdom, treasure, and crown.
He wants to destroy my family tree, from root to branch."

Simorgh replies, "O noble warlord,
Do not allow your heart to be distressed.
You have to let me set my sight
On Rakhsh and the noble world seeker."

Zaal summons Rakhsh and Rostam.
At the sight of the hero on the mountaintop,
The bird of serene heart says to him,
"O powerful elephant, who hurt you so?
Why did you engage in a battle with Esfandiar

And enflame your breast in a caustic blaze?"

Zaal replies to Simorgh, "O charitable one,
Since you show us your divine visage,
Tell me where in the world I may find a place of shelter
Should Rostam not be mended.
Sistan will be turned into a barren land,
The den of lions and leopards.
Our race will be destroyed to its root.
What shall we do now?"

The bird observes the wounds,
Searching for a way to heal them.
She extracts eight arrow heads from Rostam's body
And sucks the blood of his wounds with her beak.
Then she rubs her wings on them,
And immediately Rostam regains force and vitality.

Simorgh says to him, "Take care to rest for one week.
Dip in milk one of my feathers to brush over your wounds
And to dress them."

Then Simorgh proceeds to heal Rakhsh in the same manner,
Passing her beak along the right side of the horse
And plucking six arrows of steel from his neck
So that no part of his body remains wounded or distorted.
Rakhsh's nickers make the giver of crowns smile with joy.

Then Simorgh says, "O hero of elephantine stature,
You are more glorious than all the court's noblemen.
Why have you sought battle with Esfandiar,
The noble, invincible prince?"

Rostam replies, "Had he not spoken of chains and bonds,
I would have never accepted to fight with him.
Death and dying is a more endurable fate
Than the inability to engage in battle."

Simorgh replies, "There is no shame should Esfandiar
Lower your head into the dust, for he is a valiant son of a king,
A pure-blooded warrior, owner of divine royal majesty.
If you make a pact with me to renounce battle,
To refrain from sizing yourself up against Esfandiar

At the time of fight and retribution,
Tomorrow, pay him homage, plead with him,
And offer him your body and soul for ransom.
If when his hour has arrived, he disdains your excuses,
I will furnish you a way of salvation,
To carry your head high up to the sun."

Rostam rejoices at this speech, rejecting thoughts of war.
He replies, "I shall not fail to follow your instructions,
Even if my head were to fall prey to a shower of swords."

Simorgh continues, "By way of friendship,
I shall reveal to you the secrets of the sky.
Anyone who sheds the blood of the bold Esfandiar
Will become prey to destiny. Never will he find
Deliverance from his suffering for as long as he lives.
He will not be able to hold on to his treasures.
Misfortune will plague him for the rest of his life,
And when he departs, he will find,
In the other world, only grief and misery.
But if you have decided to follow my advice,
I shall make you as strong as your enemy.
I shall teach you tonight a marvelous secret
And close your mouth to evil words."

Rostam replies, "I am in agreement with your discourse.
Tell everything you wish to share with me.
The world will endure, but we shall depart.
Our words only will remain as evidence of us.
After my death, I wish to leave a good name."

Simorgh says, "Go and climb on Rakhsh,
Your brilliant horse, and take the shining blade.
Travel in the direction of the Sea of Chin,
All the while praising the Creator.
Do not wander on the long and windy road.
I shall transport you there myself.
You will find a massive tamarisk tree,
Nourished with grape extract.
I shall show you what part of the tree to use
As a club to strike down your adversary's head."

Rostam hears this and straps himself,

Climbs swiftly on Rakhsh, and gallops to the sea.
He notices the air obscured by Simorgh's silhouette.
He dismounts at the water's edge.
The bird full of pride descends through the air to his side.
Rostam spots a tamarisk with roots in the ground
And top branches reaching into the sky.

The powerful bird perches on the tree
And shows Rostam a dry path.
The scent of musk emanates all around.
The bird commands Rostam to draw closer,
Rubs his head with her wing, and says to him,
"Take the straightest, longest, slimmest branch.
The fate of Esfandiar is attached to this arrow of tamarisk.
Do not make light of this stick. Level it with the flame,
Search for a good old arrow of steel,
Attach it with two points and three feathers to the stick.
With it you will succeed in plunging Esfandiar to his end."

Rostam cuts one of the branches,
Then abandons the water's edge to return to his palace.
Simorgh continues to be his guide on the road,
Gliding above his head and conversing with him:
"Now if Esfandiar provokes you in battle,
Beseech him with gentleness and righteousness,
Never making use of any kind of ruse.
Kindly speech may lead him to change his mind.
And remember ancient times, for you have often
Painstakingly and devotedly served the kings.
If he refuses to listen to your excuses,
If he wishes to treat you like a worthless man,
Then bind your bow, place your tamarisk arrow
That you have saturated in wine,
Guide your two hands on a direct line with his sight,
Like a man would do who worships the tamarisk.
Destiny will guide this arrow straight to his eyes,
For that is where he is most vulnerable.
You will meet with success as long as you remain calm."

Simorgh prepares to take her leave of Zaal,
Holds him in a tight embrace,
Then happily dashes into the air.

After watching Simorgh fly away,
Rostam lights a fire and unbends the stick.
He affixes two sharp blades to it,
And, once finished, he fastens three fletchings.

27 | Rostam Returns to Battle Esfandiar

The first light of day beams over the mountains
And advances timidly amid the receding obscurity.
Rostam seizes his battle gear and prays to the Creator.
He sits on his horse's saddle, as restless as an elephant.
He advances in this manner,
As if a ship sailing on the River Nile.
He nears his noble troops to ready them for war.

Approaching the illustrious Iranian army,
The hero, still in search of a way out, sits tall and cries,
"O man of lion heart, how can you rest peacefully
While Rostam has saddled Rakhsh?"
Then he adds, "Rise from your sweet sleep
To fight against vengeance-seeker Rostam."

Upon hearing him, Esfandiar equips himself, rather
Discouraged by the little harm his weapons produced.
He says to Pashootan,
"A lion's courage weighs little against a sorcerer.
I did not think Rostam had the strength to walk home,
Burdened by helmet, armor, and coat of mail.
Rakhsh, his charger, whose chest was covered
With the steel of my shots, is now dashing free of injuries.
I have heard that Zaal raises his hands toward the sun
And that he surpasses all magicians when he is angry.
Wisdom has no power in comparison."

Pashootan replies, eyes brimming with tears,
"May worry and defeat befall your enemy!
Why are you discouraged today?
Did you not sleep last night?
What happened to intensify the quarrel?
I do not know which of the two of you
Has been abandoned by fortune,

Since you come to face new struggles."

Esfandiar, the hero, dons his armor,
Seizes his weapons, and cries out to Rostam,
"May your name vanish from the world!
O man from Sistan, have you forgotten
The bow of the warrior prince eager for battle?
The way I injured you last night
Left you weak and unable to think or plan.
You must have been healed by the magical arts of Zaal.
Without him, a coffin would have claimed your corpse.
Now you come after practicing black magic
And wish to fling yourself into battle with me.
But today I shall shatter your limbs in such a way
That Zaal will never again lay his sights on you alive."

Rostam replies, "O Esfandiar, royal warrior,
You are never satisfied with battle.
You must fear the Creator, World Master.
Do not attempt to lower your heart
And your wisdom into the dust!
I do not come today to engage in a clash.
I come to present my excuses, to save my name and honor.
Why would you fight against me with bad intentions?
Why would you close your eyes to reason?
I urge you in the name of Zartosht, the just,
In the name of his holy faith, in the name of Nooshaazar,
Of the divine grace and majesty that rests on kings,
In the name of the Sun and the Moon, in the name
Of the *Zand Avesta*, to renounce the path of perdition.

"Forget the words spoken long ago.
They are like fur that unravels on one's body.
Come to visit us in my home once again.
Allow your desire to take my life to pass.
I shall open the doors to ancient treasures,
Which I have amassed for many long years.
I shall load up beasts of burden for your treasurer.
Then I shall leave with you to appear before the king,
If such is your command.
I shall deem as just anything he decides,
Whether he declares me a free man

Or settles to burden me with chains.
Reflect on the words of an ancient wise man:
          'Do not befriend an ill-fated star!'
Let fortune remove your desire to fight.
Why have you cultivated a stone heart?
Why do you ceaselessly wish to fight?
I swear by Yazdan that you will glorify your name
By detaching yourself from battles, rancor, and injustice."

Esfandiar says, "I do not make use of deceit on battle day.
You continuously speak of home and palace,
You seek to calm your inflamed features,
But if you wish to remain alive,
Agree to be confined to the shackles."

Rostam returns, "O King, do not speak unjustly!
Do not dishonor my name and yours.
Nothing but trouble will come out of this fight.
I shall give you thousands of gems worthy of a king,
And bracelets, earrings, and chains.
I shall give you thousands of young slaves with soft lips,
Who will stand before your throne night and day.
I shall give you thousands of maidens from Khalokh,
Whose youth and beauty will be the ornament of the crown.
I shall open the doors to the treasures of Saam,
Nariman, and Zaal, O exceptional man!
I shall gather it all and place it at your feet,
Then bring men from Zabolestan
Who will all act upon your command
To destroy your enemy on the day of battle.
Then I shall stand before you as your slave
And present myself before Goshtaasp,
Who pursues me with his grudge.
O prince, banish hatred from your heart.
Do not turn your body into an ambush for the deev.
You have ways to bind me other than with chains.
Make use of them, for you are king and believer.
Chains will leave on my name an eternal stain.
It does not suit you to assume a nefarious mien."

Esfandiar replies, "How long will you continue
To speak meaningless, worthless words?

You urge me to leave the path of Yazdan
And disobey the king, world guardian,
But anyone who drifts from the king's command
Is certain to deceive the Creator.
Speak to me of only chains and war,
And cease your foolish discourse."

28 | Rostam Shoots an Arrow Into Esfandiar's Eye

Rostam realizes that pleas are ineffective with Esfandiar.
He tells him to summon Pashootan as a witness:
"He must know that I am proposing forgiveness
Without having committed a wrongful act.
He must know that fight and vengeance
Did not originate from me and that
I have never swerved off the righteous path."

Esfandiar laughs and says, "O noble warrior,
What excuses will you muster to deceive me?
Pashootan is not far from here and is aware of everything."
He presses Pashootan to draw closer.

At the sight of him, Rostam is surprised
And says to Pashootan, "O renowned man,
No matter how much I insisted that we refrain from war,
Esfandiar insisted on rejecting my pleas.
You have seen and witnessed my show of servitude.
But he appears weary of life.
If he falls to his demise at my hands,
You will recount the events to every assembly:
That Rostam pleaded and begged at length
To avoid a skirmish, but Esfandiar doggedly refused."

Esfandiar cries out, "Let us not speak.
Our affair has extended beyond discussion.
Come and let us see what you can do.
In the world, you have acquired name and disgrace."

At these words, Rostam realizes that his end is near.
He draws an arrow of tamarisk wood,
Having soaked its tip of steel in some wine.

Once the arrow is placed on the bow,
He lifts his head toward the blue and says,
"O holy Creator of Sun and Moon,
You are the Donor of wisdom, majesty, and strength.
You perceive the pureness of my heart,
My thoughts, and my power.
You know how much effort I have exerted to calm
Esfandiar and distract him from engaging in fight.
You are a spectator to his injustice and how lavish
He is in his expression of battle and courage.
Do not observe my actions as punishable offenses,
O Creator of Moon and Mercury."

When Esfandiar becomes aware that Rostam is lingering,
He says, "O famed Rostam, are you weary of fight?
You will soon see the piercing arrows of Goshtaasp
Of lion heart and the tip of steel of Lohraasp."
He shoots an arrow toward Rostam's war helmet,
Exhibiting his expert skills in archery.

Rostam hastens to affix the arrow to his bow,
In the way Simorgh instructed him.
He aims straight at Esfandiar's eyes and lets the arrow fly.

The world plunges into darkness for the famous prince
As his eyes are stitched together by the double-pointed arrow.
The flames of hatred are promptly extinguished.
His cypress tree stature sagging and collapsing,
Strength abandons him, and he loses consciousness.
The head of the king, Yazdan worshipper, bows down.
His bow from Chaadj escapes his grasp.
He seizes the neck and mane of his black steed,
And his blood reddens the dust of the battlefield.

Rostam says to Esfandiar,
"You have born the fruit of the bitter seed of enmity.
You are the one who claimed,
        'I am an indomitable and bold warrior.
        I shall bring down the dome of sky.'
I endured eight wounds from your arrows of poplar wood
Without lamenting, for the sake of name and disgrace.
A single arrow has caused you to lean

Down on your celebrated charger.
In an instant, your head will fall into the dust,
Plunging your mother's loving heart
Into the deep, dark abyss of grief."

At this moment, the illustrious king tumbles
Headfirst off his horse. He remains thus for some time,
Then he regains consciousness and sits in the dust to listen.
He seizes the arrow by its end and plucks it out.
It is covered in blood from tip to feathers.

Meanwhile, Bahman learns of the tarnished imperial glory.
He rushes to Pashootan and says to him,
"This battle has taken a dreadful turn.
The body of the elephant warrior is in the dust,
And the world is nothing more for us than a dark ditch."

The two of them rush on foot from camp to battlefield,
Where they find the warrior prince, chest covered in blood,
Holding in his hand a bloodstained arrow.

Pashootan tears at his garments,
Scatters dust over his head, bellowing and crying.
Bahman rolls in the dirt, rubbing his cheeks in warm blood.

Pashootan cries, "Who, among believers and noblemen,
Can understand the secrets of the world?
Only the Creator of soul, space, Saturn, Venus, and Sun.
A man such as Esfandiar, who valiantly
Handled the sword in the name of faith,
Who purified the world from evil idol worshippers,
Who has never acted wrongly or unjustly, perishes
In his time of youth, his royal head tossed in the dust
While the mean-spirited Goshtaasp, who fills the world
With grief, who afflicts the hearts of free men,
Lives a long and peaceful life away from battlefields."

The young princes hold Esfandiar close to their chests
And wipe off the blood from his face.

Pashootan howls and cries over him,
His cheeks stained with blood, his heart full of anguish.
He says, "Alas, Esfandiar, world master of royal race!

Who is responsible for weakening this war mountain?
Who overthrew this furious lion?
Who plucked off the beautiful tusks of this elephant?
Who has stopped the flow of the River Nile?
Who dimmed the light of the dazzling sun?
Who lowered the status of our king to dust?
Who despised the king and extinguished the noble flame,
Consuming relatives and kin?
What evil eye bore on the royal race?
Anyone who acts in malicious ways will suffer retributions.
What happened to your heart, your wisdom, your faith,
Your power, your fate's star, and your devotion?
What happened to your expert ways of war?
What happened to your beautiful voice,
So gentle in times of feast?
You purified the world of ill-meaning characters,
Fearless in the face of lions and deevs.
Now that the time is here for you to enjoy all that,
I find you lying here, with the dust as your nurse.
Damned be the crown and throne!
May I never remember the warrior rider
Who flung you into the dust!
May the throne and crown be the inheritance
Of the treacherous Shah Goshtaasp!"

The wise Esfandiar replies with sensible words:
"O blessed prince, do not despair over my fate.
This is the share handed to me by the sky and the moon.
Any living being must one day accept dust as a resting place.
You must not lament my death.
Where are Fereydoon, Hooshang, and Jamsheed now?
Wind produced them one day,
And a breath carried them away.
My ancestors of pure race, proud, elected men,
Have departed, leaving behind vacant seats.
No one remains in this passing dwelling.
I have greatly struggled in the world, at times openly,
At times secretly, providing guidance to men
And establishing the foundation of Yazdan's path.
Once divine word acquired splendor by my efforts,
We rendered powerless the hand of Ahriman.
Destiny stretched out its lion claws,

And there was no way of escape.
My hope is that in paradise my heart and soul
Will collect the fruit of the seeds I have sown.
The son of Zaal did not conquer me through his valor.
Observe this tamarisk branch that I hold in my hand.
Simorgh and Rostam, the scheming,
Are the ones responsible for my demise.
Zaal, who is acquainted with spells and incantations,
Made use of magical arts to craft this weapon of wood."

Hearing Esfandiar's account,
Rostam writhes and weeps in pain.
Weary and burdened, he approaches Esfandiar.
He says to Pashootan with deep sorrow,
"When a man displays courage, he must be remembered.
It was said once:
        'It is best not to drift off the path of valor.'
The evil deev continuously dispenses
Grief and suffering as my share in life.
As long as I can remember, since the day I cinched my waist,
I have challenged wrong and injustice.
Never did I come across an armor-bearing horseman
Of the stature and strength of Esfandiar.
Once I was able to escape at nightfall,
Once I witnessed his bow, his chest, and his ring of shots,
I searched for a solution to push me out of my predicament.
I did not wish to submit to his commands.
I found a way to hold his life in my hands with my bow,
And when the time came, I shot my arrow.
If fate wished for him to live, I would not have succeeded.
When the time comes, one must leave this dark earth,
And no precaution can prolong a single breath.
I was only an instrument hastening his fall,
But I shall endure the shame of having used this arrow
Of tamarisk in stories and songs for all eternity."

29 | Esfandiar Communicates His Last Wishes to Rostam

Esfandiar says to Rostam, "My life comes to its term.
Do not evade my presence now.
Rise and come to my side.
I have changed my intentions.
Please honor my instructions and my last wishes
For the sake of my most precious son.
Make use of your power to fulfill my requests."

Rostam hears Esfandiar out.
He sheds shameful blood tears,
Moaning and lamenting in a soft voice.

Meanwhile, Zaal, after hearing the news,
Rushes forth like wind out of the palace.
Zavaareh and Faraamarz depart like mad men.
Everyone searches for signs of the outcome of battle.

Shouts rise from the battlefield
To dim the light of the sun and moon.
Zaal says to Rostam, "O my dear son,
I shed tears for you in the agony of my heart,
For I have learned from sages, wise men, and astrologers
That the one who spills Esfandiar's blood is to perish,
That he will find on earth nothing but grief and gloom,
And that in the other world, likewise,
His fate will be dismal."

Esfandiar further addresses Rostam,
"O glorious hero, you are not the cause of my demise.
This was my destiny and what was meant to be.
No one knows the mysteries of this revolving dome.
Listen to my words: You are only an instrument.
Neither Rostam nor Simorgh, neither arrow nor bow
Has prompted my fate, only Goshtaasp, who said to me:
        'Go and burn down the land of Sistan.
        Go and conquer and annihilate Nimrooz.'
His only goal was to hold fast to army, throne, and crown,
While seeking a way to make me disappear.
Now accept Bahman, my illustrious son, my confidant.

Nurture him like a father and remember my words.
Keep him happy in Zabolestan near you,
And do not listen to the talk of wicked men.
Teach him how to lead a battle, how to sit at a banquet,
How to hunt in the desert, how to drink wine and converse.
Teach him how to use a mallet, how to play music,
How to make use of power, and how to enjoy life.
Jaamaasp, may his name be cursed,
And may he never succeed in life,
Has predicted that Bahman will be my successor
And a most powerful king.
Whoever emerges from the seed of Bahman
Will immortalize our race."

Rostam rises, places his right hand on his chest,
And says, "Even if I die, I shall keep my word.
I shall obey all your commands without fail.
I shall place Bahman on the illustrious ivory throne,
Lower on his head the heart-illuminating crown,
Fasten my belt of servitude around my waist,
For he will be my king, and I shall remain his subject."

At Rostam's words, Esfandiar replies, "O ancient hero,
Take the son when the father is deceased.
Know, as Yazdan is my witness, as true faith is my guide,
That despite all your glorious deeds and exploits,
Despite all the kings you have guarded and defended,
Your beloved name will be dishonored and defiled.
The world will fill with cries of outrage,
Indignation pointing at you for causing my death.
My heart is aggrieved, but the Creator commanded it."

Then Esfandiar turns to Pashootan:
"I have only one request, and that is for a shroud.
Once I have left this transient dwelling,
Organize my troops and take the direction of Iran-Zamin.
When you arrive at court, tell my father as follows,
          'When one is powerful, one must not make excuses.
           The world obeyed you;
           Your name was engraved on all the seals.
           I had expected more from you.
           What happened is a reflection of your dark soul.

I aligned the world with my sword of justice
And purified it from the deeds of malicious men.
Once true faith was established in Iran,
Power and kingdom were my expected rewards,
Of which you had ensured me in the presence of noblemen.
Yet, in secret, you conspired to send me to my death.
You can now be satisfied, for the deed is accomplished.
Stay calm, and sit on the throne with peace of mind,
Since you no longer have cause to feel threatened by me.
Keep your thoughts of death at bay,
And order feasts in the royal palace.
Yours is the throne; mine are menaces, war, and death.
Yours is the crown, while I contend with coffin and shroud.
But a wise old peasant bard once said
That not even bow and arrow can escape death.
Do not place your trust on treasure, crown, and throne.
I shall await you on the road, and when you arrive,
We shall go together before the Supreme Judge.
We shall speak and listen without pause.'

"After Goshtaasp's hall, go to my mother and say,
'This time, death has come to contest with your son.
An armor is nothing but wind in the face of arrows
Able to pierce through mountains of steel.
Come soon to join me, O compassionate one,
And do not afflict yourself over my condition.
Do not condemn your soul or expose your face in public.
Do not attempt to catch sight of me
Once my face is enveloped in the shroud.
The aspect of my mien will only deepen your grief,
And no man of sense would approve of such a thing.'

"Then tell my sisters and my wife, clever, valiant women
Who languish in secret with thoughts of me:
'O wise and virtuous women,
I send you an eternal farewell.
My father's throne disparaged me.
The sacrifice of my life
Is the key that unlocks his treasures.
Pashootan is on his way to him
To blacken his dim heart.'"

He speaks, then sighs deeply and whispers,
"Goshtaasp is my only persecutor."
At that instant, his pure soul exits his body,
And his punctured corpse falls back into the sand.

Rostam, in his grief, shreds his clothing
And cries out, heart full of anguish, head covered in dust:
"O valiant rider, grandson of a warrior king,
O son of king, my name was once glorious in the world,
But Goshtaasp prepared for me a miserable end."

After weeping for a long time, he addresses the deceased,
"O King, you failed to have an ally in the world.
May your soul enter paradise!
May your enemies collect their harvest!"

Zavaareh says to him, "O noble one,
Do not accept prince Bahman; be wary of him.
Have you not heard the story of the wise peasant bard,
Borrowed from an ancient book, about the lion cub?
If you raise one, his teeth will grow sharp.
He will acquire strength and soon cease to obey,
For he will be fixated on catching prey, and the first one
On whom he will pounce will be his nursing father.
The two lands will resound with evil passions,
And Iran-Zamin will be the first to suffer,
For it has lost a king. It has lost Esfandiar.
But then misfortune will befall you.
Bahman will bring bad luck to Zabolestan,
And the aging leaders of Kabol will tremble with fear.
Be assured that once he bears the crown,
He will seek to avenge the death of Esfandiar.
After your death, this vengeance-seeking warrior
Will reach to capture Zabolestan to merge it with Iran."

Rostam replies, "No one can escape the dome of sky,
Neither evil men nor virtuous ones.
I have made a decision that reason may approve,
And righteous men will remember.
If Bahman wishes to act in evil ways,
He will have cause to apprehend the twists of fate.
But you must not allow your passion to pass on misfortune."

30 | Pashootan Takes Esfandiar's Coffin to Goshtaasp

Rostam requests the building of a beautiful coffin of steel
With a pall of Chini brocade. He stuffs the inside with tar,
On which he pours musk and ambergris.
He prepares a shroud of golden cloth,
And the entire gathering bursts into laments.

After enfolding the brilliant chest of the king in the shroud,
He places a turquoise diadem on his head.
The cover is riveted over the narrow coffin,
And this royal tree, having borne such beautiful fruit,
Is allowed to gently wither and fade.

Rostam brings forty camels with covers of Chini brocade,
Of which one bears the royal coffin
While the rest march on the left and the right.
Before them and behind marches a procession of troops
Who claw their cheeks and tear their hair,
Tongues and souls muttering the king's name.
Banners are torn and overturned, kettledrums are silenced.
Everyone is dressed in either purple or dark blue.

Pashootan marches at the head of the troops.
The mane and tail of Esfandiar's black steed have been slashed.
On the inverted saddle hang Esfandiar's battle mace,
His celebrated helmet, coat of mail, tunic, and headgear.

As the procession departs, Bahman remains in Zabolestan,
Tears of blood flowing from his lashes.
Rostam takes him to his own palace
And tends to him as would a father.

The illustrious Goshtaasp receives the news
That Esfandiar's head does not exist anymore.
His clothes are in shreds,
His forehead and diadem lower to the dust.
Miserable cries emerge from the palace.
The world fills with the name of Esfandiar.
The news spreads throughout Iran.
Rulers cast off their diadems into the distance.

Goshtaasp says, "O my son of holy faith,

The era and the world will never again see your equal.
Since the time of Manoochehr, no man has been so lofty.
You have soaked your sword in blood, purified our faith.
You have held rulers everywhere in their places."

The noblemen of Iran, indignant toward Goshtaasp,
Shed their respect for him, crying out in a loud voice,
"O man of cursed destiny, you sent a prince like Esfandiar
Into Zabolestan to preserve your throne?
Seated securely at court holding on to power,
You delivered him to death
Only for your eagerness to hang on to the crown.
May your head be ashamed to wear the Kianian crown!
May your star hasten to depart!"

They leave the audience hall.
Palace and royal court are covered in dust.

When Esfandiar's mother and sisters receive the news,
They exit the palace with his daughter,
Heads bare, feet sullied with mud and dust,
Robes hanging as scraps over their bodies.

Pashootan advances on the road, consumed by grief,
Walking before the coffin and the black charger.
The women fall on him, blood flowing from their lashes.
They grab the hem of his robe and cry,
"Remove the lid of this narrow coffin.
Show us, at least from a distance, the body of the deceased."

Pashootan is deeply saddened amid the women
Who holler and scrape the skin off their faces.
He addresses the blacksmiths and tells them,
"Bring me a sharp file, for I am a lost man."
He opens the cover of the narrow coffin
And resumes his lamentations.

Once they glance at the kingly face
And the black beard wrapped in musk,
The veiled women with curly hair,
Hearts so deeply aggrieved, faint.
As they regain consciousness,
They walk away from the king's coffin,

Approach his black steed, all the while sobbing,
And they stroke its head and neck with affection.

Katayoon, Esfandiar's mother,
Spills blood tears on the horse,
For she knows that the king died in the saddle.
She says, "O steed whose trail was doomed,
It's on your back that the Kianian prince was killed!
Whom will you now carry into battle?
Whom will you hand over to the whale?"

The women hang on the horse's neck
And scatter dust over its head.
The procession's laments intensify
And grow so loud that they reach the clouds
As Pashootan enters the king's palace.

He approaches the throne, refraining from kissing it
And from bowing before King Goshtaasp.
He says in a loud voice, "O leader of wicked men,
There are signs of your imminent fall!
Look at the harm you have caused to your own son.
You have destroyed the fortune of the land of Iran,
Inciting rulers everywhere to moan and lament.
You have forgotten your sacred nature; reason deserted you.
Yazdan's admonitions will come for you.
Your illustrious son, your support, has perished.
From now on, your hand will clutch nothing but wind.
You have cast your son to death to preserve your throne.
May your eye never again witness throne and good fortune!
The entire kingdom is full of your enemies and evil men.
The royal crown will not be yours for long.
You will be cursed on this earth and, on the day of judgment,
Your actions will be deeply examined and evaluated."

He speaks and turns to face Jaamaasp, crying,
"O evil, crooked man, you swear only by falsehoods.
Your deceitful ways will tarnish your splendor.
You instigated enmity among the Kianians,
Eliciting one to engage in fight and strike the other.
Your wisdom is to teach crime,
Diminish good, and multiply acts of evil.

The seeds you have sown will one day bear fruit,
Whether visible or invisible.
A mighty prince has perished by your cunning words,
And the era of powerful men has passed.
You guided the king down a devious road,
O old man devoid of brain, reason, and good intentions!
You told him that the fate of the noble Esfandiar
Was in the hands of the glorious Rostam."

Pashootan says this and eloquently repeats
The advice and the last wishes of Esfandiar.
He relates how he bequeathed his son Bahman to Rostam
And discloses his brother's secrets.

The king listens to his son's last wishes
And deeply repents for the way he treated him.

Once the noblemen leave the palace,
Behaafarid and Homay enter,
Acutely aggrieved by the death of their brother.
They tear out their hair before their father,
Scrape at their cheeks in grief and say, "O famous King,
What thoughts have you on the fate of Esfandiar,
The first to avenge Zarir
And to remove the deer from the lion's claws?
He defended us against the Turks,
Brought order into your empire.
However, presuming true the words of a slanderer,
You attached him to columns by heavy yoke and belt.
Once he was enchained and held captive,
Our grandfather was killed and our army perished.
Then, when Arjaasp traveled from Khalokh to Balkh,
New calamities befell us from the evil Tooranian.
He led us from palace to street, face bare,
Though we had always been covered and veiled.
In Nooshaazar, Arjaasp extinguished the fire of Zartosht,
Killed Lohraasp, and seized the empire.
You witnessed there the valiant actions of your son,
The way he reduced the Turks to smoke, wind, and dust,
And returned us to you from the impregnable castle.
He was the guardian of your host and your kingdom.
But you sent him into Zabolestan, giving him advice,

While you intended for him to perish
As a decoy to elevating your throne.
His death now fills the world with grief and anguish.

"Neither Simorgh nor Rostam nor Zaal killed him.
Only you are responsible; only you realized the deed!
Do not mourn him so. You are the murderer.
You have to be ashamed of your white beard,
For you sent your son to his death
In the selfish hope of clinging to the throne.
Many kings ruled before you, worthy of majesty,
But none of them ever imagined
Propelling a son or a relative to his death.
If your son wished to inherit the royal crown,
You were the one who took kingship from Lohraasp.
You traveled in the direction of Rum,
Full of fury and distress, like a criminal in flight.
Until the moment Lohraasp handed you the crown,
Your days were dark and full of hardships.
He never killed you or cast you to the fire.
He only bestowed the crown and throne upon you.
You were the one who, for some reason,
Trivial or crucial, wished for your son to die."

Goshtaasp says to Pashootan, "Rise
And pour water over my daughters' fire to calm them."

Pashootan leaves the king's audience hall,
Taking the women with him. He says to his mother,
"Why do you knock at death's door with such passion?
He is resting peacefully. His mind is still,
For he was weary of this land and its master.
Why do you afflict your heart for him
Whose dwelling is now paradise?"

The mother accepts the advice of her son full of piety
And allows him to exert on her
The influence of divine justice.

For one year, all the homes of Iran
Resound with cries and laments.
For many years more, tears are shed over the arrow
Of tamarisk and over the spells of Zaal, son of Saam.

31 | Rostam Sends Bahman Into Iran

Meanwhile, Bahman remains in Zabolestan,
Spending time in the hunting preserves,
Enjoying wine in the rose garden.

Rostam teaches the vengeful youth
To ride, to drink, and to hold court.
In all things, he treats him as a son, smiling at him
And holding him close to his heart day and night.
He remains unaware of the affairs of the world
And what events are to unfold.
The only thing one attracts from an enemy is enmity.
In the end, no matter what are your good deeds,
You will only experience malice and hostility from him.

Once his actions correspond to the promises
Rostam made to Esfandiar, Goshtaasp no longer
Has a pretext to cultivate vengeance.
Rostam writes the king a letter, full of pain,
In which he reminds him of the memory of his son.
He begins with praise of the One
For whom repentance overrules vengeance.
He adds, "The Creator is my witness;
Pashootan can attest to it.
I made every effort possible to change
Esfandiar's mind and turn him away from battle.
I placed my land and treasure at his feet.
I would have rather accomplished more challenging deeds,
But destiny dictated for Esfandiar to remain unflinching,
No matter how full my heart was with grief
And, at the same time, with deep affection for him.

"Such is the rotation of the sky.
No one has the ability to change the will of fate.
Now I have by my side this young man
Who yearns to possess the world
And who brings me more good fortune than Jupiter.
I have taught him everything a king needs to know.
I have paid the debts of reason,
According to his father's last wishes.
If the king desires to accept my repentance

And to promise me to forget this fatal arrow,
I shall surrender my heart and soul for him,
My treasury and crown, my mind and my skin."

Once this letter reaches the world king,
He finds himself isolated from the noblemen.
Pashootan arrives and gives testimony,
Repeating Rostam's words, recounting his anguish,
The advice, and his talk of treasury and land.

The heart of the king softens toward the world hero,
And his affliction lifts significantly.
He immediately writes a response
And plants a tree in the royal garden, saying,
"How could the rotation of the lofty dome of sky
Bring destruction to a man who turns to moderation
And who advances on the path of wisdom?
Pashootan gave me the testimony you asked for,
And you have filled my heart with goodwill.
Who could shirk the wishes of the dome of sky?
The wise man does not dwell on the past.
You are as you have always been and even grander.
You are ruler of India and Ghennooj,
And if you need even more, throne or seal,
Sword or helmet, all you have to do is ask."

The messenger returns the reply in haste,
As commanded by the king who is pleased,
His worries and grief convert to joy.

In this way, some time passes.
The prince, son of Esfandiar, grows tall in stature.
He is wise, well educated, and strong of build.
He bears the blessed diadem higher than all the kings.

Jaamaasp knows, by ways good and wicked,
That kingship belongs to Bahman.
He says to Goshtaasp, "O beloved King,
You must direct your gaze to Bahman and care for him.
He possesses knowledge his father wished him to acquire,
And he has become a brave and brilliant man.
He lingered a long time in a foreign land,
And no one has ever read him a letter from you.

Would you write to Bahman? Such a missive
Will bring him the sentiment of a tree in paradise.
You have in Bahman a noble heir
Who can make you forget your grief over Esfandiar."

Goshtaasp receives this discourse with joy and
Commands the blessed Jaamaasp to write two letters:
The first one to the battle-seeking warrior.
"I give blessings to Yazdan, O Rostam, world hero,
That thanks to you we are happy, our soul is at peace.
My grandson, more dear to me than my own life,
More renowned in knowledge than Jaamaasp,
Has learned, by the influence of fortune,
The rules of conduct and of wisdom,
And I wish for you to send him back to me."

The second letter he writes to Bahman,
"As soon as you read this dispatch,
You must leave Zabolestan without delay,
For I have a deep longing to see you."

After the scribe reads the king's letter to Rostam,
The hero, a friend of wisdom, rejoices.
He gives Bahman all the contents of his treasury:
Coats of mail, shining swords, horse strappings,
Bows and arrows, maces and Indian sabers,
Camphor, musk, ambergris and fresh aloe,
Stones, gems, gold and silver, horses, fabrics,
Youthful slaves, belts, golden bridles,
Two golden cups filled with gleaming rubies,
Taazian horses with saddles of leopard skin,
Gem-embroidered saddles and reins,
One jewel-encrusted crown,
One golden torque inlaid with emeralds.
Rostam gives Bahman the lot, and the bearers of gifts
Evaluate them before Bahman's treasurer.

Rostam escorts the young prince for two stations,
Then he sends him on his way to the king.

At the sight of his grandson,
Tears of blood stream down Goshtaasp's face, and he says,
"You must be Esfandiar himself, so alike you are to him!"

He finds the prince calm of mind and a keen observer,
And assigns him the name of Ardeshir, for he is a hero,
Full of strength, ambition, intelligence, knowledge, and faith.
When he stands, the tips of his fingers reach below his knees.

Goshtaasp tests him for some months
And cannot cease to admire his tall stature.
In drills on the public square, in feasts and in hunts,
Bahman proves himself to be the most accomplished,
Just as his father, Esfandiar, once had been.

Goshtaasp can hardly tolerate the absence of his grandson,
Continuously yearning to be in his company.
He reflects, "I was in despair, I was mourning,
And the Creator brought me Bahman to comfort me.
May Bahman live eternally,
Since I have lost my noble son of invincible stature!"

The story of the battle of Esfandiar comes to an end.
May his majesty the king reign forever, free from worry!
May the world always stand at his command!
May his heart dwell in joy and his crown be lofty!
May the necks of his enemies be ensnared by the noose!

The Adventure of Rostam and Shaghaad

1 | The Beginning of the Story

The story of Esfandiar, as told by earnest men,
Ends here as we reach the story of Rostam's death,
Drawn from a book containing his family's ancient tales.

There lived an old man by the name of Aazaad Sarv,
A man who dwelt in Marv, at the house of Ahmad, son of Sahl.
He possessed a book of kings, the *Khodaay Nameh*.[76]
Holder of a warrior stature, a knowing heart, an eloquent mind,
And a tongue nourished with ancient words,
He could trace his origins back to Saam, son of Nariman,
And was well versed on the subject of Rostam's battles.

I shall now relate what I learned from him
So that I may weave together these stories.
If I stay long enough in this passing dwelling,
My soul and my wisdom will be my guide,
And I shall finish this ancient book
To perpetuate my name and memory in the world.

In the name of the world master, King Mahmoud,
Abul Ghassem, splendor of crown and throne,
Master of Iran, Tooran, and India,
He shines light on the world like Rumi silk.
His generosity has exhausted an abundance of gold,
And his knowledge has amassed a wealth of glory.

He is a powerful prince, and once the countless years pass,
Men of sense will acclaim him, his battles,

◇◇◇◇◇◇◇◇◇◇◇◇◇
76 *Khodaay Nameh*: Compilation, in the language of middle Persian Pahlavi, of the
history of Persian kings during the time of the Sassanian King Khosrow in the 6th
century CE; the information came from the memory of Zoroastrian priests as well as
the *Avesta*.

His gifts, his hunts, and his feasts.
The world is filled with the memory of his just deeds.
Happy is the witness to his crown, his court, and his host!

I find myself burdened: My ears and feet refuse to serve me;
Poverty, scarcity, and the years have snatched my strength.
Destiny, the enemy, has enchained me, leaving me
To heave deep sighs on my misfortune and this harsh year.
Day and night, I invoke divine blessings on his majesty,
Giver of justice, and the entire nation joins me,
With the exception perhaps of scoundrels and evil men.
Since he sat on the Kianian throne, he shut tight
The doors of vengeance and tied up the hands of evildoers.
He makes men tremble when they commit excess,
Even when they think they are protected by high rank.
He is generous toward reasonable men
Who do not attempt to surpass measures assigned to them.

I shall praise him in the world to glorify his name
And to remember him for as long as men exist
With this book of ancient kings,
Of noble and valiant horsemen of long ago,
A book full of feasts and battles,
Instructions and embellished words, full of wisdom
And faith, guidance toward moderation and caution,
A book that can serve as guide in the other world.

Although many things can please the king
And be of service to him today,
This book will surely serve as a memory of his reign,
For it will be inseparable from the story of his life.
I hope that the king will reward me with dinars,
For I wish to bequeath, after my death,
A memory of the treasures of the famed King of Kings.

Now I shall return to the words of Sarv,
Who shines in Marv in the house of Sahl.

2 | Rostam Travels to Kabol
to Help His Brother Shaghaad

Here is a tale I have heard from an old and wise man
Full of talent, eloquence, skills, and memories.

Zaal has, in his female chambers,
A slave able to sing and play a musical instrument.
This young woman gives birth to a son
Who shines so bright as to dim the moon's glow.
He resembles Saam, the horseman, in appearance
And stature, and the hero's family is thrilled by it.

Illustrious astrologers and sages arrive
From Kashmir and Kabol, their Rumi astrolabes in hand.
These men, who explore science and worship Yazdan,
Assess the will of the stars
And the fate reserved for the fair-faced boy.

Once they discover the unfolding of his life,
They find themselves astonished by the dismal results.
They glance at each other and tell Zaal, son of Saam,
"O successor to a family favored by the stars,
We have worked hard to calculate the secrets of the skies,
But they are not well disposed toward your son.
At the onset of maturity, once the fair-faced child
Has acquired strength and courage,
He will destroy the race of Saam, son of Nariman.
He will put an end to the throne, fill Sistan with turmoil,
And turn upside down the land of Iran.
Everyone's days will turn bitter,
And you will not survive long after that."

Zaal is afflicted by the news.
He implores Yazdan, Justice Giver:
"O Guide, the revolving dome is beneath your feet.
In all matters, You are my support and my shelter.
You teach me wisdom and the right path to follow.
You have created the firmament and the stars.
May we always nurture hope for happiness!
May we fulfill our dreams and live in peace!"

The leader gives his son the name of Shaghaad.
The mother keeps him even after he is weaned,
As his beauty and refinement steal her heart.

He speaks and observes everything.
Once he is a grown man, Zaal sends him to Kabol
And its king, who is a young man, as tall as a cypress tree,
A valiant rider, skilled in the use of mace and noose.

The King of Kabol observes him
And sees that he is worthy of crown and throne.
He rejoices at the sight of him and of his high birth,
And offers him his daughter's hand.
He presents the wedded couple
All that is worthy of them from his treasury.
He tends to Shaghaad with care, like a bright apple,
So that he has nothing to fear from the stars.

The noble leaders of Iran and India recount
Tales of Rostam and the tribute of cowhide
Demanded every year from the land of Kabol.

The prince of Kabol assumes that since Shaghaad
Is now his son-in-law, Rostam, master of Zabolestan,
Need no longer raise the matter of tribute.
But once the time arrives, Rostam's men request payment,
Which deeply offends the rulers of the land of Kabol.

Shaghaad is wounded by his brother's actions,
But he speaks to no one of it, except secretly
To his father-in-law, "I am weary of the world,
And I refuse to express deference to my brother
Since he has no shame in acting this way toward me.
What difference does it make to me: an older brother
Or a stranger, a mad man or a wise one?
Let us devise a plan to draw him into our nets,
A deed that will exalt our standing in the world."

They confer with each other, hoping to rise to the moon.
According to the words of a wise man,
Whoever commits evil acts will soon repent.

One night, the two men find themselves unable to sleep.

Until sunrise, they elaborate on ways to make
Rostam disappear and to fill with tears Zaal's heart.

Shaghaad says to the King of Kabol,
"If we wish to execute justice,
We must prepare a feast, convene noblemen,
And bring wine, music, and singers.
While we drink wine, you will speak to me coldly,
And in the midst of your speech, you will insult me.
Thus poorly treated, I shall depart for Zabolestan,
To complain about the King of Kabol.
At the court of my brother and my father,
I shall tell them that you are a coarse man of poor race.
Rostam's fury will mount, and he will wish
To rush to our illustrious land to avenge me.
You will select a hunting site on the road,
And you will dig up ditches large and deep enough
To receive the bodies of Rostam and Rakhsh.
You will garnish the bases with long spears
And shining blades, their ends pointing up,
Their handles firmly planted into the ground.
If you wish to put an end to your grief,
You should dig up ten ditches rather than five.
Bring there one hundred able workers,
Prepare the ditches, and cover them up.
Do not utter a word of the matter to anyone,
Not even to the moon."

The king departs, his reason gone astray.
He prepares a feast just as the foolish youth advised.
He convenes noblemen of Kabol, great and small,
And offers them well-served and well-displayed spreads.

Once they have dined, they gather in an assembly.
Wine and singers are summoned,
And heads fill with the effects of the royal wine.
Shaghaad begins his unpleasant discourse,
Saying to the King of Kabol,
"I come from a rank higher than anyone else here.
Rostam is my brother and Zaal my father.
Who could boast a more illustrious lineage?"

The King of Kabol, pretending to grow infuriated,
Retorts, "How long am I to keep such a secret?
You are not from the race of Saam, son of Nariman.
You are not Rostam's brother, not even his cousin.
Zaal and Rostam have never spoken of you.
How would they then recognize you?
You are a slave's son, a guard at the palace gate.
Rudaabeh will never call you Rostam's brother."

Shaghaad's heart tightens at these words,
And all incensed, he leaves for Zabolestan.
He travels with a number of riders from Kabol,
Heart full of hatred, lips full of sighs.
He arrives at the court of his blessed father.

At the sight of his son's face, his tall stature,
His royal airs, and strong limbs,
Zaal receives him tenderly and questions him.
Then he sends him to Rostam, world hero,
Who rejoices at the sight of him,
Finding him wise of mind and serene of spirit.

He says to him, "Only powerful and valiant men
Grow from the linage of Saam and Nariman!
How did your affairs go with the King of Kabol?
What does he say of Rostam of Zabolestan?"

Shaghaad replies, "Never mention his name!
Once upon a time, he was kind to me
And blessed me every time he set his sight on me.
But now, every time he drinks wine, he seeks quarrel.
He wishes to raise his head above everyone else.
He insulted me in front of the court
By revealing my inferior birth and saying,
          'Until when will you speak of tribute to me?
          Can we not confront Sistan about it?
          I shall no longer call Rostam by his name!
          I am beneath him neither in value nor in nobility.
          As for you, you are not the son of Zaal.
          Even if you were, at least he deems you as worthless.'
My heart filled with grief to be treated
So disrespectfully right in front of the leaders.

Later, he chased me out of Kabol.
I had no choice but to leave, face pale with anger."

At these words, Rostam bursts out,
"Nothing is ever hidden. Do not fear him or his land.
Cursed be his nation! Cursed be his diadem!
I shall kill him for this speech.
I shall make him and his kin tremble with fear.
I shall place you on the throne
And fling his good fortune into the dust."

Rostam assigns Shaghaad the grand palace,
Keeping him close and showering him with honors.
He selects a number of valiant warriors from his army,
Those who distinguished themselves in battle,
And commands them to prepare to depart
And march from Zabol to Kabol.

Once everything is set and troops are mobilized,
The warrior's heart is appeased.
Shaghaad comes to Rostam and says,
"Do not think of war with the King of Kabol.
If I were to merely trace your name on water,
The entire land would lose sleep and rest.
Who would dare appear to fight with you?
And if you march, who would dare await you?
I am convinced that he is already repenting,
Hoping to prevent the consequences of my departure.
He will certainly dispatch a great number
Of renowned leaders to Kabol to plead for mercy."

Rostam says, "It is natural. I shall not need an army
To lead a campaign against Kabol.
Zavaareh with one hundred renowned horsemen
And one hundred foot soldiers will suffice."

3 | The King of Kabol Calls for Ditches, and Rostam and Zavaareh Fall Into them

As soon as the ill-omened Shaghaad leaves Kabol,
The king departs for the hunting site with able warriors.
They excavate and dig trenches beneath the road,
Garnishing the bases with spears, javelins, and swords,
And fixing their handles into the ground.

Then, with great care and art,
They conceal the openings to make them invisible
To both human eye and stallion eye.

As Rostam hastily takes the road,
Shaghaad sends a horseman to tell the King of Kabol
That the world warrior is on his way without a host
And that he must go to greet him and ask forgiveness.

The leader of Kabol leaves the city,
Tongue as sweet as honey, heart bitter with poison.
But once his eyes fall on Rostam's figure,
He dismounts from afar, removes his Indian headdress,
And advances, head bare and hands on his forehead.
He removes his boots, lamenting and shedding blood tears.
He bends low to the ground, face resting on the black dust,
And asks forgiveness for what he said to Shaghaad:
"If I, your slave, was foolish enough to get drunk
And arrogant enough in this altered state,
Forgive my crimes and treat me as you always have."

He approaches barefoot,
Head filled with vengeance and heart with ruse.
Rostam forgives him, grants him new honors,
Permits him to cover his head and feet,
To climb on the saddle and to march away.

There is, across from the city of Kabol,
A green, leafy place, a pleasant setting
Where there is water, shelter, and foliage.
They unload the supplies in this area.

The king asks for provisions and prepares for feast.

He asks for wine and music,
And sits princes on royal chairs.
Then he says to Rostam, "If you would like to hunt,
I have a place where wild beasts wander in herds
In fields that abound with deer
And mountains that swarm with wild rams.
Anyone with a speedy horse like yours
Is certain to catch deer and doe.
You must not travel through this region
Without visiting this charming site."

These words and the prospect of a field
With streams, deer, and doe entice Rostam,
For what is meant to bring a man to his end
Excites his heart and perverts his judgment.

Such is the action of this ever-changing world.
Never does it reveal to us its secret.
The whale in the sea, the leopard in the desert,
The valiant lion with sharp claws, fly, ant, and elephant,
All are equally affected by death.
None can remain living when its time is up.

Rostam asks for Rakhsh to be saddled
And for the flight of sparrows, hawks, and falcons.
He places his royal bow in its sheath.
Shaghaad runs at his side.
Zavaareh, with a few men from the noble assembly,
Accompanies the mighty warrior.

During the hunt, Rostam's escort spreads out,
Some running over the mined areas,
Others over firm ground.
Zavaareh and Rostam find each other,
By way of destiny, on a road strewn with ditches.

Rakhsh sniffs the newly stirred up ground
And curls up like a ball, rearing up, bucking,
Fearing the odor of the ground
And shredding it with his hooves.
Rakhsh proceeds in a way as to stride two ditches.
Rostam urges his steed to advance,
Destiny blinding the eye of wisdom.

His anger stoked, he raises his whip to strike Rakhsh.
The terrified charger regains momentum.
Constricted between two ditches
And exerting himself to tempt fate,
The horse cannot escape and falls into the traps,
Incapable of either holding on or struggling on.

The bottom of the ditch is spiked with sharp blades.
Courage is useless and escape impossible.
The sides of the valiant Rakhsh are torn apart.
The chests and legs of the powerful hero are pierced.

Still, by means of courage, Rostam frees his body
And falls over the side of the ditch.

4 | Rostam Kills Shaghaad and Dies

Rostam opens his eyes, and, despite his wounds,
He turns to face the malicious Shaghaad,
Realizes that he is his mortal enemy
And the one responsible for his demise.

Rostam says to him, "O evil brother of cursed fortune,
It is by your deed that this happy land is to be barren.
You will repent and tremble at the consequences.
Never will you have the chance to attain old age."

The wretched Shaghaad replies,
"The revolving dome is treating you as you deserve.
Why did you shed blood for so long, hang so many men,
Attack and destroy so many lands?
The time of your death is approaching,
And you will perish at the hands of Ahriman."

At this moment, the King of Kabol arrives from the desert,
Finds the hero fatally injured, notices that his wounds
Are not dressed, and says to him, "O illustrious leader,
What happened to you in the hunting preserves?
I shall depart in haste to fetch medicine men,
Shedding blood tears for your pain.
I hope that your wounds will heal and that

I shall no longer need to flood my cheeks with tears."

Rostam replies, "O cunning man of evil race,
The time for medicine men has passed for me,
But do not shed blood tears over my death.
No matter how long one lives, one must die in the end.
The rotation of the skies assails all forms of life:
I am not a man more glorious than Jamsheed,
Who was sawn in two by Zahaak;
I claim no more glory than Fereydoon
And Kay Ghobaad, famous kings of illustrious birth;
No more glory than the evil Afraasiyaab,
Whom Kay Khosrow split in two.
Once the time of Siaavoosh arrived,
Garooy of Zerreh slit his throat with a dagger.
These were glorious Iranian kings, valiant lions in battle,
But they all departed while we remained,
Maintaining our stances on the road like fierce lions.
Faraamarz, my son, the joy of my eyes,
Will come and will request an account for my death."

Then he adds to the evil Shaghaad,
"Now this plight is upon me, do not refuse my request.
Draw my bow and two arrows, and hand them to me.
I must not allow a lion, roaming in search of prey,
To find me and pounce on me.
My bow could serve me well.
If I can avoid being torn apart alive by a lion,
My time will come, and I shall lie in the dust."

Shaghaad reaches in the quiver for the bow,
Pulls to test the bowstring. Then, delighted
At the prospect of his brother's imminent death,
He extends it within Rostam's reach.

The latter grabs the bow with strength,
Yet squirming from the agony caused by his wounds.
Fearing the shots,
Shaghaad runs to take shelter behind a plane tree
Over which many years have passed,
Hollow inside, still heavy with leaves.
The impure Shaghaad hides cowardly behind it.

Rostam sees his position, raises his arm,
And, wounded as he is,
Sends a shot pinning Shaghaad to the tree,
In a sense comforting his dying heart.

The wounded Shaghaad cries out,
But Rostam allows him little time to feel the pain.
Rostam says, "Praise the Creator who gave me
The power to avenge myself before my death.
I remember how I have devoted my life to justice.
You gave me the strength to effectuate vengeance
On this disloyal, disgruntled man prior to my death.
Absolve my sins and forgive my wrongdoings.
You are the Support and the Giver of blessings.
I have assumed my life's path
As your prophet and your faith have taught me.
My spiritual path has always been pure.
I may die with courage and peace of mind.
Welcome me into heaven. I am yours
And you may see me with complete clarity."

He says this and his soul exits his body,
Leaving the assembly to shed tears of grief.

Zavaareh tumbles down into another ditch
And perishes while his riders, great and small,
Perish alongside him.

5 | Zaal Learns of the Murders of Rostam and Zavaareh, and Faraamarz Brings His Father's Casket

Only one of the renowned riders escapes,
Traveling at times on foot and at times on horseback.
He returns to Zabolestan
And recounts that the mighty warrior hero
Lies weak in the dust with Zavaareh and his escort,
And that none of the others evaded the enemy's ambush.

A cry of anguish rises over Zabolestan,
A furious cry against Rostam's foes
And specifically against the King of Kabol.

Zaal scatters dust over his arm.
He tears at his face and chest, crying,
"Alas, our hero of elephantine stature!
If only my body were encased in a shroud instead of his!
Alas, the illustrious and valiant dragon!
Alas, Zavaareh, glorious lion!
The cursed Shaghaad uprooted the royal tree.
Who would have thought a vile fox could scheme
Against a lion in a land of vengeance?
Who remembers a blow of this intensity from destiny?
Who remembers hearing of such an act from a teacher,
That a fox's cunning words would have the power
To prevail upon a lion warrior?

"Why did I not die miserably prior to them?
Why must I remain in this world, a memory of them?
What benefit to me are life,
Its pleasures, food, rest, and fame?
Alas, the warrior hero, vanquisher of lions, brave victor!
Alas, the shining prince of the lineage of Nariman!
I desire neither life nor name at this moment,
For the seed of Zaal has been severed
With the death of Rostam, warrior, lion defeater,
World conqueror, and guide.
A deep, dark soil lifts from my soul.
Who would have dreamt of such an evil act,
An act to render dim my body and soul?
If I were to level a mountain into a valley,
If I were to convert the waters of the Jayhoon to blood,
How will I ever avenge your death?
No amount of blood in the world
Is equal to one drop of yours, so precious is it.
As long as you lived, you upheld the world.
Now you are gone.
Who will assume the responsibility?
Now that your warrior belt is in shreds,
The world, for me, is nothing but a fistful of dust."

He sends Faraamarz with his host to attack the king,
Draw out corpses from the ditches,
And impose reasons to grieve on the world.

As Faraamarz enters Kabol, he finds the city deserted.
The noblemen have vanished, so terrified
Were they about the death of the world vanquisher.
All the city dwellers bolt to leave, grieving Rostam,
Feeling as if they are being skewered over a flame.

Faraamarz finds the hunting grounds and the ditches.
At the sight of his father's face, he hollers a lion roar.
Rostam's corpse, sprawled on the ground,
Is caked with dust and blood. He deplores,
"O lofty hero, who is responsible for your demise?
May the guilty man be damned!
May he wear a headdress of dust instead of helm!
To Yazdan and to your life,
To the dust of Nariman and Saam, the rider,
I shall never again unfasten the knots of my chain mail!
I wish to avenge the hero of elephant stature
And punish all the disloyal men,
The ones who cooperated and conspired,
Their belts fastened in the name of hatred.
They are at fault for our misfortune today.
I shall not allow a single one of them to survive,
Not even the ones who instigated the plots.

He commands a resting bed
To be placed beneath the royal tree,
One covered with silk cloth and various garments.
He removes the hero's belt and royal tunic.
They bathe the deceased in warm water,
Gently wash his chest, arms, beard and body.
Ambergris and saffron are burned beside him,
And his wounds are sewn tight.

Faraamarz pours rosewater on Rostam's head
And spreads pure camphor over his body,
Which is then enveloped with a sheet of golden brocade,
Surrounded by roses, musk, and wine.
The man sewing the shroud spills blood tears
As he combs the deceased's camphor-white beard.

The body surpasses the length of two beds.
Is it the body of a man or a tree diffusing shade?

A beautiful coffin is built from teak,
Ornate with golden nails and ivory figures.
Its joints are anointed with tar,
Covered in turn with musk and amber.

Next, Zavaareh, Rostam's brother,
Is pulled out of the ditch.
His wounds are sewn, his body is washed,
His silk shroud stitched.
Skilled carpenters build him a coffin
Made from the trunk of an elm.
Faraamarz pours musk, camphor, and rosewater
As Zavaareh is nested in his ultimate lodging.

Next, Rakhsh's corpse is lifted, washed, and shrouded.
The world will never see a horse of his strength and stature.
Two days are required to properly outfit
The deceased stallion and load him on an elephant.

From Kabolestan to Zabolestan,
The world is overwhelmed by grief.
Everywhere, throngs of men and woman pour out,
Allowing little room for others to squeeze in.
The two coffins are passed from hand to hand.
The number of people holding them make
The caskets appear light in the air, and in this way,
Never touching the ground, they make their way
To Zabol in the span of two days and one night.

The entire world fills with laments.
It is as if the desert has reached a boiling point.
Voices are squelched by the strident cries of grief.

A grave is prepared in Zaal's garden,
Its crest reaching the clouds.
Two golden thrones are placed side by side,
To form the resting place of the auspicious hero.
A third one is placed next to them,
Upon which reclines Zavaareh.

Servants, whether free men or pure-hearted slaves,
Blend a mixture of musk and dust,
Scatter it at the feet of the elephantine warrior, and cry,

"O famous one, why must you call for musk and amber?
Why do you no longer take your seat at the hour of feast?
Why have you ceased to wear your Babreh Bayan in war
And ceased to distribute golden treasures?
It is as if you despise and scorn all of that.
May you be happy in joyous paradise,
For Yazdan molded you with justice and valor!"

They close the door to the grave and take their leave.
In this way, the hero, whose head rose so high,
Disappears from the face of the world.
They dig up a trench in front of Rostam's resting place
And settle Rakhsh's corpse into it.
It is as if the hero is bestriding his noble steed.

What can you ask of this fleeting sojourn
That starts in joy and ends in suffering?
You will eventually turn into dust,
Even if you were made of steel, no matter
If you are a spectator of the true faith or an Ahriman.

While you live, favor truth and righteousness,
In the hopes of attaining your dreams in the other world.

6 | Faraamarz Drives an Army to Avenge Rostam and Kills the King of Kabol

Once his father's mourning is complete,
Faraamarz commands an army to exit onto the plain.
He opens the doors to Rostam's residence
And equips his troops with weapons and goods
From his father's collected treasury.

One early morning hour, at the sound of trumpets,
Brazen kettledrums and Indian bells,
He leads his host out of Zabolestan toward Kabol,
Causing the sun to vanish from the world.

The King of Kabol hears of the approach of troops
From Zabolestan and gathers his scattered army.
The earth is encased in iron,

And the air dims to the color of indigo.

Faraamarz and his troops advance.
The faces of sun and moon pale.
Once the two armies confront each other,
The world fills with the clash of war and warriors.
The mass of horses is so great
And the black dust they raise so thick
As to make lions go amiss in the forest.
A gusting wind brings clouds so dark
They blur the distinction between sky and ground.

Faraamarz lunges out of the ranks,
Without taking his eyes off the king.
He flings himself swiftly into the heart
Of the enemy host with a few of his troops.
The riders fill the world with dust,
And the King of Kabol is taken captive.

His powerful warriors disperse. The brave men of Iran,
Akin to wolves, weigh them down in pursuit.
They kill many Indian warriors,
Many more brave and illustrious men from Sindh.
The ground of the battlefield is soaked in blood.
The armies of India and Sindh disband, defeated.
Renouncing the defense of their lands and homes,
They abandon their women and children.

Faraamarz orders the King of Kabol to be hurled,
Covered in blood, into a tower carried by an elephant.
He leads him, hands tied, to the hunting grounds,
To a site where ditches had been dug up,
Along with forty of the king's parents and worshippers.

He takes a strip of skin off the king's back.
Once he is bare, he hurls him into the ditch, headfirst,
Body covered with dust, mouth full of blood.

Faraamarz asks for his forty relatives to be burned.
Then he walks toward Shaghaad,
Lights a fire as large as a mountain, and burns his body,
The plane tree, and the surrounding grounds.
As the host arrives in Kabolestan,

They upturn the land with their hands.

Having thus executed the unjust prince,
Faraamarz appoints a new King of Kabol.
He exiles any member of the ancient family who does
Not recognize the investiture drawn out by his sword.

He exits Kabol, heart wounded and saddened,
The light of his day obscured before his eyes.
The lands of Zabolestan and Bost are in mourning.
There is not a single piece of clothing
That has not fallen to scraps.
The inhabitants advance to meet up with Faraamarz,
Chests torn apart and cheeks flooding with tears.

7 | Rudaabeh Loses Her Mind
Over the Death of Her Son

The land of Sistan mourns for one year.
Everyone is dressed in either blue or black.

One day, Rudaabeh says to Zaal,
"Show evidence of your grief for Rostam.
Since the sun shines on the world,
There never was a more gloomy day!"

Zaal replies, "O foolish woman, if I fast, fear of famine
Would be more harrowing than mourning for a son."

Rudaabeh becomes enraged and utters an oath,
"I shall from now on take neither rest nor food,
Not until my soul reunites
With the soul of the hero of elephantine stature."

For seven days, she abstains from consuming food,
Secretly communicating with the soul of Rostam.
Her eyesight dims from fasting, her valiant heart wavers,
And her heroine stature shrinks.
Everywhere she goes, a handful of slaves follow
For fear that she would hurt herself.
At the end of a week, her reason is lost,

And in a state of folly she converts her grief into feast.

She walks into the garden while everyone sleeps
And spots a dead serpent in the water.
She extends her hand, seizes the serpent's head,
And is on the verge of biting into it.

One of her chambermaids snatches it from her in time
And enfolds Rudaabeh's head close to her chest.
She guides her away from this impure place
And toward her apartment in the palace.
They sit her on her seat, bring a spread with delicacies,
And she proceeds to eat her fill.

Then they spread a soft blanket beneath her,
And she rests from her grief and weariness,
From mourning and the worry caused by her wealth.
Upon awakening, she asks for more nourishment,
And her maids bring her a variety of fares.

Once her reason returns, she says to Zaal,
"Your spoke the truth. When one is deprived of food,
One may confuse bereavement with banquet.
Rostam has left us, and we shall follow him.
Let us trust the Creator's just ways."

She donates her hidden treasures to the poor
And addresses the divine spirit in prayer,
"O most glorious One above name, time, and space,
Purify Rostam's soul of any offense he may have committed.
Give him a place in the other world, in your paradise.
Allow him to enjoy the fruit of what he has sown here!"

8 | Goshtaasp Abandons the Throne to Bahman and Dies

Now that the story of Rostam ends with his death,
I shall have to turn to other stories.

Goshtaasp feels that his fortune has dimmed.
He calls Jaamaasp to court and says to him,

"Esfandiar's death has so troubled my days
That I do not enjoy life for a single moment.
The star that pursues me fills me with sorrow.
Bahman will succeed me on the throne of royalty
And have at his side Pashootan as minister.
Stay loyal to him and obey his command.
Serve him as guide, for he is worthy of throne and crown."

He hands over to Bahman the key to his treasury
And says to him, sighing bitterly,
"My work on earth has ended,
Its flow has risen above my head.
In my reign of one hundred and twenty years,
Never did I see my equal in the world.
Now exert great effort and be a just ruler by acting
According to justice: You will thus live free of grief.
Honor wise men and keep them close to you.
Render the world black for evil men; act with integrity.
Righteousness makes depravity and lies disappear.
I give you throne, diadem, and treasury,
Having long endured worry and weariness."

Soon after he says this, life exits his body.
His entire past ceases to bear fruit.
A coffin of ivory and ebony is built for him,
A crown is hung above the throne.

His share of life was great joy as well as deep suffering.
He drank poison after having been nourished with honey.
If such is life, then where is the joy?
When one reflects on the fact that after life
The poor man stands on equal footing with the king,
Then where is indeed the joy?

Enjoy the seeds you sow and do not surrender to evil.
Lend an ear to the words of the wise man.
Our companions have marched ahead,
And we have stayed and told many ancient stories.
The one who has walked and arrived at the station,
The one who seeks virtue will find happiness.
May you encounter only good fortune
If you listen to the words of an ancient sage!

Now I shall occupy myself with the travails of Bahman
And recount for you the ageless tales.

PART TWENTY

The Ninety-Nine-Year Reign
of Bahman, Son of Esfandiar

The Thirty-Two-Year Reign
of Homay, Daughter of Bahman

The Twelve-Year Reign of Daaraab,
Son of Bahman and Homay

The Fourteen-Year Reign
of Dara, Son of Daaraab

The Ninety-Nine-Year Reign of Bahman, Son of Esfandiar

1 | Bahman Avenges the Death of Esfandiar

Bahman ascends to his grandfather's throne,
Fastens a royal belt, and engages in charity and giving.
He presents the army with gold and silver,
Rewarding its leaders with provinces and borders.

After some time, he brings his attention to vengeance.
He convenes a gathering of wise noblemen
And skilled warriors, and addresses them:
"O men of serene minds, young and old,
You are familiar with the fate of Esfandiar
And the sky's auspicious and inauspicious rotations.
You are familiar with Rostam's deeds
And those of Zaal, the aging sorcerer.
You know that, secretly or overtly,
Faraamarz reflects only on exercising retribution.
My head is filled with grief, my heart with blood,
And my mind is continually occupied on settling the score
For the deplorable deaths of Nooshaazar and Mehrnoosh.
Furthermore, Esfandiar, who renewed the glory of kings,
Was killed in Zabolestan, plunging animals, wild or tame,
And forest creatures into the senseless woes of grief.
Portraits hanging in the palace continue
To shed tears over his brutal murder
As well as on the bloodshed inflicted
Upon our young and valiant cavaliers and noblemen.

"No hero of pure race will hide in the shadows
And allow his name to be buried beneath the dust.
One's future may be auspicious
When he emulates the exploits of King Fereydoon,
Who, to avenge the blood of Jamsheed,

Made Zahaak disappear from the world.
Manoochehr led a mighty host against Toor and Salm,
Traveling from Amol to Chin to avenge his grandfather.
Everywhere, upon his passage,
Heaps of corpses leveled mountain to plain.

"When Kay Khosrow rose to power,
He drenched the earth in a sea of blood
By punishing Afraasiyaab for his father's death.
My father sought to retaliate for Lohraasp's spilled blood.
I find myself in a similar predicament with a similar duty.
After his father died, Faraamarz raised his head to the sun,
Entered Kabol to avenge Rostam, and destroyed the land
Until the ground disappeared beneath a flow of blood
And horses trampled the amassed cadavers.
I am even more worthy of executing retribution,
Since I launch my steed to fight elephants and lions.
I shall avenge Esfandiar, unmatched rider warrior.
What are your thoughts? What is your reply?
Attempt to give me advice that will bring me luck."

The army leaders and allies of the king listen
To Bahman and cry, "We are your loyal slaves.
Our hearts are full of affection for you.
You know better than anyone what happened long ago.
You are the most powerful warrior.
May your will be fulfilled in the world!
May you reach the heights of fame and glory!
No one will challenge your command, for who would
Dare breach the covenant that binds us to you?"

The warriors' shouts intensify the king's ardor.
Everyone makes preparations to travel to Sistan,
Wishing and longing for nothing else.

Trumpets resound at dawn.
Dust rises from the motion of troops
And tints the sky in shades of ebony.
On the road marches a glorious host,
One hundred thousand sword-bearing riders.

2 | Bahman Enchains Zaal

Having reached the banks of the Hirmand,
Bahman selects a noble envoy to send to Zaal, son of Saam.
He charges him with various messages:
"Esfandiar's death renders life bitter to me, as well
As the murders of Nooshaazar and Mehrnoosh,
Two noble princes of renowned lineage.
I shall now seek vengeance to free my heart of wrath.
I shall turn the river of Zabol into a sea of blood."

The envoy approaches Zaal and repeats the message.
Grief and sadness infiltrate the leader's heart.
He replies, "If the king wishes to reflect on Esfandiar's death,
He will realize that it was the undertaking of fate
And that my soul has dwelt in anguish ever since.
You witnessed what happened, good and bad,
Yet you have only benefited from my feats.
Rostam submitted to Esfandiar's command.
You saw that his soul was the very slave of obedience.
But your father, this noble and powerful prince,
Was reaching the end of his life.
At that time, he treated Rostam ruthlessly.

"Valiant lions and dragons in the forest
Do not escape the claws of fate.
Without a doubt, you are familiar
With the courageous deeds of Saam the rider
And his lifelong heroic feats until the time
Rostam was of age to draw his sword.
The high deeds of Rostam on the field of honor
And his battles occurred within the sight of his ancestors.
He nursed and nurtured you like a most humble parent.
In the army, he was at the head of the most noble warriors.
Now he is gone, having perished miserably,
Leaving Zabolestan in a state of bereavement.
If you wish to renounce battle,
If you wish to reflect graciously on our affairs,
If you wish to come here, forget your wrath.
Calm the land by your kindness and compassion.
All the wealth and dinars of Saam,
Golden belts and golden bridles, I shall lay at your feet,

For you are king, and your herd consists of noblemen."

Zaal offers the messenger a horse, dinars, and gifts.
The noble envoy returns to the side of the king
And reveals to him all that transpired at Zaal's court.

The blessed Bahman listens to him
But refuses to accept Zaal's excuses.
He grows infuriated and proceeds
To invade the land, his soul chagrined,
His head full of vengeance, his heart full of sighs.

Zaal, son of Saam the rider, advances to meet him
On the road with Sistan's most illustrious men.
He nears Bahman, dismounts, and acclaims him:
"This is a moment of mercy, the day when one
Is to purify one's heart and expel any remnant of grief.
Here I am, Zaal, the son of Saam the rider,
Bowing humbly before you.
I beseech you, by the services tendered by my family,
By the cares we have taken during your childhood,
Show some clemency and do not bring up the past.
Act with sweeping gestures, but do not seek
To stir up dust and avenge the deceased."

These words serve only to trigger Bahman's fury.
In this way, Zaal fails to achieve his goal,
And he finds himself immediately bound up
With heavy chains by order of the king.

Bahman refuses to listen to either treasurer or minister.
A great deal of gold is loaded onto camels
And taken from Zaal's palace, along with dinars,
Unspoiled jewels, thrones, and assorted carpets;
Dinnerware of solid gold, golden crowns,
Trays of solid silver, earrings and belts;
Taazian stallions with golden bridles,
Indian swords with golden sheaths,
Clothing and chests full of dinars, musk and camphor;
Slaves, sacks filled with gold and silver,
All items painstakingly amassed by Rostam,
Wealth given to him by lords and kings.

Bahman plunders the land of Zabolestan
And distributes purses of dinars and crowns to his men.

3 | Faraamarz Is Defeated by Bahman

Faraamarz receives news at the border of Bost.
He is afflicted and prepares to avenge his grandfather.
He assembles an army and takes the road to court,
Remembering Rostam's life and battles.

News of his approach
Troubles Bahman on the imperial throne.
He asks for the preparations of loads, orders his troops
To climb on their steeds and march toward Guraabeh,
Where they are to remain for two weeks.

Faraamarz advances with his host and soon faces the enemy.
Bahman's troops are stationed so innumerable
That the brilliant sun can no longer distinguish the earth.
The sound of clarions and trumpets resounds
To make the hearts of boulders shake.
The sky washes the face of the world black with tar.
Arrows plummet from the dark void like hail.
The blows of axe and the twanging of bows
Stir up the ground even more than the sky.

For three days and three nights,
Beneath the light of the sun or the gleam of the moon,
A shower of blows falls on the battlefield,
Blows of heavy mace and steel-tipped swords.
A fog of dust lifts into the air from the motion of troops.

On the fourth day, a fierce tempest blends day into night.
The world king is delighted at the advent of the storm
As the wind wails toward Faraamarz.
Bahman pursues the thick clouds of dust,
His cutting blade gripped in his hand.
He carries out destruction on the enemy host.

Sword-bearing warriors from Bost, Zabolestan, and Kabol
Turn their backs on Faraamarz and shamefully decamp.

Not a single noble and proud rider remains.

The field is strewn with heaps of corpses
From both sides, tossed one upon another.

Faraamarz, with a few select men eager for battle,
Holds the vanguard, his body punctured by cuts.
He is a lion man, the son of a lion man.
He is aware that this day is a day of calamity,
That his time has come, and such is the trap of destiny.
He says, "I have flung myself into the dragon's jaws.
I do not see myself escaping this day alive.
But I shall acquire here, with my mace and cutting sword,
A name that will linger until the day of resurrection."

He lunges to penetrate the army core
In such a way as to fall close to the king.
He assails and slays a number of leaders,
Illustrious men and champions in war.

The warriors are troubled at the sight of him.
They launch a mass of troops against him.
The riders surround him.
The furious lion grows weary from his wounds.
His charger, weakened by the points of arrows,
Wavers and falls to the ground, exhausted.

Nevertheless, Faraamarz seizes his heavy mace
And continues his feat of vanquishing brave warriors.
But he has lost so much blood that his strength
Abandons him, and he is forced to stop.

In the end, he falls captive to enemy hands,
Who lead him from the battlefield to Bahman.
The hateful king observes him for some time,
But the face of the warlord cannot make him
Resolve to take mercy on his life.

Bahman commands the gallows to be set up.
They attach Faraamarz alive to the rope and hang him.
This man of elephantine build lowers his head,
And the illustrious Kianian assails him vengefully
And kills him with a shower of arrows.

4 | Bahman Liberates Zaal and Returns to Iran

The valued Pashootan, the king's advisor,
Is deeply aggrieved by all the carnage.
He rises in front of the world master and says,
"O just and righteous King,
If your heart longed and plotted for vengeance,
You have at last achieved it,
And there is nothing more to be done here.
Do not command further plunder, slaying, and war.
Cease to instigate clatter and chaos.
Fear in the Creator, and show your shame before us.
Reflect on the rotation of the skies
That raises one above the highest clouds
And lowers the other into the depths
Of anguish, powerlessness, and abjectness.
Remember that your father,
World master and the army's glory,
Sought his grave in the land of Nimrooz.
Rostam did not hunt in Kabol, to fall
To his demise in a lowly, treacherous trench.

"O noble King, as long as you live,
Abstain from causing harm to a highborn man.
When Zaal, son of Saam, son of Nariman,
Will murmur complaints in his state of captivity
To the almighty Creator, you will have reason to fear,
No matter how auspicious your star may be.
One must take his case before the Creator.
Rostam, the guardian of the Kianian throne,
Did not cower in the face of hardships and battle.
Your crown was handed to you by Rostam,
And not by Shah Goshtaasp nor Esfandiar.

"Take into account the era
From Kay Ghobaad to the wise Kay Khosrow,
By whose sword they received power and empire.
The race of Saam was held in veneration by everyone.
Let go of the chains, if you are a sensible man.
Turn your heart away from unjust and evil acts."

After hearing Pashootan out, the king

Repents at the thought of the ancient deeds.
A proclamation is declared from his tent pavilion:
"O just and wise warriors, prepare for departure.
Refrain from further pillage and killing!"
The king dictates that Zaal be freed of his chains
And be provided with much counsel.

By the order of the pure minister and advisor,
A somber vault is constructed for Faraamarz's corpse.
Zaal is liberated from prison and returned to his palace.

Meanwhile, the noble Rudaabeh cries bitterly.
She exclaims, "Alas, Rostam, so valiant, so heroic,
Grandson of illustrious and bold Nariman.
When you were alive,
Who even conceived of Goshtaasp as world king?
Now, treasures are plundered, Zaal is held captive,
And his son has been miserably slain at the points of arrows.
Woe be to the eyes that witness such a wretched fate.
May the earth be freed from the race of Esfandiar!"

Her complaints are reported to Bahman and to the blessed
Pashootan, who is troubled for Rudaabeh.
His cheeks pale, he says to Bahman,
"O young King, you sit on the throne
Like the new moon in the center of the firmament.
In the early morning hours, send away your host.
This affair has become strenuous and dangerous.
May the evil eye never reach your crown!
May every day pass in feast for you!
It is not suitable for the King of Kings
To remain at length in the residence of Zaal."

As the mountains take on hues of sandarac,
The sound of timpani is heard at the palace gate.
The king drives his army from the land of Zabolestan
Toward the land of Iran, land of the brave.

Then he sits joyously on his throne to rest,
Governing the world according to the rules of justice.
He distributes to the poor a wealth of silver.
He brings happiness to some and dissatisfaction to others.

5 | Bahman Weds Homay and Gives Her
the Succession of the Throne

Bahman has a lion-vanquishing son they call Sassan.
He also has a daughter named Homay,
Skilled, knowledgeable, and pure-minded.
Though her name is Homay, they call her Chehrzaad.
The sight of her is her father's delight.
Because of her unrivaled beauty, Bahman decides to wed her.
Such a custom is accepted in the faith of Pahlavi.[77]

This bright moon soon finds herself with the king's child.
In her sixth month, she suffers greatly.
At the sight of her pain, Bahman's health deteriorates
To the point of finding himself on his death bed.

He summons his wife and his auspicious noblemen,
Offers them seats of power, and says,
"Here is Chehrzaad of pure body.
She has not enjoyed much happiness in life.
I bestow to her the crown, the sublime throne,
my treasury, my wealth, and the army's command.
As owner of this crown and belt,
She will succeed me on the throne,
And her successor will be the child
She secretly bears, whether a boy or a girl."

Sassan's mind is troubled by his father's words.
For three days and two nights,
He directs his shame toward another empire like a leopard.
In his despondency, he charges toward the city of Nishapur,
Wishing to be far away from his father.
His goal is to wed a woman from an influential family
While keeping his identity undisclosed.

He finds a woman, grows fond her,
And cherishes her more than his own life.
When she finds herself expecting a child,

◇◇◇◇◇◇◇◇◇◇◇◇◇
77 Inbreeding was acceptable in pre-Islamic Iran and preferred under Zoroastrian
rule. With the advent of Islam, marriage between parents and children and between
sibling was considered incestuous. But it was acceptable for cousins to marry, and it
remains so today.

He refrains from revealing his lineage.
This woman of pure body gives birth to a beautiful child,
A son to the noble Sassan, son of Bahman.
His father also names him Sassan
And passes away suddenly, soon after his birth.

Once this child matures into a man,
He sees in his dwelling only poverty.
He gathers a herd of horses roaming around mountain
And plain and belonging to the King of Nishapur.
He remains at the side of the king as a shepherd,
His home the mountain and the plain.

Now I shall return to the matter of Homay,
Who accedes to Bahman's throne after his death.

The Thirty-Two-Year Reign of Homay, Daughter of Bahman

1 | Homay Abandons Her Son Daaraab Inside a Box on the Euphrates River

Bahman dies of illness at his daughter's court.
Homay, soul charmer, is filled with grief
And mourns her father and husband for days.

She finally emerges, places the crown on her head,
And begins a new life bringing about new customs.
She receives her warriors at court,
Opens the door to the treasury, and distributes dinars.
She surpasses her father in wisdom and justice,
Spreading prosperity throughout the world.

She says, "May this crown be blessed!
May my foes' hearts be plucked out!
May good deeds be my lifelong work!
May no one endure hardship and suffering!
I shall bring wealth to the poor.
The world's noble and wealthy men
Will never have to fear the loss of their fortunes."

She enjoys the imperial throne and being world ruler.
As the time of childbirth nears, she hides from city and army.
She gives birth to a son without telling anyone,
Deeming his birth auspicious only if kept secret.
She summons a wet nurse,
A pure and holy woman, humble and beautiful,
To whom she secretly entrusts her son.
When questioned about her child's fate at court,
She would answer that he had passed away.

She bears the royal crown and sits on the throne,
Happy and victorious. At the slightest adversarial threat,
She dispatches a host to fight.

Anything that occurs in the world,
Whether good or bad, never evades her awareness.
She continues to rule with justice and righteousness
To maintain order in a world that is safe and fair
Under her rule, where everyone everywhere praises her.

In this way, eight months pass.
Her son begins to resemble the deceased king.
Homay orders a carpenter to construct a beautiful box
Out of dry wood to serve delicate matter.
It is to be covered in layers of tar and musk,
The interior chamber softened with Rumi brocade,
And a coating of wax applied to its exterior.

Then the queen places inside a mattress full of pearls,
With a layer of gold, carnelian, and stones of chrysolite.
A jewel worthy of a king is attached to the infant's arm.

At a time when the child falls into a deep slumber,
The nurse of nimble hands places him inside the box,
Wrapping him warmly with a blanket of Chini silk.
They caulk the lid with glue, amber, wax, and musk.
In the middle of the night, a few men silently lift the box
And carry it to the Euphrates River,
To gently deposit it in the rushing waters.

From the shore, the two men follow with their eyes
The box gliding in the current like a boat.
Soon they have to run to keep up with its motions.

As the sun rises over the mountains,
The box is found lodged on the riverbank,
Near a sort of makeshift wash house
Made narrow by a wedged boulder.
A laundryman rushes to pull it out of the water.
He opens it and lifts the wrapping to discover,
To his great surprise, a baby nestled within.
He covers the box with laundry and hastily takes it,
Heart joyous and hopeful, spirit charmed.

At the castle, the two men recount to the baby's mother
How they witnessed the man pick up the box.
The cautious world queen says to them,

"You must keep this secret to yourselves."

2 | The Laundryman Raises Daaraab

The laundryman returns from the river
At an unexpected hour. His wife tells him,
"What a nice harvest you bring!
You return with damp laundry.
Is anyone willing to pay you for the job?"

As it is, the heart of the laundryman
Is devastated by the death of a child,
And his wife does not cease lamenting the loss,
Her cheeks scraped, her soul dim.

The husband says to her, "Be sensible.
You will see that you need no longer weep.
If my worthy mate wishes to keep this matter secret,
I shall tell her all that transpired today.
I spotted a box in the canal,
Near the stone where I beat and rinse my laundry.
When I opened the box, I found a child nestled within.
I shall show him to you.
You will want him once your eyes catch sight of him.
We had a baby boy who did not live long.
He died, and now we find ourselves unexpectedly with a son.
He is covered in brocade and precious jewels."

He deposits the laundry and lifts the lid of the box.
At the sight of the child, his wife is greatly astonished.
She summons the graces of the World Creator.
She discovers a shiny face, akin to the face of King Bahman,
In the midst of cloths of silks and brocade.
The child is surrounded by jewels and gems.
At his feet are stones of carnelian and chrysolite.
Crimson dinars are on his left, stones of rubies on his right.

The woman immediately offers the child her engorged breast.
She is delighted with this infant able to charm her heart.
The beauty of the baby and the wealth in the box
Make her abandon her grief.

The laundryman says to her,
"We must always love him as we love ourselves.
He is the son of an illustrious man
Or perhaps a world king."

The woman adopts the baby as her own.
On the third day, they give him the name of Daaraab,[78]
Since the river had functioned as his cradle.

One day, the woman, who, in her wisdom,
Discusses all sorts of matters with the master of the house,
Says to him, "What will you do with all the jewels?
Wisdom must be your guide in this matter."

The laundryman replies, "O my dear mate,
Hidden gems serve me just as much as dust.
Better for us to leave this town,
Distance ourselves from danger and misery.
Let us go and live in a city where no one knows us,
Where no one knows if we are poor or powerful people."

At dawn, the laundryman prepares for their journey.
They depart without telling anyone of their destination.
They carry Daaraab in their arms,
Taking with them only jewels and gold.

The laundryman leaves his city, travels sixty farsangs,
And selects a home in a different nation.
He settles in a foreign city, appearing to be a rich man.
He approaches a distinguished nobleman
To trade a precious stone for fabrics, gold, and silver.
He continues in this manner until, after some time,
His supply of gemstones is depleted.
Besides the red ruby attached to the baby's arm,
There is nothing left inside the box.

His wife, in all matters his guide, says to him one day,
"Your wealth permits you to refrain from working."

The husband replies, "O my respected mate and advisor,
You can call profession any trade.

◇◇◇◇◇◇◇◇◇◇◇◇◇◇
78 Daaraab: *Aab* means water; *daar* means from.

What is better than a profession?
It is the beginning of something.
Let us raise Daaraab to be pure and kind,
And we shall see the fruit of our actions."

They bring up the child with such affection
That never does a harsh wind reach him.
After the skies revolve around Daaraab's head for some years,
He becomes a noble and strong young man.
He wrestles in the street with youths older than he,
But none of them comes close to his build and power.
All the children ganged up against him appear feeble
In comparison, and so they begin to fear him.

The laundryman bemoans their behavior,
And his hopes dissipate.
He tells the boy, "Beat this laundry on the stone.
It is not shameful for you to learn the trade."

But every time, Daaraab runs away,
And the laundryman sheds blood tears.
He spends half of his time looking for Daaraab
In the city and in the countryside.

One day, the father finds him, bow in hand,
His chest expanding according to the rules,
His thumb armed with the ring.
He seizes the bow from him and coldly says,
"You rascal of a child, you dream only of battle.
Why do you always fool around with bow and arrow?
How could you be so wicked so early on?"

Daaraab replies, "O father, you trouble my waters.
You keep me from attaining fame and glory.
Put me in the hands of wise men.
When I have learned the *Zand Avesta,*
Then you will teach me a trade and morality.
But for now, do not expect me to be serious."

The laundryman criticizes him at length,
Then entrusts his education to masters.
Daaraab learns the sciences, acquires dignity,
And ceases to misbehave and merit reproach.

In the end, he says to his adoptive father,
"O father, I shall never be a laundryman.
Do not allow your affection to cause you grief.
Allow me to become a good equestrian."

The laundryman searches for an able horseman,
Skilled with handling reins and launching a horse,
A renowned man from whom
Daaraab learns all the necessary skills for riding.
He learns how to hold bridle, spear, and shield,
How to urge a horse to flip on the battlefield,
How to emply mallet, bow, and arrow,
And how to steal oneself from an adversary.

The skills he acquires are so valuable
That leopards dare not approach him in battle.

3 | Daaraab Asks the Wife of the Laundryman for His Origins and Declares War on Rum

One day, Daaraab says to the laundryman,
"I have a secret I dare not admit, not even to myself.
You have always expressed affection for me,
Yet my features do not resemble yours in any way.
I am astonished when you call me son
And when you make me sit next to you in your store."

The laundryman replies,
"Your words make me relive ancient adversities.
If your ambition is greater than my condition,
Seek your mother, for your secret belongs to her."

One day, the laundryman leaves early for the river.
Daaraab closes and bolts the door, grasps his sword,
And enters his mother's room. Brandishing his blade,
He says, "Do not try to lie to me or keep me in the dark.
Answer my questions honestly.
What is my relation to you both? What is my birth?
Why do I live with a laundryman and his wife?"

In her terror, the wife asks for mercy

And invokes the protection of the Supreme Master.
She replies, "Do not spill my blood.
I shall answer all your questions."

She relates to him, in great detail and in absolute truth,
The entire story of the box holding the small infant,
Of the dinars and gems worthy of a king.
She adds, "We were mere laborers
And did not have the benefits of a distinguished family.
Thanks to the wealth we found on you,
We were able to acquire all that we presently have
And to emerge from a crippling condition.
We are your slaves and will obey your orders.
Reflect on what you desire.
We are at your command, body and soul."

Daaraab is confused at these words.
He collects himself to contemplate his next move.
After some time, he asks,
"Is there anything left of the fortune
Or has the laundryman drained it all?
Is there enough to purchase a horse
In this lowly state we are in?"

The woman replies, "There is more than enough.
There are coins, an orchard, and some lands."
She hands over the dinars she possesses
And presents to him the precious stone.

Daaraab buys a noble stallion, a cheap saddle, mace and noose.
Heart troubled, he approaches a border guard,
A sensible, powerful man of sound advice.
The commander treats him well and with honor.
Fortune turns favorable for him.

It so happens that a host arrives from the land of Rum
And destroys this beautiful border territory.
The commander is killed in battle,
And his troops are left to disperse without a leader.

When Homay receives the news that Rumi warriors
Have invaded the land, she commands Rashnavaad,
A leader of the lineage of warriors,

To deploy troops against the Rumi perpetrators
And to convert the land to flatland by sword.

Rashnavaad instantly mobilizes an army,
Fixes the place of gathering, and pays tribute.

Upon hearing the news, Daaraab rushes to enlist.
Once numerous troops have gathered from all sides
And corps after corps rush to participate,
Homay exits her imperial castle,
Surrounded by her chiefs, loyal advisors of pure thought.
She surveys the troops as they parade before her
And observes each man closely,
Questioning him on his name and rank.

After some time engaged in the review of troops,
Her eyes at once fall on Daaraab, noble of mien,
Tall of stature, mace of steel on his shoulder.
It is as if he fills the plain with his presence
And the earth buckles beneath his horse's hooves.

At the sight of his chest and his features, able
To charm any heart, milk flows from her maternal breast.
She asks, "Where does this horseman come from,
With such arms, shoulders, and lofty stature?
He appears brave, noble, and skillful in war,
But his weapons are not worthy of him."

After admiring Daaraab's beauty,
She approves the army's outfit.
She selects a day for the entry of the leader's campaign,
According to the stars and to the rules,
And once the army chiefs are unanimous,
They take away the troops.

Homay dispatches sentries to avoid secret maneuvers,
To be aware of the proceedings, open or covert,
Good or bad, to avoid being tormented
By possible mishaps and calamities.

The army advances from station to station.
The earth is covered with troops.
The sky is black with dust.

4 | Rashnavaad Learns the Truth About Daaraab

One day, a tempest rises that troubles Rashnavaad.
Thunder roars continuously, rain and lightning ensue.
The air whisks about, the ground floods, and the sky growls.
Men run in every direction to escape the deluge,
Attempting to set up tents on the plain.

Daaraab is troubled, having no shelter, no friend, no guide.
He seeks refuge from the torrents and comes across
Some ruins in the midst of which is an ancient, lofty dome.
Though battered over time by the elements,
It still stands, royal and tall.

He finds cover in this dilapidated structure,
Alone, deprived of help or companion.

As he makes the rounds of the army,
Rashnavaad passes the damaged dome
And hears a voice rising from the terrifying ruins:
"O decrepit vault, watch over this Iranian king,
Who owns neither tent nor friendly companion,
Who took shelter beneath your ceiling and fell asleep."

Rashnavaad reflects that this must be
Either the sound of thunder or a gust of wind,
But he hears the voice a second time:
"O dome, do not shut wisdom's eye.
You shelter the son of King Bahman.
Do not fear the rain, but pay attention to my words."

Hearing the voice a third time,
Rashnavaad's heart constricts.
He says to a reasonable man, "What could this be?
Someone must enter this place to see who is asleep
Beneath its dome and to determine the source
Of the voice so alarmed and anxious for his life."

Inside they find a young man appearing intelligent,
Bearing a warrior's mien.
His clothing and his horse are drenched.
In this wretched state,
He has made the dark, cold ground his resting place.

Someone reports to Rashnavaad what was observed.
The heart of the leader warrior leaps at the account.
He commands the youth to be immediately
Awakened by a loud and commanding voice.

They enter the dome and say,
"O sleepy man, awaken from your slumber."

Daaraab rises and mounts his horse.
Just as he does so, the dome collapses behind him,
And he closely evades being crushed.
What a remarkable phenomenon!

The queen's army leader looks Daaraab up and down.
Rashnavaad says, "Here is a marvel that confounds me.
We cannot conceive of anything more miraculous!"

He takes off right away toward his own camp, saying,
"O unique Creator, Justice Giver, no one in the world
Has ever seen or heard of such a miracle."

He calls for clothing and the preparation
Of a large tent to rest in.
He lights a fire as large as a mountain,
In which he burns aloe, musk, and amber.

When the sun reveals its head over the mountain crest,
The leader prepares for departure.
He commands the wise men who serve him
As guide to ask for a full set of clothing,
A golden-harnessed Taazian steed,
A belt, and a sword with a golden sheath.

He gives it all to Daaraab, questioning him:
"O man of lion heart, O seeker of glory,
Who are you? What is your lineage? Where is your land?
Reveal to me your origins in absolute truth."

Daaraab reveals to him all that he knows,
Just as the laundryman's wife had related to him,
On the matter of the box, the red jewel at his arm,
The dinars, and the brocade worthy of a royal warrior.
Finally, he recounts to the army chief

The story of his rest and slumber in his hiding place.

Rashnavaad expedites an envoy, to whom he says,
"Go as fast as wind, and bring back the laundryman,
His wife, the gemstone, Venus and Mars."

5 | Daaraab Fights the Rumi Army

After this order, army chief Rashnavaad departs
And brings his troops to the border of Rum.
He entrusts Daaraab with the vanguard.
Armed with vengeful, poisonous spears,
They lead a fierce campaign against Rum.

The border guard advances on his side.
The troops from two kingdoms meet each other,
And the dust of battle instantly stirs.
A wild brawl begins, and a torrent of blood is spilled.

Daaraab, at the sight of the vast host,
Flings himself like a wolf and kills so many Rumi men
That it is as if the sky brandishes a sword.
He continues to strike, as fierce as a lion,
A whale-like weapon in his clutches,
A dragon firmly planted beneath him,
Until he penetrates the Rumi camp as a mad lion.
Propelled by an urgent drive and with his sword
As his only guide, he covers the ground with enemy blood.

He returns victorious to the noble Rashnavaad,
Who showers him with blessings:
"May the queen's army never be robbed of your presence!
When we return to our nation
From this war against the land of Rum,
You will receive from the queen many rewards
In horses and treasure, thrones and helmets."

The army spends the night preparing for war,
The warriors diligently polishing their weapons.
When the sun raises its head above the darkened heights
And the earth is lit by a majestic torch, two hosts advance.

The dust they stir obscures the light of day.

Daaraab launches himself against the enemy
And abandons the reins to his fervent charger.
He allows no one from the Rumi camp to remain alive.
Only a few brave warriors escape the stroke of his sword.
He enters the army core like a wolf and scatters the troops.
Then he assails and wins over the right wing,
And he brings back much armor and loot.
He breaks the ranks of the Rumi troops.
None of the warriors retains the courage to carry on.

The brave men of Iran valiantly jump
Like lions in the traces and kill many Rumi warriors.
The blood converts the dust to mud on the battlefield.
Among the enemy, Daaraab kills forty bishops
And returns holding a cross in his hand.

Rashnavaad observes Daaraab's astonishing feats.
The heart of the hero leaps with joy.
He blesses him, praises him, and showers him
With even more expressions of friendship.

Night descends.
The world deepens in shades of tar.
They abandon the battlefield.

The leader Rashnavaad rests in the Rumi camp.
He unfastens his coat of mail.
He distributes precious items to his company.

He sends someone to Daaraab to say,
"O man of lion heart, always obliging and esteemed,
Look among these valuables and see what pleases you.
Distribute the rest according to your heart's impulse,
For you are more illustrious than was Rakhsh's master!"

Daaraab is pleased with the message.
He selects a spear from the heap
And returns the rest to Rashnavaad with a message:
"May you always be happy and victorious!"

The moment the sun's face gives way to darkness

And the sky dons its velvety black silken robe,
Rashnavaad sends sentries on the plain to patrol.
Their cries erupt like earthquakes,
Forcing roaming lions to scamper off.

As the sun lifts its golden shield, warriors awaken.
The brave men of Iran dress in armor
And lunge in pursuit of the Rumis,
Reigniting the blaze of battle with their sharp swords.
They burn cities, demolish and devastate the land.
The Rumis are annihilated,
And no one speaks further of this realm.

A great cry of distress rises among the Rumi warriors
As they leave the place that charmed their souls.
This war constricts the world,
And the Caesar's heart fills with hostility.
The face of his noblemen pale.

An envoy arrives at the side of Rashnavaad to tell him:
"May the fair queen remain within the limits of justice!
Those who longed for war are now weary.
The fortune of the land of Rum has dimmed.
If you ask for tribute, we shall obey and pay.
We are willing to draw a new treaty with you."

The Caesar sends a variety of offerings,
Chests filled with gold, and many slaves.
The leader accepts the gold and untouched jewels.

6 | Homay Recognizes Her Son

The acclaimed Daaraab and Rashnavaad
Travel joyously in the direction of Iran's court.
At one of the stations, they come across the ruined dome
In which Rashnavaad had found Daaraab sleeping.
The laundryman and his wife arrive with the gemstone,
Trembling with fear at the thought of being mistreated.

Rashnavaad summons them to his side.
They appear, invoking Yazdan's protection.

The leader questions them in detail.
They recount from memory the story of the box,
The fortune within, and the pure untouched stone.
They recount with pain the education of the child,
The trouble they faced, and the worries they sustained.

Rashnavaad says to them,
"May you both be victorious and happy!
No one in the world has ever seen such a marvel,
Nor has anyone heard such an astonishing tale."

Rashnavaad of pious heart writes a letter to Homay
On the subject of Daaraab, of the storm,
Of the place where Daaraab took shelter,
And of his feats and heroics on the battlefield.
He relates the account of the laundryman and his wife,
The story of the box, the jewels, the voice he heard,
And the fear that ensued when the dome collapsed.
He recounts everything up to the time
When Daaraab climbed on his horse.

He expedites a messenger, as swift as wind,
With the letter and the red jewel, saying,
"You must gallop in tandem with the wind!"

The envoy rushes off like a gust of storm,
Reaches Queen Homay, and delivers the letter
And the jewel, and summarizes the account he received.

Homay reads the letter and observes the gem,
And warm tears rush down her cheeks.
She recognizes the young, handsome hero
With rosy spring cheeks and a tall stature,
Whom she saw the day she reviewed the army.
She recognizes him as her innocent, noble son,
The valuable branch of her bountiful lineage.

Sobbing, she says to the envoy,
"A new ruler is about to reign upon the world.
My mind continuously agonized over his fate.
I never ceased to have qualms over the empire's destiny.
My heart was full of trepidation before the Supreme Judge,
Since I displayed signs of ingratitude and impiety.

The Creator had given me a son, whom I did not recognize,
A son I cast away into the rapid flows of the Euphrates River
After fastening this very jewel to his arm,
A son already mistreated, deprived of a father.
Now Yazdan returns him to me with a glorious name,
Acquired in the footsteps of Rashnavaad."

She showers the people of the land with a wealth of dinars.
Precious stones are blended with wine and musk
To give alms to those in need.

For one more week, Homay opens her silver treasury
And distributes to the fire temples of the land,
Dwellings of the *Zand Avesta* and the feast of Saddeh.
She widens her reach to spread her generosity
Out into the far corners of the provinces.

On the tenth day, early in the morning,
The leader Rashnavaad, in the company of Daaraab,
Revealing to no one their secret,
Arrive at the queen's court with noble warriors.

7 | Homay Places Daaraab on the Throne

The queen lowers the draperies of her audience hall,
Allowing no one entry for the duration of one week.
The world mistress prepares a golden platform,
Two thrones inlaid with turquoise and lapis lazuli,
A crown inset with precious gems, worthy of a king,
Two bracelets, an exquisite torque set with jewels,
And a royal robe of golden brocade embroidered with gems.

An astrologer, seated before the queen,
Scans the stars to find a propitious day.
On the morning of the fourth day of the month of Bahman,[79]
The queen receives Daaraab at court.
She fills a cup with rubies and another one with yellow gold.

Upon Daaraab's entrance into the audience hall,

79 Bahman: The eleventh month of the solar year.

The queen approaches him, receives him majestically,
And pays homage to him by showering him with royal stones.
Blood tears spill from her cheeks onto her breasts.
She holds the young man close in her arms,
Kisses him, and strokes his face with her hand.
Her eyes fixed on his features,
She leads him to the golden throne.
Once Daaraab is seated, his mother kisses his face,
Lifts the royal crown, and places it on his head.
She announces to the world his right to bear the diadem.

The splendor of the crown on Daaraab's head
Touches Homay, and she begs forgiveness:
"Please forgive my past deeds. Dismiss them
To youth, fortune, and other womanly thoughts,
Your father's passing, the court being vacant.
If my actions caused you harm, do not give in to them.
May you always have a seat upon the throne!"

Daaraab replies to his mother,
"You originate from the race of monarchs.
It is not surprising that your heart simmered with ambition.
Do not bemoan a poorly thought-out undertaking.
May the Creator grant you divine grace!
May your enemies' hearts fill with anguish!
What occurred in the past will be my future glory
And will never be erased from the tablets of history."

Homay invokes divine blessings upon him
And cries, "May you live as long as the world exists!"

Then she commands the grand wise master
To summon sages from many provinces,
As well as illustrious, sword-wielding warriors,
And ask them to pay homage to the famous world master.

They summon divine grace on the king's crown
And scatter gems on the new throne,
And Homay recounts her secret deeds
And their distressing, damaging consequences.
She adds, "Remember that he is the only heir
Left in the world to King Bahman.
You must obey him, for he is the shepherd

While brave warriors are the sheep.
Power, crown, and royalty are his,
For he is the support of the people."

A clamorous cry resounds welcoming the proclamation.
The assembly acknowledges the new royal branch.
Everyone scatters countless jewels on the king
And watches him disappear beneath the heaps.
The world is renewed with joy and justice.
No one lends further thought to pain and worry.

Homay says to the wise men, "O illustrious sages,
I abandon to him what firmly held my attention
During the thirty-two years of my reign:
The imperial throne and my treasury.
Now live in peace, be happy, and obey him."

Daaraab is placed on the throne,
Joyously sporting the crown,
When the laundryman and his wife approach him.
They say, "O young king,
May the Kianian throne be your delight!
May your enemies turn into slaves!"

Daaraab asks for ten pouches of gold and precious gems
And five selections of various clothing, and offers the lot
To the two who raised him with much effort.
He says, "Go and resume your profession as laundryman.
Apply yourself to your trade. Perhaps one day
You will come across another box with a baby."

They emerge from Iran's royal palace,
Uttering blessings on him in a common voice.
The laundryman returns to his wash basin
At the riverbank in the countryside.

The Twelve-Year Reign of Daaraab, Son of Bahman and Homay

1 | Daaraab Founds the City of Daaraab-Guerd

Let us implore the benedictions of the Creator
On the world king, Abul Ghassem, the sun-faced ruler,
Who brings joy to his people
Through his justice and generosity,
King of Kings Mahmoud, blessed with good fortune,
Owner of crown and throne.
He is driven only by truth and righteousness.
May his crown shine upon the world!
May he remain young as long as there is youth!
May he live for as long as there is life!
What does the poet say, the aging bard,
On the reigns of Goshtaasp, the valiant Bahman,
Illustrious heroes of pure intentions,
Of Daaraab and the ways in which Homay acted?

On the Kianian throne, Daaraab cinches his waist,
Ready for battle, and opens his hand to give liberally.
He says to his prudent and illustrious wise men,
"I have not yet conquered the world with my labors,
Yet the Creator placed the crown upon my head.
Never has there been word in public or in secret
Of a destiny more astonishing than mine.
I can only be worthy of it by exercising justice,
So that I am remembered and glorified after my death.
No one must suffer at my hands.
I wish to be exalted and to amass vast wealth.
May the earth be harvested in the shelter of my reign!
May my subjects' hearts be happy with my rule!"

People come from rich and inhabited lands,
From India to Rum, with presents and offerings
To benefit from the king's benevolence.

One day, he leaves his court to survey
His herds of steeds roaming freely in the fields.
He travels from the plain to the mountain,
Where he sees a deep and wide river.
He summons skilled experts from Rum and India
To assess one of the riverbanks, where a canal
May be forged to transport water to various lands.
Once the deed is done, he commands men
To build nearby a prosperous city to be named
Daaraab-Guerd. Its walls quickly go up.

He has a holy fire kindled on the mountain crest,
And fire worshippers gather there in hordes.
Artisans from all forms of life come to finish
The construction of his city.

Then Daaraab sends countless troops in various directions
To protect the world against any possible adversary.
He liberates his people from fear of evil men
And splits in half the hearts of evildoers.

2 | Daaraab Vanquishes Shoaib's Army

One hundred thousand Taazian spear-riders
Arrive with their leader, Shoaib,
An illustrious man from the Ghotaib lineage,
To raise the black dust over the land of Iran
And, with their power, seize the crown and throne.

The Iranian king summons such a vast host
That estimating the number of troops would be in vain.
The warring men confront each other.
The world fills with terror.
The earth can hardly bear their weight.
The mass of men leaves no space to pass or walk.

A deluge of javelins and arrows
Converts the ground into a blood-filled lake.
Cries rise on all fronts.
Heaps of corpses mount here and there.
The battle lasts three days and three nights,

Constricting the world for the wounded.

On the fourth night, the Arabs turn around and retreat.
Shoaib is killed, and their fortune dies with him.

Numerous Taazian stallions with saddles of poplar wood,
Numerous lances and spears, helmets, and coats of mail,
Abandoned by the withdrawing army,
Fall into the hands of the world king, son of Homay.

He distributes horses, spears, swords, and helmets to his troops.
Then he picks out a leader to guard the border,
One able to hear and speak the language.
He sends him to collect tribute from the land of spear-riders
For the present year as well as for the past.

3 | Daaraab Battles Filghoos and Weds His Daughter

Daaraab leaves the field of spear-riders to travel to Rum,
Where he leads a war on cultivated lands.

Filghoos, King of Rum, writes a letter
To his ally the King of Rus[80] with the news
That the son of Homay is on his way with a vast host.

The Rumi ruler remembers the events
That occurred long ago. He mobilizes an army
Of renowned warriors from Amoorieh.[81]

As Daaraab invades the land, he forces
The brave Rumi warriors to surrender the border,
But Filghoos and his leaders emerge
From Amoorieh bold and eager for war.

Two great battles ensue in the span of three days.
On the fourth day, as the illuminating sun rises,
Filghoos and his host abscond,
Leaving no one bearing a Rumi helmet on the field.
Their women and children are taken captive.

◇◇◇◇◇◇◇◇◇◇◇◇◇
80 Rus: Ancient name for Russia.
81 Amoorieh: A Rumi city that no longer exists but would be in present-day Turkey.

PART TWENTY

A great number of their warriors are killed by arrows.

They run away from Daaraab, fleeing to the cities,
Where only two-thirds of them return.
The other troops are either dead or wounded,
Spears wedged into their backs.

They retreat behind the walls of Amoorieh.
A great number of them wish to settle for peace.
An envoy is dispatched by Filghoos,
A sensible, wise man, gracious and soft-spoken.
He brings with him slaves, crates of gold,
And two boxes full of gems worthy of a king.
Here is the message it contains:
"I plead with the Creator to be my Guide.
Let us end this struggle with a feast.
Let us turn our dim hearts away from war.
In all things, one must exercise virtue and humanity.
Lies and greed only lead to one's demise.
If you seek to conquer Amoorieh, which is my capital,
Be careful, for my heart simmers
To maintain my name and my honor.
I shall engage in battle, even if the time calls for feast.
Act in the manner suitable for kingship,
As your father was king and his son succeeds him as king."

Daaraab listens, summons his noblemen,
And discusses with them the affair, adding,
"What are your thoughts?
Filghoos wishes to safeguard his honor."

The council invokes divine blessings on him and says,
"O insightful King of pure faith,
The King of Kings is the authority.
He will decide which course of action to take.
This ruler has a daughter of cypress stature,
With cheeks as rosy as spring.
Nowhere in the world does one find
A more charming person, not even in Chin.
She shines in the midst of idols like a gleaming gem.
Should his majesty set his sights on her,
She would greatly please him.

She is a lofty cypress tree that he would yearn
To transplant into his own garden."

The king summons the Rumi messenger
And says to him all that he learned from his friends,
Telling him, "Return to the Caesar and say,
        'This is how you can safeguard your honor.
        You have in your night chambers a young woman
        Who is the diadem on the forehead of queens.
        She is the one you call Nahid,
        Whom you have placed on the golden throne.
        Send her to me as tribute from Rum
        If you wish to remain in possession of your land.'"

After hearing him out, the envoy departs
As swift as wind to report back to the Caesar.
Filghoos is overjoyed to be offered
A son-in-law of royal descent.

They debate at length on the nature of the tribute
And what Rum is able to afford.
In the end, they agree that the king will receive
Every year from the Caesar, in the month of Mehr,
Ten thousand golden eggs and various precious gems.
Every egg must weigh forty mithqals,[82]
And the gems are to be of great value.

Filghoos liberally distributes jewels
To various governors of cultivated Rumi provinces.
Then he commands his learned men and border owners
To construct the road and dismiss all other matters.

The noblemen, each bearing an offering,
Depart with the king's daughter.
A golden litter is set up for her.
Slaves, worthy of diadems, are selected as her escort.
Ten camels are loaded with Rumi brocade,
Embroidered with gems and pure gold,
And three hundred more are loaded with carpets
And the necessary baggage to make the voyage.

◇◇◇◇◇◇◇◇◇◇◇◇◇◇
82 Mithqal: Unit of weight equivalent to 4.25 grams, often used to weigh precious
metal.

The beautiful Rumi princess sits in the golden litter.
A bishop and a number of priests serve her as guides.
Behind Nahid are sixty young women, as beautiful as idols,
Bearing diadem and earrings, each holding in her hand
A golden cup brimming with royal jewels.

The bishop hands over the princess to Daaraab
And the jewels to his treasurer to assess.
After that, Daaraab does not linger on the battlefield.
He returns his host to the land of Iran,
Happily taking the direction of his palace in Pars
With his fair-faced woman able to charm dim hearts.
Once there, he places the crown of power on his head.

4 | Daaraab Returns Nahid to Rum, and She Gives Birth to Eskandar[83]

One night, as the moon is asleep at the king's side,
Decked in jewels, all color, scent and beauty,
It so happens that she breathes heavily,
And the King of Kings is repelled by her stench.
He turns his head away and withdraws his face.
His eyebrows knitted with worry, he despairs.

An ingenuous and sensible man examines the queen
Until he finds an effective remedy that burns her mouth.
He grinds a certain plant with the name of Eskandar.
He applies the ground mixture to Nahid's palate
And burns it down as she sheds copious tears.
The queen's bad breath is gone; her palate is burned.
Despite the scent of musk that she exudes,
Daaraab remains distressed, and his love wanes
As his heart has grown cold toward this woman.
He sends her away, returning her to Filghoos.

Though she is with child, Nahid speaks of it to no one.
After nine months, she gives birth to a son as bright
As the shining sun whom she calls Eskandar because
Of his stature, his beauty, and the fragrance his chest exudes.

◇◇◇◇◇◇◇◇◇◇◇◇◇
83 Eskandar: The Persian equivalent to Alexander.

She believes this name will bring good fortune
Since the herb called Eskandar cured her of bad breath.

Her father, Filghoos, King of Rum, declares to noblemen:
"A Caesar is born of my lineage!"

No one utters Daaraab's name.
Eskandar is deemed the son and the Caesar the father,
For Filghoos is ashamed to admit
That Daaraab was the one who sent his wife away.

At the time of Eskandar's birth from his holy mother,
The grandfather is given the good news.
In his stables is a pale-colored mare, fast and
Tall of stature, who could be trusted in times of need.
On the same night, she gives birth to a white foal
Bearing the breast of a lion and short pasterns.

The Caesar raises his arms to the sky at the news
Of this birth, which he considers a good omen.
At dawn, he asks for the child and the mare to be decked,
And he gently strokes the foal's mane.
This creature has the same age as Eskandar.

The sky revolves for some time,
And years go by, times both happy and sad.

Eskandar grows accustomed to thinking
Like a king and speaking like a warrior.
The Caesar cheers him on even more than his own son
And enjoys passing time decorating his warrior chest.

Eskandar acquires prudence and learns worldly affairs.
He is smart, solemn, and sagacious.
Filghoos names him his successor.
Eskandar is kind and loving toward him.
He learns kingly duties from his master.
It is as if he is born to exercise justice,
Occupy a throne, and found an empire.

Meanwhile, as Nahid returns to her father,
Daaraab weds another woman, from whom is born
Another son, full of majesty and power

But one year younger than Eskandar, Nahid's son.
On the day of his birth, they assign him the name of Dara,
With wishes for his fortune to surpass his father's.

After twelve years, Daaraab's fortune and force decline.
Homay's brilliant son feels a pull toward another dwelling.
He unites his noblemen and wise men, and speaks to them
At length on the subject of the throne of power:
"The time has come for Dara, son of Daaraab,
To be your benevolent guide.
Listen to his counsel. Obey his will.
Put your heart's delight in the execution of his commands.
The royal throne does not belong eternally to anyone.
When a new joy enters the scene, one must swiftly depart.
Make every effort to be kind and just.
Remember me with fondness."

He murmurs his last words, sighs,
And this leaf of a pomegranate tree
Pales and fades, light as the flower of fenugreek.

The Fourteen-Year Reign of Dara, Son of Daaraab

1 | Dara Succeeds His Father on the Throne

After mourning his father, Dara,
A young man full of wrath and seriousness,
With a tongue sharper than his sword,
Elevates the Kianian crown to the sun.

He takes his seat on the throne and declares,
"O army leaders, highborn, valiant warriors,
I have no need for anyone who dwells in a lowly state.
I shall refuse access to the throne and crown
To those who wallow in a state of despair and misery.
If I discover someone who has disobeyed me,
May his body long to disclaim his head!
If any of you allows falsity to rule over his soul,
I shall pluck his heart out with my sword.
If anyone possesses treasure,
I want him to enjoy the fruits of his labors.
I have no need for guide or counselor,
For I am your guide and counselor.
I am the author of all your heart's joys.
Your nourishment, your portions,
And your duty come from me.
Power, command, empire, and world are mine."

He summons a wise scribe and speaks to him at length.
They compose a biting letter in the name of Dara,
Son of Daaraab, son of Bahman, dispatched
To every prince in every independent province:
"Anyone who fails to observe my will and command
Will witness my ability to make heads fly.
Obey my orders no matter what they are:
Whether it is to take another man's life
Or to surrender your own."

He opens the doors to his father's treasury,

Mobilizes troops, and dispenses up to eight dirhams
Per month to some, instead of the usual four.
To others, he gives a cupful of dirhams,
And to others, washbasins packed with them.

He distributes coins, gold, silver, strappings,
Armor, swords, and heavy maces.
He assigns a region to each worldly leader.
He empowers one of his illustrious chiefs
With the jurisdiction of the borders.
Every warrior is given something of value.

From every land, from every ruler and prince,
From India and Rum, from the Faghfoor of Chin
To the Tarkhan, envoys arrive bearing gifts and tribute.
No one dares stand up to or challenge Dara.

He builds a city he calls Zarnoosh,
And everyone in the land of Ahvaz rejoices.
He treats the poor with justice
And opens his treasury to many who beseech him.

2 | The Death of Filghoos
and the Accession of Eskandar

Around this time, Filghoos dies.
The land of Rum plunges into a state of affliction.
Eskandar climbs onto his grandfather's throne.
He aspires to reign with justice and benevolence,
And endeavors to enchain the hand of evil.

There lives an illustrious Rumi man,
Revered by everyone, the wise Arastalis,[84]
Who is prudent and extremely ambitious.
This sensible man presents himself at court
To engage in conversation with him:
"O blessed King, beware of your actions,
Or else your fame will taper before your people.
The imperial throne has seen many a ruler,

◇◇◇◇◇◇◇◇◇◇◇◇◇◇
84 Arastalis: Aristotle.

But it does not remain for anyone.
Every time you say,
        'I have arrived, I no longer need a guide,'
Every time you disregard the counsel of wise men,
You will be deemed the most foolish person.
We come from dust and are born to return to dust.
Our bodies belong to the earth.
If you act with generosity and righteousness,
You will govern with much happiness
And your reputation will outlive you.
On the other hand, if you act with ill intention,
You will reap the fruits of misery,
And you will not sleep in this world peacefully.
A king glorifies himself by virtuous deeds.
No one ever attains happiness with evil acts."

Eskandar approves of these words.
He draws near the eloquent sage and attempts
To follow his advice in all matters, whether in feast
Or in battle during the sweeping actions of war.
He receives him every day with renewed joy
And offers him a seat next to him.

One day, a Persian messenger, dispatched by Dara,
An articulate man of peaceful heart,
Arrives to demand tribute for the cultivated lands.
He delivers the message to Eskandar,
Who is pitched into a fit of fury.
He replies, "Return to Dara and tell him,
        'This tribute is a thing of the past.
            The hen that lays golden eggs has died
            And has taken with her the funds necessary to pay.'"

The response frightens the envoy, who rushes away
And quickly disappears from Rum.

Eskandar gathers his leaders and speaks of earlier deeds:
"Man, no matter how good his intentions,
Cannot surrender to the revolving dome.
I must force the world to submit to my will.
I must experience all there is of good and ill fortune.
Prepare yourselves, leave your lands,

Renounce any sort of recreation.
We must engage in rebuilding Rum."

The noblemen bow down, faces brushing the ground.
They say, "We are your slaves,
Ready to sacrifice our heads at the Caesar's command."

Eskandar opens the doors to his grandfather's treasury
And instructs the army to be at the ready.
They gather herds of horses roaming free
And bring them in from the plain.
Anyone on foot is supplied a horse, weapons, and gifts.

At dawn, a great rumor rises from the young king's
City and palace to spread across the land.
Eskandar marches off brandishing a banner
With a handle of bamboo, sporting the image of Homa.
Turquoise in color and with writing in red, it reads:
 "We are friends of the blessed cross."

From Rum to Egypt, Eskandar drives an army
With pomp and circumstance, clarions and trumpets,
An army so vast ants and flies cannot cross its path.

The King of Egypt leads a vengeful host toward them.
Two hosts from two sides meet.
They engage in battle for seven days.

On the eighth day, the Egyptians are vanquished.
Eskandar bars the road to the defectors.
At one blow, so many prisoners are seized that
The hands of the conquerors are too few to restrain them.
So much wealth is seized
That the horses can barely carry the loads:
Maces, horses, strappings, coats of mail,
Indian daggers, golden belts and golden bridles,
Egyptian swords of golden sheaths, brocade, and dinars.
A great number of riders, renowned and illustrious,
Surrender by pleading for mercy and protection.

Eskandar prepares to invade the land of Iran.
He feels as if he has a lion's heart and a warrior's hand.

At the news of an army marching from Rum
Toward his empire, Dara musters a host so vast
That countless spears obstruct the wind's path.
Troops ride out of Estakhr toward Rum
In the hopes of invading the land from the border out.

Dara leads his host to the edge of the Euphrates,
With troops more numerous than blades of grass.
They settle on the riverbank in a way as to make
The water disappear beneath the mass of armor.

3 | Eskandar Visits Dara as His Own Ambassador

The moment Eskandar hears of the approach
Of the enemy host, he marches off to meet its commander.
There is a space of two farsangs between the camps.
Eskandar convenes his noble leaders,
Who relate to him Dara's words and message.

After listening to his counselors,
Eskandar says, "I have but one option,
And that is to approach him as an ambassador.
This is the only way to gauge his secrets."

He asks for a belt encrusted with jewels worthy of a king,
A royal robe finely trimmed, a noble horse of golden bridle,
And a sword with a golden sheath to hang on the saddle.
He selects an escort of ten eloquent Rumi interpreters
And exits his camp at first light.

Once in the presence of the illustrious Dara,
He dismounts and pays tribute to him.

The world master asks him to approach, questions him,
And offers him a seat near his throne.

The Iranian noblemen are in awe of Eskandar
And secretly praise him because of his astounding
Beauty and nobility, his stature,
His majestic mien, and the force of his limbs.

Eskandar sits for a moment, then rises

And delivers the message from the Caesar.
He begins by invoking divine grace on Dara:
"O glorious King, your will is obeyed everywhere.
I have no desire to fight with his majesty,
Neither do I wish to remain in Iran for long.
I long to tread the earth and see the world.
My intentions are right and good,
In view of the fact that you sit on the throne of Iran.
But if you refuse me passage through your land,
Reflect on the fact that I cannot roam like a cloud.
You have marched against me with a host,
Without having knowledge of my innocent intentions
Or anything that concerns me and my land.
If you declare war on me, I shall fight you.
I shall not exit your land without dealing severe blows.
Select a day for battle, do not miss the rendezvous,
And do not forsake your resolve.
I shall not recoil and retreat before a prince,
No matter how vast his host."

Dara observes the courage and the wisdom,
The eloquence, the dignity, and the stature of the envoy.
It is as if this man is Dara himself,
Seated on his ivory throne, in all his majesty,
With his bracelets, torque, and crown.
He replies, "What is your name, and what is your birth?
In your appearance and on your forehead,
I observe the imprint of the Kianian race.
You appear to be greater than a simple subject.
I have a sense that you may be Eskandar.
It is obvious from your features, stature, and words
That the skies have groomed you to bear the crown."

The envoy responds, "Never did such a thing occur,
Neither in times of peace nor in times of war.
In Eskandar's court, there are plenty of eloquent men
Who are the crown on the heads of wise rulers.
How would a renowned king from a powerful land
Come to deliver his own message?
Eskandar is too sensible
To diverge from his forefathers' strict rules.
My master charged me with this missive

In accordance with royal ways and customs.
I have thus delivered it, just as I received it."

A dwelling worthy of the envoy's rank is prepared.
Once the spread is served, the Iranian king
Asks his chamberlain to summon the envoy,
Who is assigned a seat suitable to ambassadors.

After supper, an assembly is formed with wine and music.
Eskandar drinks and places the empty cup to the side.
The amount of wine poured is excessive.

The cupbearer tells Dara,
"Your guest is inseparable from his cup."

The king commands that he ask him why.
Upon the king's insistence, the cupbearer enquires,
"O man of royal mien, why do you hold on to your cup?"

Eskandar replies, "Because cups are given
To ambassadors, men of decent reputation.
If the Iranian custom is otherwise,
Return the cup to the king's treasury."

Dara laughs at this custom and asks for a cup
Full of jewels fit for a king and topped with a ruby
To be given to the alleged ambassador.

At that moment, the men who had left for Rum
To demand tribute return to the palace
And respectfully approach the king at the banquet.
Their leader recognizes the features of Eskandar
And tells King Dara, "This is the Caesar himself,
The man who sits on the throne with scepter and crown.
When the king commanded us to ask him for tribute,
This man grew infuriated and treated us indignantly,
Dangling the threat of war over our heads.
I fled his kingdom in the dark night.
Never did we see anyone like him in Rum.
He boldly entered our land to spy on your army,
Your fortune, your throne and crown."

The king hears out his envoy and closely observes Eskandar.

But the latter comprehends what is happening.
He awaits the close of the day and the sun's descent.
Then he marches toward the entrance
To the king's pavilion, climbs on his valiant horse,
And tells his illustrious riders of auspicious star,
"Our lives now depend on our steeds.
If they grow weary, we are lost."
They launch their horses of winded feet
And bolt out of the world master's camp.

When Dara finds out Eskandar has disappeared,
He sends his guards into his enemy's tents.
But at their arrival, the prudent king had left,
For his fortune is not asleep,
As is the fortune of the Iranian king.

Dara sends one thousand brave horsemen after Eskandar.
They lunge like wind but find no trace of him in the night.
They encounter an enemy patrol, and they return,
Having gained nothing but the weariness of a long chase.

Once Eskandar is back in his tent pavilion,
The Rumi leaders gather around him.
In the dark night, they find their king gratified
And, before him, eight cups full of precious gems.
He says to the warriors, "Enjoy this favor from fate.
This cup is a conquest, led at the risk of my life.
The stars dutifully obey my command.
I have counted the number of his troops,
Which is well below what we had heard.
Draw your swords of battle; advance on the field.
Our bodies will exert effort in this war.
It will be a weariness that will reward us
With the kingdom and its treasury.
The Creator is my support I embrace good fortune."

The warriors acclaim him:
"May the earth flourish under the Caesar's rule!
We offer you the sacrifice of our bodies and souls.
Such is our eternal loyalty to your highness!
Who would dare compare himself to you,
In courage, in stature, or in stateliness?"

4 | Dara Wages War on Eskandar and Is Vanquished

The sun lifts its head above the crow's dark night.
Brightening the earth with its golden torch.
Dara, world master, mobilizes his army,
And the earth is enveloped in a veil of tar.

The king bids his troops to cross the Euphrates.
They advance on the plain in greater numbers
Than there are blades of grass.

Eskandar, once aware of the approach of the Iranians,
Asks for the beating of drums and leads his Rumi host.
The earth is a mountainous sea of dust,
So numerous are the weapons, warriors, coats of mail,
Indian swords, chargers, horses, and strappings.

The two hosts form their lines of battle.
The sun draws its heat from daggers.
Before the troops are the elephants,
Who set the ground in motion like the flow of the Nile.
The valiant riders form a row behind the elephants,
Each having renounced his life.

It is as if the air weeps blood,
Forcing the earth to boil beneath the tears.
The din of clarions and bells makes the ground leap.
You would think the world is a mountain of tar
As the dust blackens the face of the sky,
And the air fills with the clamor of horses' neigh,
The leader's shouts, and the crashes of heavy mace

For seven days, the warriors, full of ardor,
Battle each other face to face.
On the eighth day, a black dust stirs into the air,
Rendering the sun the color of lapis lazuli
And covering the eyes of the Iranian warriors in a way
That they can hardly perceive the ground on the battlefield.

Dara, world master, turns his back to flee,
And, with him, his brave warriors
Leap into the rushing waters of the Euphrates River.

Eskandar's troops pursue them.
One side suffers defeat; the other is jubilant with victory.
At the edge of the river, countless Iranians are killed.
The Rumi host deserts the riverside
And triumphantly returns to camp.

5 | The Second Battle of Dara and Eskandar

Expanding the space between his host and Eskandar,
Dara sends riders to all corners of the land,
Convenes leaders and noblemen from Iran and Tooran,
Distributes wealth, and calls upon the treasurer.

At the start of the new moon, he prepares a fresh host
And fills the heads of illustrious men with trust.
He returns to the river, crosses it with troops,
And settles on the large plain.

At the news, Eskandar sets his troops in motion,
Marching toward Dara, leaving the baggage behind.

As the two hosts come face to face,
The entire world is seized by the heat of war.
For three days, the battle progresses with such violence
That no place is left for the countless corpses.
Under an auspicious star,
Eskandar is once again victorious.

Many Iranians are killed and many abscond,
But the Iranian king continues to fight awhile longer,
Until he realizes that fortune has decidedly forsaken him,
As he is left clutching only wind and shame.
Seeing that the sun and moon refuse to assist him,
He deserts the battlefield in deep pain.

Eskandar follows him, as swift as dust,
Giving continuous thanks to the World Creator.
Heralds precede the army with proclamations:
"O misguided subjects, do not fear any harm.
My troops have no qualms with you.
Remain in your homes and live in peace.

Gather your faith in Yazdan for nurturing your life
And body, and for being spared by the Rumi troops,
Even if you have dipped your hands in blood."

The Iranian warriors, reassured, turn to Eskandar
For protection and turn their hopes in the direction of Rum.
Eskandar goes onto the battlefield, gathers the loot,
And distributes the valuables to his troops,
Who feel renewed, rewarded, and bedecked.
The Rumi king remains in this land
To rest for some time with his men.

World ruler Dara arrives in Jahrom,[85]
The seat of his treasury.
His noblemen return to him, full of grief.
Fathers weep over the loss of sons.
Sons weep over the loss of fathers.
The entire nation of Iran is filled with lament,
And a deluge of tears spills from eyes.

From Jahrom, Dara takes the direction of Estakhr,
Which is the glory of the land of Iran.

Messengers are dispatched to all corners
To reach noblemen and army warriors.
Everyone gathers at the king's court.
Dara sits on a golden throne
With his loyal subjects around him.

In his sadness, he says to the Iranians,
"O powerful men, wise and prudent champions,
Tell me how to proceed under these circumstances."
He weeps for a long time, then adds,
"It is far better to die today in glory
Than to continue on while the enemy rejoices.
During the time of my ancestors,
The Iranian kings demanded tribute every year,
And the Rumi Caesars complied in every way.
But today, the fortune of our people is jeopardized
By Eskandar, who seeks royal power and conquer domination.
He proclaims himself sovereign

◇◇◇◇◇◇◇◇◇◇◇◇◇
85 Jahrom: A city in the Iranian province of Fars.

By placing the crown on his head.
But even that is not enough for him.
His intention is to convert the land of Pars into a sea of blood.
He will reduce men, women, and children to captivity,
Allowing neither young nor old to remain in this land.
If you wish to come to my aid, I shall overturn
Our pain, our worries, and the threat of ruin."

Having fallen victim to the powerful Rumi warriors,
The king's men tremble for the destruction of Iran.
"Today, we are the prey and they are the leopards.
We are the ones forced to flee in every fight.
We must support each other
So that we may seize the lost provinces.
Anyone who wishes to withdraw from this battle
Must fight nevertheless, even if only for the love of life.
Otherwise, give up your wishes on the world.
Rum has become Zahaak, and Iran is Jamsheed."
He says this while shedding bitter tears of grief,
His cheeks pale, his lips a depe shade of blue.

The noblemen, full of sense, rise to answer him.
A cry of anguish echoes over the audience hall:
"We have no desire for an empire devoid of king!
We shall engage in battle, constrict the world for our foes.
We shall tie together the hems of our coats of mail
And conquer all, to gain either tomb or empire."

Seeing his troops and noblemen voice
Their readiness to surrender hearts and lives for war,
Dara distributes weapons and dinars to them.

6 | The Third Battle of Dara and Eskandar, and Dara's Flight to Kerman

As Eskandar learns of the actions of Dara
And how he sits upon the throne,
Shining as bright as the moon's diadem,
He leads his army out of Iraq and advances,
Invoking Yazdan's name in the Rumi language.
His host has neither middle nor end,

Yet fortune is not propitious to Dara,
Who prepares to meet Eskandar.
He marches out of Estakhr with a host so massive
It is as if the earth cannot bear the weight
And the sky is hindered by the motion.

The two hosts converge, forming two lines of warriors
Armed with spear, mace, and sword.
On both sides rises a clamor so loud
It pierces the ear of the dome of sky.
The ground becomes a sea of blood
Shed by brave world warriors.
The field of vengeance is strewn with headless corpses.
Fathers forget their affection for sons,
And the turning skies show no mercy.

Night falls, and with it Dara's defeat is undeniable.
The Iranian ruler marches with his host to Kerman
And saves his life from the grip of the enemy.

Eskandar, dressed in armor for a last attack,
Travels to Estakhr, the diadem of kings
And the glory of the province of Pars.

A powerful voice announces at the palace gates:
"O noblemen, you are the people's guides.
Anyone who asks for shelter from the Creator,
To avoid the consequences of his actions,
May remain under my protection.
You will recognize this if you are my friends.
We shall be generous toward the wounded.
We shall not spill the blood of our enemies.
We shall refrain from touching anyone's valuables.
We shall direct our intelligence toward the just,
For the Master of Victory has rewarded us with majesty,
Power, and the crown of the King of Kings.
On the other hand, anyone who refuses to obey
Our commands will find himself in the dragon's jaws."

Eskandar distributes the goods
Collected on the battlefield to the troops.

Once Dara arrives in Kerman, he recognizes

PART TWENTY

That two-thirds of his warriors are missing.
Cries of grief are heard among his brave noblemen.
There remains no one wearing a helmet.

He gathers the wise leaders
And the warriors who fought alongside him.
Each man is in a state of anguish and tears,
His misfortune consuming him like a blaze.

Dara says to them, "It is surely our fault
That the sky has treated us so poorly.
There has never been a greater defeat than ours.
The ancient sages have never conveyed such a story.
Iranian women and children are held prisoner.
Our dim hearts have been struck by the stars,
Our bodies punctured by piercing arrows.
What do you think? What means do we have
To force repentance upon our enemies?
We possess neither land nor throne,
Neither crown nor kingship,
Neither child nor treasury, neither arms nor army.
We are lost, unless the Creator grants us mercy."

The surviving noblemen cry bitterly before the king
And say, "O king, we are stung by the blows of fate.
We are in such a state that the troops no longer try,
As the waves of misfortune rise above our heads.
Fathers have lost sons, and sons have lost fathers.
Such is the fate brought to us by the skies.
Our mothers, sisters, and daughters
Are held captive at the hands of Eskandar.
Your veiled women, who feared so for your life,
All the treasures of your powerful ancestors
In your possession without contest,
All the noble daughters, the Kianian wealth,
Have fallen into the hands of the Rumis.
We no longer have the ability to hold off Eskandar.
We cannot fight against him with weapons.

"Our only resource is to face him with moderation,
For the crown of power remains for no one,
And the turning skies will pass over him as well.

This knowledge belongs to any man of sense.
Offer him your surrender and multiply sweet words.
We shall see how this affair will conclude.
The rotation of the dome of sky evades human calculation.
Write him a letter that will make his dark soul reflect.
Anyone who can stoke the blaze of eloquence
With burning words may, with the use of ruse,
Clear himself of an ominous demise."

Dara listens to this advice
And follows it, as suits the ways of kings.

7 | Dara's Letter to Eskandar Asking for Peace

The king summons a skilled scribe,
Who arrives with paper and black musk.
Heartbroken and pained,
Eyes full of tears, cheeks pale, the king dictates
A letter in the name of Dara, son of Daaraab,
Addressed to the lion-conquering Caesar, Eskandar.

After exalting the Creator, Giver of good and poor fortune,
He says, "No matter how wise one is,
One must surrender to the rotations of the sky.
It hands us joy and fear in turn, placing us
At times on a pedestal, at times to be condemned.
All good originates from Yazdan,
Who is aware of things revealed and concealed,
Who is my shelter and the receiver of my gratitude.
A world victor must have a strong connection to the Creator.
It was not courage that drove us to battle.
It was the sky's will, the actions of the Sun and Moon.
Now we suffer the consequences, our hearts full of grief.
What more can one hope for from the blue dome of sky?

"Should you wish to consent and agree to a treaty,
Should you wish to renounce a subsequent attack,
I shall send you my wealth, amassed
During the eras of kings Goshtaasp and Esfandiar:
Bracelets, torques, and earrings; Kay Khosrow's throne;
A golden crown, a helmet, a coat of mail, and a golden belt.

I shall send even what I acquired through my labors.
I shall be your support in war,
And the day you summon me, I shall not delay.
It would be natural for you to return to me my family,
My veiled women and my children, whom you detained.
A world master must not seek vengeance in this way.
Captive women can only bring scorn
And dishonor upon the glory of a powerful king.
When victorious, show mercy, add to world virtues.

"Upon reading the letter, the master of wisdom,
Familiar with the art of discourse and insight,
Will find himself of the same accord.
Let us ask our friends about the dispute
Between Daaraab and Filghoos on Mount Koos,
And the actions of Daaraab with his mighty sword
Against the land of Rum and against the Rumis.
The arrival of Filghoos and his peaceful words
Softened Daaraab's heart of steel,
Softening it and making it as malleable as wax.
They reached a peace accord, each retired to his kingdom
And respected the terms for a long time.
Once you are victor, you may renounce vengeance.
Your name will retain its divine magnificence."

Dara asks for a race camel and an emissary,
To whom he hands over the letter and says,
"You must travel in tandem with the wind!"
The envoy departs and travels in haste from Kerman
To the court of Eskandar, Dara's wicked rival.

Eskandar reads the letter and says,
"May reason be the mate of Dara's soul!
Anyone who touches his family, his veiled women
And his children, will have for a throne a casket's planks.
Either that or his head will hang on a branch.
Yazdan forbids us to cause them any harm
Or to demand wealth as ransom.
If you wish to enter the land of Iran,
I consent. Royalty will be yours,
And never shall I violate my promises to you.
I shall breathe only to the rhythm of your will."

Eskandar writes a reply to the letter.
It is as if he has planted the tree of grandeur:
Its fruit is of pure praise. Its crest reaches the sun,
And its roots dig deep into the dark dust.

The race camel takes off as swift as a vessel on the sea,
For the envoy recognizes the distress in Dara's heart.

8 | Dara Is Killed by His Viziers

Dara is surprised at the contents of the letter.
In the end, he says, "To appear before the Rumi ruler
Secured in my belt would be a sadder state of affairs
Than to be confronted by death itself.
The grave is more enticing than enduring shame.
A wise man once said,
        'When the tide rises on the sea,
            A drop of rain does not affect it in the least.'
I have been the support of everyone in battle.
But being reduced to such distress,
I clearly see that only the Creator can rescue me."

Unable to find allies, near or far, he composes a letter
To Foor, full of supplications, humility, and grief.
He begins with proper homage to the World Master.
Then he writes, "O King of India,
You are wise, sensible, and clear-minded.
You must be aware of my fate by now
And of the calamities that have befallen me.
Eskandar has brought a host from Rum
And leaves me neither barren desert nor cultivated land,
Neither family nor son, neither crown nor fortune or army.
If you wish to assist me and push back the threats
To my empire, I shall send you jewels,
The likes of which you have never seen.
Never again will you need to gather wealth.
Furthermore, you will rise as the most illustrious,
Most glorious man among the world's noblemen."
He dispatches a camel as swift as wind to Foor.

Aware of Dara's machinations,

Eskandar asks for the blare of trumpets,
The drum of timpani, and the din of Indian bells.
He leads an army out of Estakhr in a way
As to make the sun drift astray in the sky.

The clamor of troops rises to the clouds.
Valiant men no longer enjoy a moment's rest.
Eskandar forms army ranks according to the rules.
The air darkens and the earth disappears.

On his side, Dara drives his host, but his troops,
Heartbroken and weary of battle, have no will to fight.
The fortune of the Iranians is decidedly on the decline.
They refuse to engage in war with the Rumis.
It is as if wild lions have transformed into foxes.
The leaders ask the enemy host for protection,
And though they once owned the pride of glory,
They are left to contend with the shame of defeat.

Dara, witness to this, absconds wistfully
With his three hundred illustrious riders,
The most valiant and glorious warriors of Iran.

Dara has two famous viziers with him on the field.
One is a wise man named Maahiar. The other is Janoosyar.
The moment they discern the hopelessness of the situation
And the once-powerful star of Dara's glory being crushed,
They say to each other, "This wretched man
Will never set his sights on his throne and crown again.
We must pierce his chest with our daggers
Or strike his head with an Indian sword.
Then Eskandar will reward us with a province.
We shall be the diadem on the kingdom's head."

In this way, the two viziers escort Dara,
One an advisor and the other a treasurer,
One standing on the king's left, the other on his right.

Night deepens its black shades. A storm stirs the air.
Janoosyar reaches for his dagger
And quickly stabs his master's chest.
The head of the illustrious king reclines,
And his company abandons him.

9 | Dara Relays His Last Wishes to Eskandar and Dies

The viziers march over to Eskandar and tell him,
"O victorious and joyous king,
We have surprised and killed your enemy.
The royal throne and crown have abandoned him."

At Janoosyar's words, Eskandar says to Maahiar,
"Where is the enemy you have slain? Show him to me."

The two viziers walk ahead of the Rumi king,
Whose heart is wrathful and distraught.
At Dara's side, Eskandar observes him
And sees that his chest is flooding with blood
And his face is as pale as the flower of fenugreek.
He commands the horses be taken away
And for someone to keep watch on the two viziers.

As swift as wind, Eskandar dismounts
And places the head of the wounded man on his thigh.
He observes Dara and notices that he can speak.
He rubs his two hands on the wounded man's face,
Removes the imperial crown from his head,
Unfastens his warrior coat of mail,
And laments at the fact that he is not a physician.

He says, "May you find some solace,
And may your adversary's heart quiver in fear!
Rise and take your place on a golden seat.
If you can muster the strength, climb on your horse.
I shall assemble healers from India and Rum.
I shall shed bitter tears over your state of misery.
I shall return to you empire and throne,
And as soon as you are healed, we shall depart.
I shall immediately hang your murderers at the gallows.
When old men recounted your demise last night,
My heart was enflamed and my lips emitted cries.
We both come from the same root, branch, and family.
Why would we destroy our race for the sake of greed?"

Dara listens to him and murmurs weakly,
"May wisdom always be your mate!

The Just Creator will reward you for your kind words.
First, you said that Iran is mine, with throne and crown,
But I am closer to death than to the royal throne,
Which is now vacant from the presence
Of the one whose fortune is on the decline.
Such is the final outcome of the revolving dome:
Its feasts convert into grief, its triumphs into defeat.
Abstain from proudly saying,
      'I am superior to this noble army.'

"Know that both happiness and pain come from Yazdan.
Remain grateful to the Creator as long as you live.
I am a fine example of what I am telling you.
My story is a warning to everyone.
I possessed such power, many kingdoms and treasure.
No one had cause to suffer under my rule.
I owned so many weapons, noblemen, chargers,
So many crowns and thrones, children and allies.
So many hearts were touched by my reign.
The world and the era stood as slaves at my feet.
This period lasted a long time; fortune was mine.
Now look at me, stripped of joy, crushed by assassins.
I despair for my children and my family.
The world turns black to me. My vision has obscured.
None of my kin have come to my rescue, and
My hope rests in the Creator, who equally cares for all.
Here I am, wounded, lying on the ground.
The world captured me in its net of destruction.
Such is the custom of the vault of sky.
Whether you are king or warrior,
Power is yours momentarily, and then it passes
As it is the chosen prey pursued by death."

Eskandar sheds a torrent of blood tears on the king,
Who is wounded and lying sprawled on the ground.
Dara, at the sight of this heartfelt grief and the tears,
Says to him, "Do not weep so.
Your tears do not have the power to heal my wounds.
My part in the fire is now only the smoke.
This is the fate reserved for me by the Creator,
Who once upon a time favored me.
Listen to my last wishes, from beginning to end.

Receive them favorably and execute them wisely."

Eskandar replies, "Command!
Tell me everything, for you have my solemn oath."

Dara speaks quickly and communicates, point by point,
His last wishes, saying, "O illustrious prince,
Always maintain fear of the World Master,
Creator of time, earth, and sky,
Creator of the weak and the powerful.
Take good care of my children, my allies,
My delightful veiled women.
Ask for the hand of my daughter of pure body,
The one her mother named Roshanak,[86]
Light of the world, and give her the joy of the throne.
My daughter will not draw gossip on you,
And even our worst enemies will not slander her.
She is a princess, the king's daughter.
Her wisdom makes her the crown of dignified women.
I hope that she will give you a glorious son,
Who will renew the name of Esfandiar,
Make the fire of Zartosht shine again,
Hold the *Zand Avesta* in his hands,
Observe the feasts and festivals, Saddeh and Nowruz,
Honor the fire temples, Ormazd, and the day of the Sun,
Purify his soul and face in the waters of wisdom,
Reestablish the customs of Lohraasp and the Kianian cult
Observed by Goshtaasp, treat noblemen with nobility,
Make our religion flourish everywhere,
And bring good fortune all around."

Eskandar replies, "O King of lion heart and rightful speech,
I shall accept your advice and your last wishes,
And will remain in this land only to fulfill them.
I shall execute these designs with wisdom as my guide."

The world master takes Eskandar's hand into his,
Laments painfully, places the other's palm on his lips,

◇◇◇◇◇◇◇◇◇◇◇◇◇
86 Roshanak: Name of Eskandar's wife in Ferdowsi's legend; historically, one of
Alexander's wives was Roxana, a Bactrian princess, while his Persian wives were
Stateira II, daughter of Stateira I and Darius III of Persia, and Parysatis II, daughter of
Artaxerxes III of Persia.

And says, "May the Creator be your shelter!
I abdicate the throne to you and travel to the dust,
Surrendering my soul to the holy Yazdan."

He speaks, and his soul exits his body.
The assembly sheds bitter tears.
Eskandar tears his clothes
And scatters dust over the Kianian crown.
He builds a tomb according to Persian custom
And rules, worthy of the status of Dara.
The bloody corpse is washed with clear rosewater
And prepared for its eternal sleep,
Dressed in luxurious Rumi brocade,
Embroidered with jewels and pure gold.
The body disappears beneath a layer of camphor,
And from then on, no one shall ever again
Catch a glimpse of Dara's face.

Eskandar places the tomb on a golden platform
And a crown of musk on the head of the king.
He lays Dara in a golden coffin,
Shedding over him a torrent of tears.
They raise the box to pass from hand to hand.

Eskandar walks at the head of the procession,
Followed by the brave leaders whose eyes flood with tears.
He feels as if his skin is parting with his body.
He places the royal coffin on the platform,
Closely observing Kianian custom.

After this, Eskandar asks for gallows to be raised.
One bears the name of Janoosyar, the other of Maahiar.
The two wretched men are attached there alive,
Two king murderers hang with their heads below.
The soldiers arrive from camp, each gripping a stone.
They toss the stones aiming at the two,
Killing them miserably and shamefully.
Cursed be the one who murders a king!

In view of Eskandar's actions to punish
The king's murderers, the Iranians offer homage
To him and pronounce him world king.

10 | Eskandar Writes a Letter to Iran's Noble Leaders

A man of high rank travels from Kerman to Isfahan,
The city where Iran's noblemen have settled.
He approaches the king's veiled women
With a message of greeting from Eskandar
And a report of the incidents leading to Dara's end:
"Neither friend nor enemy
Can rejoice at the death of a legitimate king.
You must know that today I am to replace Dara,
Who has disappeared while I continue to live.
His glorious deeds have been many.
Do not allow your hearts to grieve excessively.
We all belong to death, whether king or commoner.
For as long as we live, we all follow the same road.
Honor us by traveling to Estakhr with provisions
In order to formalize the alliance we are entering into.
I shall allow you to live in joy and health,
And peacefully prosper in the land of Iran."

A letter is dispatched to each province and each prince,
Written by Eskandar, son of Filghoos, world seeker,
Stating that any resistance will be met with punishment.

A similar letter is written to leaders and valiant warriors,
To wise men and ministers of the land of Iran,
Full of forgiveness and praise.
The end of a Chini reed is dipped in amber ink
To scratch words in praise of the Justice Giver:
"Creator of all that is visible and invisible,
Whose will propelled the world out of the void;
Creator of this world and the other,
Whose command warrants questions
Neither for the why nor for the how.
When you see the rotation of the skies,
Describe Yazdan as powerful and wise,
According to Whose command everything occurs.
We are slaves who stand before the Divine Master.
May blessings shower the brave leaders of Iran!
May blessings spread over each
And every one of you, no matter your rank!
We aspire only to acts that are true and just.

"In the midst of victory, I endured a huge blow.
In the midst of feast, a great calamity befell.
But I swear by the Master of the sublime Sun
That I did not mean to threaten Dara's life.
His enemy emerged from his own court:
One of his servants and not a stranger.
The latter has received his due punishment:
He chose to execute evil crimes
And has been duly castigated and condemned.
As for you, seek justice and remain obedient.
Have your souls be the guarantors of your loyalty.
If you wish to obtain the sky's favors
And receive from me gold, slaves, crowns, and thrones,
Obey my command and your soul
Shall not stumble into a ditch.
My shining heart mourns the death of Dara.
I shall make every attempt to comply with his last wishes.

"Anyone who presents himself at my court
Will receive gold, honor, throne, and headdress.
If he wishes to dwell in peace in his palace,
He only has to be faithful to his duty toward me.
Send to my treasury any tribute due me,
And from here on, no one need suffer trouble and grief.
You will mint currency in the name of Eskandar.
You will fulfill your duties
And a breach of your pact with me,
Will incite the wrath of the Creator.
You will maintain the palaces of prior kings
According to ancient customs.
Sentries will guard the marketplaces to bar humiliation.
The borders will be protected at all times,
Showing in this manner your value,
For value does not exercise ravages.
May you remain happy and prosperous!

"From every city, send a lovely, wise, and modest slave,
One worthy of my golden harem, aware of our faith,
Who will make the journey willingly.
She will dwell in my women's chambers,
Where her purpose will be to serve kingship.
The foreigners who pass my states walk peacefully

And live soberly, their hearts exempt from vice.
Referred to as Sufis, they are content with poverty.
Put them at the head of those who may request.
Inscribe their names at the top of your lists.
If you find an oppressive governor who plunges
Men into misery, break the unjust heart,
Cut off the roots, and destroy the branches.
I shall seek and find all the world's deceitful men
And hang alive at the gallows anyone who wishes
To turn happy beginnings into distressing ends.
Strengthen your hearts with justice and generosity.
Place upon your heads the crown of noble sentiments.
In the end, your days will pass,
And time will draw an account of your steps.
Anyone who refrains from obeying my orders
Will find himself within reach of grievous retribution."

He travels from Kerman to Estakhr
And places on his head the glorious Kianian crown.

Abstain, as much as possible,
From seeking to discover the world's secrets.
Destiny will unexpectedly turn its back on you.
Learn wisdom in this life and, in the other,
You will enjoy its fruits, which you have sown.

PART TWENTY-ONE

The Fourteen-Year Reign of Eskandar

1 | The Beginning of the Story:
Eskandar Sits on the Throne of Iran

Glory to Yazdan, Creator of world, space, and time,
Creator of peace and labor, Creator of beginning and end.
The sky, time, and space are divine elements
That languish or flourish according to divine will.
Everything, from the smallest fetus to the throne of sky,
Is witness to divine existence.
Do not call World Creator any other being,
For no one else can make the distinction
Between the revealed and the unrevealed.

May Yazdan's grace shine on the prophet Muhammad,
Who celebrates Ali the most among his assembly,
An elite gathering of pure and virtuous men.
Now let us double our blessings on the Creator
And praise the crown of the King of Kings,
Whose good fortune reflects on the light of the moon.
Generous world master, majestic and just,
The era is pleased to listen to his commands.
Master of mace, sword, and the labors of war,
Master of rest, crown, and treasure,
Prudent, wise, and holder of solemn word,
Young of years yet mature in wisdom,
The glorious king discerns the good
And credits the Creator for his crown.
Jupiter borrows its gleam from his glory.
We are proud to live beneath the shelter of his wings.

The world has never seen a crowned ruler of the stature
Of Mahmoud, King of Kings, distributor of gold.
The world has never seen a prince more worthy of the throne.
He makes the celestial dome echo with his battles.
He scatters jewels when he engages in feasts.
In his wrath, he splits boulders and makes the sky tremble.
He is king from father to son, and the spheres
Of the sun and the moon take pride in him.
May his name remain eternally!

May he gather the world's power in his hands!

I began this book in tribute to him and his glory,
His magnificence and his wisdom.
I owe my illustrious name on this earth to him.
May fate help him succeed in his undertakings!
His glance brings a glimmer to the crown.
Fortune is his shield against misfortune.
Virtuous men and world kings owe their happiness to him.
His prosperity illuminates the air as it spreads abundance.
The earth is the glorious footboard for his throne.
In battle, he is the wild elephant.
In feast, he is the sky of loyalty and pledge.
When his soul casts lightning in festivals,
The waves surge on the sea of his generosity.
Lions are his prey in the hunt,
Where game and wild beast plead for mercy.
The boom of his mace on the day of battle
Shreds the lion's heart and splits the leopard's skin.
May his head remain young, his heart full of justice!
May the world never be deprived of his diadem!

I shall circle back now to my stories,
Transcribe them to verse according to ancient traditions.

Once settled on the throne, Eskandar says,
"May reason be the mate of every king's soul!
Only the Creator may enjoy enduring victory.
A king who has no fear is an evil king.
Our good and bad fortune will pass over us,
As no one escapes the claws of time.
Anyone who comes to this court asking for justice,
Let him enter the audience hall, either now or at night.
He will receive a reply as soon as he submits his request.
Since the One who grants triumphs has given me power,
Since the Creator opened the door to victory,
My subjects, whether they dwell in mountains or deserts,
On the seas or in the cities, will have their share.
I shall demand no tribute for five years
Unless from someone who claims to be my equal.
I shall donate in abundance to the poor and
Abstain from taking from those who possess little."

Eskandar utters these words, his heart longing for justice.
A universal cry rises over Iran to bless the world king.
Then the gathering disperses,
And the king sits to consult with his advisors.

2 | Eskandar's Letter to Delarai, Mother of Roshanak

Eskandar summons a scribe,
Who arrives with a Rumi reed and Chini silk.
The scribe proceeds to sharpen his reed,
Then writes a letter to Roshanak's mother:
"May the Creator grant you the reward of virtuous people!
May you receive your soul's serenity after such hardships!
I have already written to you with more detailed counsel.
As your husband's days came to an end
And he perished at the hands of a servant,
I laid him to rest in a royal casket and in royal manner,
Acting in every way as it suits stately convention.
Before we engaged in battle, I pleaded for peace.
He did not grant me an accord.
Fate did not plan to have him live longer.
I have avenged his death with the slaying of his foes.
I hope that the Creator has received Dara in paradise
And given him a place among men of virtue.
I hope that he has accepted the means
To strike his enemies with toxic arrows.

"No one escapes the grips of death.
Death is the autumn wind, and we are the autumn leaves.
Now the entire world awaits your command.
Many witnesses have heard Dara express his last wishes
And his desire to see me wed Roshanak. He said,
        'You will never find a wife of her stature.'
Send her to me in haste escorted by servants,
And by her nurse, noblemen, and rulers of Iran.
Perhaps she can appease my restless heart.
Isfahan is as prosperous as in ancient times.
Send skilled guards. Keep fair and honest overseers,
Those named by Dara, son of Daaraab.
If you do not wish to live in Isfahan,
The land of Iran awaits your command.

Fill your heart with devotion and assign to me
The title of Dara before the entire world."

The scribe writes a similar letter to Roshanak
In the name of the powerful world master,
A letter he begins with worship of the Creator,
Wise World Master, Crafter of every creature.
Then he adds, "Only pure children
Are born from the lineage of kings.
Prudent, affectionate, soft-spoken, and chaste,
Your father promised you to me before he died,
Taking with him a most glorious name.
When you arrive at my night chambers
And the women's dwelling, you will be my queen.
You are the first woman and the ornament of the throne,
The shining splendor of glory, name, and fortune.
I have written a letter to your mother
So that she may send you to me in a worthy manner,
With the pomp and honor of the king's daughter.
You will be preceded by the grand vizier of Isfahan,
Followed by crown-bearing slaves, elephants with litters,
And escorted by the special person
Who nurtured you with milk and honey.
Come to me in trust. Join my women's chambers,
Where you will be considered Queen of Queens.
May the purity of your heart remain your ally!
May the dwelling of kings remain your retreat!
If the revolving dome endowed you with so much,
I hope that it will keep evildoers bay."

A wise man arrives as swift as wind
And relates the king's words to Delarai.

3 | Delarai's Reply to Eskandar

Delarai hears the message and sighs deeply.
She sheds blood tears for her father, Dara,
Who is now beneath the dust. She calls the scribe and,
Cheeks damp with blood, dictates a reply,
Full of sensible and auspicious words.
She begins in praise of the Justice Giver,

Master of rest, virtue, and good counsel.
Then she adds, "We prayed to the sky's Creator,
Giver of struggle, rest, and compassion,
To have mercy on the life of Dara and spread his glory,
Our tongues unceasingly muttering his name.
But now that his time has passed
And he has for throne the wooden panels of his coffin,
I wish you nothing but happiness in your life,
Along with power, victory, and majesty.
I wish for the world to submit to your command.
I shall express these sentiments openly to everyone,
For I have heard the stories of how you have exhibited
Tenderness in your feats and exploits.

"May the sky rejoice for your soul's virtues,
For Dara's coffin and for the punishment
Of Maahiar and the evil Janoosyar.
The one who spills the blood of kings
Will not have the chance to exist on earth for long.
Furthermore, I am aware that you spent your days
In the pursuit of peace, but kings need not pay homage.
It is improper to demand an act of submission
From a crowned head. We consider you the King of Kings.
Though our sun has departed, you are now our moon.
May the world bend to your will!
May your name endure engraved in royal palaces!
Dara mentioned a union with you and Roshanak,
A union that will enlighten our hearts.
My daughter stands as your slave, as we all are,
Bowing down before your command and majesty.
Since the world king singled you out,
No one would dare disobey.
We have composed a letter like the rose garden in paradise.
The world master selected you, and we shall not defy him.
We have written to illustrious and powerful men
And warriors that you will assume Dara's command,
And no one is to take up arms against you."

She hands over slaves and crates of gold to the messenger,
Along with a share of all the jewels in her treasury.
The Rumi envoy returns to Eskandar
To give an account of what he has seen and heard,

And to describe the splendor of the court and the throne,
Which appeared as if Dara were still sitting upon it.

Eskandar rejoices at these words
And peacefully lowers the Kianian crown on his head.

4 | Eskandar Sends His Mother, Nahid, to Bring Roshanak to Rum

Eskandar summons his mother, Nahid, from Amoorieh
And repeats to her Dara's last words, adding,
"Travel to Delarai and speak softly to her of the union.
Observe Roshanak in the women's chambers,
And once you have seen her,
Shower her with one thousand blessings from me.
Offer her torques, bracelets, earrings,
And a crown worthy of a king inlaid with gems.
Offer her one hundred mules loaded with carpets
And ten camels loaded with golden Rumi brocade.
Draw thirty thousand dinars from the treasury
To be placed in the crates for offerings.
Bring three hundred young Rumi women and, if necessary,
An even greater number, each with a cup in hand,
As is the custom for beautiful ladies-in-waiting.
Take with you on the road slaves, and mind every detail
In terms of planning, crowns, and royal pomp."

Closely following Eskandar's instructions,
The king's mother departs with ten learned men
Of sweet speech as interpreters.
As she approaches Isfahan,
Many noblemen advance to meet her.
Delarai exits her palace with her retinue
To receive Nahid most solemnly and welcome her in.

They toss so many coins over the vestibule
That men come to regard the money as vile.
They gather in the audience hall
With the noble leaders and the queen's advisors.

Delarai prepares a beautiful dowry for the bride,

PART TWENTY-ONE

Causing many a merchant in the marketplace to prosper.
The camels in single file form a pressing mass
Intertwined over many farsangs with their loads
Of gold and silver tableware, ornaments, attires,
Bolts of fabric for dresses, carpets for dyeing and for gifts.
Included are Taazian steeds of golden bridles,
Indian swords of golden scabbards, coats of mail,
Helmets, strappings, a mass of golden weapons,
Heavy maces, ready-to-wear wardrobes,
And a vast array of textiles such as the world has never seen.

Palace slaves are summoned, forty litters are decked.
In the shade of a parasol and surrounded by slaves,
Roshanak happily takes her seat on a golden litter.
From Delarai's palace to halfway to Rum,
All is jewel and brocade, horse and helmet.

In proximity of the town of Estakhr,
Every illustrious resident comes to meet the procession.
The city is adorned. Everyone smiles for the new queen,
But inwardly their hearts mourn the deceased ruler.

Dinars are tossed on Roshanak's brocade parasol.
Pure musk is distributed over her litter.
As the moon-faced princess enters the royal chambers,
Eskandar contemplates her at length.
He observes her lofty stature and her fair features.
It is as if wisdom itself has molded her with affection.

The king's mother places her on a golden throne.
Eskandar spills his soul to her
And sits at her side for seven days,
Discussing a variety of subjects, great and small.
He gazes at her thoroughly, viewing how
She is endowed with grandeur, gentleness,
Wisdom, modesty, and propriety.
His heart opens to allow him to fall in love.

Countless gifts are offered to her from the land of Iran,
Gold and jewels worthy of a queen.
The Iranian warriors hail Eskandar and his queen.
One can see on the earth only justice and abundance.
Barren lands flourish with new growth and greenery.

5 | The Dream of the Indian Keid, King of Ghennooj

Now, in the language of Pahlavi,
I shall turn to the storyteller's account,
To another tale that will astound you.

There lives a king in India by the name of Keid,
Intelligent, farsighted, and of joyous disposition.
He possesses a wise heart and a warrior's mind,
A royal demeanor and the gift of divine glory.

For ten consecutive nights, he has vivid dreams.
Reflecting on such a marvel,
He convenes eloquent, judicious sages from India,
Describes to them his dreams, and demands a reading.

None of the wise men are able to interpret for him.
Their hearts dim, fill with worry, and their cheeks pale.

One of them says to Keid, "O wise King and royal heir,
There is an illustrious man named Mehran,
Who has reached the ultimate boundary of knowledge.
His residence holds neither food nor comfort.
He lives in the midst of wild beasts,
Nourishing himself on mountain herbs.
He considers men like us as barely human.
He dwells with sheep and deer, keeping at a distance
From men and comfortable places of rest.
He is free from harm, for he worships Yazdan
And in turn is favored by the divine.
You may go and consult with him."

King Keid replies to the wise man,
"Is there no other way of evaluating dreams?"
Provided with no other lead, he climbs on his horse
And departs, attracted by Mehran's reputation.
The wise men escort him, fearing to displease him.

The world ruler addresses Mehran in a polite manner:
"O Yazdan worshipper, you dwell in the mountain,
Rubbing shoulders with wild rams. Listen to my dreams,
Interpret them, and exhibit your sagacity.
O holy man full of intelligence, know that one night

I fell asleep peacefully, alone, without thought or haste.
After more than half the night passed, before dawn,
I had a dream of a structure resembling a lofty palace
In which there were formidable elephants.
The palace had no doors,
Only a narrow opening on its façade.
A terrible elephant emerged effortlessly from it,
Its body turning up on the outside
While its trunk was trapped on the inside.

"The next night, in that same palace,
I saw a man usurp the vacant ivory throne.
He placed on his head the illuminating crown.
On the third night, I restlessly dreamt of four men
Tugging at the four corners of a beautiful linen cloth.
Their lips blue from the strain, they continued
To pull tirelessly, but the unrelenting cloth did not tear.
In the fourth place, O illustrious Mehran,
I saw a body of water, a man longing for a drink,
And fish that spilled water over him.
His head turned away from the water
As he leapt away, and the water chased him.

"What do you say of this dream, O benevolent one?
On the fifth night, my soul met a city
On the water's edge where the residents were blind.
They did not seem to mind their blindness,
And the city shone with beauty, commerce, and trade.
On the sixth night, O powerful and noble man,
I saw a city where every inhabitant was sick.
They questioned a healthy man on his well-being,
And he replied with a question,
          'How are you in the midst of this suffering,
          Your bodies ill, your hearts full of anguish?'
The feverish man is moved by these words
And asks for remedies to treat the sick.
Past the middle of the seventh night,
I saw a horse grazing in a meadow.
He had two feet, two hands, two heads,
And two sets of teeth to chew with.
However, his body had not the means
To pass and expel the ingested food.

"On the eighth night, O holy man,
I saw three barrels, side by side on the ground.
Two were filled with water,
But the one in the middle was ugly
And had been dry for many years.
Two kind men poured fresh water into the middle one,
Drawn from the brimming barrels.
No matter how much they extracted,
The level of the water never lessened
While the edges of the empty barrel remained dry.
On the ninth night, I saw a healthy cow on the grass,
Reclining in the sun, near a source of water.
Before her was a skinny calf, miserable looking.
Though feeble and sickly, the calf nursed the robust cow.
If you listen to my tenth dream,
You will not tire before I finish this account.
I saw a spring of water in a large field
From which rose a palace with a gazebo.
The entire field was covered with water and moisture.
But the edges of the stream were barren and dry.

"I hope that you will succeed in your reply
In revealing to me the secrets of the future."

6 | Mehran's Reply to Keid

At the end of Keid's discourse, Mehran says,
"Do not concern yourself about these dreams.
Your reputation will not be diminished,
And your kingdom will not suffer from them.
Eskandar will mobilize a vast host,
Led by warriors from Rum and Iran.
If you wish to maintain your status,
Be vigilant and do not seek war with him.
You have four incomparable wonders in your possession,
Valuable things that no one has ever set his sight upon:
First, your daughter who resembles a sublime paradise,
Whose presence brings luster to your diadem;
Second, a wise hermit, whom you hide from everyone
And who reveals to you the secrets of the world;
Thirdly, an illustrious physician, whose name

Is well known because of his vast knowledge;
And finally, a cup in which the water you pour
Is never affected by heat from either sun or fire
And from which one can drink
Without altering the volume.
These four valuable assets are the key
With which you may appease Eskandar.

"When he arrives, remain calm; avoid a fight,
If you wish that he not linger in your land.
You cannot contest with his troops, his means
Of carrying out war, and the power of his empire.
After having thus guided you on how to proceed,
I shall now explain to you the meaning of your dreams.
You saw a house with a narrow opening,
From which emerged an elephant,
Though its trunk was caught in the hole.
This house represents the world.
The elephant is a faithless king of unjust actions,
Of untrue speech, who is king in name only.
You dreamt of a throne rejected
By one and acceded by another.
Such is the way of this perverse world:
It takes from one to bestow to another whose soul is vile
And whose body is weak, whose heart is lost in greed
And whose mind is lost in gloom.
When the king's heart is aggrieved
And his lips are full of trivial words,
His subjects have no access to happiness.
When one day he goes, his name will remain in shame.

"Next, you saw a canvas stretched by four pure men.
The thin fabric could not be torn,
No matter the extent of the effort exerted.
This canvas represents faith, and each of
The four men is intent on being its sole guardian.
The first of these religions
Is the worship of fire by poet bards
Who hold the barsom[87] by observing a whispered prayer.
The second religion is the religion of Moise, called Judaism,

---

87 Barsom: Sacred twigs used in ancient Zoroastrian ceremonies.

Which commands one to venerate a single divinity.
The third is the pure faith of Younis,[88]
Who brings justice to the king's heart.
The fourth is the holy faith of the Taazian.[89]
Later, a renowned man from the land of spear-riders,
Holy and good-tempered,
Will proselytize the cult of Yazdan on four sides,
Which lifts the heads of sensible men from the dust.
The four men struggle against each other as rivals
And will continue to compete in the name of religion.

"Fourthly, you dreamt of a man who,
Despite his thirst, runs away from the source
And from the fish that offers him water.
There will be a time when a holy man will be treated
With contempt for drinking the waters of knowledge.
He will be diminished like the fish in the sea
While the head of the evil man will rise to the Pleaides.
He will summon the thirsty ones to water,
But no one will answer him within reason.
Everyone will abscond from the knowledge seeker,
And crowds will curse him.

"In the fifth place, you saw a city full of life and gaiety,
People coming and going, selling and buying,
But it was as if fate had sewn shut their eyes.
Being blind, they could not distinguish each other.
There will come a time
When the world will be in such a state,
Where learned men will serve the ignorant.
The intelligent one will be confused and mistreated,
For the tree of wisdom will not bear fruit
And will shower foolish people with praise,
Standing before them in adoration.
But they will be aware of the lies
And will feel dishonored by this sort of servitude.

"In the sixth place, you saw a weak, invalid man
Question another of strong health.

◇◇◇◇◇◇◇◇◇◇◇◇◇◇
88 Younis: Or Jonah, reference to Christianity.
89 Taazian: Arabs, reference to Islam.

PART TWENTY-ONE

A time will be upon us when the poor
Will appear wretched in the eyes of the wealthy.
He will turn around the affluent in despair,
But nothing will be offered to him.
He will sacrifice himself as a servant without salary
Or a slave of no value, for he was never purchased.

"In the seventh place, you saw a horse with two heads,
Unable to pass any waste through his body.
This is a sign that a time will come when men will be happy
For the slightest crumb, yet never will they be satiated.
The poor man, a friend of learning, no matter
How illustrious he may be, will receive nothing.
These men will think only of themselves
And not wish to come to the aid of others.

"In the eighth place, you saw three barrels,
Two full, and one empty and dry.
A time will be upon us when the poor man will be weak.
Spring clouds full of moisture
Will conceal the sun from the poor
But will not shower them with rain.
Their hearts will split with grief.
The rich will reward each other with gifts,
Treat each other in amity and with gentle words,
But the lips of the deprived man will be dry,
And his days will be plunged into dark nights.

"Your ninth dream was the one where the healthy cow
Sucked the teat of the skinny, sickly calf.
When Saturn enters in the sign of Libra,
The world will come under the rule of power.
The affairs of the sick and the poor will waste away,
While the healthy, wealthy ones will ask for more.
Never will they share their fortune;
Never will they attempt to alleviate the suffering.

"Finally, you saw a waterless source and, all around,
Fragranced musk and dried-up waterways.
There will be a period when a king will rule,
And learning will exit his person.
His dark soul will be full of sorrow.

The entire world will be afflicted by the labors he will impose.
People will be impoverished by the treasures he will amass.
He will continually mobilize new troops
To help him increase the glory of his crown.
But in the end, nothing will remain, neither host nor king.
A new throne will be raised to guard the world against evil,
And from its heights will shine
The king's majesty bestowed upon him by the Creator.

"Today, it is the era of Eskandar,
The crown on the heads of kings.
When he comes, give him your four wonders,
And I believe he will not ask for more.
If you satisfy his desires, he will pass without stopping,
For he is a sensible man who wishes to learn.
There does not exist in the world among kings
His equal in good counsel, knowledge, majesty, and worth.
He is victorious in all things and at all times."

Keid listens to Mehran's words,
And the aging world appears to him renewed.
He approaches him, kisses him on the eyes and forehead,
And departs happily, confident and heart at peace.

King Keid takes his leave of Mehran with his escort.
He returns to his palace and spreads his name
And fame throughout the world.

7 | Eskandar Drives His Host Against Keid

Eskandar glances at the land of Iran and realizes
That he is the undisputed master of the throne.
He drives his army toward the Indian Keid,
Traveling through various roads, deserted and populated.
Everywhere Eskandar stops, the doors open for him.
Everyone he passes appears far inferior to him,
And he wears his headdress higher than the planet Venus.

He reaches the stronghold named Milad by the bold Keid.
He gathers his troops in this location,
And they occupy the entire region.

A scribe is summoned to compose
A letter to Keid in the name of Eskandar,
A ruler eager to capture his prey, a victorious,
Highborn king, master of sword, jewel, and crown.
He begins in praise of those whose hearts
Are purified by knowledge and who select
The least menacing option in their affairs,
For they wish to enjoy the fruits of their labors,
And they live in fear of and pray to the holy Creator:
"They know that their seats are dependent on my will,
And that I am the shelter of the victorious World Master.
I write you this letter to bring light into your heart.
Once your scribe has read it to you,
Do not place it peacefully aside.
Do not sleep on this matter.
If it arrives by night, do not wait for daylight.
Instantly prepare to obey my instructions.
If you refuse to act according to my command,
I shall be forced to trample beneath my feet
Your head, your throne, and crown."

8 | Keid Sends a Reply to Eskandar

Once the letter reaches Keid, he calls the king's envoy,
Showers him with compliments,
And treats him with graciousness,
Placing him on a seat of honor close to him.
He says, "I am delighted to hear these instructions.
Never shall I avoid my duties to your king.
But I shall not rush to his side in this manner,
Without having made preparations
And before having elevated my head.
Neither the World Creator nor the world king
Would approve or retain a good opinion of me."

He immediately summons a scribe equipped
With an Indian reed and a sheet of Chini silk
To composes a reply as flowery as a garden in paradise.
He begins in praise of the Creator, Master of victory,
Master of fate, generous, and fair,
Giver of courage, justice, and high deeds.

He then continues, "May the heads of virtuous men
Never turn away from the illustrious king!
We shall never refuse anything
To the ruler of army, crown, and sword.
I have in my possession four wonders that no one
Has ever seen, neither in public nor in secret.
No one after me will acquire anything like them.
If the king commands, I shall send them to him
For his regalement and delight.
In addition, I shall travel to pay homage
To his majesty as his slave, should he so desire."

9 | Eskandar Sends the Envoy Back
to Enquire About the Four Wonders

The messenger travels as swift as wind with the letter
And relays to Eskandar what he heard.
The king says, "Return to the illustrious prince.
Ask him the nature of the four wonders, the like
Of which no one has ever seen in public or in secret.
We have experienced most things in the world,
And the sky will not wish to extend the sphere of creation."

The envoy leaves the side of the king,
Rushes on the road as swift as fire, and says to Keid,
"The king wishes to know the nature of these
Four wonders that no one has ever possessed,
For anything one cannot gaze at
Might as well be as if it never existed."

Keid dismisses the visitors from his audience hall
And sits with his advisors. He assigns a place
To the messenger and addresses him respectfully:
"I have a daughter hidden from everyone.
If the sublime sun would gaze at her,
It would be eclipsed by the face of this noble child.
The curls of her mane are laces as black as pitch.
Her two lips exhale the scent of milk.
The cypress tree appears twisted next to her stature,
And when she speaks, she scatters pearls.
Her face and her features make one lose one's mind,

But her knowledge is suited for instruction.
All decked out, she is the picture of modesty.
Never has the world seen such beauty and charm.
She is the daughter of a king who worships the Creator
And bears a heart full of refinement and humility.

"Next, I own a cup in which you can pour wine or water,
And if you sit in revelry with companions for two days,
The surface of the drink remains at the same level.
It is a marvel, for the liquid within never drains,
No matter how much one drinks.

"In the third place, I have a physician who can detect
A man's malady by just examining a drop of urine.
He stands before the throne for years.
The king, world master, will be exempt
From suffering any illness during his life.

"Finally, the fourth wonder, that I keep from crowds,
Is a wise man who stands at my side
And who can predict to the king,
According to the rotating sun and shining moon,
All that will occur in the future."

The illustrious messenger returns as swift as wind
To Eskandar, whose heart blossoms like a rose.
He says, "Can the world place a price
On these four wonders, if what he says is true?
If he sends them to me, my soul will rejoice,
And I shall refrain from crushing his land.
I shall then take my leave in fairness and amity."

10 | Eskandar Sends Ten Wise Men to Observe Keid's Four Wonders

Eskandar selects a number of Rumi men,
Full of sense, wisdom, and good intentions.
He writes a letter with many expressions of flattery,
With apologies, scent and ornament:
"I am sending ten trustworthy noblemen to you.
They are experienced, skilled, and conceal my secrets.

They have wisdom, patience, and have seen the world.
These guides will not digress from your sensible counsel.
Show them the four wonders, and keep them
In your palace for as long as they remain.
Once I have a letter from my virtuous observers
To attest to the evidence of the four things
Never seen by anyone, I shall write you a letter on silk
To pronounce Keid as King of India for as long as he lives."

The ten Rumi sages travel in haste to the Indian ruler.
Once at his side, Keid questions them
And carefully listens to their replies.
He receives them graciously
And prepares a beautiful dwelling for them.

The next morning, at the first light of day,
As the sun draws its sword of battle,
The king's daughter is dressed and adorned,
Though a moon needs no adornment.
The king asks for a golden throne
Bejeweled with Chini trimmings.
The young, sun-faced princess climbs on the throne
And shines more brilliantly than Venus in the sky.

The ten old sages full of wisdom arrive, their tongues
Full of sweet words, their minds full of curiosity.
The king sends them to the young princess
As requested by Eskandar, son of Filghoos.
The sages are astounded at the sight of the royal daughter,
Her luminous cheeks, her crown and throne.
Their stance weakens, as stunned as they are,
Lips full of praise for the Creator.
They find themselves unable to leave her side,
Unable to force their glance away from her.
After a long time, someone calls them to the king.

The Indian ruler says to the Rumi men,
"Why did you remain still for so long?
She is a human being to whom
Every star has bestowed a part of its beauty."

One of the Rumi sages replies,
"O King, no one has ever beheld

A more beautiful painting than your daughter.
Each of us feels as if he has not had a chance
To contemplate her long enough.
There is no human creature as exquisite as she.
We shall each sing her praises to the king."

The sages sit together with paper, ink, and reed.
Each writes what he observed in a way
As to make the paper disappear beneath the ink.
Then a rider departs as swift as wind from Milad,[90]
To take the letters of the old men to Eskandar.

The king is astonished at the contents of the missives
And each description of various aspects of the princess.
He replies, "Bravo, old sages, you have glanced at paradise!
Now return to me with these four marvels,
And do not ask more of Keid.
Hand over to him my certificate of protection,
And take the road with my beautiful mistress.
No one will ever be allowed to harm Keid,
For he has given me my due share in the world."

11 | The Ten Wise Men Bring the Four Wonders to Eskandar

The envoy departs from the verdant land
And takes the direction of the Rumi wise men.
Once they have received the king's reply
From the travel-weary rider,
They present themselves at Keid's court
In a most magnificent audience hall.
They read the reply to their letters
And the message of the proud ruler.

The King of India is pleased and relieved
To be out of harm's way.
He elects one hundred Indian men,
Intelligent, eloquent, and of sweet speech.
He opens the doors to his inherited treasury,

◇◇◇◇◇◇◇◇◇◇◇◇◇
90 Milad: Or Malad, appears to be a region in India, north of today's Mumbai.

Selects among his most precious possessions:
Bracelets, a throne and crown,
Jewels, textiles, and fineries.
Three hundred camels are loaded with these:
Ten camels bear dinars and ten more dirhams;
There is an opulent litter of green aloeswood,
Inlaid in gold and fine stones;
Ten elephants loaded with a golden throne;
One elephant covered in a sumptuous saddle
On which is seated the beautiful young lady,
Who sheds blood tears as she takes the road
With the sage and the medicine man.
An illustrious leader carries the famous cup
That once inebriated the noblemen of the Indian court.

As the young woman enters the king's apartments,
Head crowned with her black mane
And her hair's curls hovering over her moon face
Like a trellis over a flower of Arghavan, she resembles
A tall cypress tree surmounted by the moon's sphere.
No one dares glance her way.
Her eyebrows form a delicate arch,
Her charming eyes are as beautiful as narcissi in paradise,
Her hair waves naturally and without assistance.
It is as if she had been molded by a pomegranate tree.

Eskandar observes her height and mane, her face and mien.
He thinks, "She must be the beacon of the world."
He quietly pays homage to the benevolent World Master,
Creator of the sky and Creator of such stature and face.
He commands sensible Rumi warriors to sit around him.
Then he solemnly asks for the hand of the princess,
According to the rites and the laws of the Messiah.

He scatters over her so much gold and dinars
From his treasury that the moon
Can hardly clear a path through it.

12 | Eskandar Assesses the Sage Philosopher

Once the affair of the tall cypress tree is complete
And a palace worthy of her class and rank is equipped,
Eskandar turns to the sage to determine
How science would assist him in a fight.
He sends a messenger to the serious philosopher
With a cup full of melted cow butter to say,
"Rub this on your limbs, hips, loin, chest, back, and arms.
Then rest until you are delivered from lassitude.
Then you will fill my mind and brains with knowledge."

The wise man observes the butter and says,
"This riddle is not for me."

He inserts one thousand needles into the butter
And sends it back to the king.

The world king considers the needles
And secretly summons blacksmiths.
He commands them to melt the needles
And to make a metal disk, which he then sends to the sage.

The latter glances at the disk, polishes its dark surface,
And converts it into a shining, rust-free mirror.

In the dark night, they take the mirror to Eskandar,
Who withholds his secrets from everyone, even the wind.
The mirror is positioned in a humid place,
Where it blackens and tarnishes.
At this point, it is returned to the learned man,
And in this way, the riddle of the metal is extended.
The wise man proceeds to polish the metal
With a substance that will protect it from humidity.
Once it shines like water, he returns it in haste.

Eskandar observes the mirror and summons the sage,
Whom he sits close to him and questions.
He speaks to him first of the cup of butter.

The wise man replies, "The butter does not penetrate skin,
And you wished to show that you have more knowledge
Than all the philosophers of the land.

But my reply was that the mind of a learned and pure man
Can penetrate the smallest details,
Like a needle pierces the core of bones.
The seeker who digs even deeper into the mysteries
Is like a needle able to infiltrate solid stone.
But one cannot evade the presence of a stone.

"On this subject the king said,
          'When a heart is blackened
          By battle, feast, spilled blood,
          And by continuous struggles against an enemy,
          How could a subtle but sharp conversation
          Find its way into a gloomy soul?'

"I replied to you that my sweet eloquence,
My mind, heart, and cautious reason provide me
With words more loose than a strand of hair,
While your heart is no more tarnished than metal.
To that you replied,
          'Years have passed in such a state, and my heart
          Has weathered from the excess of spilled blood.
          How could this darkness dissipate?
          How could I unravel words in this gloom?'

"I rejoined,
          'According to my knowledge of things divine,
          Were your heart wicked from the beginning of time,
          Nothing would have the power of tarnishing it
          Once I rub it to shine as bright as clear water.'"

The words of the sage philosopher please Eskandar,
Who finds himself growing fond of him.
He commands his treasurer to bring robes,
Gold and silver, and a cup of fine jewels.

The sage looks at his gifts and says,
"I possess an invisible gem
That can provide you with anything you desire.
It has no adversary and is nothing
Like the valuables of the companions of Ahriman.
Guards do not ask me for salary to watch over it.
When I travel, I do not fear the threat of thieves,
For wisdom is my guardian by night,

And reason is my mind's diadem by day.
One must have wisdom, knowledge, and virtue.
Deviance opens the door to decadence.
In any circumstance, the king provides me
With plenty of food and clothing.
What pleasure may I gain in possessing more
By becoming the custodian of his fortune?
Command for these riches to be taken away,
And may wisdom be your soul's guide!"

Eskandar is stunned by the actions of this man
And reflects for some time. Then he says,
"From now on, the Master of Sun and Moon
Will not find me at fault, for I shall assume
Your wisdom, advice, and gainful words."

13 | Eskandar Assesses the Indian Medicine Man

Eskandar summons the medicine man
Able to detect an illness from a drop of urine.
He says to him, "What is the source of illnesses
That make one shed tears for the pain they cause?"

The physician answers, "Anyone who eats excessively,
Anyone who does not count the bites he consumes
Will not remain healthy for long. One is valiant
Only when one takes care of one's well-being.
I shall now concoct a remedy for you
From various herbs collected from here and there.
It will help you maintain strong health.
You will no longer need to wash your body
With various medicines. Your appetite will increase,
But you will not suffer from excess consumption.
It will bring color back to your face,
Provide you with a clear mind.
If you agree to my words, you will enjoy
An abundance of healthy blood and bone marrow.
Your body will grow in vigor; joy will fill your heart.
Your rich mane will never turn gray,
And white hair will be banished from the world."

Eskandar replies, "I have never heard of such things,
Nor have I seen anything of this nature among kings.
Formulate this elixir, and be my guide in this world.
I shall buy you at the price of my life
And shelter you against any harm caused by potential foes."

He offers him garments of honor and nice gifts,
And raises his status above other physicians.

The soft-spoken medicine man travels to the mountain
With a number of servants well versed in the sciences.
He can make the distinction between poison and antidote.
He asks for a vast quantity of plants from the mountain,
And, rejecting those that do not serve him, he selects
The beneficial ones to mix into a medicine to suit his needs.

With this plant extract, he rubs the king's body
And holds him in good health for months and years.
As a result, Eskandar sleeps little
And willingly passes his nights in debauchery.
His chest is keen on women,
And his head seeks a soft spot to rest upon.
In this way, the king grows feeble,
For he pays little care to his health.

One day, the physician observes, in a drop of urine,
Signs of this weakening state. He says to the king,
"A young man may grow weak living with women.
I think you have not slept in three nights.
Tell me; do not hide this from me."

Eskandar replies, "I shine with good health,
And my body does not feel any abuse."

The wise Indian, worthy of praise,
Does not settle for this response.
At the advent of night, he scans his books
And composes a remedy against waning vigor.

That night, Eskandar sleeps alone
Without a moon-faced companion at his side.
In the morning, the physician arrives,
Observes him, and examines a drop of urine.

He tosses away the remedy, sits in joy, reaches for the cup,
Summons a spread, musicians, and wine.

The king says to him, "Why did you toss aside
The medicine that you prepared so laboriously?"

He says, "Because his majesty last night
Did not seek the company of a woman
And spent the night alone, O King.
When you sleep alone, there is no need for remedy."

Eskandar smiles, approves, and says,
"May the world never be deprived of India!
It appears that all the competent physicians
And wise astrologers are gathered there."

He gives the prudent physician pouches of gold,
A black stallion with golden bridles, and says,
"May your tongue always be
The interpreter of your pure wisdom!"

14 | Eskandar Puts Keid's Cup to the Test

Eskandar asks for the yellow cup full of fresh water.
From morning until night, everyone drinks from it.
But no matter how much they sip,
The level of the liquid does not drop.

The king says to the philosopher,
"Keid has no equal in the world. From here on,
We shall abstain from calling this land India
But refer to it as the dwelling of Keid the sorcerer.
Though it appears like a simple cup on the surface,
There must be some sort of trick to it. Come now,
Do not conceal the reason for this wonder.
How is it that the water constantly renews itself?
Is this phenomenon a product of the stars
Or of the ingenuous art of the Indian people?"

The wise man replies,
"O King, do not dismiss this cup.
We have labored on it for many years.

We have pained over it and suffered much.
Astrologers from every land and every nation,
Where lived an illustrious noble or learned man,
Stood at Keid's side day and night as he crafted this cup.
They observed the turning of the stars
And spent many days at work.
Take, for example, a magnet that attracts metal.
In the same way, this cup attracts sweet water
From the dome of sky. It draws water as it empties,
And no man is able to solve this mystery,
No matter how piercing his eyes may be."

The wise man's speech pleases the king.
Profiting from it, he says to the old men of Milad,
"I shall not break my peace accord with Keid
As long as I remain on earth. You must obey him.
Since I have received these four precious wonders,
We shall never make further demands on him."

Eskandar asks for two hundred pack animals
To be loaded with precious objects,
To which he adds one hundred bejeweled diadems.
He buries his stockpile of gold
And pure untouched gemstones in the mountain.

Once the riches are holed up, no one ever sees them again.
Only the memory lives on in the person of Eskandar.

15 | Eskandar Launches His Host
and Sends a Letter to the Indian Foor

Eskandar swiftly launches his army from Milad
And takes the direction of Ghennooj,
Leaving his wealth in the land of Keid.

He arrives at the side of Foor
And writes a letter breathing battle and war,
A letter from Eskandar, King of Kings,
Son of Filghoos, who either ignites the fire
Or provides prosperity and affection,
To Foor, leader of the Indian army of Sindh,

Possessor of a powerful star.
He begins in praise of the Creator,
Who has always lived and will live on forever:
"The empire, throne, and crown remain for the one
To whom Yazdan grants a victorious fortune,
While the one he wishes to demoralize
Will be in a state of confusion,
Unreachable by the luster of the magnificent sun.
You have, without a doubt, heard of the gifts
Divine grace has awarded us on this earth,
In terms of triumphs, fortune, majesty,
As well as the crown and throne of the King of Kings.
None of these gifts will remain; my days will pass,
And another will come to enjoy the royal legacy.
In this center of the moon's orbit and
The narrow circle of earth, I must rest assured
That I leave behind the memory of a good name
Rather than one drenched in shame.

"When they bring you this letter,
Fill your dim soul with an incliniation for justice.
Climb down from your lofty throne, and mount
Your charger, without deliberating with your advisors.
Demand my protection and abstain from evading
Your fate, for anyone who indulges in deceit
Does not prompt his affairs to reach a proper conclusion.
If you stray for an instant from my command,
If you insist on exhibiting your power and prowess,
I shall, quick as a flame, direct a vast host
Of the bravest warriors, with me at the lead,
And you will repent for delaying your submission."

The scribe links this beam of words together, and,
Once complete, the letter is secured with Eskandar's seal.
A messenger is dispatched to Foor's court, as swift as wind.

Upon his arrival, Foor speaks of banquet and battle.
The leaders gather around his throne as the letter is read.

16 | Foor's Reply to Eskandar's Letter

Once cognizant of the illustrious king's message,
The ferocious Foor bursts into a fit of anger.
He instantly composes a bitter response,
Hence planting a tree in the garden of vengeance.

He begins, "One must respect and fear the pure Creator.
One must refrain from uttering foolish words.
The one who boasts will find himself without resource.
You call me to your side without modesty.
Is your wisdom not ashamed of your pride?
It would be one thing if it were Filghoos who had written,
But you are the one who instigates troubles.
You think you have triumphed over Dara and are so great,
But the revolving dome had grown weary.
A breed abandoned by fortune
No longer follows the advice of wise men.
Furthermore, the struggle with Keid appeared only
A game, and you now act as if kings are your prey.

"Never did the Kianians of ancient times
Address us with such offensive letters and words.
My name is Foor, from the lineage of Foor,
And we never paid attention to the Caesars.
When Dara asked for my help, I could tell
That his mind and fortune had been shaken.
Nevertheless, I sent him war elephants
And encouraged him with my words.
But when he perished at the hand of his slave
And, with it, brought down the fate of the Iranians,
Once Dara disappeared from this world,
What was meant to save him
Became for you a miraculous cure.
If misfortune befell him at the hand of an evil vizier,
Why does this propel wisdom to vacate your mind?

"Do not be so keen on this battle with me.
It will not be to your advantage.
You will witness war elephants and troops so numerous
The wind will not find passage through the plain.
You think only of your own aggrandizement;

Your nature resembles that of Ahriman.
Do not sow the seeds of greed in the world.
Fear the setbacks and the woes of destiny.
With this letter we wish to fulfill our duty
And to turn your heart in the direction of virtue."

17 | Eskandar Leads His Army Against Foor

Upon receiving the response,
Eskandar instantly selects warriors,
Skilled men, aged in experience but young in years.
The earth disappears beneath a vast host
That departs in the direction of the Indian Foor.
The sea and the roads are no longer distinguishable.

Eskandar leads his troops around the mountain,
Then across the sea, arduous terrains, and roads.
The enthusiasm of his warriors fades
As they grow exhausted from the passage.
Their pace slows down from the journey's ordeals.

One night, as they arrive at the station,
A crowd gathers at the king's side, crying,
"O Rumi Caesar, O King of Chin,
The earth buckles beneath your host's weight.
Neither the Faghfoor of Chin nor the King of Sindh
Nor Foor the Indian seeks to battle with you.
Why must you exterminate your troops
In this land that has no value
And on such challenging roads?
Not a single horse remains with vim and vigor,
Not one on which we could battle valiantly.
If the army ever returns from these conflicts,
Neither cavalier nor foot soldier will find the way.
Until now, we have been triumphant
In every instance, against every enemy host.
But today we face mountain and sea,
And yet we are not weary of life.
Do not drench in shame our names.
No one is foolish enough to fight with water and stones."

Eskandar is aggrieved by these words.
He bursts out and overturns his plans.
He says to them, "Rumi men do not find themselves
In a position to speak of these matters.
When we traveled from Iran to Rum,
Everything was gardens and lush greenery.
Out of every one hundred warriors of ours,
Not one was killed, and our expenses did not increase.
The land of Iran is ours.
What more could you ask from the Creator?
Dara perished at the hands of his own servants.
Not once did you witness the sight of a wounded mate.
I shall continue on my way without you.
I shall crush beneath my feet the dragon's breath,
And you will see how this miserable Foor
Will fail to participate in either battle or feast.
When I return, I shall take the direction of Rum
And subjugate the surface of the earth with my courage.
The Creator is my Protector, the Iranians form my host,
And I need not seek the goodwill of a Rumi man."

Having thus exhaled his fury, the king listens
To the army leaders as they beg forgiveness:
"We are the Caesar's most devoted slaves.
We trample the earth to his command.
If our horses desert us, we shall fight on foot.
If the earth is converted into a sea of our blood
Or if flat lands are transformed into mountains,
No one will witness our backs on the day of battle,
Even if we were to fight with sky, mountain, and stone.
We are your slaves; command is yours.
How could we afflict you, since our lives are yours?"

At these words, Eskandar strategizes a new plan.
He selects thirty thousand armed Iranians.
Behind them, he places armor-bearing Rumi chiefs,
Brave and keen on war, with forty thousand riders,
Experienced and skilled in battle, to trail the Iranians.

Behind them march the Khazar leaders,
Renowned, valiant, illustrious men.
Next, the Caesar selects innumerable Taazian troops

From Syria, Hejaz,[91] and Yemen. Behind them he positions
Dagger-wielding, world-conquering Egyptian riders,
Twelve thousand illustrious spear-holding horsemen
Turning the valleys and plains into a mass of steel.
Sixty illustrious astrologers and wise men escort him
To forecast the outcome of battle.

At the news of the approaching host, Foor finds a battlefield.
He rallies troops on a site overrun by a mass of elephants.
His army line stretches the length of four miles,
With elephants in the vanguard and warriors past.

A number of spies return from India to Eskandar's side.
They approach the world king to say,
"There are countless elephants in the enemy host,
And they will break your line of battle.
They extend for two miles.
Our riders will not dare attack them,
And if they do, they will not return,
For these elephants bear horns that rise to the sky,
And they fall under the protection of Saturn."

They draw elephants on paper
And pass the image to Eskandar.
The king asks the wise men to build an elephant of wax
And says, "Which one of you has a mind fine enough
To invent a way to vanquish these creatures?"

The wise men sit to seek a way out of danger.
Then the king gathers an assembly of blacksmiths,
Those at the head of artisans, more than
Three thousand from Rum, Egypt, and Iran.

They construct a war horse with bridles,
Straddled by a cavalier made out of steel.
They secure the joints with nails and copper solder.
They polish the cavalier and his horse,
And, after having filled the interior with oil,
They haul them on wheels to Eskandar.

Eskandar is delighted with the invention.

◇◇◇◇◇◇◇◇◇◇◇◇◇
91 Hejaz: A city in the western part of the Arabian Peninsula.

The wise king knows how to benefit from it.
He commands his men to proceed to build
More than one thousand similar horses and riders.
Who has ever seen an army of steel riders
Mounting steel chargers dappled, bay, gray, and black?

At the end of the month, the work is complete
With the aid of these men full of resources.
Eskandar marches off, wheeling his host of steel
With riders that appear keen and ready for battle.

18 | The Battle of Eskandar With the Indians and the Death of Foor

Once in proximity of Foor,
Eskandar studies from afar his riders and his host.
The clatter and the dust of war rise on both sides.
The warriors, eager for battle, advance.

Someone ignites the oil within the horses of steel,
And the Indians strike their foreheads in awe.
With the flames, the steel horses are set in motion.
Enemy troops shout a roaring cry at the sight.
Elephants are infuriated by blows of metal hooks.
They loop around their trunks the burning riders,
A phenomenon that deeply confounds their drivers.
The entire Indian army retreats, and the war elephants,
Noble and fierce, thus repelled by men of steel,
Withdraw in haste behind the troops.

Eskandar pursues the enemy host, as swift as wind,
Until the light of day fades and the armies
No longer are able to see well enough to fight.

Then the king, world seeker, dismounts
With his Rumi warriors between the two mountains.
He sends patrols in every direction and takes care
That the enemy has not the chance to surprise them.

As the golden ingot of the sun's shining throne appears,
The world turns into an enormous white crystal.

The sound of trumpets, fifes, and Indian bells rises.
The two hosts prepare for battle,
Raising to the sky the points of their spears.

Eskandar, a Rumi sword in hand,
Advances in the midst of the two lines.
He sends a cavalier to summon Foor from afar and say:
"Eskandar arrives at the vanguard wishing to see you.
He will speak to you and listen to you.
If your words are in line with justice,
He will be happy to concur with you."

Foor rushes out of the army core.

Eskandar says to him, "O illustrious one,
Our two hosts are shattered by the battle.
Creatures, wild and tame, are devouring human brains,
And the hooves of horses grind human bones.
Why is it always up to the armies to kill each other
Or to return when they survive?
We are two brave youths, eloquent and wise warriors.
Let us secure our belts and fight each other,
Since we must determine who will rule over the realm.
The champion will be the owner of troops and kingship."

Foor listens to the Rumi king, accepts the bargain with joy,
And replies, "This complies with our customs and path.
We shall fight without our hosts."

Foor considers himself as powerful as a lion
And the charger beneath him as fierce as a dragon,
While he deems Eskandar a rider of lesser status,
Slim as a reed, covered in a thin coat of mail,
And handling what appears to be a feeble mount.

The two warriors grab their daggers
And advance into the middle of the two hosts.

At the sight of this man reminiscent of a mad elephant,
Mounting a horse as large as a mountain,
And brandishing his sword like a dragon,
Eskandar regrets having agreed to battle.
Though he fears for his life,

He stiffens and launches himself into the arena.

At that moment, a great cry rises from the rearguard.
Alarmed, Foor swivels head, eyes, and ears in its direction.

Taking advantage of Foor's loss of focus,
Eskandar advances like a gust in a whirlwind of dust,
Strikes the lion man with a blow of his sword
Above the chest, and severs his shoulders, head, and neck.
The body tumbles off the horse and onto the ground.

The head of the Rumi army reaches the sky.
Its warriors rush to the side of Foor
With the sound of clarion and timpani of lion skin.
The earth is covered in steel,
And the sky is the color of ebony.

A voice echoes in the plain: "O righteous men,
You are the flower of the land of India,
The head of the Indian Foor lies in the dust,
And his elephantine body is torn to bits.
Who will you be fighting for?
Why so many blows, why so much clatter?
Eskandar represents to you what Foor once was.
It is to him that you must address banquet and feast."

The Indian warriors march with a common exclamation.
They take in Foor's head sullied with mud and blood,
His body slashed by the point of the sword.
A sorrowful cry rises over the troops.
They toss away their weapons and appear
Before the Caesar, lamenting, heads covered in dust.

Eskandar returns their weapons to them
And addresses them with benevolent words:
"If Foor the Indian has died here,
Your heart must not surrender to concern.
I shall welcome you better than he has.
I shall drive away fear from your hearts
And distribute his wealth and treasure to you.
It would be sinful for me to hand it over to my troops.
The Indian population will prosper,
As I shall dispense countless crowns."

From there, Eskandar climbs on the throne of Foor.
On one side, there is pain and mourning;
On the other, banquet and feast.

Such is the way of this passing dwelling.
One day it gives you joy, the next sorrow.
Enjoy your assets, and reserve nothing for tomorrow.
Why should you leave what you have amassed
With great labor for another to possess?

The Caesar remains on the throne for two months
And distributes Foor's wealth to the troops.

There lives a nobleman, a powerful Indian hero
By the name of Sevorg, whom Eskandar places
On the throne and says, "Never hide your gold.
Give generously and enjoy what you have in hand.
Do not attach yourself to this transitory crown and throne.
At times Eskandar rules; at times Foor.
At times one dwells in pain and anger,
At times in feast and banquet.

Sevorg distributes gold and silver to his host,
And spreads joy to the leaders of the land.

19 | Eskandar Makes a Pilgrimage to Kaaba[92]

Once the army is aggrandized with riches
And a short time of rest passes, Eskandar's heart
Flutters with trepidation, and he feels the urge
To travel to the sacred site of Kaaba.
The sound of timpani is heard in the early morning hour,
And the air is rendered as bright as the rooster's eye
By the countless spears and silken banners
That shine like stars with hues of red, yellow, and purple.

After having brought joy to some and sadness to others,
Eskandar departs with treasure and crown toward
The holy home Abraham built with effort, with elephants

◇◇◇◇◇◇◇◇◇◇◇◇◇
92 Kaaba: In pre-Islamic times, it was a holy site of pilgrimage for Taazian Bedouin
tribes and idol worshippers in Mecca, an important city and a center for trade.

Marching to the sound of sad laments as well as jolly clarions.
The Creator gave this dwelling the name of Beit Al-Haram,[93]
Within which dwells the true divine path, and said,
"It is *my* house because it is holy and a blessing to you
Until you are called to the Creator's side,
For the World Master requires neither dwelling
Nor nourishment, neither object nor rest nor compliment.
It is a place of worship since the day it was constructed,
And, since then, it has accrued divine memories."

World conqueror Eskandar marches toward Kadesia,[94]
Passing through Jahrom, in the province of Pars.

At the news, Nasr, son of Katib,
From whom Mecca draws its glory and splendor,
Comes to meet him with his warrior leaders,
His valiant, spear-brandishing cavaliers.

A rider arrives in haste from Mecca to the side of Eskandar
And says, "This renowned man who is on his way
And who demands throne, treasury, and rulership
Is a descendant of Ismail, favorite of the stars,
The son of Abraham the patriarch."

Nasr appears before Eskandar, who receives him well
And assigns him a seat of honor. Nasr is filled with joy
And recounts his origins, elaborating on his secrets.

Eskandar says, "O prince of pure heart and fair speech,
Aside from you, who are the brave men of this tribe?"

Nasr responds, "O world-conquering King,
Khozaa is the powerful leader of this city.
When Ismail departed from this world,
Kahtan, the world victor, emerged from the desert
With a vast sword-bearing host
And unlawfully seized the land of Yemen.
Many innocent men from our race were maimed,

<hr>

93 Beit Al-Haram: Meaning House of Allah. Brings us to the era of Ferdowsi himself
rather than ancient times.
94 Kadesia: Or al-Qadisiyah, a historical city in southern Mesopotamia, in
today's Iraq.

And the prosperity of this tribe perished.
But Kahtan was not acceded by the World Creator,
And his path to the sublime road of sky was curtailed.
Once he turned into dust,
Khozaa, harboring no fear for the divine,
Arrived to unjustly trouble the fate of men.
The holy home and all of Yemen are in his hands.
He casts his nets in the Red Sea.
He has turned his back on the true way,
And no longer knows the path of justice and virtue.
His heart retains no memory of Yazdan.
He holds the world tight in his fist,
And the race of Ismail suffers from oppression."

Eskandar proceeds to sentence to death
All the members of the family of Khozaa.
He executes them and skins their heads,
Allowing to remain neither foe nor friend.
He seizes Hejaz and Yemen with his skills
And the aid of his brave sword-wielding men,
And returns to power the descendants of Ismail,
Who are able to reclaim their lineage.
Then he returns on foot to the holy site,
And the descendants of Ismail come to him joyous.
At every step he takes, his treasurer distributes dinars.

Once he arrives at the palace gates,
He gives Nasr abundant gold and wealth,
And all those who had been poor
Or had been forced into labor prosper.

20 | Eskandar Drives His Host to Egypt

The king leads his host away from this site,
Takes the direction of Jeddah,[95] not lingering there for long.
He commands his army to build many vessels and boats.
The ambitious world-seeker prince travels
From Jeddah to Egypt with his troops.

◇◇◇◇◇◇◇◇◇◇◇◇
95 Jeddah: A port city in the Arabian Peninsula by the Red Sea.

Ghabtoon is then King of Egypt,
And the number of fighters surpasses the imagination.
When he learns that a proud and victorious defeater
Is on his way, he marches off to greet him
With a procession consisting of many slaves,
Pouches filled with gold, a crown, and a throne.

Eskandar is pleased to see him and pays no attention
To the words of Ghabtoon's wicked enemies.
He remains in Egypt for one year,
Until he and his troops are well rested.

The land of Andalusia is governed by a queen,
An intelligent woman, leader of a vast army,
Ambitious and generous, whose name is Keydafeh,
Fortune having granted her glory and her heart's desires.
She selects among her troops a rider able to draw
And perfectly reproduce a subject's face.
She says to him, "Present yourself to Eskandar,
But refrain from disclosing my name or my land.
Observe him, his attention, his speech, his manner,
His demeanor, and how he sits upon the throne.
Draw his portrait from head to toe,
Representing his color, his face, and his stature."

The artist obeys the queen and climbs on his horse,
Ready to execute her orders.
He travels from Andalusia to Egypt, as swift as a courier.
He observes Eskandar, the noble Caesar,
And every time he does, whether on the throne
Or on horseback, he takes paper and Chini compass
And draws his portrait, then departs in haste.

At the sight of Eskandar's image, Keydafeh grows
Troubled and hides the picture with a deep sigh.
She reflects, "This man will trample the world,
Making use of weapons as well as wisdom.
Anyone who appears before him to fight
Will not have the chance to enjoy life on earth."

Meanwhile, Eskandar asks Ghabtoon,
"Who is comparable to Keydafeh in the world?"

Ghabtoon replies, "O King, there is no prince
So powerful anywhere in the world!
No one can estimate the number of her troops
Unless he examines at length the books.
No one equals her in wealth, power, dignity,
Kindness, virtue, wisdom, and benevolence.
The city she has built out of stone
And which a leopard is unable to snatch
Is four farsangs in length and in width.
If you ask the sum of her fortune,
It exceeds any conceivable measure,
And rumors of it have traveled the world."

21 | Eskandar's Letter to Keydafeh

Eskandar summons a scribe to compose a letter
From Eskandar, King of Kings and world conqueror,
To Keydafeh, wise queen, whose power and supremacy
Have awarded her a glorious reputation:
"Let us first offer benediction to the Master of Sun,
Source of the Moon's light and the revolving dome,
Just Creator, Giver of justice and prosperity.
I do not mindlessly wish to usurp your throne.
I simply recognize your merit and your dignity.
I hope to brighten your gloomy thoughts
With this letter, and I hope that
You will then proceed to send me tribute.
You must appreciate the foolishness of opposing me.
Do exhibit caution and foresight,
And demonstrate your power and your pure faith.
Should you make use of ruse in this affair,
You will bring a change of fate only upon yourself.
You may wish to reflect upon the examples of Dara and Foor:
You need not search far to find a lesson."

Once the wind dries the ink, a seal of musk is affixed,
And a racing camel departs by the order of the glorious king.

Upon reading the letter, Keydafeh is surprised.
In her reply, she elaborates on praise due Yazdan:
"Distributor of justice, Creator of the world and dome of sky,

The One to assign good and ill fortune,
The One who granted you victory over the Indian Foor,
Dara, and the noblemen of Sindh.
But such victories have emptied your head.
You compare me to them.
As a result of your conquests,
You place the crown over your head,
But my dignity and my power, my army
And imperial treasure confirm my superiority.
How could I obey a Caesar?
How could I tremble in fear of his threats?
Before me are stationed thousands of warriors.
Heading each battalion of one hundred men is a ruler.
If I were to summon all of my subjects,
There would be no seat left in this land.
When they cross the border to engage in battle,
Each army leader has a wealth of loot in his reach.
Why do you utter such excessive words?
Dara's fall has filled your head with vainglory."

The queen appends her golden seal on the letter
And dispatches a camel as swift as wind.

22 | Eskandar Travels to Andalusia and Captures the Castle of King Faryan

Eskandar reads the letter,
Immediately asks for the blare of trumpets,
And sets his army into motion.
He marches diligently for one month
And arrives at a border governed by King Faryan,
Owner of army, treasury, and vast power.
He possesses an enormous fortified city,
Its walls so high that cranes cannot reach its heights.

Eskandar gathers the troops at the walls.
He summons engineers to bring catapults and mangonels.
In one week, the noble army captures the fortress
And occupies the city.
Then Eskandar enters the square
And commands the end of the bloodshed.

PART TWENTY-ONE

There lives in this town a son of Keydafeh,
Named Keydroosh, son-in-law and favorite of Faryan,
Who has given him his noble daughter to wed,
Thus glorifying his name and stature.
This youth is the sole recipient
Of Faryan's attentions and affections.

During this occupation, King Faryan is killed.
Such was his destiny in the world.
Keydroosh and his wife are taken captive
At the hands of a man named Shahrguir.

Eskandar knows who this man is.
He seeks to find a way out of his predicament.
He calls his vizier to his side,
A powerful man of intelligence, named Bitghoon,
And hands him command, throne, and crown.
He says to him, "I shall offer you a bride.
I shall call you Eskandar, son of Filghoos.
You will place yourself before my throne
In the manner of kings, and when I stand before you,
Covered in my armor, you will command
The bold executioner to cut off the head of Keydroosh.
In all humility, I shall advance to ask for mercy.
You will dismiss the crowd from the audience hall.
I shall double my prayers,
And you will grant him clemency."

The king's vizier is embarrassed.
He cannot understand the mystery behind this affair.
The world king says to him, "This must remain our secret.
You will call me to your side like a messenger.
You will bet at length on Keydafeh,
Then you will send me to her side with ten riders
To say,
        'Go without delay, and return a reply to my letter.
        Bring Keydroosh to accompany me.'"

Bitghoon replies, "I shall do as you command
And execute this ruse according to your instructions."

As the sun draws its sword and night retreats in fright,
Bitghoon sits on the throne, face red and heart disquieted.

Eskandar appears before him, dressed in armor,
Having closed the door to the audience hall
And opened the path of deceit.

Shahrguir brings Keydafeh's son, captive
And shedding copious tears, hand in hand
With his beautiful wife, who shines in beauty.

Bitghoon asks brusquely, "Who is this man?
Why is he shedding tears of grief?"

The young man replies, "Calm yourself.
I am Keydroosh, son of Keydafeh,
And here is Faryan's daughter, my only spouse,
Who has never stepped outside the women's chambers.
I had left to take her to my palace
And to take care of her as if my own life,
But then I fell captive to the grip of Shahrguir,
Heart wounded by the stars and body by arrows."

At these words, Bitghoon's head is troubled.
His heart fills with blood under the pretense.
He jumps up in fury and says to the executioner
Of high deeds: "Dust must envelop these two beings.
Slit their throats with your Indian sword,
Husband and wife, bound up as they are."

A disguised Eskandar approaches, kisses the ground,
And says, "O King, O descendant of the Caesars,
Would you kindly show them mercy?
Such a thing would raise your head above all peoples.
Why would you cut off, in a bout of fury,
The head of an innocent man?
The Creator would not approve of such a thing."

The cautious Bitghoon replies,
"You have rescued and freed two beings."
Then he turns toward Keydroosh and says,
"You are saving your head,
Which was already far from your shoulders.
I shall now send your savior with you.
He will explain to your mother all that I have to say.
If she accepts to send me tribute,

All will be well and no one will fear the threat of war.
Take care of my generous vizier, who will give
Your mother a choice between banquet and battle.
Act toward him as he has acted toward you,
For the heart of a noble man feels the need to be discharged.
When he receives the reply to my letter from the queen,
Protect his return with your care."

Keydroosh replies, "I shall loosen from him
Neither my gaze nor my heart nor my ears.
I shall take care of him as if my own life,
For he is the one who returned to me
My life, my wife, and my world."

23 | Eskandar Visits Keydafeh as Ambassador

The world-conquering king selects
Ten illustrious Rumi men to suit his needs,
Advisors able to keep a secret.
He says to them, "During the journey,
You will only address me as Bitghoon."

Keydroosh takes the head of the procession.
Eskandar does not lose sight of him
And continuously listens to him.

Their powerful chargers gallop like fire.
They reach a mountain of crystal,
Dotted with all sorts of fruit trees and plants.
After crossing this mountainous terrain,
They continue on the road through the queen's land.

Keydafeh, aware of the approach of Keydroosh,
Listens attentively, for it concerns her son.
She takes the road to meet up with him
With a cortege of powerful and blessed men.

As soon as he discerns his mother,
Keydroosh dismounts to express praise and affection.

Keydafeh orders him back on his steed,
And they take the road together, holding hands.

Keydroosh recounts all that transpired,
Cheeks pale at the memory of what occurred
In Faryan's city, and the fact that diadem,
Throne, army, and treasury have been lost.
"The man who is approaching saved my life
And my wife's life from the clutches of Eskandar,
Son of Filghoos, who had ordered our execution.
Now you must do all that he asks of you.
Attempt to give him a reply that conforms
With the fulfillment of my promises."

Her son's account greatly distresses Keydafeh.
She sends for the messenger, receives him graciously,
Offers him a noble seat, and questions him.
A magnificent dwelling is prepared for him, and
She offers him all sorts of dishes, clothes, and carpets.

He spends the night in rest, and the next day,
At daybreak, he visits the queen's court.
The servants raise the curtain and allow him
To pass through the main gate with his horse.

He sees Keydafeh on the ivory throne,
A crown of garnet and turquoise on her head,
Surrounded by numerous slaves,
Dressed in a tunic of golden Chini brocade
And a golden vest embroidered with eyelets of gems.
Her face as resplendent as the sun,
She sits on a throne held by crystal columns,
And before her are slaves adorned with torques
And earrings, wearing boots embellished with fine jewels.

Eskandar is confounded and murmurs
Yazdan's name numerous times,
For he sees a throne next to which
The kingdoms of Rum and Iran count for nothing.

Eskandar approaches the queen
And kisses the ground in the manner of a devious man.
Keydafeh observes him and immediately recognizes him.
She receives him, questions him, and invites him to sit.

Once the shiny sun reaches the horizon,

PART TWENTY-ONE

The time of the audience for strangers has passed.
She asks for spreads, musicians, and wine.

Long tables of teakwood, encrusted in ivory
And inlaid with golden stars, are set up.
Countless dishes are served,
And once they are consumed, ample wine is poured.

Keydafeh asks for gold and silver cups,
And the guests drink to her health.
As they sip the wine, the queen takes a moment
To observe Eskandar more closely.
She says to her treasurer, "Bring me, just as it is,
The brilliant bolt of silk on which is a charming portrait.
But do not touch it rudely with your hand."

The treasurer obeys her command and hands her the silk.
She studies it attentively, then she glances at Eskandar
And is amazed at the resemblance between him
And the portrait, immediately recognizing him
As the Caesar, commander of a glorious army.

She also recognizes that he is deceiving her
By making himself his own envoy before her court.
She says to him, "O powerful man, come here
And relay to us Eskandar's message."

He replies, "The world king has spoken to me
In the presence of the land's noblemen
And has charged me with a missive for Keydafeh,
Queen of pure heart:
          'Seek only righteousness in the world.
          Guard yourself from avoiding our command,
          And observe the wise treaty we propose.
          If you allow duplicity to dwell in your heart,
          I shall launch an army to shatter you and your host,
          And to burn down your entire land.
          Everywhere I find hints of your skills,
          And I do not wish to rush to engage in war.
          You are blessed with insight and a pure life.
          The world trusts your subtle wisdom.
          Now if you refuse to pay tribute and fees,
          You will have cause to fear.

If you recognize that you are not powerful enough
To resist me, you will find me benevolent and fair,
As long as you remain distant from falsehoods and lies.'"

Keydafeh flinches at these words and understands
That her only course of action is silence. She says,
"Return to your palace, and rest with your friends.
I shall give you my reply tomorrow
And will advise upon your return."

Eskandar withdraws to his chambers.
He passes the night to avoid impending difficulties.

As the brilliant torch of sun raises its head
Above mountain crests and plains
To gleam like a golden, silken cover,
Eskandar presents himself at the queen's court,
A smile fixed on his lips, a heart black with worry.
The master of ceremonies spots him,
Interrogates him, and presents him to the queen.

He finds the audience hall filled with people.
He observes the queen's throne made of rock crystal,
Encrusted with carnelian and chrysolite,
With a frame of precious royal stones.
The platform is made of sandalwood and aloeswood,
And the columns are covered with onyx and turquoise.

Eskandar is in awe of this sight,
Full of majesty, splendor, and power.
He cries out, "I find here a palace
To which worshippers will never find an equal."

He advances with dignity toward the queen.
A golden throne is placed for him.
Keydafeh tells him, "O eminent Bitghoon,
Why are you so astonished by this palace?
Are there no such places in the land of Rum
That this poor country surprises you?"

Eskandar replies, "O Queen,
Do not disparage or deride your home.
Your head rises above the heads of kings,

For your sea is a mine of precious jewels."

Keydafeh smiles at Bitghoon, and her heart rejoices.
She dismisses everyone, asks the pretend envoy
To sit closer to her, and says to him,
"O son of Filghoos, are feast and battle,
Prosperity and adversity indifferent to you?"

Eskandar pales at the queen's words.
His soul is afflicted, his cheeks blanch as he replies,
"O wise queen, you must not speak so.
Why do you seek to collect tribute from me?
Who is the responsible party who led you on this path?
I give thanks to the nurturing Creator
Who keeps us alive that at this moment
I am not in the company of one of our court's noblemen.
What you recounted, on the subject of the Caesar,
Is as if my soul is being severed from my body.
I am Bitghoon, O world mistress,
Do not call me son of Filghoos."

Keydafeh says, "Exempt your lips from such discourse.
I am certain you are Eskandar.
If I were to place your portrait before your eyes,
It would confirm this fact and you would cease
To search for an expedient and attempt to be calm."

She retrieves the square of silk and places it before him.
It is a beautiful portrait of King Eskandar himself.
The latter bites his lips, the day dims for him,
And he says, "I certainly hope that no one
Is around who may be concealing a sword."

Keydafeh replies, "If you had a sword hanging
On your chest's harness, neither your strength
Nor your sharp blade would serve you well.
You would have neither a battlefield
Nor an open pathway to flee."

Eskandar says, "A prince who wishes to conquer the world
With his courage must not retreat before danger.
A man without heart will never reach the heights of power.
If I had my weapons at this time,

This entire palace would turn into a sea of blood.
I would kill you and stab myself before my enemies."

24 | Keydafeh Advises Eskandar

Keydafeh has a fit of laughter on his account,
His courage, and his angry words. She says to him,
"O lion King, do not boast at length about your valor.
It is not your power that helped you overcome
The Indian Foor or Dara, son of Daaraab,
Or any of the warriors of Sindh.
The days of these mighty rulers were meant
To come to an end, and the stars favored you.
Now you are proud of your audacity
Because you have become master of world and era.
Know that happiness comes from Yazdan,
To whom you must give thanks for your life.
You said that world wisdom belongs to you,
But what price can you draw from your acumen
If you throw yourself into the dragon's jaws,
If you sew your shroud in your days of youth,
And if you act as your own envoy?

"I am not accustomed to either shedding blood
Or foolishly contending with a powerful man.
A king able to do as he wills acts as generously
As a sage, with a sense of justice.
Anyone who spills the blood of a king
Will find in his tomb only intense fire.
Therefore, remain here in trust,
Then depart joyously.
When you return, assume new habits.
Do not go anywhere as your own emissary,
For even the dust knows that you are Eskandar.
There is no mighty world ruler
Whose portrait is not in my possession,
Painted in this fashion on a piece of silk.
I entrust these to the care of a prudent man
And submit them to the science of astrologers,
To learn whether to trust or fear the individual.
When a judicious king shows compassion,

Men and women of the era will sing his praises.

"Furthermore, as long as you stay here,
I shall call you Bitghoon and, consequently,
Will seat you further from my throne,
So that no one will suspect your secret,
Your name and your fame.
Then I shall dismiss you, treating you with kindness.
But you must be cautious and promise to never express
Enmity or reflect evil thoughts for my sons,
My land, my family, and my allies.
Furthermore, you must promise to recognize me
As an equal and as the rightful sovereign of this nation."

Eskandar rejoices at her discourse.
Her words free him of worry and assure his safe return.
He swears by the Justice Giver, all powerful,
By the faith of the Messiah, and the sword of battle,
"That I will always act fairly and kindly
Toward your land, your sons and your relatives,
For as long as they are around,
And will never seek to deceive or undermine them."

Once the oath is taken, Keydafeh says,
"There is one thing I must warn you about.
My son Teynoosh has little respect
For my wisdom and my advice.
He is a conceited man, Foor's son-in-law.
He must not suspect your identity, from near or far,
Although you are very close friends,
For he will wish to avenge the death of Foor
And would make the sky fall onto earth in battle.
Now return to your palace content,
And do not think about life's tragedies."

25 | Eskandar Is Cautious With Teynoosh

Eskandar leaves, his heart feeling as high as a mountain.
Even the wise man worries about the dangers of death.
Keydafeh had the power to erase his frown,
And he does not think to deviate from her will.

He remains still for the night. The next day,
Early in the morning, he exits his palace
And enters the queen's audience hall.
She is decked out on the throne, surrounded
By flowers and members of her court.
Above the hall are ornaments of ivory and gold,
A variety of precious gems inlaid in gold.
Around the queen are musk-scented bouquets,
And before her stand her two sons, respectfully,
Teynoosh, the horse-conqueror, and Keydroosh.
Both are caring and attentive to their mother.

The youngest son says to Keydafeh,
"O Queen of fortunate star, dispenser of justice,
Act in a way that Bitghoon departs content,
With a guide to avoid anyone mistreating him
On the road or taking him for an adversary.
He is the one who saved my life, more precious
To me than anyone in this resplendent world."

His mother replies, "I shall honor him
And be sure to follow your advice."

The queen addresses Eskandar:
"Reveal now your secret. Tell us your wish.
What are Eskandar's plans? What are his orders?
What do you know of his desires?"

The disguised envoy replies, "O illustrious Queen,
I am in your presence for too long. Eskandar told me,
        'Depart and ask of Keydafeh tribute for her land.
        If you delay your return, I shall send my host.
        I shall leave her neither land nor crown,
        Neither throne nor daylight,
        Neither peace nor royal dignity.'"

26 | Teynoosh's Anger Toward Eskandar

At these words, Teynoosh is unleashed like a fierce wind.
He says, "You wretched, foolish man, you will cease
To be considered a member of the human race.

Do you not know before whom you sit?
Do not place yourself thus before the queen
And diverge insolently from her commands.
Your head is full of anger and arrogance.
You don't even disclose the identity
Of the king in whose name you speak.
You must display the respect due her majesty,
Or else I shall cut off your head
Like one plucks an orange off a branch.
This very night, I shall display your head
To the army in vengeance for the death of Foor."

His mother bursts out at him as she sees that his mind,
Eager for battle, is wandering off the subject.
She says to Teynoosh,
"He does not speak on his own behalf.
You must not speak and act so rudely."

Then she turns to point at Keydroosh and says,
"This man, Bitghoon, saved your brother's life
And is responsible for bringing him here.
Now speak of him in a more gentle manner."

The son exits the hall, wrathful,
His eyes burning with his heart's blood.

Keydafeh whispers to Eskandar,
"Teynoosh is an unreasonable, foolish man.
We must not allow him to covertly plan a strike.
We must take care and reflect on a course of action.
You are knowledgeable and worldly.
Contemplate a solution to this predicament."

Eskandar replies to her, "What you say is true,
But you must call Teynoosh back."

The world mistress summons her son
And sits him in the glorious court.
Eskandar says to him, "O renowned man,
If you wish to attain your heart's desires,
It is best for you to remain calm.
I do not resent you for what has occurred.
I accept all your words. I am the one who suffers

Most from the injustice of Eskandar, who remains
Peacefully on his throne with the crown on his head.
Meanwhile, he sends a majestic queen someone
To collect tribute so that any harm and injury
Provoked by his enemies fall on my shoulders.

"O prince, listen to my advice.
Refrain from animosity.
Know that I am well enough upset at him
And have nurtured the thought of killing him.
I shall seize him and bring him to you.
Once the world is free of his presence,
I shall be on my way.
You are not cognizant of my skills and abilities.
I shall rush to take him the reply
And come up with a proposition for him.
If I seize him by the hand and bring him to you
In a way that he is not escorted by troops,
You will find him free of sword, throne, and crown.
What will be my share of this kingdom?
How will you prove to me your gratitude?"

Teynoosh replies, "I hear you; we must act swiftly."
He turns to the envoy: "It all depends on you
And if you execute the plan I propose.
If you act in good faith, I shall give you part of the treasure,
Crates of gold and all the rest, stallions, royal servants.
As for me, I shall remain at your service.
You will be world master and know total happiness.
You will be my vizier and my treasurer in this land."

Eskandar rises from his seat to take
The prince's hand to conclude the settlement.

Teynoosh asks him, "How will you successfully
Accomplish this deed, by what sort of ruse?"

Eskandar says, "Once I take leave of the queen,
You must travel the road with me, with an escort
Of one thousand illustrious riders from your host.
I have spotted a forest along the road.
I shall place you there as ambush with your troops.
I shall outpace you to travel to the king,

Where I shall observe his evil mind.
I shall tell him that Keydafeh sends him
So much wealth that he will never want for anything,
And Teynoosh, her older son, sends his greetings.
But the queen's envoy declared that he dare not
Present himself before the king with his army.

"I shall say to Eskandar,
        'If it pleases his majesty
        To journey with his wise men to Teynoosh
        And his companions, he will receive the riches there.
        Teynoosh will show himself
        Once he sees you without a host.'
When Eskandar hears my golden words,
He will not suspect a devious plot.
He will place himself beneath the shelter of the trees.
He will ask his treasurer for crown and throne.
Rest at peace on the outcome of fate, for, at that moment,
You may surround him with your valiant escort.
This will be your chance to execute vengeance,
A time to reach your purpose
And aggrandize your name and status.
Once you are able to seize him, I shall belong to you.
I shall be, if so you wish, the guardian of your land.
My affairs will prosper, my wishes will be fulfilled,
And you will bring back vast treasure, slaves, and horses."

Teynoosh rejoices at these words.
He sits as tall as a noble cypress tree and replies,
"I hope that the brilliant light of day will dim for him
And that he will fall unexpectedly into my trap
As retribution for the blood he has spilled in the world:
The blood of Dara, son of Daaraab; princes from Sindh;
And, of course, the blood of Foor, valiant Indian king."

Keydafeh hears the conversation with Eskandar
And perceives the ruse with the eye of wisdom.
She smiles secretly to herself, hiding her coral lips
Beneath her delicate silken dress.

Eskandar takes his leave, his mind replete with worry.

27 | Eskandar's Pact With Keydafeh and His Return to His Host

Eskandar spends the long night seeking a way out.
As the sun displays the embroidered hem
Of its Chini robe, lifting from earth its golden banner,
And as the glistening purple silk of night vanishes,
Eskandar presents himself before Keydafeh.
The chamberlain receives him according to custom.

The world master dismounts and enters the queen's hall.
Visitors and strangers are dismissed,
And the ambassador appears before the queen.

At the sight of her on the throne, Eskandar says,
"May Jupiter be your wisdom's companion!
By the faith of the Messiah and the righteous word,
By Yazdan the all-knowing, Witness to our language,
By the worship and cult of the powerful cross,
By the life and head of the redoubtable queen,
By the belt of priests and by the holy spirit,
I swear that from here on, the land of Andalusia
Will never catch sight of me.
I swear that I shall never send a host to invade it
And never contrive any sort of ruse against you.
I swear that I shall never cause any harm your sons,
Nor command any other to do so.
I swear by my life that I shall never oppress you,
That I shall treat your friends as brothers
And revere your throne like the holy cross."

In this oath, Keydafeh observes the fairness of his heart
And the sincerity of his pledge and commitment.
She asks for golden seats to line the hall
And to deck the area in grand Chini style.
She summons noblemen of blessed star
And invites them to sit on the thrones.

Then she convokes her two noble sons,
Her parents, and her allies, and she says,
"One must avoid pain and suffering in this fleeting world.
I hope the rotation of fate will guard me

From a share of vengeance and fight.
Eskandar will never tire of battle,
Even if he were to slaughter the sky.
He wishes to engage in war against us to plunder
Our treasures, yet all the wealth in the world
Is not worth the price of countless hardships.
I desire neither a fight with him
Nor to plunge my kingdom into a state of turmoil.
I shall give him a sensible reply,
Shower him with honors, and advise him at length.
But if, despite my counsel, he insists on battle,
If he disregards the connections
And the duties that bind him to me,
I shall march against him with my host
In a way as to make sky and earth take pity on him.
But the attempt he has made will not bring ill luck,
And we must hope that our friendship will endure.
What do you say and what is your reply?
Give me valuable and blessed advice on this affair."

All the noblemen raise their heads to reply,
"O Queen full of justice and nobility,
No one remembers a monarch worthy of comparison.
You only speak the truth. Happy are those ruled by you!
If the king gains your friendship,
What better outcome could a wise man ask for?
He will not attempt to seize your treasures,
And he will not wish to afflict you at the price of them.
If a ruler such as Eskandar comes from Rum
And converts with his sword the land into a sea of blood,
Exits your court with invaluable presents,
Still all the wealth in the world is not worthy
For him to engage in war.
We only wish to maintain peace in our land.
The name of a war-starved man is never celebrated."

The queen listens to the words of her advisors of pure heart.
She opens the door to her treasury and asks
For a golden torque, bracelets, and her father's crown,
The likes of which no one in this city has ever seen.

She says to the envoy,

"This crown with its gems is above all value.
No one has ever possessed such a priceless piece.
Eskandar is worthy of this royal crown.
I am fond of him as much as I am fond of my own sons."

Keydafeh possesses a throne made up of seventy pieces
That could only be assembled by a single skilled man.
The pieces are tightly fitted together,
The tips of the wood delicately mortised with gold.
The extremities of the legs are shaped as dragon's heads,
And no one can estimate the value of the inlaid gems.
There are at least four hundred jewels worthy of a king
And as many garnets, of which two,
The color of a pomegranate bud, weigh one mithqal each.
There are four hundred raw emeralds, as green as rainbows.

Forty camels are loaded with clothing.
The heart of the woman bestowing
Such treasure is as vast as the depth of the sea.
She asks for loads of five hundred elephants,
The length of many miles, more than four hundred
Splendid leopard skins called Berber,
And one thousand speckled suedes,
Full of beauty and richly colored.
Then she calls for one hundred hunting dogs,
Fast as arrows and able to outrun gazelles,
Two hundred buffaloes driven by slaves.
Next come four hundred ebony thrones
Bedecked in brocade and silk,
Four more of fresh aloeswood, so rich
They are the envy of the sun and of the color gold.

From the palace, she further orders
One hundred noble harnessed stallions
And adds them to the gifts and presents.
Finally, she asks for one thousand swords,
Indian sabers, battle armor, and two hundred helmets.
She relays her instructions to her treasurer:
"Without delay, count everything for Bitghoon,
And tell him to prepare for departure tomorrow at dawn."

As daybreak lifts its shiny banner and

The violet-colored firmament borrows a shade of white,
The earth is fresh and the mountain rose-colored.
At that time, timpani beat at the palace door.
Eskandar climbs on his horse,
Having obtained permission to return home.

The valiant Teynoosh puts order to his escort,
Treks from the great square to Keydafeh's palace,
And says to her, "Farewell, dear mother,
May your mind remain young!
May your head be the weft of the cloth
With the sky as the link!"

He marches from station to station to the camp
Of the illustrious Eskandar, ally to good fortune.
The latter asks for the loads to be placed in the woods,
Where they find a running source of water and trees.
He says to Teynoosh, "Remain calmly here.
When you have rested sufficiently, lift the cup.
I shall depart to fulfill my promises.
I shall act in every way most loyally."

Eskandar retires to his pavilion, where his troops gather
With shouts of joy to adorn the imperial crown.
They had despaired, unsure whether they would
Ever set their sight on their illustrious leader again.
The entire host blesses him in a common voice
And bows down to the ground at his feet.

The king selects one thousand of the most illustrious
Rumi noblemen, avid for battle, and they depart,
Dressed in chain mail and armed with bull-headed mace.
They form a battle line
Around the periphery of the woods.

Eskandar then shouts a cry: "O audacious man,
Do you wish to fight or to run away?"

Teynoosh trembles and regrets the plans and designs
He had once deemed so wise.
He says, "O noble-minded King,
Praise is more worthy than quarrel.
This is not what you promised my mother.

Did you not say that you will not stray off the path?
Execute a good deed as you did
With my brother Keydroosh. Act in good faith."

Eskandar replies, "O King, why do you bend
In the midst of such beautiful company?
You have nothing to apprehend from me.
Do not allow fear to enter your heart.
I shall not cause harm to any member of your family.
I shall not violate our treaty with Keydafeh,
For vile is the king who breaches a truce."

Teynoosh dismounts instantly, in great distress.
He kisses the ground, and the world master
Takes his hand, fulfilling his promise.

Eskandar says, "Do not be troubled, give in to joy.
I hold no grudge against you in my heart.
I have placed my hand in yours, in the presence
Of your mother seated on her golden throne.
I promised you that I would place your hand
In the hand of the king, world master.
Today I have fulfilled such promise,
For vain words do not suit a monarch.
I am Eskandar, and back then it was Eskandar
Who gave you his good intentions.
Keydafeh was well aware that the hand you held
Belonged to the Rumi king."

The Caesar commands a servant to place a throne
Beneath the shelter of a blossoming tree.
He asks for a spread, for musicians and wine.
They revel in wine the color of a red tulip.
He distributes gold and silver to his companions
And, to those who merit them, crowns and belts.

He says to Teynoosh, "Do not linger in these woods,
Far from your land. It is not a site worthy of you.
Tell Keydafeh in my name,
          'O wise Queen and world mistress, farseeing
          And cautious, I shall be loyal to my oaths
          For as long as I live, and my soul
          Will remain full of affection for you.'"

28 | Eskandar Visits the Land of Brahmins[96]

Eskandar drives his host away from the area
And marches in haste to the land of the Brahmins,
Where he wishes to learn the ancient customs
Of these men devoted to abstinence.

With news of the approach of the king and his host,
The pious Brahmins emerge from the mountain.
They write a letter to Eskandar, king of wise men,
Beginning by conjuring the names of noblemen,
From the World Master to the world king:
"May his majesty be forever victorious!
May his wisdom and his power always expand!
O valiant King, Yazdan has given you this vast world.
What do you seek in our impoverished land,
The home of divine servants?
If you are in search of treasure,
It would appear that reason fails you.
One finds patience and wisdom here,
Two qualities that infuse our hearts with tranquillity.
No one can take patience away from us,
And never did wisdom cause harm to anyone.
You will find here only a bare flock,
Dispersed by rain and snow, and if you linger long,
You will have to consume the seeds of wild herbs."

The envoy, wearing around his waist
A belt of roots and plants, reaches Eskandar.

Eskandar observes him, reads the letter,
And decides to remain innocuous and fair.
He stations his army around the town
And advances with a few notable Rumi men.

The holy men respectfully advance to meet him,
Carrying with them certain valueless objects,
For they have neither treasure nor seeds nor crops.
Everyone summons blessings upon the world king.

96 Brahmins: See footnote 13.

Eskandar observes the Brahmins, listens to their acclaim.
He sees that they walk barefoot, and bare of body and head.
Though they are naked,
Their souls bear the fruits of wisdom.
Their clothes consist of leaves and herbs,
And their meals of wild seeds,
Though their land is full of game.
They are unfamiliar with battle and feast.
They eat and sleep in the mountain and the desert,
Gathering in naked groups everywhere.

Eskandar asks, "How do you sleep, eat, and rest?
How do you tolerate the dust of battle?
What is your share of happiness in this world?
For the sky does not separate the poison from the antidote."

One of the wise men replies, "O world conqueror,
Never do we speak of glory and battle.
We have no need for clothing, bedding, or prepared food.
Since man is born nude from his mother's breast,
He must not be sensitive in dress,
As he will return to the dust unclothed.
This world is only a place of fear and misery.
The ground is our bed, the air is our covering,
And we keep our gaze fixed on the road,
To determine what sort of fate awaits us.

"The ambitious man strains himself with much effort
To attain something that is not worth the exertion.
One day he must leave this fleeting sojourn
And abandon his crown and treasure.
He will be accompanied only by his good deeds
While his head and throne will rest in the dust."

Eskandar asks, "Are there in the world
More things visible or more things concealed?
Are there more people alive or more deceased?"

The Brahmin replies, "O King,
If you count one hundred thousand dead,
You will not find a man alive in proportion to these.
Happy are those who do not succumb to hell.
But this man living now must also die.

Each one of us dies to leave a place for another."

Eskandar asks whether land or water
Prevails in the world where the sun shines.

The Brahmin replies, "O King,
Water is the guardian of the land."

Eskandar asks, "Who is awake and aware?
Who is the greatest sinner on earth?
For some men live while others move around
Without knowing why they wander on earth."

The Brahmin replies, "O pure-hearted King
Who seeks to investigate the mysteries,
The one aware is the one who has few desires.
The greatest sinner is the powerful man
Who hungers for vengeance
And whose greed makes him lose his mind.
If you wish to know him well,
Take a look at your own body.
The earth submits to your will.
It is as if the turning sky is your parent.
Yet you still want and search for more.
Can you safeguard yourself for the dim dust?
Greed has become your soul's hell.
Let us hope that my words will help you
Renounce your attachments and inclinations."

Eskandar asks, "Who is the master of our souls?
Who is our permanent guard against evil?"

The Brahmin replies, "It is greed that is master,
It is the essence of vengeance and the soul of sin."

Eskandar asks, "What is the nature of greed,
Since one must mourn the desire to boost oneself?"

The Brahmin replies, "Greed and need are two deevs
Who perpetually conceive lengthy calamities.
One of them has lips parched by misery, the other
Spends nights in an abundance generated by insomnia.
However, misfortune will capture both as prey.

Happy is the one whose soul is open to wisdom!"

As Eskandar listens to these words,
His face turns yellow as the flower of fenugreek,
His cheeks pale, and his eyes shed tears.
But his smiling features contract as he asks,
"What do you need from me?
I shall not spare my wealth for you,
And never shall I hesitate to fight for you."

One of them replies, "O glorious King,
Close for us the door of old age and death."

The king replies, "It is of no use to appeal to death.
How can you remove yourself from the sharp claws
Of this mighty dragon whom you will never escape,
Even if you were made of solid steel?
A youth, no matter how valiant,
No matter how long he remains on earth,
Cannot escape the grips of old age."

The Brahmin replies,
"O wise and powerful King, world master,
Since you know that we have no means
Of avoiding death and since there is no suffering
More cruel than old age, why do you
Put so much effort into conquering the world?
Why do you foolishly strain
To smell the poisoned flower?
The hardships you endured will remain after you,
But the fruits of your labors and your treasury
Will change hands and be dispatched to your enemies.
You weary yourself to labor for others.
This shows a lack of sagacity
And clearly brings light to your stupidity.
White hair is the messenger of death.
How can you wish to remain alive?"

The enlightened king says, "If a servant,
By the grace of the Creator, has escaped my wars,
He would nonetheless perish by the sky's provisions.
Neither the wise man nor the warrior can fend off
His destiny, no matter how persistent his attempts.

Furthermore, those who succumbed in my wars
Or whose days were shortened by the stars
Were worthy of their fates by their actions
And by the blood they spilled,
For an unjust man cannot escape.
They have been stricken by divine justice
When they strayed off the path of wisdom.
No one can elude divine will
Or discover the workings of this world."

Eskandar distributes gifts and does not
Remain in the presence of the Brahmins for long.
He departs without causing harm to anyone
And resumes his eastward trek
Eager to explore new lands.

29 | Eskandar Reaches the Far East Sea and Witnesses Strange Phenomena

From the land of the Brahmins, Eskandar arrives
At a site with an exceptionally vast and deep sea.
Men wearing veils over their faces like women
Approach, dressed in robes and decked in color and scent.
Their language is neither Arabic nor Pahlavi,
Neither Chini nor Turkic or Persian.
They live on fish alone, as they have no access
To the outside world to gather supplies.

Their strange appearance surprises Eskandar.
He invokes the name of Yazdan in his native Rumi tongue.
All at once, a mountain emerges from the water,
Humid and fresh, and as yellow as the sun.

Eskandar asks for a speedy boat,
For he wishes to observe this mountain.
One of the philosophers says to the king,
"There is no path leading to the vast sea.
Wait until a lesser person has a chance to investigate."

Thirty men, half Rumi and half Persian,
Sit on the boat and navigate across the waters.

They discover that the mountain is a yellow fish
That, at the moment the crew approaches,
Pulls down the vessel with a sudden movement
And makes it disappear into the depths.

Eskandar and his troops, transfixed by the sight,
Murmur the name of the Creator.

The Rumi philosopher says to Eskandar,
"Science is a most valuable thing.
Through it, a wise man becomes king among kings.
If you had left and had perished, the heart of our host
Would have wallowed in blood."

He drives the troops away from this site
And arrives at the edge of a beautiful lake
Surrounded by poles of bamboo so enormous
They appear to be large trunks of plane trees,
Measuring more than ten cubits in thickness
And forty cubits in height.
All the houses of this land are built out of bamboo,
And the ground buckles beneath the weight.
It is impossible to remain long in these thickets,
For no one could drink the brackish water there.

Eskandar journeys past this lake and finds deep waters.
The land is beautiful, the water like honey,
And the soil exhales the scent of musk.

The army takes some food and prepares to pass the night.
But a great many restless aquatic snakes emerge,
As well as scorpions the color of fire from the forest.
The world dims and constricts for the sleepers.
On every side die countless sages, wise men, and warriors.

Hundreds of boars armed with long tusks,
As sharp as diamonds, and lions more massive than bulls
Attack from all sides, allowing no hope of escape.

The troops retreat, away from the water's edge.
They set ablaze the bamboo forest and kill so many beasts
That they find it hard to carve a path through.

30 | Eskandar Reaches the Land of Habash[97] and Triumphs in Battle

From there, the sun-faced king
Marches to the land of Habash.
He finds it to be rendered black like a raven's plumage,
For the inhabitants themselves are black with eyes of fire.
They form a host of huge, robust men,
Bearing naked bodies and imposing statures.

At the sight of enemy dust stirred in the distance,
They shout cries that rise above the dark clouds.
They unite in masses of thousands and thousands,
And the king's eyesight dims at the spectacle of them.

They come for Eskandar and kill countless warriors.
They brandish bones in lieu of javelin and spear,
Which they hurl at the men.

The king commands his troops to dress in battle armor.
The people of Habash rush uncovered into the fight,
But they are overwhelmed by the troops
Who resemble lions and massacre a huge number.
Those who survive flee from the battleground.

So much blood is spilled
That the earth resembles the Sea of Chin.
Valleys and mountains are stained in red.
Everywhere are heaps of cadavers,
Which they cover with brushwood and scrub
To subsequently smolder in a blaze.

As night descends, one could hear rhinoceroses howling,
Their crash drawing closer.
Eskandar dons his chainmail and helmet.
Each creature is larger than a buffalo.
The one at the lead is larger than an elephant
And sports a horn and body as dark as indigo.
It kills a great many renowned warriors

◇◇◇◇◇◇◇◇◇◇◇◇◇◇
97 Habash: Or al-Habash, an ancient part of eastern Africa situated in present-day
Ethiopia.

And submits to repeated attacks
Without turning its back on its attackers.
In the end, it is defeated by a shower of arrows.
This elephant vanquisher resembles a mountain of steel.

From there, Eskandar hastily leads his army away,
Invoking the name of Yazdan, Justice Giver.

31 | Eskandar Nears the People With Pliable Feet and Kills a Dragon

Upon his arrival in the land populated
By the people with pliable feet,
Eskandar notices that many of them possess
Neither horse nor armor, neither sword nor mace,
Yet every warrior has the stature of a cypress tree.

He hears a deafening sound, akin to thunder,
Coming from the host of naked men running
On their knees and bearing a resemblance to deevs.

Eskandar's troops advance, ready for battle
And vengeance, striking blows of arrow and sword.
Their brilliant day turns into night.
They toss large stones through the air
That whistle like autumnal wind through trees.

Once the number of men with pliable feet decreases,
Eskandar rests and retreats with his troops.

He marches swiftly to a city where one
Can distinguish neither center nor border.
The inhabitants approach him respectfully
And with open hearts, wanting for nothing.
They come with carpets, clothing, and a variety of food.

Eskandar receives them in friendship
And addresses them questions,
Assigning honor according to rank.

The king asks his warriors to settle on the plain.

PART TWENTY-ONE

The land turns into a spread of silk
With tent pavilions dressed on the plain,
And army camps scattered around.
Soon the newcomers engage in feast and revelry.

They continue to rest and feast for some days.
This worldly host, experienced in the ups
And downs of battle, has a chance to ease up.
Eskandar awaits the propitious day
When he can march his army away.
He questions the right moment but receives no hint of it.

He spots a mountain that rises to the stars,
As if it is reaching to pluck out the sky.
The men who dwell there are few in numbers,
And they do not remain on the location at night.

Eskandar asks them which road leads to it
And how he could have his troops traverse it.

They bless him and say, "O illustrious King,
There is a way to cross this mountain,
Should a guide dare do so,
But on the opposite slope resides a dragon
Whose acrid venom would subjugate a wolf.
Your host could not march past him unharmed.
The smoke of his poison climbs to the moon.
His mouth spews flames, and his two loops
Form nooses able to capture elephants.
No one in the city dares attack him.
Every night, he requires five buffaloes for sustenance.
We purchase these and take them up to the boulders,
Carrying them, full of mistrust,
Terrified that he may come on this side
And cause harm to countless people."

The valiant king selects a few of his men
And tells them to refrain from feeding the dragon.

As the time of his meal passes,
The dragon fiercely advances to their side.
Eskandar asks his warriors to shower him with arrows.
The dragon storms forward and,

With its breath, inhales a few of the men.

Eskandar, son of Filghoos, asks for drums and timpani.
They light a number of fires here and there.
Fearful of the sound of the instruments,
The beast retreats to his side of the mountain.

Once the sun raises its head over the house of bull,
The song of the lark is heard in the rose garden.
Eskandar distributes silver from his treasury
And asks for five buffaloes. He kills them and skins them,
While leaving some of the pelt attached to the heads.
With this ruse, he returns courage to his kind men.
They stuff the buffalo skins with poison and oil,
And blow air into them to inflate them.
Hand in hand, they take the direction of the dragon
As the skins are lifted and carried by shifts of men.

As they near the dragon, Eskandar notices
An object that appears to be a black cloud
With a blue tongue and two blood-red eyes.
Its jaws splutter flames, ravaging everything in sight.

With a slight sense of relief
And observing the dragon uneasily, the men send
The buffaloes rolling down the mountainside.
The beast quickly swallows them all, body, skin, and flesh.
The poison infiltrates its form, saturates it,
And pierces the intestines to invade its brains.
The dragon strikes its head against the boulders repeatedly.

Eskandar's host sends a shower of arrows raining on him,
And this massive mountain, able to eat wild beasts, falls.
The troops pass by the creature, deeming it a vile thing.

Eskandar then leads his army to a lofty mountain
That strikes with awe the bravest men.
With good eyesight, one could see from afar its crest,
As pointy as the blade of a sword.
At the top is a golden throne,
Placed away from people and crowds.
On it sits an old man, bearer of majestic mien,
Even after his death. He wears a coat of brocade,

And his head bears a crown inlaid with various gems.
Surrounding him is abundant gold and silver.
No one could pass him and go beyond.
Anyone who climbed up to him,
To ask this dead man for something,
Would tremble, no matter how intrepid he may be,
And would instantly succumb to death.

Eskandar climbs to the crest, fixes his gaze on the dead man
Covered in gold and silver, and hears a voice saying,
"O King, you have ended your career.
You have destroyed royal thrones.
You have raised your head above the vault of sky.
You have slain your enemies and many a friend.
It is time. It is your time to depart."

At this voice, the king's cheeks shine like torches,
And he leaves the mountain, wounded at the heart.

32 | Eskandar Encounters Marvels in Haroom,[98] the City of Women

Eskandar departs with his noble Rumi men
And marches toward the great city of Haroom,
An unguarded city entirely occupied by women.
Each resident has a woman's breast on the right of the body,
A breast similar to a pomegranate rolled on a piece of silk,
While the left breast is as flat as a man's breast,
Easy to dress in armor on battle day.

The proud king arrives with his Rumi men
At the gates of Haroom City.
He writes a letter according to the rules of law,
As suits a man of noble birth,
Composed by the King of Iran and Rum,
And addressed to the rulers of the land of Haroom.

He begins in praise of the Creator of the celestial spheres,
From Whom we receive favors, justice, and affection:

◇◇◇◇◇◇◇◇◇◇◇◇◇
98 Haroom: A fictional city with only women as residents.

"Anyone endowed with a sensible mind,
Anyone who does not waste his life away
In frivolous endeavors, is aware of my high deeds
And the far reaches of my dominion.
Anyone who refuses to submit to my command
Is certain to meet the dark dust for his final rest.
I do not wish to leave a single land unexplored.
If I come to you, it is not to fight or to obtain wealth
But with the sole purpose of furthering my knowledge.
My soul is keen on peace, justice, and the will to feast.
If you possess a wise man, prudent and learned,
Allow him to read this letter full of sound counsel,
And may the noblemen of your land
Prepare to come and greet me on the road,
An act for which no one will have reason to repent."

He dispatches one of his wise Rumi philosophers
To Haroom with the letter full of sweet words.
Close to the city, he sees only women.
The entire host is outside the city walls,
Standing on the plain to contemplate the Rumi visitor.

The residents with good counsel gather to listen
To the reading of the letter by a learned woman.
Once they consider its contents and the king's intentions,
They sit down to compose a reply:
"May you live eternally, O renowned King!
We have your envoy sitting before us
And have read your letter from beginning to end.
In the first place, about your mention of kings,
Your war victories and your past battles,
Know that if you bring a host to the city of Haroom,
You will see neither earth nor soil.
The city contains uncountable streets, pathways,
And neighborhoods, each populated by ten thousand
Women who sleep in coats of mail lined with silk.

"The expansion of our numbers restricts us.
None of our women has a husband,
For we choose to remain veiled virgins.
Anywhere we travel, we find only deep waters.
Any woman who leans toward marriage

PART TWENTY-ONE

Is banished and cast into the deep waters,
Which she must cross in fair or stormy weather.
Once married, if she gives birth to a daughter
And if this child takes the ways of women,
Seeking color and perfume,
She may not leave her place of birth.
She may breathe in the air of the sky sublime.
But if she has the ways of a man of tall stature,
Then she may join our community in Haroom.

"On the other hand, if the mother gives birth to a son,
He will not find a place among us.
Every night, ten thousand virgins
Keep watch on the water's edge.
We place a golden crown higher than Gemini
On the head of those who overthrow
A lion-man from his horse on the day of battle.
Thirty thousand women are in our midst,
Wearing crown and golden earrings
For having defeated a proud and valiant man.

"You are powerful and of an illustrious race.
Do not close the door to glory and fame.
Rumors will spread that you fought women,
That you lost and shamefully fled the battlefield.
It would be a source of great humiliation for you
That will not be forgotten, for as long as the world exists.
But if you want to come with Rumi noblemen
And take a tour of the city of Haroom,
If you act with justice and courtesy,
You will be received with benevolence and feast.
Should your actions and intentions prove otherwise,
We shall meet you with a host
That will eclipse the sun and moon."

The reply to the king's letter complete,
A woman is elected as messenger.
She takes the road wearing a crown and a robe
Worthy of a queen, and is escorted by ten beautiful women.

As they solemnly near the king on horseback,
He sends a cortege to receive them.

The illustrious woman hands over the letter
And relays the contents of the missive.

Eskandar, in view of the reply, selects a sensible man
Of penetrating intellect to send a message:
"May wisdom be your minds' companion!
Neither king nor nobleman remains
On the surface of the earth who is not my inferior,
No matter how powerful or fortunate he may be.
Camphor dust or black dust,
Feast or battle are equal to me.
I did not come with elephants and timpani,
And an army that would make plain and mountain
Quiver beneath our stallions' hooves, to fight women.
If you come to greet me, I wish to visit your city.
As soon as I have toured the sites,
I shall not linger but shall lead my host away.
I wish to observe your customs and ceremonies,
Your majesty, your power, and your equestrian skills.
I shall question you in secret on your affairs and habits,
How there could be so many women living without men,
And how you replace those who die.
I wish to uncover the answers to these riddles."

The messenger departs and repeats these words,
Unveiling the secrets to the women.
The most powerful of them consult with each other
And reply, "We shall select two thousand women,
Eloquent, educated, and aware.
Every group of one hundred carries ten crowns
Inlaid with precious jewels, and together
There will be two hundred crowns worthy of a king.
We have weighed them, one after the other.
We have placed them in a pile, and each
With its fine stones weighs more than three ratals.[99]
Once we have news of the king's approach,
We shall set out on the road to meet him, for we know
The reputation of his wisdom and majesty."

The female envoy departs and relays the reply

◇◇◇◇◇◇◇◇◇◇◇◇◇◇
99 Ratal: A measure of weight equivalent to 12 to 16 ounces.

PART TWENTY-ONE

And all the words imprinted with insight.

Eskandar leaves the station and guides his army,
Astonished by the affair of these women.
After traveling for two stations, a great storm rises,
And snow falls to cover the valley and mountaintop.
A great number of the king's servants perish
From the cold and the snow on the journey.

They travel through two more stations swiftly
In severe cold and icy weather, and arrive at the city.
There arises a heavy smoke and a black cloud.
It is as if the army is treading through flames.
Chain mail burns the shoulders of the riders.
The earth smolders beneath the horses' hooves.
Challenges persist until they reach a city with residents
As black as night, their frames jet black, the color of soot,
Their slobbery lips the color of obsidian, their bleary eyes
Blood red, and their mouths spewing flames.

They lead numerous elephants bearing gifts to the king.
They say, "We summoned the snow and the fierce storm
To prevent you from journeying our way.
Never before has anyone ventured here.
You and your army are the first."

Eskandar remains in this land for one month.
Once king and host are rested,
They take the direction of the city of women
In haste and with joyous hearts.

Eskandar crosses the water and perceives
Two thousand women with crowns and earrings.
There is a forest with running water and trees,
A fortunate site that charms the soul.
The women prepare a feast in its meadow,
Spreading lush, colorful carpets and embroideries.

When Eskandar enters the land of Haroom,
Women rush to him from all corners,
Bearing crowns, clothing, jewels, color, and scent.

Eskandar welcomes the women's hospitality.

As night makes way to day,
He enters the city, examines it attentively,
Informs himself on all sorts of things, great and small,
And remains there until he unveils its mysteries.

33 | Eskandar Marches Westward

After having enquired on all sorts of subjects,
After having inspected the sea,
Eskandar leads his army westward
And comes across a huge, fortified city inhabited
By formidable, red-faced people with yellow hair,
Powerful and most skillful in battle.
When, upon his command, they appear before Eskandar,
They bow and strike their heads with their hands.

Eskandar asks their leaders,
"Which one of you can divulge to me your wonders?"

An old man replies, "O auspicious lion-conqueror,
On the other side of the city is a fountain,
Filled with the finest water we know,
But no one can drink from it.
When the brilliant sun is positioned directly above,
It disappears into the deep waters.
Behind this source, the earth dwells in darkness,
And everything we observe in the world is invisible there.
I have heard endless tales about this dark fountain.
An intelligent man, worshipper of Yazdan, spoke to me
Of the source, saying that it is referred to as the water of life.
This man of serene mind told me, "Anyone who drinks
From the source will never die, for it flows straight
From paradise and purifies your sins when you bathe in it."

Eskandar asks, "How do horses travel to this dim land?"

The worshipper replies, "One must ride to it on a foal."

Eskandar asks for herds of horses wandering freely
Through camp and pastures, and he selects
Ten thousand four-year-old colts to serve him.

34 | Eskandar Searches for the Elixir of Life

Eskandar departs gaily with his host,
Calling to his side prudent noblemen.
He marches until he arrives at a city
Where there is neither middle nor end
And which contains all that he needs,
Full of gardens and public space, palaces and structures.

He remains there, and the next morning, at dawn,
He takes the direction of the source, without an escort.
He stays until the sun pales and disappears.
By the grace of the pure Creator,
He witnesses the marvel of the shiny orb
Disappearing into the dark, bottomless fountain.

He returns to camp, reflecting deeply.
At night, he invokes the name of the World Master.
Then he directs his thoughts to another source
That the wise man named the fountain of life.

After having prayed to the Creator,
He selects from his host the most patient men,
Asks for enough provisions to last forty days,
And marches swiftly, eager to discover new wonders.

He commands his army to remain in the city,
Then he seeks a guide and finds him in Khezr,[100]
The leader of the people's noblemen.
Khezr becomes his adviser, and Eskandar
Follows his command on the journey,
Abandoning to him his heart, life, and good faith.

The king says to him, "O prudent man,
Let us quickly reach our destination.
If we arrive at the fountain of life,
We shall stand there at length in worship.
One does not die when one educates one's mind,
Entrusts oneself to the Creator,
And follows the road of wisdom.

◇◇◇◇◇◇◇◇◇◇◇◇◇
100 Khezr: Believed to have been a messenger and prophet, guardian of the sea.

I have with me two garnets that will shine
In the night the moment they perceive the water.
Take one of them and walk before me,
And take care of your soul and body.
The other will serve me as a torch on the road.
I shall enter this darkness with my escort,
And we shall see what the Creator hides there.
You are my guide, and Yazdan, who is my shelter,
Will lead me to this source of water."

They set out on the road in search of the fountain of life.
An immense cry of exaltation rises on the plain.
They abandon provisions at every station.
They march for two days and two nights, fasting.
On the third day, two roads appear in the darkness,
And the king loses track of Khezr.

The prophet continues on the road toward the source,
Raising his immortal face toward Saturn.
He washes his head and body in the limpid water
And seeks no other protector than Yazdan the pure.
He drinks and rests, then swiftly returns,
Praying and praising the Creator.

35 | Eskandar Converses With the Birds

Eskandar approaches a land where light reigns.
He sees a lofty, shining mountain.
Four columns of aloeswood are planted on its crest,
Rising to the clouds, each holding a large nest
In which sits a magnificent, green bird.
The four birds on four columns speak in Rumi
And call out to the victorious world ruler.

The Caesar hears their voices,
Climbs to the top, and approaches the birds.
One of them says to him,
"O King, you revel in hardships.
What are you after in this temporary dwelling?
If you raise your head to the vault of sky,
You will have to sadly return.

Now that you are here, tell us, have you witnessed
Structures built of reeds or golden bricks?"

The king replies, "Both of these houses exist:
Ones made of reeds and others of golden bricks."

The bird climbs down, troubling the Yazdan worshipper,
And retorts, "Have you ever heard in the world
The cries of drunken men and the melody of songs?
What about the sound of musical instruments?"

Eskandar replies, "Joyous men will not think much
Of a man who, by the decree of fate,
Has never taken part in revelry,
Even if he poured out his soul and heart to them."

The bird climbs further down his column of aloeswood
To land on the ground and ask, "What prevails,
Justice and righteousness, or scarcity and lies?"

Eskandar replies, "The one who seeks knowledge
Will rise above everyone."

The bird leaps to the column from the ground,
Cleans its claws with its beak, and asks the Caesar,
"Why do pious men dwell in mountains in your land?"

The king replies, "When a man follows the holy path,
He has no other dwelling but that of the mountain."

The bird, in good and serene humor, climbs back up
To its nest, sharpens its beak with its claws,
Assured that the Caesar would not commit him to death.
It commands him to ascend to the mountain crest
And see what he can find there
And what would make the happiest man shed tears.

36 | Eskandar Sees the Angel Israfil[101]

At these words, Eskandar scales the mountain,
Without an escort, to explore its crest.
He finds Israfil, trumpet in hand, head in the air,
Mouth full of wind, eyes full of tears,
Awaiting the moment when Yazdan would tell him,
"Let there boom the blare of the trumpet!"

At the sight of Eskandar on the mountain,
He shouts a cry as loud as thunder and says,
"O slave of your greed, do not exert yourself so!
One day, your ear will be stricken with a loud sound.
Do not go through so much trouble
To hold on to crown and throne.
Prepare to leave and abstain from further efforts."

The king replies, "Fate has given me a share in life
For which I must always move about and travel the world."

He climbs down the mountain, lamenting
And adjuring the Creator, Giver of virtues.
Then he resumes his march on the dark road,
Preceded by his guides.

As the host is enveloped in darkness,
A cry emerges from the black mountain:
"Anyone who picks up a stone
Found beneath his foot will have cause to repent,
And he will repent just the same if he does not.
He will end up vainly seeking remedy for his ailment."

The troops listen to the words, each growing concerned
About future troubles whether he picks a stone or not.
One of them says, "This pain comes from our sins.
You will regret if you take a stone from the road."

Another says, "We must grab a small piece and hope
That we will suffer neither pain nor fatigue."

Some of them take stones, others do not,

◇◇◇◇◇◇◇◇◇◇◇◇
101 Israfil: One of four angels equivalent to Raphael or Uriel; angel of music.

And yet others take tiny ones in laziness.
As they exit the land of the source of life
And reach the plain, darkness dissipates,
And each man attempts to convince himself
Of the truth of the matter when only lies seem to appear.

The chest of one fills with stones of ruby,
Another one with rough gemstones.
Those who grabbed only a few deeply regret it,
For having scorned the abundance of chrysolite.
And those who refrained from taking any are most
Regretful for having turned down precious jewels.

37 | Eskandar Travels West to See Marvels and Builds the Dam on the Way to Yajooj and Majooj[102]

Eskandar remains two weeks on the plain
And, after having rested, resumes the march with his host.

He turns to the west wishing to cover all the roads.
On his way, he finds a beautiful city
That appears to be immune to wind and dust.
At the beat of timpani from the backs of elephants,
The city's noblemen advance for two miles to meet the king.
The world seeker receives them with favors
And elevates their heads to the sun.

He asks whether this land conceals a unique wonder.
They lament to the king about the rotations of fate:
"We have before us a rather dreadful quandary
That we shall explain to the auspicious king.
This mountain, with its crest touching the clouds,
Fills our lives with distress, grief, and blood.
Our souls are wounded by Yajooj and Majooj
To such an extent that it plucks out our hearts.
When a group of these people arrives in our land,
We are left with worry and pain, unable to sleep.
They spread chaos and mayhem in our cities.
They appear to be camels with black faces

◇◇◇◇◇◇◇◇◇◇◇◇◇◇
102 Yajooj and Majooj: Two tribes in Manchuria.

And black tongues, eyes the color of blood,
Teeth in the shape of boar tusks, bodies obscured by fur.
Who would dare stay in their company?
Their chests are dim, their ears are like elephant ears,
And when they lie down, they use one ear as a pillow
And the other as a covering for warmth.

"Every female gives birth to one thousand babies.
How can we estimate their numbers?
They gather in herds like animals,
And they dash sprightly as deer.
In spring, when the green sea boils and the clouds
Cast thunder to draw large dragons out of the waves,
The air fills with the roar of lions.
The clouds drop serpents upon the mountains.
These people come in herds to feed on the snakes,
Year after year, and their chests and limbs expand.
The rest of the year, they live off the vegetation,
Searching for herbs everywhere and storing them.
During the winter cold, they lose weight,
And their voices grow feeble like pigeon voices,
While in the spring, nourished by serpents,
They howl gruffly like wolves.

"If the king could find a means to free our hearts
From worry, we shall shower him with abundant
Praise that will remain on earth for a long time.
Make a show of your power and save us,
And for that you may need the help of Yazdan."

Eskandar takes pity on them and reflects for a time.
Then he replies, "I can offer you vast treasure,
And your land will furnish aid and the necessary measures.
I shall reduce this race to order by my wisdom
And with the assistance of the Creator, Giver of virtues."

The people reply, "O King,
May misfortunate be kept at bay!
We are your slaves in everything you desire.
We shall be your loyal servants as long as we live.
We shall bring to you everything you require,
For we have no higher interest and desire than this."

PART TWENTY-ONE

Eskandar inspects the mountain, taking with him
A group of sages and philosophers.
Then he summons blacksmiths and asks them
To bring copper and bronze, heavy hammers,
Quicklime, stones, a great quantity of wood,
Everything required to complete the work.

The necessary materials are brought to him
In masses that exceed all measure.

Once everything is set and the plan is well thought out,
The master blacksmiths and expert masons rush
From all over the world to Eskandar's side to help him.

From every nation arrives a group of skilled men.
They build two walls, one on each side of the mountain,
From base to crest, each one hundred cubits wide.
One layer of coal is placed one cubit high,
Then a layer of iron in the middle,
A layer of copper, and finally a layer of sulfur.
This is a most elaborate plan executed in line
With the arts and the manners of Kianians.

They proceed with layer upon layer of various metals
Until it is a compact whole from ground to uneven crest.
A large quantity of tar and oil is poured
Over the entire thing, as well as a mass of coal that is
Then set aflame while one hundred thousand blacksmiths
Fuel the fire by order of the victorious king.

Wind blows from the mountain, and the heat of the flames
Sends tremors of fear among the stars.
The wind and the labor of the blacksmiths
Continue for some time as they brew together
The materials and make them melt with the heat.

Then the world is freed from Yajooj and Majooj,
And the earth is a place where one can settle and live.
This famous dam built by Eskandar
Saved the world from evil men and quarrels.
It is five hundred cubits high
And more than one hundred cubits wide.

The noblemen pay homage to the king and say,
"May time and space never be deprived of you!"

They bring valuables from their land in great quantity.
The king declines their gifts and departs,
Leaving the world astounded by his deeds.

38 | Eskandar Encounters a Dead Man in the Palace of the Topazes

Eskandar continues his march diligently for one month,
Until king and host find themselves exhausted.
In the end, he arrives at a mountain
With no trace of either wild beast or men.
On the mountaintop he sees a crest of lapis lazuli
On which sits a lofty palace made of stones of topaz.
Inside the palace are crystal candelabras,
And in the middle is a source of salt water.

A fine red stone serves as a lamp.
It is placed on fabric as black as a raven's plumage.
The light reflection of this lamp falls on the water,
And the gem lights the entire palace like the bright sun.

Near the source of water are two golden thrones
On which an unfortunate being rests.
He has the body of a man, the head of a boar,
And is miserably dead on this proud throne.

His head rests on a pillow of camphor.
A cover of brocade is enveloped around him.
Anyone who visits this palace to stir things up
Would tremble as life would be extinguished there.

A voice rises from the source of salty water:
"O greedy man, do not act foolishly!
You have seen many things that no one has witnessed.
Now you must turn your horse's bridle away.
Your life is reaching its end,
And the royal throne is without a king."

Eskandar is alarmed by the voice and retreats
To return to his camp, as swift as smoke.
From there, he rushes his troops, invoking the Creator.
He leaves the site of the mountain, taking the road
To the desert, preoccupied, his soul unsettled,
His mind afflicted, his eyes shedding copious tears.
He is followed by his host and preceded by his guides.

39 | Eskandar Encounters the Talking Tree

By way of the desert, Eskandar reaches a land with joy,
For he can hearken in the distance the voices of men.
The place is one massive garden
Where hearts rejoice in every delight.

The noblemen of the city meet him on the road.
They receive him, bless him,
And shower him with gold and gems.
They say, "O King, your visit blesses us with honor.
Never did a host visit this land,
And never has the name of king been uttered here.
Now that you are here, our lives are yours.
May you enjoy a serene mind and a healthy body!"

Eskandar is happy to be in the presence of these men.
He rests from his weariness of road and desert.
He asks them, "What wonder may I observe here?"

His guide replies, "O triumphant, benevolent King,
There is one wonder the likes of which no one
Has ever seen or heard of, in public or in secret.
It is a tree composed of two trunks joined in growth.
Such a marvel must not remain unknown.
One of the trunks is male, the other female.
This tree speaks, has large limbs,
And is quite beautiful and fragrant.
At night, the female speaks and exudes a scent.
As soon as day appears, the male's voice is heard."

Eskandar departs with his Rumi riders,
Accompanied by the land's noblemen.

He asks them when the tree speaks the loudest words.

The interpreter replies, "When nine parts of the day
Have passed, one of the trees will begin to talk,
And the propitious king will hear its voice.
At night, the female part speaks,
And the leaves and trunk exhale the scent of musk."

Then he asks, "When we pass the tree,
What wonder shall we encounter, O blessed man?"

The interpreter says, "Once you pass the tree,
You will no longer remain uncertain of where to go.
There is no place beyond the tree.
The guide calls it the limit or the end of the world."

The king continues his march with the fortunate Rumis.
At the speaking tree, he finds the ground burning hot
And the soil disappearing beneath the skin of wild beasts.
He asks his interpreter, "What are these pelts?
Who has skinned wild beasts in such a fashion?"

The interpreter replies,
"This tree has a great many worshippers.
When they come here to pay homage,
They search for food and live off the flesh of wild beasts."

When the sun arrives at its zenith in the vault of sky,
Eskandar hears a sound from above,
Coming from the leaves of the lofty tree.
It is an unpromising sound, full of terror.
He is frightened and asks the interpreter,
"O prudent man, what are the leaves saying?
For they stir the blood within my heart."

The other replies, "O blessed King,
The limbs of the tree say,
        'Why is Eskandar in constant motion,
        Traveling the world in such a fashion?
        He will soon straddle the road of departure.
        When two times seven years of his reign are complete,
        He will be forced to abandon the imperial throne.'"

PART TWENTY-ONE

Eskandar sheds tears of blood, and his heart fills with grief.
He does not open his lips and anxiously waits until midnight,
The hour when the leaves will speak.
Then he asks again, "Reveal to me the secret of the words.
What is this other branch saying?"

The interpreter discloses, "The female branch says,
        'Why do you tire yourself so in this vast world,
        So full of greed you are, so desirous for possessions?
        Why do you trouble your mind so?
        You are obsessed with the passion to tour the world,
        To trouble men, and eliminate other rulers,
        But you don't have much time left on earth.
        Do not dim the light of your day.'"

The king says to the interpreter,
"O man of pure heart, question him on the fatal day.
Will I be present in the land of Rum?
Will my mother see me alive again or only at the time
When she is forced to dress my face in a shroud?"

The talking tree replies, "Hurry and leave right away.
Neither your mother nor your relatives in Rum,
Nor your nation's veiled women will ever see you again.
Death will strike you in a foreign land,
And the stars will mock your crown and throne."

At these words, Eskandar steps away from the tree and,
Heart wounded by the sword of fate, returns to camp.
The highborn heroes depart to prepare gifts for him.
There is a shining armor, as long as the River Nile
And wide as elephant skin. There are two fish teeth,
Five cubits long, that a man could barely lift,
Coats of mail and rich brocade,
One hundred enormous golden eggs,
Each weighing one hundred mahns in silver weight,
And a golden rhinoceros inlaid in precious stones.

Eskandar accepts the gifts and leads his army
Out of this land, shedding tears of blood.

40 | Eskandar Visits the Faghfoor of Chin

From there he takes the direction of Chin,
Elevating the noblemen to the Pleiades.
He travels from station to station for forty days,
Until he arrives at the sea where they dress
The tent pavilions with silk brocade and
Where host and leader engage in rest.

One day, he asks a scribe to write a letter
In the name of Eskandar, world conqueror,
Full of all sorts of compliments and threats.
The scribe composes and completes the letter and,
Once folded, Eskandar departs as if he is the envoy,
Selecting as guide a man aware and liberated,
Who is at one with him and whom he can direct.
He entrusts the army's command to the leader
And takes with him five Rumi men full of wisdom.

As soon as the Faghfoor learns that an envoy
Approaches Chin, he sends an escort to meet him.
Eskandar advances proudly on the road.
He arrives at the Faghfoor's grand palace,
Observes the valiant cortege of troops.
Eskandar climbs down from his portico to join the emperor.

Eskandar nears him quickly and pays him tribute.
He remains in the audience hall for a long time.
The Faghfoor receives him graciously, asks after
His health, and assigns him a magnificent residence.

As the brilliant torch appears above the mountains,
Eskandar brings a parade horse decked in brocade.
The Faghfoor calls the king's messenger.
Eskandar speaks befittingly, hands over the letter,
And delivers the message of the Caesar.

The letter, in the name of the King of Rum,
World master and leader of all borders and all lands,
On whom rulers invoke benedictions, is addressed
To the Faghfoor of Chin, ornament of provinces.
The letter begins with thanks from servants

To the World Creator, World Owner who ties all bonds,
Guide of all and Master of purity and benevolence.
Then it continues: "My command for Chin
Is that this land prosper and refrain from fight.
We constricted the world when we engaged in battle
With Foor; with Dara, who was world king;
With Faryan the Taazi; and so many other princes.
Travel from east to west and you will find no one
Who diverges from my command.
The sky knows not the number of my troops,
Unless Mercury, Venus, and Sun keep count.

"If you breach my orders in any way,
You will bring misfortune not just upon yourself
But also on your people and on your land.
When you have read this letter, prepare your tribute.
Do not be troubled and do not struggle.
If you come here, you will find me in the center of my army.
I shall receive you as a friend who bears me affection.
I shall leave you the crown and throne,
And you will suffer no harm on the part of fate.
If you delay in leaving your land
And coming to visit your king here,
If you wish me to leave you unharmed,
Send to my treasury all that there is in Chin
Of rarity and new valuables, golden crockery,
Swords, steeds, rings, bolts of fabrics, slaves,
Ivory thrones, rich brocade, torques, and crowns.
Send away my host, and enjoy the security
Of throne, treasure, and headdress."

The Emperor of Chin is angered by the letter,
But he restrains himself and stays quiet.
Smiling, he addresses the envoy, unaware that
He is Eskandar: "The sky is your king's companion.
Tell me what you know of his mien, his stature,
His valor, and his manner of speech."

The envoy replies, "O Emperor of Chin,
Know that there exists no one like Eskandar.
He surpasses the imagination by his courage,
His wisdom, his kindness, and his intelligence.

He has the stature of a cypress tree
And the strength of an elephant.
His generosity is as vast as the flows of the Nile,
His tongue is a sharp sword, and his sweet words
Make eagles swoop down from mountaintops."

The Faghfoor changes his mind.
He asks for wine and spreads to be set in the garden.
They enjoy the feast and drink until the day dims
And the heads of the drinkers are troubled by wine.

The Emperor of Chin says to the envoy,
"May Jupiter be your king's ally!
Tomorrow morning, I shall reply to his letter
And render brilliant the day before your eyes."

Eskandar, as the envoy, departs from the emperor's hall,
Half drunk and holding in his hand a citron.

As the sun raises its head under the sign of the lion
And the sky vanquishes night, Eskandar visits
The Faghfoor, his heart relinquishing any ill thought.
The Faghfoor questions him: "How was your night?
Yesterday, you left somewhat inebriated."

He asks for a scribe to bring paper, musk, and amber,
To write a warm reply to Eskandar's letter.
They cover the page with Chini ornaments.
It begins with homage to the Justice Giver,
Who grants us courage, justice, and virtue,
Creator of wisdom, abstinence, and faith.
"May divine blessings be showered on the King of Rum!
Your envoy of sweet speech has arrived with the letter.
We have read and conferred with our noblemen.
As for what we have learned from the battles
And the misfortunes of Dara, son of Daaraab,
Of Faryan and of Foor, whom you vanquished,
You triumphs render you the shepherd
While world rulers unite to form your herd.
Know that it was a gift of the Master of the Sun and Moon
And not the effect of your courage and number of troops.
Once a prince's time has passed, what difference
Does it make if he dies in feast or on the battlefield?

PART TWENTY-ONE

The day they fell into your hands and succumbed
Was the term that fate had decided upon.
One cannot extend or curtail the moment timed by destiny.
Try not to deem yourself superior to them,
For even if you were made of steel,
Your time would still come up, without a doubt.

"Where are Fereydoon, Zahaak, and Jamsheed?
A hurricane blew over them
And snatched their breath away,
Transporting them to the land of nonexistence.
I do not fear you, yet I shall not attack you,
For my head is not full of pride like yours.
Our customs invalidate the spillage of blood,
And my religion prohibits me from causing harm.
You call me to your side, but you will be disappointed.
I serve and worship Yazdan, not a particular king.
I send you more wealth than you desire,
For I shall not argue over due generosity."

Eskandar feels his cheeks burning.
The effect of the Faghfoor's words strike his heart
As if it has been pierced by an arrow's tip.
He reflects: "I shall never be seen again,
Traveling the world in secret."
He returns from the audience hall to his residence
And prepares for departure.

The proud Faghfoor opens the door to his treasury.
He feels no regret for the donations he is about to make.
He asks for fifty crowns inlaid with stones, ivory thrones,
One thousand camels loaded with gold and silver,
One thousand more heavy with heaps of Chini brocade,
A variety of silken fabrics, camphor,
Grey amber, aloeswood, and musk.
He asks for the pelts of squirrel, ermine, and sable,
And pouches of musk, two thousand each.
The man who despises wealth breathes more easily.

The Faghfoor's clever treasurer loads them.
Then they add to the count one hundred
Beautiful stallions with silver and gold restraints,

Three hundred servants with golden belts,
And three hundred red-skinned camels,
Laden with Chinese curiosities.

He selects a serious one of sweet words from among
The older Chini men and commands him to go to Eskandar
With greetings and missives, and to announce to him
That the noblemen of the land will pay homage to him
For as long as he stays on the border of Chin.

The Chini man goes on the road with Eskandar.
Who could have thought
That Eskandar's envoy is the king himself?
When the boatman spots him, he rises abruptly
And proceeds to deploy the sail.

The royal vizier arrives with troops to meet the king,
Who recounts the success of his ruse.
The troops bless Eskandar and bow low before him.
Then the Chini man, understanding that the king
Has disembarked, runs to him lamenting.

Eskandar says to him, "No need to excuse yourself.
But do not reveal all this to the Faghfoor."
He rests during the night, and in the early morning
He sits solemnly on the royal throne.

Handing out gifts to the Chini escort, he says to him,
"May wisdom be your mind's companion!
Go to the Faghfoor, and tell him that I respect him.
If he wishes to visit us here,
The entire land of Chin belongs to him.
If he wishes to go elsewhere,
Nothing prevents him from doing so.
I shall rest for some time,
For one cannot walk swiftly with a vast host."

The envoy departs like wind, taking the message
From the Caesar of Rum to the Faghfoor of Chin.

41 | Eskandar Arrives in the Land of Sindh and Engages in Battle

The king remains in place for one month.
After feeling restored, he resumes his march with his host.
They trace their steps back from the Green Sea,[103]
They cross deserts and long stretches of land,
From station to station, until they arrive in Chaghvan,[104]
A magnificent city, home of a magnificent palace.

The highborn men and leaders of Chaghvan,
Endowed with name and intelligence,
Come to greet the king with gifts and offerings.

Eskandar immediately interrogates them
On the marvels of their land.
The most eloquent among them replies,
"O King, we know of no site worthy of you.
Here reign poverty and grief.
If you go further, you will hold nothing but wind."

Disappointed, the king abandons Chaghvan
And takes the direction of Sindh with his host
When the riders of the land encounter them
With reinforcement from India.
Those still mourning the death of Foor,
Standing staunch in their resolve to shed blood,
Bringing with them elephants bearing Indian bells.
The sound of weapons resounds and blends
With the blare of trumpets.

One of the Sindhi is named Bendah,
An illustrious rider, intelligent and powerful.
The two hosts fall upon each other in a general melee.
The earth converts into a mountain
With heaps of fallen men, and, at nightfall,
There remains no Sindhi standing on the plain.

Eskandar launches his troops in their pursuit.

◇◇◇◇◇◇◇◇◇◇◇◇◇
103 Green Sea: Must be a sea in the Far East, perhaps the Sea of Japan.
104 Chaghvan: A city in the Far East, perhaps Changwon in South Korea.

Eighty-five elephants, golden crowns,
Swords, and various valuables fall into their hands.
Women, children, and older people approach the Caesar,
Crying and saying, "O prudent King,
Be vigilant. Do not surrender this land to fire.
Refrain from killing the children,
For in the end, your days will pass.
Happy is the one who tramples the earth
Innocently, without causing harm to anyone."

Eskandar displays neither affection nor pity
For the wounded, and a great many women
And children, men young and old, are taken captive.

From there, he travels to Nimrooz by way of Bost.
Once arrived, he purifies the world of enemies.
Then he marches to the land of Yemen, eager
To possess the world and trailed by a glorious host.

The King of Yemen and his leaders hear of his approach.
They present themselves to him,
Bearing gifts worthy of him in value and beauty.
Ten camels are loaded, five with Yemeni bolts of fabrics,
Five with dinars, and ten more with dirhams, for anyone
Who owns wealth will have a heart free of worry.

Then there are one thousand baskets full of saffron,
Abundant textiles of brocade and clothes,
A cup of chrysolite from the Yemeni treasury,
And eighty-five unpierced pearls; a cup of lapis lazuli
Containing sixty topazes, topped with ten ruby gems.

He gives the lot to his servants uttering blessings, and
They arrive with offerings and gifts before the king's tents.
Eskandar questions the king as suits custom.
He receives him well and asks him to sit near his throne.

The King of Yemen invokes the grace of Yazdan and says,
"May you and your retinue be victorious!
I shall be happy if you can remain here for two months
So that you and your host may rest from the journey."

Eskandar utters blessings on him and says,

"May wisdom always be your companion!"

In the early morning hours, the King of Yemen
Returns, and the world fills with the clatter of his host.

42 | Eskandar Drives an Army to Babel[105]

Eskandar drives his host toward Babel,
Making the world disappear beneath the dust.

They tread for one month, without rest.
In the end, they approach a mountain,
Its crest invisible to human eyes,
For its summit is concealed by a dark cloud
And appears to rise to nearly touch Saturn.

One cannot find a path to climb on any side.
The king and his troops are confounded.
They scale the steep incline with much effort.
The most agile among them is put to the test.

Exhausted from their ascent, they come to a point
Where they observe a deep sea on the other side,
Next to a lush plain, at the sight of which
The troops jump up and down with joy.

They descend toward the body of water,
Invoking the name of the World Creator.
They encounter everywhere countless wild beasts,
And the men subsist solely on game.

From afar, they perceive a robust, wild man with a dark,
Hairy body and two enormous elephant ears.
The riders seize the man and drag him to Eskandar,
Who takes one look at him, stunned.
He conjures up the name of Yazdan, examines him
Curiously, and asks, "What sort of man are you?
What is your name? What do you find in these waters?
What is your intention? What is your desire?"

◇◇◇◇◇◇◇◇◇◇◇◇◇◇
105 Babel: Or Babylon, ancient city in Babylonia, which is situated in today's Iraq.

The other replies, "O King, I was named
Gooshbastar by my father and mother."

Eskandar asks, "What is at the center of the water
Where the sun rises?"

He replies, "O King, may you live eternally glorious!
There is a city as large and beautiful as paradise.
It is as if the earth does not participate in its design.
You will find there neither home nor palace
Constructed from any other material than fishbone.
In the citadels, you will find dazzling paintings
Representing the faces of Afraasiyaab,
Brighter than the sun, as well as portraits of the warrior
Kay Khosrow, showing his grandeur, courage, and customs.
But everything is painted on fishbones.
Neither dust settles here nor is there soil.
If the glorious king commands,
I shall march to the city without an escort."

Eskandar tells the man with giant ears,
"Go and bring back one of the inhabitants
So that I may observe something new."

Gooshbastar delivers the message of the Caesar.
Then he departs with seventy wise men, young and old.
They are dressed in attire made of silk and fur.
Each wise old man holds a golden cup full of pearls.
The youths hold crowns and bow low
Before the Caesar to pay him homage.

They sit together through the night, speaking at length.
The men say, "We are in possession of the treasury
Of Kay Khosrow, one worthy of you."

Eskandar swiftly heads toward Iran,
Crossing the body of water.
He observes and explores cities, lands, and markets.
Finally, he arrives at the door of the dwelling
Housing the treasure of Kay Khosrow,
A treasure full of crowns, golden thrones,
Diadems, bracelets, and belts, so much so
That a man cannot fully estimate its value.

He seizes the entire collection to take with him
And happily returns to his host and his camp.
They rest through the night, and, at the cock's crow,
The sound of timpani rises at the Caesar's entrance.

43 | Eskandar's Letter to Arastalis
and Arastalis's Reply

Eskandar marches off toward Babel,
Making the earth disappear beneath his army's weight.

He feels his end approaching, and the day dims for him.
He thinks that he must leave no one in the world
Of royal lineage who may one day drive his host
Against Rum and conquer this cultivated land.

Having devised this stratagem, he writes to Arastalis:
"I have a sense that I must annihilate world leaders
From the lineage of the highborn.
I have traveled through seven nations,
And many a nobleman has fallen into my traps.
And now, the thought of my pending death
Dims the light of my day."

He commands anyone from the Kianian race
To make preparations and appear at his court
While banishing from their hearts mistrust of him.

Upon receipt of the letter, the wise Arastalis,
Terrified, immediately composes a reply,
Flooding the paper with his tears,
As if the tip of his reed is made of his eye's lashes.
He writes: "We received the world king's letter.
His majesty must abstain from an evil strategy.
Do not give consideration to this action.
Do give alms to atone for your thoughts.
Be careful and surrender to Yazdan.
Sow only seeds of goodness in the world.
We all belong ultimately to death
From the moment we are born,
And we concede our lives without defense.

"No one can successfully take royalty with him.
Each king departs relinquishing power to another.
Take care not to spill the blood of noblemen,
For you could be cursed until the day of Resurrection.
If there remains no king on the throne of Iran,
Armies of Turks, Indians, Slavs, and Chinis
Will rush on all sides to exercise vengeance
And subsequently threaten the land of Rum.
We must not allow a single man of Kianian race
To be hurt in any way, not even by a gust of wind.
Summon leaders and noblemen,
Offer them feast, guidance, and banquet.
Assign each prince a land worthy of his rank,
And draw up a list of noblemen's names
From whom you have taken without giving back.
Do not give one power over the other.
Refrain from assigning the title of world king.
Turn all the Kianians into a shield for your land
If you wish to prevent hosts from invading Rum."

Upon receipt of the reply, Eskandar hurries
To execute his new plans and his new ideas.
He convenes the most valuable noblemen
And assigns them each a place according to status.
He draws a certificate in which each person
Vows to refrain from expanding, even a little,
The part assigned to him in the world.
These renowned rulers are given the title
Of Moolookeh Tavayef or King of Tribes.

That night, Eskandar arrives in Babel,
Where he finds the noblemen delighted to see him.

At that moment, a woman gives birth to a child
Who astonishes anyone who sets his sights on him.
He has the head of a lion, the hooves of a horse,
The chest and shoulders of a man, and the tail of an ox.
This monster dies at birth, so much the better,
For never did a woman give birth to such an offspring.
The child is taken to the king, who observes him
Carefully and in a state of bewilderment.
He takes him for a bad omen and says,

"The earth must cover such a race."

He summons a great number of astrologers
And speaks to them at length of the dead infant.
The sages are frightened but conceal
Their impressions from the blessed king.
He grows angry toward them and says,
"If you hide anything from me,
I shall instantly cut off your heads!
You will end up with lion jaws as your shrouds."

Observing the ruler's fury, the astrologers tell him,
"O glorious King, you were born
Under the constellation of the lion.
It is well known to noblemen that you have seen
The infant with the head of a lion upon his death.
Your rule is on the decline, and the world
Will stir with troubles for a long time
Until a new king settles on the throne."

The astrologers concur with this forecast,
Providing explanations for the clues that guide them.

Eskandar grows concerned; his mind and reason droop.
He replies, "There is no remedy for death.
My heart is not troubled by the fact
That I may not be granted a lengthier life.
The time that we are allotted on this earth
Can be neither reduced nor extended."

On this very day, he enters the city of Babel anxious,
For he senses his forthcoming misfortune.

44 | Eskandar's Letter to His Mother and His Last Wishes

Eskandar calls a skilled scribe,
And reveals to him his heart's deepest secrets
So that he may compose a letter to his mother:
"It is impossible to conceal the warnings of death.
I feel as if I have lived my portion of existence.

The time that we are allocated on earth
Can be neither reduced nor stretched.
Do not afflict yourself on my demise,
For death is not a novel thing.
Anyone born must one day die,
Whether he is king or commoner.
I shall tell Rumi noblemen that, upon their return,
They are to only listen to your advice and command.
I shall insist that no one disobey you.

"I have assigned a province
To every Iranian who posed a threat to the Rumis.
Once they take possession of their respective states,
I hope that their greed will not usher them to Rum
And that our land will not be subjected to further peril.
Once I am dead, you will dispose of my body in Egypt
Without neglecting any of my last wishes.
Every year, disburse one hundred thousand
Of my dinars to hard-working farmers.
If Roshanak gives birth to a son,
He will perpetuate his father's glory.
No other person but him must rise to kingship,
For he will make the land of Rum flourish.
But if at the time of labor she gives birth to a daughter,
Have her wed the son of Filghoos, to whom
You will give the title of son and not son-in-law
And through whom you will keep my memory alive.

"You will send back Keid's daughter to her father,
Honorably and in complete confidence.
You will hand her chests of gold
And return to her her beloved slaves.
You will prepare a litter for the road.
At the time of departure, you will send her back to India
With her diadems and jewels, the gold and silver
That she brought with her from her father.
I have put an end to all my affairs here in good faith.
Now I am left to prepare for my death.
Please respect and follow my strict instructions,
And refrain from adding anything to my words.

"To begin with, I wish for you to prepare a golden coffin

And a shroud of Chini gold for my head,
Stuffed with amber and worthy of my person.
May no one recoil in the care for my corpse.
You will fill all the slots of my coffin with tar, camphor,
Musk, and gray amber. First, you will pour honey,
Which you will cover with a sheet of Chini brocade,
Over which you will place my body, and then cover my face.

"You, my mother full of wisdom,
Follow my advice to the end of your days.
Take everything you need from what I brought back
With me from India and Chin, from Tooran, Iran,
And the land of Mokran, and distribute the excess.
I ask you to be reasonable, O my kind mother,
To maintain a state of serenity,
To refrain from debasing your own body,
For no one remains eternally in this world.
Without a doubt, your soul will join mine
When the end of your days arrives.
Peace is a greater virtue than affection.
Only the weak let themselves surrender to passion.

"You have loved me for months and years.
Now pray to Yazdan for my loving soul.
Assist me with your invocations and prayers.
Look and find someone in the world
Whose soul has been spared from death.
May my soul be your soul's slave!
May your remaining days be joyous!"

Once the letter is sealed, Eskandar sends
A speedy courier to travel from Babel to Rum
With news of the eclipsed imperial glory.

45 | Eskandar's Death in Babylon and His Burial in Eskandarieh[106]

Upon hearing of the king's condition,
The world dims in the eye of noblemen.
They take the direction of the throne of power,
And the region fills with noise and clatter.

Rumors of the army's emotions reach Eskandar,
Rumors that he senses the culmination of his days.
He asks for his throne to be carried
Out of the king's palace and into the field.

Warriors are deeply troubled at the sight
Of their king, his cheeks drained of color.
The entire plain resounds with cries,
As if they are boiling over in a fierce blaze.
Everyone laments: "Our luck has run dry,
For the king disappears from among the Rumis.
The rotation of the sky that brings us this fatal day
Will convert the land of Rum into a vast, arid plain.
Our foes have obtained the object of their desires.
They have attained the goal toward which they rushed.
The world will turn bitter for us.
We shall cry out in pain openly and secretly."

In a feeble voice, the Caesar mutters, "Have the care
And the humility to follow my last wishes
If you long to continue to enjoy your souls and bodies.
You have a duty to fulfill when I am no longer here.
Your turn will come not long after me."

He says this and his soul exits his body.
This king, who defeated myriad hosts, exists no more.

Unanimous cries emerge from his host, shredding
The air and merging with the throb of timpani.
Everyone scatters dust upon his head.
Blood drips from hearts through their eyes' lashes.

---

106 Eskandarieh: Or Alexandria, an ancient Egyptian city founded in 331 BCE by
Eskandar (Alexander the Great).

They set the palace on fire
And cut the tails of one thousand horses.
They place saddles upside down on chargers.
It is as if the earth itself hollers and weeps.

They carry the golden coffin onto the plain,
Their laments piercing the sky.
A bishop washes the body with musk and rosewater,
Sprinkles camphor over it, and weaves a golden shroud.

People continue to sob for their illustrious king.
They take his corpse, wrapped in Chini brocade,
And soak it in honey from head to toe.
Then they close the lid of the narrow coffin.
This noble tree, which once spread its shade
Far and wide, disappears as he is set to rest.

You will not linger long in this passing dwelling.
Why then do you reach for the royal throne?
Why do you boast about your valuables?

They pass the coffin hand to hand across the plain.
The sound of two voices is heard, one in Rumi,
The other in Persian, discussing the subject at length.

The Persians agree: "He must be buried here,
Since this is the realm of kings.
Why should one travel around the world with a coffin?"

One of the Rumi leaders replies,
"I do not wish him buried here.
If you deem fair what I say,
Eskandar must return to his native land."

A Persian man speaks to say,
"Anything you may say counts for nothing.
I shall show you a meadow dating back to ancient kings.
It is the site of a mountain so lofty
Not even vultures have access to its crest,
Which the wise and aged men call Khorm.[107]
There is there a forest and a source of water,

◇◇◇◇◇◇◇◇◇◇◇◇◇
107 Khorm: Perhaps refers to Khorma, a village in today's northern Iran.

And when one asks a question at the sight,
The reply comes from the mountain in a voice
Heard by the entire crowd.
Take an old man there and take the coffin.
The old man will address a question,
And the reply will come from the mountain
To give you advice that will bring good fortune."

They depart, running like mountain sheep
For the meadow that bears the name of Khorm.
They ask the question and receive the reply:
"Why do you keep a royal coffin for so long?
Eskandar's homeland is Eskandarieh,
A city he founded and lived in during his life."

The troops hear the voice and leave in haste,
Taking with them the king's wooden coffin.

46 | The Wise Men Mourn the Death of Eskandar

After Eskandar's casket is taken to Eskandarieh
And placed on the plain, the world falls victim
To strife and all sorts of chatter.

Children, men, and women gather around the casket,
So vast in numbers that a counter
Would make an estimation above one hundred thousand.

People shedding tears of blood observe Arastalis at the lead.
He places his hand on the narrow coffin and says,
"O King, worshipper of Yazdan, now that this coffin
Serves you as dwelling, where is your wisdom,
Your knowledge, and your acumen?
Why have you fallen prey to dust in the days of your youth?"

The wise men of Rum gather, and one of them says,
"O elephant of brazen body, who slaughtered you?
Which man is seeking to seize your seat?
Where was your vigilance and your good sense?"

Another man says, "You collected so much gold.
Where is it now? You cannot even take it with you."

Another man says, "No one was able to escape you.
Why did you have to shake hands against death?"

Another man says, "You are now resting from your labors.
This is the reward reaped by the one
Who chases after treasures and empires."

Another man says, "When you appear before the Supreme
Judge, you will then collect the fruits of your harvest."

Another man says, "The one who spills the blood of kings
Will find himself stripped of power."

Another man says, "For a long time you were a rough gem,
And we shall soon find ourselves in a similar situation."

Another man says, "You left the world so quickly
That you remain like a rough gemstone."

Another man says, "When the World Master sees you,
You will be taught what you did not learn here."

Another man says, "Since men have never escaped death,
It is best not to extend a hand to aggrandize oneself."

Another man says, "O King, whose head is higher than
The Sun and Moon, why do you hide your face from us?"

Another man says, "A skillful man struggles
To maintain himself free of excess troubles.
O man full of virtue and valor,
The coffin's gold has vanquished you."

Another man says,
"You have wrapped yourself in golden brocade;
Your beautiful features are now concealed.
Free your face from this golden sheet, for the crown,
Bracelets, and ivory throne make claims on you."

Another man says, "You have been stolen from your slaves,
Your moon-faced Chini and Rumi servants,
And hold in your arms abundant gold.
Know that gold and brocade do not suit kings."

Another man says,
"Now the one who questions the dead will ask you,
    'Do you remember what your master said?
    Why did you spill the blood of noblemen?
    Why were you so relentless in battle?
    Did you not see that all the noble leaders who left
    Took with them nothing but their good actions?'"

Another man says, "Your days have passed,
And your tongue is mute. Anyone who witnessed
Your crown and throne will have to give up ambition.
Power remains for no one; not even you could hold on to it.
One must not seek to plant the tree of power."

Another man says, "Your deeds are swept away by wind.
The heads of leaders are freed from your tyranny.
You are now traveling to a sublime court,
A world where sheep and wolf are separated"

Another man says,
"Why did you exert yourself in this fugitive dwelling?
A narrow casket, the extent of your wealth,
Is the compensation for your labors.
You may wish to hear the sound of clarions,
But you must content yourself with confinement."

Another man says, "When your host returns,
You alone will remain on the vast plain.
Without a doubt, you will follow each departing warrior
And will be consumed with lengthy regrets."

47 | Eskandar's Mother and Wife Mourn His Death

Eskandar's mother rushes out,
Presses her cheek to his head, and says,
"O glorious King, virtuous, auspicious world master,
Though you are close to us, you have traveled far
From your land, your army, and your people.
May my soul be your soul's slave!
May the hearts of those who rejoice in your death perish!"

Next arrives Roshanak, full of grief, who says,
"O King of liberated men, where is the world master
Dara, who established order on the earth?
Where are Khosrow and Ashk?
Where are Faryan and Foor, princes of Sindh?
Where is the King of Shahrzoor?
Where are the other rulers whose heads,
On the day of battle, were banished to dust?
You were mighty as a cloud bursting with hail.
I believed you were exempt from death.
You witnessed so many battles, wars, and executions.
When you attacked at times alone, at times with a host,
It appeared as if you received a pass from fate,
Something we kept hidden even from your inner circle.
You caused the world's noblemen and rulers to vanish.
You brought down the crown of the King of Kings.
The tree you planted was beginning to bear fruit.
Now I find you united with dust as your only friend!"

Once the sun, the sky's crown, descends and disappears,
The warriors, weary of such talk place the casket in the ground.

The world unfearingly raises a hurricane like a breath.
One finds neither justice in it nor injustice or oppression.
One comprehends neither the means nor the goal,
And neither the poor man nor the king is exempt.
One must attempt to be benevolent, humane,
Valiant, compassionate, and joyous.
Beyond that, I see no part in the world for you,
Whether you are lowly or illustrious.
But if you leave behind a poor reputation, you will be
Refused divine pardon as well as access to paradise.

Such is the custom of this ancient world.
Eskandar departs while words endure.
He succeeded in killing thirty-six emperors.
Look and see what he retains in his fist.
He founded and built ten beautiful cities
That are today razed and reduced to weeds.
He undertook a question no one had ever posed,
And the horizons recount the legend of Eskandar.
That is all. Speech is precious,

More valuable than anything, unlike an old palace
Falling to ruin beneath the ravages of rain and snow.

I conclude here the story of Eskandar's dam.
May all things occur for the best and in the interest of joy!
May the world king's heart subsist in bliss,
And his body be sheltered from harm!

48 | Ferdowsi's Grievance With His Age and His Fate

O sublime dome of sky, giver of joy to dim hearts,
Why do you afflict me so in my old age?
When I was young, you held me to your breast.
In my declining years, you forsake me with contempt.
The happy rose of my cheek is yellowing.
The silk of my life converts into thorns of sorrow.
The cypress tree, growing lofty in the garden,
Is bending over, and this shining lamp is dull.
The black summit is covered with snow,
And people can detect the failings of the poet king.

You have been like a mother to me, but now
I shed tears of blood on the pains you inflict upon me.
You have neither faith nor wisdom,
And your dark paths fill me with terror.
I wish you had never raised me,
Or, if you had, you had never oppressed me.
Once I am free of this darkness,
I shall recount to the Supreme Judge your offenses.
I shall complain about you before Yazdan the pure,
Shouting cries and covering my head with dust.

Fate found me miserable in my old age
And doubled the hindrances.
The sublime lofty sky replied to me,
"O grumbling old man, you complain
Without having suffered any hardship!
Why do you attribute happiness and misfortune to me?
You are greater than me in every way.
You nourish your mind with knowledge.
You eat and sleep and choose your dwelling,

And you can freely seek the path to good and evil.
I am powerless in all the things you speak of,
And the Sun and Moon ignore them as well.
Ask guidance from the One who has created the way,
Who has created night and day, Sun and Moon,
The One and only being whose existence is not a mystery,
Whose actions have neither beginning nor end,
And upon whose order all things are born.
Anyone who claims otherwise is a foolish man.
As for me, I am a slave shaped by the divine Creator,
Acting upon divine command and united by divine bonds.
Turn to Yazdan, who is our shelter.
Ask with moderation all that your heart desires.
Know that there is no other Master of sky,
No other who makes Venus, Moon and Sun shine.
Divine grace has been granted to Muhammad's soul
And to every single one of his companions.

49 | In Praise of Sultan Mahmoud

Let us praise the world king who equally revels
In feast, battle, and the acquisition of knowledge,
Abul Ghassem, insightful king,
Whose path is through the path of wisdom,
Who designs within the guidelines of prosperity.

May his heart find eternal joy
And remain free from pain and worry!
Illustrious and blessed Mahmoud,
Through whom grandeur exists,
The King of Kings of Iran and Zabolestan,
Master of all the territories from Ghennooj
To the border of Kabolestan,
Mahmoud of auspicious purpose,
The illustrious one who glorifies royal power,
May he, his army, his kin, and his land be exalted!
May his powerful army leader, the eminent
Emir Nasr, be blessed, for he renews the epoch,
And his existence brings joy to the revolving dome.
His name is victorious, as victorious is his fortune.
His arrow can pierce through a tree.

When the army is commanded by Abul-Muzaffar,
Its head will rise to reach above the moon.

May the king's body evade harm!
May he always lean on a vast treasure!
May his host's leader dwell in joy, retain a shining heart,
And find security with abundant wealth!
May the dome that revolves for time immemorial
Never negate its affection for the royal family!
May they, father after father, son after son,
Proudly bear the crown of royalty and victory!

May the king be blessed on this fourteenth day
Of the month of Shavaal,[108] for his goodwill
In regard to waiving, for one year, taxes and tributes
Due by men of faith and awakened worshippers.
This directive has renewed the times of Anushiravan[109]
And established our affairs in good order.

After a long period of time,
After the veil of justice has spread,
He will be rewarded for his just and generous deeds
And will receive a robe of honor from the sky
That will prevent him from gaining in years
And will allow him to retain the crown of kingship.
May his head be youthful, his body free from pain!
May the magnitude of his soul
Appear loftier than the revolving dome!
No one will turn down my predictions,
No one willing to count the months and years of my life.

Be watchful and make sure that this book of kings
Will remain as a banner above the heads of wise men
Until the end of time, a vestigial seed
From the lineage of Kiumars to continuously
Be blessed, acclaimed, and admired by all.

Anushiravan, son of Ghobaad, once said:
"If a king fails to follow the path of justice,
The wheel of providence will turn black for him.

◇◇◇◇◇◇◇◇◇◇◇◇◇
108 Shavaal: Tenth month of the Islamic calendar.
109 Anushiravan: Or Khosrow I, Sassanian King who ruled from 531 to 579.

Not even the stars will consider him an apt ruler.
Injustice is a letter of testimony for kings
Who have troubled and tormented the innocent."

May the lineage of the creative, the wise, the just
Continue to live on earth for all eternity!
No one remains here forever,
But the renown of good deeds will always linger.

Where are Fereydoon, Zahaak, and Jamsheed?
Where are the Taazian princes and the Iranian kings?
Where are the noblemen of the Sassanian Empire,[110]
From the descendants of Bahram[111] to the Samanid dynasty?[112]

Zahaak was the most despicable and despised king,
For he was faithless, impure, and unjust
While the auspicious Fereydoon, praised by all,
Conquered all the admiration and the acclaim
Upon his departure from the world.
His name lives on in perpetuity.

Words endure in the world as inheritance.
Words are more valuable than royal jewels.
Never is an unjust man praised, never those who link
Their joy to the acquisition of throne and treasure.
The objects of their ambition perish,
And no one will utter their names again.

Upon this letter from the benevolent king,
May he enjoy his glorious throne forever!
All the people have exited their homes
And have marched to the fields where they pray
For his majesty, their prayers rising beyond the skies,
As they cry: "May the crowned head live on!
May his star of good fortune shine gloriously on him!
May he be surrounded by his good deeds!
May his name be sung and written on walls and palaces!
May the names of his kin, his troops, and his land be blessed,
And blessed be his stature and royal demeanor!

◇◇◇◇◇◇◇◇◇◇◇◇◇
110 Sassanian Dynasty: Ruled Iran from 224 to 651.
111 Bahram: Sassanian king.
112 Samanid Dynasty: Ruled Iran from 819 to 999.

APPENDIX

Glossary of Names

Aabteen: Fereydoon's father; killed and served as a meal to Zahaak's snakes. (Vol. 1)

Aarash: Iranian warrior in the army of Kay Khosrow. (Vol. 3)

Aarezooy: Daughter of Sarv, King of Yemen, and wife of Salm, son of Fereydoon. (Vol. 1)

Aaveh: Son of Samkanan and descendant of Fereydoon; ally of Kay Khosrow in the great battle with Afraasiyaab. (Vol. 3)

Aayaas: Of Chin, warrior ally of King Arjaasp. (Vol. 3)

Aazaad Sarv: Lives during Ferdowsi's time in Marv, owns the *Khoday Nameh,* one of the sources for *The Shahnameh,* and is a man who can trace his origins to Saam, son of Nariman. (Vol. 3)

Aazarafrooz: Son of Esfandiar whose brothers are Bahman, Mehr-noosh, and Nooshaazar. (Vol. 3)

Afraasiyaab: King of Tooran-Zamin and son of Pashang (son of Zaad-sham). Father of Karookhan, Sorkheh, Jahn, Shiddeh, Gurch, Afraasi-yaab, Faranguis, and Manijeh. Killed by Kay Khosrow. (Vols. 1-3)

Afraasiyaab: Son of Afraasiyaab; Tooranian warrior. (Vol. 3)

Aghriras: Brother of Afraasiyaab and Garsivaz. Killed by Afraasiyaab. (Vol. 1)

Aghriras: Tooranian leader who fights in the great war (not to be con-fused with Afraasiyaab's brother). (Vol. 3)

Ahran: Rumi nobleman who weds the third daughter of the Caesar. (Vol. 3)

Ahriman: Dark spirit whose goal is to promote division and chaos.

Ajnaas: Tooranian warrior in Afraasiyaab's army. (Vols. 1-2)

Akhvaast: Tooranian warrior. Killed by Zangueh in the battle of the heroes. (Vols. 2-3)

Akvan Deev: A threatening creature that resembles a deev with a black stripe across its back. Killed by Rostam. (Vols. 2-3)

Alkoos: Tooranian warrior in Afraasiyaab's army. Killed by Rostam. (Vol. 1)

Alvaah: Zaboli warrior in Rostam's retinue. Killed by Kaamoos. (Vols. 1-3)

Andariman: Tooranian warrior and brother of Afraasiyaab. Killed by Gorgeen in the battle of the heroes. (Vols. 1-3)

Andariman: Brother of King Arjaasp, Biderafsh, and Kohram. Killed by Esfandiar. (Vol. 3)

Anushiravan: Or Khosrow I, Sassanian king who ruled from 531 to 579. (Vol. 3)

Arastalis: Aristotle, whom Ferdowsi places in the land of Rum; advisor to Eskandar. Historically, Aristotle was Alexander the Great's tutor up to the time he ascended to the throne in 336 BCE. (Vol. 3)

Ardeshir: Bijan's son and Giv's grandson; Iranian warrior in the army of Lohraasp. (Vol. 3)

Ardeshir: Prince, with brother Shiddasp, sons of King Goshtaasp. Killed by Arjaasp's troops. (Vol. 3)

Ardeshir: Tooranian warrior in the army of Arjaasp. (Vol. 3)

Ardeshir: Name given by King Goshtaasp to Bahman, son of Esfandiar. (Vol. 3)

Ardeshir: Son of King Bahman, also called Sassan. (Vol. 3)

Arjaasp: King of Tooran; his parentage is somewhat unclear but most likely is the son of Garsivaz (son of Pashang). Killed by Esfandiar in the impregnable castle. (Vol. 3)

Arjang: Deev and army commander in Mazandaran. Killed by Rostam. (Vol. 1)

Arjang: Son of Zerreh and brother of Garooy; Tooranian warrior in the army of Tajov. Killed by Tous. (Vol. 2)

Arjasp: Tooranian leader in the army of Afraasiyaab. (Vols. 1-2)

Armail: With brother Garmail, saves intended victims of Zahaak's serpents. (Vol. 1)

Arnavaaz: Daughter or sister of Jamsheed; concubine of Zahaak, then wife of Fereydoon and mother of Iraj. (Vol. 1)

Ashkeboos: Ally of Afraasiyaab from Kushan who fights Rohaam and Rostam. Killed by Rostam. (Vol. 2)

Ashkesh: Of the family of Ghobaad and leader in the Iranian army under the rules of Kay Kaavoos and Kay Khosrow. (Vols. 1-3)

Aspanooy: Slave under the command of Tajov, Afraasiyaab's son-in-law. (Vol. 2)

Baanoogoshasp: Rostam's daughter and Giv's wife. (Vol. 2)

Baarmaan: Tooranian warrior, son of Viseh (son of Zaadsham). Killed by Ghaaran. (Vol. 1)

Baarmaan: Tooranian warrior killed by Rohaam in the battle of the heroes. (Vol. 2-3)

Baazoor: Tooranian sorcerer. (Vol. 2)

Bahman/Ardeshir: Esfandiar's son and King of Iran; his grandfather Goshtaasp also calls him Ardeshir (some Persian editions of *The Shahnameh* refer to him as Ardeshir); marries his daughter Homay/Chehrzaad. (Vol. 3)

Bahraam: Son of Goodarz and Iranian warrior under the rules of Kay Kaavoos, Kay Khosrow, and Lohraasp. (Vols. 1-3)

Bahraam: Name of a number of kings who ruled in the Sassanian period. (Vol. 3)

Barteh: Iranian warrior and leader of the family of Tavaabeh under the rule of Kay Khosrow. (Vols. 1-3)

Beed: Deev in the army of Mazandaran. Killed by Rostam. (Vol. 1)

Behaafarid: Daughter of King Goshtaasp; sister of Homay and Esfandiar. (Vol. 3)

Behzaad: Siaavosh's horse, then mastered by Kay Khosrow. (Vol. 2)

Behzaad: King Goshtaasp's stallion. (Vol. 3)

Bendah: Sindhi leader. (Vol. 3)

Biderafsh: Powerful Chini/Tooranian leader in the army of King Arjaasp and his brother. Killed by Esfandiar, son of Goshtaasp. (Vol. 3)

Bijan: Son of Giv and Baanoogoshasp, Rostam's daughter; Iranian warrior under the rule of Kay Khosrow. Loses his life in the blizzard after Kay Khosrow disappears. (Vols. 1-3)

Bitghoon: Eskandar's vizier who disguises himself as the Caesar. (Vol. 3)

Bivard: Ruler of Kaat and ally of Afraasiyaab. (Vol. 2)

Booraab: A Rumi blacksmith. (Vol. 3)

Boossepaas: Father of Kooh; Hoomaan pretends to be him when he meets Rostam. (Vol. 2)

Borzeen: Iranian warrior and son of Garshaasp. (Vols. 1-2)

Borzvila: Ally of Afraasiyaab in the last great battle. (Vol. 3)

Brahmin: Guide and teacher of the Hindu caste. (Vol. 3)

Caesar of Rum: Various Rumi rulers and allies of Afraasiyaab in wars. (Vols. 1-3)

Changgesh: Ally of Afraasiyaab who fights Rostam and is killed by him. (Vol. 2)

Daaraab: Son of Homay and Bahman who is raised by the laundry-man and his wife; husband of Nahid of Rum and father of Eskandar and Dara. (Vol. 3)

Damoor: Tooranian warrior who lends a hand in the slaying of Siaavosh. (Vols. 2-3)

Dara: Son of Daaraab and half-brother of Eskandar. (Vol. 3)

Deev: Child of Ahriman, also referred to as Eblis; represents the material or physical embodiment of Ahriman; a fragment of the dark spirit.

Delafrooz: Descendant of Kay Ghobaad and Iranian warrior in the army of Kay Khosrow. (Vol. 3)

Delarai: Wife of King Dara and mother of Roshanak, Eskandar's wife. (Vol. 3)

Eblis: Name synonymous with Ahriman and deev. Eblis is one of the many physical manifestations of Ahriman.

Elias: Son of Mehraas, King of Khazaria. Defeated by Goshtaasp, son of Lohraasp. (Vol. 3)

Emperor of Chin: Ally of Afraasiyaab. (Vol. 2)

Esfandiar: Son of Goshtaasp and Katayoon, and brother of Pashootan, Behaafarid, Shiroo, Nivezaar, Shiddasp, and Farshidvard; his sons are Bahman, Mehrnoosh, Aazarafrooz, and Nooshaazar. Calls himself Khorraad at the impregnable castle. Killed by Rostam. (Vol. 3)

Eskandar: Persian equivalent to Alexander; son of King Daaraab and Nahid of Rum, and half-brother of Dara; marries Roshanak, daughter of Dara. (Vol. 3)

Faghfoor: Title given to the rulers of Chin, or China, who govern under the authority (jurisdiction) of Afraasiyaab or Tooran-Zamin. (Vols. 1-3)

Faraamarz: Rostam's son and Iranian warrior under the rules of Kay Kaavoos, Kay Khosrow, King Lohraasp, and King Goshtaasp. Killed in vengeance by King Bahman. (Vols. 1-3)

Faraanak: Fereydoon's mother and Aabteen's wife. (Vol. 1)

Faranguis: Afraasiyaab's daughter, wife of Siaavosh, and mother of Kay Khosrow who later marries Fariborz, son of Kaavoos. (Vol. 2)

Farghaar: Skillful warrior who defends Afraasiyaab. (Vol. 2)

Farhaad: Grandson of Goodarz; Iranian warrior under the rules of Kay Kaavoos and Kay Khosrow. (Vols. 1-3)

Fariborz: Son of Kaavoos and brother of Siaavosh. Loses his life in the blizzard after Kay Khosrow disappears. (Vols. 1-3)

Farrokhzaad: Adoptive name of Goshtaasp, son of Lohraasp, during his stay in Rum. (Vol. 3)

Farshidvard: Tooranian warrior and leader in Afraasiyaab's army; son of Viseh (son of Zaadsham). He and his brother Lahaak are killed by Gostaham, son of Gojdaham. (Vols. 1-3)

Farshidvard: Son of King Goshtaasp and Esfandiar's brother. Killed by Kohram. (Vol. 3)

Fartoos: Ruler of Chaghan; ally of Afraasiyaab. Killed by Fariborz, son of Kaavoos, in the great war. (Vols. 2-3)

Fazl: Son of Ahmad, or Abbas Fazl bin Ahmad; minister of Sultan Mahmoud during the time of Ferdowsi. (Vol. 3)

Fereydoon: Sixth king and son of Aabteen and Faraanak; father of Salm, Toor, and Iraj; great-grandfather of Manoochehr. Dies of old age. (Vol. 1)

Filghoos: Caesar of Rum and father of Nahid, who weds King Daaraab. (Vol. 3)

Five Chambermaids: Rudaabeh's servants. (Vol. 1)

Foor: Leader of the Indian army of Sindh. (Vol. 3)

Foorood: Son of Siaavosh and Jarireh (Piran's daughter). Killed by Bijan. (Vol. 2)

Fooroohal: Iranian warrior in Kay Khosrow's army. (Vol. 3)

Gargooy: Iranian warrior in King Goshtaasp's army. (Vol. 3)

Garmail: With brother Armail, cook in Zahaak's kitchen. (Vol. 1)

Garooy: Son of Zerreh; descendant of Toor and Tooranian warrior responsible for Siaavosh's death. Killed at the order of Kay Khosrow. (Vols. 2-3)

Garshaasp: Father of Nariman, father of Saam and Borzeen; warrior in Manoochehr's army. (Vol. 2)

Garshaasp: Son of Zu and tenth King of Iran who rules for nine years. (Vol. 1)

Garsivan: Tooranian warrior. (Vol. 3)

Garsivaz: Son of Pashang and Afraasiyaab's brother, responsible for Siaavosh's death; father of Andariman, Arjaasp, Biderafsh, and Kohram. Killed at the order of Kay Khosrow. (Vols. 1-3)

Garukhan: A family that supports Kay Khosrow in his great battle against Afraasiyaab. (Vol. 3)

Garzam: Tooranian warrior in Afraasiyaab's army. Killed by Giv. (Vol. 1)

Ghaaloos: Rumi emissary and advisor of the Caesar. (Vol. 3)

Ghaaran: Son of Kaaveh; brother of Kashvaad; Iranian warrior and chief. (Vols. 1-3)

Ghaaran: Ruler of eastern lands and ally of Kay Khosrow in the great battle against Afraasiyaab. (Vol. 3)

Ghabtoon: King of Egypt during the time of Eskandar. (Vol. 3)

Gharaakhan: Tooranian warrior who serves Afraasiyaab. (Vol. 3)

Ghobaad: Son of Kashvaad (son of Kaaveh); Iranian warrior in Manoochehr's army; not to be confused with Kay Ghobaad. Killed by Baarmaan. (Vol. 1)

Gholoon: Tooranian warrior in the army of Afraasiyaab. Killed by Rostam. (Vol. 1)

Ghool: Name meaning giant; witch defeated by Esfandiar in the fourth stage of his quest. (Vol. 3)

Ghorcheh: Tooranian warrior in the army of Afraasiyaab. (Vol. 2)

Giv: Son of Goodarz, grandson of Kashvaad, husband of Baanoogoshasp, and father of Bijan and Goraazeh; Iranian leader and warrior who serves under Kay Kaavoos and Kay Khosrow. Loses his life in the blizzard after Kay Khosrow disappears. (Vols. 1-3)

Gojdaham: Iranian warrior, defender of the White Castle, and father of Gostaham, Gordaafareed, and Hojir's wife. (Vols. 1-3)

Golbaad: Tooranian warrior killed by Zaal. (Vol. 1)

Golbaad: Tooranian warrior and leader in the army of Afraasiyaab. (Vol. 2-3)

Golgoon: Goodarz's horse. (Vol. 2)

Golgoon: Lohraasp's horse. (Vol. 3)

Golrang: Fereydoon's horse. (Vol. 1)

Golrang: Fariborz's horse. (Vol. 2)

Golshahr: Piran's wife and mother of Jarireh. (Vol. 2)

Goodarz: Iranian leader who serves under Kay Kaavoos, Kay Khosrow, and Lohraasp; son of Kashvaad (son of Kaaveh); has 78 sons and grandsons. (Vols. 1-3)

Gooshbastar: Strange and hairy man Eskandar encounters on his way to Babel. (Vol. 3)

Goraazeh: Son of Giv (son of Goodarz); Iranian warrior under the rules of Kay Kaavoos and Kay Khosrow. (Vols. 1-3)

Gorazm: Iranian swarrior of Kianian lineage in the army of Goshtaasp. Killed by King Arjaasp's troops. (Vol. 3)

Gordaafareed: Iranian female warrior who fights with Sohraab; daughter of Gojdaham (of the family of Goodarz). (Vol. 1)

Gorgeen: Son of Milaad and Iranian warrior in the armies of Kay

Kaavoos and Kay Khosrow. (Vols. 1-3)

Gorgsaar: Commander of King Arjaasp's host. Captured and later killed by Esfandiar. (Vol. 3)

Goshtaasp: Son of Lohraasp, King of Iran; marries Katayoon, daughter of the Rumi Caesar; father of Esfandiar, Shiroo, Nivezaar, Shiddasp, Farshidvard, and Behaafarid; conceals his identity behind the name Farrokhzaad in Rum. (Vol. 3)

Gostaham: Son of Nozar; brother of Tous (different from Gostaham, son of Gojdaham). (Vols. 1-3)

Gostaham: Young son of Gojdaham and brother of Gordaafareed (different from the son of Nozar). (Vols. 1-3)

Gueraami: Son of Jaamaasp, Goshtaasp's minister. Killed by Arjaasp's troops. (Vol. 3)

Gurch: Afraasiyaab's fifth son and Tooranian leader. (Vol. 3)

Haaroot: Angel who along with the fairy Maaroot comes to earth to teach spells. They lose access to heaven because of their sins and are imprisoned in Babel. (Vol. 2)

Heshoo: Rumi guardian of the shores. (Vol. 3)

Hirbad: Sudaabeh's servant. (Vol. 2)

Hojir: Son of Goodarz; Iranian warrior and Gojdaham's son-in-law. (Vols. 1-3)

Homa: Large and powerful bird in Persian mythology, symbol of happiness; similar to the griffin or the phoenix. (Vols. 1-3)

Homay: King Bahman's daughter, sister of Ardeshir/Sassan, also called Chehrzaad; marries her father, Bahman, and they have a son, Daaraab; upon Bahman's death, she rules as queen for thirty-two years. (Vol. 3)

Hoom: A devout descendant of Fereydoon who lives humbly as a hermit in a mountainous cave. (Vol. 3)

Hoomaan: Tooranian leader, son of Viseh (son of Zaadsham). Killed by Bijan. (Vols. 1-3)

Hooshang: Second King of Iran; son of Siaamak; rules for forty years. (Vol. 1)

Hooshdeev: Malicious Tooranian warrior under the command of King Arjaasp. (Vol. 3)

Hormozd: Or Ormazd, another name for Creator. In the ancient Persian solar calendar, each day had the name of a deity instead of a number. Each name evoked a concept. The division then was not based on a seven-day week but on a thirty-day month.

Illa: Unclear whether he is Afraasiyaab's son or grandson; Tooranian warrior. (Vol. 3)

Iraj: Youngest son of Fereydoon and Arnavaaz; brother of Salm and Toor; grandfather of Manoochehr. Killed by his brothers. (Vol. 1)

Iraj: Ruler of Kabol and ally of Kay Khosrow in the great battle against Afraasiyaab. (Vol. 3)

Israfil: One of the four angels equivalent to Raphael of Uriel; angel of music. (Vol. 3)

Jaamaasp: Astrologer and guide to Goshtaasp. (Vol. 3)

Jahn: Tooranian warrior, Afraasiyaab's son and advisor. Overthrown by Rostam in Gang but survives and is offered the rulership of Tooran-Zamin by Kay Khosrow, who forgives him. (Vols. 2-3)

Jamsheed: Son of Tahmures and fourth King of Iran who rules for 700 years. Killed by Zahaak. (Vol. 1)

Jandal: A wise envoy sent by Fereydoon to find three sisters to marry Toor, Salm, and Iraj. (Vol. 1)

Janoosyar: Vizier and treasurer of King Dara who conspires with Maahiar to kill the king. Killed by Eskandar. (Vol. 3)

Jaranjas: Tooranian leader who fights for Afraasiyaab in the great war. (Vol. 3)

Jarireh: Siaavosh's wife and Foorood's mother; eldest daughter of

Piran. (Vol. 2)

Jooyaa: A warrior leader in the army of the King of Mazandaran. Killed by Rostam. (Vol. 1)

Kaafoor: "Man-eater" Tooranian who dwells in the city of Bidaad. Killed by Rostam. (Vol. 2)

Kaakooleh: Descendant of Toor and Tooranian warrior. (Vol. 3)

Kaakooy: Descendant of Zahaak who battles Manoochehr. Killed by Manoochehr. (Vol. 1)

Kaaloo: Tooranian warrior in the army of Afraasiyaab. (Vol. 2)

Kaamoos: Ruler of Kushan and Afraasiyaab's ally in war. Killed by Rostam. (Vol. 2)

Kaaveh: Father of Kashvaad and Ghaaran; blacksmith who leads the opposition against Zahaak. (Vol. 1)

Kaboodeh: Servant of Tajov, ruler of Gorooguerd. Killed by Bahraam. (Vol. 2)

Kahaar: From Kahan, an ally of Afraasiyaab. Killed by Rostam. (Vol. 2)

Kahtan: Conqueror of the land of Yemen. (Vol. 3)

Kalaahoor: Warrior rider in the army of the King of Mazandaran. (Vol. 1)

Karkoo: Warrior and ally of Afraasiyaab. (Vol. 2)

Karkooy: Salm's grandson and a relative of Zahaak on his mother's side. Killed by Saam. (Vol. 1)

Karookhan: Afraasiyaab's eldest son and Tooranian leader. (Vol. 3)

Kashvaad: Son of Kaaveh and brother of Goodarz; Iranian warrior and soldier in Manoochehr's army. (Vols. 1-2)

Katayoon: Daughter of the Rumi Caesar; marries Goshtaasp, future King of Iran, and gives birth to their son, Esfandiar. (Vol. 3)

Katib: Father of Nasr, ruler of Mecca at the time of Eskandar's visit. (Vol. 3)

Kay Aarash: Son of Kay Ghobaad. (Vols. 1-2)

Kay Aarmin: Son of Kay Ghobaad. (Vol. 1)

Kay Ghobaad: Descendant of Fereydoon and eleventh King of Iran who rules for one hundred years; father to four sons: Kay Kaavoos, Kay Aarash, Kay Pashin, and Kay Aarmin. (Vol. 1)

Kay Kaavoos: Son of Kay Ghobaad and twelfth King of Iran who rules for 150 years. (Vols. 1-3)

Kay Khosrow: Son of Siaavosh and Faranguis, and grandson of Kay Kaavoos and Afraasiyaab. (Vols. 1-3)

Kay Pashin: Son of Kay Ghobaad. (Vols. 1-2)

Kebord: Tooranian warrior. (Vol. 3)

Kehila: Tooranian warrior. Killed by Manoochehr in the great war. (Vol. 3)

Keid: Indian King of Ghennooj.

Ketmaareh: Iranian warrior and son of Ghaaran. (Vol. 3)

Keydafeh: Queen of Andalusia. (Vol. 3)

Keydroosh: Son of Keydafeh and son-in-law of King Faryan; brother of Teynoosh. (Vol. 3)

Khashaash: Important warrior in King Arjaasp's army. (Vol. 3)

Khazar: Semi-nomadic person from the land of Khazaria. (Vol. 3)

Khazarvan: Tooranian warrior in the army of Afraasiyaab. Killed by Zaal. (Vol. 1)

Khezr: Messenger and prophet, guardian of the sea. (Vol. 3)

Khojabr: Tooranian warrior in the army of Afraasiyaab. (Vol. 1)

Khorraad: Iranian warrior in the army of Kay Kaavoos. (Vols. 1-3)

Khozaa: Descendant of Abraham and leader of Mecca; Eskandar executes him and his entire family. (Vol. 3)

Khuzan: Ruler of the land of Pars and Iranian warrior leader who fights alongside Kay Khosrow. (Vol. 3)

Kiaanoosh: Fereydoon's brother. (Vol. 1)

King Faryan: Ruler of a fortified city on some border between Egypt and Spain, and father-in-law of Keydroosh, Keydafeh's son. (Vol. 3)

King Firooz: Descendant of Kay Ghobaad and ruler of Gharchehgan; ally of Kay Khosrow in the great battle against Afraasiyaab. (Vol. 3)

King of Chegel: Warrior leader in King Arjaasp's army. (Vol. 3)

King of Egypt: Ally of the King of Haamaavaran. Killed by Zavaareh in the battle with the three nations. (Vol. 1)

King of Guran: Ally of Kay Khosrow in the great battle against Afraasiyaab. (Vol. 3)

King of Haamaavaran: Father of Sudaabeh, wife of Kay Kaavoos. Killed by Rostam to save Kay Kaavoos. (Vol. 2)

King of Kabol: Father-in-law of Shaghaad, Zaal's son. Killed by Faraamarz, Rostam's son. (Vol. 3)

King of Kerman: Ally of Kay Khosrow in the great battle against Afraasiyaab. (Vol. 3)

King of Khotan: Afraasiyaab's ally in war. (Vol. 3)

King of Khuzan: Ally of Kay Khosrow in the great battle against Afraasiyaab. (Vol. 3)

King of Mazandaran: Ruler of a kingdom of deevs who captures Kay Kaavoos and is then killed in Rostam's epic seven-stage quest. (Vol. 1)

King of Mokran: Afraasiyaab's ally in the great war. Killed by Tokhaar and Tous. (Vol. 3)

King of Rus: King of Russia. (Vol. 3)

King of Shaam: King of Syria and ally of the King of Haamaavaran. Captured by Rostam in the battle with three nations (Vol. 1)

King of Sindh: Ally of Afraasiyaab. (Vol. 2)

Kiumars: First King of Iran who rules from a mountaintop for fifty years. (Vol. 1)

Kohram: Tooranian warrior. Killed by Barteh in the battle of the heroes. (Vols. 2-3)

Kohram: Brother of King Arjaasp, Andariman, and Biderafsh. Killed by Shiddasp, son of Goshtaasp. (Vol. 3)

Kohram: King Arjaasp's eldest son. Killed by Esfandiar. (Vol. 3)

Kolbaad: Son of Viseh; Tooranian warrior. Killed by Fariborz, son of Kaavoos, in the battle of the heroes. (Vol. 3)

Konaarang Deev: Guardian of a rocky, desolate place on the way to the White Deev's dwelling. (Vol. 1)

Kondor: From the land of Saghlaab and an ally of Afraasiyaab in war; warrior in the army of King Arjaasp. (Vols. 2-3)

Kooh: Assumed name used by Hoomaan to trick Rostam; son of Boossepaas. (Vol. 2)

Kundrow: Zahaak's minister. (Vol. 1)

Lahaak: Son of Viseh (son of Zaadsham); Tooranian warrior and leader in the army of Afraasiyaab. He and his brother Farshidvard are killed by Gostaham. (Vols. 2-3)

Laundryman: Finds Daaraab, son of Homay and Bahman, floating in a box on the river and raises him with his wife. (Vol. 3)

Lohraasp: Iranian warrior in Kay Khosrow's army who is named King of Iran by Kay Khosrow; son of Arvand Shah (descendant of Kay Pashin, descendant of Kay Ghobaad), and father of Goshtaasp and Zarir. Killed by Arjaasp's troops. (Vol. 3)

Maah Aafareed: One of Iraj's wives and Manoochehr's grandmother. (Vol. 1)

Maah-e Aazaadeh Khooy: Daughter of Sarv, King of Yemen, and wife of Toor, son of Fereydoon. (Vol. 1)

Maahiar: Vizier and advisor of King Dara who conspires with Janoosyar to kill the king. Killed by Eskandar. (Vol. 3)

Mani: Iranian prophet who wrote the holy book of Manichaeism, *Arjang,* also known as *The Book of Pictures.* He preached throughout the land of Persia in the third century BCE. (Vol. 3)

Manijeh: Afraasiyaab's daughter and Bijan's wife. (Vol. 1)

Manoochehr: Seventh King of Iran and grandson of Iraj who rules for 120 years; son of Pashang and *Nameless.* (Vol. 1)

Manoochehr: Son of Aarash and warrior from Khorasan; ally of Kay Khosrow. (Vol. 3)

Manooshan: Ruler of the land of Pars and Iranian warrior leader who fights alongside Kay Khosrow. (Vol. 3)

Manshoor: Ruler of Chin and ally of Afraasiyaab. (Vol. 2)

Mardaas: Zahaak's father, ruler in Mesopotamia. Killed by Eblis. (Vol. 1)

Mardooy: Tooranian warrior in the army of Tajov. (Vol. 2)

Mehraab: Ruler of Kabol and father of Rudaabeh; descendant of Zahaak. (Vols. 1-2)

Mehraas: King of Khazaria. (Vol. 3)

Mehran: Wise man with deep foresight who advises the Indian Keid.

Mehrnoosh: Son of Esfandiar and brother of Bahman, Aazarafrooz, and Nooshaazar. Killed by Faraamarz. (Vol. 3)

Milaad: Father of Gorgeen and Iranian hero in the army of Kay Kaavoos and Kay Khosrow. (Vols. 1-2)

Mirin: Wealthy Rumi descendant of Salm who marries the second daughter of the Caesar. (Vol. 3)

Moolookeh Tavayef: Meaning "King of Tribes"; name assigned to any minor ruler.

Mother of Siaavosh: Descendant of Fereydoon and granddaughter of Garsivaz. (Vol. 2)

Nahel: Tooranian warrior. (Vol. 2)

Nahid: Daughter of Filghoos, Caesar of Rum; wife of King Daaraab and mother of Eskandar. (Vol. 3)

Nameless: Daughter of Maah Aafareed and Iraj; granddaughter of Fereydoon; wife of Pashang, mother of Manoochehr. Ferdowsi does not assign her a name. (Vol. 1)

Nameless: Wife of Kay Kaavoos and mother of Siaavosh; granddaughter of Garsivaz. (Vol. 2)

Namkhaast: Evil sorcerer at the court of King Arjaasp. (Vol. 3)

Nariman: Great Iranian warrior in the army of Manoochehr; Saam's father and Zaal's grandfather. (Vols. 1-2)

Nasr: Son of Katib; ruler of Mecca at the time of Eskandar's visit; he is a descendant of Abraham. (Vol. 3)

Nastaar: Guardian of the Rumi Caesar's stables. (Vol. 3)

Nastihan: Tooranian warrior; son of Viseh (son of Zaadsham). Killed by Bijan. (Vols. 2-3)

Nastooh: Son of Goodarz and Iranian warrior. (Vols. 2-3)

Nastooh: Tooranian commander who fights for Afraasiyaab in the great war. (Vol. 3)

Nastoor: Son of Zarir, son of Lohraasp; King Goshtaasp grants him his daughter's hand. (Vol. 3)

Nivezaar: Son of King Goshtaasp. Killed by Arjaasp's troops. (Vol. 3)

Nooshaazar: Esfandiar's son; his brothers are Bahman, Mehrnoosh, and Aazarafrooz. Killed by Zavaareh. (Vol. 3)

Nozar: Son of Manoochehr and eighth King of Iran who rules for seven years; father of Tous and Gostaham. Beheaded by Afraasiyaab. (Vol. 1)

Ostaghila: Ally of Afraasiyaab in the great battle. (Vol. 3)

Palaashan: Tooranian warrior and Afraasiyaab's army leader. Killed by Bijan. (Vol. 2)

Pashang: Iranian warrior from the seed of Jamsheed; Fereydoon's nephew (his brother's son), selected by Fereydoon to marry Fereydoon's *Nameless* granddaughter; father of Manoochehr. (Vol. 1)

Pashang: Son of Zaadsham and father of Aghriras, Afraasiyaab, Garsivaz, Andariman, Sepahram, Kohram. (Vols. 1-3)

Pashootan: Son of Goshtaasp and Katayoon, and brother and advisor of Esfandiar. (Vol. 3)

Philosopher: One of the wonders of the Indian Keid who is given to Eskandar as a tribute. (Vol. 3)

Physician: One of the wonders of the Indian Keid who is given to Eskandar. (Vol. 3)

Pilsam: Son of Viseh (son of Zaadsham) and brother of Piran; Tooranian army leader. Killed by Rostam. (Vols. 1-2)

Piran: Son of Viseh (son of Zaadsham) and brother of Pilsam; Tooranian army leader. Killed by Goodarz in the battle of the heroes. (Vols. 1-3)

Poolaad: Of Ghondi; ruler deev in the army of Mazandaran with hooves as feet. Killed by Rostam. (Vol. 1)

Poolaad: Tooranian warrior. (Vol. 2)

Poolaadvand: Fierce Tooranian warrior who dwells in the mountains of Chin. Killed by Rostam. (Vol. 2)

Pormaye: Cow that nurses Fereydoon. (Vol. 1)

Pormaye: Fereydoon's brother; same name as the cow that nurses Fereydoon. (Vol. 1)

Rakhsh: Rostam's horse. Killed by Shaghaad, Rostam's brother. (Vols. 1-3)

Rashnavaad: Warrior leader in the army of Queen Homay. (Vol. 3)

Rezvan: Keeper of paradise. (Vol. 2)

Rivniz: Tous's son-in-law and brother-in-law to Zarasp; Iranian warrior, has forty beautiful sisters. Killed by Foorood. (Vol. 2)

Rivniz: Youngest son of Fariborz; grandson of Kaavoos. Killed by the Tooranians under Kaavoos's reign. (Vol. 2)

Rivniz: Son of Zarasp and Iranian warrior, "worshipper of Aazargoshasp." (Vols. 2-3)

Rohaam: Son of Goodarz and brother of Giv, Bahraam, Hojir, and Shiddush; Iranian warrior under the rule of Kay Kaavoos and Kay Khosrow. (Vols. 1-3)

Rooeen: Son of Piran (son of Viseh) and Tooranian warrior. Killed by Bijan in the battle of the heroes. (Vols. 1-3)

Roshanak: Daughter of King Dara and Delarai, and wife of Eskandar; name of Eskandar's wife in Ferdowsi's legend; historically one of Alexander's wives was Roxana, a Bactrian princess, while his Persian wives were Stateira II, daughter of Stateira I and Darius III of Persia, and Parysatis II, daughter of Artaxerxes III of Persia. (Vol. 3)

Rostam: Iranian world hero and son of Zaal and Rudaabeh; marries Shahrbaanoo; father of Faraamarz and Baanoogoshasp. Killed by his brother Shaghaad. (Vols. 1-3)

Rudaabeh: Daughter of Mehraab and Sindokht; wife of Zaal and mother of Rostam. (Vols. 1-3)

Saam: Iranian warrior and head of Manoochehr's army; Nariman's son and Zaal's father. (Vol. 1)

Saaveh: Relative of Kaamoos and warrior ally of Afraasiyaab. Killed by Rostam. (Vol. 2)

Saaveh: Warrior in Esfandiar's army. (Vol. 3)

Sabbaah: King of Yemen and ally of Kay Khosrow in the great battle against Afraasiyaab. (Vol. 3)

Saghil: Rumi prince, son of the Caesar, and brother of Katayoon. (Vol. 3)

Sahi: Daughter of Sarv, King of Yemen, and wife of Iraj, son of Fereydoon. (Vol. 1)

Salm: Son of Fereydoon and Shahrnaaz; brother of Toor and Iraj. Killed by Manoochehr to avenge Iraj's death. (Vol. 1)

Samanid Dynasty: Ruled Iran from 819 to 999. (Vol. 3)

Samkanan: Warrior in the army of Kay Khosrow in the great battle; father of Aaveh. (Vol. 3)

Sanjeh: One of the deevs in the service of Mazandaran; guard of the mountain on the path to the White Deev. (Vol. 1)

Sarv: King of Yemen and father of the three maidens who marry Fereydoon's sons Toor, Salm, and Iraj. (Vol. 1)

Sassanian Dynasty: Ruled Iran from 224 to 651. (Vol. 3)

Sassan: Named Ardeshir, son of King Bahman and brother of Homay/Chehrzaad; father of Sassan. (Vol. 3)

Sassan: Son of Sassan (son of Bahman). (Vol. 3)

Sepahram: Brother of Afraasiyaab and Tooranian leader. Killed by Hojir. (Vols. 2-3)

Sevorg: Indian leader assigned to rule by Eskandar. (Vol. 3)

Shaavaran: Father of Zangueh. (Vols. 1-2)

Shabaahang: Farhaad's white horse. (Vol. 2)

Shabdeez: Mehraab's horse (Vol. 1)

Shabdeez: Ghobaad's horse (Vol. 1); Giv's horse. (Vols. 1-2)

Shabrang: Bijan's horse. (Vol. 2)

Shaghaad: Rostam's brother born from Zaal and a musically inclined slave. Killed by Rostam. (Vol. 3)

Shahpoor: Iranian warrior who serves the kings from Fereydoon to Lohraasp. (Vols. 1-3)

Shahrguir: Warrior who takes Keydroosh and his wife captive near Spain. (Vol. 3)

Shahrnaaz: Daughter or sister of Jamsheed; concubine of Zahaak; later wife of Fereydoon and mother of Salm and Toor. (Vol. 1)

Shahrbaanoo: Giv's sister and Rostam's wife; mother of Faraamarz. (Vol. 2)

Shamaasaas: Tooranian warrior in the army of Afraasiyaab. Killed in battle by Ghaaran. (Vol. 1)

Shammaakh: Ruler of Syria and ally of Kay Khosrow in the great battle against Afraasiyaab. (Vol. 3)

Shamiran: From Shakni, an ally of Afraasiyaab. (Vol. 2)

Shangal: From India, an ally of Afraasiyaab. Killed by Rostam. (Vol. 2)

Shiddasp: Minister under the rule of Tahmures. (Vol. 1)

Shiddasp: Son of King Goshtaasp and brother of Ardeshir. Killed by Arjaasp's warrior. (Vol. 3)

Shiddeh: Also referred to as Pashang. Afraasiyaab's son and Tooranian leader who fights in the great war. Killed by Kay Khosrow. (Vols. 2-3)

Shiddush: Son of Goodarz (son of Kashvaad) and Iranian warrior serving the kings from Manoochehr to Kay Khosrow. (Vols. 1-3)

Shirkhoon: Guide of Zabolestan in Zaal's retinue. (Vol. 3)

Shiroo: Son of King Goshtaasp. Killed by Arjaasp's troops. (Vol. 3)

Shirui: Warrior in Toor's army. (Vol. 1)

Shiruye: Iranian warrior and general in Manoochehr's army. (Vol. 1)

Shiruye: Iranian warrior in Lohraasp's army and grandson of Giv. (Vol. 3)

Shitarakh: Tooranian warrior. (Vol. 2)

Shoaib: Taazian leader from the Arabian Peninsula from the lineage of Ghotaib. Killed by Daaraab's troops. (Vol. 3)

Siaamak: Son of Kiumars; father of Hooshang. (Vol. 1)

Siaamak: Tooranian warrior. Killed by Goraazeh in the battle of the heroes. (Vol. 3)

Siaavosh: Son of Iranian Kay Kaavoos and descendant of Tooranian Garsivaz. (Vol. 2)

Simorgh: Bird of knowledge that rescues and raises Zaal. (Vol. 2)

Sindokht: Mother of Rudaabeh; wife of Mehraab. (Vol. 1)

Sohraab: Son of Rostam and Tahmineh. Killed by Rostam. (Vol. 1)

Sooroosh: Archangel able to hear and relay divine messages. (Vols. 1-3)

Sootooh: Sorcerer in the service of King Arjaasp. (Vol. 3)

Sorkheh: Afraasiyaab's son and Tooranian leader. Killed at the order of Zavaareh. (Vol. 2)

Sultan Mahmoud, Abul Ghassem: Ghaznavid ruler of Iran (999-1030) during Ferdowsi's later years.

Tabah: Tooranian warrior in King Arjaasp's host. (Vol. 3)

Taazi/Taazian: Bedouins or tribes living in the land of Arabia or Mesopotamia (between the Tigris and the Euphrates), also "field of warriors" or "field of spear-riders"; worshippers of the Black Stone or Kaaba, as given by the prophet Muhammad; symbolic rather than cultural, national, or geographical.

Tahmineh: Wife of Rostam and mother of Sohraab, daughter of the King of Samangan. (Vol. 1)

Tahmures: Son of Hooshang, third King of Iran, and Deev-Binder who rules for thirty years. (Vol. 1)

Tajov: Ruler of Gorooguerd, a province of Tooran-Zamin; of Iranian lineage but also Afraasiyaab's son-in-law. (Vol. 2)

Taliman: Iranian warrior in Nozar's army (Vol. 1); ally of Kay Khosrow (Vol. 3).

Tarkhan of Chin: A title the Turks and Iranians use to refer to rulers who fight with the Tooranian army against Iran-Zamin. (Vols. 2-3)

Tavaabeh: Name of a family of warriors loyal to Iranian Kay Khosrow, led by Barteh. (Vol. 2)

Tevorg: Sentinel who watches over Afraasiyaab's city. (Vol. 2)

Teynoosh: Son of Keydafeh and brother of Keydroosh. (Vol. 3)

Tokhaar: Warrior in Foorood's army and Foorood's advisor. (Vol. 2)

Tokhaar: Ruler of Dahestan and leader in Kay Khosrow's army from the noble race of Vashmeh. (Vol. 3)

Toor: Son of Fereydoon and Shahrnaaz; brother of Salm and Iraj. Killed by Manoochehr. (Vol. 1)

Tous: Son of Nozar, brother of Gostaham, and commander of troops under Kay Khosrow; bearer of the Kaaviani banner and the golden boots. Loses his life in the blizzard after Kay Khosrow disappears. (Vols. 1-3)

Turks: The Turks of *The Shahnameh* are nomadic tribes moving through the lands east of Iran with no relation to today's Turkey, which sits west of Iran and which was established in the 11th century upon the conquest of the Turks by the Byzantines. (Vol. 1-3)

Turkish boy: Servant of Zaal during his courtship with Rudaabeh. (Vol. 1)

Tuvarg: Tooranian warrior. (Vol. 3)

Ulaad: Ruler of a land in the fifth stage of Rostam. Ultimately, Rostam makes him ruler of Mazandaran. (Vol. 1)

Ulaad's guardian: Unnamed guardian of the field owned by Ulaad. (Vol. 1)

Varaazaad: King of Sepijaab and a brave warrior who fights for Afraasiyaab. Killed by Faraamarz. (Vol. 2)

Vashmeh: Name of a family, led by Tokhaar, ruler of Dahestan, ally of Kay Khosrow in the great battle. (Vol. 3)

Viseh: Father of Piran, Pilsam, Nastihan, Kolbaad, Baarmaan, and Hoomaan; Tooranian army leader and Afraasiyaab's minister. (Vols. 1-2)

White Deev: Leader in Mazandaran. Killed by Rostam. (Vol. 1)

Wife of the laundryman: Raises Daaraab, son of Homay and Bahman, with her husband. (Vol. 3)

Witch: Woman who helps Sudaabeh prove her innocence. (Vol. 2)

Yazdan: Plural of Yzad (divine), encompasses all of divinity, Creator of all that is manifested, unmanifested, and all that is yet to come into existence.

Yzad: Singular of Yazdan, Divine Creator.

Zaadsham: Afraasiyaab's grandfather and Pashang's father. (Vols. 1-3)

Zaal: Saam's son; Rudaabeh's husband and Rostam's father; also called Dastan-e Zand by Simorgh and Zaal-e Zar by Saam; father of Shaghaad. (Vols. 1-3)

Zahaak: Son of Mardaas and fifth King of Iran who rules for one thousand years. Captured by Fereydoon. (Vol. 1)

Zangaleh: Tooranian warrior. Killed by Fooroohal. (Vol. 3)

Zangueh: Son of Shaavaran and Iranian warrior under the rules of Kay Kaavoos and Kay Khosrow. (Vols. 1-3)

Zarasp: Son of King Manoochehr and brother of Nozar; Kay Khosrow's treasurer. (Vols. 1-3)

Zarasp: Son of Tous (son of Nozar) and brother-in-law of Rivniz. A warrior under the rule of Kay Khosrow. Killed at the hands of Foo-rood. (Vol. 2)

Zarir: Son of Lohraasp; and brother of Goshtaasp. Killed by Biderafsh, Arjaasp's brother. (Vol. 3)

Zartosht: Zoroaster or Zarathustra, Iranian prophet who lived in the sixth century BCE. (Vol. 3)

Zavaareh: Rostam's brother. Killed by Shaghaad. (Vols. 1-3)

Zerreh: Father of Garooy and Arjang; Tooranian warrior. (Vol. 2)

Zhendehrazm: Son of the King of Samangan and brother of Tah-mineh; uncle of Sohraab. Killed by Rostam. (Vol. 1)

Zirak: A wise man who interprets Zahaak's dream of Fereydoon. (Vol. 1)

Zohir: Iranian warrior in the army of Kay Khosrow. (Vol. 3)

Zu: Son of Tahmaasp, descendant of Fereydoon, and ninth King of Iran who rules for five years and dies at the age of 86. (Vol. 1)

THE KIANIAN KINGS: LINE OF SUCCESSION
From Kiumars to Kay Kaavoos

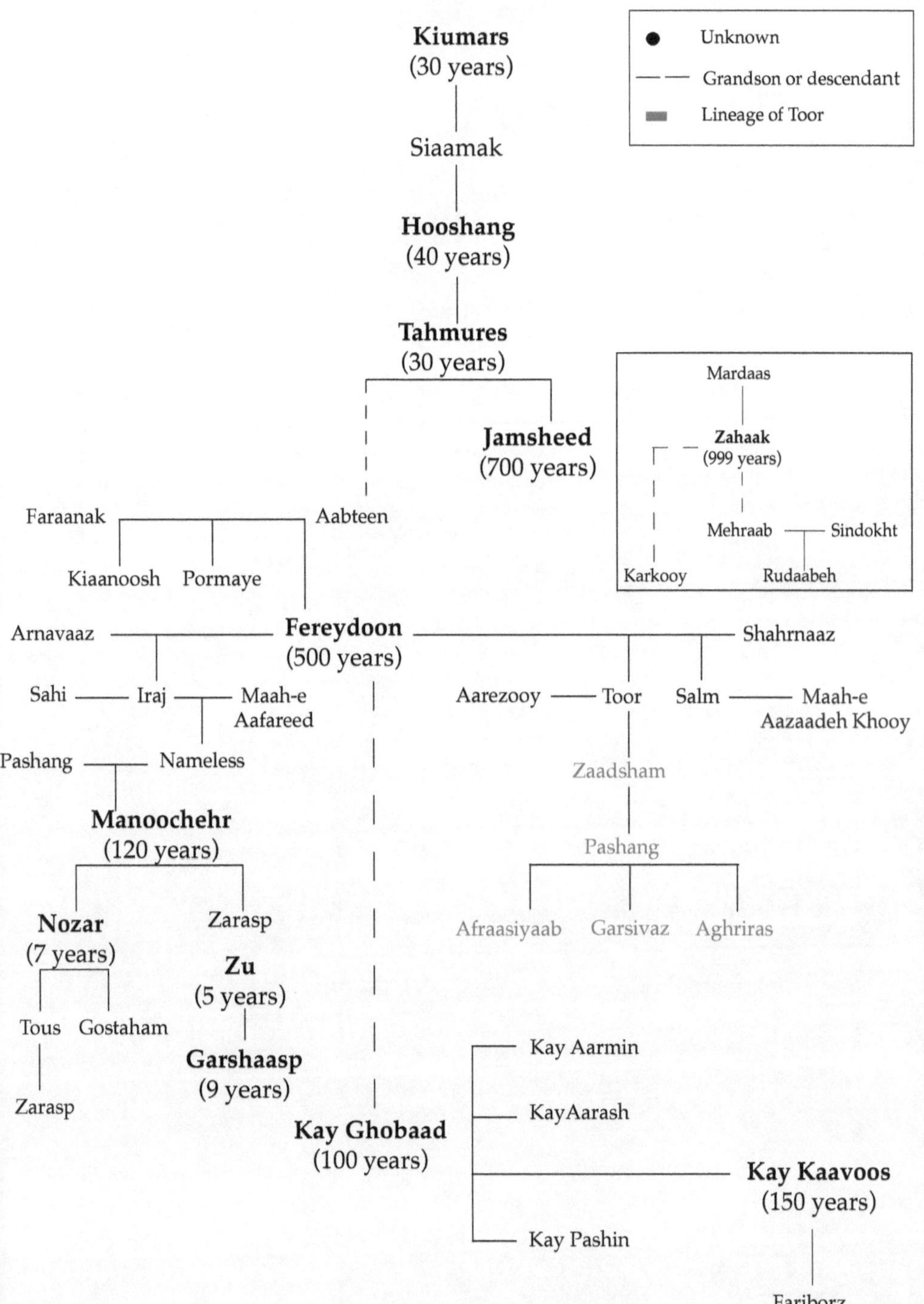

THE KIANIAN KINGS: LINE OF SUCCESSION
From Kay Khosrow to Eskandar

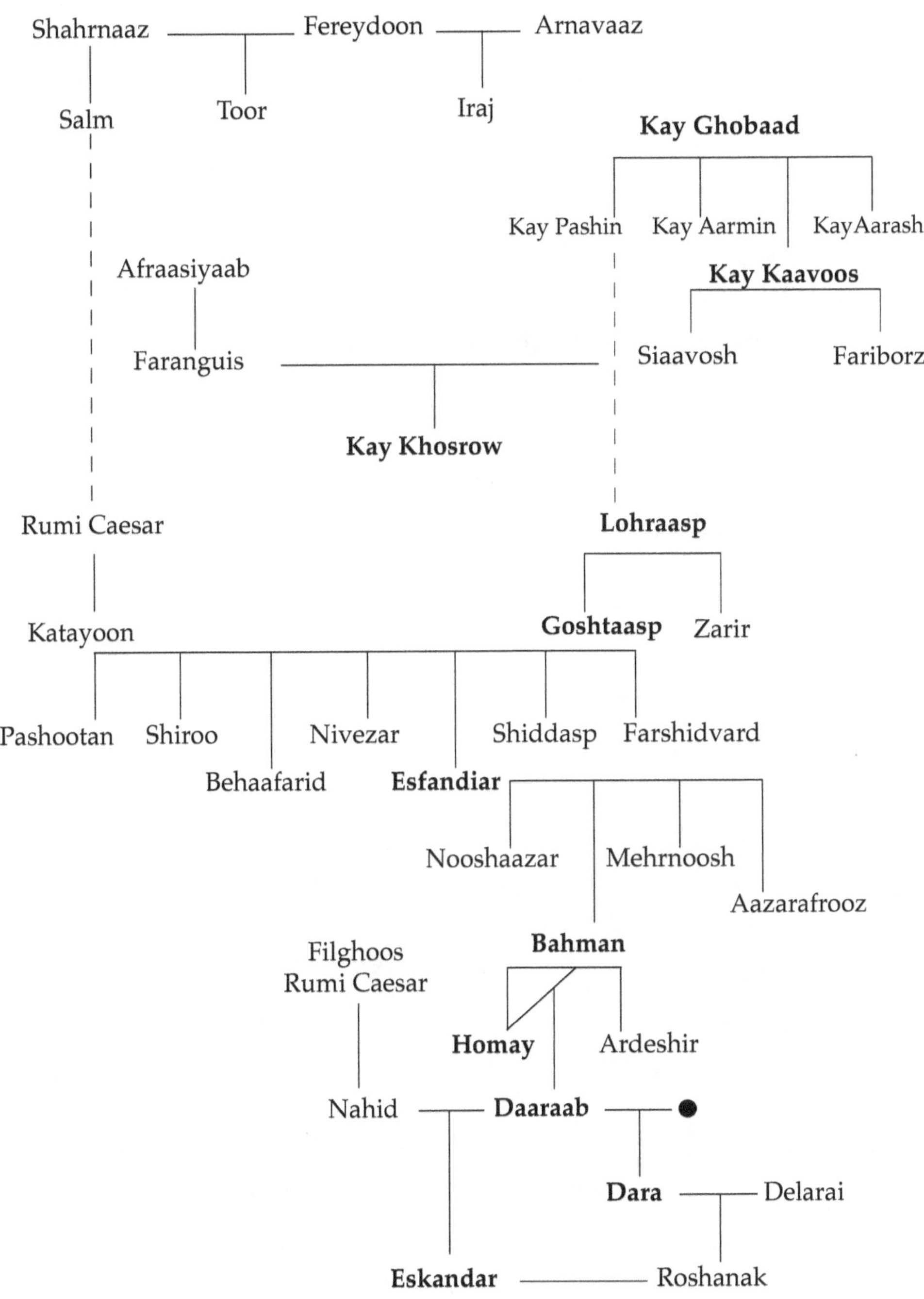

THE IRANIAN HEROES: LINE OF SUCCESSION: Kianian Period

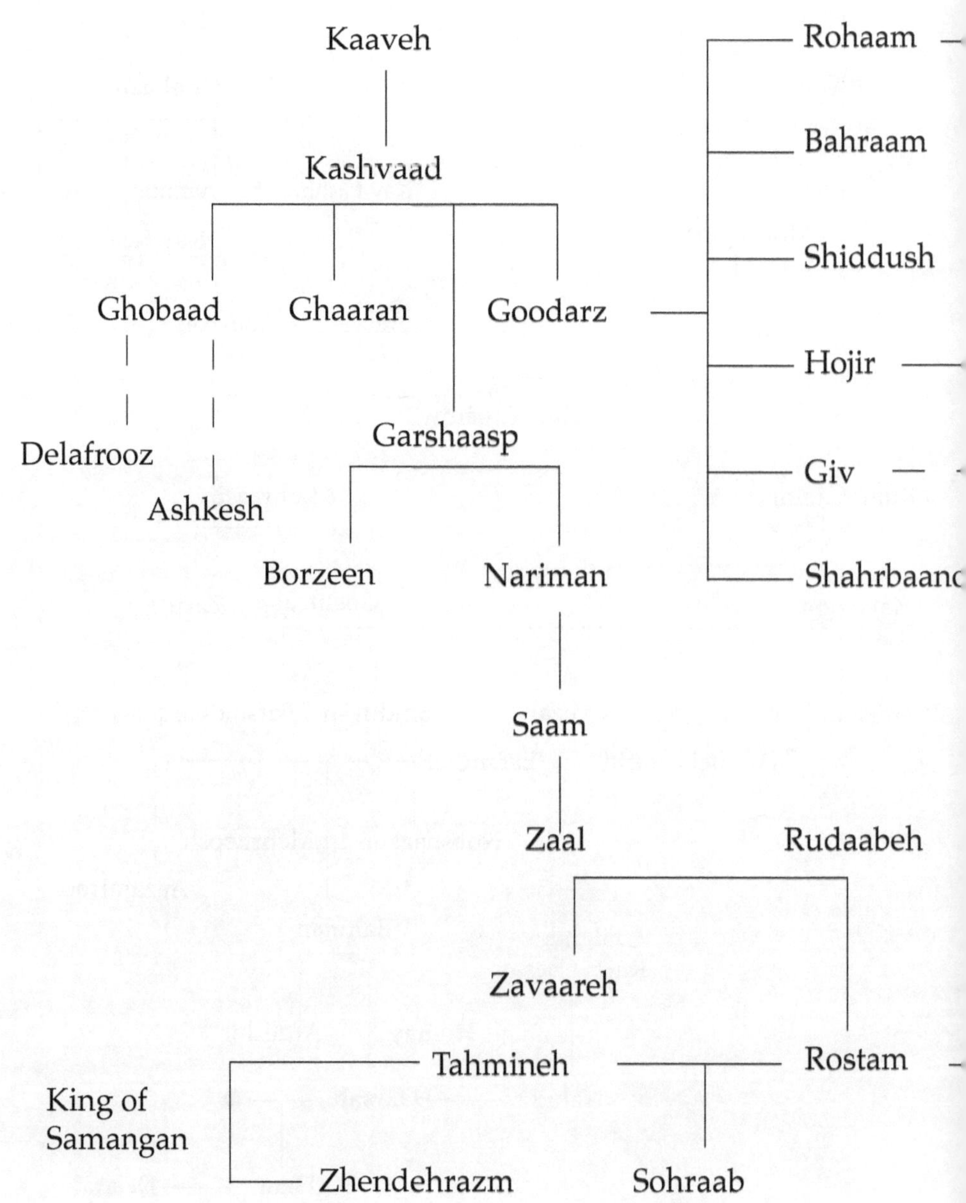

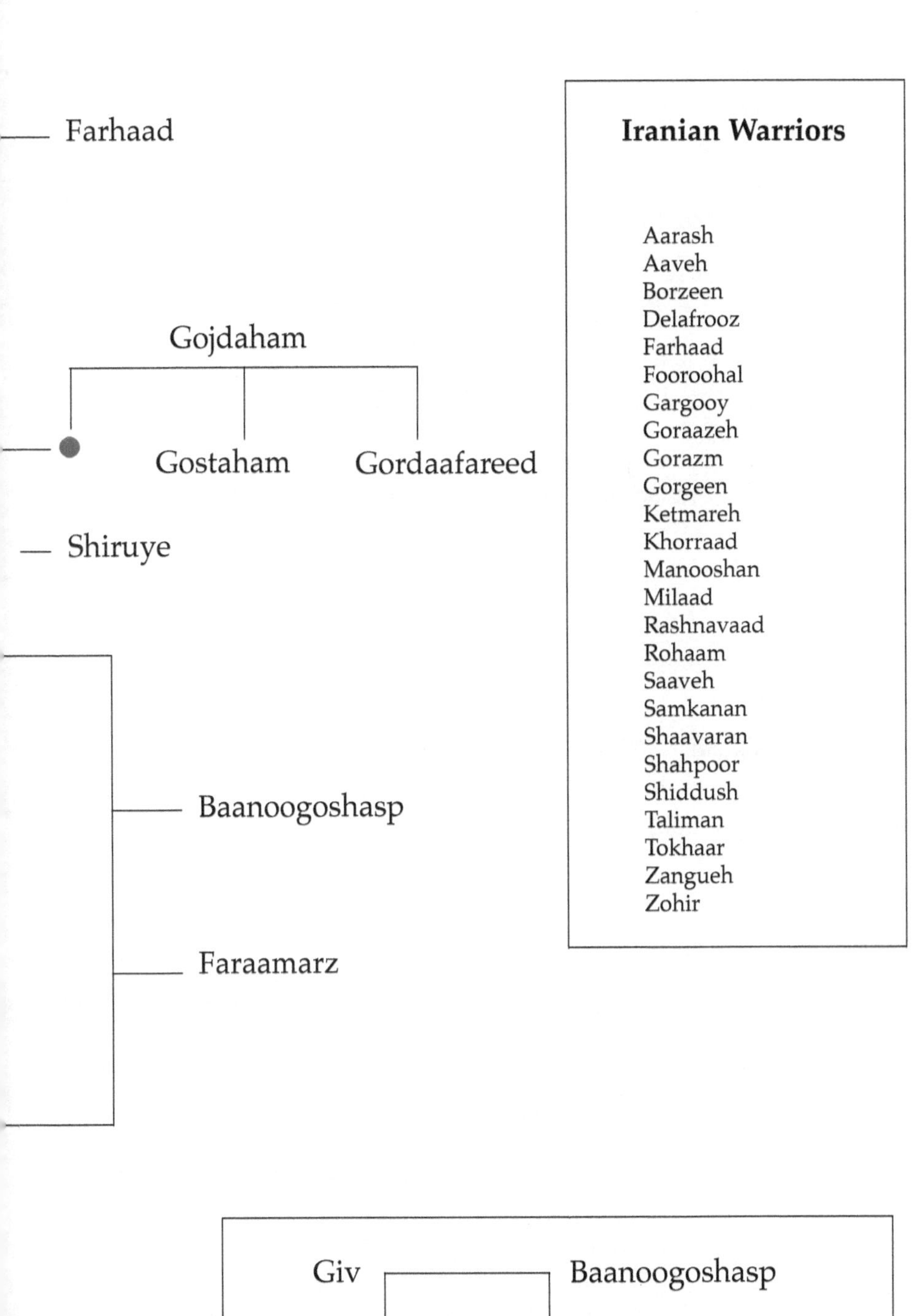

THE TOORANIAN KINGS AND WARRIORS: LINE OF SUCCESSION Kianian Period

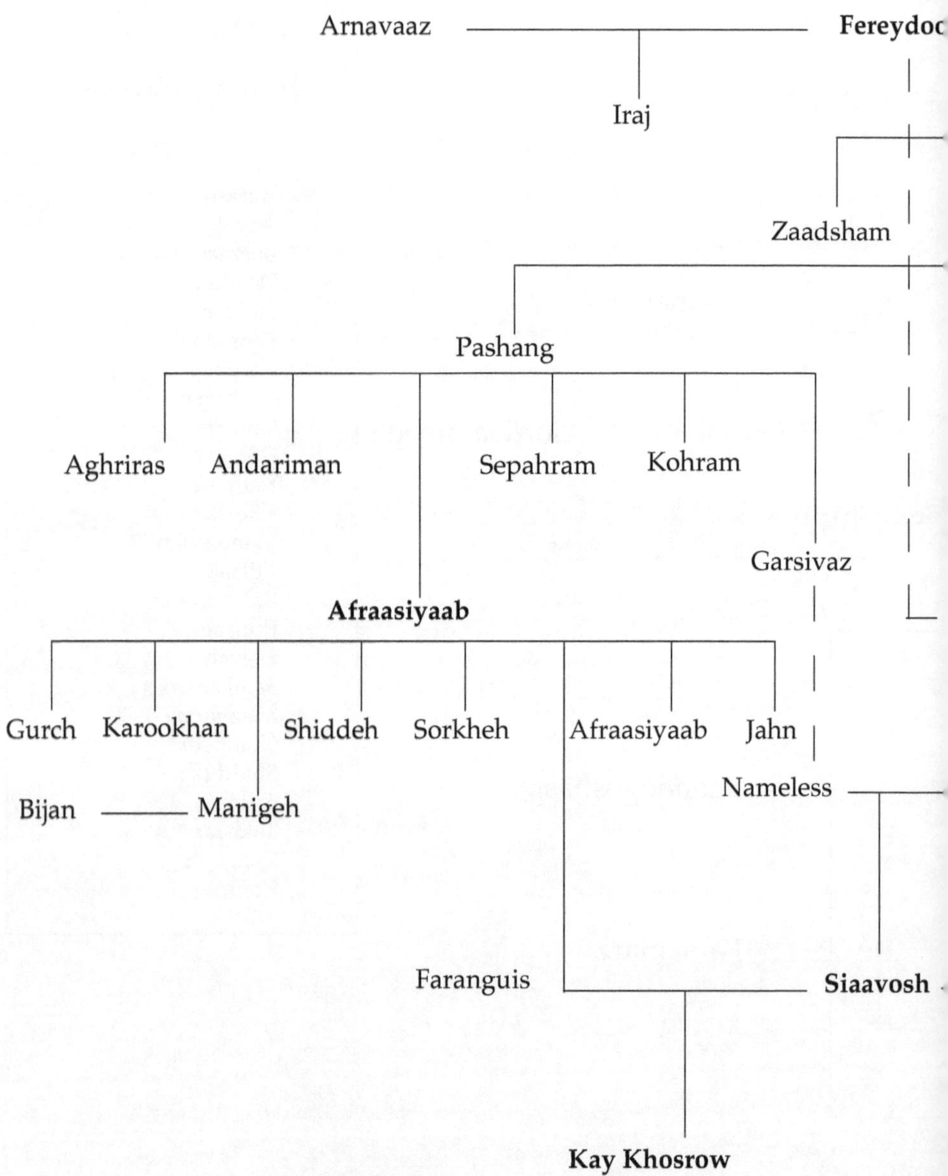

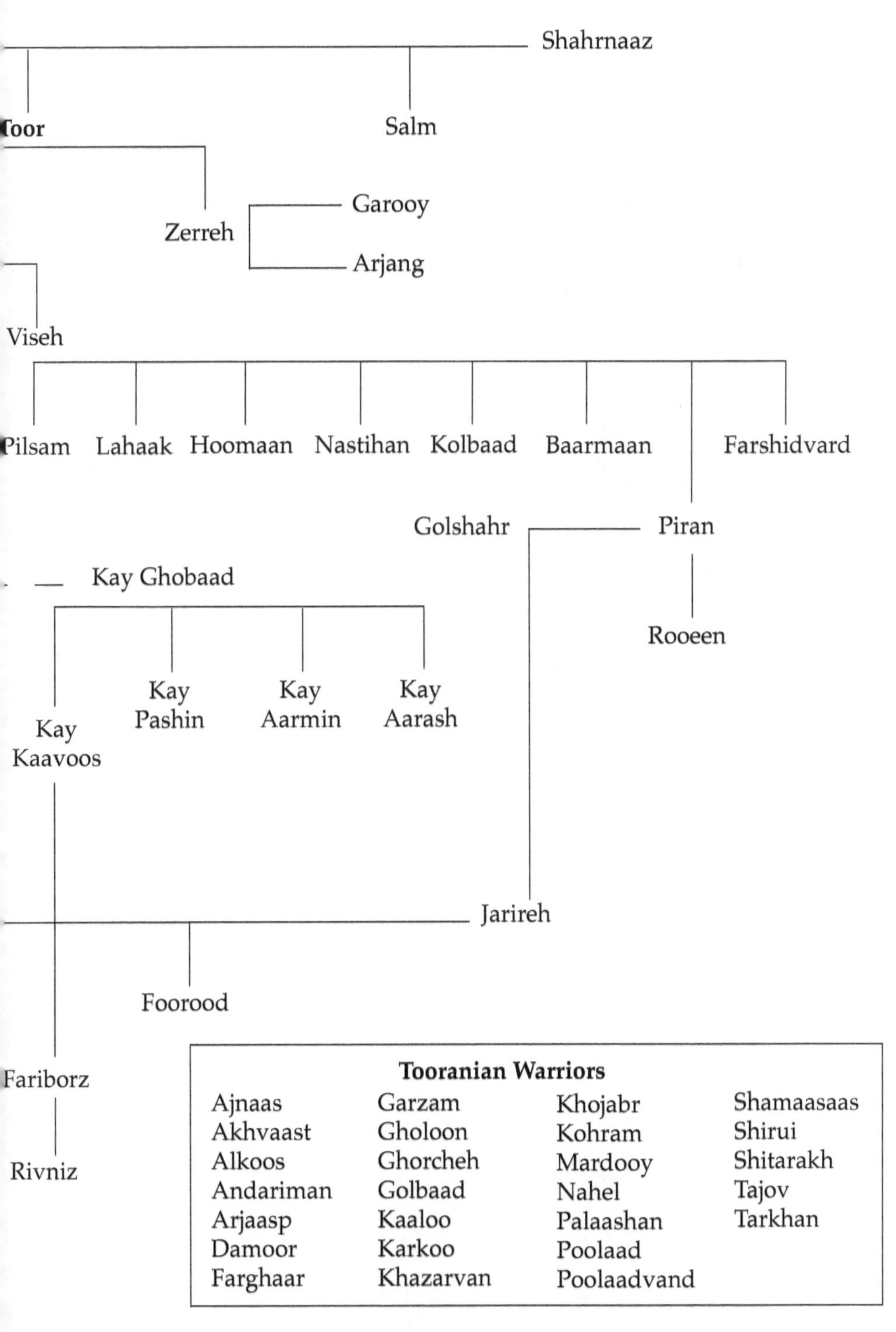
Shahrnaaz
Toor
Salm
Zerreh
Garooy
Arjang
Viseh
Pilsam
Lahaak
Hoomaan
Nastihan
Kolbaad
Baarmaan
Farshidvard
Golshahr
Piran
Kay Ghobaad
Rooeen
Kay Pashin
Kay Aarmin
Kay Aarash
Kay Kaavoos
Jarireh
Foorood
Fariborz
Rivniz
Tooranian Warriors
Ajnaas
Akhvaast
Alkoos
Andariman
Arjaasp
Damoor
Farghaar
Garzam
Gholoon
Ghorcheh
Golbaad
Kaaloo
Karkoo
Khazarvan
Khojabr
Kohram
Mardooy
Nahel
Palaashan
Poolaad
Poolaadvand
Shamaasaas
Shirui
Shitarakh
Tajov
Tarkhan

THE TOORANIAN WARRIORS:
Under the Reigns of Afraasiyaab and Arjaasp

Afraasiyaab's Warriors

Aghriras	Kebord
Ajnaas	Khazarvan
Akhvaast	Khojabr
Alkoos	Kohram
Andariman	Mardooy
Arjaasp	Nahel
Borzvilla	Nastooh
Damoor	Ostaghilaa
Farghaar	Palaashan
Garzam	Poolaad
Gholoon	Poolaadvand
Ghorcheh	Shamaasaas
Golbaad	Shirui
Illa	Shitarakh
Jaranjas	Siaamak
Kaakooleh	Tajov
Kaaloo	Tarkhan
Karkoo	

Arjaasp's Warriors

Ayaas
Ardeshir
Biderafsh
Garsivan
Gorgsaar
Hooshdeev
Khashaash
Kohram
Sootooh
Tabah
Tuvarg
Zangaleh

Glossary of Geographical Markers

Aarman-Zamin: On the border of Tooran-Zamin and Iran-Zamin.

Ahvaz: A city in southwest Iran; capital of the province of Khuzestan.

Alaanan: Region in northwest Iran, north of the Aras River.

Alborz, Mount: Regarded as holy in myths and legends. In geographical terms, it stands in northern Iran.

Almas River: Perhaps beyond the borders of Tooran-Zamin.

Amol: A city in Iran where Fereydoon resides before taking residence in his capital city of Tammisheh. Situated in the Mazandaran Province, near the Alborz mountains

Amoorieh: A Rumi city that no longer exists but would be in present-day Turkey.

Amu: A city near Amu Darya (Jayhoon River).

Andalusia: Southern region of Spain.

Andaraab: A city in present-day Afghanistan.

Ardabil: An ancient city in northwestern Iran.

Arman or Arman-Zamin: On the border of Tooran-Zamin and Iran-Zamin.

Aroos: Name for the treasure Kay Khosrow collects in the city of Tous; Persian word that means bride.

Arvand: A river also known as the Shatt al-Arab River. It begins at the confluence of the Tigris and Euphrates rivers.

Asprooz, Mount: Perhaps a mythical mountain on the way to Mazandaran where Kaavoos is blinded by the deevs.

Azerbaijan: A region in northwestern Iran.

Baamian: A city in present-day Afghanistan.

Babel: Or Babylon, ancient city in Babylonia that is situated in today's Iraq.

Badakhshan: In today's northeast Afghanistan and southeast Tajiki-stan.

Baghdad: Capital of Iraq.

Bait-Al Moghaddas: Jerusalem; meaning pure city.

Balkh: A city in Iran-Zamin, situated in today's Afghanistan.

Baluchistan: A province in today's Iran bordering Pakistan and Af-ghanistan.

Barda: A city in present-day Azerbaijan that once was the capital of Caucasian Albania.

Barein: A city in Iran-Zamin.

Bidaad: Meaning unjust, also referred to as "city of battle"; a city built by Toor with spells and magic in Tooran-Zamin and populated by man-eaters.

Bost: A city and river east of Sistan; situated in today's Afghanistan and now named Lashkargah.

Borz: Another name for Mount Alborz.

Bozgoosh: Area on the way to the dwelling of the White Deev.

Bukhara: A town in Tooran-Zamin; ancient city situated in today's Uzbekistan.

Chaadj: A city in Tooran-Zamin; near today's Tashkent in Uzbekistan.

Chagal: A city in Tooran-Zamin, in today's Turkestan region.

Chaghan: Also Chaghaniyan, land independent of Iran-Zamin or

Tooran-Zamin; a region in Afghanistan north of the River Jayhoon; ruled by an ally of Afraasiyaab.

Chaghvan: A city in the Far East, perhaps Changwon in South Korea.

Chalus: A seaside town on the Caspian Sea; may refer to Mount Koos or Caucasus.

Chegel: Name of a Turkish tribe famous for the beauty of its people.

Chin: China; Generally refers to lands to the east of Iran, as Rum represents the lands to the west. In later stories, Chin is part of Tooran-Zamin.

Daaraab-Guerd: A city founded by King Daaraab.

Daghooy: Hunting plains near the border of Tooran-Zamin.

Dahestan: Presently located in Turkmenistan and Iran.

Dahr: Land outside the borders of Iran-Zamin or Tooran-Zamin.

Dajleh: Arabic for Tigris River.

Damavand, Mount: The highest peak on the Alborz mountain range.

Dambar: A place in today's eastern Afghanistan.

Damghan: A city east of Tehran.

Eram: A Persian garden in Shiraz, Iran; also a heavenly garden in the desert; it is said to appear to the traveler like a mirage.

Eskandarieh: Or Alexandria, an ancient Egyptian city founded in 331 BCE by Eskandar (Alexander the Great).

Estakhr: An ancient city in southern Iran in the Pars Province, north of Persepolis; seat of Kashvaad's palace.

Faariaab: A city in present-day Afghanistan.

Farab: An ancient city on the Silk Road in present-day Kazakhstan.

Fasghoon, Forest of: A forest in Rum (perhaps fictional) where a fierce wolf "with the body of a dragon and the strength of a whale" dwells.

Fort Bahman: A fortress on the border of Iran-Zamin and Tooran-Zamin.

Gang: May be an ancient city on the edge of the Sayhoon River (Syr Darya); seat of Afraasiyaab.

Gang-Behesht: Same as Gang-Dej, the city built by Siaavosh.

Gang-Dej: A fort city built by Siaavosh past the Sea of Chin.

Ghaaf, Mount: A mythical mountain often depicted in images as encircling the world.

Ghaaran, Mount: Perhaps a fictional mountain somewhere in Iran.

Ghajghaarbaashi: A town in Tooran-Zamin, situated in today's Turkey.

Gharcheh: A city in Iran-Zamin.

Gharchehgan: Land around Gharcheh in Iran-Zamin.

Ghatan: A city located in present-day Afghanistan.

Ghaznein: A city in Iran-Zamin, in present-day Afghanistan.

Ghennooj: A city near or in India.

Gholoo, Mountain of: Unclear of the location but in Tooran-Zamin.

Gholzom, Sea of: The Red Sea, between Egypt, Saudi Arabia, Sudan, and Yemen.

Ghom: Or Qom, a city between Tehran and Isfahan.

Ghoor: A province in Afghanistan.

Ghoz: A city in Iran-Zamin.

Gilan: A province in today's northwestern Iran bordering the Caspian Sea; Iranian warrior shields often come from this region.

Gilan, Sea of: Caspian Sea.

Golzarioon: A fictional river in Tooran-Zamin.

Gombadan, Fortress of: A castle in Iran where Esfandiar is locked up for some time at his father's order.

Goozganan: A city in present-day Afghanistan.

Gorgan: A city in northern Iran; capital of the Golestan Province.

Gorganj: Land in the region of Khaarazm.

Gorgsaaran: Meaning "land of the wolf," marks the border separating Iran-Zamin from Mazandaran.

Gorooguerd: A province of Tooran-Zamin.

Green Sea: Probably a sea in the Far East, perhaps the Sea of Japan.

Guraabeh: Burial site of Saam, the hero.

Guran: In today's Lorestan Province of Iran.

Haamaavaran: Perhaps a fictional land; perhaps a reference to Yemen.

Hamaavan, Mount: Site of retreat for Iranian warriors in Tooran-Zamin.

Habash: Or al-Habash, an ancient part of eastern Africa situated in present-day Ethiopia.

Halab: Equivalent to the city of Aleppo in today's Syria; once part of the Persian Empire during the Achaemenid period.

Hamaavan, Mount: A site of retreat for Iranian warriors in Tooran-Zamin.

Haraah: A region ruled by an ally of Afraasiyaab; perhaps al-Harrah in today's western Saudi Arabia, near Jordan.

Hari: A city in Iran-Zamin, situated in today's Afghanistan.

Haroom: A fictional city of women where each resident has a male breast and a female breast.

Hejaz: A western region on the Arabian Peninsula.

Herat: Or Hari, a city in Iran-Zamin, situated in today's Afghanistan.

Hirmand: On the border of Iran and Afghanistan.

Hirmand River: Flowing through Sistan and through today's Afghanistan.

House of Goshtaasp: Fire temple founded by King Goshtaasp.

Impregnable castle: The residence of Arjaasp in the land of Chin.

Iran-Zamin: Land of Iran.

Isfahan: A city in Iran, south of Tehran; seat of the hero Giv, where he receives Kay Khosrow upon his arrival in Iran-Zamin.

Jahrom: City in the Iranian province of Fars.

Jaram: A city situated in today's Afghanistan.

Jayhoon River: Also known as the Oxus River and Amu Darya; located in present-day Afghanistan.

Jeddah: A port city on the Arabian Peninsula by the Red Sea.

Kaasseh Rood: Perhaps a fictional river in Tooran-Zamin.

Kaaba: Meaning "cube" in Arabic, in pre-Islamic times, it was a holy site of pilgrimage for Taazian Bedouin tribes and idol worshippers in Mecca, an important city and a center for trade. After Islam, it became a shrine at the center of the Great Mosque. Muslims everywhere face its direction at the time of their prayers; some believe that it was built by Abraham and his son Ismail.

Kaat: Capital of Khaarazm, or Chorasmia, in ancient times, situated in west-central Asia, south of the Aral Sea.

Kabol: A city in today's Afghanistan.

Kadesia: A region on the Arabian Peninsula.

Kahan: Land independent of Iran or Tooran; its ruler is Kahaar, ally of Afraasiyaab.

Kalaat: A city in present-day Afghanistan.

Kandahar: A city in today's southern Afghanistan.

Karkh: Name for the ancient western section of Baghdad.

Kashaf: A city in northeastern Iran.

Keemaak, Sea of: Most likely the Caspian Sea.

Kerman: A city southeast of Tehran.

Khaarazm: Or Chorasmia; in present-day Tajikistan and Afghanistan, south of the Aral Sea.

Khalkh: Region in present-day Mongolia.

Khalokh: A town in the land of Tooran.

Khargaah: A border town or area near the Jayhoon River and part of Tooran-Zamin.

Khataah: A city near Chin.

Khazar Sea: Caspian Sea.

Khazaria: Land northwest of the Caspian Sea occupying today's Uzbekistan.

Khoonehye Asiran: A city in the district of Ahvaz built by King Shahpoor to house Rumi prisoners. The name means "the dwelling of prisoners."

Khorasan: Region in today's northeastern Iran.

Khorm: Perhaps refers to Khorma, a village in today's northern Iran.

Khotan: A town on the southern side of the Silk Road between China and the west; situated in Tooran-Zamin and ruled by Piran.

Khotlan: A city in Maavaronhar.

Khuzan: A small village in today's Alborz Province of Iran.

Kimaak, Sea of: Kimaak was the name of a Turkic tribe; may refer to the Ural River, which discharges into the Caspian Sea.

Konaabad: A city in Tooran-Zamin.

Konaabad, Mount: A mountain in Tooran-Zamin

Kondaz: Pahlavi name for the city of Paykand near today's Bukhara.

Kooch and Baluch: Kooch is a village in today's Iran; Kooch and Baluch are two tribes near Baluchistan, Iran.

Koos: Caucasus.

Kushan: A mountainous region in today's China.

Laadan: In present-day Ukraine; site of a battle where the Iranians lost heavily to the Tooranians.

Maachin: Comprises greater China.

Maavaranhar: An area near the Jayhoon River and part of Tooran-Zamin.

Mai: An area in today's eastern Afghanistan or Indian subcontinent.

Margh: A city in today's south Khorasan Province of Iran.

Marv: A city in Iran, situated in today's Afghanistan.

Mayam: A fictional river or sea.

Mazandaran: Residence of the deevs and the White Deev in *The Shahnameh* including Gorgsaaran; a non-geographical realm that in no way references the present-day province in northern Iran bordering the Caspian Sea.

Mehr Borzeen: Iranian fire temple established by Goshtaasp Shah.

Milad: Also Malad; appears to be a region in India, north of today's Mumbai.

Milad Castle: Residence of the Indian Keid.

Mokran: In Iran-Zamin and in the coastal region of today's Baluchistan, in southern Iran.

Naarvan: An area in northern Iran, perhaps in present-day Mazandaran.

Navand: A village in northwestern Iran where shines the flame of Barzeen.

Nimrooz: Capital of Zabolestan or Sistan; served as the prime meridian until Europe gained strength and made the switch to Greenwich, England.

Nishabur: A city in Iran-Zamin, situated in today's Afghanistan.

Nohbahaar: Buddhist temple in Balkh.

Pars: A province in southern Iran with Persepolis as capital.

Pashan: Perhaps in present-day India; site of a battle where the Iranians heavily lost to the Tooranians.

Paykand: Or Baykand; a city in Tooran-Zamin, near today's Bukhara (Uzbekistan).

Raibad: A city in Tooran-Zamin

Rey: The oldest city in the province of Tehran; today it is part of the capital city.

Rum: Name of regions west of Iran; Byzantium, eastern Roman Empire.

Rumi: Adjective meaning from Byzantium.

Saghilaa, Mount: Appears to be a fictional mountain in Rum.

Saghlaab: Land outside of Iran-Zamin and Tooran-Zamin; land of the Slavic people; ruled by Kondor, ally of Afraasiyaab.

Sagsaar: East of Afghanistan.

Sagsaaran: Or Sistan, is in today's eastern Iran and southern Afghanistan, near Baluchistan; also named Sakastan.

Samangan: Land in ancient times and a province in present-day Afghanistan.

Samarkand: A city in Tooran-Zamin, a destination on the Silk Road, and in present-day Uzbekistan.

Sari: A town in present-day Mazandaran; once the capital of Iran.

Saroj, Desert of: Region in Iran-Zamin; unclear of the location.

Sea of Chin: Reference to a body of water in the Far East.

Sea of Sindh: May refer to the Gulf of Oman, south of the Sindh Province, or perhaps the Sindhu (Indus) River.

Sepad, Mount: Appears to be a fictional mountain in Kalaat.

Sepand, Mount: Meaning sacred, holy.

Sepijaab: Land in Tooran-Zamin close to the Jayhoon River.

Shaam: Syria.

Shahd, Mount: Unclear location, perhaps in India.

Shahd River: May be a reference to the Arvand River, also known as the Shatt al-Arab; in today's southern Iraq.

Shaheh: A city in today's Khuzestan Province of Iran.

Shakni: Land outside of Iran-Zamin and Tooran-Zamin ruled by Shamira.

Shangan: A city around the border between Iran-Zamin and Tooran-Zamin.

Shirkhan: An area in Damavand in western Iran.

Siaavosh-Guerd: A city built by Siaavosh in Tooran-Zamin on land given to him by Afraasiyaab.

Sindh: A province in the southeastern part of India.

Sindhu River: Indus River in India.

Sistan: A province in today's eastern Iran and southern Afghanistan, part of Baluchistan; same as Zabolestan.

Soghdi: A region in Tooran-Zamin.

Sughd: A town in Tooran-Zamin; perhaps in northern Mongolia, near the Chinese border.

Taleghan: A city in the Alborz mountain range.

Tammisheh: Fereydoon's capital in northern Iran; in Mount Koos (meaning Caucasus).

Taraaz: Or Taraz, a city in Turkestan famous for its beautiful women; also a river in today's Kazakhstan.

Tarmaz: A town on the edge of the Jayhoon River, on the border between Iran-Zamin and Tooran-Zamin.

Tartar: Situated in Tooran-Zamin, in today's Azerbaijan.

Tehran: Present-day capital of Iran since 1786.

Tooran-Zamin: Land of Toor and his descendants Pashang and Afraa-siyaab; also referred to as Turkestan.

Tous: An ancient city in the province of Khorasan in Iran; also the city where Ferdowsi lived and worked.

Transoxiana: Also referred to as Maavaran-nahr (Arabic). It is in the land of Tooran beyond the Jayhoon (Oxus) River and covers the region in today's Uzbekistan and Tajikistan, and parts of Kyrgyzstan and Kazakhstan.

Turkestan: Land of Turks east of Iran; also referred to as Tooran-Zamin.

Urmia, Lake of: A saltwater lake in the northwestern part of Iran.

Viseh-Guerd: A city in Tooran-Zamin named after Piran's father, Viseh; ancient city in northern Afghanistan.

White Castle: A castle defended by Gojdaham and his children in Iran-Zamin, near Tooran's border.

Yajooj and Majooj: Two tribes residing in Manchuria and causing mayhem across the neighboring lands.

Zaabeh, Mount: Perhaps a mythical mountain in the Alborz mountain range.

Zabol: Capital of Sistan, or Zabolestan; a province in today's eastern Iran, part of Baluchistan.

Zabolestan: Also Sistan; land ruled by the hero Nariman and his descendants Saam, Zaal, and Rostam; in today's southern Afghanistan.

Zam: A city around the border between Iran-Zamin and Tooran-Zamin.

Zarnoosh: A city built by King Dara in the region of Ahvaz, in southwestern Iran.

Zerreh, Sea of: Situated in southwestern Afghanistan.

The World
of
Ferdowsi's Shahnameh

Ural River

KHAZARIA

Terek River

Caucasus
Mountains
Koos

Black Sea

Caspian
Sea
Sea of
Gilan

Konaaba

RUM
Byzantium/
Constantinople

Dahestan
Tartar

Yerevan
ARMENIA

Gorganj

AZERBAIJAN

Amoorieh

Nassibin

Nahravan

Barda

Khorm

Tammisheh

Naarvan

GILAN

Navand

Bastam

Nisha

Halab

Ghebchaagh

Deylam

Shooraab

Ardabil

Chalus

Gorgan

HAMEDAN

Mount Zaabeh

GOLESTAN

Tigris River/
Dajleh

Khuzan

Mount
Alborz

Amol

Sari

GORGSAAR

MAZANDARAN

Mount Damavand

Damgh

Euphrates River

LORESTAN

Rey

Bozgoc

Jerusalem

Guran

Taleghan

Tehran

Shemiran

Mount Asprooz

Karkh

Baghdad

Shirkhan

Kufah

Ctesiphon

Khorram Abad

Ghom

Margh

IRAN-ZAMIN

Babylon

Mada'in

Arvand River/
Shatt al-Arab

MESOPOTAMIA
ASSYRIA

Shushtar

Ahvaz

Isfahan

Ghobaad/Awan

Zargh

Land of Taazian
Haamaavaran
Egypt
Nile River

Estakhr

Kerman

Shiraz

KAARZI

Mokran

PARS

YEMEN

Bahrein

Jahrom

Zarnoosh

Kojaran

Persian Gulf

The markings on this map are mere reference points to
the story and may not be historically accurate

RUS/RUSSIA

Mazandaran
Residence of the deevs and the White Deev
in The Shahnameh including Gorgsaaran;
a non-geographical realm which in no way
references the present-day province in northern Iran
bordering the Caspian Sea.

Dambar

Syr Darya/
Sayhoon River

Khalkh

Aral
Sea

Khotlan

Farab

MAAVARANHAR

SOGHDI

Kaat

Paykand

Samarkand

Soghd

Bukhara

Mai

Khargaah

Taraaz

Kushan Mountains

Chaadj

Chagal

TOORAN-ZAMIN

Amu Darya
Jayhoon/Oxus

Khataah

Maimargh

ARMAN-ZAMIN
COSHMAIHAN

Ghabchaagh

CHIN/CHINA

Amoy

Marv

Bukhara

Samangan

Tous

Tarmaz

Andaraab

Khotan

Balkh

Badakhshan

Kashaf

Baamian

Dambar

Faariaab

GHOOR

Kabol

KHORASAN

Ghaznein

Ghatan

Herat/Hari

Jaram

Zam

Hirmand

Chaghan

Nimrooz

Bost

Zabol

Kandahar

ZABOLESTAN

Kalat

SISTAN

River Hirmand

Firozabad

Sorsan

BALUCHISTAN

Sindhu River/
Indus River

INDIA

Ghennooj

SINDH

Sendal

Milad

Sea of Sindh

Glossary of Persian Words

Aab: From *aaberoo,* meaning honor, nobility, and integrity; code of honor.

Aaban: Eighth month of the solar year.

Aazar: Ninth month of the year and ninth day of the month.

Aazar Borzeen: Fire temple founded by Lohraasp.

Aazargoshasp: Divine, holy, eternal flame of the Zoroastrians; a revered fire temple for kings and warriors during the Sassanian times in Azerbaijan.

Andisheh: Thought.

Ard: The twenty-ninth day of any month is the day of Ard in ancient Iran.
Arrash: Unit of measurement corresponding to the length of the forearm, from fingertip to elbow.

Ayeen: Divine principle or code of human life; path and purpose that reflects all that encompasses the divine, free of barriers set by culture, geography, dogma, or religion.

Babreh Bayan: Armor that is worn only by Rostam. Uncertain about its meaning. Literally refers to leopard skin. Other interpretations refer to beaver skin or dragon skin. It is meant to be waterproof and impenetrable.

Bahman: Name of the second day of the month and the eleventh month of the solar year.

Bahraam: Mars.

Barzeen: Zoroastrian fire temple with an ever-burning flame situated in Khorasan, in northeastern Iran.

Bidaad: Meaning unjust.

Daad: Infinite justice; justice that is non-judgmental and unchange-able for it is divine, constant, eternal; different from human justice that is encompassed by a strict set of laws.

Deev: Son of Ahriman, also referred to as Eblis; represents the materi-al or physical embodiment of Ahriman; a fragment of the dark spirit or demon.

Dehghan: Farmer; keeper of land and crops, of rain and sun, and all that grows; keeper of ancient wisdom, poet, and bard.

Dinar: Gold coin.

Dirham: Silver coin.

Esfand: Twelfth month of the Persian solar calendar; begins in Febru-ary and ends in March; also the name of the plant and herb rue; also meaning sacred or holy, as in *Sepand*.

Farr: Divine grace; state of consciousness holding infinite grace of light and life.
Farsang: Ancient unit of measure equivalent to 6.24 kilometers or 3.88 miles.

Gohar: Essence.

Homa: Large and powerful bird in Persian mythology, symbol of hap-piness; similar to the griffin or the phoenix.

Jaan: Life force, soul, spirit.

Kaavian: Belonging to Kaaveh, the blacksmith, who leads the oppo-sition against Zahaak. The Kaaviani banner is made of the cloth of blacksmiths with the colors red, yellow, and purple representing the two ends of the color spectrum as well as the center color.

Kamand: Ancient unit of measure.

Kay: King.

Kherrad: Wisdom; Eternal Wisdom; absolute, pure consciousness.

Kianian: Royal; from *kian,* meaning royalty.

Kushti: A sacred belt or girdle worn by Zoroastrians around their waists; it has 72 interwoven white strands of sheep's wool representing seventy-two chapters of a part of the *Avesta.*

Mahn: Reference to a form of weight measurement in the ancient Middle East, around 3 kilograms or 6.6 pounds; so 600 mahn is equivalent to 1,800 kilograms or 3,968 pounds.

Mehr: Complex word that includes deep eternal love, affection, compassion, mercy; also the seventh month of the Iranian calendar.

Mehregan: A festival and memorial to Fereydoon, still celebrated today on the Mehr day of the Mehr month of the year.

Mithqual: Unit of measuring weight equivalent to 4.25 grams; often used to weigh precious metal.

Naam: Divine essence, what is contained in space; also defined as "name."

Nowruz: New Day, the Persian New Year, still observed by Iranians of all religions during the spring equinox on or around March 21.

Pahlavan: Noble hero, paladin, warrior, fighter for the cause of *mehr;* guardian of crown and throne, soldier of light.

Pahlavi: Or middle Persian; literary language during the Sassanian rule until the advent of the modern Persian language.

Pishdaadian: Meaning the era prior to the rule of law. The dynasty comprises the first Persian kings: Kiumars, Hooshang, and Tahmures.

Ratal: A measure of weight equivalent to 12 to 16 ounces.

Raai: Will or thought (*andisheh);* intellect or knowing that works in favor of universal time, not human or chronological time.

Saddeh: Festival to celebrate Hooshang's discovery of fire in *The Shahnameh;* meaning one hundred, it marks one hundred days before Nowruz; it is a celebration of overcoming darkness.

Sepand: Same as *esfand,* meaning sacred or holy.

Sitir: Form of measure equivalent to 75 grams.

Sokhan: Divine Word, ultimate truth.

Teer: Mercury.

Yazdan: Creator of all that is manifested, unmanifested, and all that is yet to come into existence. Plural of Yzad (divine) encompasses all of divinity.

Zamin: Land of; for instance, Iran-Zamin means land of Iran.

Zand Avesta: *Avesta* is the Zoroastrian holy scripture; *Zand* is the interpretation of it.

The Persian Calendar

Based on the solar calendar, the months are named after twelve divinities and correspond to nature's cycles and the signs of the zodiac:

Spring:
Farvardin – Aries; the first month of the year begins with Nowruz, the first day of spring and the spring equinox.
Ordibehesht – Taurus; spans the months of April and May.
Khordaad – Gemini; third month of the year.

Summer:
Teer – Cancer; Mercury; the fourth month begins with the summer solstice.
Mordaad – Leo; fifth month of the year.
Shahrivar – Virgo; sixth month of the solar year.

Fall:
Mehr – Libra; the seventh month begins with the fall equinox or Mehregan.
Aaban – Scorpio; eighth month of the year.
Aazar – Sagittarius; ninth month of the year, ends with the winter solstice or Yalda.

Winter:
Dey – Capricorn; tenth month of the year.
Bahman – Aquarius; eleventh month of the solar year.
Esfand – Pisces; twelfth month of the year.

This translation would not have been possible without the selfless and unwavering dedication of Soudabeh Araghi who spent countless hours with me revising the entire final manuscript. I am immensely grateful for her truly heroic contribution, which played an instrumental role in completing this significant work.